ROUTLEDGE LIBRARY EDITIONS:
ECONOMETRICS

Volume 4

THE STATISTICAL METHOD IN ECONOMICS AND POLITICAL SCIENCE

THE STATISTICAL METHOD IN ECONOMICS AND POLITICAL SCIENCE

A Treatise on the Quantitative and Institutional Approach to Social and Industrial Problems

P. SARGANT FLORENCE

Routledge
Taylor & Francis Group

LONDON AND NEW YORK

First published in 1929 by Kegan Paul, Trench, Trubner & Co. Ltd.

This edition first published in 2018
by Routledge
4 Park Square, Milton Park, Abingdon, Oxon OX14 4RN
605 Third Avenue, New York, NY 10017

Routledge is an imprint of the Taylor & Francis Group, an informa business

British Library Cataloguing in Publication Data
A catalogue record for this book is available from the British Library

ISBN: 978-0-8153-9640-6 (Set)
ISBN: 978-1-351-14012-6 (Set) (ebk)
ISBN: 978-0-8153-5422-2 (Volume 4) (hbk)
ISBN: 978-0-8153-5425-3 (Volume 4) (pbk)
ISBN: 978-1-351-13351-7 (Volume 4) (ebk)

Publisher's Note
The publisher has gone to great lengths to ensure the quality of this reprint but points out that some imperfections in the original copies may be apparent.

Disclaimer
The publisher has made every effort to trace copyright holders and would welcome correspondence from those they have been unable to trace.

The Statistical Method in Economics and Political Science

A Treatise on the Quantitative and Institutional
Approach to Social and Industrial Problems

By

P. SARGANT FLORENCE

*M.A. (Cambridge), Ph.D. (Columbia), Professor of Commerce
in the University of Birmingham, late University Lecturer in
Economics and Politics at Cambridge University, Author of
'Economics of Fatigue and Unrest,' 'Overpopulation,' 'Economics
and Human Behaviour,' etc.*

LONDON

KEGAN PAUL, TRENCH, TRUBNER & CO. LTD.

NEW YORK : HARCOURT BRACE & COMPANY

1929

Printed in Great Britain at
The Mayflower Press, Plymouth. William Brendon & Son, Ltd.

PREFACE

THIS treatise on " the quantitative and institutional approach to social and industrial problems " is addressed to all students of economics and political science who find theories unsatisfactory without the test of fact ; and to all students of statistics who find figures or mathematical technique barren without application to life. These students may be just general readers pursuing their interests for interest's sake ; they may be learners and apprentices in research wanting additional training in theory and technique ; or they may already be specialists or teachers who find the survey and solution of social questions impossible without recourse to statistical exposition.

In appealing to such a wide audience two courses were open. The more congenial plan was to assume optimistically that those interested in statistics were also familiar with economic and political theory, and that those interested in economics and politics were also familiar with statistical technique, and to confine myself, accordingly, to working out the possibilities of co-operation between theory and technique. This plan has in fact been followed in devoting a special part of the book, entitled Statistical Fieldwork, to a systematic and somewhat original statement in general terms of the principles and methods of applied statistics.

But experience in teaching advanced students, and in reviewing works of those in later life, has shown me the necessity of facing the fact that statistical technique and economic and political theory have traditionally been taught apart. I have, therefore, taken little allied knowledge, either mathematical, economic or political for granted, and have left no technical term or method, no theoretical conception or law unexplained or unillustrated.

Such a comprehensive policy, I am well aware, runs two proverbial dangers : that of teaching grandmothers to suck eggs, and that of breaking the camel's back.

To save the grandmothers I have separated into Parts II, III and IV, respectively, the methods of statistical measurement ; the principles to be followed and fallacies to be avoided in applying these measures to economic and political fields ; and the resultant

v

construction of a statistical economics and politics. Grandmothers at home in statistical measurement may thus, if they choose, concentrate upon economic and political applications; and grandmothers at home in economic or political theories may devote themselves to the statistical groundwork. Moreover, in teaching the methods of statistical measurement—the egg most often sucked—I have not attempted to go beyond the minimum requirements. I am concerned that the economist and political student shall not miss the wood for the trees, and I make no attempt to compete with (and indeed constantly cite) the many excellent textbooks detailing the mathematical theory of statistics that have recently appeared in England and America.

On the camel's behalf, I have tried to lighten load by illustrating the methods of statistical measurement with instances relevant to the economic and political theory discussed later; and to shorten time by ample cross-referencing. This treatise may, in fact, be used as an introductory manual of realistic economics, administrative science and comparative politics. All the various subjects that are statistically approached are indexed not only in the usual alphabetical order, but also systematically in order of logical development. And all the more elementary statistical terms and methods used are brought together for brief definition and illustration in a statistical glossary.[1]

Apart from developing methods of fieldwork and attempting to present within the covers of one book a balanced synthesis of fieldwork, statistical measurement, and realistic applications, this treatise attempts to break new ground in the direction indicated by the Economics and Political Science of its title. The " and " is not a mere additive symbol. It refers to the conception, set forth in Chapters III and IV, of an organic relationship between the two sciences, that involves functional analysis, institutional interpretation, and a more workmanlike approach to questions of organization such as division of labour and the control of industry. Humble students of business administration and industrial or commercial organization, will be agreeably surprised to discover the terms upon which their subject is admitted into the intimate circle of the orthodox social sciences.

It is with the utmost gratitude that I record the generous co-operation of old colleagues at Cambridge. Early chapters were read and criticized most helpfully by the late Mr. Frederick Lavington and the late Mrs. Dorothea Braithwaite; by Mr. Maurice Dobb, Mr. G. F. Shove, and Mr. R. B. Braithwaite; and the final manuscript most thoroughly overhauled by Mr. J. L. Cohen, Mr. Austin

Robinson and Mrs. Joan Robinson. What good friends could do, they did ; they are not responsible for my many conscious, and perhaps unconscious, heresies. I also owe a special debt of gratitude to Miss Portia Holman for her aid in systematizing text, tables, and glossary. And at many a moment of crisis my wife has stepped in to lend a hand, typing, preparing manuscript for the printers, correcting punctuation, yea, and even spelling.

P. SARGANT FLORENCE.

THE UNIVERSITY,
  BIRMINGHAM.

---

[1] The table of CONTENTS, also, outlines the augument of each chapter section and *indicates the page where any given section is to be found.*

The following abbreviations have been used in references to periodicals :

Ec. Jl. Journal of the Royal Economic Society.
J.R.S.S. Journal of the Royal Statistical Society.
J.A.S.A. Quarterly Publication, later called Journal, of the American Statistical Association.

CONTENTS

PART ONE

MOOD AND MATTER OF STATISTICAL ENQUIRY

The function of economics and political science is the study and discovery of fact in the indicative mood, free from moral implications, and from optative and imperative attitudes. Scientific knowledge must first be obtained before it can be applied to produce the results desired for the good of mankind.

In the pursuit of knowledge, the primary function of statistics is to describe item facts summarily. Such descriptions may substitute experience for the assumptions all too prevalent in economic and political thought, particularly as to the actual workings of social institutions. But statistical methods also aspire to verify the generalizations of economic and political theory, or to suggest pertinent generalizations of their own for theory to interpret. The supposed inferiority of the statistical approach compared to deductive reasoning as an education in mental discipline is questionable, and on the score of practical interest its realism justifies a place for applied statistics in all university curricula.

Outline of the thesis and plan of the whole treatise.

§1 *The Division of Labour in Social Research.* The actual system of specialization now prevailing in the social sciences is discussed, and lines of demarcation are suggested that distinguish economics and political science proper, political economics, and economic politics.

§2 *Political and Exchange Economics.* That subjects actually included in Economics are all connected with acts of exchanging, and focus at the outset upon individual behaviour as against a deductive approach, avoids the impression that economic events occur automatically. The part of political science that we call Political Economics deals similarly with the acts of compulsion by threat of

PART TWO

THE STATISTICAL MEASUREMENT OF ECONOMIC AND POLITICAL DATA

CONTENTS

PAGE

PART FOUR

SKETCH FOR A STATISTICAL ECONOMICS AND POLITICS

CONTENTS

LIST OF TABLES

The Statistical Method in Economics and Political Science

PART ONE

MOOD AND MATTER OF STATISTICAL ENQUIRY

CHAPTER I

THE FUNCTION OF ECONOMICS, POLITICAL SCIENCE, AND STATISTICS

ECONOMICS and the adjective economic have recently become distinct, in their implication, from economy and the adjective economical. To practise economy and to have an economical outlook refers to a particular, and usually approved, " business-like " variety of behaviour or set of opinions ; to practise economics and have an economic outlook refers to the dispassionate study of all or any varieties of behaviour of a certain sort. Similarly politic like economical refers to a particular, approved, variety of behaviour, and the dispassionate study of all or any varieties is called political. What sort of matters are studied by economics and political science, and how these are related to kindred matters, will be discussed in Chapters III and IV ; here it is the mood of approach, not the matter, that is at issue.

Economics and political science have as their function the study of various forms of " economic " and " political " behaviour or opinion. They may form part of an attempt deliberately to improve the behaviour of mankind, and may claim to be sciences that can be applied in certain particular ways to beneficent practical uses. But, though they must take account of other people's opinions of right and wrong, economists and political scientists cannot alone and unaided recommend particular approved varieties of behaviour or opinion, for the reason that in the ultimate analysis they cannot judge what constitutes improvement or when a process is beneficent and worthy of approval.

B

Take a simple statement of economists which, whether correct or incorrect, will be intelligible to politicians :

A reduction in the population of settled countries tends to increase wealth per head.

Does this necessarily indicate what beneficent procedure to adopt ? Many persons would desire larger populations for their respective countries rather than mere increase of wealth per head, and until the desideratum is agreed upon there can be no practical policy. Three distinct stages in the deliberate procedure are in fact distinguishable, each cast in an appropriate mood, the Indicative, the Optative, and the Imperative.

The Indicative is the mood of science stating a fact. A reduction in the population tends to increase wealth per head.

The Optative is the mood of ethics or morals and its ideals or desires are ultimately independent of scientific statements. They may run : Oh ! that our population were big ; or else, Oh ! that wealth per head were increased.

The Imperative is the mood of the practical " economical " or " politic " statesman or publicist ; but the practice deliberately commanded or advocated must depend upon the indicative statement and also upon the optative wish. It is only if the first proposition is considered true, and also if the increase of wealth per head is considered good and desirable, that the imperative may ring out,

Let the population be reduced !

These different moods can and should be separated.[1] Whatever their conduct, utterances, or opinions as private persons with the full allowance of human emotions and sentiments, there ought to be at least some authors devoting themselves to research and scientific discovery, who take their studies as seriously as do physicists, biologists, or anthropologists ; and who, however keen to improve the lot of man, will be content to state their conclusions in the indicative mood and to eschew ethical valuation and practical precept. The embryonic and parlous state of economics and political science to-day, and the many controversial issues still unsolved, is primarily attributable to the admixture of moral implications with scientific observation in the author's thought, and in the communication of his thought to reader or audience.

[1] I speak here in the imperative mood not as an economist or political scientist, but as one advocating the economical and politic organization of human thought. See my *Economics and Uplift*.

Moral implications—the intrusion of ideals about social service and sin—obstruct and confound learning by distracting the audience, by misleading the audience, and sometimes by confusing the author himself.

The author's moral outlook may not tally with that of the reader, and if the author mixes that outlook with his statements of fact, the latter though perfectly true, may be rejected or resisted along with the former as mere propaganda. However intelligible the author's scientific conclusions, a "foreign" ethical code or an unfamiliar sense of sin will be a source of distraction; and communication with his audience may thus be entirely or partially baulked by his peculiar moral ideals.

Admixture with moral outlook may render statements of fact unintelligible to the audience. When some action is considered desirable and called good, or any of the fifty synonyms of good, by the author, and another action is considered a sin and called bad, or any of the hundred synonyms of bad—one simply resulting in the fulfilment, the other in the baulking of the author's peculiar plans and desires—the reader or auditor may remain ignorant of the precise nature of the desires referred to. Probably, he will unconsciously suppose that what he (the reader or auditor) happens to consider desirable or the reverse is what the author is referring to by " good," " bad," etc. Here communication with his audience is vitiated by the author's ideals and moralizings being misunderstood, and the audience is misled.

Finally, as a result of compounding ethical and moral considerations with a purely indicative attitude, the author may actually mislead and confuse himself. If definitions are based on ethical distinctions they may cut across and blur the purely factual distinctions, and if the author enunciates " principles " that might be indicative or optative or imperative in mood, he may well deduce fiction from them rather than fact.

Turning from criticism to a constructive plan, I suggest that economists and political scientists should leave the " shocked missionary stage " and imitate modern anthropological writings in their amoral attitude to social life. This attitude, applied to the solution of the problems of to-day, allows the economist and political scientist to co-operate more freely with—because independently of—practical statesmen and reformers.

This treatise, in short, assumes the function of economics and political science to be the study and discovery of fact in the indicative mood, leaving these facts open and public, to be used in conjunction with other moods for the good of mankind.

The statistical approach to Economics and Political Science must therefore be justified and valued according as it fulfils these scientific functions either in advancing research and learning or in advancing education and the power to learn.

The phrase that rankles most among statisticians ambitious to advance learning and research is that statistics prove nothing, but "merely describe." What is implied by this term of contempt ? On the most severe interpretation "merely descriptive" means descriptive merely of an isolated fact. Some individual perhaps lived to be 150 years old, or Blue Books may tell us that the population of London in 1901 was 4,536,063 souls. But statistics, though made up of this sort of thing, are not this, any more than a house is merely a set of bricks. Populations of single towns and individual's ages are the data or "item cases" ; but vital statistics do not begin till rates and averages are calculated, nor population statistics till curves of growth and other comparisons are instituted. The essence of the statistical approach is summarization of the numerical data, the measurement of their general value or range of value, and of their degree of variation ; and if by description is meant the mere recording of isolated and unrelated facts, the inconsequent retailing of anecdote, then statistics is *not* mere description.

"Mere description" may, however, be given a wider reference. It may, while excluding generalization and inference, yet include this numerical *summarization* that reduces masses of item cases and stray information to manageable proportions.

Even in this sense of description, works of "mere" description are often dismissed as unworthy of the attention and beneath the consideration of thinking persons. Yet under certain circumstances, I venture to submit, a wider knowledge of the facts such as statistical summaries would give is the one thing needful to change merely *thinking* persons into scientific investigators. These circumstances are all too often present in the case of English economists and political scientists.

There are certain summaries of facts such as the form of the actual distribution of wealth between classes of individuals, or the standard types of consumption of various social classes, which economists should not merely take under notice by consulting some reference book or otherwise refreshing their memories, but which they must all the time keep at the back of their heads or at least "paste in their hats." Otherwise things, often inaccurate things like equality of opportunity, will be too much taken for granted. In England taking such things for granted is peculiarly dangerous owing to the odd method of educating the class from which most economists and political scientists are drawn. Boys are deliberately segregated from girls and from their own families for eight months in the year, and owing to the expense of this education they are automatically kept apart from the sons of poorer parents. At the most impressionable ages they obtain no first-hand experience of the behaviour of half their own class or of any member of what they come to consider a lower class but which, be it remembered, constitutes at least four-fifths of England's population. Unless they have family and working-class problems and conditions described, middle-class young men may well remain in ignorance ; and should they proceed to argue deductively, introspectively, and from limited premises " out of their heads," they may not only delude themselves but lead others astray.

English classical economists preached thrift unceasingly to the working-classes in blissful ignorance of the probability (revealed in vital statistics) that savings of earnings would result in curtailment of bare necessaries in the way of food, housing, or education. English classical economists were also responsible for the idea that birth rates depended on married men's ratiocination as to their power of supporting additions to the family, and that in consequence birth rates would vary positively with increases in wages and other forms of income. The bare statistical *description* of the course of birth rates in the different classes since 1870 has been sufficient to dispose of this.

A further characteristic of the primarily classical education of the well-to-do Englishman is its attempt to make him a gentleman who shall regard a life of business activity as materialistic, sordid, and somewhat vulgar. " The average person is not interested in Industry " was the first sentence of an essay turned in to me by one fresh from a " public school." It is not surprising that Mr. Gordon Selfridge has a hard task in getting the " romance " idea of business across the English footlights.

While the perfect English gentleman should not go into business, the upright American citizen will not touch politics. Hence in one country or the other economic and political behaviour tends to be studied as an exercise in dialectic, to the neglect of the actual *modus operandi* of economic and political institutions. The behaviour of joint-stock companies and corporations, of boards of directors and factory managers, or of committees of municipal councils is left severely alone, though a statistically summarized description of their practice and experience would correct many assumptions taken for granted, and shift economics and political science from a merely speculative and rhetorical basis to a basis of fact.

Here I rest the case for mere description in the sense of summarized information about specific events. The claims of statistical method for a further extension of its frontier in the world of science are more controversial. "The theory of statistics," writes J. M. Keynes,[1] "can be divided into two parts which are for many purposes better kept distinct. The first function of the theory is purely *descriptive*. It devises numerical and diagrammatic methods by which certain salient characteristics of large groups of phenomena can be briefly described; and it provides formulæ by the aid of which we can measure or summarize the variations in some particular character which we have observed over a long series of events or instances. The second function of the theory is *inductive*. It seeks to extend its description of certain characteristics of observed events to the corresponding characteristics of other events which have not been observed. This part of the subject may be called the theory of Statistical Inference."

Let us suppose systems of piece-wage payment are under discussion. Description might consist in a statement of what amount of wages were paid for specific amounts of output under several different systems. This would be a description in the most elementary sense of a mere inventory of unrelated bits of numerical information. But description might also include a summary history of piece-wage systems, or a review of many systems in one or several industries in the form that such and such a system is the most frequent or is typical. This would be a description in the sense of a statistical summary, and for the reasons just adduced it appears to me of scientific value. But description might go further. Differences, changes, or variations in piece-wage systems may be described in conjunction with differences, changes, or variations in some other describable character such as output; and the way these two characters, wage systems and output, vary together may be " described " in a numerical expression such as a coefficient of correlation.

Though near the frontier this does not imply trespassing on the territory of inference as distinguished by Mr. Keynes. We simply note that at various factories piece-wage system A has on most days been observed to be associated with a higher output in the case of a majority of employees than system B, but nothing need be inferred as to the effects of systems A and B elsewhere and elsewhen.

Yet, though not in themselves an inductive proof, these statistical descriptions of an association or correlation are a step in induction.

[1] *A Treatise on Probability*, Chapter XXVII.

The description of the " characteristics of the observed events " may be extended to " the corresponding characteristics of other events which have not been observed," i.e. may be generalized if precautions are taken in what I shall call the statistical " field-work," and if extension of the descriptions is supported on grounds of common-sense or accepted theory, as well.

Thus if mere informative descriptions of one set of facts are not justified for their own sake, they may be justified when laid beside other such descriptiors or beside plausible theoretical conclusions for the purpose of tracing causal relationships. Few economic or political circumstances and events can have their causes explained or their results foreseen without reference to statistical descriptions of, for instance, the business cycle, or the distribution of wealth, or the age-distribution, or the distribution of personal abilities in the population, or without reference to statistical descriptions of the general trend of birth and death rates, or of the actual mechanism of governmental or industrial organization. Economics and political science study the phenomena of a variegated and fluctuating world and these phenomena cannot be understood *in vacuo*, isolated from description of their mundane context.

Hitherto I have been speaking of the function of the statistical approach in economic and political *research*. But it may be argued that though statistical method is useful in establishing the truth about phenomena and in giving the business man and the bureaucrat a technical knowledge and grasp of his material not otherwise obtainable, yet that is no reason for teaching the statistical approach in schools and universities. The deductive method of argument, it is often held, is the better training for the mind, a better mental gymnastic and discipline. Against this view I would plead that it is better for the mind to face facts and to start with accurate data than to start with assumed premises.

The assumption that all men aim to increase their incomes or wish to exercise power over others undoubtedly possess far-reaching economic and political implications, and the unfolding of such implications, other things being assumed equal, is no doubt a healthy exercise in logical ratiocination. Yet such straight-laced assumptions are inclined to inculcate " slick " thinking, instead of training the faculty for weighing evidence, for exact observation, and for systematic classification. If it is mental discipline that is wanted, generalization by collection and comparison of real cases occurring amidst the welter, complication, and uncertainty of economic and political life, is likely to entail greater mental effort than deduction from single-minded economic men or straight-thinking voters in a stationary state. Clear definitions must be framed and consistently adhered to, irrelevant circumstances distinguished from the relevant, and the *perspective* of indirectly and directly, probably and improbably, relevant factors perpetually kept in view. And when the observed cases refuse to obey a law one has confidently begun to formulate the moral qualities of honest and dispassionate self-criticism are called into play while the student learns the unreasonableness of nature, particularly human nature, which resists all his personal predilections and desires. The stern dictates of inductive science surely impose discipline enough !

If in accordance with modern educational theory, however, less stress is laid on exacting the discipline and more on eliciting the interest of the pupil, there is no question that real cases and problems falling perhaps within the personal experience of the pupil have a wider appeal than a hypothetical construction. When applied to a concrete situation the value of mathematics and logic becomes obvious even to the normal schoolboy. The function of economics and political science is to advance knowledge on matters of direct importance to human welfare ; the function of statistics and the statistical approach is to make sure that this knowledge, and the minds growing into this knowledge, are objective, realistic, and precise. The plan by which the statistical approach proposes to fulfil its functions may now be set forth.

CHAPTER II

THE STATISTICAL METHOD SET FORTH

THE aim of this treatise is constructive, and the construction is attempted mostly with existing materials and in accordance with existing plans. My main thesis is that materials are lying about, and plans are not executed owing to lack of co-operation between builder and architect, and I propose to explore the possibilities of co-operation and synthesis.

The material thus to be built with is the actual observed behaviour and reaction of individual persons, and the actual observed functioning of institutions. These particular doings and events cannot, however, lead to accurate description and generalization unless there is statistical measurement and summarization on systematic lines. The scope and close interrelation of the economic and political sciences that are to be statistically "approached" are (Chapters III and IV) set forth systematically therefore, by reference to the aspect of human behaviour, reactions, and customs upon which these sciences focus. Economics deals mainly with the terms of exchange, the stimulus of and reaction to price. Political science deals with the customary organization of compulsion but may extend to the "organization" of anything, including exchange.

The plans of the new construction are the accepted theories of economics as developed by Marshall, and the accepted analysis of comparative politics so far as such exists. These theories must be tested by the light of statistical measurement, or conversely, they may serve to interpret independent statistical summarizations. This mutual verification and interpretation, however, is checked not merely by the unfamiliarity of the theorist with statistical technique and the difficulties of handling the figures mathematically after they are obtained, but it is checked more powerfully by the difficulties of fieldwork in collecting, classifying, and applying the statistics relevantly to the problem at issue.

My object is not merely to state difficulties but also to help in their solution. Preaching and practising a consistent nomenclature I shall explain (Part II) as simply as possible, without resort to algebra, the standard mathematical technique applicable and

9

significant in the widely variable, complicated, and qualitatively differentiated doings and situations of man. The principles of classification and orientation demanded by qualitative differences and complexities will be (Part III) set forth together with the principles and precautions to be observed in representing qualities through quantitative index numbers. Finally I shall discuss statistical and non-statistical methods of causal interpretation such as isolation of factors, experiment and introspection, with a view to avoiding specific fallacies.

Thus equipped the statistical investigator may tackle (Part IV) the intricacies of economic theory, once this theory is modified in the direction of flexibility (Chapter XV) to suit statistical requirements. The statistical approach (Chapter XVI) starts from item facts but (Chapter XVII) may use established theories as plausible working hypotheses. Eventually statistically tested theories or theoretically interpretable statistics may perhaps (Chapter XVIII) be found to rest upon a solid and exact physical or psycho-physiological basis.

In political science there is no body of accepted theory but merely some functional and structural analysis, and the statistician must build up his own theories (Chapters XIX and XX) empirically by the correlation of varieties of structure, procedure, and transactions, and by the correlation of varieties of objectively distinguishable procedures such as ruling, work-sharing, and manning.

The general argument of this treatise is given in greater detail in the Table of Contents ; and cross-references to the various subjects dealt with is provided by the systematic index (Chapter XXI) which lists these subjects in the more or less logical order conventionally adopted by economic and political text-books. Finally an explanation of all the elementary statistical terms that are used will be found conveniently set forth in a glossary appearing as an appendix.

CHAPTER III

§1   *The Division of Labour in Social Research*

THE study of mankind has assumed proportions so vast that it is now attacked by specialists piecemeal, and the economist and political scientist are but two such specialists. There are many drawbacks in division of labour among those investigating social questions, yet in view of the limits to the lives, endurance, and energy of all human beings and to their very various capacities division of labour is necessary and inevitable. The practical question is how to split up the study most expediently.

The study of man may be regarded as two-dimensional. Mankind has been observed by historians " chronologically," *along* periods of time, and has also been observed sectionally *at* any one period. The first may be called the historical, evolutionary, genetic, or longitudinal view, the second the cross-sectional view.

The most obvious principle in the division of labour is that practised among the historians of specializing in one particular stretch of their longitudinal view. One authority will know all there is to know about human history in the Middle Ages ; another will take up the tale at 1485 ; another will carry on with this general history from 1815, and so on to the present time, like runners in a relay race.

But if all ages of man, all the stretches of human history, are to be apprehended in some sort of chronological order, this is humanly possible only by studying the genesis and evolution of one sort of activities or a few allied sorts. Historians who do not confine their researches to the course of events in one period, usually specialize, therefore, in one topic or subject as economic, constitutional, military historians, or as social historians or genetic sociologists.[1]

---

[1] Though the derivation of the word does not imply it, English sociology appears customarily to take the longitudinal view. It is defined as a " science occupied with the principles which underlie human society considered in a condition of development." This conception of sociology is not, however, usual in Germany or America, and the adjective genetic or evolutionary must be added when referring to the longitudinal study of general social development.

For any intensive cross-sectional view of mankind the same topical division of labour is necessary as in the longitudinal view, particularly if it is intended to compare the same activity in different cross-sections. Accordingly there is now a science of comparative politics and comparative ethics, and there are economists, jurists, military authorities all concerned with one form or a few allied forms of human activity, and that not necessarily historically but often isolated as far as possible from the accidents of time and place.

Furthermore there are some investigators of human activity particularly in primitive periods who, like archæologists, ethnologists, or philologists, confine themselves to one method of approach or one source of evidence. So few remains are left by extinct primitives, and so little conversation is possible with the primitives even when not extinct, that it is here the mere technique of collecting data that becomes a special problem. Archæologists base their theories mainly on material remains, anthropologists on actual contact with primitives, ethnologists on head-measurements and physical traits, philologists on words and speech-forms and so on. In studying primitive phases a separate science is thus formed by each distinct possible source of evidence.

Social data, in short, have been divided up between specialists on several conflicting principles :

1. According to the source and type of evidence used.

2. According to the topic ; e.g. the type of social relationship or activity studied.

3. According to the chronological epoch or phase of development ; e.g. ancient, primitive, medieval, modern.

In modern epochs or civilized phases distinguished on the third, chronological, principle, further subdivision is generally carried out according to the second or " topical " principle. Each of these special sciences looks at a different topic or aspect of human activity, has a different focus and scope, and uses all sorts of evidence at all times to throw light upon its particular topics. The characteristics and limits of the several " scopes " are not always clear, though practice is usually clearer than definition, theory, or precept. In the present chapter I propose to examine the objective marks by which topics are assembled under the scope of Economics, or distinguished as the topics of Political Science ; and to discuss the advantage to a co-ordinated social research of contracting, extending, splitting up, or amalgamating these various "scopes." In the next chapter will be examined the very real (but often academically neglected) relation of these economic and political topics to the other facts of social life appearing on the horizon of their scope.

Economics appears to be distinguished from political science in two respects :

(1) In respect of the kind of power, stimulus, or sanction propelling the human actions described.

Economic behaviour consists in voluntary exchanging, e.g. buying and selling, and is a response to things (goods, services, or money) with various prices or exchange values. It is *im*pelled and encouraged by the prospect of getting something wanted more, *in exchange* for something wanted less, and *dis*pelled and discouraged by the contrary deterrent prospect ; it is a reaction positive or negative to the sanction of the market.

Political behaviour is a response to customs, laws, and commands with various penalties attached. It is *com*pelled usually by the deterrent prospect of punishment, personal or financial. It is a reaction, usually negative, to the sanction of society or the State.

Early Victorian political science, under the inspiration of Austin, was chiefly concerned to identify the persons or body of persons possessing the ultimate power of compulsion. We need not enter into the various theories of such "sovereignty." We can admit that certain actions are compulsorily enforced, and can investigate the terms of deterrence without discussing in whom precisely (e.g. in what organs of the State) ultimate authority is vested.[1]

(2) The less consciously formulated line of separation between economics and political science is more difficult to explain, though its tacit employment has determined the actual division of social sciences to a greater extent, perhaps, than the division by sanction. While economists have concerned themselves with the immediate TERMS of voluntary exchange, i.e. what amounts of one commodity will exchange for what amounts of other commodities, political scientists have not greatly bothered about the terms of deterrence, i.e. what severity of command, what threats of what penalty will prevent what crimes or legal wrongdoings, but have specialized in the complementary question of the organization of compulsion, the question of the structure and activities of the institutions (persons or group of persons) by, through, or within which commands and compulsory powers are exercised.

These two methods of dividing up social studies are at cross-

[1] For the modern view on these matters, cf. H. J. Laski, *Grammar of Politics*, Chapter Eight, XI.

purposes. There are questions that are economic as judged by both criteria, such as the question—Why do people exchange goods at such and such prices ? There are subjects purely political as judged by both criteria, such as the question—How is the police or judicial authority appointed ? But there are other subjects of enquiry that are economic judged by one criterion, political judged by the other.

A diagram may clarify matters to those readers who can, or prefer to, visualize relationships :

TABLE IIIA

DIFFERENTIATION OF POLITICAL AND ECONOMIC SCIENCES

	The Sanction of Compulsion (Political)	The Sanction of Voluntary Exchange (Economic)
The Terms (Rates and Quantities) Involved (Economics)	1. Political Economics What are the penalties by which observance of laws is compelled and why ? (Administrative Science)	2. Economics (Pure) What are the prices and amounts at which goods and services exchange and why ?
The Organization Involved (Politics)	3. Politics (Proper) Who fixes penalties and by what acts ? (Forms of State Organization)	4. Economic Politics Who fixes prices (wages, etc.) and by what acts ? (Forms of Business Organization)

The problems placed in the two *vertical columns* marked Political and Economic follow the method of division based on the ultimate sanction. The problems placed respectively in the two horizontal rows (marked as Politics and Economics) are divided up on the second principle of distinguishing the nature of the institution and organization from the actual terms involved. Now the problems in box 3, i.e. in the political column and the political row, are clearly political, and the problems in box 2, i.e. in the economic column and the economic row, are clearly economic ; and scientific attention has tended to concentrate on these " purely " political or " purely " economic boxes. Nor is the reason for this concentration far to seek. Clearly if men observe laws and a certain code of customs, the persons or institutions who possess, or are to be entrusted with, the power of compulsion, and their precise organization, must be very carefully watched. Hence where social relations are governed by compulsion it is the institution of the governing party that requires special study, and in the political column there looms out in particular the study of the institutions of State government. The adjective political and the substantive politics are in fact generally used as equivalent to " pertaining to " and " study of " State government. But where the social relation is one of exchange no such obvious importance attaches to the constitution of either party to the exchange. It is the conditions and terms of the exchange itself that is of chief interest.

The less pressing problems of " Political Economics " that may be more easily distinguished as Administrative Science and " Economic Politics " (distinguishable as Business Organization), included in boxes 1 and 4 respectively of Table IIIA, are sometimes considered the proper study of the political, sometimes of the economic specialist, and sometimes of special specialists. The precise method of allotment would not matter if the result were merely some duplication and poaching. But in fact, parts of these territories have been almost entirely neglected, and other parts though cultivated have not been brought into fruitful and scientifically profitable relationship with contiguous territories.

§2 Political and Exchange Economics

The focal point of pure economics was taken to be the actual terms of exchange between buyers and sellers trading on a market.[1] A typical text-book of economics may contain introductory chapters, " books," or parts, defining the scope and conceptions of economics, describing the agents of production and discussing, usually only philosophically, consumption and the satisfaction of wants,[2] but there is always a general examination of Value and Exchange,[3] Distribution,[4] Money and the Mechanism of Exchange,[5] and International Trade.[6] Subsequent divisions that seem optional are Taxation,[7] Labour Problems,[8] and Industrial Organization.[9]

---

[1] Cf. my Economics and Human Behaviour, pp. 12 ff. and 52 ff., for a discussion of current but misleading definitions of the scope of economics.
[2] Taussig, Principles of Economics, Book I; Marshall, Principles of Economics, Books I–IV; J. S. Mill, Principles of Political Economy, Book I; Seligman, Principles of Economics, Part III, Book II.
[3] Marshall, Principles, Book V; Taussig, Book II; Mill, Book III, Chapters I–VI; Seligman, Part III, Book I.
[4] Marshall, Principles, Book VI; Taussig, Book V; Mill, Book II; Seligman, Part III, Book III.
[5] Marshall, Money Credit and Commerce, Books I and II; Taussig, Book III; Mill, Book III, Chapters VII–XVI; Seligman, Part III, Book IV.
[6] Marshall, Money, etc., Book III; Taussig, Book IV; Mill, Book III, Chapters XVII–XXII; Seligman, Chapter XXXII.
[7] Taussig, Book VIII; Mill, Book V.   [8] Taussig, Book VI.
[9] Taussig, Book VII; Marshall, Industry and Trade.

The division of economics universally present that is entitled *Value*, deals with the terms on which articles (goods or services) exchange in the short and long run both under conditions of competition and of monopoly, wherever the agents of production are fairly mobile. The division on *International Trade* also deals with the terms on which articles exchange, modified by supposing labour and to some extent capital to be immobile, as they actually are between different countries. *Distribution* deals not with actual distribution of wealth between individuals (still less with the delivery of goods from producer to final consumer) but with the terms of exchange for the use (during specified periods) of certain factors of production—land, labour, capital, and management. It is the value and the terms of exchange of the use of each of these factors that is discussed in separate chapters under the familiar titles rent, wages, interest, and profits, respectively.

Most of the introductory and optional divisions of an economic text-book also focus attention upon terms of exchange at least as a starting point. The divisions dealing with labour, with industrial organization, and the agents of production are interested chiefly in the economic efficiency of these " factors " or institutions ; that is in the exchange value of their output as compared with their (economic) cost. The prevailing poverty of the labourer, the limited extent of his consumption and purchasing activities, is attributed to the low exchange value of his work compared to the exchange value of the wants he may wish to satisfy. The huge profits of certain business organizations are put down to the high exchange value of their aggregate production when compared to their low costs per unit of output, reduced by the economies of the division of labour, large-scale operation, integration, etc.

Among the topics optionally discussed in economic text-books, taxation is the only one that is not contingent upon the voluntary act of exchange. Though taxes have many and interesting economic consequences, and are beloved by economists as exemplifying an easily understood form of cost with a problematical incidence, thxes are not exchange values. A realistic investigation of tax problems belongs properly to political, not exchange economics, and is discussed in §3.

The fact that economics focuses upon the act of exchange must continually be stressed, if the place and relationship of economics to other studies of human behaviour is to be understood.

Definitions of the scope of economics frequently fail to suggest that economics is a science of human behaviour. " The study of wealth " does not mention, and scarcely implies, the existence of human beings at all. And other definitions where wealth is taken not as a material good but as some state of consciousness, a form of happiness or welfare to correspond as well as to rhyme with health,[1] fail to give the idea of objective *activity* and reaction.

Now these " wealth " types of definition are no mere aberration but are symptomatic of the traditional approach to the study of economics. They start out with presumptions such that most men's dominant motive is to acquire maximum utility, or the maximum net balance of utility over disutility either in the sense of a (net) maximum of what is good for him or a maximum (net) sum of satisfaction ; and from these abstract presumptions of (enlightened or unenlightened) self-interest that consciously weighs gains against losses and is liable to reach margins of doubt, normal values and prices are " deduced " without inductive testing. The events of the market and the activity of exchanging to which, after all, actual prices and exchange-values owe their very being, tend to be looked upon as a mere automatic and uninteresting reflex of the interplay of motives and estimates of utility or disutility.

This criticism of deductive economics is a commonplace.[2] But curiously enough the leading critics of orthodox economics fall a prey to the same phantasmagoria when they omit to observe actual behaviour. There are descriptions by J. A. Hobson of the conditions underlying business activity, that must make manufacturers rub their eyes in wonder at their own efficiency and at the joyous simplicity of running to capacity.[3] And these supposed conditions are made the basis of precise deductions and a complete new system of Economics, that is quite as old-fashioned as any orthodox theory in its failure to emphasize values and prices as an outcome of a peculiar form of human behaviour called exchanging.

The aspect of human behaviour seen by " Political Economics " (box 1 of Table IIIA) is analogous to the pure economic aspect. The focus of Political Economics is the same question of the relative terms of stimulus and reaction. The terms are not relative prices, but the relative terms of the penalty stimulus compelling men to observe laws and customs and to react within their bounds.

If the compulsion to observe laws and customs by penalizing violations of them consisted in deterring men by exacting or inflicting various amounts of money in fines, or so many days' detention

---

[1] E. Cannan, *Wealth*, Chapter I.

[2] And I shall not pursue the matter here. Those unfamiliar with the method of deductive economics and the criticisms levelled against it may be referred to my *Economics and Human Behaviour*, esp. §§1 and 2.

[3] Hobson, *Free Thought in the Social Sciences*, e.g. p. 120.

in prison (longer or shorter " terms ") or so many stripes, or so much hard labour, an exact political parallel could be obtained to the economic scale or schedule of prices. Comparatively early in its existence society thought out a complicated tariff of penalties in terms of one kind of penalty only, to take the place of the life for a life, eye for an eye, principle which involved (among other inconveniences) payments in more than one set of terms. The Anglo-Saxon system of wergild, for instance, commuted all possible forms of penalty (death, mutilation, torture, etc.) into terms of monetary fines only.

" The amount of the Wergild varied, according to a graduated scale, with the rank of the person slain. For a ceorl it was fixed at 200 shillings ; for a lesser theyn, 600 shillings ; for a King's theyn 1200 shillings. The wer of an ealdorman was double that of a King's theyn ; that of an Atheling three times, that of a King usually six times as much. For bodily injuries a bot was payable, being highest in amount where any disfigurement ensued."[1]

" Every man's life had its value, and according to that valuation the value of his oath in the courts of justice varied, and offences against his protection and person were atoned for."[2]

The modern German States seem to have kept up these exact and relentless but uniform terms of *quid pro quo* in compelling observance of laws ; and an investigation of local police court reports in England would probably demonstrate customary penalties for venal offences such as speeding, riding without lights, cheeking policemen, etc., along a single scale of fines or terms of imprisonment.

When men are to be deterred from more severe crimes the penalties are of different kinds and along a number of different scales, and the system is analogous to economic bartering in kind, rather than a money economy where the stimuli to sell are all of one kind.

There is, to begin with, the distinction between direct punishments by the State as a result of a criminal suit, and damages or reparation obtained by the plaintiff as a result of a (successful) civil suit. Sidgwick did not think the difference fundamental,[3] however. Both procedures are used as a stimulus to what the modern psychologist would call a negative reaction, i.e. non-repetition of the unlawful (civilly or criminally actionable) behaviour, and in some cases the mere enforcement of reparation may be

---

[1] Taswell–Langmead, *English Constitutional History*, Chapter I.
[2] Stubbs, *Constitutional History of England*, Vol. I, Chapter VI.
[3] *Elements of Politics*, Chapters VIII and IX.

adequate for purposes of prevention. Secondly, the preventive measures adopted in a modern State are of different kinds. Exile (unless the victim is an alien), outlawry, or ostracism is no longer legally resorted to ; but in the punishment of crimes the State still uses physical punishment ranging from birching to the extreme capital punishment of death, imprisonment with or without hard labour, money fines, and surveyance.[1]

But judicial precedent and penology, "the science concerned with the processes devised and adopted for the repression and prevention of crime," has ranked these various kinds of penalties in some sort of order of deterrence as degrees along one scale of severity. Jurisprudence in fact frankly distinguishes some classes of crimes, as torts and felonies, merely according to the severity of the penalty meted out.

What severity of penalty will balance what severity of wrong-doing or crime, may be, and has been, excogitated by deductive political science in much the same way as deductive economics speculates about the equilibrium of prices.

If the human calculator familiar to theoretical economics is also assumed here, these pains and penalties should " on principle " be so adjusted that they are *just* severe enough to deter all men from committing the crime or wrong at that " price." If a more realistic view is taken and wide variability admitted in resistance to temptation among different individual persons, the principle may be stated as so to fit punishment to the crime that all but the habitual or hopeless criminal is deterred. Otherwise, the stimulus may be much *more* severe than is necessary to secure law-abiding reaction among normally constituted persons.

Such were the principles on which Jeremy Bentham worked out his legal systems,[2] and which found vent in the Workhouse Test of the 1834 Poor Law. Life in the Workhouse was to be *just* so unpleasant that all but those genuinely unable to find work, even at starvation wages, should be deterred from entering. A passage or two from Sidgwick's *Elements of Politics* is worth quoting as an illustration of the utilitarian method of reasoning from set principles.

" It is a difficult matter to determine satisfactorily the right degree of punishment for any given offence. It is easy to say, with Bentham, that it ought to be sufficient to deter, and not more than sufficient.

[1] " In Britain during the year 1922, 572 persons were flogged or whipped, 32,049 persons were sentenced to imprisonment or penal servitude, 416,025 were fined and 30,363 kept under surveyance either in schools and institutions or under recognizances or on probation." *Howard Journal*, April, 1925.
[2] *Theory of Legislation*, Penal Code, Part Third ; esp. Chapter II, " Proportion between Offences and Punishments."

But our general knowledge of the variations in human circumstances and impulses would suggest—what experience amply confirms—that no punishment whatever can be relied upon to be adequately deterrent in all cases. Murder and manslaughter, burglary and larceny, have continued to harass society through all changes in the allotment of punishment; and no change is likely to put an end to them. Now, impulsive crimes we cannot hope to prevent by any intensification of punishment until human nature is fundamentally altered : but crimes planned in cold blood are matters of calculation, and it does not seem impossible that it should be made unmistakably a man's interest, on a cool calculation of chances, not to commit a crime. Since, however, the attainment of this result depends not only on the amount of punishment, but also on the chances that the criminal (1) will be caught, and (2) will be condemned if caught, it may easily happen that in a community where the police is ill-organized, and the judges liable to be corrupt or inefficient, the required adjustment of interests cannot be effected : the uncertain chance of the maximum punishment which humanity admits may not be enough to outweigh the prospective profit of the crime. For the same reason, in societies where similar governmental defects exist in a less degree, an increase in the efficiency of the police and judicature will often enable intensity of punishment to be reduced without increasing crime.

" The difficulty of adjusting amount of punishment to gravity of offence, in a manner adapted to meet all variations in human nature and its circumstances, affords a strong argument for increasing heavily the severity of punishment at each repetition of any kind of deliberate crime : since the fact that a man, after suffering the punishment of an offence committed in cold blood, proceeds to commit another offence of the same kind, is tolerably conclusive evidence that in his particular case the punishment already inflicted was not sufficiently deterrent." ...

" Avoidance of excess in punishment is important, not only in order to inflict no more pain than is needed—which, of course is to be aimed at from a utilitarian point of view—but even more in order that different degrees of punishment may all be adequately deterrent, where the criminal has choice of alternatives of crimes, differing in degree of mischievousness. It is of fundamental importance that a man should always have adequate motive to refrain from committing each successive part of any possible complex offence ; or a greater offence instead of a lesser. Punishment, therefore, should be so chosen that clearly greater punishments may be allotted to more mischievous crimes.

" This is one argument for attaching capital punishment to murder alone : so that (e.g.) the thief or burglar may have an adequate inducement not to commit murder even when it would give him an additional chance of getting off."[1]

The parallel should not be missed between weighing an uncertain chance of punishment against " the prospective profit of the crime," and the calculations of the economist's entrepreneur as to his chance of gain and normal profits.

The economist argues that the possible gains of the entrepreneur

[1] Sidgwick, *Elements of Politics*, Chapter VIII, pp. 122–4.

who risks capital must outweigh his losses to such an extent that the average of net gain (from losses and gains combined) is considerably greater than a normal interest on safely invested capital, plus a normal remuneration for management.[1] Similarly the political scientist argues that a penalty must involve a considerably greater loss on the criminal or wrongdoer generally when he is caught or detected than the extent to which he is likely to gain on the average. Where, for instance, the crime is theft of property or evasion of taxes, the penalty, falling on those detected, of a pecuniary fine unaccompanied by any significant disapproval among those with whom the criminal mixes, must on principle be very much greater than the amount stolen or withheld.

Consideration of further refinements in such checks and balances excogitated by the Benthamites must be omitted. We are merely concerned to establish : (1) that there exists a group of problems analogous to economic problems of price, centring on the question what amount of deterrence is exercised or threatened by government to obtain a given degree of performance or observance of laws or customs by individual persons ; and (2) that this group of problems has hitherto only been attacked by the methods, so familiar in economics, of deducing " principles " from psychological assumptions of man's reasonableness and enlightened calculation. This method is, however, being questioned in Political Economics or Administrative Science much as it is in pure economics. Human Nature in Politics[2] certainly calculates still less on general principles of utility and cost than does Human Nature in Economics.

It was questioned by Sidgwick himself whether *crimes passionelles* are much deterred by the severity of the penalty, and it is questionable whether even professional burglars and pickpockets coldly calculate and weigh the penalty if they are detected, against the probable amount of " swag " they can get away with if not detected. The picture of Bill Sikes vaccillating on the *margin of doubt* whether to burgle and take a risk or stay safely at home is perhaps a little thin. The need for inductive investigation of the conditions of legal " right and wrongdoing " is just as strong as in the case of economic activities ; and police statistics, judicial statistics, the " overt " acts so dear to lawyers, and many fiscal enumerations are ready to hand, to help in forming generalizations of scientific value.

---

[1] See below, Chapters VII and XVIII.
[2] Graham Wallas' book with this title was perhaps the first to introduce this scepticism, current among psychologists and practical politicians, to the notice of academic political science.

In pure economics the data are (or should be) facts actually observed or anticipations of facts actually elicited. Similarly the data of political economics (or administrative science) are (or should be) the amounts or intensities of the punishments actually imposed or actually expected, and the actual extent of observance of the law that this degree of imposition (overt or expected) stimulates.[1] Political, like Exchange Economics, should, in short, observe people's actual reactions in relation to the actual stimulus of any situation.

§3   *Scope of Political Economics as Administrative Science*

There have been several lines of human activity hitherto appropriated for study by pure Economics, which are more easily approached through a political science including within its purview both the administrative and organizational problems connected with the exercise of the compulsory sanction.[2] This false assignment prevails, for example, in certain branches of Public Finance.

The study of Public Finance, central and local, is usually taken to include the investigation of problems connected with the following public activities:

I. The Raising of State Revenue.

A. By State trading, i.e. by the State participating in the production of articles for exchange.

B. By taxation, and loans ultimately paid for out of taxation.

II. The Expenditure of State Revenue.

A. Productive: i.e. ultimately to increase the trading revenue of the State.

B. Non-productive, as grants and bounties paid for out of tax revenue.

Now economics can deal with the problems of the terms of State-trading. When the State is engaged in producing, buying, or selling goods and services on the ordinary market (activities IA and IIA), the State government is subject to the same conditions as competitive or monopolistic private traders. But taxation (activity IB) is " the compulsory expropriation and forced payment for advantages not necessarily accruing to the taxed person," and in spite of their almost universal inclusion in economic text-books taxational activities are politically sanctioned and must be studied as such (and placed in boxes 1 and 3 of Table IIIA). At least three of the four

---

[1] E.g. the data of Table XIXA, Chapter XIX.
[2] A political science covering the left half of Table IIIA.

maxims or canons of taxation enunciated by Adam Smith are of the exact Political Economic, i.e. Administrative Science type. They plead for convenience, certainty, and economy in collection and their purport is mainly administrative efficiency, to avoid impracticability, friction, evasion, and non-observance of the law.

The essential condition of taxation is not the voluntary exchange of goods and services, but the fact that governments compel payments from individuals without necessarily giving them personally any utility in exchange. In the title of his chief work Ricardo distinguished the *Principles of Political Economy* AND *Taxation*, and most of the leading writers on taxation, though often adopting divergent definitions of their subject, agree in excluding taxation from the scope of economics proper,[1] together with other branches of Public Finance. The argument need not therefore be elaborated. It is only when taxation or expenditure out of taxes (e.g. grants and bounties), or when loans made in anticipation of taxes affect, say, the distribution of wealth, or when taxes, bounties, or loans affect exchange values or the conditions underlying exchange values, e.g. by restricting consumption or production just as any other cost might, that economists, as such, can evolve theories of "incidence," "shifting," "the discouragement of saving," "dynamic effects," and so forth.[2]

Taxation is the non-trading revenue of government, and its converse, the non-trading expenditure of governments, is also a question for political science, rather than for economics. The money forcibly collected issues in grants to encourage or compel something to be done that would not be impelled by mere exchange, but which the community wants to have performed. Museums are maintained by the State and by municipalities though the fees charged do not cover expenses and private enterprise would fail to reap any profit thereby. And obviously the poor have to be relieved, if at all, without *their* giving anything in exchange.

[1] "The science of finance is indeed in one sense a part of economics, but in another and better sense a quasi-independent science. The attempt to treat the problems of finance in a few chapters at the end of a treatise on economics, as do most of the English works, is bound to be unsatisfactory in the extreme." E. R. A. Seligman, *Principles of Economics*, Preface to the Fourth Edition.

See also Bastable, *Public Finance*, Introduction, I, §7. Bastable adds a footnote to the effect that examination of the treatises of Rau, Roscher, Wagner, and Cohn support his statement. "The financial sections of the treatises . . . are in fact independent works, and may be studied quite apart from the other sections."

[2] For an economic treatment of taxation, i.e. the effect of taxation on the National Dividend—a sum of exchange values—see Pigou, *Public Finance*.

Similarly there is no question of voluntary exchange under any system (such as was possibly the full communism[1] of the earlier Bolshevik regime) where goods are so rationed[2] that each individual is given a specified amount according to his physiological or other needs, and no transfer is permitted between individuals. If exchange is not allowed and does not occur, no exchange value can actually emerge and there is no material for the economist to work upon. If he revolts against a communistic world that revolutionizes his science, the economist does so not as a scientist, but emotionally as one imprecates a faithless mistress. Self-effacement either quietly or, if he feels he must protest, by some sort of *hara-kiri*, is the more dignified course.

The universal proscription of voluntary exchange is not, however, likely to occur among the bourgeois states of our generation. All the practical schemes for nationalization that have been mooted still require, by the variety of sanctions and forms of organization they propose, the co-operation of the pure economist with the political economist (of administrative science) and with the political scientist proper.

Political Science proper would be concerned with the form of organization of the controlling body whether a department of State, a semi-public corporation, a committee of a municipal council, or a regulated company.[3] Pure economics would be involved in so far as the trading principle were adopted, but in so far as national services were performed compulsorily, or revenue was obtained by compulsory taxation and the services provided free to consumers, questions of administrative science or political economics would be raised. Important work such as road-making, education, or relief of the poor cannot be " met " by charging a price to individual consumers even in a developed individualistic society such as ours. Here there are no " prices " or exchange-values to hand, but that is no reason for neglecting the scientific investigation of the comparative *efficiency* of various kinds and amounts of penalty, in moving men to perform or finance (to various amounts) those important social activities and services.

---

[1] Prof. Gustav Cassel uses " Communism " in this precise sense. *Theory of Social Economy*, Chapter III, §11.

[2] The rationing system adopted for certain articles by capitalist countries during the late war merely fixed maximum amounts for each individual. Within these limits each individual could voluntarily buy or sell what amounts he chose.

[3] The great variety of possible forms of State control are discussed in Chapter XX, §7.

§4 *The Scope and Importance of Economic Politics*

The neglect accorded to Political Economics or Administrative Science has also been meted out to Economic Politics, the study of business and industrial organizations, but in the body of this treatise, particularly Chapters XIX and XX, the institutions and societies between or within which exchange is effected will be duly analysed and statistically approached.

Scientific investigation is here concerned not as in pure Economics with the kinds and amounts of stimulus actuating men's various kinds and intensities of behaviour, but with forms of behaviour itself. This behaviour is not merely to be casually alluded to as the inevitable condition or consequence of normal economic motives, but must be described in detail and accurately summed up as of lively interest in itself, and of the utmost importance in any economics pretending to analyse exchange-values in specific markets.

The old-fashioned economist's habit of describing the actions of groups of human beings in the *passive* voice or in the third person singular, and NEUTER at that, is symptomatic of his nebulous ideas as to the actual organization and procedure of economic institutions.[1] Students of economics are so infected by this mechanistic view that a certain proportion allude fairly regularly in examinations to the *automatic* breeding of the working-classes, usually as an example of the delicate (and fortunate) adjustments of supply to demand in this, our well-equilibrated world. Again, who is it that actually changes the price of any article when it is changed ? On the organized stock and produce exchanges the actual process of fixing and changing prices is fairly obvious, and so it is at a sale by auction ; but the process is not clear when the article passes or has passed through the hands of merchants, wholesale and retail, as most articles do before reaching the final consumer. And the person or persons who have the initiative in adjusting retail prices in shops are probably very different when the article is monopolized or is a proprietary article, than when it is a " staple " article produced competitively. But this important and interesting type of information is not usually vouchsafed in economic text-books. The usual wording is that " prices are fixed " or " are determined," etc., not that " So-and-so decides or would probably decide to change prices." " When people talk about supply and demand," says Keynes in his *Scope and Method*, " they sometimes forget that these are themselves phenomena depending upon human will."

[1] Some political scientists fall into a similar cliché when they vaguely allude to social " movements " without realizing that it is men and women who are moving and moved.

Supply and demand refer to a certain body of actual or potential "suppliers and demanders," persons whose human vagaries may very effectively modify events. The supply of cash in the hands or stocking of a miser is no supply economically, and a business organization may not always adjust supply to demand on the approved model of the alert business man. "Consulting experts in business organization testify," we are told,[1] "that practically every large concern they enter is honeycombed with prejudices, jealousies, and cliques which must be analysed and taken account of before purely efficiency measures can be suggested."

The more enlightened economic text-book of to-day is usually introduced with a detailed survey of economic institutions, such as large-scale production, vertical and horizontal combination,[2] monopolistic combines and trusts; and reasons are given for supposing size, combination, and monopoly to make—or not to make—for efficiency and economy.[3] And wherever economic theory has been most successful it will usually be found that account has been taken of the relevant institutional factors. The operations of the banking system, the money market, and the stock and produce exchanges usually have chapters or at least paragraphs devoted to them in the body of economic text-books; and the existence, organization, and activities of these institutions is admitted to affect prices. As a result the economic interpretation of the terms offered and accepted by banks, financial houses, stock-jobbers, etc., is often convincing, and is even occasionally read and listened to by the business men concerned.

Recently under the stimulus of Mr. and Mrs. Sidney Webb and of Mr. G. D. H. Cole the organization of Trade Unions has also been noticed. In their classical work *Industrial Democracy*, the Webbs consider Trade Unions under the main headings: Structure (Part I), Function (Part II), and Theory (Part III). The "theory" is largely a question of economic consequences, but structure and function are words that are, of course, familiar in the analysis of the political State.[4]

---

[1] Z. C. Dickinson, *Economic Motives*, p. 12. This certainly agrees with my own somewhat limited experience of large business organizations.

[2] E.g. Taussig, *Principles of Economics*, Book I; Clay, *Economics for the General Reader*.

[3] Taussig, *Principles*, Book VII. Marshall, *Industry and Trade*, Book III. This study of the "Protean" shapes of modern trade combinations and monopolies was not published till 1920, however, some thirty years after the first appearance of Marshall's *Principles*.

[4] Terms like structure and function borrowed from physiology have often suggested fatuous political analogies. For instance, "No body can be healthful without exercise, neither natural body nor politic; and certainly to

As a result of the application of this political analysis to the working-class movement, the new theory of wages is no longer a mere skeleton or apparatus of thought, but classifies and considers the effect upon wages, salaries, and terms of employment of actual working-class (and professional class) practices such as restriction of entry and the collective bargain. The terms of the wage bargain, and of fees too, are no longer considered as automatically settled by quasi-mechanical forces, but account is taken of the effect of organization in changing bargaining power, and of the effect of social institutions in controlling the supply or demand of labour and skill of various grades.

The most glaring omission in economic text-books, as far as economic organization or politics is concerned, appears to be the absence of any study of the ordinary species of industrial organization. The business firm and its satellite factory or factories are connected institutions that are taken for granted, yet it is they who usually exercise such organized authoritative control as does exist within the competitive industrial system. This absence of any quasi-political analysis of industrial organization accounts, I think, for much of the obscurantism and vague aspiration of economists' contribution to the problem of industrial control.[1]

An industry consists usually of numerous businesses or firms, and each firm may possess several factories. But it is the firm that controls and effects a combination of definite amounts of capital, management, and labour. Productive Associations, Co-operative Production, or Co-partnership schemes attempt to obtain labour, capital, and management to some extent from the same class of

a Kingdom or estate a just and honourable war is the true exercise." Or this from Rousseau's *Contrat Social* (II, iv.) : " Comme la nature donne à chaque homme un pouvoir absolu sur tous ses membres, le pacte social donne au corps politique un pouvoir absolu sur tous les siens." And even when free of physiological implication, the word function, in particular, is used in political science in a confusing number of different senses (See Chapter XIX §1). The word is apparently indispensable, but strict watch must be kept over its use.

[1] Two distinct types of Industrial Control are often confused : so-called Market Control where prices and amounts exchanged are " determined " by circumstances, by the higgling of buyers and sellers ; and organized authoritative control *within an organization* such as the firm or factory, where prices and output are " determined " by somebody's " fiat " though always with reference of course to cost of production or conditions of the market. The use of the verb determine for both types of control appears to be a source of further confusion among laymen, if not among professed economists ; and economists have already seen the necessity of distinguishing internal from external economies according as these are determined within the organization or by outside circumstances such as the localization in the same town of plants controlled by different organizations.

persons ; but under the " capitalist " English joint-stock company, or American corporation, these three " factors of production " are usually provided by different groups of people. Two of these groups find a representation WITHIN the organization through the Board of (managing) Directors and the General Meeting of (capitalist) shareholders ; but the fact that the third group (labour) is left to organize itself if at all OUTSIDE the firm (in Trade Unions, etc.) gives rise to the likelihood of trouble and is of the utmost political interest.

Political analysis applied to the industrial firm would focus first upon the SIZE of the firm as measured by the number of persons employed, or possibly the amount of the Capital invested, or the values of the output per year[1] ; and the CONSTITUTION of that firm as measured by the number of its local operating units—shops or plants or factories. Size and constitution may be considered structural or morphological questions. The firm is formed of so many factories and individual persons as the animal body is of so many organs, limbs, or bones.

Let us in this introductory outline neglect the functioning of the *firm* and proceed to the structure and function of the constituent local factories of which the firm is found to be formed.[2]

The events of a political nature that I see in a factory are, first, a number of persons of different antecedents, age, sex, or race associated in a " going concern." The acts of some of these persons mark them out as a managing, governing, or ruling staff (a hierarchy of managers, superintendents, and foremen) issuing orders ; the usual behaviour of the other persons consists, more or less, in carrying out those orders. These persons I also see in groups of specialized occupations acting in co-operation. I observe, in short, item acts of co-ordinated and co-operative behaviour on the part of individual members of an organization. The political aspect of the factory also exhibits individual men joining and others leaving the organization. Though the organization may be the same, the " personnel " is continually changing, there is continual wastage and continual recruitment and " manning." Some men stay on, their tenure of office is long ; others stay but a brief while and if they are in the majority, one may consider the factory group as only loosely associated and as lacking in " stability." And even when men have joined the society or organization constituted by

[1] Cf. Chapter V §3, X §1.
[2] The organization of the firm is too complicated to use as an introductory illustration of the statistical approach. It is discussed at length in Chapters XIX and XX.

the factory, it does not follow that men will always attend. There are scheduled times for foregathering and mustering, but there may be individual persons who do not observe the schedule, who do not man the plant from day to day. They attend irregularly, absent themselves, or " lose time."

The political view of a factory can now be summed up and pushed further with the help of the physical parallel. The enumeration (which can often be statistical in form) of the number and types of members in the organization (its SIZE), and of the various hierarchical and co-operating groups of parties (the CONSTITUTION of the organization), may be called a question of MORPHOLOGY or STRUCTURE. But the more interesting questions politically are FUNCTIONAL : (1) the mutual interaction of the several hierarchical parties, the process or procedure of ruling or management, issuing and observing orders ; (2) the mutual activity of co-operation between the various occupational parties, the vertical or horizontal division of labour, the degree of gangwork or combination of labour, etc. ; (3) the movement of men in and out of the organization and their attendance. A close physical parallel to these three questions of human interactions and mutual behaviour, though it proves nothing, may illustrate the distinction : (1) the control of the body by the nervous system ; (2) the specialization of function between the several bodily members ; and (3) metabolism and the ingestion and excretory system. These three questions may thus be grouped as questions of *physiology* as against *anatomy ;* the answers to such questions would describe the *functioning* of the factory organization as against its structure.

But a further group of questions come into view, which the word FUNCTION, though not FUNCTIONING, often includes. I refer to the action of the organization as a whole towards the outside world. This distinction, most important, as we shall see, in all social research, is brought out in a mechanical metaphor by the distinction between the (inner) mechanism of a machine and the external work the machinery accomplishes. The group of persons known as a factory are up against more or less intractable material conditions which may, for instance, inflict accidental injuries upon them, and they are up against external social conditions and restrictions. The work of the group consists in producing or carrying through (in spite of these material and social conditions outside the group[1]) various kinds and quantities of output, services, or transactions.

---

[1] If we are considering a system of factories controlled by one " multicellular " firm, the external conditioning society of any one factory is that firm, and the factory's external social relations or transactions are largely

Now the immediate aim of the political scientist looking at
factory organization is to describe and compare the representative
types and varieties of factory structure, of factory functioning
(manning—ruling—co-operating) and of " external " factory work
or transactions ; and the practical value of the analysis of the
behaviour of a factory group into these several " functions "
(functionings) and transactions is, that it allows him to compare
the *alternate* types and varieties of each of such functions.   One
variety of ruling cannot usefully be compared with one variety of
co-operation ; there must be a comparison of like but alternative
activities and policies.   This " functional " analysis is thus a
necessary step in all comparative politics.   It should be followed
by functional synthesis.   The political scientist of industry should
look for representative combinations of the alternate varieties of
factory structure and work, with alternate ways of manning, ruling,
and co-operating within a factory.   If found comparatively frequently, these combinations may be considered compound types
or systems of organization.

Is a combination of a system of many factories each of large size,
low labour turnover, paternalistic " staff," rather " functional "
rule, and highly developed division of labour, typical in the work
of making standardized motor cars sold in open market ?   Is, in
short, the Ford organization a representative type or tending to
become so ?   Or is there no discernible type and merely equally
frequent varieties ?   Or to take the singly controlled farm whose
size is small, and where labour turnover and absence are low, rule
customary rather than authoritative, and division of labour rare.
Does this farm constitute a predominant type in agriculture, or
merely one of several equally frequent varieties ?   These are the
sort of questions that a science of industrial organization should
answer, and can answer largely by means of statistical summarization.

For the depiction of the structure, functioning (mechanism), and
transactions (work) of typical factories much useful statistical
material is ready to hand.   Inventories or censuses are taken at

identical with the firm's inner relations or functioning. This methodological
conception is fundamental to any political analysis, but is difficult. It is
developed at greater length in Chapters XIX and XX.

The factory is ruled by the firm and is one of the co-operating parties of
the firm. If it were the firm itself that was under consideration, its external
social relations or transactions would chiefly consist in exchange activities on
the market, selling various kinds of products or services to customers, and
buying, probably from producers of raw material. It is this very point that
the factory is part of an organization engaged in exchanges, that makes the
study of the factory group one of *economic* politics.

given times of the total number and sorts of men and women employed in individual factories or in industry as a whole,[1] and the proportion is found in which they are distributed among the various hierarchical ranks, grades of skill, or occupations.[2] Continuous records are kept of accidents that occur to the personnel, of the persons moving into and out of employment (i.e. records of labour turnover), and of the time lost by absence of persons in employment. Many material conditions and events are also measurable, and often measured. There are uniform units on which to reckon such as the common economic denominator of money, and in modern large-scale production there are often standard outputs, standard conditions, and files of standardized records of the *matériel* no less than the *personnel*.[3] If we are dealing with more than one factory or firm there are numbers of similar businesses where behaviour must, and can be, averaged or segregated into distinct varieties and types,—where acts recur in some kind of sequence ; and these typical courses of behaviour may be associated or correlated with the types of transaction, the kinds of industry and trades, in which the business is engaged.

From the standpoint of the purely economic or administrative science, the most interesting features of a factory are the various inducements offered that succeed in getting a certain proportion of men to sign on and to stay, to attend punctually, to be trained, and to carry out orders, e.g. producing various quantities of output of standard quality with a minimum of accidents. Statistics of labour turnover, lost time, output, and accidents may be regarded as reactions to stimuli acting through the human factor's fatigue and unrest, and may be taken as tests of the efficiency of stimuli such as higher wages, expenditure on welfare work, cost of improved ventilation, etc. etc. That is how such statistics were mainly used in my *Economics of Fatigue and Unrest*. But the standpoint of political science, apart from its administrative side, looks beyond this relation between stimuli and reactions. Its focus is always upon the organization of the persons who are offering stimuli or reacting thereto, and in this case it is upon the structure, functioning (mechanism), and work of the factory personnel. The behaviour appearing as the " functioning " of the factory is the manning of the organization, the managing of the men, and their division of the labour among themselves ; and statistics are available to

---

[1] E.g. Table VA.
[2] E.g. Florence, *Economics of Fatigue and Unrest*, Table 2.
[3] Chapters XIII and XIV op. cit. are devoted to standard forms of record for these purposes.

measure types and varieties of these three sorts of functioning as well as types and varieties of structure and work.

To sum up. The common species of industrial firm or factory, though it lies at the very heart of the industrial system, has not received the close political analysis accorded to the State, and more recently to the Trade Unions and to combination of firms. This outline of a systematic study of industrial organization was worth developing therefore for its own sake as tracing the most important branch of " economic politics." But it was developed also to illustrate the connection and affinities between the sciences (as I see them) of economic politics and politics proper (i.e. State organization) on the one hand, and the science of political economics (i.e. State administration) on the other.

In all these disciplines three rules prescribe the matter and method of investigation.

First, it is the overt, visible, audible, acts of men, the actual facts, events, utterances, or elicited expectations which we observe. In political science proper, it is particularly difficult to escape from a paper constitution or a law that may be a dead-letter, and to attain to the real activities and expectations of man and the real facts of his situation. A reading of legal documents must not take the place of the reading of Blue-books that show the extent to which laws " work," nor can it replace actual experience, questioning, and observation on the spot. In the factory it is much easier to focus without distraction upon the actual individual behaviour of individual persons. And it is the individual person who is the " atom " of political science.

Secondly, the study of factory behaviour illustrates in a simple way how individual acts may be classified according to their functional part in the general organization, so that alternative varieties of the same kind of function can be usefully compared.

Finally, the study of an institution of which there are numerous instances all varying to some extent in their characteristics, obviously requires the use of statistics in depicting simple and compound types, or predominant varieties. Though statistics are helpful in describing typical combinations of the antecedents and opinions[1] of members of a constitutional State government, yet we can hardly hope to obtain a " typical " European State[2] as we do

---

[1] Table IXB, Chapter IX.

[2] Though I notice " Factors determining the extent of popular participation in elections in typical European States " as a project for research originating in Chicago.

a representative firm or factory. In short, the extension of political science to the mundane affairs of everyday organization, together with behaviour as the focus, and a functional classification for comparative purposes, leads inevitably to a statistical form of enquiry.

CHAPTER IV

§1 *Political, Economic, and Social Behaviour*

THE focus and scope of the economic and political sciences which are to be statistically approached are now defined. These sciences investigate the terms and organization of compulsory enforcement and of exchange. Exchange and enforcement are simply activities, ways of behaviour, of certain persons, groups or societies of persons ; but there are groups of persons with social activities and " ways of behaving " other than exchange and enforcing.

Most men and women are not conscious when they are doing something economic, or when something political, or when something that is neither one nor the other. Their doings and activities of all sorts (however academically distinguishable) are thoroughly mixed up and intricately bound together. Their political and economic activities, if any, will be affected by their " other " social activities, and these " other " social activities will in turn affect their own or other people's political and economic activity. In this treatise, in short, political and economic activities have been somewhat arbitrarily selected for study, and this selection by no means exhausts the possible social activities of the community when social is used in the widest sense of the word.

Familiar social institutions and organizations that do not use or involve either the sanction of compulsion or that of exchange are the church, the family, smart Society with a big S, convivial and political clubs and parties, and even business organizations when a spirit of goodwill, emulation, and " jollying along " reigns within.

The sanctions or stimuli exercised in these institutions are positive and negative. They consist of encouragements as well as discouragements : approval or disapproval by one's " set " and the fear of being ostracized and cut, or if one merely commits a *faux pas*, laughed at ; the feeling of duty done, or the sense of sin and the fear of hell-fire and other religious deterrents from twinges of conscience to papal excommunication ; the incentive of honour with its various degrees from fame and glory through mediocre respectability to *dis*honour and self-abasement ; the stimulus (positive and negative) of reciprocal relationship with one's fellows,

INTERRELATIONS 35

also felt in various degrees from active power over others through degrees of mutual co-operation[1] to servitude.

The optative, moralistic mood is specifically (Chapter I) excluded from our scientific attitude. The word moral may therefore be used in its original sense, as in Moral Science, to refer to these socially exercised yet non-political and non-economic sanctions.

The word social is also applied to all kinds of human doings and activities whether these have anything or nothing to do with organizations and sanctions, political, economic, or moral. The " Social " history that is now read, even in British public schools, as a sort of antidote to the text-book " histories " about the schemes, gestures, and fates of those economically, politically, morally, or otherwise powerful, refers to the lives and doings of plain, ordinary, average men.

But the organization of exchange, and *a fortiori* political organization, occupies only a small part, if any, of the time of ordinary plain men and women. They are not as a rule engaged in the organization of anything either by political, economic, moral, or other means.

Psycho-physiologically, man and woman have certain elementary needs and wants ; they indulge in sexual and social intercourse and consume clothes, houses, fuel, and food to satisfy their several wants. Civilized man, primitive or modern, embroiders upon these wants and cultivates the arts, decorative, æsthetic, technical, and social. He develops education, knowledge, culture ; standards of cleanliness, hygiene, comfort, and leisure ; and codes of etiquette, manners, (positive) morality and (substantive) law governing the various mutual relations of individual members of the community as such.

Social customs, actual " fare " or modes of life, standards of living, technical and artistic achievements remain to be investigated, therefore, quite apart from the various forms of organization and the various sanctions through which, or in spite of which, this civilization may have been achieved.

It is evident that if certain social activities are to be labelled political and economic and placed in special boxes, shelves, at least, must be provided in the same cabinet on which to lay all these *other*, closely connected social doings.

In Table IVA I have sketched the design of such a cabinet. The four boxes of Table IIIA remain in the same relative position ; but between boxes 1 and 2, containing facts about the terms of

---

[1] There is also the alternative middle ground of complete independence. Some people, like the Miller of Dee, " Who sang from morn till night, I care for nobody, no not I, and nobody cares for me," appear to prefer the absence of any degree of social reciprocity.

the political and economic sanctions, lies a shelf conveniently numbered 1½ to contain data about the terms of other sanctions ; the non-economic non-compulsory "moral" incentives, motives, and impulses to act. And between boxes 3 and 4, containing facts about the political organization of the State and facts about the organization of industries, businesses, and markets lies a shelf conveniently numbered 3½ to contain data about the organization of societies using only "moral" pressure. Below this no separate boxes are arranged. There is simply one long shelf numbered 5 to contain facts about the non-political, non-economic social customs and technical achievements of civilized man. Each shelf with the boxes (if any) on the same tier may be referred to as a "horizon" or "level."

Now I am inclined, for scientific purposes, to place more importance on the distinction between the horizontal level of any social activity than on the vertical division (by boxes and shelves) to which the activity may belong. I shall refer to the three levels hitherto distinguished, as (I) that of the sanction level with boxes and shelves 1, 1½, 2, or, since economics is here the leading type of science, the quasi-economic level ; as (II) that of the organization level, with boxes and shelves 3, 3½, 4, or (since political science is the predominant type) the quasi-political level ; and as (III) the level of positive, substantive, achievement and civilization, the purely sociological level.

TABLE IVa

HORIZONTAL AND VERTICAL GROUPING OF SOCIAL DATA, AND THE SPECIAL SCIENCES BY WHICH THEY ARE STUDIED

		(The *Political* Sanction of Compulsion)		(The *Economic* Sanction of Exchange)
	The Study of Terms *Quasi-Economic Level* (I)	(1) Terms of compulsion, by Administrative Science	(1½) Terms of other (Moral) Sanctions	(2) Terms of Exchange, by Pure Economics
The Study of Institutions	The Study of Organization *Quasi-Political Level* (II)	(3) Political Organization, by Political Science Proper	(3½) Other (Moral) Organizations	(4) Economic Organization
	Level (III)	(5) Positive Laws, Customs, Achievements, Fare, etc., studied by Sociology, Jurisprudence, etc.		

The homogeneous character of all activities placed on the middle level is particularly evident. The organization of a business firm or of a Trade Union or of a church has so many affinities to the organization of the State, their structure and functioning (government, manning, and division of labour) are so similar in character, that many all-important analogies and distinctions will be missed if different investigators continue to work each in separate compartments.

A further coalition usefully adopted is that between the two lower levels. If we except the purely technical achievements of man involving no social relations, it is this " area " that appears to be referred to by the adjective *institutional*, now so fashionable in American academic circles.

An institution may be (1) an organized society or group of persons like Parliament, a factory, or the Workhouse, and the proper study of political science, or (2) it may be a mere social custom like the institution of marriage. And an Institutional Economics is one that takes account not merely of economic organization but of political and " moral " organization, and of " mere " customs and social achievements as well. It is an attempt to consider terms of exchange in the light of all the surrounding social activity and to view the social system as an integral whole.

§2 *Integral Action of the Social System*

Those whose business it is to study social behaviour, its terms of fulfilment and achievement, must for convenience file their data in pigeon holes, boxes, shelves, compartments, and departments. But let them beware of splitting their minds up into pigeon holes and compartments like the useful but prosaic cabinet of Table IVA. To the mind's eye this cabinet should be at least three dimensional and its three levels regarded as different *aspects*. Any form of human behaviour recorded in the cabinet does not belong exclusively to one level but may be focused from at least three standpoints, i.e. may present at least three " scopes " or aspects. A person's behaviour may appear as economic, as a question of sanctions seen, say, from the front (or back) ; but there will also be political " sides " to it, questions of organization ; and seen from the bottom or top it may wear a sociological aspect and appear a question of mere custom or achievement.

One of the chief tasks of realistic social research is to see *all round* the subject, to observe the *relations* between various appearances from different aspects. The danger of referring political and economic appearances or phenomena to different dossiers has already been indicated and specific reference was made to the intimate relation between Administrative Science, Economics, and Political Institutions; and between Economics and Economic (trade and business) Institutions. Here we shall emphasize the close relationship between appearances strictly economic and political (and boxed as such), and behaviour apparently only social (and temporarily shelved).

Every single form of social activity, say that of building a cathedral or of performing rites within it, involves relationships between varieties of behaviour on the several levels of shelves and boxes separately distinguished. There is the technical achievement (Level III) of ritual and cathedral building; there must be an organization of the group of persons (Level II) performing the work technically necessary; and there must be some sort of sanction or incentive (Level I) propelling the group towards ritual and building. Each level (or shelf) is a complementary aspect and must be considered in turn, but at each level, that of technical achievement, organization, or sanctions, there are alternate ways of behaving, to be investigated by the appropriate science.

An achievement social rather than technical, is the negative custom of not drinking alcohol. Among the puritanically inclined the sanction may be merely moral, a sort of social taboo; among the poor in a State that imposes high taxes on alcohol it may be merely economic; while in the United States of America the sanction, like that of the medieval sumptuary laws prescribing the lower orders not to wear silk stockings, is legal (and constitutional) compulsion. Which of these sanctions is the most effective in obtaining a 100% or even 90% " dry " achievement is matter for investigation by a quasi-economic science (Level I) of stimulus efficiency.

Or take the positive reaction, the achievement of drinking. Alcoholic drinks, let us suppose, are freely obtained on economic terms; but the organization making *and/or* exchanging them for money may be an individual, a company of private capitalists, a co-operative society, a club, or the State government itself. What different results follow from each of these various ways of behaving is a matter for investigation by a quasi-*political* science (Level II) of organization.

Any form of social behaviour,—building, ritual, drinking, or not drinking—can thus be investigated from a number of standpoints and presents different facets or aspects accordingly. While the economic and quasi-economic focus is upon the relation (level or aspect I) between the terms and intensities of reaction and stimulus, the political or quasi-political focus (level or aspect II) is upon the reacting persons and organizations.

These different aspects of behaviour are complementary but each aspect offers a number of alternate ways of behaving. The activity of education may be instanced. To educate children parents and educators must be (I) stimulated, must be (II) organized, and must have (III) some technique or mode of education. These three aspects of education co-exist and are complementary, but each aspect presents a variety of possible alternate stimuli, organizations, and patterns of reaction.

I. Educators may be stimulated by money or love. Parents may be left to pay, or education may be free, or, if that does not stimulate, school attendance may be made compulsory.

II. Education is given by church organization, State organizations, semi-public organizations like universities and the English public schools, and private organizations or individuals.

And (III) obviously, the mode and type of instruction, the curriculum, is subject to every sort of variation.

Education is but one of the many social activities that are provided in different ways, on different terms, and by different organizations. Experience as to the effect of each of these alternative policies should be collected and sifted by the appropriate special science, sociological, economic, or political; at the same time the specialists involved must not forget that they are merely studying complementary aspects of one and the same individual, integral, social activity.

§3 *The Institutional Interpretation of Economics*

When conditions of exchange are obviously affected by some peculiar institution, the modification is often dismissed by economists in some convenient phrase like " friction " or " stickiness " ; and friction and stickiness are more likely to upset sheer deductions from the assumption of a calculating economic man than all the fifteen (or twenty, or three) instincts rolled into one that have been suggested as an alternative assumption.[1]

It is perhaps superficial to point to the importance of the commercial morality and trade customs of the time and place ; tipping or not tipping, bargaining in shops and bazaars or not bargaining, the degree to which the rule of *caveat emptor* is pushed ; notions of a just or customary price, a fair day's wage for a fair day's work ;

[1] Cf. my *Economics and Human Behaviour*, pp. 102 ff.

the habit of accepting commissions and taking rake-offs, squeezes, and perquisites. These customs are possibly variable and their effect uncertain, but when it comes to compulsorily sanctioned laws such as rights of property and inheritance, the tenure of land, freedom of contract or the amount of governmental interference in financial or industrial affairs, the very foundations of economics are brought in question.[1]

The possibilities of investigating by statistical methods the intricate interrelations of terms of exchange with non-economic sanctions and with non-economic institutions will be discussed at a later stage.[2] Here it is the bare recognition of the existence and importance of such relationships that must be argued, and the surest method of pleading is to refer to two or three leading problems that occur in the interpretation of wage rates. Wage rates are labour's terms of exchange (and are a part of the data filed in box 2 of Table IVA), but they are affected among other influences (A) by non-economic terms and sanctions (data filed in box 1 and shelf $1\frac{1}{2}$) ; (B) by the peculiar institution of the family (data filed in shelf $3\frac{1}{2}$) ; and (C) by the standards of life prevailing in various classes (data filed in shelf 5).

A : *The relation between wages, the main terms of exchange for work, and other non-financial terms.*

" The attractiveness of a trade," wrote Marshall, " depends on many other causes besides the difficulty and strain of the work to be done in it on the one hand, and the money-earnings to be got in it on the other," and he proposes the expression *net advantages* to refer to the " true reward which an occupation offers to labour . . . calculated by deducting the money value of all its disadvantages from that of all its advantages."

Investigation may show that an honourable career—in the service of one's country—will be chosen in preference to a more highly paid but merely respectable business position. It may be found that consciously or unconsciously honour and social approval are felt as a compensation for sacrifice of pay and are accepted in lieu thereof.

Expert observers maintain that a girl will be moved to accept work in a public tea-shop in exchange for less pay and keep than she will accept for similar work as a private parlour-maid. To the constraint and claustration of private employment is added the continual supervision by one's mistress, and this dependence on the caprice of others, this lack of status acts as a deterrent. It is

---

[1] Ely, *Property and Contract in their Relations to the Distribution of Wealth.*
[2] Chapter XVIII §§5, 6.

stated that the waitress finds " publicity " and a social life exciting, and will react to these allurements as though they were equivalent to economic values. Though honour and sociability may not be considered the prime motive power, yet they act as " lubricants " in facilitating acceptance of trade terms.

There is good evidence that the independent farmer in America, or the peasant proprietor in France, or the small independent shop-keeper in England, are all willing to labour for lower pay per unit effort than is the agricultural or commercial " employee " continu-ally subjected to the authority of others. Apparently they find other advantages and inducements in their terms of work beside that of mere payments in exchange for output.

B : *The relation between wages and the institution of the family.*

Fathers of families expect a family wage and since most work-men either are, have been, or expect to be fathers of families, an effective majority of all male Trade Unionists will insist on a family wage being written into their " collective " bargain with the employers. They meet the employers in a solid front with an agreed common rule for which all are prepared to strike if necessary. Not so among women. Among working women there is not one standard upon which a sufficient majority can agree and force upon the minority. For there are probably as many girls industrially employed who are living with their parents and not wanting full keep, as girls and women living alone or trying to keep themselves and support dependents to boot. There can be no agreement to strike for wages sufficient to meet the heavy demands upon the women supporting others, and any wage adequate to their needs that may be secured is likely to be undercut by the low standard of requirements of girls partially supported by others.

A further influence exerted by the family upon the economics of women's employment is due to the fact that people usually move in families. Where the husband moves there also moves the wife and daughters, and since the husband's and father's wages are usually greater than that of wife and daughters it is favourable terms of employment for him that tends to determine the location of the whole family. Men and women arrive as *joint products* of which the woman is the mere *by-product*.

Clearly the interpretation of the differences of men's and women's wages for work apparently similar must hark back to the institution of the family. If greater equality is desired changes must probably be introduced into family arrangements, but inductive investigation of the actual and probable effects of such rearrangements upon wages are not to hand.

C : *The relation between wages and salaries and the fact that several standards of living and education are found in every community,* i.e. *the fact that society is stratified into classes.*

In England this stratification is so marked that novels and treatises about the lower strata[1] read like books of foreign travel, and descriptions of the haunts and habits of the poor, their family budgets and social amenities, whether these are paid for or obtained free,[2] are as useful and necessary to the economist bred among the richer class, as Baedeker's guide books are to the rich tourist.

Stratification is obviously a bar to that mobility in the agents of production assumed by the economist, and a difficulty in any theory of a *general* wage-level. The theory of non-competing groups or grades has been introduced in modification, but economists do not seem very clear as to the number, limits, or distinguishing marks of any of the grades, and little or no attempt has been made to investigate the matter further.[3] Henderson, for instance, merely reproduces Marshall's distinction between (a) automatic, (b) responsible manual labour, and (c) automatic and (d) responsible brain workers which Marshall himself copied from the American sociologist Giddings.[4]

As a result of social immobility, over-populated classes with higher birth rates tend to remain over-populated and their members tend to remain ill-paid. Wealth tends to remain unequally distributed, and this in turn limits the exchangeability or vendibility of the more expensive types of goods and affects the very focus of economic science, namely the quantities and prices at which goods can be put on the market.[5]

These institutional interpretations of differences in wages are

[1] E.g. Robert Tressall, *The Ragged Trousered Philanthropists* ; Richard Whiteing, *No. 5, John Street ;* Booth, *Life and Labour of the People in London ; The Equipment of the Workers*, by members of St. Philip's Settlement, Birmingham, etc.

[2] Neglect of free goods, facilities, and surroundings will often mar a comparison of modes of life in different countries. The English working class probably fares worse in this respect than that of Germany (cf. Florence, *Economics of Fatigue and Unrest*, pp. 56–61), and thus the difference in the standard of living of the two countries is not as wide as appears at first sight.

[3] E.g. by finding the actual degree of mobility or migration between members of different social groups, the extent of intermarriage, mixing in schools, in social entertainments, pooling of information, etc.

[4] *Political Science Quarterly*, Vol. II, pp. 69–71.

[5] The relation of the pure economic data of box 2 to the economic politics data of box 4 and the politics (proper) data of box 3 was discussed in Chapter III ; their relation to other sanctions, to non-economic institutions, and to mere standards of life (compartments $1\frac{1}{2}$, $3\frac{1}{2}$, and 5) are now under discussion and this example completes, therefore, the illustration of the different *types* of interrelations between economic and all other social data.

simply cited as examples of the importance of institutional causes in a great number of problems that appear, on the surface, purely a matter of economic or quasi-economic sanctions.

We may revert to the still embryonic science of *industrial organization* discussed in Chapter III §4. Suppose it is desired to know the causes of, to interpret, differences in output or accidents per man per hour between different factories in the same industry possessing the same sort of technical equipment. The possible causes are economic, as differences in the wage paid ; or quasi-political, as differences in the structure, manning, specialization, and management of the factory organization ; or they may be simply such institutional, customary, factors as the hours of work, the intensity of work, and the other working and living conditions of the factory hands. To understand these conditions as they are found to-day and as they may be found to-morrow it is necessary to know something of the growth of the modern industrial system, the resort to machinery and other scientific inventions, the extension of division of labour, and the spread of the large factory, factory town, and big business. It is necessary also to realize the implication of the capitalist system of control and the various modifications of such a system " let alone " that have gradually been introduced by the institution of the State and the Labour Movement.[1]

Many of these institutional conditions and modifications, for instance the hours of labour, the monotony, regularity, and repetitiveness of the occupation, the size of the factory, the standard of living, and the membership of Trade Unions, are statistically measurable and the task of institutional interpretation may therefore be set out by correlating numerical variations in *personnel* behaviour (e.g. in output and accidents) with numerical variations in institutional conditions. But we are anticipating. . . .

§4 *The Economic Interpretation of Social Institutions*

While the institutional interpretation of economics still wears the charm of novelty, the economic interpretation of social institutions, considered historically or otherwise, is *vieu jeu*. The plan

---

[1] An attempt at such preliminary orientation is given in the first three chapters of my *Economics of Fatigue and Unrest*. To quote my introduction, ". . . Phenomena of industrial fatigue and unrest (are not) intelligible without some orientation in modern economic organization. The fatigue— or unrest—of the medieval handicraftsman or of a slave in the household system of the Roman empire presented problems entirely different from those uppermost to-day."

has not been neglected, academically, so much as spurned[1] and rejected.

The academic doctrine[2] that economics should keep to its own sphere and not interpret events in other spheres, begs the question whether it has a sphere. My view, as explained in §2, is that there is no specifically economic form or line of behaviour, but that economics simply focuses upon one aspect of behaviour. This being so, economics must co-operate with the social sciences focusing upon the other aspects ; there must be continual cross-references and cross-interpretations. Types and varieties of feature seen along the economic aspect must be interrelated with types and varieties of feature of other aspects.

Several illustrations of the interrelation of the economic with the political aspect will be given in this treatise as a matter of course and without apology for an apparently materialistic outlook. Success in elections is linked up, for instance, with the money spent by the rival candidates (XIII §3) ; the occupations of members of Parliament is enquired into (VI §1) ; and systems of justice are correlated with the economic stage of development (XX §9) of a people. Interpretation of political activities is not exclusively economic, however, and particular attention is paid to psychological and even (XIII §2) psycho-analytic theories. For it is clear that the relationship of varieties of social life and institutions with events and behaviour of an economic nature (connected, that is, with the terms and organization of exchange), is not to be dogmatically denied any more than affirmed.

Measured observation of the varieties of human behaviour is required, free from the assumptions and deductions of speculative philosophy that start from one single aspect of a man, and free from the academic delimitation of the whole subject into " spheres of influence."

Enough has been quoted to demonstrate the need for an inductive, observational, not to say statistical, liaison between general sociologists, political scientists, and economists.

The subject is so vast and human powers so meagre that division of labour must prevail among investigators of man's social behaviour, but exclusive specialization should be looked upon as a necessary evil rather than cherished as an object of professional pride. There

---

[1] Largely because of its association with Karl Marx. Marx was also a pioneer in institutional interpretation but this did not " get " the public's " goat " or fire its imagination (according to class) as did the economic interpretation. Cf. M. H. Dobb, *Capitalist Enterprise and Social Progress ;* Max Eastman, *Marx, Lenin and the Social Revolution.*

[2] E.g. Ellwood, *Sociology and Modern Social Problems.*

is a common aim to describe and account for human behaviour, but this consummation can only be reached by distinguishing several aspects of any form of behaviour for different specialists to investigate, by studying varieties and tendencies of behaviour exhibited from each aspect, and then relating the varieties and tendencies of one aspect with the varieties and tendencies of the others. Economic, political, and sociological features may be separately focused, but only with a view to a more complete ultimate correlation and integration.

§5 Summary and Thesis

Division of labour is a necessary evil in social research, and care must be exercised that the several specialists are co-ordinated, and that they co-operate conveniently for the advancement of the science along inductive lines.

Once the data have been collected from various sources of evidence, investigations not aiming purely at the historical view must divide up the study of man " topically " according to the aspect of social activity that is looked at.

Various specialists, the economist (pure and simple), the political scientist (proper), the jurist, and the sociologist, have already chosen a particular focus and scope for their attentions, and in surveying the remaining aspects of human behaviour we have tried for the sake of scientific continuity to reserve to each of these principals his chosen rôle. The line of reservation most consciously recognized refers to the kind of stimulus or sanction that provokes human behaviour. Political Science is concerned with the exercise of various compulsory powers, economics deals with prices and amounts voluntarily exchanged at various prices.

But there is a more important line of demarcation between specialists' preserves, dictated by the difference in the specific ability and technique required of the specialist, no less than by the affinities in the topics studied. That line lies between the study of the relation of behaviour to stimulus, and the study of human behaviour itself. The word reaction refers to the subjects on both sides of the line ; but while investigations of " economic " type focus upon the problem of what terms or intensities of stimulus will set off what terms or intensities of reaction, investigations of political or institutional type look at the groups and kinds of persons re-acting, and their organization and mutual interaction.

This plan of specialization, though unconsciously adopted in practice, has not hitherto, to the best of my knowledge, been consciously recognized.

The definitions consciously set forth make either the purpose or the inner psychological mechanism employed the distinguishing mark of the various social sciences ; or they distinguish these sciences according to the field of objects studied. Economics is said, for instance, to deal with man's rational behaviour, his adjustment of means to ends,[1] or his conscious organization[2] for the purpose of satisfying wants ; or economics is said to deal only with material objects or only the business " field."

The first two of these distinguishing marks appear to me to have the great fault in distinguishing marks, of not being observably distinguishable. If economics, political and other social sciences are to be founded on observation, it is essential that one should be able to observe what data are relevant, but the degree of reasonableness or consciousness of any act is not readily noted off-hand, and different observers would certainly differ in its assignment.

Material objects, to refer to the other proposed marks of economics, are perhaps distinguishable from spiritual, and the ordinary business of life from conviviality and the pleasures thereof ; but dealing with these matters neither distinguishes economics from other sciences, nor indicates the whole scope of economics. There is a physics and chemistry of all material objects as well as an economics, and there is an economics of Art as well as of business and the provision of material objects.

Different forms of human behaviour cannot, in short, be divided into spheres or " fields " of study either according to the motive (if any) of behaviour inside the person's mind (if any), nor according to the degree of materiality (if any) of the object (if any) about which the behaviour concerns itself. The principle of division must be that of different aspects of the same form or line of behaviour, economics or quasi-economic, political, or sociological. In any case the features of each aspect upon which a realistic economics, political science, or sociology focuses attention are the actual reactions of persons,—not nominal or legally or conventionally supposed contracts and arrangements of general application that are perhaps never fulfilled. It is individual persons as members of society, their individual acts and utterances and the specific stimulus to specific intensities of reaction in act and utterance, that enter the scope of observation and focus attention.

But division of labour among the experts must not imply segre-

---

[1] Knight, in *The Trend of Economics*, edited by Tugwell.
[2] Hawtrey, *The Economic Problem*.

gation of these reactions, and the final task of economics and political science is to trace the relationship between varieties and tendencies " featured " by the economic and political aspect, with the features of the sociological aspect.

Now in the investigations of these sociological features statistical methods have been freely admitted.   There are vital statistics of the births, marriages, illnesses, and deaths of persons during a *period* of time, and of their distribution at any point of time according to residence, age,[1] sex, race, religion, physical and mental condition,[2] conjugal status and family relationship.[3]   There are statistics also of persons' modes of life, their family budgets, housing conditions, concentration in cities,[4] hours of work,[5] kinds of occupation, education, income,[6] etc.   And there are statistics of persons' more exceptional behaviour, their migrations, divorces, crimes, civil litigation, etc.   A statistical formulation, therefore, of the economic and political features would assist to bring them into relation with the sociological features already statistically measured.   But mere " graphical " description of the multitude of various unit reactions of a multitude of individual persons soon becomes compendious and unwieldy.   Geography and demography we know from childhood as an inventory of names of countries, capitals, mountains, rivers, peoples, and of figures and facts about them.   If we are to proceed to a scientific discipline like geology or sociology, accurate summarization of the itemized individual ways of behaving into varieties and tendencies and combinations of behaviour must follow, and this must proceed by statistical methods of measurement.   Man's social behaviour must be approached inductively, starting with observation of the individual behaviour of the individual man ; but this approach if it is to be of any general scientific value must also be a statistical approach.   This is my opening thesis.

[1] Table VIE, Chapter VI.   [2] Table VIA.
[3] See Carr-Saunders and Jones, *The Social Structure of England and Wales*, for a systematic statistical presentation of sociological data.
[4] Table VIIIc.   [5] Table VID.   [6] Table VIc.

PART TWO

THE STATISTICAL MEASUREMENT OF ECONOMIC AND POLITICAL DATA

CHAPTER V

LANGUAGE AND TYPES OF STATISTICAL MEASUREMENT

§1   *Conditions of Statistical Measurement*

" STATISTICS can prove anything " is probably the first thought that will occur to the reader. Whether this gibe is the result of mature experience or simply a type of the free association of words elicited by the psycho-analyst seeking his patient's complexes, depends on the sort of statistical reasoning the reader may have encountered. Certainly, statistics have been used to prove almost anything *and* everything, but so have general deductions from " reason," " common-sense," " human nature," and " the lessons of history." Reasoning based on statistics is perhaps more dangerous because the statistical material used may be quite accurate as far as it goes and may, by the reliability of its source, its detail, and its verifiability, lend a suspicious plausibility to the theories it is supposed to confirm. It is in the method of treating and applying the statistical material that the fallacy or fallacies usually occur; and attention will be concentrated on the devising of summary statistical measurements (Part II), and on the application of these devices to economic and political investigations (Parts III and IV).

The question of the accuracy and authenticity of various sources of statistical material will not be dealt with. There are several reference books that may be consulted and many allusions in statistical journals to the difficulties of census-takers, registrars, tax-inspectors, and other collectors of statistical data.[1] It is, for instance, well known that the ages of women, as returned by themselves on the census forms, tend normally to understate the truth

---

[1] E.g. A. L. Bowley, *Elementary Manual of Statistics.*

and cannot be accepted at face value. Other records, though not each individually accurate, may not show any particular bias and their errors cancel out. In an investigation of factory accidents I found the officially recorded time of report at dressing station, though usually slightly later than the officially reported time of the actual occurrence of the accident, to be occasionally five minutes or so earlier. A special sample investigation of the time of occurrence of accidents, however, and of the reliability of the method of recording those times, did not show any special bias to error in one direction, except a bias for *rounding out* in putting down the nearest full hour or quarter hour[1] in preference to odd but accurate minutes.

The materials out of which statistics is built are obtained either personally or from documents and records, and their original source is either simple observation of facts, acts, and utterances " in situ," " from the life " without specific tampering with conditions, or the source may be set observation, or " elicitation " of reactions (motor, verbal, etc.) to specially devised tests or questionaries, or to experiments in specially constructed laboratories. Each source of observation has its own particular difficulties. There is an art, for instance, in asking fool-proof and shame-proof questions, and in knowing when not to ask questions at all. Each source of data has its own special liability to biased or chance error and falsification, but we shall leave these preliminary difficulties of " authentication " in the care of the antiquarian, the scientific historian, the scholar pursuing the Higher Criticism of his documents, and the immediate observer, recorder, and collector of the material. The data of the statistician, the facts that are given him, we shall take to be authentic, and accurately observed at source and accurately recorded.[2]

The object of statistical measurement is, in the simplest terms, to obtain a summary but numerically accurate *description* of some point at issue, and wherever possible to specify numerically the reliability or degree of accuracy of such a summary for the purpose of *generalizing* or prediction. Statistical measurement begins when particular cases have supposedly been accurately observed and recorded, and proceeds to describe certain characteristics of these cases in the mass. The names and the full characterization of the individual cases are dropped and their personalities are merged as

---

[1] *U.S. Public Health Bulletin*, No. 106, p. 135. This source of error is of common occurrence in statements of age, cf. Bowley, *Elements of Statistics*, Part I, III, 1.

[2] The statistician should not omit to state the source of his data, the time, place, name of observer, and, where not obvious by inspection, the number of observations made.

mere units in an aggregate figure. This process[1] makes it possible to obtain summary yet accurate descriptions of the variable characters of a multitude of multiform facts and events which the human mind could not otherwise comprehend; and from these descriptions it is often possible to generalize.

Most authoritative definitions of statistics, besides alluding to (a) observation of actual "appearance" in (b) man's social behaviour, allude also to the characteristics of (c) massed data and (d) expression in numerical quantities or figures. For instance:

" Die Statistik unternimmt es, die 'Massenerscheinungen' (characteristics a, c) des menschlichen Gesellschaftslebens (b), um sie zu unserer Erkenntnis zugänglich zu machen zahlenmässig (d) zu erfassen."[2]

" La science de l'homme vivant en société (b) en tant qu'elle peut être exprimé par les chiffres (d)."[3]

" The systematic statement and explanation of actual events (a) and the laws of man's social life (b) that may be obtained from those on the basis of quantitative observation (d) of aggregates (c)."[4]

The contrast between (a) the statistical argument from appearances, from what is "sensed" and the deductive intellectual argument, as also (d) the quantitative character of their results, was alluded to by the very founder of statistical method, Sir William Petty. " Instead of using only comparative and superlative words and intellectual Arguments, I have taken the course (as a specimen of the Political Arithmetic I have long aimed at) to express myself in terms of Number, Weight or Measure; . . . to use only Arguments of Sense."

The original reference of the word statistics was not political arithmetic, but simply detailed comprehensive descriptions of State facts and activities.[5] Statistics always involved mass observation of social behaviour, a sort of permanent Statesman's Year-Book, but did not originally involve numerical expression in figures. As the word is used to-day, however, the chief condition that distinguishes statistical from the other inductive descriptions hitherto discussed (in Chapters III and IV) is *numerical* measurement. But this does not necessarily imply that the characters observed must be numerically measurable or quantitative. It is sufficient if

---

[1] Concrete and practical examples of this process of boiling down detailed factory records and observations into tables of statistics is given in my *Economics of Fatigue and Unrest*, pp. 390–1, and Chapters XIII and XIV.
[2] Zizek, *Fünf Hauptprobleme der Statistischen Methodenlehre*.
[3] M. Block, quoted in *Encyclopædia Britannica*.
[4] Translation from Von Mayr, loc. cit.
[5] Cf. Yule, *An Introduction to the Theory of Statistics*, pp. 1–5.

qualitative characters are manifested by a number, mass, or series of similar items.

§2 *Inaugural Conceptions and Vocabulary*

A halt must be called at this point to insist upon the distinction between what may be called a character or characteristic (words I shall use interchangeably), and what I shall venture to call a quality. Statistical explanation is difficult enough without the added confusion of the capricious terminology forced upon statisticians by the dictates of popular usage or literary style. Heat and cold might equally stylishly (or stylelessly) be referred to as two " characters " of the " quality " temperature, or as two " qualities " of the " character " temperature. But a consistent style must be adopted and it is the *latter* form of address that I shall choose. Heat and cold will be referred to as qualities of the character temperature ; short and tall as qualities of the character height ; and inhabiting the U.S.A. or Russia *as qualities of the character* or characteristic " inhabiting."

To avoid the congestion and collision of ideas inevitably consequent upon inconsistency in the reference of terms, this preliminary rule of the road may be laid down.

Rule I. *Temperature, height, habitat, sex, birth rates, and the outcome of events shall be referred to as a character in respect of which qualities are differentiated as hot and cold, tall and short, the U.S.A. or Russia, male and female, high or low birth rates, success or failure.*

A character may be one person's or a group of persons' " situation," " lot," or " fortune " ; the person's age (Table VIE) or the size of a group (Table VA) *at any one time.* Or character may relate to a man's behaviour and activity or the stimuli befalling him ; the sort of penalty he receives (Table XIXA), his hours of work (Table VID) and output (Table VIB), or the money he makes (Table VIC), or the money a group makes (Table VIIB), during any period. Character, in short, is not to be confined merely to a static latent condition " in " man or group at a given moment.

Rule I sees us safe through an initial bottle-neck. But a narrower and more perilous terminological traffic-jam looms ahead.

The chief confusion in the preliminary terminology of statistics arises from the fact that two sets of varying quantities or figures are often, though not necessarily, involved in the field of observation. When we say that " the population of the U.S.A. or Russia is so-and-so much," only one sort of quantitative measurement is presented. But when we say that 179 students were about 69 inches tall, 139 about 70 inches, 108 about 71 inches, and so on, varying numbers and figures are presented to measure the exact degree of height as well as to measure the "vogue," "population," or "frequency" of that height. In statistical language height can be said to be a variable character or, for short, a variable. This use of numbers in two connections (and the consequent confusion) does not occur where the character is only differentiated in quality; when, as statisticians say, the characteristic is merely an "attribute" as green, blue, pink; or a denizen of the U.S.A. or Russia; or male or female in sex.

The distinction between characters that have merely qualities and those that are quantitatively measurable is not a hard and fast line of demarcation. There are many qualities that can be ranked as grades in some sort of consistent order or hierarchy without the use of any precise quantitative measure : black—grey—white or (on the hierarchical model of private, corporal, sergeant, lieutenant, captain) unskilled, semi-skilled, skilled, learned. These ranks when placed in a consistent order of merit, importance, magnitude, etc., are known as *isotropic*, all equally (ισος) turned (τρεπειν), facing the same direction. Sometimes the correct order is not given at the outset and it is the task of statistical measurement to find the order empirically.[1]

To avoid the confusion of several sets of quantities, the quantities of a character may therefore be thought of as isotropic qualities. When specific heights of quantities of persons are mentioned in quantities of inches, a given *range* of inches may be considered as a quantitatively valued quality, and instead of saying so-and-so many persons were between so-and-so many inches high, to say so many were short, so many medium, so many tall, etc.

The distinction between quantitatively and qualitatively differentiated characters is not clear cut. Nor is the distinction vital to the existence of statistical measurement. Numerical measurements, as we have seen, can be made even when the character is not a variable, but an attribute having qualities but no quantities. In short, *the sine qua non* of statistical measurement is enumerable uniform items.

The preliminary vocabulary of statistics must therefore include reference to quantitatively differentiated characters as in Rule II, and also to the instance or item as in Rule III.

Rule II. *When a character is measurable only qualitatively statisticians name it an attribute ; when it is measurable quantitatively, as temperature along a scale of degrees, statisticians name it a variable.*

[1] Cf. Chapter VIII.

Instead of quantities of a variable character it is common to speak of amounts or extents of that character, and the quantities, amounts, or extents that actually occur are often referred to as great or small, high or low, severe or slight, etc. *Both quantity and quality of a character may conveniently be referred to as the value[1] of that character.*

Rule III. *The things which manifest the several values (quantities or qualities) of the character or characters to be measured, and manifest them with varying but quantitatively measurable frequency, may be named the statistical specimens, instances, or " items."*

The usual organization of the field of observation is that similar items are observed each of which " counts as one " unless specifically weighted, and that each of these items manifests various degrees or qualities of the character or characters to be described. The items may be concrete things, persons, groups of persons, and events,[2] or they may be abstract dimensions, units of weight, length, volume, time, or space, economic or physical values, either commonly recognized and conventional or, like ton-miles, quets, male eating-units,[3] etc., newly thought out for the purpose in hand.[4]

The characteristics manifested by these items may or may not be measurable in quantities or degrees like the age of a person or a date or an economic value, but for the purpose of statistical measurement there must be quantitatively enumerable similar items that have each of them, for all the observer knows, an equal opportunity of manifesting any of the possible values. The item " person " tells us nothing about his height that is not equally likely of another " person " and it is in this respect that the items are similar.[5]

---

[1] Since we have put behind us all ethical, moralistic senses of value in Chapter I.

[2] Married couples may be observed in order to find the difference between age of husband and age of wife. In this case the two ages are characters (with quantitative values) of the item couple. Or the context, striking a match, may be observed to find how hard a rub is followed how quickly by a flame. In this case the hardness of rub and the quickness of flame are two characters (with quantitative values) of the item striking a match.

[3] See Chapter X §1.   [4] See Chapter IX §1.

[5] Zizek, in his *Fünf Hauptprobleme*, also stresses the importance of certain inaugural conceptions in statistics and refers to them in a consistent nomenclature.

" We must recognize that the characteristic of statistics, their own particular language, is not figures—these show no peculiarities and can be obtained by means of the simple arithmetic, but the peculiar conception (Begriffe) to which these figures relate." While Zizek's Erhebungsmerkmal appears to be the equivalent of my *character*, Erhebungseinheit (or Zahlenheit, the unit of counting) is the equivalent of my *item*. Zizek also stresses the conception of the Aussagen, the various forms of the statistical statement and Gruppen or classes. These I deal with later in Chapters VI and IX.

The relationship between the observer and his field and the references of the terms item, character, value, frequency, may be indicated in a diagram.

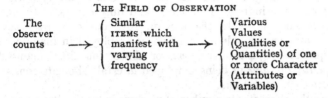

THE FIELD OF OBSERVATION

| The observer counts | → | Similar ITEMS which manifest with varying frequency | → | Various Values (Qualities or Quantities) of one or more Character (Attributes or Variables) |

§3 Types of Statistically Measured Issues

Numerical expressions are sometimes sought for their own sake. The population of London is a matter of pride to the Cockney megalomaniac ; Jack Hobbs' number of centuries or batting average is of absorbing interest to the cricket enthusiast. The exact number of ants in a given ant-hill is thrilling to the naturalist. But as an instrument in scientific research, numerical measurement is used to set up some kind of comparison. Even the Cockney, the cricketer, and the naturalist must have some standard of comparison or, at least, some method of realizing the dimensions of the feats and features they glory in. A population of over six million, an average of 65·53 runs, a hill of a hundred thousand ants is surely uninteresting unless one has some idea of the possibilities and actualities in size of towns, in batting records, and in pullulation. And to the scientific investigator the comparison must have a certain relevancy to an issue. The statement that in 1901 the population of London (County) was 4,536,063, but that of Great Dullpuddle 1537, is certainly a comparison, but it has no " point," it settles no " issue."

Statistical measurements are not as a rule obtained for their own sake. There is some point at issue which it is desired to illustrate or demonstrate by a comparison ; and the sort of issues that statistics can describe, or about which statistics can make generalizations or predictions, appear to fall into three main types. There are issues about a single character at any time or place ; issues about tendencies or consecutive changes in a single character, from time to time, or place to place ; and issues about the degree and kind of relationship or association between two or more characters. The inaugural conceptions already named are appropriate to the description of political and economic tendencies and relationships no less than in the description of *single* political and economic characters. They form a sufficient vocabulary even when two or more sets of variable characters are dealt with.

(1) In the statement[1] about a single (quantitatively measurable) character that " in the United States in 1914 out of 7 millions returned as employed in manufacture, 5·4 millions or almost four-fifths were employed in establishments of more than fifty workers," the item is the individual employee and fully expressed the statement would run : " In the U.S. in 1914 out of a *frequency* of 7 millions *item* individuals returned as employed in manufacture, a frequency of 5·4 millions *items* or almost four-fifths manifested the *quality* or *value* of being employed in establishments consisting of more than 50 workers."

Here the character is number of workers in establishment and all the possible values are reduced to two ranges or classes of value. The frequency is then measured with which all the values within each range are manifested ; i.e. the employees that constitute the items are *distributed* according as they were employed in establishments with over 50 workers, or in establishments with 50 workers and under.

Wherever the character involved is quantitative there is a possible alternate method of summarization which is most popular. An *average* value is computed to represent the general position or *incidence* along the scale of value of the exact quantities of the character manifested by the items taken as a whole. This may or may not be supplemented by a summary measure of the dispersion of these values over the scale. There are various methods of calculating the average value (detailed in Chapter VI), but the method giving the most realistic result (though not necessarily the least arbitrary method) is to select the most prevalent or frequent quantity of the character, i.e. the value manifested by more items than any other value. But whether it is this " mode " that is quoted or some differently computed average the connection of the average value with the relative frequency of all the values manifested must never be lost sight of or missed. Though less summary, a frequency distribution giving the comparative frequency or *frequency coefficient* of each value (quantity or range of quantities) distinguished, is always nearer to the facts than an average, and often more significant. In the United States in 1914 the seven million wage-earners were counted in 275,791 establishments, and the average size of establishment as calculated by the arithmetic mean number employed was therefore 26. But this is not a particularly typical sort of size.

Besides being calculable only when the values of a character are quantities (one could not speak of an average nationality or

[1] Florence, *Economics of Fatigue and Unrest*, p. 27.

occupation) the average often fails to present a summary of all the facts, particularly when the deviation of quantities is wide and the whole distribution skew.[1] The popular lay view that statistics deals only with averages cannot be too strongly repudiated.

Statistical measurement starts out with the recognition of the infinite variability of facts and events and uses averages only when they are justified by the form of that variability.

(2) In the measurement of tendencies or changes over time and place, the lapse of time and the distance in space can be considered (and I think should be considered) simply as a character manifested, with other characters, by the item under observation. *This local or temporal character is always quantitatively measurable* as dates, distances, etc., and its specific values can therefore be placed in a consecutive isotropic order. In its simplest form a tendency is measured by comparing the number (frequency) of specified items at specified consecutive stages, positions, or points of time or space. The number of tons of beer consumed by the community or the number of convictions for drunkenness is observed *from year to year* or at least at different dates in some kind of " isotropic " sequence. The following statement of changes in the distribution of employees among establishments of various sizes may be regarded as a measurement of the frequency of item individuals manifesting contrasted quantities of *two characters*, namely, (*a*) size of the establishment (in number of workers) where they were employed, (*b*) time (in years) when the enumeration was made.

" In Germany establishments maintaining one to five persons as assistants employed 3·6 million persons in 1907 as against 2·6 millions in 1882 ; but between these years the numbers employed in factories having 6 to 50 workers increased threefold from 1·2 to 3·7 millions ; and the number employed in factories containing over 50 persons increased more than threefold, from 1·6 to 5·2 millions."[2]

The issue consists in contrasting the distribution of two specified years whose distance in time is measurable. The years are placed in order of their " occurrence " to show the tendency of *growth* in large-scale production. It is not the actual frequency of employees in 1882 and 1907 that is the point at issue, but the change in the distribution of employees, in the comparative frequency of employees in large, small, and very small establishments respectively between the two years. The frequency of employees in each size of establishment might be represented as the same number, say 100,

---

[1] See Glossary, §§10, 15.
[2] Florence, *Economics of Fatigue and Unrest*, p. 27.

for the first of the two time-values without disturbing the issue ; on the contrary, it would clarify the issue. The exact change is more clearly expressed by saying that the number of employees in the two larger sizes of establishment increased 309%, just over threefold, and 325%, or three and a quarter fold, than by saying that the increase was from 1·2 millions to 3·7, and 1·6 millions to 5·2.

TABLE Vₐ

Size of Establishment measured in number of Workers employed	Millions of Individuals employed in Establishments of specified size		Comparative change in the Frequency of such Individuals		Approximate Size of Establishment where average Individual was employed	
	1882	1907	1882	1907	1882	1907
1 — 5	2·6	3·6	100	138 ⎫		
6 — 50	1·2	3·7	100	309 ⎬	5	45
Over 50	1·6	5·2	100	325 ⎭		
All Sizes	5·4	12·5	100	231		

When changes and tendencies of characters that consist in quantities are described, it is usual, though more arbitrary and artificial, to give an average quantity of the character at each date or place. Table Vₐ shows that in 1882 almost exactly half (2·6 out of 5·4 millions or 48·2%) the number of individual workers were employed in establishments where five or less were at work, and we might calculate the average *type* of establishment in which any employee might find himself, to be one employing just over 5 workers. In 1907, since over two-fifths (5·2 out of 12·5 millions or 41·6%) were employed in establishments with more than fifty at work, this average or type might be calculated as one employing something short of 50—say 45 workers.

In this case where only two widely scattered years are compared, an average to take the place of a frequency distribution is artificial almost *ad absurdum*. Averages can be justified only where realistic accuracy must be sacrificed to limits of space and to limitations in the time, patience, and intelligence of the reader ; where, for instance, tendencies in the size of establishment are traced over a long series of years and compared in the same table with other tendencies—say, the increase in output or capital value per establishment.

[1] Florence, *Economics of Fatigue and Unrest*, p. 27.

(3) When it comes to measuring the relationship, the inter-dependence, if any, between the quantitative or qualitative values of two (or more) characters of the same item, the issue consists in comparing the frequencies of all the possible associations or combi-nations wherever or whenever observed.

Among the figures displayed in Table IXF the individual " date " of the years is irrelevant to the issue. The change of prevalent values or frequencies during a specific lapse of years is not the issue, but the connection of price with the amount produced at that time ; the forty years are the items each manifesting the two characters to be correlated,—a particular average price of corn and a particular average amount produced. The year is simply the " tie " between price and amount produced, and is counted as one unit of frequency in the appropriate box of the table.

Again, the attempt is often made to demonstrate industrial fatigue by showing a fall in the output of the last hours of a con-tinuous spell or day of work. Here the hours are the items observed and these items combine two characters : (a) the production of output, (b) the previous duration of work since the beginning of the spell or day,—the age (in hours) of the working period. Both characters (a) and (b) are variables, i.e. have values quantitatively measurable—(a) in terms of units of output, (b) in terms of hours of work—and their variations are relevant to the issue. The point at issue is whether the values of one character (units of output per hour) tend to fall, and if so how much and according to what law, when the values of the other character (previous hours of work) rise (i.e. whether there is a negative correlation between the values of the two characters) ; or whether the values are independent, i.e. show no *particular* relation one toward the other.

§4   *Tabular and Graphic Presentation*

The original Rules of the Royal Statistical Society allege that " the statist commonly prefers to employ figures and tabular exhibitions," and for the sake of visual comprehension and saving space, tables and graphs are an inevitable part of the statistician's argument. Some of these " exhibitions " have in the course of time been given conventional names such as the Correlation Table, the Frequency Curve, the Regression Line, the Periodogram ; and it is important to complete the account of the preliminary nomen-clature of statistics by showing the relation of these differently named tabular " exhibitions " to the various types of issue already differentiated.

Many of the more practical text-books on statistical method devote chapters to graphical and tabular presentation,[1]—indeed there are entire books written on the subject.[2] These technical problems need not delay our statistical approach any more than the preliminary problems of collection and authentication of data ; but warnings must be given against identifying any one type of issue with any one particular form of tabular or graphic presentation.

Three issues have been distinguished, but the characters involved may be either qualitatively or quantitatively measured. This complication results in seven methods of presenting those issues each with specifically named (though not always formally distinct) tabular or graphic exhibits.

I *Frequencies* of Values of Single Characters

A Character Qualitatively Valued : The Frequency Table
B Character Quantitatively Valued : The Frequency Distribution or Curve

II *Tendencies* of Values of Character through Quantitative Measures of Time or Space

A Character Qualitatively Valued : The Tendency Table
B Character Quantitatively Valued : The Periodogram, Time or Space Series

III *Relationship* of Values of Two or More Characters

A Both Characters Qualitative : The Association Table
B One Character Quantitative : The Contingency Table
C Both Characters Quantitative : The Correlation Table

I A The comparative frequencies of different *qualities* of one character can be shown in a column or row of item figures as in Table XIX A, the frequencies of " reappearances " among young persons who have undergone different qualities of punishment. This is the sort of issue that is presented graphically by lines, areas of different magnitude, or by pictures of men, animals, beer-barrels swollen to the correct proportionate size ; an enormous bearded and booted Russian, for instance, inflated to twelve times the content of a Dutchman in breeks and sabots to show the comparative population. The chief purpose of graphical presentation of this sort of issue is to tickle the imagination of school children

---

[1] E.g. Boddington, *Statistics and their Application to Commerce.*
[2] E.g. Karsten, *Charts and Graphs* (734 pages !).

and adults mentally of school age, or to impress the tired business man or the bored politician. Graphs or pictures help the initiated but little in realizing the comparative frequencies (or tendencies in frequencies) of merely *qualitative* differences.

IB The values of a single quantitative character are summarized either in one average appearing as one figure in a table or they are summarized in a frequency distribution appearing as one array (row or column of figures in a Table) (cf. Tables VI, A, B, C, D, E), or graphically as one frequency polygon or area enclosed by a frequency curve. This curve is usually constructed by making the vertical height of the curve (the ordinate) measure the frequency of the consecutive quantities or ranges of quantity of the character, while the quantities themselves are marked off horizontally (as *abscissæ*) along the base.[1]

IIA Comparative tendencies through time or space in different *qualities* of one character are tabulated by resort to several columns or rows of figures each representing successive stages.[2] The rows in Table VIIIB, for instance, show the changes in the comparative frequency of different qualities of political opinion, i.e. Liberal or Conservative, held by members of Parliament at successive periods.

IIB Quantitative tendencies through time or space are presented either as one array of average quantities, e.g. one average for each year (as in the original column of figures in Table VIIID),[3] or as several frequency distributions (e.g. one distribution for each year as in Table V or VIIIA). The appropriate graph is an area bounded by a polygon or *curve*, often called a periodogram or histogram. This is usually constructed as Table VIIIc (which is unconventional in applying to space rather than time), to measure the distance in time or space horizontally as abscissæ along the base and to measure the average quantitative values of the other character (i.e. average persons per square mile) vertically, as ordinates.

IIIA The comparative frequency of the association of various qualities in two or more characters of one set of items is presented in an Association Table like Tables IXA or XIIIc. There are rows and columns, but neither the headings of the columns nor the cross-heads of the rows are necessarily in any consecutive isotropic order.

---

[1] Cf. Glossary §14.

[2] When several rows or columns of figures appear in a table they may simply be additive, that is they may merely add to the evidence about the same issue supplied by the first row or column. In Table XIXB, for instance, figures in Columns A and B are to be read simply as samples each helping to throw light on the comparative frequency of the same qualities of punishment.

[3] The remaining columns are simply derived from the first column and are not even additive.

IIIB and C. The comparative frequency of the association of quantities of one character with *qualities* of another is usually presented in a contingency table like Table IXc or IXB.

The comparative frequency of the association of quantities of one character with quantities of another is usually presented either in a correlation table like Table IXF, or in a Regression Table like Table IXE which summarizes, by means of averages, the frequency distribution of the quantities of one character when the quantities of the other character are approximate to given stages, i.e. fall within certain consecutive ranges of value. Except for this very summary regression table, these tables with several columns and rows of figures not additive or derived one from another, are similar in form to those presenting issue IIB, but the reading is different. Whereas a tendency to change over time or space is read by comparing the figures in the same row or the same column, the association, contingency, or correlation table can only be read intelligibly by a comparison of *all* figures in whatever row or column ; the eye must roam into every " box " of the table.

This difference in the area of comparison makes a difference in graphical presentation. To show changes in frequency distributions a number of periodograms might be drawn, one for each class (e.g. small, large, and very large establishment in Table VA) ; their relative height at the various periods of time would exhibit sufficiently the points at issue. For the graphical presentation of the issue of relationship, however, a *three*-dimensional relief map would be required : consecutive points along length and breadth to denote the values of the two variable characters, depth or height (or colour might be used as in orographical maps) to denote the varying frequency.

§5 *A Summary and Review*

There are three main types of statistically measurable issue : (1) The frequency of various values of one character at any time or place ; (2) The tendency of the values of one character to vary over a sequence of times and places ; (3) The relationships, associations, correlations, or contingencies between the various values of two or more characters. When tabulated or graphically presented these several issues are confused by the fact that when values are quantitatively measurable (i.e. when the character is variable), one average quantity is computed to summarize the general incidence of a whole array (column or row) of figures or of a whole curve representing many frequencies. *One* array (or curve) may therefore represent the frequency distribution of a single character, or if the character consists in measurable quantities, it may represent the tendency of its average quantity to change over time or place, or it may represent the regression (the "law" of correlation or contingency) of the average quantity of one character with certain "stages" in the quantity of the other character. Similarly *several* arrays (rows and columns) of figures may represent the frequency distribution of one character at different times or places, or the association, correlation, or contingency between the values of two or more characters at any time or place. Which issue is represented depends upon the direction of comparison. In the tendency table figures are compared only one way at a time ; in the correlation table there is an all-ways comparison.

It is the type of issue itself, not the form of its presentation that matters, and the chapters that follow will be devoted in turn to the measurement of the three main statistical issues.

But the calculation of frequencies, tendencies, and relationships are often undertaken with a view to making generalizations from the measurements of observed data, to cover data not observed. Tables and graphs displaying observed facts may not merely illustrate and describe these summarily, but may attempt to *transfer* the summary to other situations ; and summaries of the point at issue may have a *kick* in them to force that point, like a *spur*, upon further unobserved facts. But these generalizations and prognostications are all subject to uncertainty and the measurement of uncertainty must be broached in a separate chapter (VII) immediately after the discussion of the first issue. The uncertainty of generalizing each of the further issues may then be discussed briefly toward the end of the appropriate chapter.

Human nature is capricious, impatient, fickle, vacillating, and inconsequent, liable to vagaries, non-conformity, false optimism, panic, unrest. Men are not consistently rational as the old deductive economists would have them be, but creatures (though again not consistently) of instinct and habit. It is impossible to deduce from any one consistent theory of man's nature what he will do or how he will behave and react, and scientific investigation must begin with the observation of actual doings, behaviour, and reactions and proceed to generalize by inductive methods.

Economic and political reactions, the aspects of human activity which are to be approached by statistical methods, appear odd, heterogeneous, diverse, dissimilar, idiosyncratic, contrarious, anomalous, variegated, irregular, errant, desultory, entangled, complicated, unrelated, unexpected. It is the object of statistical measurement to bring some kind of scientific order out of chaos, consistency out of variability, and regularity out of apparent irregularity ; to seek some degree of uniformity, succession, interdependence, and certainty.

The statistical measurement of the frequency of values of a single character shows how far there is an approximation to one or a few particular values, and when values are quantitative how far the form of frequency distribution may be defined. Even when using the phrase normal distribution statistical measurement does not deduce a normal value from a few simple presumptions, but tries to summarize the apparently multiform, dissimilar, complicated variations of the character. The statistical measurement of tendencies in the values of a single character shows whether there are any predominant movements, or stabilities, or recurrencies among the flux of events and apparently wanton changes. It is not an attempt to escape from details as is the orthodox economist's conception of a tendency, but an attempt to summarize those details. The measurement of the relationship or association between the values of two or more characters, shows how far all complex occurrences, synchronisms, coincidences, and other observed combinations are temporary, local, and individual entanglements and how far the values of certain characters are more or less generally wedded and persistently associated. Theoretical economists use tendency to refer to persistent associations as well as to temporal or spatial movements ; but here also the statistical method, starting out from the observed facts, is clearly different from the deductive method based on assumption and presumption. The measurements of risks and uncertainty show whether there are any probabilities more likely to be true than not among the chances and flukes of everyday life. The argument is not *a priori* on given assumptions of the odds, but *a posteriori* on previous experience of situations as far as observably similar.

CHAPTER VI

THE SUMMARY MEASUREMENT OF A SINGLE CHARACTER

§1 *The Frequency of Qualities and the Distribution of Quantities*

THE characters that statistics attempt to measure summarily are either attributes with two or more alternative qualities, or variables of different quantity. Though both qualities and quantities may be called *values* or varieties of the character, statistics clearly cannot summarize matters so definitely where characters are merely qualitative. The statistical treatment of any one qualitative character is indeed confined to two lines of approach ; the measurement of the absolute or comparative frequency of each alternative quality and, where there are more than two qualities, the ranking of these qualities in some consistent order.

Political Science is more limited than Economics to qualitative characters and an example of the statistical summarization of single qualitative attributes may be drawn from membership of the House of Commons.

Table IXB groups members of Parliament of either party from 1832 to 1867 in respect of their occupation. Members of Parliament are the statistical items, occupation the statistically measured character ; and the chief object of the table is to display the comparative frequency (in items) of each occupation. The most frequent group is that of landholders, while the working-class is not represented at all. These findings are interesting enough in themselves, particularly if the figures of the parliamentary " representatives " are related to the frequency or " population " of the same occupation in the country at large. But when Liberal members of Parliament are distinguished from Conservative it becomes possible to arrange or rank the qualitatively distinguished occupations in respect of their Conservativeness or Liberalism. Omitting Radicals, 504 army and navy M.P.'s out of 921, or 53·5%, were Conservative ; landholding members of Parliament were just under 50% Conservative ; shareholders 49·7% Conservative ; lawyers 38·4% Conservative ; and so on, followed in order of Conservatism by the professional (civil servant, independent, and salaried) group, by financiers and merchants, and finally by industry. Such a list is often called isotropic because the qualitative values or varieties of the characters are ranked or ordered in the same specific direction, and in this case the direction is Conservatism. And here the isotropic order of qualities was not evolved *a priori*, but found empirically by statistical observation and tabulation.

When it comes to the observation of a quantitative character we may speak of a distribution of items over its quantitative values, and the character itself is called a variable.

The numerically measurable (quantitative) characters of the economic and political world are variable in at least two ways : (1) It is seldom the case that any one quantitative value of the characteristic is universally prevalent to the exclusion of other values. Wealth is unequally or variably distributed in the sense that not every individual or family observed has an income of the same value. The frequency curve is not just one upstanding peak at one particular value. (2) It is seldom the case that all values have the same frequency. There are not an equal number of poor, middle class, and rich as some leader-writers would have us believe. For wealth is also unequally and variably distributed in the sense that there are not the same number of individuals or families enjoying (or suffering from) each specific value or range of value of income. There are a far greater number of poor than of persons with incomes of moderate value, and a far greater number of the middle sort than of the very rich. The frequency curve is not a flat plateau equally high at all values.

The form of variation of economic and political variables, the " distribution " of their values, usually lies somewhere between these two cases. Sometimes the form of distribution approaches the first case. The hours of work in the manufacturing industries of England are to-day (1929) almost *in*variably of the value of forty-eight per week. Here one could almost tell the truth without statistical expressions and simply say that men work forty-eight hours a week in manufacturing industries.

Sometimes, truth approaches the second case. Where immigration of adults is taking place to replace the native born who are gradually diminishing with advancing age, remarkable equality in number may be found in the several age-groups up to thirty years of age.

The male white population of the U.S.A. in 1910, for instance, was unusually equally distributed over the various ages up to the age of thirty : Under five years, 4·7 millions ; five to nine years of age inclusive, 4·2 millions ; ten to fourteen years of age, 4·0 millions ; fifteen to nineteen years of age, 4·0 millions ; twenty to twenty-four years of age, 4·0 millions ; twenty-five to twenty-nine years of age, 3·8 millions.

Here again a statement to the effect that there were about as many persons of one age as of another up to the age of thirty would be free from statistical phrases and yet manage, perhaps, to approach the truth.

These cases are as near as we can get to exceptions that prove the rule of a variability in economic and political characters. Statistical description is necessary if this variation is to be described. Sometimes the variability is one that can be reduced to a simple formula, and this may form a convenient starting-point.

§2 *The Normal Distribution*

A frequent form of variation in physical and biological characters is a frequency distribution where there is neither one value almost universally observed, nor yet an equal number of items manifesting each value. The frequency curve is neither completely upstanding nor completely flat. Yet there is regularity in its irregularity. There is a curve with a fat belly in the middle and a tail at one end and a slim head at the other ; a curve also like the shape of a bell or a cocked hat. Instead of the *one* value there is a more or less central typical representative or *average* value, and instead of an equal number of items at different values there is a narrower or wider scatter or *deviation* of items at values above and below the average or typical value. And this scatter follows a regular course. There are as many values above as below the average and the distribution is symmetrical, there are fewer values deviating widely from the average than values deviating only slightly, and the rate at which the wider deviations become fewer is reducible to a formula.

This distribution is the result that will most probably occur by chance where the values actually distributed are themselves the sum or chance combination of a number of component characters, each varying in value independently one from another (Glossary §18) like the plus and minus errors of an unbiased calculator. And as this is theoretically taken to be the " normal " situation, the curve is usually called the normal probability curve or curve of normal error.

Theory apart, many basic physical characteristics such as the height of men are distributed in this way. And mental characteristics too, such as the " general intelligence " gauged by Professor Burt's tests, appear to follow the same curve.

" From the numerous results obtained from the widespread employment of intelligence-scales, one fact of deep social significance emerges—the vast range of innate individual differences. A famous clause in the American Declaration of Independence proclaims that all men are created equal. In the psychological sense as distinct from the political, not only are men created unequal, but the extent of the inequality surpasses anything before conjectured. In a survey carried out upon all the children in a representative London borough—a census covering more than 30,000 cases—it was found that, within the elementary schools, the mental ratios might vary from below 50% to above 150% ; that is to say, the brightest child at the age of ten had the mental level of an average child of fifteen, while the dullest had the mental level of a little child of only five.

TABLE VIA

DISTRIBUTION OF INTELLIGENCE AND VOCATIONAL CATEGORY

Level of Intelligence (in mental ratio)	Educational category or school	Number of children (in percentages)	Vocational category	Number of male adults (in percentages)
1. Over 150	Scholarships (university honours)	0·2	Highest professional work	0·1
2. 130–150	Scholarships (secondary)	2·5	Lower professional work	3
3. 115–130	Central or higher elementary	13	Clerical, technical, and highly skilled work	12
4. 100–115	Ordinary elementary	35	Skilled work. Most minor commercial positions	27
5. 85–100	Ordinary elementary	35	Semi-skilled mechanical work. Poorest commercial positions	36
6. 70–85	Dull and backward classes	13	Unskilled labour and coarse manual work	18
7. 50–70	Special schools for mentally defective	1·5	Casual labour	4
8. Under 50	Occupation-centres for the ineducable	0·2	Institutional cases (imbeciles and idiots)	0·2

Over this vast scale the distribution of intelligence is neither flat nor yet irregular ; it follows a simple mathematical law. Its frequency conforms to the so-called ' normal curve,' and the abnormal and defective are found to constitute no isolated types, but to be simply the tail-end of a chance distribution. Probably all or most of our mental capacities are distributed in the same fashion.

Since variations in intelligence are so wide and so continuous, it becomes convenient to divide the entire population into about six or eight separate classes or layers. A classification of this kind, worked out empirically, for children, is already implicitly embodied in the organization of our various schools. A second classification can be drawn up, on an analogous basis, for adults, and will be found, in the main, to reflect the amount of difficulty and responsibility entailed by their several occupations. It is interesting to find that the proportionate number of individuals falling into the parallel sections tallies pretty closely both for adults and for children."[1]

If the physical and mental characteristics of man are distributed in this normal curve, we might expect many of the characters of the acts or works of men also to be distributed in this way.

Table VIB on page 70 shows the hourly output of a group of factory employees working on exactly the same job during the same hours. They were not specially selected for the job nor were they restricting their output ; on the contrary, they were women (mostly widows) not belonging to a Trade Union and " all out " to earn as much as possible at the rather scanty piece-rates offered them.

In this distribution there is clearly a more or less typical hourly rate of output about half-way between 2·2 and 2·8 lbs. per hour centring, say, at 2·5 lbs., and the number of hours when any specified output was made (i.e. the frequency) tapers off as the specified output deviates further from this typical value. And this " tapering " takes place at about the same rate or gradient on either side except for a marked " shrinkage " −0·6 and −0·8 from average.

The frequency of outputs between 2·0 and 2·2 lbs. (two classes below the class with the typical value) is 245 ; the frequency of outputs between 2·8 and 3·0 lbs. (two classes above that with the typical value) is 252. And five classes above and five classes below the typical value have each a frequency of 35 items. The distribution is more or less symmetrical and the typical value is near the centre of gravity of the whole distribution ; yet the mere statement

[1] Cyril Burt, *Presidential Address*, Section J, British Association for the Advancement of Science, 1923.

TABLE VIb

Fourteen Women Charging Small Buttons Over a Period of
4 Weeks to 4 Months—10 Hours' Plant U.S.A.[1]

Range of Value of Hourly Output	Number of times specified hourly output produced by any person	Deviation of·centre of range from rough Arithmetic Mean (2·5 lbs.)
Less than 1·4 lbs.	23	—
1·4 up to 1·6 lbs.	35	−1·0 lb.
1·6 up to 1·8 lbs.	59	−0·8 lb.
1·8 up to 2·0 lbs.	128	−0·6 lb.
2·0 up to 2·2 lbs.	245	−0·4 lb.
2·2 up to 2·4 lbs.	319 ⎫	−0·2 lb.
2·4 up to 2·6 lbs.	351 ⎬ 992	0·0 lb.
2·6 up to 2·8 lbs.	322 ⎭	+0·2 lb.
2·8 up to 3·0 lbs.	252	+0·4 lb.
3·0 up to 3·2 lbs.	194	+0·6 lb.
3·2 up to 3·4 lbs.	101	+0·8 lb.
3·4 up to 3·6 lbs.	35	+1·0 lb.
3·6 lbs. and above	16	—
All Values	2080	—

of any typical or average value—the arithmetic mean, to be precise, is 2·529 lbs. per hour—is obviously not a sufficient description of the facts ; less than half the items (992 out of 2080) have values in the (three) classes of value nearest the average value. To summarize the facts accurately, some measure must be given of the dispersion or scatter of the values above and below this average value.

Statistical theory has elaborated several measures of dispersion (Glossary §§10 and 11). The simplest and most intelligible device is to state the deviation above and below the average value within which the values of half the items fall. In Table VIb this deviation is slightly over 0·3 lb. ; obviously, half the items (1040) have values ranging slightly wider than the 992 items scattered 0·3 lb. round 2·5, from 2·2 to 2·8 lb. When items are ranked in the order of their values, the *quartiles* are the values of the items ¼ and ¾ of the way along the ranks (Glossary §9). Thus the quartiles exactly

[1] Florence, *Individual Variations in Efficiency*. Weltwirtschaftliches Archiv, Kiel, January 1924.

enclose the values of the middle half of items, and it is customary to take half the range between the quartiles as a measure of deviation called the *semi-interquartile range*. More exact and more frequently used measures of deviation, such as the average deviation and the standard deviation, are detailed in the statistical glossary (§11).[1] The rationale of their formulæ is not so obvious and they need not be described in detail here ; the interquartile range sufficiently conveys the general idea of a dispersion or deviation measure.

The deviation measure is particularly important in describing the normal curve, since it is a property of this distribution that once the average and the deviation measure are given, the whole curve can be drawn *ex hypothesi*. If half the items have a value within $1/x$th of the average value (i.e. if the semi-interquartile range measure of deviation is x), then it is possible, if the distribution is " normal," to state the relative frequency of all the values along the scale without specifying any further measures.

§3 Skew Distribution and the Problem of Averaging

The distribution that is apparently normal in the physical and mental characters of individual persons, and possibly in the direct outcome of such characters (e.g. output), is not, I think, quite so normal in economic and political life generally. By taking thought, man may not add to his stature, but (probably by not taking thought) he *does* add to his weight, and it is ominous for the study of man's more conscious activity that the weights of men are distributed abnormally[2] and that there is a bias toward heaviness.

Table VIc on page 72 gives the distribution of incomes in the U.S.A. ; a distribution clearly most " abnormal." It is not the moderately rich, the middle class, that are most numerous, but almost the poorest class.

Here there is not merely wide variation in the character under review, but variability in its very variation. There is no possibility of reducing the variation to any consistent formula.

A distribution such as that of wealth (Table VIc) is said to have a skew ; it is lop-sided, for the number or *frequency* of items at each value does not taper off equally or symmetrically on either side as we recede from the more or less typical values. Tapering occurs

---

[1] In Table VIB giving the distribution of hourly outputs, the average deviation would be (roughly) the sum of all the deviations regardless of sign, i.e. $0.2 \times 319 + 0.2 \times 322 + 0.4 \times 245 + 0.4 \times 252 + 0.6 \times 128 + 0.6 \times 194$, etc. etc., divided by 2080, the total number of item hourly outputs.

[2] Yule, *Theory of Statistics*, Table IX, Chapter VI.

TABLE VIc

DISTRIBUTION OF INCOME AMONG PERSONAL INCOME RECIPIENTS

United States of America, 1918[1]

Classes of Value of Income	Frequency within Class	Cumulative Frequency
	Thousand Recipients of Incomes of specified Class	Thousand Recipients of Income in and *below* specified Class
Below Zero	200	200	200
$ 0— 500	1,828 ⎫		2,028
$ 500— 1000	12,531 ⎬ 14,359		14,559
$1000— 1500	12,498 ⎫		27,057
$1500— 2000	5,222 ⎬ 17,720		32,279
$2000— 3000	3,065		35,344
$3000— 4000	953		36,297
$4000— 5000	430		36,727
$5000— 6000	234		36,961
$6000— 7000	143		37,104
$7000— 8000	94		37,198
$8000— 9000	66		37,264
$9000—10,000	48		37,312
Over— $10,000	257		37,569
All Incomes	37,569		37,569

only on the positive side of high incomes and the skew is termed positive.[2] At the negative end there is simply a landslide forming a regular "cliff" between the frequency of $500—$1000 incomes and that of incomes between 0 and $500.

Is there any one value that can be spoken of as the typical average income per family or person? If arbitrarily we took the arithmetic mean income as the typical value the frequency of items distributed below that value would far outnumber the frequency of the higher values. The arithmetic mean is given as $1543 a year, but the figures in column 3 of Table VIc show that out of the $37\frac{1}{2}$ million items there are 27,057,000 with incomes less than $1500,

---

[1] *Income in the United States*, National Bureau of Economic Research.

[2] Several different devices have been set forth by statisticians for measuring the direction and the comparative degree of skew. The simplest formula (Glossary §16) is to add the values of the upper and lower quartiles (in this case $1574 + $833 = $2407), subtract twice the median (in this case 2 × $1140 = $2280), and divide the remainder ($2407 − $2280 = + $127) by the difference of the quartiles ($1574 − $833 = $741): the "coefficient of skewness" thus calculated is $+\frac{127}{741}$: there is a *positive* skew of + ·17. This is only a model calculation to illustrate the application and applicability of measures of skew. The extensive taper at the positive end of the scale would be measured more significantly in the coefficient of skewness making use of the deciles, which are given below, or in the coefficient $\frac{Mean - Mode}{Standard\ Deviation}$. (See Glossary §16).

let alone less than $1543. Judging from the number of those receiving incomes between $1500 and $2000 there are probably relatively few persons with this "average" income. The most typical range of income in the sense of that most frequently occurring (i.e. the *modal* range) is obviously a great deal lower and appears in fact (*op. cit.* Table 25) to be $900 to $1000.

The arithmetic mean is clearly no satisfactory summary indication of the facts of the case and other formulæ must be used to obtain some average figure of income. The mode itself might be used, but while the arithmetic mean is unduly influenced by the high but infrequently found values, the mode, at about $1000 in the American distribution of wealth, is completely uninfluenced by the wider positive deviations.

A useful compromise between mode and arithmetic mean is provided by the median (Glossary §9), the value on each side of which are half the items when the items are ranked in order of their value. In the distribution under review this median value is $1140, i.e. there were as many persons with incomes below $1140 as with incomes above that figure ; and this is perhaps as exact a summary of the typical income as can be obtained. But obviously it is, taken alone, quite an inadequate summary of the facts. Nor will the additional information supplied by some measure of the average deviation give all the significant features of the distribution.

The semi-interquartile range is $\dfrac{\$1574 - 833}{2}$, viz. $370 ; and the *relative coefficient of dispersion* based on this measure (the range divided by the value of the midpoint between the quartiles, see Glossary §13) is $\dfrac{1}{2}\dfrac{370}{(833 + 1574)}$, i.e. ·31.

This points to a relatively narrow or upstanding dispersion and gives no representation of the long "taper" at the positive end, i.e. among the richer members of society,—the comfortably "well-to-do," to use their own modest euphemism. The skew-measure must be added (Glossary §16), or better still, a statement of the actual value of the quartiles and lower and upper *deciles*, i.e. (Glossary §17) the values of the items $\frac{1}{4}$, $\frac{3}{4}$, $\frac{1}{10}$, and $\frac{9}{10}$ of the way along the ranks, when items are ranked in order of their values.

The position of these measures is obtained from column 3 of Table VIc where the frequency is cumulated. 37,569,000 Recipients of Income are numbered in all. The lower (or first) decile is the income of the $\dfrac{37,569,000 \ th.}{10}$ recipient in order of income, i.e. the

3,756,900 th. ; and the upper or ninth decile is the income of the $\frac{37,569,000}{10} \times 9$ *th.* recipient, i.e. the 33,812,100 th. The lower decile falls somewhere in the \$500–\$1000 income class but nearer to \$500 ; approximately[1] at \$600. The upper decile falls in the \$2000 to \$3000 income class almost exactly,[2] at \$2300.

The values of the quartiles have already been given.

These five significant values serve to summarize the whole distribution :

	Values	Deviation from Median
Lower (1st) decile	\$600	540
Lower (1st) quartile	\$833	− 307
Median	\$1140	0
Upper (3rd) quartile	\$1574	+ 434
Upper (9th) decile	\$2300	+ 1160

A comparison of the deviation of the two quartiles or the two deciles from the median, immediately displays the positive skew in the greater deviation of the two positive values from the median as contrasted with that of the two negative values.

§4 *The Prevalence of Skew Distributions*

Skew distributions are often to be expected in the statistics of human events and social behaviour for at least four sorts of reasons :

(1) There are often limits imposed on the value of a character at one end of the scale and not at the other. The most obvious example occurs in the measurement of the time taken to perform certain acts. Man cannot run a hundred yards much quicker than in nine or ten seconds, but he can run, walk, or stroll it in any number of seconds or minutes at the positive end of the scale.

Measuring the time taken in successive repetitions of minor industrial operations, Dr. A. H. Ryan and I found a positive skew to be almost invariable,[3] so much so that the arithmetic mean had to be abandoned as a measure of the typical speed of the operation and the median substituted.

I examined the coefficients of dispersion and skewness (Glossary

---

[1] *Income in the United States*, Table 26.

[2] *Loc. cit.* Note that the frequencies of the values within each income-class are not equal, but decrease with increased values as does the whole distribution.

[3] See *U.S. Public Health Bulletin*, No. 106, Chapter IX.

§§13 and 16) obtained on as many as 45 series of uninterrupted repetitions of a lathe operation (2599 repetitions were included in all), and I worked out the percentage values of the significant deciles and quartiles relatively to the median.

Upper (9th) decile	+ 108·31%
Upper quartile	+ 103·57%
Median	100·00%
Lower quartile	97·01%
Lower (1st) decile	94·47%

The extremely narrow deviation from median is the statistical feature that first strikes the eye. It is a measure of regularity in timing, symptomatic of rhythmical activity, and will be discussed later.[1] The other interesting feature is the narrowness of the deviations on the negative side when compared with those on the positive side, a skew symptomatic of the physiological limit to speeding.

(2) In the distribution of output already given (Table VIB), a whole hour's output is the statistical item and the table does not show the probably skew distribution of times taken in individual repetitions of the operations, the charging of one button, *during* the hour. But even hourly totals of output are affected when the limits to speed are not only set physically and naturally, but also by human contrivance.

Statistics of hourly output or of the average output of a group of individuals[2] sometimes show a queer negative skew in their distribution which is in striking contrast to the distribution shown in Table VIB. If there was some agreement among workers to restrict output and not to produce more than a given amount, a landslide would obviously appear at this value in the frequency curve, with few items beyond the value on the positive side. The curve, in short, would show a negative skew, just as though the possible rate of output were obstructed by the mechanical or physiological conditions of production.

(3) Skewness in the quantitative variation of human acts may result not from the deliberate contrivance of the agent himself, but from the deliberate selection of the agent by some other " superior " person, or by dint of natural forces.

The selection of the fittest involves presumably the rejection of the unfittest, that is, the cutting away of the extreme negative

[1] Chapter VIII §3.
[2] Cf. *J.A.S.A.*, Sept. 1920, pp. 299–303 ; *U.S. Public Health Bulletin*, No. 106, Chapter IV, etc.

values. This process would tend to produce a positively skewed distribution of characters of the selected group, and a negatively skewed distribution of characters of the rejected group.

For some reason or other a short stature is considered unmilitary in spite of its obvious survival value in trench and guerilla warfare. Men below a certain height are rejected by the recruiting sergeant ; men above the normal are (all the more) joyfully accepted. The result is a positively skewed height distribution among armed forces.

Similar results should follow wherever vocational selection is adopted in industrial occupations or wherever candidates must pass some sort of entrance examination.

In the final examinations of Universities it is usual to distinguish three or more classes of success, yet it is often not the second or middle classes that are the most populous and have the highest frequency, but the third or lowest class. Presumably the normal frequency curve of ability established by Burt and others has been truncated more or less successfully[1] by the entrance examination. Half the belly representing the high frequency at the mode and all the tail of negative values has been severed and what is left is the slim head admitted to the first and second classes and the upper half of the (stout) body admitted to the third class.[2]

(4) The " dint " of natural forces may also effect a skew in the quantitative variation of human conditions and fortunes. A skew distribution (in this case again a positive skew) is inevitable in the ages of a population not recruited by immigrants, if the absolute number of births remains fairly constant. Apart from immigration there cannot be more people of thirty alive than were born thirty years ago, and in fact the misfortune of premature death sees to it that there should be considerably less. If as many (or more) are born this year as were born thirty years ago it follows that those aged thirty must be less " frequent " than those aged 0 to 1 ; and similarly throughout the age groups, the older the fewer.

If age implies experience the combined effect of death and the selection of the naturally more able would be cumulative in producing a positive skew in the holding of offices requiring skill and experience. The hierarchical principle of " the higher up the fewer " might conceivably be justified in this way by a statistical political science.

---

[1] Only more or less because some candidates were probably ploughed in their finals who should have been included in the truncation—others involved in truncation might have, finally, got " through."

[2] See, however, Peterson, in *American Journal of Political Science*, 1928, p. 758, who appears to assume a normal distribution of ability among students.

§5 Bimodal and Discontinuous Distribution

In Table VID showing the number of hours per week worked by men hired by the month on American farms, there are two typical values. There is a concentration of men working 60 to 64 hours a week but a second smaller concentration of men working from 48 to 56 hours per week. The arithmetic mean is 58·8 hours, a value almost completely unrepresented (there were only 155 cases of hours of work from 56 to 60 a week), and the median is much the same value.

A summary description of the hours worked must be in terms of modes. A 60 to 64-hour week is one mode representing 33% of all items and a working week of 48 to 56 hours is another mode, representing a further 28% of cases.

Beside bimodalism or multimodalism this table exhibits the greatest irregularity in the successive frequencies. The curve has not only two peaks but is jagged and serrated along most of its edge. Such an irregular silhouette is of frequent occurrence in statistics of human behaviour, owing to the preference of mankind for certain values picked out along the scale. The preference is often one for round numbers. It may be surmised from Table VID that a week of exactly 60 hours or of exactly 48 hours was a favourite arrange-

TABLE VID

HOURS OF LABOUR OF AMERICAN AGRICULTURAL WORKERS[1]

Second Quarter of 1921—Farms making Reports

Ranges of Hours worked per Week	Number of Males hired by the Month working specified Hours	
Under 40 . . .	102	
40 and over, but under 44	326	
44 ,, ,, 48	139	
48 ,, ,, 52	786 } 2nd Mode	
52 ,, ,, 56	665	
56 ,, ,, 60	155	
60 ,, ,, 64	1682 → 1st Mode	
64 ,, ,, 68	302	
68 ,, ,, 72	347 } 3rd Mode (?)	
72 ,, ,, 76	425	
Over 76 . . .	265	
	5194	

[1] Abridged from Table XLIII, Willford I. King, *Employment Hours and Earnings in Prosperity and Depression*, New York. National Bureau of Economic Research.

ment. In fact the six full day week would make all multiples of six more likely to occur as the weekly hours than would other figures. This probably accounts for the apparent unpopularity of the 44 but under 48, and the 56 but under 60 class; neither of them contains a multiple of six.

The same *discontinuity* in frequency is observable in many other statistics of human behaviour. Terms of discount offered by banks during any period are often quoted at certain rates but not at others that seem equally likely *a priori*. If 7% frequently occurs, so may 7½% and 8%, but not 8½%, 9% may occur only to a limited extent, 10% frequently, 11% not at all but yet occasionally 12%.[1]

Though possibly *natura non facit saltum*, as Marshall inscribed his "Principles,"[2] *human* nature certainly does jump, and the exercise of human control is often visible in the complicated multi-modal form of frequency distributions.

§6 *The Beggary of Literary Summarization*

A literary description would obviously be futile in all forms of distribution except those completely flat where all values are equally frequent, and those completely upstanding or thin where there is but one value to be found. And the introduction of the word "average" which literary standards now perhaps permit, would be of little avail unless the distribution were "normal," and of not too wide a deviation.

Graham Wallas quotes[3] an attempt on the part of a Permanent Secretary to the Irish Local Government Board to describe certain facts to a Royal Commission, in a more or less literary form.

"I don't say there are not second-class clerks (who are recruited at 18) equal to first-class (who are recruited at 23), nor do I say that all first-class clerks are on the same footing as regards ability; but there is undoubtedly a line of demarcation, which anyone dealing with administration easily detects, between first and second-class clerks."

"His phraseology," comments Graham Wallas, "is obviously unsatisfactory, but if he had merely said that 'on the average' first-class clerks are abler than second-class clerks, he would not have told the Commission that which he wanted to say, viz., that, if the ability of the members of the first and second class were

---

[1] Beckhart, *Discount Policy of the Federal Reserve System*, p. 395.
[2] The quantum theory now throws doubt upon even Nature's pedestrian continuity.
[3] *The Great Society*, Chapter X.

plotted on ' polygons of variation in respect to ability,' the two polygons would be similar, but that the first-class polygon would be superior to, though overlapped by, the second class. This is the kind of statement which we all want to make a dozen times a day about sections of every biological species from human beings to cabbages, and I know of no existing words in which it can be said which are both short and clear."

Graham Wallas is thinking of polygons (i.e. frequency curves or distributions) of more or less similar form. When the form is different, of various deviations and various skews, and perhaps with various numbers of modes, literary description falls shorter yet of what it " wants to say." Yet, however ungainly the narrative may be, any self-respecting social science must endeavour to describe summarily and accurately the widely scattered, lop-sided, and often humpy distribution of the characteristics of human behaviour, reactions, and situations generally.

The positively skewed distribution of the wealth and income of individuals within a community has already been noticed ; and it is probably of paramount importance in economic and political life that this happens to be the form of wealth-distribution. Yet most economic text-books give it only such a passing nod of acquaintance as suspiciously betokens a desire to cut.

Another character fundamental to economic and political activity is the duration of human life. Mr. Shaw has dramatized, and prefatorially described, the consequences of a longer *average* of human existence ; but what of the statistical distribution of ages-at-death among Methuselahs ? If a large number of them died young by accident before their long education had been complete, the unrequited cost to the community would be heavy and the quiet and passionless efficiency desiderated by Mr. Shaw greatly endangered. If again senescence were to set in after the age of, say, 300 and a large proportion lived on, senile, they would " improve " the average age at death, but not the productiveness and amenity of the new order.

The average age at death is no complete indication of the fact and consequence of a longer or shorter span of human life, and often, indeed, the distribution of " spans " is so abnormal that it is impossible to lay down definitely what this one particular average age is. The disagreement that exists due to the different methods of argument or the different points of view adopted, is an illuminating commentary on the difficulties of accurate summarization.

§7 *Conflicting Summaries of Age at Death*

The *average* age at death may be stated (according to the method of computation) as anything from half a year to about 80 years of age. Three points of view may be contrasted : (1) The realistically statistical. (2) The summary wisdom-while-you-wait, nutshell view. (3) The argument by deductive implication.

(1) The realist looks first to the frequency distribution. During the years 1906-10 those states and cities of the United States where registration is compulsory (The U.S. " Registration Area ") reported that 139,015 persons died annually in their first year, 29,523 in their second, 12,802 in their third, and so on downwards till the ages between 10 and 14, when about 2162 died on the average at *each year of age*. The absolute number of deaths then rises with age till between 65 and 69 the number averages about 8733 for *each* year of age ; then (owing to the continually decreasing " frequency " of those alive at the higher ages) the number of deaths falls again in consecutive years of age till between 90 and 94 deaths average only about 1020 for each year of age. The curve as a whole thus shows a bimodal distribution, with a high " spire " at 0 to 1, and a low mound with flattened crest at 65 to 69 ![1]

The one yearly age at which most people died was the first year of life, and if one value is to be named as the most typical age of death it must be the mode 0 to 1. But the realist will consider that no single average value can represent the facts.

The English statistics of deaths for 1923[2] of which Table VIE, column 2, gives an abridgement, shows the same sort of distribution. There is a pronounced mode in the first years of life, but there is a second mode with a flattened crest in the sixties and seventies. The lowest point of the " trough " in deaths occurs between ages 10 and 14, and the exact crest of the second mode between 70 and 74, five years later than in the American figures. A sufficient selection of age-classes is presented in Table VIE to show both these " turning points," the dip of the trough and the peak of the crest. For comparative purposes columns 3 and 4 exhibit deaths in England and America for each age group as a percentage of all deaths.

(2) In the American distribution for 1906-10, exactly 50% of the deaths are reported as occurring at ages under 39, so that the *median* age of all who died at that period might be computed by the statistician in a hurry at about 39 years. In the English

[1] *Statistical Abstract of the United States*, 1918, Table No. 54.
[2] *The State of the Public Health*, Annual Report of the Chief Medical Officer of the Ministry of Health, 1923.

distribution for 1923, 41% of the deaths occurred to persons *under fifty*, and 53% to persons *under sixty*, and the median age may be computed as about 57.[1] Yet these particular ages are nowhere near the top of any crest in the frequency curve. Death at these ages is in real life comparatively infrequent and the summary " nutshell " average most unreal.

(3) The death-rate in England and Wales to-day (1924–28) is roughly $12\frac{1}{2}$% per 1000 ; that is, one person dies every year among every 80 persons. It might be supposed, therefore, by the *deductively minded*, assuming a static State and a series of " ifs," that persons on the average live to 80.

TABLE VI_E

POPULATION AND DEATHS AT CERTAIN AGES

Ranges of Age	England and Wales, 1923[2]			U.S.A. 1906-10
	Population (Millions)	Deaths— Actual Number	% of Deaths at All Ages	% of Deaths at All Ages[3]
0– 4	3·6	78,574	17·6	27·3
5– 9	3·2	7,228	1·6	2·3
10–14	3·6	5,892	1·3	1·5
15–19	3·6	9,024	2·0	2·6
60–64	1·4	35,242	7·9	5·7
65–69	1·0	40,739	9·2	6·1
70–74	·7	44,100	9·9	6·1
75–79	·4	40,333	9·1	5·5
80–84	·2	29,132	6·5	3·9
Total at All Ages (including 20–60)	38·4	444,786	100·0	100·0

Obviously if there are eighty people evenly distributed in age (i.e. each at one-yearly age up to 80) and one of them dies every year and is replaced by a new-born babe, the average age of the

[1] This striking international contrast is partly due to the arbitrary method of nutshell statistics, partly to the gap in the years compared during which there was progress in the reduction of deaths in both countries, partly to the differences in the age-constitution of the two populations. Fewer died old in America because, owing to recent immigration of young people, there were relative fewer old people alive. A better test of comparative healthiness is the number of years' expectation of life of a child at birth. This, unlike the median or mean age at death, is not affected by the particular age-distribution of the living population.

[2] Report of the Chief Officer of the Ministry of Health, 1923.

[3] *Statistical Abstract of U.S.*, 1918.

whole group will continually rise unless it is the person aged 80 who dies. Every year each of 79 survivors becomes one year older— the average age advances exactly one ; and the only fact that can exactly counterbalance this and keep the average age of all the 80 constant, is the substitution of a child of 0–1 for an octogenarian who dies. If each age is equally represented at the beginning, and if this age-constitution among the living keeps constant year to year, and if the average age at death is also constant from year to year, then a death-rate of $12\frac{1}{2}$ per thousand, i.e. one death in 80, *must* imply an average age at death of 80.

The average age of death (i.e. the median age) in England to-day has been calculated above as something like 57. This divergence from the theoretical 80 is due chiefly to two statistically measurable divergences in the assumptions underlying the theory. The " if " clauses of the last paragraph fail to correspond with the facts in respect of the evenness and constancy of the distribution.

(a) Those living are *not* distributed evenly over all ages as Table VIE, column 1 makes clear. Population is more " frequent " in the earlier ages. Roughly speaking 40% of the population of England ($36\frac{1}{2}$% to be exact) are aged 0–20 years, 30% are aged 20–40 years, 20% 40 to 60, and 10% are over 60. This is a peculiarly uneven distribution and death will consequently tend to occur at lower ages than might otherwise be expected.

(b) The age-constitution among the living is far from constant. More babies of 0 are continually being born and surviving the early dangerous age than the total numbers of persons dying. In 1922, 780,124 were born (of whom about 50,000 would die before one and an aggregate of 75,000 before five), but only a total of 486,780 died at all ages in England and Wales. This accounts for the failure of the average age of the living, and hence the average age of the dying, to approximate to the death-rate expectation as much as it might *in the same year* if the facts under (a) were the only departure from the static theoretical conditions.

The average age at death is of the utmost importance in estimating man-power and national efficiency ; and it is clearly not to be computed without a thorough grounding in the statistical measurement of variability. It will not do to assume an even, " flat " distribution of ages among the living, nor yet a normal distribution about an average age either among the quick *or* the dying. Nor will it do to assume static conditions from year to year either in the total number of the population or in its average age.

This introduces the issue of the statistical measurement of

changes, "dynamic" as opposed to "static" problems. Before considering these issues in Chapter VIII, however, something must be added to the chronicle of human variability. For human affairs are not only variable but most uncertain in their variation.

CHAPTER VII

RISK AND UNCERTAINTY

WHERE there is wide deviation and a skewed or bimodal form of distribution, the average value of the character, whether mode, median, or mean be used, obviously becomes of less importance ; and even the deviation and skew measures and the table of quartiles and deciles, often prove inadequate to summarize the significant facts. The description of the ages at which deaths occur is such that there is no one age somewhere near the middle of the scale of ages which can be used to describe the general character of the facts, the " usual " age of death. In the distribution of wealth among Americans (Chapter VI §3) the ninth decile is $2300, and no higher value is given in the Summary Table. Yet it is only incomes of a value above this that can be said to afford much above a merely " decent " working-class standard of living. The well-to-do are relatively so few (in fact, not one-tenth of the population even in America), that they fall out of the summary picture given by the deciles altogether ! It is only in the close meshes of the upper percentiles (Glossary §9) that they are prevented from slipping through the investigator's net.

But this does not imply that summary statistical measurements must be abandoned. The enquiry must return to the original starting-point of the relative frequencies of values, i.e. qualities or ranges of quantity. The question asked at the outset and emphasized at the end of the last chapter was not what summary values best represent all the item values, but, when certain ranges of values along the scale are specified, how many items or what proportion of the whole number of items manifest values within each specified range.

§1 *Risks and their Frequency*

The summary but accurate statements that statistics strives to reach are not confined to the statement of an average value, or of an average deviation, or of a coefficient of skewness descriptive of the whole distribution. Instead of a whole frequency distribution

84

of values being specified and a representative value required, the original form of the statement may be worded to specify a certain range of values and to require statistics to show its proportionate or absolute frequency. The question might be what exact proportion of income recipients receive over $2500 a year. More usually it is pauperism, at the other end of the scale, that is under investigation. And here, also, it is not the *average* income of working-class families that is the important issue, but the number or proportion of families with incomes *below* a certain standard value of income.

In England employers are not legally compelled to compensate their workers for accidents resulting in less than four full days' absence from work, and the important question for them is not the *average* number of days lost by accident per worker employed,[1] but the proportion of days lost by reason of accidents of a specific degree of severity, i.e. resulting in the loss of more than three working days ; and it is, in fact, the frequency with which such losses occur for any one group of workmen that determines the premiums charged by insurance companies.

Pauperism, and compensatable accidents, are extreme events or involve extreme values, and they are also evils, and to such the word " *risks* " is currently applied.

But obviously a statistical description of the relative frequency of happy events is equally feasible, and equally important. The winning of a race for which perhaps a dozen other horses have been entered, is presumably an event of high value for those connected with the winning horse ; and if as a result of a statistical description of the horse's previous " form " people laid bets at certain odds, one might logically speak of their betting on the *risk* of the horse *winning*.

In practice it is uncommon to use risk in this way. Instead, popular speech indulges in the extension of the reference of " risk " from extreme (evil) values to extreme infrequency.

A premature death is a risk in the sense of an extreme value (the defunct was *in extremis*), an evil occurrence, and also a relatively unusual occurrence. Industrial insurance involves the promise to pay compensation and benefit when some emergency occurs that is not merely extremely severe but relatively infrequent, e.g. an accident severe enough to entail the loss of a given number of days' earnings.

But insurance companies speak blithely of " good " risks as well

---

[1] This average might actually come out lower than the prescribed number of days qualifying for compensation, and it would then look as though no compensation at all need be paid.

as bad risks, signifying thereby not that the thing risked is at all pleasant or that the value is extreme, but that the prospects or probability of a risk being *realized* in a given case is relatively *slight*. A man of unusual health for his age is a " good " subject to insure against the risk of premature death because he will probably live longer than the average of his age-class on which the terms of his insurance (the premiums, etc.) are based.

By a linguistic practice that Ogden and Richards[1] call the *utraquistic subterfuge*, the same word risk and also the word probability may refer to the terms of a bet or speculation, i.e. whether the odds or chances are even, six to one, ten to one, etc., or may refer to the subject-matter of the bet or speculation, i.e. the eventuality whose chances of realization are calculated and on which the odds are laid. This eventuality may be what we have called a quality (e.g. winning or not winning), or it may be quantitatively and numerically defined as the " odds." When the calculation deals with the chances, say, of £1000 or £2000 worth of damage being done by fire, or of a horse doing the course in a *specified* number of minutes, the usual confusion supervenes by reason of the double set of quantitatively measured " risks," one referring to the quantitative frequency of item occurrences, the other to the quantitative values that may occur.

As a further complication, probability, if not risk, may also refer to the degree of certainty with which the exact chances can be expected and estimated, the degree, for instance, to which any particular horse's form CAN indicate the correct odds to lay.

It should be obvious by this time that any inherent difficulty there may be in measuring probability or risk by statistical methods is greatly increased by terminological ineptitudes. Every notion referred to has *several* words referring to it, and every word *several* references.

§2   *A Reformed Terminology*

The situation most convenient for purposes of discussion would be one in which every notion had one symbol that referred to no other notion. If we suppose a word or symbol to be a husband and the thing referred to to be a wife, the most convenient situation can be described as one of monogamy. But the actual situation is one of complete promiscuity. Every husband (each word) has several wives (or references), every wife (or reference) several husbands

---

[1] *Meaning of Meaning*, p. 239.

(or words to refer to it) ; and nearly all the husbands of any one wife are also husbands to the other wives and most of the wives of any one husband are also wives to the other husbands.

To clarify the relationships it is best to isolate (in a box to be called A) the use of " risk " referring to the specified (usually extreme) value or range of values of a certain characteristic whether it is considered good or evil. This value (quantity or quality) corresponds to the *eventuality* whose proportionate frequency or exact chance of occurrence or realization is enquired into, the *subject-matter* of a prediction, speculation, bet.

Setting aside this eventuality or subject-matter, the ideas *about* the eventuality that are referred to so promiscuously, are of two kinds. There is (B) the frequency with which the eventuality is realized or may be expected to be realized relatively to other qualities or quantities of the same character ; a frequency which finds expression in the terms of a bet or an insurance policy, the " odds " laid and the " chances " estimated. And there is (C) the degree of certainty of this relative frequency being realized.

But both kinds of reference (B and C) may be made on any and all of three psycho-physical levels.

(I) There is, in theory at least, an exact physical chance or frequency of realization of a specified value, which would be known if all the " universe " of items concerned could be observed and measured, or all the factors in the situation gauged. The condition of gauging all the factors is approximately reached in the experimentalists' laboratory, and is approached outside the laboratory when instruments are specially constructed, like a roulette board and ball, or dice, to eliminate bias. If a perfectly constructed " unloaded " six-faced die is thrown a number of times, *a priori* the chances are that any one face must turn up in one-sixth of the total tosses, that is, must have relative frequency of $16 \cdot 7\%$. The reliability of this chance is in the long run, when the tosses form a sufficient number of instances or items, 100% ; and what number of items is sufficient to ensure $x\%$ of certainty is one of the problems of " probable error." In mere observatory work without control of instruments as in the laboratory or without *a priori* knowledge strength lies in numbers. The exact relative chance or coefficient of frequency of any value of a character can only be certainly known if all items manifesting the character are observed. But this is impossible. Only a *sample* of all the items is usually available for statistical measurement.

(II) The chances of an eventuality being realized, its expected frequency of occurrence, must be calculated from the values of an observed sample of items as far as circumstances allow, and the degree of reliability or unreliability of this calculation also calculated. On this level one may speak of actuarial or statistical expectation,[1] and actuarial or statistical reliability.

(III) There are purely psychological, subjective expectations about the outcome of eventualities ; hopes, fears, beliefs as to one's degree of " luck " depending largely on temperamental idiosyncrasies ; and on the same level are subjective degrees of assurance or doubt, with which such beliefs may be held—degrees of " credit " attached to such imaginings.

The level and relationships of these several references may be pictured in a diagram for the benefit of those who profit by such devices.

TABLE VIIA

ANALYSIS OF THE VARIOUS MEANINGS OF PROBABILITY

A.		B.	C.
	I.	Physical chances or frequency of realization of eventuality (or specified value) if *all* the items observed or *all* factors known.	100% Reliability, Certainty, etc.
The Specified		(Also called inherent Probability.)	in the long run.
Value, Risk, or Eventuality (also called the Probability.)	II.	Actuarial chances or frequency of realization of the eventuality (or specified value) expected on basis of *sample* of observed items. " The risks of a risk." (Also called the Probability.)	Various intermediate degrees of { Certainty, Credibility, Precision, Reliability, etc. (Also called the degrees of Probability.)
	III.	Chances or frequency of realization of the eventuality (or specified value) psychologically expected on no physical basis. Hopes, fears, beliefs, creeds, faiths.	100% Unreliability, Uncertainty, etc. (though the conviction and assurance of the " faithful " may be almost infinite.)

Many words like risks and probability will be noticed to occur in more than one compartment of the diagram. A system of monogamy —one man one wife in one apartment—whatever may be thought against it in real life, is certainly to be desired in the marriage of symbol and reference to produce scientific offspring. In cases of

---

[1] Mathematical expectation is used in this sense by Prof. Pigou, e.g. *Economics of Welfare*, ed. I, pp. 497–8 : " The mathematical expectation of earnings." But the epithet mathematical might apply equally well to Level I.

doubt as to their reference I propose to supplement these errant words, or words under suspicion of errancy, by signs in brackets indicating their position or box in the Table : i.e. A, B I, B II, B III, C I, C II, C III.

The distinctions between the seven entries in the diagram are not intended to be revolutionary, and consciously or unconsciously they are continually being made—in fact, they *have* to be made—by every economic and social investigator who wishes to save his work from the consequences of linguistic debauchery.

In "An Approach to the Theory of Business Risks " (*Ec. Jl.*, 1925) Lavington defines Risk as an " unrelieved probability of loss." This definition is on the middle level (II), but two pages further Lavington proposes slightly to amend this definition of Risk " by defining it not as the (actuarial) probability, but as the (individual) expectation of loss." This refers the reader to the lower level of the business man's (possibly quite unfounded) hopes and fears (B III) about the prosperity of the undertaking, and it is obviously on this level that a part of profits and interest may be said to be a payment for taking risk or bearing uncertainty or both.

Lavington then proceeds to distinguish uncertainty (C) from risk (B) : " There are, then, these two things : the expectation of loss known as Risk . . . and the likely error of that expectation known as Uncertainty," and he proceeds to argue that both are associated with economic losses. A business man either insures against risks or makes an allowance for risk which he includes in his expenses of production.

" The spinner learns the cost of momentary stoppages due to broken threads, the potter the proportion of his wares injured in the processes of firing, the shipowner the wastage of his property on the seas ; and each trade gradually forms its rough estimate of the degree in which the operation of its plant will fall short of its full productive efficiency as a result of the irregular demands of its markets. As the average value of these Risks is gradually revealed, that value passes more and more certainly into expenses of production, and the realized money costs of Risk are recovered more and more surely from the consumer. But in fact, of course, this tendency is not fully effective. The range of imperfectly foreseen events extends from the calculable average of the spinner through the partially known fluctuations in market conditions and the chances of Trade Disputes to occurrences increasingly uncertain in their incidence and increasingly important in their effects. And the result is that the entrepreneur is exposed to the disturbing influence of events whose realized costs may differ widely from his expectation."

To the physical sciences " Level III " may be of little importance, but in all sciences dealing with human nature the level of fancy and imagination figures as largely in the content or " copy " of the science as Levels I and II should figure in its method.

Modern business is largely concerned in anticipating demand, and in the absence of mathematical estimates of demand business men's (perhaps undue) optimism or pessimism about the realization of profitable eventualities is the controlling factor in the speed of the industrial machine. The political machine, too, is largely controlled by expectation of the way the cat will jump. Electoral results in a democracy are notoriously uncertain, and popular (and even " inside ") prediction cannot be said to have gained any remarkable success. Nor do autocrats appear to have been any more successful in gauging the public opinion on which their tenure of office ultimately depends.

They, and party organizers in a democracy, would give a good deal to be able to turn their mere hopes and fears into probabilities and improbabilities, i.e. fairly reliable estimates of their exact chances.

Hopes, fears, doubts (B III) usually diverge wildly from the actuarial expectations (B II). Londoners' fears in the German air raids on their town were ridiculously greater than was justified by the actual proportion hurt by bombs (B II) ; on the other hand the hopes of survival by men in the trenches were probably higher than was actuarially justified. And these opinions are usually held with an assurance that is *inversely* correlated with their actuarial certainty or uncertainty. The more unreliable a faith actuarially, the less, usually, the Doubt of the believer.

Though one function of statistical methods is " mere " description, the same or similar methods may also be used for prediction and can to some extent reduce wild speculation to a tame and cool calculation of chances.

Mr. Lavington's spinner and shipowner have reduced certain of their risks to actual figures which can be included in their estimates of costs of production for the following year or for any specific new contract that is being bid for. But the transition from observed past to unobserved future is often beset with pitfalls and the business man must realize what he is doing. He is attempting to get away from mere psychological states of mind (Level III) about issues that are alive and pressing for solution, and to reach physical certainty through his limited experience of facts that are past, and often dead and gone. He is trying to combine physical accuracy with generalization about the *inconsequent* variable facts of economic life, and it is the intermediate level that demands further attention.

The word probable, though often used on Level I (as in the " physical or inherent probabilities of the case," column B), is principally used on Level II. On this level its reference may be either to Column B or C, and usually it refers to a combination of both. It is occasionally also used for the actual eventuality under discussion (A). As a result it is possible to make such a statement as that *this probability is probably improbable,* i.e. this particular eventuality is fairly reliably calculable as relatively infrequent.

But there is a further complication in the use of the word probable. Specifically, *probable* also refers to a *particular degree* of probability of the eventuality being realized (B) or of this expectation being reliable or not (C).[1]

To predict that some eventuality will probably be realized (B) is to assert something less than that it will *always* or *generally* be realized, but something more than that it is equally likely to be realized or not realized. One cannot say at one and the same time it will probably rain or it will probably not rain. To say that an eventuality is probable means in popular usage *much* more than that it will be *sometimes* or *possibly* realized; " usually " is, in some contexts, the nearest equivalent. And, again, to say that the expectation or prediction is a probable one (C), lies between saying that it is certain and reliable, and that it is uncertain and unreliable. Curiously enough, while in respect of the actual chances probable refers to *more* than an equal chance, in respect of the degree of reliability " probable " does refer to some medium, fair degree of reliability which in the expression " probable error " definitely denotes equally likely to be correct as not.

The following diagram on page 92 ranks in a rough order the degrees of frequency statistically expected (B II) and the statistical reliability of that expectation (C II) as commonly stated in ordinary language.

Relatively high frequency or relatively low frequency (i.e. infrequency) of realization (or occurrence) may be combined with stronger or with weaker degrees of certainty or reliability; and

---

[1] In my own terminology, probable is one quality in respect of the character probability, just as frequent is one quality in respect of the character frequency, i.e. it is the opposite of the quality infrequent. Cf. Chapter V, Rule 1.

	Degree of Frequency of Realization (B II)			Degree of Certainty or Reliability (C II)
That the Eventuality or Risk will	always generally *probably* (usually) sometimes *possibly* never	be realized is		uncertain possible plausible *probable* (as often as not true) *certain*

what is commonly referred to by the shorthand expressions, " probability," " improbability," " possibility," and " plausibility," are combinations of these two sets of degrees. Frequent use will be made of these expressions, and their reference, therefore, I shall give here in full as a terminological rule additional to the three rules in Chapter V :

Rule IV. *An eventuality which is moderately (or fairly) reliably expected to be realized with relatively high frequency, may be called a probability.*

An eventuality which is moderately reliably expected to be realized relatively infrequently may be called an improbability.

An eventuality which is rather unreliably expected to be realized with relatively high frequency may be called a plausibility.

An eventuality which is rather unreliably expected to be realized either *with relatively low frequency* or *with any unspecified frequency may be called a possibility.*

§3 *The Statistical Estimate of Probabilities*

How does the statistical method formulate, or rather how does it fill in the formula of a probability involving considerations pertinent to columns A, B, and C in Table VIIA ?

(A) The eventuality speculated about may be a mere qualitative distinction such as success or failure, but it can be a value or range of values specified quantitatively. Often this range of values includes all values at the extreme end of the whole scale of values, and when it is the " wrong " end, e.g. death at or before forty, the eventuality is, as we have seen, usually called a risk. But it is also possible that the eventuality whose occurrence or recurrence is speculated about is some more or less average range of values at the centre of the scale.

(B) To calculate the chances of an eventuality being realized, say that a male person twenty-five years of age will (a) die before he is forty or will (b) not die till he is over seventy-five, is just the sort of problem that the practical statisticians called actuaries delight in ; the chances of realization can, for a given place and time, be stated in exact numerical terms. As far as England and Wales from 1901 to 1910 is concerned, the answer to (a) is 9·1% to (b) 26·6%.[1]

What is the basis for such calculations ?

Where there is no *a priori* knowledge of what the relative frequency of the different values should eventually be (as there is in dice-throwing), the chances or " statistical expectations " (B II) are based on the actually observed or " experienced " frequency, or the actually observed or " experienced " average (B I). With no source of knowledge except observation we can only know what to expect from what has already been experienced or sampled under similar circumstances. Therein lies the practical importance of statistical description of existing experience or samples of experience.

If, on the other hand, economics and politics are deduced from some " inside " knowledge of human motive like an *a priori* knowledge of the possibilities of dice-throwing, experience and its summing up are of subsidiary importance. Even if a six had turned up five times in the experience of twenty throws of one unloaded dice, I should still be chary of taking 3 to 1 against, for I know *a priori* (whatever the actual but limited experience may be) that the " inherent " physical chances are 5 to 1 against.

If I know that the dice is loaded I shall still, if I am wise, bet according to my " inside " knowledge, not according to my experience of the first few throws.

But Economics and Political Science cannot, in my view (Chapters III and IV) rely on an *a priori* assumption. Man is not a loaded dice always trying, calculating, reasoning to turn up a high value and turn down a low ; at least we have no certain, inside, knowledge that this is so, and we must judge partly at any rate by previous experience. The simplest statistical expression of past results is a statement of *the comparative frequency of a specified range of values*.

An average value seems an obvious device to describe summarily the various observed values of a characteristic, but from the point

---

[1] Newsholme, *Vital Statistics*, p. 253, Table B.

of view of prediction of values as yet unobserved, the average wears a more complicated aspect. The average of the value of any character of sample items is the value from which the observed values deviate least. It is, therefore, for the unsampled items (or the whole set of items) not necessarily the true value but simply the most probable value of that character. *The arithmetic mean*, to be precise, appears as a value such that when the plus and minus deviations therefrom of all the item-values are summed, they cancel out ; it appears also as the value from which the standard deviation of any distribution of item-values is least (Glossary §11). The *median* appears as that value from which the plus deviations are equal in number to the minus deviations. The *mode* is by definition the most frequent value, i.e. the one value individually most probable.

But though deviations from the average value calculated in one way or another are less than from any other value, it is quite possible that no one item-value may be identical with the average value (unless the mode is used), if this average value is stated with great exactitude. The more measurements are refined the more the probability of their occurrence is reduced. Among a thousand men it would be most improbable for any one man to measure exactly 5 ft. 7·32753 inches, though this might be the exact median or mean. To calculate probabilities for practical purposes, therefore, it is more convenient to think of approximations, e.g. to specify a sufficiently wide range round the average or any other representative value and to estimate the number of cases (i.e. the frequency of items) having values within those specified limits. In short, the *exact* average value is abandoned for a specified *range* of values, and the statistical results on which prediction or generalization is made can be reduced to one identical form, a statement of the *comparative frequency of* a specified range of values.

"A statistical generalization is always of the form : ' The probability that an instance taken at random from the series S will have the characteristic ϕ is p.' "[1] For example, the probability that any number taken at random from a series of numbers will have the characteristic of being odd is $\frac{1}{2}$. Oddness is a quality ; but statistics are also required to estimate the probable occurrences of eventualities of quantitative value, and this complicates the form of statement. Statistical generalization will in this case be of the form[2] : The probability that an instance taken at random

---

[1] J. M. Keynes, *A Treatise on Probability*, p. 412.
[2] Expressed in the terms I defined in Chapter V §2. Note that Keynes uses the term characteristic where I use quality, quantity, or value.

from the series or set of items, S, will have the value or range of value a is p_1, that it will have the value b is p_2, that it will have the value c is p_3 . . . and so on . . . where a b c . . ., etc., are values or ranges of value of the character ϕ.

(C) With what degree of reliability (certainty or uncertainty) will a specified range of value be realized with any given frequency ? How certain are the chances of this eventuality occurring ?

Where there is no *a priori* knowledge, the statistical estimate of chances of an eventuality or range of values being realized (B II) is based on the observed frequency of realization of that eventuality or value in a sample or samples (B I). Similarly the statistical measure of the *reliability* or uncertainty of that estimate (C II) is based on the observed *stability* in the frequency of realization of the eventuality or specified range of value in *successive* samples (C III).

The reliability is the greater, on the one hand, the greater the number of items observed, and on the other, the lower the deviation from estimated expectation of the frequencies of the specified range of values in each sample.

According to the 7th English Life Table based on the experience of 1901–10, the eventuality that an Englishman of twenty-five will die before he is forty is expected to be realized in about 9·1% of cases. In other words, among Englishmen aged twenty-five the ninth percentile value of age at death is about forty (Glossary §9).

But the reliability of this expectation depends on the number of Englishmen observed for the purpose of the estimate and the deviation that samples of them showed. If the observations were collected in separate samples of a hundred, and if among the first hundred observed 18 died and among the second hundred none, giving an average expectation of 9, expectation will be less reliable than if 8 died among the first hundred observed and 10 among the second—also giving an average expectation of 9. And obviously the more hundreds observed to average 9 deaths the more reliable that figure.

When quantitative characters are dealt with, it is often the reliability of an *average* value that is required to be calculated. In calculating the frequency of approximation to an average value, it is convenient, as already explained, to specify any required limits round the average value and to estimate the relative frequency of items with values within the range of those limits. The problem of the reliability of an average and of any specified range of value is thus cast in the same form.

Theoretically a full statistical statement of risk and uncertainty should contain three numerical measures : The specified range of value betted on, the odds or chance of its realization, and the degree of certainty or reliability of these odds. In practice, instead of first specifying some definite limits or range either at one or other end of the scale or round the average (e.g. height within half an inch plus or minus of average), the chance or comparative frequency of realization is given conventionally as a standard (say, half or nine-tenths of the total items) and the various ranges of values within which this exact proportion of cases may be expected to fall are then calculated according to the number of observations made and the observed degree of deviation experienced. In order to gain a measure of certainty and reliability, we lose in simplicity and definiteness. We can no longer specify one definite range of value and find its exact frequency of realization, but must be content with the standard frequencies of various ranges, unspecifiable at the outset.

The measure of reliability called the *Probable Error* (Glossary §19) finds for any number of observed samples or items the range of values within which half the item-values are likely to fall, i.e. the range of values the frequency of realization of which can, considering the evidence, be *reliably* expected to be 50%, and on the realization of which in any given case the betting should be even odds. Where the distribution of item-values is " normal " this range of eventuality can be calculated fairly accurately. Moreover we know in this case (see Table in Glossary §18) that if on the observed, sampled evidence 50% of items manifest values with a range from " Q " above to " Q " below the average, then 95·7% will manifest values within a range from 3Q above to 3Q below average.

Calculation of the probable error of the average of an observed sample distribution of values, drawn from a large group of values, in foretelling the average of the whole group mostly unobserved, is based on some very simple considerations. One unobserved item *might* manifest a value anywhere along the whole scale of values. In other words, the *possible error* of the expectation might be almost any amount within the limits of the scale. But values of a *number* of hitherto unobserved items similar, similarly situated, and of similar magnitude to those already observed as a sample will not, on the average, show anything like the possible error. To begin with there will be some small errors " mixed in " which will tend to dilute the possible wide errors to an average consistency of error ; the average error of this number of new items will tend toward the average deviation of the originally observed sample of items. In the second place, some of the number of new, hitherto unobserved item-values will be above the original average value, others will be below ; and by cancelling out, the average of distributions of these unobserved values will " fluctuate " or deviate from the sample average by an amount less than the average deviation of the observed sample distribution. Thirdly, in a normal distribution the deviations above and the deviations below expectation respectively should not only tend to show the same average but *should be equally frequent.* Thus the greater the total frequency of observed or sampled items, the more likely it is that the probable error of expectation based on the observed average will be only a fraction of the observed deviation measure, whether the average deviation, or the semi-interquartile range, Q, be used for this purpose.

Mathematical theory shows that in the normal distribution, the probable error of the average is the semi-interquartile range divided by the square root of the total frequency of observed items. Suppose, then, the manufacturer employing the women charging buttons (Table VIB) wants to know with what certainty he can rely in the future upon the rate of production of the fourteen women being maintained, when conditions are the same. He knows the average of the preceding period was 2·529 lbs.

This exact figure, of course, is not likely to be reproduced in the future, and anyhow, what the manufacturer wants to know is what he may *reliably* expect in round numbers.

The evidence before him already summed up in the interquartile range is that in 50% of *separate instances* the rate of output was little less than 2·529 — ·300 lbs. per hour, i.e. 2·229 lbs., or more than 2·529 + ·300 lbs. per hour, i.e. 2·829 lbs.

Now in the future one or several women may be in exceptionally good form in some of the hours, or a number of hours may be exceptionally favourable for some of the women—as indeed they were recorded to be in the observed distribution. But there is an equal chance that some of the women may be " off-colour " and the hours unfavourable to production. These values of *individual instances* will cancel out and the future average value is likely to be *more* certain than the interquartile range of item-values indicates, i.e. the expectation of an hourly output within the interquartile range 2·529 — ·300 lbs. to 2·529 + ·300 lbs. is likely to be more than 50% certain.

If all the item-values, i.e. hourly outputs of each woman, are independently determined,[1] the employer may safely calculate that

---

[1] This cannot be assumed off-hand since, e.g., one woman's illness may affect all her hourly outputs for a considerable period.

H

the rate of output is as likely as not to average within the range $2 \cdot 529 \pm 0 \cdot 300$ lbs. divided by the square root of the number of such instances $= 2 \cdot 529 \pm \dfrac{0 \cdot 300}{\sqrt{2080}} = 2 \cdot 529 \pm \cdot 006$. This is the range of probable error or 50% certainty, but if a standard of 95·7% certainty is required the employer can only be assured that the output will average within the range $2 \cdot 529 \pm 3 \left(\dfrac{0 \cdot 300}{\sqrt{2080}} \right) = 2 \cdot 529 \pm \cdot 020$.

If when the new output is actually observed, its average is found to be outside these wide limits, the investigator is justified in speaking of a *significant* difference between the averages of the new and the original sets of output. The two sets are not, apparently, *random samples* of the same conditions. New and different conditions affecting the output appear to have supervened. Thus the probable error is useful not merely in estimating or predicting the limits within which, or without which, summary measures of the same character as yet unobserved are with equal probability likely to fall ; but is useful also in discriminating between differences that are significant and are worth further investigation, and those that are attributable simply to fluctuations in sampling.

Normal distribution is probably the exception rather than the rule among political and economic values, and even where the distribution appears normal (without any strong *a priori* reason) caution must be exercised in measuring degrees of reliability by means of the probable error formula. Yet to quote one authority :

" It can be shown mathematically that even when the form of distribution is distinctly non-normal the ordinary rules for finding the probable deviations hold with an approximation close enough for practical purposes, and experimentation with different forms of distribution bears out the mathematical conclusions."[1]

§4 *Social Insurance and Business Risks*

It is the law of large numbers, the increased *certainty* of an estimate when a large number of items is covered, that encourages all forms of insurance against the occurrence of some eventuality. And " social " insurance against the eventuality of increased poverty or the complications due to poverty is gaining the attention of all practical economists and politicians.

[1] Carl J. West, *Introduction to Mathematical Statistics.*

Social insurance, as such, does not directly affect "chances" and risks,[1] it does not diminish total frequency of the eventualities insured against. It does not directly diminish the proportion of deaths, the amount of sickness or unemployment, or the number of accidental injuries among wage-earners. It does not directly reduce the probability or chance of occurrence of these eventualities to any one workman. But it *does* make the expectation of the given frequency of the economic losses involved more certain and uniform.

Of a large number of working men the chances or expectations are, say, that ten out of a hundred will be unemployed at any one time; but of any one particular group of a hundred the actual occurrence of this proportion is uncertain.

Even if all individuals in such groups shared the losses involved, members of one group of a hundred would lose more than members of another. But if the group of men mutually insuring one another is increased by random selection to, say, 10,000, the percentage unemployed among each of the different groups tends toward equality and uniformity.

If 10% are expected to be unemployed on the average for the country as a whole, approximately 10% of unemployment will be realized within each relatively large group of individuals selected at random. Thus if each individual within the group wanted to be completely insured against the economic loss involved, he would give one-ninth of his pay while employed as a premium in return for the assurance of benefits at full pay while unemployed[2]; and a *large* enough group could accept this bargain with fair certainty of making ends meet. Almost uniformly for every member receiving full earnings out of the common fund there would be nine members paying in one-ninth of their earnings, i.e. one man's full earnings.

But not so a small group. The same actuarial expectation of one out of ten being unemployed would be more often belied than not, and a series of periods when the lie was an exaggeration rather than an understatement would reduce the group involved to bankruptcy.

Increased certainty or *security* is obtained not only by the fact of individuals mutually clubbing together, but by the fact that each of them will usually insure over long periods. The longer the time

[1] I.e. considerations of Type B in Table VIIA. Insurance is essentially an attempt to meet the uncertainty (Type C) of a *given* risk.

[2] To be quite fair he should not when unemployed receive the usual gross pay but the usual net pay of those in employment after subtraction of the premium, and if this were arranged the premium paid by those in employment could be lessened by a fraction.

over which insurance is spread the more *certain* of realization is the mathematical expectation.

Some social eventualities, particularly those where physical and physiological factors are of prime importance, are more certain than others. Death, sickness, accidents, can all be safely " covered " by insurance companies of average business efficiency. Unemployment insurance, on the other hand, partly because the condition of random selection cannot be fulfilled,[1] is usually undertaken only by the State, Municipality, Trade Union, or Friendly Society willing, if necessary, to face a loss for the " common good." And other eventualities there are that are not suitable for insurance at any cost or on any principles.

Insurance against business risks, i.e. against the eventuality of " losing money," when " making money " in profits was the chief consideration in conducting the business, has rarely been deliberately undertaken by persons other than those conducting the business. The losses have appeared too uncertain in their comparative frequency, as well as in their value or intensity. Their frequency of realization is not uniform but depends on the circumstances of time and place, on the economic conjuncture of the particular industry, and on the personal capacity of the men conducting the business firm and their willingness to exercise that capacity,—a willingness that might suffer if profits were insured. Increased certainty of any expectation of adequate profits could only be obtained—as scientific investment experts tell us—by flinging wide the net and including many firms, many places, many industries for many years all in one gigantic scheme. Where one firm in one industry in one country over a limited number of years is concerned, the individual investor can only form an *expectation* of profit subject to the widest *uncertainty*.

Suppose a waiter in a restaurant is left a thousand pounds invested in 5% War Loan which at that time stood at par on the Stock Exchange. He knows nothing of stocks and shares and the science of investment, but feels that a bright fellow like him ought to get more than 5% on his money. He sees the lavish expenditure going on among those he waits upon, and he feels that with such excellent customers there must be money in the restaurant business. Opportunely he hears of the forthcoming issue of shares of a new hotel and restaurant company ; but, being a bright fellow, he knows he must enquire into the previous profit-making record of such companies, and he opens his *Economist* for February 4, 1922, to find the very statistical information he wants.

---

[1] And partly because of the cyclical fluctuations in Unemployment.

TABLE VIIb

ANNUAL DIVIDENDS OF TWELVE BRITISH HOTEL AND RESTAURANT COMPANIES, 1912–1921

Year				Code Number of the Individual Company[1]							
	(1)	(2)	(3)	(4)	(5)	(6)	(7)	(8)	(9)	(10)	(11)	(12)
1912–13	Nil	8	$2\frac{1}{2}$	3	11	$193\frac{1}{3}$	10	5	6	15	9	6
1913–14	Nil	6	Nil	3	11	50	10	5	5	$12\frac{1}{2}$	9	6
1914–15	Nil	Nil	Nil	Nil	8	25	Nil	Nil	$3\frac{3}{4}$	$17\frac{1}{2}$	9	3
1915–16	Nil	Nil	Nil	Nil	$2\frac{1}{2}$	75	5	Nil	$2\frac{1}{2}$	$12\frac{1}{2}$*	9	Nil
1916–17	Nil	Nil	Nil	Nil	$2\frac{1}{2}$	$133\frac{1}{3}$	6*	Nil	4	$12\frac{1}{2}$*	9	Nil
1917–18	Nil	Nil	Nil	Nil	8	150	$7\frac{1}{2}$*	Nil	6	$17\frac{1}{2}$*	9	Nil
1918–19	Nil	Nil	Nil	Nil	11	$150\frac{1}{2}$	$7\frac{1}{2}$*	Nil	10	$12\frac{1}{2}$*	10	6
1919–20	Nil	15	Nil	Nil	11	$133\frac{1}{3}$	$7\frac{1}{2}$*	Nil	15	$12\frac{1}{2}$*	10	$13\frac{1}{2}$
1920–21	Nil	8	$6\frac{2}{3}$	Nil	15	Nil	Nil	10	15	$12\frac{1}{2}$*	11	3

* Free of Income Tax.

Let us suppose that he has no conception of the circumstances that may underlie variations in business profit, but judging solely from the table of values before him he is thinking out the price at which to buy the stocks on the Stock Exchange.

He begins by calculating the average of the annual dividends declared by all the companies. From this labour he soon turns bewildered.

The rates of dividend of any company in any year vary, over a wide scale of values, from 0 to $193\frac{1}{3}$% and there is no clear central point or range within the scale where rates of dividend tend to be more frequent than at other points or ranges. There is no average value to which the majority of single values would approximate fairly closely, and which could be said to sum up the whole distribution of values. The impossibility of giving any one such representative value leads the statistically minded to sum up the facts in another way; to state the proportionate frequency with which certain given ranges of value occur.

Our enterprising waiter is not primarily interested in average results. He is frankly speculating on changes in the market value of his stock and is attempting the multiplication of his inheritance at the least possible risk of losing all. From his statistics he wants to obtain the relative frequency with which dividends are actually " passed," and the frequency with which high dividends on capital (say, a dividend of over 100%) are actually realized.

In addition to the average rate the prospective investor therefore proceeds to calculate (for the twelve companies over the nine years) the percentage of times (i.e. the relative frequency) when no dividends were paid. The arithmetic mean rate of dividend for all

[1] For actual name of Company see *The Eco omi* February 4, 1922.

the twelve companies over the nine years was 13·3%, but the eventuality of total loss of dividend was realized 40 times out of a possible 108, i.e. the realization of this unfortunate eventuality or *risk* was some 37%.

But the prospective investor wants also to know the reliability of the average dividend and of his estimate of riskiness, and in columns (1) and (2) of Table VIIc he proceeds to observe each company separately as though it were a random sample of results to see whether this " average " and this " risk " was uniform over all companies. Obviously the deviations of the separate companies from the average rate of dividend of 13·3% and from the 37% chance of total loss of dividend are enormous, and he concludes that this wide deviation between individual companies together with the relatively small number of companies under review makes the unreliability of the general average dividend of 13·3%, and of the general expectation of total loss, very high.

TABLE VIIc

SUMMARY MEASURE FOR PREDICTING PROBABLE DIVIDEND AND RISK OF
NO DIVIDEND

Based on Dividends of Twelve British Hotel and Restaurant Companies for each of Nine Years, 1912–1921

Code Number of Company[1]	Percentage frequency (chances) of No Dividend	Average Rate of Dividend on Capital for the Nine Years
(1)	100	0·0
(2)	55	4·1
(3)	77	1·0
(4)	77	0·7
(5)	0	8·9
(6)	11	101·1
(7)	22	6·0
(8)	66	2·2
(9)	0	7·5
(10)	0	13·9
(11)	0	9·4
(12)	33	4·2
Average	37	13·3

Not all businesses are as uncertain or as unreliable in average rate of dividend and average rate of *no* dividend as the British Hotel and Restaurant industry seems to have been between 1912 and 1921, and when all the firms in one industry and all types of

[1] For actual name of Company see *The Economist*, February 4, 1922.

industries are observed (a natural preliminary to scientific investment) then statistical stability may appear. Bowley[1] quotes an
investigation into 3878 companies whose average (arithmetic mean)
rate of dividend *on capital* was £4. 15s. 7d.%. Seventy-six per cent of
the companies had a rate of dividend between £3 and £6 and only
6% had no dividend. The uniformity was high, the deviation low.

Henderson[2] suggests that the risks of business enterprise are
usually of such a type that there is a large chance (i.e. the expected
frequency is high) of a " relatively small gain, balanced by a small
chance of serious loss or entire failure."

As far as dividends are used as a measure, the small sample of
an industry given above belies this view. There appears in fact
a slight chance (one company out of twelve) of making very large
profits, but a large chance of making little or no profits. The facts,
however, merit a wider extension of the statistical treatment to
which they are so admirably suited.

Henderson's statement may be put into statistically recognizable
terms. It is equivalent to the assertion that the distribution of
rates of profit about the average rate is *negatively skewed*.[3] The
negative values below the average, though fewer in number, will
be the more extreme. The risk of very low values is more frequently
realized than the " risk " of very high values.

Table XVIIj, reproduced from the report of the Royal Commission
on the Coal Industry, exhibits the losses and profits per ton of 613
British Coal-Mining undertakings in 1925. The modal[4] profit is
near 0, the arithmetic mean profit is a loss of 3d. per ton, but heavy
losses of over 5s. a ton are more frequent than heavy profits of
over 5s., as 56 to 13. This constitutes a negative skew at least at the
extremes. The evidence from other industries does not however agree.

In his evidence before the Colwyn Committee on National Debt
and Taxation Mr. W. H. Coates submitted statistics of the rate of
profit on turnover as computed for income-tax purposes. The
figures refer to corporate enterprises in cotton, wool, iron, and steel,
miscellaneous metal and food industries, and wholesale and retail
distribution for the two financial years 1912–13 and 1922–23, and
there is a certain similarity in the form of distribution of the profit
rates for the two years.

[1] *Elementary Manual of Statistics*, Chapter VII.
[2] *Supply and Demand*, Chapter VII. This also appears to be the view of
Prof. Carver in suggesting that in business the possible losses are larger than
the probable gains. See Knight, *Risk, Uncertainty, and Profit*, pp. 364 ff.,
for this and other theoretical views.
[3] Glossary §15. See the graphical representation in Pigou, Appendix to
Economics of Welfare.
[4] See Glossary §5.

In the earlier year the median rate of profit on turnover was 4·61%, the lower and upper quartiles 2·53% and 7·67% respectively, and the coefficient of dispersion based on these measures therefore $\dfrac{7\cdot67-2\cdot53}{2\times4\cdot61}=\cdot56$.[1] In the later year the median rate was 4·11%, the lower and upper quartiles 1·24% and 8·46%, and the coefficient of dispersion based on those measures therefore ·88.

In both years there was a decided positive skew. Calculated by formula B, §16 of the Glossary, the coefficient was +·19 in the earlier year, +·20 in the later year, and (see formula A) the arithmetic mean was considerably higher than the median in both years. The positive skew is also easily demonstrable for the year 1912–13, when the median was not far from 5% (4·61), by grouping companies into those securing profits below 5% and those securing profits above 5% and then dividing these groups into sub-groups : (1) heavy loss, (2) subnormal return, (3) moderate profits, (4) heavy profits. Thus a frequency distribution is obtained roughly about the median which shows that

> 0·10% of Companies had a loss of more than 5%.
> 53·33% of Companies had anything between a loss of 5% and a profit of 5%.
> 41·29% of Companies had a profit between 5% and 15%.
> 5·28% of Companies had a profit of more than 15%.

Heavy profits are more frequent than heavy losses, which are indeed most infrequent.

The hypothesis of a negative skew in business profits cannot therefore be fully substantiated from statistical returns. But it must be borne in mind that the risk of getting no profit at all, though this is only a few points below the average rate of profit of, say, 5%, may be as painful to a business man as, say, 20% profit, 15 points above average, is pleasant. Hence the economist may assert that his hypothesis is dealing in terms of psychological utilities and disutilities that do not correspond exactly proportionately to money gains and losses. *Prima facie* the economist's contention then appears beyond the ken of objective statistics. But we shall return to the matter in discussing the psychological substratum of economics in Chapter XVIII. Till then the facts as to the frequency distribution of profits must be regarded as an important first approximation to the verification or disproof of an economic theory, and one which, when it does not support the theoretical economist, lays upon him the burden of proof.

[1] Glossary §§6, 8, and 13.

CHAPTER VIII

THE MEASUREMENT OF TIME AND SPACE TENDENCIES

ECONOMICS and political science claim to draw conclusions and make generalizations about *changes* in prices, changes in institutions, changes in customs, and changes in activities generally. But to derive any general historical tendency is as difficult, if not more difficult, than to strike a representative average ; the same baffling variation is continually encountered as in attempting to summarize the facts at any single time or place.

Cannot statistical methods serve here also ? A perusal of the usual economic or political or historical text-books would suggest an answer in the negative ; knowledge of the contents of any modern statistical manual an answer in the affirmative. Can it be that text-book writers have not been introduced, or is it that they find it easier to cut their new acquaintance ? At the risk of a reputation for tactlessness I shall attempt a *rapprochement*, and shall begin where mutual acquaintance has already ripened, namely with the study of price changes and the designing of index numbers.

§1 *The Summary of Item Price-Changes*

The prices of different articles and services do not rise or fall uniformly when different years are compared, and the average degree of change which it is the object of the general price-level index number to measure[1] is true only " more or less." Wide and " abnormal " deviations may be manifest which will materially reduce the significance of the arithmetic mean conventionally used, and may necessitate the use of other forms of the average. Prices fixed over a period of years by contract or fixed by law or custom will be much slower to rise or fall, and among prices that may rise or fall heavily there is usually an asymmetrical distribution, positively skewed.[2]

" Edgeworth emphasized the fact," writes Prof. Irving Fisher,[3] " that price *dispersion upward* always or usually exceeds the price

---

[1] See below, Chapter X §2. [2] See Glossary §15.
[3] *The Purchasing Power of Money*, pp. 425–6.

dispersion downward. There is no limit to the former, but the latter is limited by zero. Statistical tests show clearly this asymmetry of dispersion. From this fact it has been argued that the best average should be one from which large deviations above it count no more than small deviations below it. This condition, whether good or ill, is not met by arithmetical averages, but is met by the geometric average and by the median which in fact usually closely follows the geometric average."

Table VIIIA, presenting changes between 1913 and 1918 in the prices of 144 articles in the United Kingdom, illustrates how the arithmetic mean of price-changes is pulled upward by the extreme positive deviations which can have no negative counterpart. The most frequently occurring (i.e. the modal) range of index numbers measuring the increase in the prices of item articles from the pre-war year to October 1916 was the range 150–199, but the arithmetic mean of these index numbers (pulled up by three quotations above 600) comes out between 250 and 299. From the pre-war year to October 1918 there is an equally serious discrepancy. The modal range of index numbers for the later date is 200–249, but the arithmetic mean pulled up by nine relative changes above 600 (the

TABLE VIIIA

DISTRIBUTION OF THE VARIOUS PRICE-CHANGES OF 144 ARTICLES WITHIN THE SAME PERIOD

1913–14 to 1916–18, United Kingdom.
(International Price Comparisons, U.S. Department of Commerce, 1919)

Price relative to that of 1913–14, July–June	Frequency of articles with specified relative Price-Change.	
	October 1916	October 1918
50– 99	3	1
100–149	38	14
150–199	Mode 53 Median	26
200–249	17	31 Mode
		Median
250–299	10	23
300–349	4	8
350–399	5	9
400–449	5	9
450–499	3	8
500–549	1	1
550–599	2	5
Over 600	3	9
All Prices	144	144
Median	177	249
Mode	150–199	200–249
Arith. Mean (approx.)	250–299	331

index number of potassium permanganate being 4597) comes out at approximately 331.

The median change corresponds closely with the mode. In the period up to October 1918 it can be measured in the Table by eye. Exactly 72 articles show index numbers below 249 and exactly 72 show index numbers above 249. Thus 249 is the median index number, compared with some number between 200 and 249 as the modal index number. In the earlier year the median index number is 177, falling midway in the modal class of price-changes 150–199. This approximation of the exactly calculable median to the less easily calculable mode, makes the median a fairer representative of the general tendency in price-changes than the widely divergent arithmetic mean value, and indeed secured its adoption by those responsible for the figures I have quoted.[1]

§2 Tracing Specific Tendencies

To describe the average rise or fall in prices throughout a number of years or other points of time is simply to sum up in one representative value all the varying values at that point in time. It is only a preliminary measurement, of the type already described in Chapter VI. The new issue now to be introduced is to compare the representative value obtained at specific individual points (e.g. of time), with a view to finding some general movement or tendency in the values of consecutive points.

To simplify matters at the outset it is convenient to settle upon one point, period, or stage, as a standard or base from which changes can be measured. Changes in the average of prices are measured from the average of prices in some base year, and this base average is usually expressed as a hundred. The average of prices in the different years are thus all expressed as ratios, e.g. percentages of the base year's. By this arrangement the exact proportional or comparative changes taking place in values are indicated clearly without the confusion attending the quotation of particular absolute values. Such an arrangement forms an integral part of the systems of *index numbers*. The other constituents of these systems, e.g. the use of sample prices of sample articles, are dealt with in Chapter X §2.

All changes or movements in the values of some character over time, place, or points of *incidence* of one kind and another, are

---

[1] Wesley C. Mitchell, *International Price Comparisons*, U.S. Department of Commerce, 1919.

subject to random or accidental movements. But often it is possible, and where possible most important, to discern some under-lying *secular trend* acting in a definite direction throughout the whole period, or "seculum," of study; or to discern some continually recurring *cyclical* or wave-like *fluctuations* completing their course in finite periods *within* the whole period of study.

Trend and cycle may both be covered by the word tendency if we guard against thinking of tendency as the abstract notion so often referred to under that title by theoretical economists. The economist's " tendency " is a course of events that will only be actually observable and measurable by an accident ; it is a result of certain assumed conditions which may not exist in fact. The statistician's tendency, on the contrary, is something that can be actually observed in the facts. It is an induction, not a deduction, a summary traced from a record of particular measurements.

Often enough the two types of statistical tendency, the trend and the cycle, are both at work. Throughout the nineteenth century business activity fluctuated in cycles of boom and slump, though there was a secular trend toward greater activity as the century proceeded, and most booms reached a height of activity a little above that of the preceding boom. The secular or cyclical tendencies must usually therefore be " extracted " out of a mixture of tendencies. Statistics may measure the rate or rates of inclina-tion of the secular trend, and three characteristics of any cycle : i.e. (1) the length of the period within which the cycle is complete, its span ; (2) the particular form or internal arrangement of the cycle or wave ; (3) the amplitude or swing of the cycle ; that is, the maximum depth of the wave, the height from crest to trough.

§3 *Cyclical Fluctuation and Rhythm*

Sometimes the *period* or span of the cycle is implicit in a theory as to its incidence. In seasonal fluctuations the year is the span or period, since the boom is taken to fall at certain specific seasons of the year, the slump at others. But in trade cycles the period is implicit only in *some* theories, such as the sunspot or harvest theory when the spots or bumper harvests are taken to fall at specific times separated by regular intervals.

Where the timing (or incidence) and span of a recurring cycle is given, the statistical investigation is relatively easy. Fluctuations that are supposed to be of yearly recurrence can be isolated by averaging the values of the same points in each recurring cycle.

The seasonal fluctuation in prices of agricultural produce,[1] in the rate of sickness,[2] in unemployment,[3] can all be isolated for separate study by averaging all the January values for different years, all the February values for the different years . . . all the December values; or all the spring, summer, autumn, winter, values respectively for the different years.[4]

Typical of the case when the span of recurring cycles cannot be implicitly surmised *a priori*, is the phenomenon of rhythm in industrial operations where the worker is more or less free to " choose his time." Here the notion of rhythm lends itself to direct statistical measurement. The term rhythm I have defined[5] and used[6] " to signify the regular and frequent repetition of a group of differentiated motions and pauses." This type of definition has the advantage that the degree of regularity and frequency of repetition are measurable statistically. The regularity of repetition is measurable by the deviation (Glossary §11) in the time-spans of successive repetitions of an operation. In lathe operations studied in an American brass factory, fifty to a hundred successive repetitions were usually made without interruptions. These " runs " were then followed by short intervals for rest, machine adjustments, etc. Within any " run," the median of the times taken by each performance of the operation was chosen as the time more nearly representing the typical speed than the arithmetic mean time. It is this median time that measures the span of the cycle, and in contrast to the span of the seasonal cycle its duration and incidence can only be discovered empirically. From this median time or speed, the *average deviation* of the times of successive repetitions of the operation was obtained, and this divided by the median gave a coefficient of dispersion (Glossary §13) which was lower the more rhythmical the operation or operator.

In many of the industrial operations studied in this way the regularity of repetition was marked. A basis or standard of comparison was formed by a simple repeated action designed to obtain a high degree of rhythm, namely, tapping as fast as possible with one finger on a tambour. Comparison of the coefficients of dispersion showed that experienced lathe operators were almost as rhythmical

[1] Cf. monthly fluctuations in egg prices, Mills, *Statistical Methods*, p. 315.
[2] Cf. seasonal fluctuations of members of Trade Unions, etc., on sick pay, Florence, *Economics of Fatigue and Unrest*, Chapter XI.
[3] Cf. *Labour Gazette*, Ministry of Labour.
[4] There are more complicated and accurate methods than this, but a bare reference to some of the recent applications of these methods in economic and political questions must suffice.
[5] Florence, *Use of Factory Statistics* (Columbia Studies), p. 112.
[6] E.g. *U.S. Public Health Bulletin*, No. 106, Chapter IX.

(i.e. as regular in repeating their time-spans) in machining fuse rings as in tapping with one finger.

Different parts of an operation, i.e. the various movements, steps, or phases which comprise a complete operation, were found to have very different degrees of speed and of rhythm (or regularity) in their time-span. This raises the question of the form or internal arrangement of the cycle, a question whose statistical solution may be taken up in connection with the trade cycle.

§4   The Trade Cycle

The regular occurrence and recurrence of trade cycles has led many economists to speak of the " Economic Rhythm." " The dominant characteristic of (the industrial) movement during the last half-century in this country," writes Prof. Pigou,[1] " is that it has taken place in a series of waves, rhythmical in character and closely similar in length." Since 1860 the intervals or spans between successive years of minimum employment as recorded by British Trade Unions making returns were 7, 10, 7, 10, 7, and 7 years respectively ; the intervals (span) between successive maxima 6, 11, 7, 7, 11, and 5 years respectively.

And within the whole cycle Professor Pigou distinguishes at least two phases, each assigned an average duration or span. The average length of periods of lessening employment being $\frac{26}{6}$ years,

and that of periods of improving employment $\frac{21}{6}$ years.

Economists usually carry this " internal " analysis of any one trade cycle yet further. Stages are differentiated such as the period of boom, the climax and crisis, the slump, the depression or retrocession, and the period of revival leading round the cycle again to the period of boom.

Within the regular trade cycle as within the regular industrial operation the " phases " are differentiated, and some at least of these steps or phases appear to have a certain regularity of their own. These observations therefore go beyond the mere investigation of the span of the whole cycle or wave, i.e. the duration of the period between crest and crest or trough and trough ; they enter into the question of the form or internal arrangement of the wave, and note that sections of the wave have also a more or less definite span recurring regularly in wave after wave.

[1] *Economics of Welfare*, edition 1, Part VI, Chapter I.

Wesley Mitchell[1] finds that "the period of decline in business cycles is decidedly more variable in duration than the period of advance ; the latter period in turn is appreciably more variable in duration than are whole cycles." For the alternate periods of business expansion and business contraction in the United States, 1878–1923, measured according to five indices of business activity, he gives the following arithmetic mean durations (Glossary §4), standard deviations (Glossary §11), and coefficients of dispersion (computing the standard deviations as percentages of the corresponding arithmetic means) (Glossary §13).

	Number of Observations	Mean Duration in months	Standard Deviation in months	Coefficient of Dispersion
Period (Phase) of Advance . . .	55	22·75	8·34	36·7%
Period (Phase) of Decline . . .	51	19·82	10·10	51·0%
Whole Cycles . .	101	42·02	12·37	29·4%

In so far as one phase is less rather than more regular in its appearance and span, the statistician has the means to find out whether this is in any way connected with failures in the punctuality of *other* phases in the same cycle. If one recurrence of any phase of a cycle or wave takes longer than is usual for this phase, will the time taken by the next or any other section or sections of the same cycle, i.e. its span, be shorter than usual, and thus " *compensate* " or redress the balance, so that the whole cycle tends to be more regular in its repetition and length of span than any of its component parts ? Or, on the contrary, is there a tendency to *cumulation* such that if one stage takes longer than usual the other stages of the same cycle tend also to have a longer span ?

Rhythm is an important element in music and one may borrow the musical term *rubato* to refer to this possible *compensation*. *Rubato*, as explained in musical text-books, " consists of a slight *ad libitum* slackening or quickening of the time in any passage in accordance with the unchangeable rule that in all such passages any bar in which this licence is taken must be of exactly the same length as the other bars in the movement, so that if the first part of the bar be played slowly, the other part must be taken quicker than the ordinary time of the movement to make up for it, and vice versa, if the bar be hurried at the beginning, there must be a rallentando at the end."[2]

---

[1] *Business Cycles*, p. 339.   [2] Grove's *Dictionary of Music and Musicians*.

In contrast to *rubato* is the *cumulative effect*, in which each of the stages of any single cycle tend to agree, all the phase-spans of one cycle being longer or being shorter than usual. In *rubato* the time of the single whole cycle approximates the average cycle time, but with cumulation the deviation of the single whole cycle from the usual period would tend to equal the sum of the deviations of its component stages.

Between *rubato* and cumulation lies an organization of the cycle such that the time or span of each of its phases is " independent " of the time or span of the others in the same cycle. There is no clear tendency for the differentiated sub-periods either to cumulate or to compensate.

Which of these three types of arrangement is followed in the *rhythm* of any cycle with differentiated sub-periods appears to me an important question to ask, before setting out upon elaborate non-statistical " explanations " and hypotheses of cyclical phenomena.

In explanation of the time or span-regularity of any industrial operation, *rubato* would appear to point toward a conscious effort to work regularly like the effort of a bandsman to be on time at the first beat of the bar however slow or fast he may have been at the minor beats ; and the discovery of such a tendency would negative the hypothesis of an unconscious rhythm on his part *during* the bar.

Similarly a statistical study of the times of phases within the trade cycle might also point to one non-statistical hypothesis as preferable to another. " There are only two sorts of causes in which we can reasonably hope that the real explanation may be found," writes Prof. Pigou.[1] " First, there are causes which, there is reason to believe, themselves recur with a periodicity corresponding in some degree with the periodicity of the general industrial movement. Secondly, there are causes the occurrence of which may be sporadic, but which, once they have come into play, do not exhaust themselves in a single act, but start wave-movements of a periodicity similar to that which our records display."

Might not the first type of cause be the more likely explanation if *rubato* were found the rule ? If, for instance, sun-spots started the boom phase of the cycle and sun-spots were regular in their periodicity, the timing of all the phases would have to be such that any irregularity in one would have to be compensated for by an opposite irregularity in the others. In no other way could the boom phase be brought round to the predetermined sun-spot time. The

---

[1] *Economics of Welfare*, edition 1, p. 804.

appearance of the sun-spots acts, in fact, as the conductor's baton does upon the wayward or forward bandsman.

Contrariwise the statistical discovery of a tendency to cumulation would appear to negative the influence of an external periodicity like that of sun-spots.

There are various means by which statistics can answer the question of *rubato*, independence, and cumulation. The simplest method is to correlate[1] the times of two given phases in the same repetition of the cycle. The period (in years) of decreasing and increasing unemployment (i.e. the rising and falling trade phases) in the six cycles cited by Prof. Pigou are 3 and 3, 4 and 7, 3 and 4, 3 and 4, 6 and 5, 2 and 3 respectively. Clearly there is a tendency to cumulation marked by a positive correlation of the periods of the two phases in any single cycle. The falling trade phase tends to be longer when the rising trade phase is longer, and vice versa.

The trade cycle is not to be spoken of with such certainty, however, as the cycle of an industrial operation. The latter is something that must sooner or later be completed and the time of its completion cannot be mistaken. The trade cycle is a tendency to be analysed out of a mass of other tendencies and, before investigating the relation of phases within the cycle, the statistician has to prove the real occurrence and recurrence of such a cycle at all. The statistical methods of analysis will be described in §8, and the items that are used as indices to trade are listed in Chapter XVI §6. Meanwhile attention must be drawn to the possibility of measuring periodic cycles in political life, and also of measuring spatial cycles in the density of population. One possibility will illustrate the measurement of amplitude, the other expand the notion of incidence.

§5 *The Political Cycle*

While economists think in terms of cycles or waves, political scientists prefer to speak of a political pendulum. A pendulum fluctuates from side to side and its " swing " gives the *amplitude* of the change, the depth of the wave from crest to trough.

It is, of course, a familiar sight in Almanacks and Year-Books to have the Balance of Parties (in England usually since 1832) displayed and commented upon as a pendular motion. Between 1868 and 1892, the regularity of the motion in England is remarkable. At exactly six years' intervals, 1868, 1874, 1880, 1886, and 1892, there were elections in which Liberals and Conservatives won

---

[1] Correlation is explained in detail in Chapter IX. See also Glossary §24.

I

alternately, and one might then have been justified in speaking of a six-year span, and even in seeking an *interpretation* of the apparent rhythm. To be sure there was an intervening election in 1885 in which the Liberal majority was perhaps out of time and tune, and since this oddly rhythmic mid-Victorian age the pendulum has gone very much awry.

The majorities may be tabulated in columns left and right of a centre of gravity, and if we assign a different *amplitude* from centre to large and small majorities, and space the years of election roughly according to the length of the interval between them (Table VIIIB), pendular motion seems far from a misnomer.

Sir Richard Martin took the Electoral Swing of the Pendulum as the subject of his presidential address to the Royal Statistical Society in December 1906. He went deeper than the mere number of Parliamentary representatives and enquired how far the swing over had " gone " (i.e. how great was its amplitude) in the votes cast by the electors in the various constituencies.

In the election of 1900 there were 210 contested seats won by Unionists. " If 5% of the majority (of voters in each constituency) had gone over, 53 of these would have been lost ; if 10% had changed, 83 would have been lost, reducing the Unionist numbers (net victories in those contested seats) to 104 and 44 respectively."

In 1906 there were 310 seats won by Liberals in a straight " two-sided " contest where conditions were not anomalous. " Of these

TABLE VIIIB

THE POLITICAL CYCLE OR SWING OF THE PENDULUM

Britain, 1865–1910

	Whig or Liberal Majority		Conservative or Unionist Majority	
	Large	Small	Small	Large
1865		67		
1868	128			
—				
1874			46	
—				
1880		62		
—				
1885	166			
1886				123
—				
1892		39		
1895				152
—				
1900				134
—				
1906	300			

we find that if 5% of the electors had changed sides, 60 seats would have been lost, and if 10% had changed sides, 123 seats would have been lost.

" These on a division would have represented 120 and 246 votes, respectively, so that the Liberal and Labour Majority, which now (December 1906) stands at 289 for the United Kingdom, would have been reduced to 169 and 43 respectively. Allowing for several isolated cases, we may safely say that the ' swing of the pendulum ' is, at the outside, a diversion of 10% of the votes of the victorious party to the other side."

The significance of the difference in the amplitude of the swing of (a) seats and (b) votes secured by different parties will be discussed further in Chapter XIX §6.

§6 *Localization and the Cycle of Town and Country*

The span, form, and amplitude or " swing " of a rhythm occurring through time is now well recognized as a fit topic for statistical measurement, and the result of such measurement daily appears in modern economic or political text-books.

What is not yet realized is the possible application of such statistical measurements to the *spatial* succession of events.

Temporal cycles consist in thicker concentrations of business activity at certain times than at others. But are not differences and variations in the geographical concentration of industries or population precisely the topic of that section of economic and political science which is devoted to localization and the growth of towns ?

Urbanization and the localization of population implies a geographical concentration of people, wealth, buildings, etc. ; but these items are not all concentrated in one spot, they are only more or less concentrated at a succession of spots. A cross-section contour map might be drawn, say, from London to Liverpool along the route of the old L.N.W.R. main line as in Table VIIIc, in which vertical height shows the relative densities of population.

Such a cross-section looks similar to the familiar graphical presentation of business cycles. Density of population is the amplitude, distance in miles is analogous to time-span, and internal arrangement is given by the sky-line of the diagram. And the facts thus represented *are* similar. The essential facts of industrial fluctuation are that at certain *times* there is a concentration of activity measured by business done or economic values changing hands per week or month ; the facts of localization are that in certain *places* there is a concentration of activity measured by density of population or wealth, etc., per acre or square mile. In both cases there are two separable questions :

(*a*) What is the amplitude, span, and form of concentration anywhere or at any time ? and (*b*) At what particular times and places does the concentration occur ? What is the precise *incidence* of the concentration ?

The form of concentration may be (1) a " core " of *high* density of population, e.g. London or Liverpool, with an outer ring of medium density which is by no means equally dense throughout its circumference ; the cross-section may, in fact, usually be a skewed distribution (Glossary §15), or the form may be (2) merely a shorter or longer stretch of uniformly *fair* density. Case (1) are cities and suburban districts ; case (2) may be called industrial areas. The

Table *VIII.c*

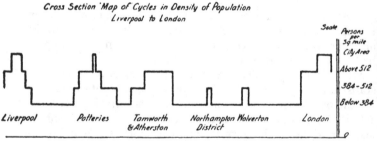

Cross Section 'Map of Cycles in Density of Population
Liverpool to London

(*From Survey Atlas of England and Wales*, Bartholomew, 1903, Plate VIII.)

incidence of such an area is shown in Table VIIIc in the Tamworth and Atherston coal-mining district. The pottery district falls somewhere between (1) and (2).

In an agricultural area of homogeneous fertility and limited transport facilities villages may be expected at certain regular intervals, and market towns at more distant yet also regular intervals.[1] This distribution might be taken as a standard. Departures at some particular place in the case of some particular industry from such a standard distribution exercise the economist's ingenuity under the title of the *problem* of the localization of industries. This problem will be pursued in Chapter XVIII.

---

[1] An example of this, in purely agricultural country, occurs on the west to east line, St. Neots—Cambridge—Newmarket—Bury St. Edmunds, or on the south to north line, Ware—Royston—Cambridge—Ely—Downham Market. These market towns are distributed at intervals not more than 17 nor less than 13 miles from one another.

§7 *The Isolation of Secular Trend and Other Tendencies*

Secular tendencies or trends are exhibited in processes of growth, progress, or decay, in learning curves, and in all *cumulative* tendencies. Such trends are not always linear ; their inclination may not be a straight line. The rate of growth, learning, etc., may be constantly accelerating or retarding, or may change from one to the other.

The secular trend, if linear, is most easily isolated or " extracted " out of a mixture of tendencies (above, §2) by the device of the moving average. " The average value for a number of years (or months or weeks) is secured, and this average is taken as the normal or trend value for the middle of the period covered in the calculation of the average."

The exact number of items to be averaged in obtaining the value of the central item depends on the object in view.

To eliminate random fluctuations the number of items need only be small; to eliminate cyclical fluctuation the number of items must at least be as great as the " span " of the cycle.

Table VIIID gives the actual bank clearings in New York City in thousands of million dollars (milliards of dollars) for a long series of years.[1] Random and accidental movements, such as the drop in the year the European War broke out, can be eliminated by averaging three years together as in column (3) ; but cyclical fluctuations cannot be eliminated by averaging less than seven or nine years together.

The averages of bank clearings for nine years centring on consecutive years given in column (4) of Table VIIID show a gradual but almost uninterrupted movement upward ; the secular trend of steady business progress—wherever it does not measure mere inflation ![2]

The same device that achieves the elimination of cyclical and accidental fluctuations also permits the *isolation* of such fluctuations.

To isolate random fluctuations each item-year should be compared with the average of the three neighbouring years given in column (3).

In 1914, for instance, the year's bank clearings were $\frac{83\cdot0}{96\cdot1}=86\cdot4\%$ of the average bank clearings of the three years 1913–14–15 ; and this relatively wide deviation downward marks the effect of the accident of war.

Of more permanent interest is the isolation of the cyclical

---

[1] Quoted from F. C. Mills, *Statistical Methods.*
[2] See Chapter X §3 for the method of eliminating this element also.

fluctuation. This is best achieved by comparing each year's three-year moving average with its nine-year moving average, in the shape of a percentage excess or deficiency. Column 5 of Table VIIID exhibits by this means the position of each year on the cycle when its record is freed from accidental oscillations. A regular succession of ups and downs will be noticed, each upward or downward phase occupying from three to five years ; up from 1897 to 1900, down from 1900 to 1903, up from 1903 to 1906, and so on. The maxima or crests of the wave-movement occur in 1900, 1906, 1910, etc., the troughs or minima in 1897, 1903, 1908, 1914 as column (6) shows.

TABLE VIIID

YEAR-TO-YEAR CYCLICAL AND SECULAR CHANGES IN NEW YORK BANK CLEARINGS, 1895–1923[1]

Year	Annual Clearings in Milliards of Dollars	Moving Average 3-Year (Non-Accidental)	Moving Average 9-Year (Secular Trend)	Percentage 3-Year compared with 9-Year $=\dfrac{(3)}{(4)} \times 100$	Excess or Deficiency of (3) over (4)
(1)	(2)	(3)	(4)	(5)	(6)
1895	29·9	—	36·9	—	—
1896	28·8	30·7	37·8	81·5	− 7·1
1897	33·4	34·7	42·5	81·6	− 7·8
1898	42·0	45·4	47·6	95·4	− 2·2
1899	60·8	51·8	52·2	99·2	− 0·4
1900	52·7	64·3	56·5	113·8	+ 7·8
1901	79·4	69·5	63·7	109·1	+ 5·8
1902	76·3	73·9	71·6	103·2	+ 2·3
1903	66·0	70·3	76·6	91·8	− 6·3
1904	68·6	76·1	78·7	96·7	− 2·6
1905	93·8	89·0	84·3	105·6	+ 4·7
1906	104·7	95·2	86·3	110·3	+ 8·9
1907	87·2	90·4	88·1	102·6	+ 2·3
1908	79·3	90·0	92·0	97·8	− 2·0
1909	103·6	93·4	94·8	98·5	− 1·4
1910	97·3	97·8	93·6	104·5	+ 4·2
1911	92·4	96·8	94·3	102·7	+ 2·5
1912	100·7	95·9	102·3	93·8	− 6·4
1913	94·6	92·8	113·2	82·0	−20·4
1914	83·0	96·1	121·6	79·0	−25·5
1915	110·6	117·7	137·0	85·9	−19·3
1916	159·6	149·2	153·7	97·1	− 4·5
1917	177·4	171·9	164·1	104·8	+ 7·8
1918	178·6	197·3	177·8	110·9	+19·5
1919	235·8	219·2	192·4	113·9	+26·8
1920	243·2	224·5			
1921	194·4	218·5			
1922	217·9	208·8			
1923	214·0				

[1] Calculated from data in F. C. Mills' *Statistical Methods in Economics*.

The device of the moving average is only a crude method of isolating or eliminating accidental or random fluctuations, cycles, and trends. Too much depends on the particular span of years arbitrarily selected from which to calculate the moving average. More refined mathematical calculations may discover an algebraic formula where such arbitrary selection has less influence. But whatever the method of calculation we must be clear as to the purpose of such a formula. Its purpose is to estimate the values of the changing character at consecutive stages of the trend or cycle, so as to " fit " the values actually observed ; or to put it conversely, the general formula or law should be such that the observed values will appear to " obey " the estimated values.

When the observed item-values at each stage have been averaged, the general course of events may appear stationary or a constant linear progress in one direction and along one line, *or* a progress in one direction at varying rates, *or* a movement which is sometimes a progression in one direction, sometimes a retrogression in the opposite direction ; and the formulæ will increase in complexity as the trend to be " fitted " departs from stationariness and sheer linearity, just as tailoring or dressmaking becomes more difficult the greater the variety of " figures " permitted by fashion.

In framing these formulæ it is the custom among mathematicians to represent the specific " stage " of time, space, etc.,[1] as X and the value at that stage of the character to be measured as Y ; a, b, c, d, etc., represent any numbers desired, but remaining constant at all " stages."

A formula of the type $y=a+bx$ will place these theoretically formulated values of y along a *straight* line. The values of y at successive stages will be in arithmetic progression. This formula, in short, will fit a strait-waistcoat to the observed figures. A formula of the type $y=a+bx+cx^2$ can place these theoretically formulated values of y along any species of line with one curve, i.e. either convex or concave. It will fit the observed figures, as a mid-Victorian corset fitted the waist or stomach. But more complicated formulæ such as $y=a+bx+cx^2+dx^3$ will allow of convolutions S and 2 and ? shaped curves to fit whole-length figures upholstered in Victorian fashion. Cyclical movements can also be summarized in algebraic formulæ of varying complexity.[2]

But there is no need to flog a dead horse, or rather to goad a very

---

[1] E.g. the value (in specified units) of the interval between the base-period and the point of time under observation.

[2] E.g. Prof. H. L. Moore, *Economic Cycles, their Law and Cause*, Chapter II, esp. " The Use of Fourier's Theorem."

live one. The technical details of the statistical summarization of time tendencies need not be enlarged upon ; they are described in a number of accessible text-books.[1]

The more complicated the formula the more closely will the derived, estimated, values " fit " the observed values ; but what the statistician gains in accuracy of approximation he loses by complexity, and this dilemma of all summarization calls for the same personal judgment and common sense as the choice of suitable averages and other measures of the distribution of values of a single character.

§8   *The Probabilities of a Tendency*

Formulæ of trends and cyclical fluctuation serve not only to summarize events past and present, and by " intra-polation " to fill in gaps in the past history, but under the title of " extra-polation " offer some indication of future probabilities. The discussion of probability, risk, and uncertainty, applied in the previous chapter to the probable frequency of a specified value or range of values of a single character regardless of time or place, can also be applied to the probable frequency of values of one character of an item at successive dates, places, or other measured stages involving varying conditions or contexts. Tendencies can be regarded as eventualities that may be betted on at various odds, long or short, with varying degrees of certainty just as much as the value of any item or the frequency of any range of values.

We specify a value or range of values of the changing character, estimate the chances or expected frequency of its realization at a given date, place, or other stage, and compute the reliability of this estimate. Or else we specify a date, place, or other stage in a statistical series and estimate the chances or expected frequency of a given value (or range of values) of the character being then realized and compute the reliability of *this* estimate.

A *probable* tendency lies in the eventuality of specified values or ranges of values occurring at specified dates, places, or stages, this eventuality being fairly reliably expected to be realized with relatively high frequency. A merely *plausible* tendency is a similar eventuality which is rather unreliably expected to be realized with relatively high frequency. An *improbable* tendency is a similar eventuality which is moderately reliably expected to be realized with relatively low frequency.

If the formula $y=a+bx$ has fitted the trend of events observed

---

[1] F. C. Mills, *Statistical Methods* ; A. L. Bowley, *Elements of Statistics.*

at several stages it may be used to forecast the most probable values at unobserved stages of the trend and these stages may occur between those observed (intra-polation), or subsequent to and beyond (extra-polation) all observed stages. In Table VIIID the secular trend from 1895 to 1913 was such that, at stages of six years, the nine-year moving average of bank clearings increased by about equal sums averaging 25·4 milliards : 26·8 milliards of dollars between 1895 and 1901, 24·4 between 1901 and 1907, and 25·1 between 1907 and 1913. A simple formula of type $y=a+bx$ might be calculated " by eye " to the effect that the average of clearings centring in any year $(y)=36·9$ (the average clearings centring in base year)$+25·4x$, where x represents the interval from base year (1895) in stages of six years.

On top of this, the cyclical fluctuation would have to be formulated and changes in the value of money—the price " level "—allowed for.[1] Then, barring accidental random movements, bank clearings might be forecast for any one year desired, though only " plausibly," with a doubtful degree of reliability.

In the prediction of business prosperity, the forecasting of price changes, and scientific advice as to profitable investment, statistical methods have in recent years become almost indispensable for reputation and prestige. Statistical " Services " are at the beck and call of the business leader ; weekly, if not daily Bulletins are issued of the state of trade and its immediate prospects ; confidential audits are undertaken by efficiency engineers and consulting experts. In consequence, methods of cycle analysis and trend tracing are expatiated upon in much detail in recent publications.

The measures of the reliability of this analysis and tracery are not always given sufficient attention. The mathematically measurable factors in reliability are the number of items observed, and the deviation of their values one from another. But what is often more important is the question of the context of the observed terms, the particular, perhaps unmeasurable, circumstances prevailing at the time, place, or " stage " of observation,—circumstances that may not recur in the future. Methods of computing mathematical reliability were described in Chapter VII ; the precautions to be taken in examining the circumstances of the observation will be outlined in Chapters X and XI as part of applied statistics or " field-work." Meanwhile one can only point to numerous failures in prognostication even under the highest auspices. Bad harvests have been foretold as a result of an expected coincidence or superimposition of unfavourable phases in several cycles of different span,

[1] See Chapter X §3.

that were no more realized in the event than the predictions of *Old Moore's Almanack* or an astrologer's horoscope. Yet, as statistical observations increase and more circumstances become measured, the degree of reliability will become more calculable, and economic and political tendencies will be assignable either as probabilities or improbabilities, rather than as the mere plausibilities or possibilities put forward by economic and political theory to-day without statistical verification.

CHAPTER IX

THE MEASUREMENT OF RELATIONSHIPS BETWEEN CHARACTERS

§1 *The Vocabulary of Relation Measurement*

ALL types of item already considered,—persons, articles of sale and other objects, establishments and other institutions,—manifest *a number* of characters, and statistical measurement is not confined to the summarization of the values of one character nor yet to the tracing of tendencies in one character through various stages of time, place, etc. Indeed, the most important issues in economics and political science are those seeking to demonstrate a relationship between the values of two or more characters manifested by various kinds of statistical item.

The statistical item or instance must not be thought of as necessarily some one nameable thing. It is often not one thing but conjoined things (or persons), such as a married couple, father and son, mother and daughter ; and the characters whose relationship, if any, is to be measured may be a character of one of the things or persons, e.g. fertility of mother, and the same, or another character, e.g. longevity, of the other conjoined thing or person, e.g. daughter. A statistical item may indeed be any set of circumstances observed or considered conjointly together, any context or " conjuncture " ; the various circumstances or members of the context or conjuncture being the characters whose relationship is at issue.

The terminology describing relationship is at present most confused, and I shall try to avoid this confusion by consistently adopting the following terminological rules which are based upon and follow up the rules stated in Chapters V and VII.

Rule V. *Two or more characters conjointly manifested by any item may be related* (dependent) *or unrelated* (independent).

One character is unrelated to (or independent of) *another if its value (quality or quantity) in any item tends in no degree to vary with variations in the values of the other character or characters conjointly manifested by the same item. Otherwise it is related* (or dependent). I shall use the words related and relationship rather than dependent or dependence, because the latter words suggest some *causal* relationship, a conception I do not wish to introduce at this stage.

Different sets of words are used according as (a) the characters are both attributes with only two alternative *qualitative* values each ; (b) both are variables with *quantitative* values reckoned in numbers of units ; or (c) one character is a variable, the other a " duo-qualitative " attribute, or one or both characters are multi-qualitative attributes. By multi-qualitative I refer to an attribute that has more than two specified qualities or " varieties." These several qualities or varieties are often quasi-quantitative in that they can be ranked off-hand in " isotropic " order, as very thin, thin, fat, fatter, fattest.

Rule VI. (a) If the relation is one between qualitative characters (ATTRIBUTES) it is usual to speak of the *qualities* (or less accurately the characters)[1] being *associated or disassociated*. If the characters (attributes) are independent and the qualities neither associated nor disassociated, we shall call them unassociated or non-associated.

(b) When quantitative characters (VARIABLES) are related they are said to be *correlated*. When quantitative characters are independent and unrelated they may be called *uncorrelated* or *non-correlated*.

(c) When qualitative characters are related to quantitative, or both or one character is multi-qualitative, they may be said to be *contingent*. When there is independence the characters may be called uncontingent or non-contingent.

Rule VII. *A relation between characters may be specifically positive* (congruent) *or negative* (inverse). *It is positive if a comparatively high value tends in some degree to occur in one character when the value of the other character is comparatively high, and similarly of low values. The relation is negative if a comparatively high value tends in some degree to occur in one character when the other character has a comparatively low value or vice versa.*

Where quantitative and quasi-quantitative characters are involved positive contingency like positive correlation can be stated in the form " the more . . . the more . . . ," or " the less . . . the less . . . " ; negative contingency like negative correlation in the form " the more . . . the less . . . ," or " the less . . . the more. . . ."

The terminology to be used may be tabulated systematically as follows :—

---

[1] Though colour of eyes and tint of hair may be said to be related it is more usual to speak of some particular quality of colour (e.g. brown eyes) being *associated* with some particular quality of tint (e.g. dark hair) or *disassociated* with some other particular quality of tint (e.g. fair hair).

Type of Characters Conjoined	Dependent (Related)		Independent (Unrelated or Non-related)
ATTRIBUTES (Qualitative Characters)	Associated	Disassociated	Unassociated or Non-associated
VARIABLES (Quantitative Characters)	Positively (Congruently) Correlated	Negatively (Inversely) Correlated	Uncorrelated or Non-correlated
ATTRIBUTES with VARIABLES	Positively Contingent	Negatively Contingent	Uncontingent or Non-contingent

§2   *Association Between Two Qualities of Two Characters*

Where neither characteristic is quantitative but both can only be said to have one quality *or* another, or two qualities positive or negative, there are four possibilities : Both qualities positive ; quality of first character positive, quality of second negative ; quality of first character negative, quality of second positive ; both qualities negative.

Each of these four possible combinations may be manifested by a *variable frequency* of observed items.   The frequency of items is not in this case distributed along one scale as a column or row, but is distributed in four compartments of a table of double entry.

Table IXA shows the distribution of imports[1] into the United Kingdom as between the four possible combinations of non-manu-factured food-and-raw-material, or manufactured goods (dis-tinguished in the character " degree of manufacturedness ") with the two qualities British and not-British distinguishable in the character " country of origin."

The question which such a table attempts to answer is whether one alternative quality of one character is particularly associated or disassociated with either one of the alternative qualities of the other character.   The economic, and indirectly the political im-portance of this question lies, as we shall see (e.g. Chapter XIX §3 and esp. §6), in the accurate statistical measure it affords of the

---

[1] Measured in economic values.   But since these values are the items whose frequency distribution is at issue, confusion must be avoided by speaking of import trade or pound's worth imported rather than values of imports.

degree of specialization or division of labour between groups and organizations of persons.

TABLE IXA

ASSOCIATION OF COUNTRY OF ORIGIN AND DEGREE OF MANUFACTUREDNESS IN THE IMPORT TRADE OF THE UNITED KINGDOM IN 1911

	Articles wholly or mainly Manufactured	Other Articles, Food, Raw Materials, etc.	All types of Article
	Actual Trade		
Foreign Origin	£145Mn.	£364Mn.	£509Mn.
British Origin	£20Mn.	£151Mn.	£171Mn.
All countries of Origin	£165Mn.	£515Mn.	£680Mn.
	Theoretical Trade if characters Independent		
Foreign	£123·5Mn.	£385·5Mn.	£509Mn.
British	£41·5Mn.	£129·5Mn.	£171Mn.

If there were no particular association (or disassociation) the same *proportion* of the food-and-raw-materials trade as of total trade would be imported into the United Kingdom *from British possessions*. The proportion of the total import trade that is of British origin is $\frac{171}{680}$ or roughly one-quarter, and therefore if there were no association or disassociation but complete "independence," one-quarter of the 515 million pounds'-worth of food and raw materials imported should be British (to be precise 129·5 million pounds'-worth) and three-quarters of foreign origin (i.e. 385·5 million pounds'-worth) ; and one-quarter of the 165 million pounds'-worth of manufactured goods actually imported should come from British possessions, i.e. 41·5 million pounds'-worth ; and three-quarters from foreign countries, i.e. 123·5 million pounds'-worth. The *actual* import trade shown in Table IXA when compared with these *theoretical* figures that might be expected on a hypothesis of independence, shows excess of 21·5 million pounds'-worth in food and raw materials coming from British possessions, and in manufactures coming from foreign countries ; and an equivalent deficit in raw materials coming from foreign countries and in manufactures coming from British possessions.

Now it is obvious that the higher this " common difference " (excess or deficit) from what would theoretically be expected if there were independence, the more the association or disassociation. The absolute difference must of course be taken relatively to the total amounts involved and for comparative purposes the measure of association or disassociation must be reduced to a coefficient with well-defined limits such as $+1$ for complete association and -1 for complete disassociation.

These conditions are satisfied by the *Coefficient of Association* (see Glossary §22) devised by Udny Yule.

$$\text{Common Difference} \times \frac{\text{Grand Total of Items}}{\text{Sum of Cross Products}}.$$

In the case under consideration this coefficient works out at

$$£21\cdot5 \text{ million} \times \frac{£680 \text{ millions}}{£(145 \times 151)M + (£364 \times 20)M}$$

$$= £21\cdot5M \times \frac{680}{21,895 + 7,280}$$

$$= \frac{14,620}{29,175} \text{ or } 0\cdot5$$

What does this statistical measure of the degree of association or disassociation allow us to state? We cannot say that food and raw materials are more frequently imported from British possessions (i.e. are of greater value) than food and raw materials imported from foreign countries (because they are not); nor (though it is true enough) is there much point in stating that the manufactures are more frequently imported from foreign countries than from British possessions. This is *equally* true of food and raw materials. But what is both interesting *and* true is that of a given trade in imported food and raw material, more of it is likely to be of British origin than in the case of an equivalent amount of manufactures. Or to put it in another way, of a given value of imports into the United Kingdom, say, one hundred pounds'-worth, sent from British sources a greater proportion (namely $\frac{151}{171}$) will be of the *food and raw materials kind* than in the case of one hundred pounds'-worth of *all* articles sent from foreign sources. Here the proportion will be not $151 \div 171 = 88\%$, but $364 \div 509 = 71\%$. In short, British possessions can be said to *specialize in exporting food and raw material* to the

Mother country as against foreign countries who *specialize in exporting manufactures* to the United Kingdom.

Specialization consists in certain persons or groups of persons doing mostly one type of work, and others mostly another type. Seldom can any person be said to do *solely* one type, e.g. only brainwork or only manual work. The large-scale farmer manages and organizes, but he also uses his hands even if it is only to tickle his pigs with a stick. If one group, said to be specializing in manual work, is much larger than another said to be specializing in brainwork, the former group may between them actually do more brainwork without contradicting the statement, just as in the table before us Britishers overseas may be said to specialize in providing food and raw materials for the United Kingdom, even though they export a smaller total value of food and raw materials into the United Kingdom than do foreigners.

Specialization, or division of labour as he called it, was to Adam Smith the starting-point—the title of Book I, Chapter I, in fact—of the *Wealth of Nations*. And in his *History of Social Development*, Müller-Lyer makes " The Development of Division of Labour " (Differentiation)[1] the outstanding tendency in social progress. " Differentiation is indeed the universal fundamental law, according to which all development proceeds, not only in the intellectual world of human culture but everywhere in animal nature." Here, therefore, is another instance of the value of statistical methods in giving an exact formulation of an idea constantly used in economics and, as we shall see,[2] in all the political and social sciences.

§3 *Relationship or Contingency between Several Qualities of Two Characters*

The statistical theory of association applies, strictly speaking, only where two values are distinguished in the two characters. Where one character is quantitative and the other qualitative, or one or both has *several* qualities, the statistical methods adopted are simply extensions of statistical association.

When a character of any item has several qualities a difficulty occurs in that these qualitative values can sometimes not be ranked off-hand into an ordered series. One of the uses of calculating contingencies is to obtain such an order *empirically* by reference to some other character of the item. For if the same item has another

[1] Heading to Book III, Chapter III.
[2] Chapters XIX §§3, 6, XX §5.

TABLE IXB

CONTINGENCY BETWEEN PARTY AND OCCUPATION OF MEMBERS OF PARLIAMENT, 1832–1867

PARTY	Army and Navy	Land-holders	Shareholders, Directors, Proprietors	Lawyers	Professional,[1] Literary	Financiers and Merchants	Indus-trialists	TOTAL
CONSERVATIVE—								
(a) Actual No. of M.P.'s	504	1946	142	258	108	323	204	3485
(b) *Theoretical Distribution*[2]	*389*	*1650*	*131*	*294*	*150*	*481*	*390*	*3485*
% Difference of (a) from (b)	+29	+18	+8	−12	−28	−31	−48	
LIBERAL—								
(a) Actual No. of M.P.'s	417	1949	144	415	230	743	674	4572
(b) *Theoretical Distribution*[2]	*511*	*2157*	*171*	*387*	*197*	*631*	*518*	*4572*
% Difference of (a) from (b)	−18	−10	−15	+7	+17	+18	+30	
RADICAL—								
(a) Actual No. of M.P.'s	14	69	29	35	23	90	65	325
(b) *Theoretical Distribution*[2]	*35*	*157*	*13*	*27*	*14*	*44*	*35*	*325*
% Difference of (a) from (b)	−60	−56	+123	+30	+64	+105	+86	
Total No. of M.P.s	935 (11·15)	3964 (47·3)	315 (3·75)	708 (8·45)	361 (4·3)	1156 (13·8)	943 (11·25)	8382
% of each occupation								100

[1] Including Civil Servants, Independent and Salaried.
[2] On assumption that political party and occupation independent characters.

character which is quantitatively measurable, then the qualities of the first, merely qualitative, character may be ranked empirically according to their association with the numerical quantities of the second character. It was by this means that the occupations of members of Parliament were ranked in Chapter VI §1 in respect of the *number* of Conservatives and Liberals respectively pursuing those occupations. The process of tabulation is identical with that of the association or contingency table. Being a landholder, for instance, is more frequently *associated* with being a Conservative M.P. than might be expected if Conservatism and landholding were independent. The basis of the " isotropic " ranking is given in Table IXB, where the actual distribution of the item-M.P.'s in the different compartments is compared with the theoretical distribution (figures in italics) to be expected if party affiliation and occupation were independent, uncontingent characters. These theoretical figures are obtained by finding the percentage of *all* members of Parliament who followed each of the groups of occupations (for instance, 11·15% army and navy, 47·3% landholders, etc., given in brackets in the bottom row of the table), and calculating what the numbers of Conservative, Liberal, and Radical M.P.'s would be " theoretically " for each occupation, if the distribution were the same as for the total of members. Thus 11·15% of the 3485 Conservative M.P.'s is 389, and this is the theoretical number of army and navy Conservatives.[1]

If the differences between the actual and theoretical number in each compartment of the table (expressed as a percentage of the theoretical number) be then compared, it will be seen that these percentage differences tend to be positive and large in the top left part of the table, and in the bottom right-hand part of the table ; but in the bottom left-hand part and the top right-hand they tend to be negative and large. In other words, army and navy men, landholders and shareholders, etc., were more frequently Conservative and less frequently Liberal or Radical, than a theory of independence between occupation and political party suggests. Financiers and merchants, on the contrary, and to a still greater extent Industrialists, tended to be more frequently Liberal and Radical ; and if occupations are listed in the order given in the headings of the table there is an obvious and consistent contingency between occupation and party. From the percentage differences shown in the table the coefficient of contingency may, in fact, be worked out by the formula given in the Glossary §23 as +·24.

[1] The percentages are given, simply, to the nearest ·05. For a more minute calculation of the theoretical figures see next table.

§4 *Relationship or Contingency between Several Qualities of One Character and Quantities of Another*

An important example of the application of the contingency table to a relationship between characters, one of which is quantitative, occurs in Prof. H. L. Moore's attempt to trace the influence of the strength of Trade Unionism in any industry upon the success or failure of strikes in that industry.[1] The table he constructs is reproduced here as Table IXc and his argument is worth giving in full.

" Inquiry concerning the influence exerted by labour organizations on the outcome of strikes may be worded as follows : To what degree is it true that the stronger the labour organizations in an industry, the more favourable to the interests of the labourers are the results of strikes that are declared by labour organizations in the industry ? In order to obtain an answer to this question, it will be necessary to agree upon some measure of strength in labour organizations, and to array the various industries of the country in the order in which labour organizations are strong, in respect to the quality of strength that is agreed upon.

From one point of view, the strength of labour unions may be measured by the degree in which the trade disputes in an industry are ordered by trade unions. If a large proportion of the strikes in an industry have their origin outside of the trade unions, it may be assumed, as a general rule, not only that trade unions are not strong when the industry is considered as a whole, but that the unions in the organized part of the industry are not strong. The fighting capacity of the organized part of the industry must be weakened, as a general rule, by the existence of a large body of unorganized labourers in kindred occupations of the same industry.

When the strength of trade unions is measured by the degree in which the strikes in an industry are ordered by trade unions, is there any relation between the strength of the unions and the outcome of strikes ordered by the unions ?

On pages 33–34 of the Report on *Strikes and Lock-outs*[2] a table is given of ' Strikes and Establishments involved in Strikes ordered by Labour Organizations and not so ordered, by Industries, 1881 to 1905.' This table supplies material for ranking the 82 enumerated industries according to the percentages of total strikes, in the several industries, that were ordered by labour organizations. For example, in the industry for the manufacture of agricultural implements, labour organizations declared 63·22% of all the strikes affecting that industry between the years 1881 and 1905 inclusively. It is assumed in the subsequent argument (1) that the control of trade disputes of an industry on the part of labour unions is proportional to the percentage of total strikes affecting the industry that are declared by labour unions ; (2) that the strength of the labour organizations of a particular industry is proportional to their control of trade disputes.

---

[1] *Laws of Wages.*   [2] *U.S. Commissioner of Labour, Annual Report.*

On pages 486-487 of the same Report there is given a table headed, 'Summary of Strikes for the United States, ordered by Labour Organizations and not so ordered, by Industries, 1881 to 1905.' The same 82 industries that appeared in the table which has just been described are enumerated also in the above 'Summary.' Furthermore, this 'Summary' gives the outcome of strikes that were ordered by labour organizations, according as the strikes succeeded, succeeded partly, or failed.

From these official data Table IXc has been constructed. The table will afford the means of measuring the relation between the degree in which labour unions control trade disputes and the outcome of strikes ordered by unions. That is to say, the table will supply an answer to the question as to whether the outcome of a strike ordered by labour organizations is in any way associated with the measure in which the labour organizations control the trade disputes of the industry. If the hypothesis is accepted that the strength of labour organizations is proportional to their control of trade disputes, Table IXc will likewise supply an answer to the question as to whether the strength of labour organizations has anything to do with the outcome of strikes declared by organizations.

The construction of the table will be made clear by an illustration. In the first column of the body of the table marked 'Below 20,' the figures 389 signify that, in all of the industries covered by the official report, 389 establishments in which strikes occurred were in industries in which labour organizations declared below 20% of the total strikes of the industry. In case of 211 of these 389 establishments the strikes failed ; in 67 of the establishments the strikes were compromised ; and in 111 of the establishments the strikes succeeded. It will be observed that the table refers only to the outcome of strikes ordered by labour organizations. All of the data in the official summary have been included except the material referring to 'domestic service' and to 'miscellaneous.'

From this table two conclusions will be drawn : (1) as to the nature of the association (i.e. contingency) between the outcome of strikes and the degree of control of trade disputes on the part of labour organizations, and (2) as to the measure of this relation.

The method employed in extracting the conclusions from the data is the method invented by Professor Pearson for the derivation of the *coefficient of mean square contingency.* An indication of the significance of the coefficient of mean square contingency, as a measure of association, is given by the following consideration : The total number of establishments in which strikes occurred is seen, from the entry in the next to the last column and the bottom row, to have been 156,459. Of this total number of establishments 53,512 were establishments in which the strikes failed ; 24,943 were establishments in which the strikes partly succeeded ; and 78,004 were establishments in which the strikes succeeded. The last column marked 'Chances' gives the ratio of these numbers, respectively, to the total number 156,459. If, now, the outcome of the strikes in the 389 establishments recorded in the first column had been similar to the outcome in the whole of the establishments enumerated, the number of the establishments in which the strikes failed would have been $(389)(\cdot3420193)=133\cdot05$; the

TABLE IXc

CONTINGENCY BETWEEN THE STRENGTH OF LABOUR ORGANIZATIONS AND THE OUTCOME OF STRIKES ORDERED BY LABOUR ORGANIZATIONS[1]

Actual Number of Ordered Strikes with Specified Outcome (and in italics Theoretical Number if Factors Independent) in Industries where Strikes were ordered in Specified Percentage

Outcome of Strike	Below 20%	20–30%	30–40%	40–50%	50–60%	60–70%	70–80%	Above 80%	Total Chance of Ordered Strikes	Relative Chance of Specified Outcome
Failed	211 *133·05*	376 *319·10*	993 *538*	905 *964·84*	11,622 *7894·49*	713 *597·17*	8345 *6908·79*	30,347 *36156·57*	53,512	·3420193
Succeeded partly	67 *62·02*	136 *148·74*	214 *250·77*	749 *449·73*	6037 *3679·78*	503 *278·35*	2463 *3220·32*	14774 *16853·29*	24,943	·1592240
Succeeded	111 *193·94*	421 *465·16*	366 *784·23*	1167 *1406·43*	5423 *11507·73*	530 *870·48*	9392 *10070·89*	60594 *52705·14*	78,004	·4985587
All Outcomes	389	933	1573	2821	23,082	1746	20,200	105,715	156,459	1·0000000

[1] H. L. Moore, *Laws of Wages*, p. 111.   For explanation of table see p. 132, opposite.

number in which strikes succeeded partly would have been (389) ($\cdot159422$)$=62\cdot02$; and the number in which strikes succeeded would have been (389)($\cdot4985587$)$=193\cdot94$. Numbers derived in this way will be referred to as the numbers given by *independent probability*.[1]

Now it is clear that the numbers actually occurring in the sub-groups differ from those given by independent probability. In case of the establishments in which strikes failed, we have in the first column $211-133\cdot05=+77\cdot95$. And in case of the establishments in which strikes were successful, we have $111-193\cdot94=-82\cdot94$. That is to say, in industries in which labour organizations were weakest,—in the sense of controlling only a small percentage of the strikes that occurred in the industries,—the outcome of strikes, in establishments in which strikes occurred, was such that there was a positive deviation from independent probability of $+77\cdot95$ in case of strikes that failed; while in case of strikes that succeeded, there was a negative deviation from independent probability equal to $-82\cdot94$.

If, in a similar manner, the column marked ' above 80 ' is examined, it will be found that, in case of establishments in which strikes failed, there is a negative deviation equal to $-5809\cdot57$, while, in establishments in which strikes succeeded, there is a positive deviation equal to $7888\cdot86$.

We find, therefore, that for weakly organized industries, the successes are fewer and the failures are more than would be given by independent probability; while for strongly organized industries the contrary relation proves to be true. These two extreme columns suggest that the outcome of a strike is in some manner related to the degree of union control of the industry, and it is required to determine rigidly from all of the data of the table the quality and the degree of association between the two variables.

The deviations from the independent probability of the same sign, or some function of the deviations may be taken as a measure of the association."

From this starting-point the coefficient of contingency described in the Statistical Glossary (§23) can be worked out.

The deviations (8) of the actual from the theoretical frequencies $211-133\cdot05=+77\cdot95$, $376-319\cdot10=+56\cdot90$, etc., are all squared, and then divided by the theoretical frequency, giving $\dfrac{77\cdot95^2}{133\cdot05}$, etc. The sum of these fractions (there will be 24 altogether) is $10,670\cdot33$. This is denoted X^2 and the root mean square coefficient of contingency " C," the square root of $\dfrac{X^2}{156,459+X^2}$, is $\cdot253$.[2]

As a result of this investigation Professor Moore draws the following conclusion :[3]

" The greater the degree in which labour organizations control

---

[1] Probability is used in this case in the sense marked B II in Chapter VII.

[2] Calculating coefficients of contingency by two different methods, Prof. Moore makes them $\cdot232$ and $\cdot30$ respectively.

[3] *Laws of Wages*, p. 116.

the disputes of an industry, the more likely is the outcome of a strike declared by labour organization to be favourable to the interests of labourers."

These methods of calculating relationship are obviously of the same nature as those directing the argument from the association table of imports (Table IXA). The distribution of items actually observed into the various compartments of the table is compared with the theoretically most "probable" distribution, supposing the two characters to be independent and unrelated.

The argument applied to two non-variable characters or attributes can thus be usefully applied where at least one of the characters is a variable.

§5 *Correlation and the Regression Line or Curve*

We may now proceed with the problem of relationship between two characters measured quantitatively, i.e. between variables. The facts may be presented in one of two different forms, one of which is merely an extension of methods already discussed.

The relationship may be presented (1) as a general tendency towards a change in the *average* of the values of one character from class to class, when items are classed according to the range of value of the other character. This is the method of the regression table. It is akin in *form* to the measurement of tendencies over time and place discussed in Chapter VIII, and it is akin in *principle* to the empirical ranking of several qualities in some isotropic order as occupations of M.P.'s in order of their Conservativeness. Or (2) the relation may be set out in the correlation table and summed up in the coefficient of correlation. This is akin in form and principle to the computation of the table and coefficient of contingency.

TABLE IXD

AVERAGE MORTALITY AMONG INFANTS OF FATHERS EARNING VARIOUS GRADES OF INCOME

(Eight American Cities, 1911–1913[1])

Range (and its Midpoint) of Annual Earnings of Father		Average Infant Death Rate per Thousand Born
$1050–1249	($1150)	64
$850–1049	($950)	84
$650– 849	($750)	108
$450– 649	($550)	126
Under $450		168

[1] Florence, *Economics of Fatigue and Unrest*, p. 345. Fathers' incomes are here graded into *equal* Ranges of Value.

(1) Table IXD shows that in a group of families observed between 1911 and 1913 in eight American cities, the higher the earnings of the father, the lower is the rate of mortality among their infants.

Only the *average* infant mortality in each *grade* or range of earnings is vouchsafed, and the table in form merely illustrates a general tendency. The income of every father is pigeon-holed into successive stages of income, similar to the stages of time or place discussed in the last chapter, and there is shown a continuous (upward) tendency in infant mortality through successive stages, similar to the growth of bank clearings in Table VIIID. This tendency is, in these non-temporal and non-spatial cases, usually called a regression. There is a *regression*[1] of infant mortality *on* father's income. Or the word co-variation might be used. Infant mortality and father's earnings co-vary (negatively) and the regression line measures the law of their co-variation.

But the same matter might have been set forth in a more graphic (though more complicated) manner if the arrangement had consisted of a table of double entry. Instead of one column of spaces for the average mortality at the different stages of income, there may be several rows one below the other (say, three, as in Table IXE) to distinguish the different grades or intensities of infant mortality conjoined in any item-family with the different grades of income, and each income grade will form a column of compartments.

TABLE IXE

REGRESSION LINE OF INFANT MORTALITY ON INCOME OF FATHER

(Illustrating Table IXD)

Infant Death Rate per 1000 Born	Annual Earnings of Father Classed				
	Under $450	$450 to $649	$650 to $849	$850 to $1049	$1050 to $1249
Over 150	(168)				
		(126)			
100 – 150			(108)		
				(84)	
Under 100					(64)

Each item-family record could then be placed in a pigeon-hole in the appropriate income column and the appropriate mortality

[1] The use of the prefix " re " to indicate merely a backward tendency, as in " reactionary," is etymologically right but inexpedient. This reference can be given by the prefix " retro," as in retrograde, or " de," as in degressive, the opposite of pro-gressive. The prefix " re " should be reserved for *any* *re*sponse or *re*-action in the sense used in chemistry. Hence regression would indicate any movement of values up or down, *in response to* a change in other, related, values.

row, and the statistician could scan and compare the relative frequency of items scattered in all the different compartments.

In each income column these items will probably be most thickly bunched in the mortality row where the average mortality for that income grade would fall. These averages, as stated in Table IXD, are inserted in the appropriate pigeon-hole of Table IXE.

They form a line tending downwards from left to right, that indicates graphically the direction of the regression tendency. As incomes get larger and vary upward (left to right) infant mortality tends to vary downward.

A formula might be obtained to sum up the particular law of co-variation similar to the formula for growth of New York bank-clearing over time.[1] Starting with a father's income round the midpoint $1150 a year (class of income $1050 to $1249), every fall of $200 in income (the x character) seems to be associated with a rise of about 20 per thousand in the infantile death rate (the y character). That is every unit rise in infantile death rate is related to a $10 fall in father's earnings below $1150. A simple though only roughly approximate formula to sum up the trend of co-variation would run

$$y = 64 + \frac{x}{10},$$

where x is the deficiency (in dollars) of father's income below the standard of $1150.

For instance, when x is 950 or $200 below $1150, y would, according to the formula, be $64 + (200 \div 10) = 84$. This theoretical value tallies exactly with the actual average value.

Again, where x was 550 y would be $64 + (600 \div 10) = 124$. The average of the value actually observed was 126.

The coefficient of correlation is a more refined measure of the same type as the coefficient of contingency. It measures the odds or chances that any specified value of one character will be persistently associated with a specified value of the other character observed in any item, i.e. the chances of agreement with or deviation from some tendency or law of relationship or co-variation, such as the regression line of infant mortality on father's earnings. While the coefficient of contingency was based upon the observed deviation from independent probability, the coefficient of correlation is based upon the observed deviations from such a given " law " or regression tendency.

The coefficient of contingency can be used to measure the relation

[1] Chapter VIII §7.

between two quantitative variables[1] as well as that between characters one or both of which is a qualitative attribute, but the coefficient of correlation cannot be applied to attributes, since it is only a relation between two *variables* that can be presented as a mathematical " regression " equation. Where the relationship of variables *is* under consideration, however, the coefficient of correlation is usually preferred by statisticians to the coefficient of contingency.[2]

It is somewhat difficult, however, for the practical economist or social investigator to see the logical connection between the formula employed and the actual purpose of the correlation coefficient. Yet in principle it is essentially the same as that of the coefficient of contingency, and the precise method of obtaining it need not exercise us here.

The elementary principle of the coefficient is a comparison between (*a*) some measure of the average deviation of the observed actual values from estimated theoretical values along the regression tendency (a measure conventionally known as the average or standard error of estimate) and (*b*) some measure of the average deviation of the observed values from their own average value.

In the case of the regression of infant mortality on father's earnings, the general tendency seemed to be an increase in mortality rates of 20 per thousand for every decrease of $200 in the father's earnings per year. But individual families would of course deviate from this general tendency, and it is some kind of average of these deviations or errors of estimate that would constitute the numerator of the primary comparison involved in correlation.

Obviously the wider the deviation or error the less close is the relationship. But this width of deviation or error may be simply due to the absolute magnitude of the values involved, and the absolute magnitude of their deviation from average. It is to eliminate this disturbing factor that the average error is divided by some measure of the average deviation.

The usual formula for obtaining the coefficient of correlation is derived from this original elementary comparison in such a way as to achieve at least two objects.

(*a*) As in the case of the coefficients of association and contingency, it was desired to peg down the coefficient of correlation to strict limits : $+1$ to measure perfect positive correlation, o to measure

---

[1] See Elderton, *Frequency Curves and Correlation*, Chapter X : The Theory of Contingency.
[2] Yule, *Theory of Statistics*, IX §6.

no correlation, i.e. independence, -1 to measure perfect negative correlation.

(b) For the sake of economy of time and effort it was desired to avoid the actual calculation of the regression tendency, the errors from which are the principal element in the measure of correlation. This short cut is feasible, but only by the use of mathematical devices, the logic of which is not obvious to the non-mathematician.

The resultant short-cut formula may be stated as follows without mathematical symbols.

The coefficient of correlation is the (arithmetic mean) average of the products of the deviations of the values of the two characters of one item from their average value, divided by the product of the standard deviations of the values of the two characters.

The full formula and an example of actual computation by this method is given in the Glossary §24.

The mathematician moves in devious ways his wonders to perform, and the sceptical or agnostic reader must refer for enlightment to mathematical text-books suitable to his case. The coefficient of correlation, in contradistinction to that of contingency, is usually very fully treated in such text-books.

The coefficient of correlation should be a measure of the utmost importance in the group of problems lying at the heart of economics, such as the relation of available and visible supply to the price of an article.

Table IXF, adapted from H. L. Moore's *Economic Cycles*, shows the " scatter " of item associations round a regression line running from top left-hand corner to bottom right-hand corner. This line is a statistical formulation of an economic law, the tendency, in fact, for prices to fall as supply increases. This fall can be observed in the table by eye.

The formula or equation of regression is y (% year-to-year change in price of (Indian) corn)$= -\cdot8896x + 7\cdot79$, where x is the % year-to-year change in the production of (Indian) corn.

For example, at a percentage change in production of corn (x) between -6 and -1, with a mid-point of $-3\frac{1}{2}$, the price (y) should change $-3\frac{1}{2}(-\cdot8896) + 7\cdot79$
$$= +3\cdot1136 + 7\cdot79$$
$$= 10\cdot9036$$

Speaking generally, in the years when the production fell most compared with that of the preceding years, prices rose most, and vice versa. In statistical language there is a regression of prices on production such that the lower the supply falls the higher rises the price.

TABLE IXf

CORRELATION OF CHANGES IN PRICES AND IN AMOUNT OF CORN (MAIZE) PRODUCED, U.S.A., 1866–1911

Number of years when specified change in production was associated with specified change in price

Percentage Change in Price per Bushel of Corn	Range and Midpoint of Percentage Changes in the Production of Corn (Maize)														
	−31 to −26	−26 to −21	−21 to −16	−16 to −11	−11 to −6	−6 to −1	−1 to +4	+4 to +9	+9 to +14	+14 to +19	+19 to +24	+24 to +29	+29 to +34	+34 to +39	Over 39
	−28½	−23½	−18½	−13½	−8½	−3½	+1½	+6½	+11½	+16½	+22½	+26½	+31½	+36½	
Over +35	3														
+35 to +30															
+30 to +25		1		3	1										
+25 to +20			1	1											
+20 to +15				1			2								
+15 to +10				1		2			1						
+10 to +5				1			1	1	1						
+5 to 0								1							
0 to −5						1	1	1							
−5 to −10		1	1		1	2	1	1							
−10 to −15					1		2			2					
−15 to −20								3	1			1			
−20 to −25								1						1	2
Over −25															3

[1] Moore, *Economic Cycles*, p. 71.

This regression appears from the table to be somewhat irregular. There is a heart-breakingly wide scatter in the middle values of the scale. At the very point given as an example of the position of the regression line, namely when the production fell $3\frac{1}{2}\%$, there is no actual instance anywhere near the estimated change in price, namely 10·9%.

On the whole, however, the " fit " is fairly close and this is reflected in a negative coefficient of correlation as high as —·789.

The measure of correlation may be based on the deviations or error, not from a straight line or " linear " tendency, but from any of the forms of " curves " that tendencies may take in accordance with the complication of their formulæ or equations. These complications were briefly indicated in discussing tendencies through time (Chapter VIII §7), and for the mathematical methods of obtaining correlation measures such as the *correlation ratio* " η " suitable when tendencies are curvilinear, the reader may refer to text-books of statistical theory.[1]

§6 *Relationship between Values of Several Characters*

Statistical measures of relationship (by association, contingency, or correlation) may seek the relation not merely between two characters such as colonies and specialization in the provision of food and raw material, or year-by-year change in price and change in supplies of an article, but the relation between several characters. The specialization of foreign countries in export of manufactured goods to England as compared with England's colonies (§1 and Table IXA) might be related to their greater division of labour as measured in the number of different occupations, or to their greater use of machinery as measured in the accumulation of capital, or to their more complete urbanization, or to their larger scale of production and organization (measured in Chapter V), or to their (e.g. Prussia's) system of limited monarchy, or of landed estates with rent-paying labourer-hiring tenant farmers. If a sufficient number of foreign countries, preponderantly exporting manufactures to the United Kingdom (e.g. Switzerland, France, Belgium), were observed as items, specialization in export of manufactured goods might be shown to be associated (positively correlated) with some of these features, but, on the whole, disassociated (negatively correlated) or unassociated (independent) with others among these features (e.g. constitutional and agricultural systems). If

---

[1] E.g. Yule, *Theory of Statistics*, Chapter X §20.

association between such specialization and certain features persisted in all or most countries or times that could be instanced, then we could claim to have disclosed a specific *type* of industrial development. The use of the word type indicates precisely such a complex or combination of specific values (quantities or qualities) in conjoined characters. Modern industrial development may probably be shown to combine comparative specialization in export of manufactures, and comparatively greater division of labour, greater use of inventions, more intense urbanization, and larger scale organization and production. Similarly, compared with the characteristics of other races a Nordic " type " of physique combines lighter-coloured hair, fairer complexion, bluer eyes, squarer build, taller stature ; and this is associated by some authors with peculiar mental characters, of which—if Nordic themselves—they are usually somewhat proud.

The arrangement of social phenomena under types was regarded by Professor Wagner as a chief stage in economics and the social sciences, next after the description of those phenomena. Some psycho-analysts speak of psychological types, others of complexes ; and in both cases the idea is that of an association of several values (quantities or qualities) occurring, recurring, and persisting, more often than might theoretically be expected from the chance or independent distribution of those qualities over countries, peoples, epochs, or other statistical items. Whether these several related characters are, like height, measurable in quantity, or are measurable in several qualities such as degrees of fairness in the complexion, or can only be distinguished by two qualities such as dark *or* fair, the degree of relationship could always be measured statistically by an extension of the principles of association, contingency, or correlation.[1]

This problem of multiple relationship presents itself perhaps most frequently in the attempt to isolate the relationship of two characters by eliminating their relationship with further " disturbing " characters. If tall stature is associated with blue eyes, is this not because a fair complexion is associated with stature and blue eyes is simply part of a fair complexion ?

The outcome of strikes, whether successful, partially successful, or a failure on the part of the strikers, was found associated in some degree with the control of the Trade Unions in the industry concerned. But the outcome is also, according to Professor Moore, associated to some degree with the duration of the strike and with the objects of the strike.

[1] Cf. Chapter XII, below.

" The greater the duration of the strike, the less likely is the outcome of the strike to be favourable to the interests of the labourers."

" It is found that a strike for the recognition of the Union has been the most likely to succeed ; a strike for an increase of wages has been the most likely to be compromised ; and a strike in sympathy with the workers elsewhere has been the most likely to fail."[1] Professor Moore is able, in fact, to rank some eight causes of strikes in the order of their expectation of success, of partial success, and failure in an isotropic order similar to the list of occupations of members of Parliament (§3) in order of their Conservatism.

These many characteristics of a strike associated with the outcome of a strike give rise to questions of interpretation.

" If labour organizations in weakly organized industries are predisposed to strike for causes that are likely to fail, while the stronger unions enter into trade disputes for more promising causes, the results that we have obtained would find their explanation not in the degree in which labour unions control trade disputes, but in the wisdom with which strong unions choose the grounds of the disputes into which they enter."[2]

But practical problems such as these mark the frontier of purely mathematical statistics and bring us close to the province of statistical " fieldwork " and interpretation to be attacked in the following chapters.

§7 The Probabilities of Relationship

The third chief stage in economic and other social sciences was, in Professor Wagner's view, " the explanation of the causes upon which phenomena (and types ?) depend."

Useful as a statistical description of economic events may be, it is not the final aim of economic science. What it is ultimately hoped to accomplish is to extend description to cover instances not yet observed with some degree of precision. If for all observations of quality A in one character we have also observed quality B to be present in another character, we want to be able to *infer* that A and B always are and will be associated ; or if this universality is impossible (as it usually is in the social sciences), we wish to know what the exact probability is that any hitherto unobserved instance of A taken at random will also have the quality B.

Such a wished-for statistical generalization when made about the

---

[1] *Laws of Wages*, pp. 120 and 124.   [2] *Ibid.*, p. 118.

association of quantitative or variable characters, is most simply expressed as a mathematical formula of the type described in discussing tendencies such as the regression of infant mortality on father's earnings (§5).

If this formula were certain, the average infant mortality of groups of families could be foretold off-hand from the particular value of their income. And formulæ of a similar kind have been advanced as practically certain by leading authorities on social affairs. Dr. Farr thought that general mortality increases with the density of the population, not in direct proportion of these densities but as their sixth root.[1]

If y represents the relative mortality of any place, and x its relative density of population :

$$\text{Then } y = \sqrt[6]{x}.$$

If one place were 729 times as densely populated and a second 64 times as densely as a third, one could forecast their probable comparative mortality rates as $\sqrt[6]{729}$ is to $\sqrt[6]{64}$ is to $\sqrt[6]{1}$, or as 3 is to 2 is to 1.

Farr subsequently modified the terms of his formula, and his thesis " under present changed conditions," to quote Newsholme, " cannot be maintained."

Formulæ such as Farr's which describe the " law " of co-variation, association, or correlation, in fact only measure probabilities, not certainties, and the same wording may represent their purport that has already been applied to the probable frequencies of certain values of a character, and to probable tendencies in time or place.

Associations or correlations of values of two or more characters of an item can be considered eventualities, with varying degrees of probability, just as much as the distribution or tendencies of values of a single character. All that was said about risk and uncertainty in Chapter VII applies equally well in this more complicated issue.

A *probable* association (or correlation, etc.) of values is an association which is moderately or " fairly " reliably expected to be realized with relatively high frequency.

A *plausible* association of values is an association which is rather unreliably expected to be realized with relatively high frequency.

An *improbable* association of values is an association which is moderately or " fairly " reliably expected to be realized with relatively low frequency.

We specify a range of value (or a quality) of one character and estimate the chances or expected frequency of its realization in

---

[1] Newsholme, *Vital Statistics*, pp. 280 ff.

association or correlation with a given range of value (or quality) of the other character or other characters, and measure the reliability of the estimate. For this purpose coefficients of correlation, contingency, and association should have attached to them, as averages have, standard mathematical measures of their reliability : standard or probable " errors " plus and minus.

The meaning of, say, positive correlations with a high coefficient and low probable error can be put in this form : Whenever the value of character A is large, it can be fairly reliably expected that a comparatively large value of character B will be realized with a frequency that is high relatively to the total frequency of the large values of B.

The coefficient of correlation gives some measure of this relative frequency ; a coefficient of $+1$, denoting complete or perfect positive correlation, would imply that all of the comparatively large values of B might be expected to be associated with the comparatively large values of A ; and the same, of course, could be said, *mutatis mutandi*, of the relatively small values of the two characters.

The degree of reliability of the expected association or relationship between characters does not depend upon the mere multiplication of the number of items manifesting the characters, but rather on the persistence or stability of the association or correlation under very different conditions and circumstances. In his *Essay on Population* Malthus examined birth rates, marriage rates, and death rates and attempted to show that his hypothesis of their relationship held true,[1] or fairly true, in all the different countries and all the different stages of civilization examined. It was safer to generalize and to prophesy the future course of events from the similarity of these differently circumstanced relationships, than from a high coefficient of association at any one time or place, or a high coefficient when all the data were lumped together.

If within very differently circumstanced groups of instances high values in character A are observed to be associated with high values in character B, in about the same proportion throughout, the chances are high (and this estimate reliable) that in hitherto unobserved groups of instances the same degree of association will be found.

But in the usual case experienced by the statistician (alas !) the degree of closeness in the correlation between the values of the two characters can only be described as "*fairly*" reliable and its

[1] See Florence, *Over-Population, Theory and Statistics.*

recurrence in the several groups or samples of items is only " *fairly* " stable, and the samples are only " *fairly* " differently circumstanced.

This raises two questions about the reliability of a correlation or association coefficient.

(1) Exactly how strict must this stability or persistence of the association or correlation be for associations or correlations of various degrees of " closeness," as measured by a higher or lower coefficient ?

Standards of tolerance or *significance* for these coefficients are calculable on mathematical considerations as such standards are for averages (Chapter VII). These methods of calculation have received their meed of attention in text-books[1] and need not detain us.

(2) How different should the conditions and circumstance be under which the degree of association or correlation is studied for purposes of generalization ?

This is largely a question of the degree of variation or the qualitative differences in the *observed* circumstances as contrasted with the degree of variation or qualitative differences likely in the *unobserved circumstances* which statistical generalizations are to cover.

It is essentially a non-mathematical problem of statistical field-work, and the answer cannot be given precisely enough for text-book purposes. Yet it is probably the more important question in the fluctuating tide and welter of human affairs and will be dealt with at some length in the chapters (XI–XIV) on Statistics Applied in Generalization, and all which that implies.

---

[1] E.g. the probable or standard error of a coefficient of correlation. Yule, *Theory of Statistics*, Chapter XVII.

PART THREE

STATISTICAL FIELDWORK IN ECONOMICS AND POLITICAL SCIENCE

CHAPTER X

STATISTICS APPLIED IN DESCRIPTION

§1 *Selection and Definition of the Statistical Terms*

IN statistical measurement the descriptive stage endeavours to summarize as accurately as possible, in " figures," the values of one character, the tendencies in these values, and the relationship between the values of two or more characters.

But *before* these numerical summaries can be undertaken it is necessary to decide, in view of the measurability of the available data, upon the most convenient and suitable characters, values, and items to illustrate or demonstrate the point at issue.

Such decisions are by no means automatic, nor arrived at by rule of thumb, but require discretion and judgment. Before statistical measures are computed, much spadework or *preliminary fieldwork* is necessary in considering the nature of the character or characters to be numerically valued ; the nature of the item manifesting the characters ; and the nature of the character's values (qualities or quantities) that are to be distinguished along the scale of variation.

These causes for consideration might be, and often are, " lumped " together as the question of the Unit. Text-books of statistical method generally reduce this part of their task to pious recommendations to the reader to define his units and then to be constant to his chosen definition. But a " unit " may refer to the characteristic, or the item, or the " degrees of value " distinguished. We may speak of measuring unit commodities in units of money, referring thereby to the fact (1) that we take single commodities as the ITEMS to be observed and enumerated[1] ; (2) that we evaluate

---

[1] This is the reference of unit when King, *Elements of Statistics*, writes : " Enumeration implies the determination of a unit the numbers of which are to be counted."

each of these items not in respect of their weight bulk or merely pleasure-giving qualities, but in respect of another character, their price in *money* ; (3) that we measure degrees of price down to the last halfpenny, a halfpenny being at present the lowest unit of money generally accepted.

Let us pick out as the point at issue not a mere " illustrative example " but a description of the facts as to the existence and growth of large-scale production and its relation to the life of the workman. Suppose further that the character of large-scaledness is to be measured by the number employed per industrial establishment.

What are the processes involved before statistical measurement can serve a useful purpose ? The preliminary fieldwork that is required may be outlined as the selection and definition of (1) the character whose values are to be measured ; (2) the qualities, classes, ranges, or degrees of value in which to present measures of the character ; (3) the items whose character is to be measured.

(1) The selection and definition of the character whose values are to be measured.

The number of employees per industrial establishment involves the selection and exact definition of two referents ; an answer to the two questions : what is an employee, and what is an industrial establishment ?

The answer to the first question may seem obvious to the casual reader, but it will not seem so to the casual *worker*, or to the statistician who has to take casual employment into account. A definition of employee is by no means to be undertaken without forethought. The relationship of employment is loose,—neither black nor white, but shaded. Some persons are employed whole or overtime, others half-time, others employed only on odd jobs. Yet the question " when is an employee not an employee ? " is one that must be asked and answered by some clear rule before any counting and figuring can begin. The degree of part-timedness that shall disqualify must be first arbitrarily thought out. But there is further difficulty. To the statistician who must go out and count the heads, the exact referent for which industrial establishment stands is of some significance. So much has been written and re-written about the importance in the life of the worker of large-scale production, that recent writers have considered the whole question too " trite " for further consideration. But how usual is it for the economist to tell us exactly what it is to which the largeness of scale refers ? Is it the industry that enlarges over the whole world, or in a particular country or town ; or is it the factory that is enlarged, or the business organization or the combination of organizations ? Different industries contain a very variable number of business organizations or " firms " run independently or in combination. Business organizations, e.g. the Ford Motor Company, Boots Cash Chemists and other " chain-stores " comprise a very variable number of factories, plants, or shops. The number of unit individuals to be counted as employed per establishment (*a*) in smaller, and (*b*) in larger establishments is clearly entirely different according to whether establishment refers to plant, firm, or combination of firms.

When the actual figures have to be obtained of the numbers employed *somewhere*, it is impossible to write vaguely about the scale or size without thinking of the size of *some*thing, and it is quite possible that an industry enlarging itself by the growth of super-factories, or super-shops like Selfridges, would not effect the economies of the multiplication of small plants under the control of a few large businesses. The phrase large-scale establishment is much favoured by economists and certainly excludes any possible reference to the scale of production of a whole town or country, or over the whole world. It does *not* tell us, however, whether largeness of a particular factory is referred to or largeness of a whole firm or combination of firms.

The confusion comes to a head in comparing the German and Austrian censuses of production when the same word " Betrieb " refers in Germany to the technically homogeneous " works," and in Austria to the business unit. Undoubtedly, says Zizek,[1] only one " Betrieb " would in many cases be counted in Austria, where the German investigation would find and count several " Betriebe."

The word used in the American census of manufactures is " establishment," but writers using and attempting to interpret the census figures appear to have wildly divergent views as to the meaning of the word. J. A. Hobson refers to the American " establishment " as a " business " or a " business unit."[2] Leroy-Beaulieu, on the other hand, identifies establishment with " plant,"[3] and Seligman identifies it with factory.[4] To be sure, the definition

---

[1] *Fünf Hauptprobleme der Statistischen Methodenlehre*, p. 31.
[2] *Evolution of Capitalism*, edition 1917, p. 114.
[3] *The United States in the Twentieth Century*, translated by H. A. Bruce, p. 173.
[4] *Principles of Economics*, edition 1916, p. 337.

officially given by the American census authorities can hardly be said to clarify matters.

> The term " establishment " comprises the factories, mills, or plants which are under a common ownership or control and for which one set of books of account is kept.
>
> If, however, the plants constituting an establishment as thus defined were not all located within the same state, separate reports were secured in order that the figures in each plant might be included in the statistics for the State in which it was located. In instances separate reports were secured for each of the different industries carried on in the same establishment.

In this uncertain atmosphere statistical investigation cannot thrive. The preparation of the soil by intelligible definition of the character to be measured is an essential part of statistical field-work. Taussig specifically tells us that " the census regards an establishment in any one place as independent and separate, even though it be owned and managed by persons or corporations having establishments of the same sort in other places,"[1] and I shall take his authority coupled with that of Seligman and Leroy-Beaulieu, and some internal evidence of the census figures themselves, as identifying establishment with *local* plant, factory, mine, mill, not with business firm.

(2) The selection and definition of qualities, classes, ranges, or degrees of value, in which to present measures of the characteristic.

This task requires particular care where the character is observed in its natural state to have a great variety of values, which must, however, be classified for summary presentation in a frequency distribution.

What shall constitute a large, largish, fair-to-medium, medium, smallish, small-scale establishment, respectively ?

Establishments cannot, for shortage of paper (if no other reason), be distinguished according to each single possible number of employees, and the values must be classed into *approximately* correct " orders " of magnitude within given intervals along the scale of values ; but obviously the smaller the number of such classes the larger the frequency of items in each class and the more summary and less precise the results. The decision as to how all these possible varieties of value shall be grouped, though it is likely to be somewhat arbitrary, should not be thoughtless. With more than fifty employees an establishment will usually be split into two or more departments and fifty units is therefore a frontier line roughly dividing establishments into two orders or qualities of

---

[1] *Principles of Economics*, edition 1911, foot-note, p. 51, Vol. 1,

magnitude, the unitary establishment and the departmented establishment.

This approximates to a qualitative evaluation ; and the question of the *classes of qualities* that are to be distinguished often looms large where the character is an attribute and not a variable. The different kinds of industries or occupations into which the census of population is to distribute its items, the different causes of industrial and other accidents, the different denominations of diseases, religions, etc., have all formed a subject of controversy exercising the acutest minds and filling Blue books with the greyest matter.

For international comparisons, or comparison between different years, or in fact any comparison between different situations, a standard definition of qualitative classes is imperative if the fallacy of equivocation is to be avoided. It is unfortunate enough when one country divides establishment according to number employed, at entirely different numbers,[1] but it is worse when exactly the same name refers to very different quantities or qualities. The eradication of a disease from a particular district has more than once been " demonstrated " by deftly dropping its name and substituting another, and many times have Englishwomen been accused of a growing tendency to idleness because in the census of 1891 daughters and other female relatives of the head of a family assisting in household duties were classed as occupied, and in subsequent censuses as unoccupied.

Statisticians responsible for these classifications often have to choose between continuing an old standardized but perhaps foolish distinction, and initiating a new-fangled but wiser distinction that may cut across the other and confuse the unwary. The dilemma is not overcome without thought, worry, and the exercise of judgment.

(3) The selection and definition of the item to be observed in respect of the given character.

The obvious presentation of the facts regarding the growth of large-scale production, and that almost universally adopted, is to make the establishment the item, and state the frequency of establishments consisting of, say, 5 or under, 6 to 50, or more than 50 individual employees, etc. But if it is desired to look at the large-scale production from the individual employee's point of view and compare large-scale employment with other characteristics of the worker's life, the individual worker must be taken as the item that manifests various characteristics. Instead of describing how

---

[1] While in Germany and America the divisions occur between establishments employing 5 or under, 6–50, more than 50, in France the classes are 1–4, 5–50, etc. See Hobson, *Evolution of Capitalism*, Chapter V.

many large and small establishments exist, the statement must be formulated as in Table VA. Each individual employee is there considered as the item and he is examined in respect of the characteristic of his affiliation to a large or a small-scale establishment, and counted as an item in one class or the other according to the answer. And the same care is required in defining employee for the purpose of counting or not counting any given worker as an item in the account, as in defining " him " to serve as a unit of characterization. The degree of part-timedness below which workers do not qualify as employees must be laid down, and once laid down strictly adhered to.

The first task of the field statistician is now complete. He has selected and defined all the units or terms involved in statistical measurement, the *items* to be observed, the *character* to be evaluated, and the *classes of values* of the character that are to be separately distinguished.

The whole process might be referred to as the selection and definition of units or simply as *classification*, if this word is taken to include the organization or creation of definite classes of qualities or quantities of a definite character, as well as the distribution of qualified items into those classes. In this preliminary work the field statistician is simply acting in the double capacity of the subordinate person that business men refer to as their filing clerk, and of the superior being who has created and organized the system of filing.

The selection and definition of classes of value or qualities of a characteristic is like organizing the boxes and compartments of a filing system in order to receive documents or other data. Each datum is first registered (or not) as a fully qualified item suitable for being filed under the definition, and its characteristic is then evaluated in the units (or qualities) as duly selected and defined also. According to their class of value or quality registered and measured, documents are assigned appropriate boxes and compartments in the general system.

There is a great advantage in combining the activities of creator or organizer and of mere file-filler. The separate compartments or boxes in the system can be thought out with a knowledge of what the possible or probable documents are with which it will be filled, and what are their probable or possible values. This knowledge will be lacking to those who, by a process of analysis rather than classification, invent filing systems with boxes and compartments all complete out of their heads. Economic boxes are too often empty because there are no qualities or quantities of a characteristic, no tendencies or associations that can be placed in those boxes.

What should a filing clerk think of her boss who ordered her to arrange compartments in his file to receive letters from names beginning with Digamma, Brp——, the exclamation mark, the swastika symbol, and the sign of the cross, with five sub-classes (*a*) St. Andrew's, (*b*) St. George's, (*c*) Maltese, (*d*) Greek, and (*e*) plus sign ? Yet these are the sort of orders economic theory is continually giving out to such of its devotees as desire to apply its interpretations to the facts and situations before them.

And what does a business man think (and say and do) of (and to) filing clerks who fail to follow their subtle yet useful system of files ? Slips and misunderstandings are continually occurring in political and economic science owing to the gulf that is set between theory and " mere " fieldwork. One generation of economists does not or cannot follow the definitions of other generations, and sometimes not even their own definitions, as muddles about the meaning of utility and welfare amply prove. How, then, can mere laymen be expected to follow ?

The invention and filling in of government forms is very much like filing ; each question in the form is in fact usually designed to elicit an answer suitable for filing in a particular pigeon-hole. Economists and political scientists should be prepared not merely to devise the questionnaires but to fill them in with all the detail demanded. In short, the units and classes they refer to and distinguish should be so selected and defined that they CAN be observed and measured.

§2 *Description by Index*

The need for imposing such discipline on any prospective organizer of scientific investigation, at least while he works " up the ladder," becomes yet more evident when we consider the fulfilment of his higher functions,—functions requiring that judgment, discretion, and arbitrary decision which the man at the top of the ladder is supposed to exercise.[1]

For it is necessary continually to question the propriety of the characteristic or items selected and defined, as a true measure, description, and representation of the real point at issue. It must constantly be borne in mind that the characters whose values statistics measures are not necessarily identical with the ultimate point or proposition to be proved, or problem to be solved.

[1] Zizek in his *Fünf Hauptprobleme der Statistischen Methodenlehre* makes arbitrary choice (Willkür) in the statistical process one of the five " main problems."

The point at issue may be identical with, or may be distant one, two, or any number of removes, from the measured terms, i.e. from the items or characters whose values are actually described. In the latter case the descriptions may be said to be indirect or vicarious, and the variation in the measured values to be a mere representative or index of the variation in the point to be demonstrated or illustrated.

In legal parlance, these vicarious measures are merely circumstantial evidence. The point at issue may be whether Jones murdered Brown. No one has borne witness to having seen the deed done, but a bloody finger-mark was found on Brown's body. Printing a finger-mark is not identical with committing a murder, it is circumstantial evidence of the deed, not the deed itself; and though the discovery of the printer is the immediate question relevant to the issue, the discovery of the murderer is the real issue in which the court is interested. Similarly the proportion of all the strikes in any industry that are ordered by a Trade Union is not identical with the relative strength of Trade Unions in that industry, but it is taken by H. L. Moore (Table IXc) as a character evidential of, representing, or *indicating* the real issue of the strength of Trade Unions in an industry.

From the standpoint of the effect of large-scale production (rather vaguely understood) upon the workers' life, the various definitions of employees per establishment that have been ventured may all be wide of the mark. The number of employees in an establishment (whatever establishment may refer to) may be a most erratic and fallacious indication even of the scale of establishment.

A chemical works or a brewery feels large to the employee at work therein, though it employs only half the men that a small-feeling confectionery works employs; and as measured by the capital invested, or the area of land covered, or the dimensions of the building, the chemical works or brewery might well be considered the larger. Machinery and mechanical forces have supplanted labour and the particular characteristic "number of employees" often fails to indicate the point at issue; capital cost, area, dimensions of establishment, or the annual economic value of the output of an establishment might be a better index. Clearly the selection of the number of employees as the character to be used for valuing scale of production requires thoughtful consideration and possibly reconsideration.

These difficulties in selecting a numerical index are in this instance mainly attributable to the lack of definition of the conception of "large-scaledness" involved in the issue. Quite as often the point at issue is clear enough, but the difficulty is to find an objective numerical index of any kind.

Economic and political issues abound that provide no direct statistical measure of the characters immediately involved. Variations in the general working capacity of a body of employees are not directly and numerically describable, but they may be indicated by variations in the output. But these variations, in their turn, are not " evaluable " in common units for the factory as a whole, and may have to be indicated by the total power consumption of all the electrically driven machines.[1]

The selection of a statistically descriptive character often resolves itself into the task of obtaining a measurable test, representative, or " index," of a less measurable character that is nearer to, but not itself, the real point at issue. Variations in power consumption may be used as an index of variations in the output of the whole factory, but this output itself is merely an indication of, not identical with, the variation in human working capacity that is the real point at issue.

Evaluation of different forms of index character in common units along one scale (as output of different kinds in terms of power of consumption) is the process familiar to physicists as calibration. Calibration frequently presents difficulties to the economist to whom the device is familiar in connection with that of weighted index numbers. To weight the different forms of working-class consumption for the purpose of an accurate cost of living index, it is necessary first to calibrate the consumption of food, clothes, housing, etc., in terms of the units of money actually found expended in typical family budgets. And there are many other economic and political uses of calibration.

Can the energy consumed in different forms of exercise be reduced to a common scale, say in terms of foot-pounds, so that the daily exercise necessary for a man's health or the effort for which wages are supposed to be paid[2] can be indicated, whatever the form of the exercise?[3] Can the food needed by men, women, and children

---

[1] Florence, *Economics of Fatigue and Unrest*, pp. 237, 240.
[2] See below, Chapter XVIII.
[3] An entertaining calculation appears in the *American Health Magazine* edited by Dr. Sargent of Boston. " According to recent English authorities the average man should do, daily, work equivalent to climbing a perpendicular ladder one-half mile, or twenty-six hundred feet, high. Ordinarily, some other more convenient method of exercise must be adopted. It has been determined that walking twenty feet on a level at the rate of three miles an hour, is *equivalent* to lifting the body perpendicularly the distance of one foot. Hence, one may, if he chooses, walk ten miles, instead of climbing a ladder half a mile high. Of course, hill climbing and mountain climbing will accomplish

of various ages be reduced to a common factor so that the requirements of differently composed families can be accurately gauged ?
Authorities claim that an adult woman needs ·8 as much food as an
adult man, and she is calibrated or weighted therefore as $\frac{8}{10}$ths of a
male eating-unit.   Similarly a child between 2 and 6 years of age
counts or weighs $\frac{4}{10}$ths of a male eating-unit, and a child between
6 and 10, $\frac{6}{10}$ths.[1]   In this way eating capacity is substituted for
persons in indicating the needs of a family in the matter of food,
and where the issue is whether or not a wage earner obtains a living
wage for his family, the substitution or " calibration " obviously
makes for greater accuracy in measuring the precise point at issue.

§3   Corrected and Composite Indices

A true index of any given character at issue may not be an
observable character, weighted or unweighted, obtainable in simple
undiluted form.   In order to indicate the exact point of interest
without adulteration from extraneous conditions not at issue, it
may be necessary to correct the observable measure by multiplying
or dividing it by some other observed and measured character, or
by adding or subtracting some such character, or by combining
several such characters.   In short, the index may be composed of
several measures and may be a product, a quotient or ratio, an
aggregate or a difference, or some combination of any of these.
Examples of multiplication occur in the composite ton-mile measure
used as an index of the volume of goods traffic on a railway ; and
an example of addition and subtraction occurs in correcting monthly
unemployment percentages for the normal seasonal flux[2] so as to
obtain the " net " general trend.

But the most usual process of correction is by division.   This
results in an index ratio, the familiar *rate* of so and so *per* something

---

the same thing as ladder climbing, and if one chooses to do the work indoors,
he may work out his task in stair climbing.   Going up and down a flight of
stairs ten feet high is equivalent to raising the body about twelve feet perpendicularly.   Hence, one might do the required amount of work by going
up and down such a flight of stairs one hundred and seventeen times.   But
first, he may do the work while standing in a corner and raising himself on
his toes.   In such exercises the body is elevated about three inches.   Hence,
four heel-raisings would be equivalent to raising the body one foot, and to
raise the body half a mile, or twenty-six hundred feet, it would be necessary
to rise upon the toes ten thousand four hundred times.''

[1] This is the Atwater scale, but not all authorities agree.   Cf. *Methods of
Conducting Family Budget Enquiries*, International Labour Office, Studies
and Reports, No. 9.

[2] See Chapter XIII §5.

or other. The precise character to be used as divisor or denominator is often fairly obvious; for instance, in cases where variation in the extraneous condition not at issue is likely to effect a variation in the index character employed, proportional to its own variation.

To use a simple illustration from the investigation and measurement of industrial efficiency. The output or accidents of a factory may be fairly certainly expected *a priori* to vary about proportionately with the number of employees at work at the time. We are not interested in measuring the numbers at work in this roundabout way, so the appropriate index must consist in output or accidents per head or per given number at work. In technical language the index must be a ratio taking into account the inherent *exposure*. The greater the number of men at work the greater *pro tanto* the exposure to output and accidents. But further correction is necessary if accidents are to be used as an (inverse) measure of working capacity. Accidents per head may be presumed *a priori* to vary more or less proportionately with the quantity of output per head. If working capacity improved between the second and third working hour of a day more output would presumably be produced. This increased activity would presumably raise the inherent mechanical hazard or exposure to accident, and would *pro tanto* result in an increased absolute number of accidents. If there is any fall in the human psycho-physiological working capacity, its effect on the absolute number of accidents per head is thus superimposed upon a mechanically determined rise in accidents; and if it is this psycho-physiological variation that is the point at issue, then this mechanical influence due to mere rise in output must be eliminated. The solution of the difficulty is to take some ratio of accidents to output as the proposed index of working capacity or incapacity, and to employ the measure *number of accidents per unit of output*.

In the instance just cited the index ratio resorted to was arrived at by *a priori* considerations of the probable effect of increased output upon accidents. Often, however, the necessary correction of the index must be specifically investigated, and found empirically. This plan has been extensively used in attempts to indicate the general course of trade. If bank clearings, or imports and exports, or tonnage of ships clearing or entering ports, are to be compared from month to month or quarter to quarter to obtain a picture of the general trend of business prosperity, the normal seasonal variation must be allowed and corrected for just as in Table VIIID the yearly random fluctuation and the cyclical fluctuations were eliminated to obtain the secular trend. If fluctuations in trade are to be measured from month to month, part of the variation is due to differences in the number of working days per month. This can be exactly, numerically, allowed for off-hand and *a priori* without inspection of previous experience, by means of a coefficient of trade per working day or per standard twenty-six working-day month.[1] But the variation from month to month goes beyond this and depends on climatic factors the precise effect of which can only be discovered empirically by averaging the experience of many previous years.

Imports of raw material into Great Britain are on the average high in November, December, and January; imports of food, drink, and tobacco high in October, November, and December; and we cannot say whether imports of raw materials and food, etc., are high in the November of any particular year compared to, say, April of the same or a previous year till we correct to allow for this month's usual or standard fluctuation.

Economic values, i.e. prices, calibrate the various articles of trade in terms of a common factor, but at the same time introduce an ambiguity since they partly indicate changes in the mere value of money. If the issue we are interested in is not the changes of the general price level but changes of the physical volume of trade, this can only be exactly indicated if the aggregate of economic values is divided by the index number measuring the level of prices. The bank clearings of Table VIIID rose violently in 1915, largely because of the inflation of prices during the war, and their rate of increase does not measure the rate of increase of the actual amount of business done. To obtain a measure of the volume of business, the figures for each date must be artificially " deflated," that is, divided by the index number measuring the general rise in prices at that date.

A more familiar correction is that employed for mortality as well as birth or marriage rates. The actual number of deaths during a year is divided by the total population, and the answer given in deaths per thousand. This death rate raises further complications. The bare number of heads in the population is too simple a denominator. The " exposure " of a group of persons to risk of death varies with the ages of the persons constituting that group, i.e. varies with the " age-constitution " of the group. If the group is composed mainly of old people, a larger number of deaths is inherently to be expected, and for comparative purposes, i.e. to compare the effect of factors other than age, the denominator of

---

[1] Cf. also my method for correcting factory output to a standard fully worked hour to allow for involuntary lost time when the operative's machine broke down, etc., Florence, *Use of Factory Statistics*.

the ratio should be higher than if among the same number of persons the young were more largely represented. In practice, by the procedure known as standardization, the death rates actually observed of each age-group are given a standard weight based upon the comparative frequency of persons within those age-groups in a standard population, and a weighted mean thus reached irrespective of the age distribution of the population actually observed.[1]

Output records of an individual employee are often computed by scientific managers as a percentage efficiency, 100 representing some fairly *feasible* output that can be expected under the known circumstances of the case. This presents another form in which an index ratio is found practically useful, namely for the computation of fair piece wages and to avoid the need for subsequent rate-cutting.[2] Suppose a fair day's work for any individual in some of the various operations to be found in a motor-car works[3] has been worked out, by time study or other scientific management methods, as

> 203 radiators to be soldered,
> or 387 axles to be ground,
> or 187 crank shafts to be ground,
> or 362 crank cases to be ground.

Suppose a fair day's wage for each of these fair days of work is taken to be 15s. Then the actual piece wages paid, if it is to be an exact measure of the relative effort and skill expended, comparing one job with another, can be arrived at by dividing the actual output of each individual on each operation by the standard fair day's work *for that operation* and multiplying the ratio so obtained by 15s.

Jones grinds 370 axles, Smith grinds 370 crank cases, but Robinson grinds only 250 crank shafts. Yet Robinson gets paid most. His efficiency ratio is $\frac{250}{187}$, i.e. 133%, and therefore his wage 133% of 15s., i.e. £1, while Smith's ratio is only slightly above 100% and

---

[1] Actuarial methods employed are described in most handbooks of statistics. Cf. Newsholme, *Vital Statistics* ; Collis and Greenwood, *The Health of the Munition Worker*.

[2] When one job is paid better per unit of effort than another, men on the other jobs are naturally disgruntled, and departmental morale suffers.

[3] The figures are based on my own investigation of an American plant that was highly standardized. Cf. *U.S. Public Health Bulletin*, No. 106, Tables 3, 5, 7. The hourly averages are multiplied by eight to give the day's output.

Jones' is slightly below, and their wages only $\frac{370}{362} \times 15$s. and $\frac{370}{387} \times 15$s. respectively.

This procedure exhibits a combination of calibration or weighting and correction of the index. The denominator calibrates the different operations of a factory, i.e. reduces them to a common scale in terms of effort and skill; and reduces the absolute figures of output of the numerator to some comparable degree of success in attaining the standard.

It is clear that index ratios can be used to meet many requirements. They can measure, like corrected index numbers, the percentage variations of one type from a " base " freed from confusion with other types; and they can measure, like death rates, the degree of mortality relative to a given population freed from the influence of absolute numbers and the age distribution. They can also measure success compared to some standard that is slightly above the average attainment or is simply some sort of average.

The denominator, in short, may be a value of the *same* character as the numerator manifested at a given " base," time, or place, or may be the average or any standard value of the *same* character against which the observed values are compared; or else the denominator consists in values of a related but *different* character, i.e. population as against births. In the first case the figures may be called comparative, in the second relative; but in all cases the denominator represents some measure of the possibilities or probabilities of the circumstances against which significant variations in the actual values are clearly discerned. There were 886,643 births in England and Wales in 1880 and 896,962 in 1910; but this apparent constancy is not by itself significant for most purposes, and it is the corresponding variation in the birth rate from 34·2 to 25·1 per thousand of population that is worth noting and remembering.

Absurd fallacies are often enough committed by neglecting the exposure or expectable probabilities of the case and comparing absolute, observed, numbers instead of corrected numbers; and the frequency of falls (or is it leaps?) into this particular pit by propagandists and newspaper reporters largely accounts for the popular disrepute of statistics. It is this *Fallacy of Absolutism* in attempting to describe characters numerically, that has led well-meaning people to assert that vaccination has shown itself more dangerous than failure to vaccinate, because more vaccinated persons fell ill of small-pox than unvaccinated persons. The facts are quite possibly true,[1] but since those in the vaccinated class greatly outnumber those in the unvaccinated class a more approximately true measure of danger to any person is the ratio of the number of cases *per person within each class*. Mark Twain was puffed with pride at the low death rate of the cities of Western America compared with those of England, but he forgot that a greater proportion of the population of Western America fell into the younger age-groups and was therefore physiologically less liable to death. It was not a matter of superior hygiene but immigration ; and he should have corrected for age distribution before describing American health so patriotically.

Even where the importance of a relative or comparative measure is realized mistakes are often made in selecting the denominator. The comparative feasibility of different jobs in a factory may be miscalculated, and the percentage efficiency of those occupied in these different jobs, and in consequence their piece wages, may be unfairly allotted. And even in the highest quarters where the uses of a ratio are well recognized, it is often found impossible to agree on any particular form. In comparing the success of different business firms the absolute amount of profits made is obviously of slight significance. Some denominator must be found to allow for the scale of the firms and its operations, and to yield a comparable rate of profit. But whether the denominator is to be the capital invested by the profit makers (which would make the bases of profit and interest indistinguishable), or the total wages bill, or both capital and wages bill or some other index corresponding more closely to the effort and sacrifice of management for which profit is supposed to be a remuneration[2]—all this is still unsettled. Yet economists continue glibly to talk of rates of profit, and *normal* rates of profit at that !

The reference of the fallacy of absolutism may be extended to cover cases of *non-significant* or *false relativity* such as this. In both cases there is a failure to correct the vicarious measure so as to describe and compare the precise point at issue significantly.

There is a marked tendency, prevalent among the over-sophisticated, to describe issues by ratios that are more misleading than a bare statement of the absolute numbers. Murders committed in certain cities of the United States are often fifty times as frequent as in English towns of the same population, but when attempting to indicate any one inhabitant's chances of a death by violence it is as well to realize that compared with other ways of dying the

[1] Cf. Newsholme, *Vital Statistics*, 1st edition, Table, p. 200.
[2] Cf. Marshall, *Principles of Economics*, VI, viii.

M

number of deaths by murder is, even in the United States, practically negligible. Alarmist descriptions of depopulation by violence are fallacious, misled (on that issue) by a *false relativism* in the index that compares the proportion of persons murdered in different countries, instead of relating murders to the numbers of deaths in general or to other methods of dying in the same country.

Sometimes a meticulously inclined factory manager will state the accidents per man in each of his departments for each week. I have known figures like ·005 or 0·333% to be given as an accurate description of the accident ratio in departments employing 200 or 300 men respectively, merely as a consequence of one accident having occurred. This is a flight from absolutism carried too far ; relativity run riot. Where small numbers are concerned, a more intelligible and significant index of the condition of affairs is obtained when both numerator and denominator are left in their native state uncorrected and un*rati*onalized.

§4   *Description by Sample*

Parallel to, and sometimes confused with, the difficulty of representative description by an accurate numerical index, is that of obtaining an accurate *sample*.

Among economists the name index number is applied *par excellence* to numerical indications of the change from time to time in the purchasing power of money (over all goods, stocks, and shares, and other items of trade), or to indications of the periodic changes in the cost of living of working-class families. But the most important and intriguing feature of these index numbers is that they are samples.

The items selected for the evaluation of the prices they manifest, are certain specified exchangeable articles (bought and sold in certain markets) that are *few* in number relatively to all the articles sold in all markets.

The prices at any given time of the specified articles are usually averaged, and this process of averaging prices at various points of time presents difficult enough problems in statistico-mathematical measurement.[1]   But there are problems yet more difficult involved in the statistical fieldwork preliminary to the collection of the figures. An index number of prices is an index in two senses. It " indicates " the *change* in the prices of the specified articles

---

[1] Discussed in Chapter VIII, and below, Chapter XIV §5.

between specified points of time and a base period ; and the change in the prices of these specified articles is supposed to indicate, in the sense of sampling, changes in the whole class of articles *relevant to the issue*. The fieldwork required includes, therefore, selecting and defining the SAMPLE of articles whose prices are to be used.

Samples are that form of vicarious or representative measure in which the values manifested by certain *items* are used to indicate the values of the same character manifested by other items, usually the complete set of items. The purposes of samples and indices are parallel. An index is a specific character whose values are observed in order to represent the values of another different character. A sample is a specific set of items manifesting a certain character whose values are observed in order to represent the values of the same character manifested by other sets of items, often the complete number of items in the class.

Sampling is very frequently resorted to merely to save time and trouble ; only a certain proportion of a whole group of items observable and measurable are selected. In such a case the selection of the items to serve as samples must be *random*, that is, the basis of selection must be a character independent and unrelated to the character to be measured.

Investigating the average length of employment of American-born and immigrant workers in an American brass works, I had no time to go through the records of all the 13,000 individual employees concerned, but took as a sample the records of those employees only whose name began with an S.[1] There was no reason to expect that workers called Smith, Stanley, Sullivan, Swabsky, Simkhovitch, etc., should stay a longer or a shorter period in the employment of the factory than workers called Brown, Jones, Robinson, Popoff, etc. The character used in selecting the sample, namely, the initial letter of the name, was independent of the character at issue, namely, length of employment, and the selection was thus random.

Where the items to be measured are of different types, as the different types of commodities purchased by working-class families, and where some of the types are known to occur more frequently, or in greater quantities than others, as purchases of bread compared with purchases of pepper, WEIGHTING of item-values is resorted to. This process is familiar in estimating the working-class cost of living, but may be applied in many other industrial, economic, and political problems. For instance, to obtain a work curve, i.e. the output of consecutive hours of the working day, representative of a whole factory, I took a census of all the various types of operations

[1] *U.S. Public Health Bulletin*, No. 106, pp. 166–9.

performed in the factory, and weighted the observed sample of work curves of each type of operation according to the relative frequency of that type in the plant as a whole.[1]

§5   Tests of the Descriptiveness of Indices and Samples

An ideal index character or sample of items should satisfy two elementary conditions : (1) The index or sample should vary proportionately with the character to be indicated or with the character manifested by the items to be *sampled*, i.e. the index or sample should be representative of the issue.   (2) The index or sample should not vary with and represent variations in some character other than that to be measured.   The index or sample must if possible represent the truth, the whole truth, and nothing but the truth about the sampled items or characteristics to be indicated.

Irregular or chance variations in character other than that to be measured that may affect the index or the sample can, of course, be excluded or cancelled out in the long run by *averaging*.   A day of unusually bad temper on the part of the foreman will probably lower the output of the department for that day—say a Monday ; but if the output of several Mondays are averaged this effect will be greatly " diluted," or if a Monday of unusually good temper happens to be included it will be entirely cancelled out.   The formula for the second requirement of a good index or sample may therefore be modified to run that the index character should not *as a rule* vary with variations in characteristics other than those to be indicated, or that the sample items should not *as a rule* manifest variations other than those manifested by the items to be sampled. In short, samples and indices should exclude and eliminate the chances of a *bias* or *regular* source of ambiguity.

Exact mathematical test of a suitable index or sample is possible where the facts at issue that are to be indicated or sampled are themselves measurable ;   that is, wherever sample and index are used to save time and trouble and not because the direct measurement of the point at issue is insuperably difficult.

In the case of index measures the test is the correlation of the index with other indices of the character, or with the character to be indicated itself.   In the case of samples the test is the agreement of the sample average with averages of similar samples, or with the average of the whole class of items, within the limits of probable error,[2] allowing for the " fluctuations of sampling."

[1] See *U.S. Public Health Bulletin*, pp. 73-75.   [2] See Glossary §19.

Once these tests are made upon a proposed index measure or sample, and the index and sample are found fully and exclusively to *represent* the points at issue, this efficient representation may be taken to hold in all similar circumstances. In their schemes for vocational selection, industrial psychologists proceed precisely on these lines. Psychological tests are invented to indicate in the course of a few minutes the mental alertness and special aptitudes of an applicant for a job. But such tests are not generally adopted before passing through the fire themselves. The tests must originally have been tested. If it is a test for aptitude in printing, experienced and skilled printers should first be subjected to the test, and the results of the test should correspond with, be correlated to, the order of merit of the printers at their actual work before the test is used in selecting new printers.

Where the characters or items to be indicated or sampled are not themselves directly measurable, as, for instance, the working capacity of factory employees, common sense and judgment must take the place of mathematical tests.

To investigate how far variable industrial conditions such as hours of labour, temperature, form of organization, have an appreciable effect on human working capacity, it is necessary to calibrate working capacity, i.e. to find some vicarious yet, if possible, complete and exclusive numerical expression for the characteristic working capacity. Indices that suggest themselves are quantity of output, proportion of spoiled work, percentages of accidents, etc., on sample days in the case of sample work and workers ; but it is seldom that a situation can be so selected that (a) the sample of output, spoiled work, accidents, can be expected to vary in exact proportion with variations in working capacity generally ; (b) that characteristics affecting output, etc., other than human working capacity, are not also varying and thus making the samples and index to vary for reasons extraneous to working capacity.[1]

One of the deepest pitfalls in the statistical method now yawns at our feet. It is very tempting to select samples and indices easily measurable, as " vicars " for a characteristic or point at issue that is difficult to measure, and then to identify the non-measurable with the measurable terms. Ellwood[2] takes the number of divorces or their percentage to the total population as an index

---

[1] To be precise, variations in the " indicand " should be the sole cause or relevant condition of variations in the index. This question of causal relationships is taken up in detail later.

[2] *Sociology and Modern Social Problems*, Chapter VII.

of the relative " immorality " of different countries, and apparently by identifying immorality and the index chosen succeeds in pointing the moral to the United States with no further trouble to himself or, I suspect, most of his readers.

The fallacies of equivocation and absolutism arising from ambiguous qualitative definition and failure to correct indices, have already been noticed. Here we reach a third class of fallacy in statistics applied to descriptive uses,—the FALLACY OF OBJECTIVISM, of confusing what is objectively measurable and measured with the actual point or problem at issue. The use of divorce cases in the same state as an objective measure of immorality from year to year has led to a sort of *fetish* worship of the number or rates of divorce as an index of the trend of morality, that is only rivalled by the index of the illegitimate birth rate.

This fallacy of objectivism or fetishism is of frequent occurrence also in money matters. The measurable growth of public expenditure on education or relief of destitution is taken as identical with the growth of education or the increase in poverty ; the sums paid for a picture as identical with its æsthetic value. Again, estimates of the cost of living are based on precisely calculated workmen's budgets which only the better-to-do and more thrifty families would keep. Money spent on beer seldom figures in the returns of these supposedly typical families, yet we know that 19,000,000 barrels of beer is not an unusual annual consumption in the United Kingdom at a cost of £9 per adult inhabitant.[1] The beer drinkers apparently do not keep accounts and are difficult to measure ; but their expenditure and cost of living cannot be assumed to be indicated by the sample accounts of the budgeteers. Again, in assessing the national income of a country the statistician is liable to select only goods and services that have measurable exchange values. During the nineteenth century the baking of bread, making of jam, growing of vegetables was to a great extent transferred from the unpaid housewife to the paid baker, confectioner, and market gardener. Some of the increase in income, measurable in market values per head, of which statisticians boast was therefore merely nominal and the increase shown is no exact indication of the real increase in the services and goods obtained.

Similarly, in obtaining indices of work capacity the operations where the output was actually observed were all of a repetitive nature, otherwise no units of output would have been obtainable. But it would be a mistake to conclude that the curve or other

[1] U.K. Statistical Abstracts.

variations observed in the output of measurable repetitive operations were representative of the curve or other variations of less measurable operations; and no amount of weighting the different types of repetitive operations can overcome this difficulty.

CHAPTER XI

§1   *The Limits of Statistical Estimation*

MATHEMATICAL devices for inferring or estimating hitherto unobserved frequencies and values and measuring the probable error of estimate have already been set forth.   These probabilities may refer to each of the various types of issue.

It may be a question of estimating the distribution of values of a single character or the average value of the character, as in the case of the output, Table VIB, of the women " charging " buttons ; or it may be a question of estimating tendencies, or of estimating associations and correlations.   Forecasting probable eventualities of all sorts in the future, or casting back to prehistoric eventualities, or estimating any other unobserved situations from descriptions of present, historic, or observed events generally, is largely a question of discriminating between what is of more general application in the situation observed and described and what is simply a particular *accident, phase,* or coincidence that will probably not persist in the unobserved situation.

The situations described in economics and political science, with their extreme variability and complexity, render such discrimination between the general and the particular especially difficult, and sometimes lift them quite beyond the scope of mathematical manœuvre.   Successful economic or political predictions and generalizations are often dependent more upon discriminating and judicious fieldwork than upon the summary and neat results evolved by " arm-chair " mathematicians " playing about " with figures without reference to their context.

The summary description in the form of a frequency distribution presented in Table VID shows that 2018 of the 5194 American agricultural workers hired by the month, that is about 39%, worked less than 56 hours a week.   Is this the most certain basis for an estimate of the hours of work on a typical American farm that we can get ?   If a particular American agricultural worker is being spoken of in casual conversation, and our opinion is solicited as to whether he works less than an eight-hour day seven days a week, can we only reply that the chances of this being the case are 39 to 61 ? Judged merely from the *figures* in the table, this answer, however uncertain, is the only possible estimate. But if we engage in a little fieldwork and go " behind " these figures, it will be found that the average number of hours worked in the Northern and Southern States of the Union is different. The arithmetic mean hours for the United States as a whole was 58·8. In the north, or to be precise the New England, Middle Atlantic, and North Central States, there was one well-defined mode in the hours worked per week—between 60 and 64 hours,[1] and the arithmetic mean was about 62½ hours per week. In the south, or to be precise the South Atlantic and East and West South Central States, the arithmetic mean hours were about 54 per week. If a calculation were made of deviation, say, the semi-interquartile range (Q), of the distribution of hours on the 3543 Northern and the 2136 Southern farms respectively, where males were hired by the month, it would unquestionably be found that the probable error (Q÷root of number of farms, Glossary §19) was less than one-third of the difference of 8½ hours between the Northern and Southern arithmetic means. This difference in hours may therefore be considered *significant*, and the Southern and Northern hours cannot be considered samples of the same general distribution. This in itself is an important result of discriminating between Northern and Southern sections. But it also follows that if before answering the question about " typical " American farm hours we may ask whether the worker is living in a Southern or a Northern State we can give the answer more reliably and with greater certainty. We can generalize about the hours of labour of Northern or of Southern agricultural labourers with more precision than about American agricultural labourers at large. There is a general type of length of working day in the Northern and, though the dispersion is wide, perhaps another type in the Southern States, but no general type throughout the United States as a whole. Thus, before the figures in the table can be used for estimation and generalization, the statistician must have an expert knowledge of the different circumstances in his field of observation, circumstances which may, as in this case, or may not, be statistically measurable. And only by fieldwork can he be saved from generalizing the average for America as a whole, and perhaps applying the peculiar bimodal and discontinuous distribution of agricultural hours in America to more homogeneous countries.

To sum up. The mathematical measures set forth in Chapters V

[1] King, *Employment Hours and Earnings in Prosperity and Depression*, Tables XLI-XLIV, 2nd or 3rd quarter of 1921.

to IX such as averages, deviations, or probable error are a necessary step in accurate generalization. But they must be used in conjunction with expert knowledge of the " field," and discrimination is constantly called for in deciding how far the existence of similar circumstances permits the summary of observed results to be applied more generally.

A mathematical average eliminates all individual deviations in the values of the character due presumably to conditions individual to the item. The average daily output of the women charging buttons for several months is not affected by variations in the foreman's daily temper or varieties in the weather ; and the output of efficient and inefficient workers more or less balances out. To this extent the average output of this particular group was the effect of general conditions, and may be, and was (Chapter VII) taken as a sample from which, by the help of the mathematics of probability, to estimate within limits the general level of output of the same workers or class of workers in the same department of the factory. But clearly this average figure could not be used to much purpose for estimating the level of output on the same job in other factories or for men or boys. To this extent the summary value obtained in any one factory can probably *not* be generalized to apply to other factories by any mathematical measures.

§2 *The Dangers of Forecast and Prophecy*

The form of estimate most often in evidence is the forecast of future eventualities. The comparison of frequency distributions at two different dates presented in Table VA describes summarily yet accurately a tendency toward the growth of large-scale factories—those employing over fifty workers increased 325% in fifteen years—and cancels out " stray " fluctuations in the size of *individual* concerns. It is, so far as it goes, a statement of a *general* tendency. But the statements about the distribution of establishments of various sizes that were made in Chapter V were confined to certain particular " situations," for instance Germany in 1882 and 1897 ; and the description involves, and takes " for granted," the existence of certain other facts general to the time and place. Germany had in 1882 a population of about 55 millions ; she had enjoyed eleven years of peace, and was just turning from a short period of increased production that had supervened after a heavy depression general to industry. There was a great deal of beer drinking among all classes generally throughout the land, and Wilhelm I was Kaiser.

In 1897 Germany had a population of about 65 millions, had been unified twenty-six years, was ruled over by Wilhelm II, and was showing prosperity and steady progress in industry.[1] Much the same amount of beer drinking was generally indulged in.

When we come to generalize we have to consider all these circumstances one by one in order to discover which of them, if any, may plausibly[2] be expected to affect the tendency to larger scale establishments that is at issue. Those circumstances that are plausibly expected to affect the issue may be called " relevant " conditions.

For the sake of argument, beer drinking, the particular Kaiser on the throne, and the existence of a throne at all, may be dismissed as irrelevant ; but population, duration of peace, the state of trade may be accepted as relevant. An investigator may wish to interpolate, that is, to estimate values at a situation or position between those actually observed, or he may wish to extrapolate, that is to estimate values *beyond* the situations observed. Suppose he wishes to extrapolate the scale of factories in Germany in 1912 and again in 1927 (to continue the fifteen-year periods). He must attempt to trace the course of the relevant conditions of population, trade, and the duration of peace, but can safely neglect beer consumption and the monarch, if any.

Arguing merely mathematically from the observation of 1882 and 1897, the millions employed in factories containing over 50 persons should in 1912, fifteen years after 1897, have been 5·2 (the number in 1897) multiplied by the rate of growth in the fifteen years previous to 1897, that is $5·2 \times \dfrac{5·2}{1·6} = 16,900,000$; and in 1927, another fifteen years on, should have been $16·9 \times \dfrac{5·2}{1·6} = 54·9$ millions.

This is of course a (very) crude mathematical estimate and its realization can only be considered as a bare possibility. It assumes (1) linear geometric progression, and (2) takes no account of the probable increase of the general or even the factory population of which the number of large-scale factory employees must be some sort of fraction. The basis for estimating these necessary modifications happens to be capable of a mathematical solution. If the figures for *more* than two years were known, a curve of progress could be drawn instead of relying on a mere hypothesis of linear geometric (or arithmetic) progression, and the formula of this curve

---

[1] Thorp and Mitchell, *Business Annuals*, National Bureau of Economic Research.

[2] Chapter VII.

might be modified by inserting some function of the *known* total factory population.

But the application of mathematically calculable refinements has its limit, and in human affairs this limit must usually be imposed when the investigation is yet far from any position from which to predict or generalize.

§3 *The Converse Fallacy of Accident*

The limits of purely statistical generalization depend upon the question how many of the relevant conditions in the situation described are, or have an influence, numerically measurable, how many there are whose influence can only be judged by non-statistical expert knowledge of the field, or simply by common sense.

Theoretical economists are prone, as we shall see (XV §1), to the fallacy of accident in " inferring of the subject with an accident that which was premised of the subject only." There are conversely all too many examples of statisticians generalizing over-hastily from figures observed at particular times and places, accidentally chosen, and illustrating the CONVERSE FALLACY OF ACCIDENT by inferring of the subject only that which was observed of the subject with an accident.

Professor Pareto has attempted to establish a *general* law or regression-line of the distribution of wealth to the effect that if the number of incomes greater than any income x is equal to N, the number greater than mx is equal to $\left(\dfrac{1}{m^{15}}\right)$ N, whatever the value of m may be. But the observations on which Pareto bases this generalization were all, as Professor Pigou points out,[1] taken in countries with certain similar accidents, namely the same particular laws of inheritance and the same particular " capitalistic " system of production. These particular " accidental " circumstances in the observed situation are probably relevant conditions affecting the distribution of wealth. The particular distribution of wealth observed cannot be generalized to apply under circumstances and situations free from these accidents.

Sometimes the necessary fieldwork involves expert knowledge of historical circumstances, and the field worker should know and be able to warn the mathematical statistician summarizing past events in his field, of any contemporary accidents that may have disturbed the sequence of his figures.

[1] *Economics of Welfare*, edition 1, p. 693.

Mr. Yule,[1] for instance, makes the generalization that the fertility of the human race may vary sufficiently to account for the present fall in birth rates (1880–1925) without reference to methods of birth control as an explanation, and in support of his contention he cites the variation in " fertility rates " per married women aged 15 to 50 experienced and recorded in Sweden in every decade between 1756 and 1885, before birth control would probably have started on any significant scale. The decade showing the lowest fertility rate was, however, that from 1806 to 1815,[2] and this extreme variation synchronized with the accident that Swedish armies participated in the Napoleonic war. This circumstance is certainly a condition relevant to the issue. " War would lower the fertility of the wives of the married soldiers serving at the front and by taking marriageable bachelors abroad would also lower the proportion of younger and naturally more fruitful married couples."[3]

The variation that Mr. Yule points to does not in any case appear great[4] when its measure of deviation[5] is compared with the corresponding measure for 1880–1925, but it is evident that these historical fertility rates per 1000 married women cannot be regarded as establishing the general possibilities of variation in human fecundity without reference to the particular and possibly accidental historical circumstances when they were observed.

§4 *The Need for Orientation*

Sufficient examples, hypothetical, fallacious, and genuine, have been cited to illustrate the importance in the process of generalization of observing the circumstances and determining the relevancy of the various circumstances observed. Among the welter of circumstances present in any " situation " statistically described, statisticians must detect, or " spot," or must have spotted for them, the conditions that are relevant in the sense that they may plausibly be expected to affect the issue in other situations to which generalization is applied. Some of the accidental circumstances that occur only in the particular situations observed may thus be relevant, and may render the distribution and tendency of values and the associations and correlations observed in that situation, of no

---

[1] *J.R.S.S.*, Jan. 1925.
[2] Mr. Yule's rate is equally low for the decade between 1796 and 1805, but when the rate per 1000 married women aged 15 *to 45* is substituted (it is a better index of fecundity) the rate for 1806–15 is very much the lowest.
[3] Florence, *Over-Population*, p. 46.
[4] Op. cit., p. 47.　　　　　　　　　　[5] See Glossary §11.

general validity, and of little value in forecasting and estimating generally.

How is the mathematical statistician to know what are the " relevant " conditions that might possibly influence the issue or influence his index or sample of the issue ? How is he to judge the probability and if possible the relative importance of their influence ?

The answer is that the general statistical practitioner relying entirely on numerical data and mathematical processes cannot be expected to combine a knowledge of mathematical technique with a proper orientation in *every* subject to which statistical methods are applicable and in *every* field where statistical issues are joined. There must be special statisticians carrying perhaps less mathematical equipment, but thoroughly conversant with the field of application.

This knowledge and judgment of the circumstances in any situation that may possibly be relevant to the issue if that situation is to form the basis of generalization, must be added to the duties already (Chapter X) required of the field worker. He must add the duty of orientation to that of classification (selecting and defining the terms of the description) and representation (finding samples and indices, where necessary, through which to obtain an accurate description).

The work of a pilot provides perhaps the closest analogy to these additional duties of the field-statistician. The first requisite in a pilot is familiarity with the chart of the particular waters upon which he plies his trade. The second requisite is ability to know the whereabouts on this chart of the particular ship he is navigating. The pilot must know how to take his bearings in the midst of the waters. He must know which of all the shoals, rocks, and currents in his waters are close at hand, " relevant factors," and therefore important to remember at a given time ; and which may be neglected. The pilot must know, thirdly, what course to navigate so as to circumvent those dangers. His duties thus illustrate the need for (a) knowledge of all conditions in the field of study, (b) judgment as to what are the relevant and what the negligible conditions in relation to the position or issue, and (c) skill in selecting a course and allowing for special conditions of wind, tide, and current that will bring the ship safe into port. The mathematical statistician appears in the rôle of captain of the ship. Competent to navigate in open waters and ready to adapt his course to typical emergencies, he is ignorant of the dangers that lurk and may emerge in *particular* waters. To return to the original land-lubber metaphor, the mathematical statistician cannot be expected to realize and avoid without map-reading, surveying, and path-finding, all the PITFALLS in the particular FIELD he is at the moment observing and describing.

It is "up to" the field worker to be fully orientated. And orientation implies something more than familiarity with a mere list or schedule of conditions possibly relevant to the issue. It implies familiarity with a chart rather than a list. It implies some notion of the force and degree of relevancy, some notion of the relative positions of the possibly relevant conditions.

Relevant conditions were defined as those circumstances in a situation that may plausibly be expected to be affecting or influencing the issue. Some of these conditions may have only an indirect influence. They only affect the issue by affecting an " intermediate " condition that does directly affect the issue. Failing light, for instance, may *directly* increase accidents by making dangerous places difficult to see, or may only indirectly affect accidents by or " through " its influence on the working capacity of the victim. Trying to see in a dim light may fatigue him and thereby or, more accurately, there-through, render him less generally alert to danger.[1] These indirect relationships may be indefinitely extended and complicated.

Though logically relevance could be surmised without thinking out beforehand any particular relationship that relevant conditions may bear to an issue : it is in practice difficult to detect or spot the conditions relevant to an issue " out of the blue " without some scheme of their degree or form of relationships in mind. And before thinking out any such scheme to apply to a particular situation and issue, it is helpful to realize all the possible forms of relationships that may subsist between conditions relevant to any issue.

Relevant conditions are those circumstances in a situation that may plausibly be expected to affect the issue. But such conditions are simply certain *values* of " *characters* " (as defined in Chapter V) or of " factors "[2] in which we do not happen to be directly or mainly interested at the moment, which do not happen to be " at issue." They *disturb* the issue but are *extraneous* to it.

At any other moment, in some other investigation, these circum-

---

[1] See Table XIIB.

[2] A matter of terminology. We speak of heat and damp or temperature and humidity of *a high value* as a *condition* of successful cotton-spinning. Temperature and humidity is not the condition ; the condition is the particular value—quantity, degree, or quality—of the characters " temperature " or " humidity " (Cf. Chapter V, Rule 1, p. 52).

Characters with such influential or relevant values are often referred to as factors. We may speak of the factor of temperature and humidity influencing cotton-spinning.

stances may become the values of the character at issue, the cynosure of the observer.

Hence to list the possible relationships between characters not merely helps to distinguish the conditions relevant and the other circumstances irrelevant to any issue, but also helps in the explanation or INTERPRETATION of that, and possibly other issues. For these relationships are none other than what are popularly known as *causal* relationships.

When " relevant " conditions are said to be conditions influencing or affecting the issue it is only a coy manner of speaking. To influence or affect a thing, is to *cause* it to be other than it otherwise would be, and conditions relevant to any issue are all those circum-stances that are in some sense causes, direct or indirect, superficial or underlying, main or contributory. Whatever influences or affects distributions or tendencies of values or observed associations between values, is in some measure a *cause* of those issues, and a possibly relevant circumstance implies a condition possibly causally related.

§5 *Summary : The Scope of Statistical Fieldwork*

The statistical approach involves a number of stages to which for remembrance' sake consonant names may be attached together with occasional subtitles. (1) Authentication or the verification of accuracy of the record. This did not detain us but was alluded to in Chapter V §1. (2) Mensuration or the summary measurement of frequencies and values, described in Chapters VI to IX. (3) Classification or definition of units. (4) Representation by index and sample. And (5) Orientation. These three latter stages are all described in Chapters X and XI under the heading of Statistical Fieldwork. The stage of orientation is particularly important in passing from description to generalization.

A statistical description is a statement that in a given situation or under certain circumstances the values of one character have such and such a frequency distribution, can be summarized in some specific average, or that the distribution or average of values has changed from so and so to such and such, or that the values of two or more characters are associated or correlated in some specific manner and to some specific degree. Description deals with what is or was. Generalization is concerned with what " might be " or at least " might " continue to be, or persist in being, in spite of variable conditions. To generalize it is necessary to show that the frequency distributions, average, time, or space changes, or associations of values continue, persist, or recur when all or at least a large proportion of the *relevant* factors differ, vary, or change in value.

Now orientation is required to make the practical distinction between irrelevant and relevant circumstances or between various degrees of relevancy, a distinction that concerns the expert knowledge of the civil servant, or of the practical man on the spot, or of a special field-statistician, rather than the technique of the mathematician. Complicated mathematical formulæ have been elaborated as a more or less general law of the different liability to accidents of different individuals in a group. The basis of these formulæ was either agreement with accident statistics of whole factories, without specifying the differences in the work of the employees who were actually observed,[1] or else agreement with accident statistics for specific operations without referring to the fact that machines doing similar work vary considerably in their action and, therefore, their dangerousness. Indeed, it would be doubtful to anyone conversant with the industrial field whether modern factories with their minute specialization, i.e. with the persistent association of one particular individual with one particular operation of specific dangerousness, is a suitable field at all for finding the variation among *persons* generally to liability to accidents. Accidents occurring to persons with similar exposure, e.g. street accidents of people using the same streets for the same periods of time, would seem much more likely to isolate the human from the very relevant but disturbing mechanical factor.

Treatises on statistical methods are inclined to be entirely devoted to the mathematical treatment of the frequencies or values of the data, without considering the circumstances under which the data were originally observed and collected, and the difficulties of their classification and representation. The omission can be understood since these difficulties are different for each special field of investigation. They are not the same in investigating family budgets as in investigating industrial disputes, industrial accidents, or the wages and hours of labour. Separate manuals must perhaps be written on the statistical fieldwork in each of these fields.[2] Yet certain

---

[1] E. M. Newbold, " Practical Applications of the Statistics of Repeated Events Particularly to Industrial Accidents," *J.R.S.S.*, 1927. The paper and the whole discussion that followed passed without any specific reference to the actual circumstances " in the field " under which the data occurred and were collected.

[2] An outline of what such fieldwork manuals would contain may be seen in the Series N (Statistics) of the *Studies and Reports of the International Labour Office*. I attempted such a *Manual for Field Research* (indeed, that was the sub-title I chose) in my *Use of Factory Statistics in the Investigation of Industrial Fatigue*.

N

general principles and possible fallacies of fieldwork can be pointed out along the lines attempted here, and the attempt is certainly worth making ; for the statistical method appears more likely to go astray in its generalizations through faulty fieldwork than through any sin of omission or commission in the highly documented mathematical technique.

The sixth stage in the statistical approach is that of Interpretation or causal explanation, and is dealt with in the chapters that follow. The " orientation " of the mathematical statistician and the detection of those circumstances that are irrelevant, relevant, or very relevant by the field-statistician, will be found to have been simply one aspect of interpretation ; for the question of relevancy involves, equally, an hypothesis of cause and effect. For interpretation, as for orientation, it is necessary to canvass the various possible forms that causal relationships may take, and this task is worthy of a new chapter.

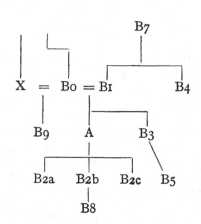

CHAPTER XII

§1 *The Genealogical Analogy*

THE most familiar device for presenting relationship is the pedigree or family tree, the chart of the relationship between ourselves and our " relatives." This analogy is particularly appropriate because it distinguishes mere association or correlation from causal relationship, and distinguishes, further, between different forms of relationship.

My face may resemble that of another person alive, or dead but preserved in a portrait. The length of our noses may be closely correlated or the colour of our eyes associated, but it does not follow that we are related—it may be a coincidence. Nor does it follow that if we are related we are related as father and son, a relationship that may be taken as the prototype of direct causal influence. We may be brothers, both effects of one or more causes, or uncle and nephew, or grandfather and grandson, or granduncle and grandnephew and so on.

B may be correlated with A but not causally related; or if causally related to A, may be a relative in any of the positions, B_0, B_1, B_2a, b, c, B_3, etc. shown on the diagram opposite, and overleaf.

B_0, B_1, B_2a, B_2b, B_2c may all be called *directly* (or immediately) and *lineally* related as mother, father, and three sons respectively of A. Of these, B_0 and B_1 are the direct (immediate) causes, and directly (immediately) relevant to A; while B_2 a, b, c, are the direct (immediate) offspring or results of A and directly dependent upon A. B_3 is directly but not lineally related, as a brother of A; it is the result of the same causes (B_0, B_1) as A is, and may be called co-dependent with A upon B_0 and B_1. B_7 and B_8 may be called lineally but indirectly (i.e. only mediately or ultimately) related as grandfather and grandson respectively of A; of these, B_7 is the ultimate but indirect cause (once removed) of A its *causa causans* and only *indirectly* relevant to A, while B_8 is the indirect result (once removed) of A, i.e. only indirectly dependent upon A.

Lineal causes and results more indirect and ultimate yet, i.e. further removed, may of course be traced like great-grandfathers, great-great-grandfathers, grandsons, etc. B5 and B4 may be called indirectly and non-lineally related to A ; a mere collateral branch. Of these, B4 is, like an uncle, a direct result of an indirect cause (B7) of A ; while B5 is, like a nephew, an indirect result of a direct cause (B1) of A. Finally, there is B9 a half-brother of A by marriage of his mother with X and the result of one cause of A (the mother B0) but not the result of A's other cause (the father B1).

A genealogical tree such as this is helpful not merely in disentangling all the relevant conditions possibly influencing the point at issue, but also in devising indices and index ratios to measure an

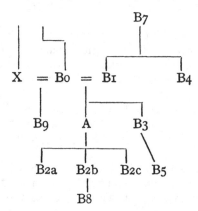

otherwise non-measurable issue, and to make certain of and test the adequacy and non-ambiguity of such indices. B2a, B2b, B2c, and B8 might form indices of A more or less adequate, like the accidents, output, and lost time forming *direct* indices of working capacity, or the power consumption that forms an *indirect* (once removed) index of working capacity through its representation of output.

Table XIIA is a rough sketch of a genealogical tree setting forth some of the correlates and the possible and plausible causal relations (causes and consequences) of an increase in unemployment in a modern industrial State.

The reference to poor harvests, undue pessimism of business men, and autonomous monetary deflation as " originating impulses," and the reference to rigid wages and prices and banking arrangements as " conditioning " causes of unemployment, are based on Professor Pigou's selection of the more important probable

TABLE XIIa

GENEALOGICAL PRESENTATION OF THE THEORY OF UNEMPLOYMENT

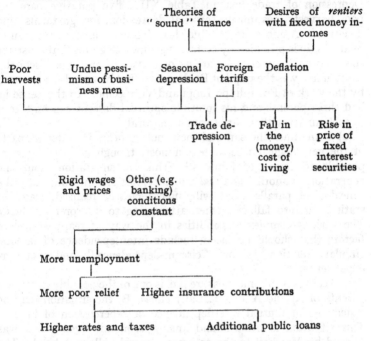

influences upon the *amplitude* of trade fluctuations.[1] I add seasonal depression which Pigou specifically excludes from the scope of his investigation[2]; and I add foreign tariffs partly to represent the class of erratic influences which, as mentioned by Pigou,[3] include inventions, strikes, changes of fashion, and wars, partly because there is a general tendency at the present time for most countries to change their tariffs in the same sense, e.g. upward, and thus to qualify tariffs as a possible cause of " a significant percentage change in the aggregate foreign demand " for any exporting country's goods.

§2 *Complex Genealogy*

The analogy of cause and effect relations with genealogical family relations has clearly two important limitations.

---

[1] *Industrial Fluctuations*, esp. Part I, Chapter XXI. Differences in wording are chiefly due to my accounting here for a specifically negative fluctuation, i.e. trade depression, not fluctuations in general.
[2] Op. cit., Part I, Chapter I.   [3] Op. cit., Part I, Chapter IV.

(1) One effect may not merely be generated by two causes like father and mother, but by three or a multiplicity of causes. Depression of trade has, in Table XIIA, five putative parents ; poor harvests, pessimism, seasonal depression, foreign tariffs, and deflation. A more useful (but less familiar) analogy to causal relationship is provided by certain ingenious diagrams that illustrate the relation between generations of artists of any one " school." Ghirlandaio was the pupil of Baldovinetti, but he was also influenced by the work of Fra Filippo Lippi and Verrocchio. In this sense he had three parents and his multiple spiritual descent can be traced in such an art without appearing unnatural.

(2) Sometimes the same phenomenon appears in different parts of the genealogical tree, a feat almost, though not entirely, impossible to scions of families.[1] This transmigration from one generation to another is a *real* difficulty, not one introduced by the genealogical parallel, and will, unless clearly realized, lead the statistician into fallacies when attempting to interpret his facts. The various complex possibilities in the way of reappearance of factors that should be faced, include interdependence of factors, circular relationship or " circum-dependence," and counter-dependence.

If B causes A in some measure (i.e. is one of the possibly numerous parents of A) and A also partially causes B, the situation may be called one of mutual interdependence or repercussion of factors. This situation is often found among economic events and was likened by Marshall to the action of several balls in a bowl. The position of each ball affects and is in turn affected by that of the others. The line of (causal) descent must here be represented

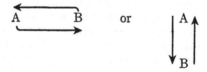

When the same fact reappears in the line of causation, but not directly and immediately,—if A causes B, B causes C, C causes D but D causes A again or the opposite of A—then we speak of an ultimately circular process. The circle may end either in cumulation or equilibration. Marshall, for instance, pointed out that if a man were unemployed he would be the poorer, and the poorer he is the

---

[1] Such cases occur where, for instance, a widow marries a relative of her first husband.

less nourished and healthy he is likely to be, hence the less industrially efficient, hence the more likely he is to be unemployed. This circular train of causation may be called cumulative because we are led after successive generations of causes to the same quality of result that we started with as a cause, often intensified in value. If on the other hand after a succession of causes and effects we are led to a precisely opposite result from the fact started with, then we may speak of an equilibrating or self-rectifying train of causation. The old classical economics was full of such providentially self-rectifying " harmonies." If wages were raised, workmen would beget more children or more would survive ; this would result after ten or fifteen years in a larger number of available labourers ; this larger supply would tend to reduce wages. Thus a rise in wages ultimately leads to a self-rectifying fall.

Sometimes the same fact *and* its opposite may appear in the same genealogical tree though not necessarily in the direct line. Discussing the effect of lighting upon industrial accidents I have pointed out the possibility of conflicting elements, and this conflict may be illustrated by means of a diagram, Table XIIB, similar in form to Table XIIA.

TABLE XIIB

GENEALOGICAL RELATIONSHIP OF ACCIDENTS AND POOR LIGHTING

Poor lighting

Eye-strain of workers   Low visibility of objects

More accidents   Less output   Lower output   More accidents

Fewer accidents   Fewer accidents

A low degree of (negative) correlation between intensity of lighting and frequency of accident would not necessarily disprove that lighting made for safety, but might plausibly be the *net* result of a number of counteracting trains of causation. Poor lighting might plausibly be correlated with a high accident rate (and also a low rate of output) through physiological eye-strain of the workers. Poor light might also be plausibly correlated with a *high* accident rate and a low output through the physical fact of lower visibility in the objects worked upon. But lower output, particularly that caused physically rather than physiologically, is likely to result in fewer accidents in any given period of time since lower output entails fewer movements. Thus the correlation of poor light with more accidents expected at first sight may be entirely or partially counterbalanced and neutralized. The detection of this relation of counter-dependence, like that of mutual interdependence, is clearly essential in any exposition of the relevant factors or interpretation in terms of cause and effect.

The practical value of distinguishing these complex relations is yet more evident in tracing what lines of causation are cumulative and what self-rectifying. A statesman satisfied with things as they are will not interfere with the self-rectifying equilibrating causes and will only depart from his policy of *laisser-faire* when cumulative tendencies appear toward a result he does not like. A progressive statesman, on the other hand, who disapproves of the results will consider both self-rectifying and cumulative relationships as vicious circles, and will concentrate his energies to break the circle at some specific point. An economic and political science that hopes to be made use of must always be on the look-out, therefore, for these complex relationships, must distinguish them from simpler forms of causal generation, and must proclaim the distinction loud and clear.

§3 *The Causal Indentation Table*

Instead of these genealogical representations of possible relatives that are cumbersome, take up some space, and are expensive in printing, resort may be had to the device of the indentation table. Here each " generation " or remove away from the starting-point is marked by leaving a wider margin on the left-hand side. The chief line of argument is seen by reading the less indented sentences :

An Increase in Unemployment
  Which plausibly results in higher insurance contributions
  And also plausibly results in more poor relief
    Which plausibly results in higher rates and taxes
    And/or which plausibly results in additional loans,
    May, plausibly, be caused by bad trade
      Which is plausibly caused by foreign tariffs
      And/or plausibly caused by poor harvests
      And/or plausibly caused by seasonal depression
      And/or plausibly caused by undue pessimism of business men
      And/or plausibly caused by deflation,
        Which is plausibly caused by theories of " sound " finance
        And/or plausibly caused by the desires of persons with fixed incomes

And plausibly results in a fall in the money cost of living
And plausibly results in rise in the prices of fixed interest and
    securities,
When combined with rigid wages and prices,
And other things are equal, e.g. banking conditions.

With each remove back to possible causes or forward to possible effects (or results) the heading is indented more and more, and as the possible causes and results are removed further and further away from the starting-point they may be called more and more subordinate. Thus a complete order or hierarchy of subordinates (like the result of inflation) and super-ordinates (like the increase of unemployment itself) and co-ordinates (like deflation and foreign tariffs and seasonal depression) is kept in mind, and may serve to interpret statistical associations between any two or more members of the hierarchy.

To avoid the long-winded repetition of " which plausibly results in or is caused by " a shorthand may be substituted. A symbol, say R, can be used for *result*, N[1] for *cause*. Indentations can then be reinforced by writing R and N smaller or in a different alphabet at each remove, as N, *N*, n, *n ;* R, *R*, r, *r*, i.e. the more subordinate the result or cause the lower the " case " of the letter or the more exotic the alphabet.[2]

§4 *Joint and Alternative Causes and Results*

Where there are several co-ordinate causes or results they may be numbered N I, II, III, or R 1, R 2, or lettered N a, N b, or R A, R B, etc. Now co-ordinate causes or results may be alternatively connected by the conjunction OR or AND/OR like the five plausible causes of bad trade or the two plausible causes of deflation ; or they may, like the plausible results of deflation, be suggested as necessarily both present and joined by the conjunction AND. An ingenious device to mark this distinction is to *letter* the co-ordinates that are plausibly alternative but to *number* co-ordinates that are suggested as plausibly supplementary or joint. These numbers and letters may vary in case and alphabet like the symbols of cause

---

[1] The excuse for this apparently arbitrary selection of signs appears later.
[2] To understand the chapters that follow immediately (XIII and XIV) it is not necessary for the reader to continue with the present chapter. In the paragraphs that follow, the scheme of tabulation and notation outlined in the foregoing paragraphs is developed and extended for the purpose of presenting systematically current economic theories and, less directly, current political ideas. Their practical connection is therefore with Chapters XV–XX.

or effect according to their degree of subordination, as N I, *N I,* *n* I, *n i,* or N A, *N A,* n a, *n a.*

TABLE XIIc

ANALYTIC PRESENTATION OF THE THEORY OF UNEMPLOYMENT

Increase in Unemployment

R A : More poor relief
      R A   Higher rates and taxes
      R B   Additional public loans
R B : Higher insurance contributions
N I : Depression in trade
      N A   Poor harvests
      N B   Seasonal depression
      N C   Undue pessimism of business men
      N D   Deflation
            n a   Theories of " sound " finance
            n b   Desires of *rentiers* with fixed incomes
            r i   Fall in money cost of living
            r ii   Rise in prices of fixed interest securities
      N E   Foreign tariffs (and other erratic circumstances)
N II : Rigid wages and prices
N III : Other things (e.g. profit) being equal

The direct causes to which an increase in unemployment is attributed in Table XIIc are examples of supplementary or joint connection. A falling off in trade (N I) will not by itself cause unemployment, runs the theory, but there must also be joined or combined with it as a *causa sine qua non* (N II) a stickiness or rigidity in wages such that wages will fall less than the exact amount required to restore equilibrium. Other things being equal (N III) is also necessarily presupposed. An example of supplementary or joint *results* is the fall in the cost of living and the rise in the price of fixed interest securities, which may both plausibly be expected to follow deflation. The conception of *alternative* results and causes is somewhat more complicated.

Unless it is intended to present rival and mutually repugnant theories as to the causes or results of a tendency or distribution of values on the same diagram, absolutely exclusive alternatives are not in question when economic and political events are measured quantitatively, but usually only alternatives in the sense of reciprocals that vary and are correlated inversely and negatively.

If tobacco is taxed the revenue of the State will probably be increased AND the consumption of tobacco decreased, but the more the one result accrues the less the other. This is the relation subsisting (see Table XIIc) between higher rates and taxes (*R A*) and additional loans (*R B*). Both may be results of more poor relief having to be paid, but to the extent to which resort is had to loans, rates and taxes will be less high, at any rate for the moment.

The same reciprocal relation in values may be supposed between the alternate co-ordinate causes. A given percentage falling off in trade (say 10%) may be due to poor harvests ($N A$) and/or to monetary deflation ($N D$) and/or to undue pessimism ($N C$).

Any one of these three causes might explain most of the amplitude of the depression without being joined or supplemented by the others. If any one of these causes were removed while the others were left unchanged, trade depression might, according to Professor Pigou, almost entirely disappear; it is not necessary that they should all be removed. It is only in this negative sense of not being necessarily joint or supplementary that causes are here said to be alternative. So far from the three plausible causes of industrial depression being mutually exclusive, Professor Pigou[1] sees "a great dream of reconciliation."

"Controversialists who have imagined themselves to hold incompatible opinions are not necessarily in conflict at all! One school of thought maintains that inequality in the harvest yields of different years is the dominant factor in industrial fluctuations; another that errors of forecast among business men are dominant; another that instability in the level of general prices is dominant. Each of these schools holds that, if it is right, the other two must be wrong. Our analysis shows that this is not so. Each of the above factors may be dominant in the only sense that is intelligible, in the sense, namely, that if it, and therefore all the effects causally due to it, were removed, industrial fluctuations, as they exist to-day, would almost entirely disappear. Of course, our analysis does not *compel* the members of these divergent schools to agree. It is open to a member of the harvest school to hold that the stabilization of prices by itself would accomplish nothing, and to a member of the stable money school to retort in kind. But none of these schools is driven by the logic of its own opinions to deny the opinions of either of the others. Harmony becomes at least *possible*, and a great deal of barren argument goes by the board."

§5 The Variety of Social Causes and Results

The method of the indentation table setting forth possible causes and results and their exact relationship may be further extended to distinguish the different types of causation that are for the moment surmised of the specific situation dealt with. In the social sciences the conscious and expressed aims, motives, intentions, and purposes of persons constitute an important variety of determining causes to be distinguished from " N " the " natural " causes.

[1] *Industrial Fluctuations*, pp. 188–9.

The policy of deflation is possibly due in part to the fact that the ruling classes, in England at least, are largely composed of persons with fixed money incomes who would gain by the fall in the money cost of living. This kind of causation is deliberate and very different to the way in which deflation more or less automatically, spontaneously, and naturally causes bad trade. It is useful, therefore, to have a separate symbol for a deliberate purposive type of cause aiming at some object and the letter O may be employed for this.

Further, when such a deliberate object exists, policies may be consciously adopted to bring the object about. These policies are not, strictly speaking, results of the object and may be distinguished by using the symbol P instead of R. O is the end, P the means, and facts connected by O and P relationships may be called a *teleological* series. And a fifth symbol M may be conveniently used where we do not wish to imply any *causal* relation but merely to distinguish the circumstances under which the causal relationships are established, the cases in which the relationship occurs. M should thus not imply any causative influence but merely the co-existent time, place, and situation, or the context or " matter " in hand. These five symbols are distinguished in ordinary language by a variety—too great a variety—of words. The translation of the symbols into ordinary variegated English proceeds as follows :

When N precedes the heading read " because of," " owing to." The fact introduced by N is the natural cause, the conditions, the agent, the determinant not specified as a deliberate purpose.

When O precedes the heading read " in order to," " for the purpose of." The fact introduced by O is the final cause, use, deliberate purpose, aim, end in view, and answers the question Why ? or Wherefore ?

When P precedes the heading read " by means of," " by." The fact introduced by P is the deliberate policy, action, method, means adopted ; and often answers the question How ?

When R precedes the heading read " with the result, consequence, effect, that." The fact introduced by R is the result, consequence, effect not specified as intentional.

When M precedes the heading read " in the matter of, case of ; *in re* . . . ; among the . . . ; as to . . . ; anent . . . ; speaking of . . . ; for example, for instance." The fact introduced by M is the circumstance under which the process of causation is supposed to take place.

The difference between alternatives or supplementaries is clear cut when employing M. M A, M B, M C, are alternative cases considered one by one. Change in the scale of production, for instance, involves either

      M A   Diminishing Returns
      M B   Constant Returns
or M C   Increasing Returns.

M I, M II, M III are the additive parts that make up the whole of the super-ordinate. Cost of Production, for instance, consists in

      M I   Wages
      M II   Interest
      M III Salaries of Management, etc.

The five symbols that are suggested were chosen because they are almost consecutive letters of the alphabet and not, like A, B, C, X, Y, Z, used in other connections ; and because most of them can be remembered as initials—R for Result, P for Policy, O for Object, M for Matter in hand, N for the Natural cause, not an object of human desire.

In the economic world of to-day events are often the unforeseen ulterior consequences (R) of the clash of natural conditions, and unorganized, independently acting individuals. There is little purposive organization in the capitalist system as a whole. " When we look outside the unit of business control, be it company, corporation, or one-man business, everything seems at first sight chaos. There is no authority vested in any body of persons to regulate the connection between these unit businesses, no conscious plan for industry as a whole. Among these businesses, working in successive stages of production, and dependent on one another for their raw materials, their equipment and their market, each looks after itself, captures markets, corners materials, conducts rate wars, and lets the devil take the hindmost. Each business, individually, must ' speculate ' on its limited stock of knowledge and take the risk of losing its capital in the struggle."[1]

The verb " to determine " thus comes to be used by the economist, in his causal interpretations, to refer to the action of " natural forces " working automatically like the forces of demand and supply " determining " prices under competition, as N determines R.

   R   *Variations in Price*
     M A   Competition
      N 1   Demand
      N 2   Supply.

[1] Florence, *Economics of Fatigue and Unrest*, p. 41.

Occasionally, however, the verb *determine* refers to a deliberate purpose on the part of some person or organized body of persons like a monopolist or monopolistic combine.

> R   *Variations in Price*
>   M B   Monopoly
>   *N*   The Monopolist
>   o   Maximum Net Profit
>   *p*   Restriction of Supply.

In the political or quasi-political world, indeed, many events are the deliberate fulfilment of expressed objects O, and the " OP " series will have to be frequently resorted to besides the " NR " series. Trade Unions (N) declare strikes (PA) or alternatively engage in political action (PB) for avowed objects (O) and these strikes or political activities have varying unforeseen consequences (R). Their degree of success is measurable by comparing their R with their O. Similarly of government policy.

A final word of caution : These distinctions among the causes and results of any factor in a situation, and between the form of conjunction of co-ordinate factors, are simply useful methods to employ in considering and expounding possible causal connections and relationships. They are not to be taken as philosophical distinctions inherent in nature, but simply as aids to thought helping to outline the exact hypotheses, the exact possibilities and plausibilities that are to be tested by statistical or other scientific methods and that are to be converted either into probabilities or improbabilities. The statistical, and non-statistical methods of testing the degree of probability of various supposed causal relationships are set forth in the next two chapters respectively.

CHAPTER XIII

In Chapter XI the desire to generalize brought us up against the need of tracing the causal relationship of all conditions *possibly* or rather *plausibly* relevant to the issue, and in Chapter XII, accordingly, were canvassed the various possible forms and degrees of causal relationship that might hold between factors. This and the next chapter are concerned with methods of interpreting the actual situation that confronts the investigator. They are concerned with the reasons for supposing some of those (possible *and plausible*) relationships between various characters to be probable and others to be improbable.[1]

If the possible and plausible relationships are viewed as a genealogical tree. we must now enquire into the sort of reasons why B1 in the tree on page 178 should be considered the putative or probable father of A ; or B3 not the direct or linear heir to B4.

§1 *The Logic of Statistical Interpretation*

At first glance it might appear that the statistical methods of association and correlation set forth in Chapter IX would settle the matter. The very name CORRELATION denotes bringing things into relation with one another and certainly most statistically measurable characters that are cause and effect must be associated or correlated. The opposite, however, does not hold. All such causes and effects are associated and correlated, but not all associated or correlated characters are cause and effect. Their causal relation may not be as direct as this or they may have no *causal* relation at all. Statistical correlation refers to the observation of some degree of co-variation or *co-incidence* between specific values of two or more characters of an item. It refers only to the logic of *events* and makes no pretensions to *interpret* the coincidence.

Mr. Yule has shown[2] that the fall in the death rate from 1866

---

[1] Cf. the reference of probability, plausibility, improbability put forward n Chapters VII, VIII, IX.
[2] *J.R.S.S.*, Jan. 1926.

to 1911 has been most closely paralleled by a fall in the proportion of marriages solemnized in the Church of England : the coefficient of correlation is +0·9512 and its probable error is small enough to justify considering this measure significant.   But can anyone say off-hand which is cause and which effect or whether there is any causal relation at all ?   Is it that solemnization of marriage in a Nonconformist chapel or registry office is conducive to superior health ; or is it, reversing cause and effect, that the longer people live the more strongly they advise their children (or grandchildren) against the Anglican ritual ?   Mr. Yule thinks that some people may suggest that both variations were due to the growth of rationalism and science—an indirect fraternal relationship ; but even this " explanation " he summarily dismisses.   " Most people would, I think, agree with me that the correlation is simply sheer nonsense ; that it has no meaning whatever ; that it is absurd to suppose that the two variables in question are in any sort of way, however indirect, causally related to one another."   Again, it cannot be taken as proven from Table IXD that the father's low earnings directly caused infant mortality in his family. Both may have been caused by inferior human stock and the relationship may have been :

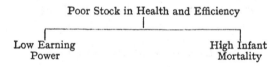

The particular association detailed in Table IXA was chosen deliberately, for the reason that it obviously does not settle the question of cause as some *associations* might seem to do.   If in winter time I always have a cold within a week of taking a cold bath, and never have a cold when I have not taken cold baths, I may infer, or at any rate I have a strong ground for inferring, that a cold and a cold bath are causally associated in a particular way.   But the fact that imports into England from British possessions over-seas are likely to be more of the raw materials type than are imports into England from foreign countries, would generally be considered a very weak ground for supposing the import of raw materials as the direct cause of maintaining over-seas possessions or for supposing the maintenance of over-seas possessions the direct cause of importing raw materials.   There may be *some* causal connection, but until history has been ransacked and political and economic motives severely cross-examined, the particular causal relationship remains dim.

The conclusion we have gradually been working up to may now be enunciated.

The statistical measure of association and correlation when combined with some test of its reliability, merely gives exact expression to one ground (stronger or weaker according to circumstances discovered later) *for supposing some causal relationship*.

The argument in favour of taking a measure of *association* between *attributes* (qualities of characters) to be any ground at all for supposing causal relationship, is that which logicians express in the Canon of Inference by the method of agreement, or rather inference by the joint method of agreement and difference. This is J. S. Mill's wording of the Canon :

" If two or more instances in which the phenomenon occurs have only one circumstance in common, while two or more instances in which it does not occur have nothing in common save the absence of that circumstance ; the circumstance in which alone the two sets of instances differ, is the effect, or the cause, or an indispensable part of the cause, of the phenomenon."

The argument for accepting a measure of *correlation* between *variables* as some ground for supposing causal relationship is expressed in J. S. Mill's Canon of Concomitant Variations.

" Whatever phenomenon varies in any manner whenever another phenomenon varies in some particular manner, is either a cause or an effect of that phenomenon, or is connected with it through some fact of causation."

The two canons are similar in principle, and for the sake of simplicity I shall discuss the logic only of inference from the association of attributes (qualities of two or more characters) either present or absent.

The translation of the Canon of Inference by the joint method in language suitable to statistical enquiry (cf. Rules in Chapter V) would run as follows :

If a frequency of *items* in which the value of one character occurs have only one value of another character in common, while a frequency of items in which the value of the first character does *not* occur have nothing in common save the absence of the value of the other character ; the value of this other character in which alone the sets of items differ, is the effect, or the cause, or an indispensable part of the cause, of the value of the first character.

In terms of baths and colds :

If three (item) weeks in the winter in which a heavy (value of the character) cold in the head occurs, have only a cold (value of the

o

character) bath in common, while twenty-three winter weeks without a heavy cold in the head have nothing in common save not taking cold baths ; the taking of cold baths in which alone the sets of instances or items (i.e. the weeks with and without a severe cold in the head) differ, is the effect or the cause, or an indispensable part of the cause, of the heavy value of the first character, cold in the head.

That this argument runs parallel to statistical association is clear from the way in which the alleged facts diverge widely from chance probabilities and indicate perfect association.

On independent probability, of the three winter weeks with cold baths, $3 \times \frac{3}{26}$ should have had colds, that is, 0 or 1, not 3 ; and of the twenty-three winter weeks without any cold baths, $23 \times \frac{23}{26}$ should have been free from colds, that is, 20 or 21, not 23, and there should have been some instead of no weeks with cold baths but no colds, and some instead of no bathless weeks with colds. The common difference or deviation of the alleged facts from these probable figures is 2 or 3, to be exact 2·654 ; and the co-efficient of association (1 measuring perfect association) is[1]

$$\frac{2 \cdot 654 \times 26}{0 + (23 \times 3)} = \frac{69}{69}.$$

Mill's wording, however, is not entirely fool-proof. In any literal sense it is absurd to speak of two or more instances agreeing *only* in the presence or absence of such and such values or qualities, for almost *any* number of instances whatever, that we might happen to select, could not fail to agree in many points of presence, and must agree in indefinitely numerous points of absence.[2]

In the case of the baths-colds associations, certainly we cannot be sure that the three weeks with cold baths and heavy colds really had only cold baths and heavy colds in the head in common, and that the twenty-three weeks had *nothing* in common except the absence of cold baths and heavy colds. Even if attention is confined to circumstances or values which might physiologically be *relevant* to the formation of colds, it will be difficult to demonstrate. Heavy clothing was probably worn all the twenty-six winter weeks and is therefore common to the three weeks ; exercise by means of lawn tennis was perhaps absent all the twenty-six weeks.

From the *statistical* standpoint these conditions *cannot* be relevant,

---

[1] See Glossary §22.   [2] Cf. Mercier, *Causation and Belief.*

or as Mill would put it, cannot be " material." Their variation or alternation cannot be associated or correlated with the absence or presence of heavy colds for the simple reason that we presumed heavy clothing and absence of tennis to be invariable throughout the winter.

The cautionary words in Mill's Canon are equivalent to saying that we must be sure that some degree of association or correlation could not be established between the occurrence of heavy colds and conditions other than that of taking cold baths. If such association might possibly be established in the case of certain conditions these conditions become " relevant." Their influence must be eliminated or controlled, and the characters at issue in the original association must be " *isolated* " before any causal relationship can be demonstrated in that association.

Circumstances and conditions are (as aforesaid, Chapter XI §4) simply values (quantities or qualities) of characters or " factors " present in the situation described, which are *not* the factors or characters mainly involved in the issue ; and the chief statistical test for possible relevancy (as it is for causation) is to take note of all those " other " characters in the situation, whose values (quantities or qualities) are varying (or altering) as the values of the character or characters involved in the issue are varying.

This test applies to all issues ; as well where the relevant conditions or the causes of a given distribution or tendency in the values of *one* character are sought, as where the association of two or more characters are " given " and secondary or further relevant conditions are feared. The application to problems of distribution and deviation and of tendency through time in *one* character, can be illustrated from the investigations of hours of labour, birth rates, and large-scale production already broached.

(*a*) The hours of farm-work in America vary widely (Table VID) and a test of what is a relevant and possibly causal factor lies in a similar wide distribution or variation on its part ; a requisite satisfied by the wide geographical distribution of workers across Northern and Southern States.

(*b*) A given variation or deviation in the ten-yearly rates of births per married women cannot be exclusively attributed to variations in sheer fecundity. These variations may have occurred during variations between peace and war that might partly account for them.

(*c*) Rapid increase in Germany's large-scale factories occurred while population, years of peace, and trade prosperity were all increasing and all of these *possibly* relevant conditions become for that reason the more *probably* so.

Thus changes, alterations, and variations in attendant circumstances paralleling or coinciding with variations in the values of *single* characters at issue, all give some ground for supposing the relevancy and causal relationship of those circumstances to that character. But only some ground.

In the sections that follow ways and means of navigating closer to the probable causal relationship (the pilot's port) will apply chiefly to issues of statistical association or correlation of *two* or *more* characters. First, it will be noted that many leading authorities in the realm of social and psychological science who appeal to the association of statistically measurable characters as demonstrating causal relationship, do not take even the elementary precautions of the statistical technique described in Chapter IX and set forth by Mill's Canons. They argue from coincidence of a few item-cases only, failing to consider and tabulate the cases of non-concomitant incidence. They look only to instances that have " circumstances in common " without enquiring whether in all other instances these circumstances are not *absent* in common. It is the fallacy of argument *by mere coincidence*.

§2   The Fallacy of Coincidence

Professor Sigmund Freud wishes to prove that the loss or breaking of a gift is largely caused by the desire to forget about the giver.

" A young man loses a pencil to which he was much attached. A few days before he had had a letter from his brother-in-law which concluded with these words : ' I have neither time nor inclination at present to encourage you in your frivolity and idleness.' Now the pencil was a present from his brother-in-law. Had it not been for this coincidence we would not of course have maintained that the loss involved any intention to get rid of the gift. . . . Dropping, breaking, and destroying things of course serves a similar purpose in regard to the object."[1]

To prove that this is anything *more* than a coincidence we should have to know very much more about this idle and frivolous young man. How many pencils or other articles associated with particular persons did he lose, drop, break, or destroy per year ? How many querulous letters did he get from his brother-in-law or other relations or acquaintances ? Exactly how many days before the loss of the

[1] *Introductory Lectures*, p. 42.

particular pencil did the letter quoted from arrive ; and what degree of proximity in time between the two events should allow us to speak of coincidence ?

Let us take half a week as a reasonable period *within* which the two events must occur to constitute coincidence.

Two questions must then occur to the scientific enquirer.

How often did the young gentleman lose things associated with particular persons without any unpleasant letter having arrived from them, less than half a week previously ; and how often did unpleasant letters come from people without his losing or breaking things connected with them within half a week ? If one unpleasant letter arrived on the average once a week from *one* among, say, twenty relations or acquaintances and the young man lost, or broke, or dropped, or destroyed something connected with one of these twenty people once a fortnight, the pure " chance " of some such " accident " following a letter by not more than half a week is likely to be realized every second fortnight. For on the average one letter should have arrived the week the fortnightly accident occurred, i.e. the week of which the day of the accident forms the centre or half-way point ; but within this period it may equally well have come in the half-week after the day of the accident as in the half-week before, and it is only of every *second* fortnight, therefore, that we can fairly predict an accident *following* the letter by half a week.

Some unpleasant letter, then, from one of twenty correspondents will precede by half a week or less the loss, dropping, breakage, or destruction of some article connected with these correspondents *every* second fortnight, i.e. every lunar month.

Let us take it that a young man remains so, for about fifteen years, i.e. from 20 to 35. Fifteen years is, to be exact, 780 weeks ; but for the sake of clarifying the illustration let us take it that the man remains young for 800 weeks, almost fifteen years and *a half*.

In the course of these fifteen years odd, the young man should (on the reasonable assumptions we have made) have received 800 displeasing letters from the twenty acquaintances, one in each of the 800 weeks covered.

There should also on our assumption have been 400 " accidents " of one kind or another (one in each fortnight) to articles connected with these correspondents, half of which, or one in each of the 200 lunar months covered, should have followed by half a week or less the receipt of an unpleasant letter from any one of these correspondents.

In the case of one-twentieth (i.e. ten) of these accidents the article should, merely on independent probability, have been an article connected with any *one* acquaintance " X," and in the case of a twentieth of these 10 accidents to articles connected with Mr. X, i.e. in half a case, the letter should have been from Mr. X himself.

The chance probabilities of this particular coincidence and of the other possible associations can be tabulated according to the standard form in Table XIIIAB.

TABLE XIIIAB

TEST OF PSYCHO-ANALYTICAL SIGNIFICANCE OF AN EVENT

Theoretical probable cross-classification of 200 item half-weeks within which accident to article connected with one of twenty correspondents follows unpleasant letter from *any one of these*

	Not a letter from Mr. X.	Letter from Mr. X.	Total
Accident to article NOT connected with Mr. X.	180¼	9½	190
Accident to article that WAS connected with Mr. X. . . .	9½	½	10
Total	190	10	200

But there should be half a chance of a similar coincidence with regard to any other of the twenty correspondents besides X. In short, there are ten (whole) chances that such a coincidence should occur in the course of the young man's youth.

Making the assumptions we have made (though they do not appear unreasonable under Viennese circumstances they can always be modified),[1] the coincidence Freud brings forward in proof of his contention can hardly be called remarkable or even unusual at all, and in the light of independent chance probability cannot even contribute a basis of a proof of a causal relationship.

Further examples of this FALLACY OF COINCIDENCE are of course of very frequent occurrence in arguments for telepathy, psychic phenomena, *et al.*

A mother dreams she hears her sailor son calling for help. This dream is said to occur at the same time as a shipwreck in which said son is drowned. And this coincidence is held sufficient to establish a causal relation, usually direct.

A wide tolerance is often exercised in the time allowed to elapse between supposed cause and effect. Mrs. Nickleby, we read, put her feet in hot bran and water somewhere about Christmas and was

---

[1] E.g. one unpleasant letter per month instead of per week would yield about two and a half chances of coincidence instead of ten and so on.

delighted to find that by Easter her cold was entirely gone. Such " tolerance " obviously allows of many chance coincidences. If the mother dreams of her sailor son every second night and he appears to call for help in every third dream, she dreams of him calling for help every six days. When the shipwreck occurs it is *bound* to happen within three days, sooner or later, of such a dream. And if a three-day " before or after " tolerance involves certainty of " coincidence " whenever the shipwreck occurs a one-day tolerance involves a one in three chance of such coincidence.

We may leave such pseudo-statistical arguments from association. They fail to tabulate the cases of incidence without co-incidence—the nights the mother dreamt of her son calling but he wasn't shipwrecked. Let us turn to genuine statistical associations.

§3 *Analysis by Partial Association* : *Isolation by Selection*

Statistical association properly tabulated in the manner of Tables IXA or IXB, implies that on the basis of mathematical and field-work investigation we may expect the relatively frequent realization of certain qualities (or ranges of value) of one character, or indices representing that character, in association with given qualities (or ranges of values) of other characters of the same item or their representatives. Let us suppose that tests of probable error type have shown that such expectations can be fairly reliably formed so that we may on statistical grounds speak of probabilities. How far can we " ground " inferences as to *causal* relationships upon such statistical probabilities ?

It is important first to review all the other possible factors in the situation whose relationships could be demonstrated by statistical association or correlation. In so-called partial association or partial correlation, methods are devised for considering the effect of one possible factor or condition at a time, and thus trying out in isolation the various possible causes of a given distribution, tendency, or co-variation.

Mr. Yule presents the following case in political science.[1] " It is observed at a general election that a greater proportion of the candidates who spent more money than their opponents won their elections than those who spent less." The details were that out of every 100 winning candidates in straight fights where for every winner there would only be one loser, 66 spent more money than their opponents.

[1] Yule, *Theory of Statistics*, edition 1919, pp. 43, 59, 364.

Cross-classification in an association table as presented in Table XIIIc is not difficult, but does it prove anything in the way of a general rule ?

TABLE XIIIc

ASSOCIATION OF SUCCESS IN ELECTION AND SPENDING OF MONEY

Actual cross-classification of two hundred political candidates according to their success and relative expenditure

	Spending more than opponent	Spending less than opponent	Total
Winning . . .	66	34	100
Losing . . .	34	66	100
Total . .	100	100	200

" It is argued," proceeds Mr. Yule, " that this does not mean an influence of expenditure on the result of elections, but is due to the fact that Conservative principles (in this particular Election) carried the day, and that the Conservatives generally spent more than the Liberals." The argument is that the observed association between winning and spending more than opponent, is due to the association of both with being a Conservative.

Two rival theories are advanced of the causal relation between the character of winning and that of spending more than one's opponent. One holds that there is a direct father-son relation between them :

Spending more than opponent
|
Winning

The other that the two are brothers :

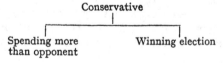

The method of settling the matter by partial association is to confine attention to the universe of Conservatives (instead of dealing with candidates of both parties together) and to compare the percentage of Conservatives winning and losing elections when they spend more than their opponents, and the percentage winning and losing when they spend less. If the proportion of Conservatives winning is greater among those spending more than their opponents than among those spending less, then spending appears to have something to do with winning in spite of the alternate explanation advanced.

From the data given by Mr. Yule we can work out the fact that the Conservatives spent more than their opponents in 80%, and less in 20%, of the contests ; and that they were winners *and* spent more than their opponents in 54·5% of all contests, and were winners *and* spent less in 8·5% of all contests.

This partial association (applying only to the Conservative *part* of the candidates) may be compared, by means of the usual association-table, to the associations theoretically to be expected on chance probability if the condition of being a Conservative was the sole deciding cause.

TABLE XIIId

TEST OF SIGNIFICANCE OF SPENDING MONEY IN ELECTION RESULT

Actual and theoretically probable cross-classification of 100 *Conservative* candidates according to their success and relative expenditure

	Spending more than opponent	Spending less than opponent	Total
Winning .	Actual 54·5 Theoretically probable 80% of 63 = 50·4	Actual 8·5 Theoretically probable 20% of 63 = 12·6	63
Losing .	Actual 25·5 Theoretically probable 80% of 37 = 29·6	Actual 11·5 Theoretically probable 20% of 37 = 7·4	37
Total .	80	20	100

It is evident from the table that the condition of spending more than one's opponent did effect an " improvement " in results over and above what was to be expected from the predominance of Conservative victories and the normally more lengthy Conservative purses. Eighty per cent is the proportion in general among Conservatives of those spending more than their opponents, so that of the total of 63 Conservative candidates who won, 80% of 63 or 50·4 should theoretically be expected to have spent more than their opponents. In fact 54·5 spending more won. And more Conservative candidates *lost*, namely 11·5, among those spending less than their opponents than would theoretically be expected, namely 20% of 37 or 7·4.

But the association of heavier expenditure with victory certainly does not appear as glaring as at first sight.

The chart of probable relationship should apparently be set forth as a combination of the two alternative charts given on page 200.

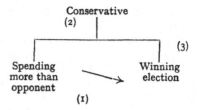

The correlation originally observed between Spending More than Opponent and Winning is explained directly (line (1) and first chart on page 200) ; and also indirectly via the fact of being Conservative (lines (2) and (3) and second chart on page 200).

The causal relationships can also be presented by means of the table of indentation.

Spending more than Opponent
    N   Being a Conservative
       r   Winning (at that particular political crisis)
    R   Winning.

In the issues usually confronting the investigator of human affairs the conditions possibly relevant are not often as few and as obvious as in this political question. The social investigator usually has to wrestle with the *multiplicity* of (possible) *causes*. This multiplicity might appear on a chart of *possible* or plausible relationships as

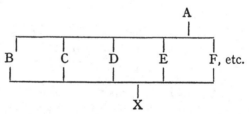

where the possible causal relationship of B to X is the issue and C to F etc. are possibly relevant causes or conditions.

The issue of the work curve is a familiar example of a multiple complex of this kind.

It is maintained that after work has continued for two hours or so, a lower rate of output per hour is observable and generally predictable in the next and later hours, and this is explained as caused by the " fatigue " of continuous hours of work gradually predominating over the effects of any other possibly relevant conditions. As the " spell " of work (of four or five consecutive hours) proceeds, it is the number of previous hours' work done that varies (increases) regularly and that alone, so runs the theory, can account for the regular variation (decrease) in the average rate of output.

If previous hours of work are to be thus generally " correlated " with the output of any hour, note should be made of the fact that, especially in afternoon spells of work, conditions of temperature and light, and the " nutrition " of the workers, also vary generally from hour to hour and may possibly have a general influence on output. In winter, the last hour of the working day is not merely the hour in which the number of previous hours of work is at a maximum, but also an hour which is generally colder and darker, as well as generally hungrier than other hours.

The factors of temperature, light, and hunger might therefore take the place of the factor of hours ; they are possible alternative causes to account for the work curve.[1] And there may be other relevant factors, that do not vary in the course of the observation. The occupation and type of work performed and the incentive to work (e.g. time or piece wages) do not usually vary from hour to hour and cannot alone account for the variation in output ; but output might possibly not fall with hours at all if the occupation were sedentary and the work light or the workers on a piece rate,[2] and though constant throughout the hours of work variations and differences in these conditions must enter into our calculations.

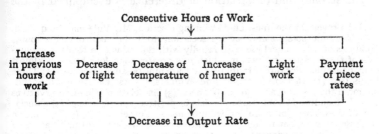

Consecutive Hours of Work

| Increase in previous hours of work | Decrease of light | Decrease of temperature | Increase of hunger | Light work | Payment of piece rates |

Decrease in Output Rate

When many conditions (i.e. many characters extraneous to the issue) may possibly be relevant to an issue such as that of the relation between hours of work and output, association and partial association of *all* the possibly relevant conditions soon become

---

[1] And might be marked NB, NC, ND where hours are NA. See above, Chapter XII.

[2] In this case light work and piece rates would be marked N II and N III where hours are marked N I.

tedious.[1] But practical considerations occurring to the experienced investigator in the field will often suggest to him that certain conditions varying or constant are *practically* irrelevant to the issue, or if relevant have not a great influence upon results when compared with the other factors, and are therefore *practically* negligible.[2] As for the remaining, probably relevant, conditions that exert a palpable influence, generalizations about the issue can be reached on the same principles as partial association by *selecting* as the universe, within which to tabulate associations, only some particular situation or parts of a situation where the significant conditions are in fact constant.

Two kinds of variation in the significant conditions may occur ; variation in the course of the observation of one situation and variation or, popularly speaking, differences between one observed situation and another. In each case the problem is to isolate the factor at issue by selecting a situation where these other things are constant or equal without, however, rejecting so many items that the number is insufficient to support any summary. In the case of the work curve, light varies in the course of the observation of any one situation. But if investigation of the work curve proceeds in the summer months, isolation is achieved by partial association, in that the association of hours of work and output is investigated within the sufficiently large universe of days when natural light does not fail, and is fairly constant during the course of the observation.

The second kind of variation or difference is exemplified in the

---

[1] To revert to the question of winning election, Mr. Yule may be quoted. " The total possible number of associations to be derived from n attributes [qualities of a character] grows so rapidly with the value of n that the evaluation of them all for any case in which n is greater than four becomes almost unmanageable. For three attributes there are nine possible associations : Three totals (e.g. (1) *All* Conservatives and Winners, (2) Association of *all* Spending more than opponents and *all* Winners, (3) Association of *all* Conservatives and *all* Spending More) ; three partials in positive universes (e.g. (4) association of those spending more and winning *among* Conservatives, (5) association of those spending more and Conservative *among* winners, (6) association of Conservatives and winners *among* those spending more) ; and three partials in negative universes (same partial associations but (7) among non-Conservatives, (8) among losers and (9) among those spending less).

" However," continues Mr. Yule, " it is not necessary in any actual case to investigate all the associations that are theoretically possible ; the nature of the problem indicates those that are required." On the political question, in fact, we only investigated the total associations numbered (1) (2) (3) and the partial association numbered (4).

[2] Unless the original intention was to study this factor specifically. We can then only regret that the results of this factor are " masked " by the results of more important factors and must seek to study the minor factor under happier circumstances in another sort of situation.

various types of industrial operations or types of wage payment that vary, not in the course of observation, but as between situations. Here isolation may proceed by arbitrarily grouping operations and wage systems, such as in the judgment of the field statistician differ only negligibly, in broad " sufficiently populated " classes, and by considering separately the association of hours and output under one or similar classes of wage payment, and upon similar classes of work. A differently shaped work curve is likely to be obtained for each selected isolated class,[1] and if the classes of, e.g., work could be graded as ranges of value along a numerical scale of heaviness or of repetitiveness,[2] relations could be traced between at least three quantitatively measured characters : hours, output, and work.

Erroneous generalizations due to lack of partial association or selection are rife and may be classed as FALLACIES OF MAL-SELECTION. The contention that most people die in their beds and that therefore a bed is the most unhealthy of places is a familiar example of failure to apply partial association where it is quite feasible and where the relationships demand it. Going to bed is a usual consequence of being ill, and dying occurs usually after a period of illness. Both phenomena are normal results of illness and to obtain a scientific proof it would be necessary to select only cases of illness, and *within* the universe of illnesses to see whether those going to bed really died in greater proportion than those not going to bed. The same solution is indicated to the problem why some health resorts have higher death rates than industrial districts. The moribund tend to go to health resorts, and before condemning these " health resorts " as fraudulent, one should select invalids, if possible of similar degree of invalidity, and find whether they do not die off at a more rapid rate in industrial purlieus.

§4 *Experimental Analysis : Isolation by Control*

Those who spend more than their opponents in elections are usually Conservative ; light varies in winter as hours of previous work increase. In neither case can the mere investigator into related and competing issues control the matter. All he can do is to select those items and cases that avoid the disturbing influence. He may investigate results only as they occur among Conservatives or only as they occur in summer months, and thus isolate the factor

---

[1] See the four types of work curve, Florence, *Economics of Fatigue and Unrest*, Table 40.
[2] As suggested in Florence, *Use of Factory Statistics*.

of spending more and of previous duration of work by process of selection of items. But there may, of course, be no items in which the relevant factors are suitably isolated by nature ; increasing hunger and continuous work may, for instance, always be joined.

The resource of physicists and chemists in such a pass is the experimental laboratory where conditions that are not naturally isolated may be artificially isolated under the investigator's own control. Now it is usually held that economic and political events and circumstances are largely uncontrollable, and that it is the impossibility of controlling the situation to suit scientific needs that makes statistical methods so essential in social research. It is not true, however, that some quasi-experimental selection may not also be used by the statistical investigator into economic and political events.

He can sometimes introduce—and if desired discontinue—a change at a time or place chosen by himself when other things are under his control, as in the notable case of Dr. Abbé, who was both scientifically minded and the manager of the Zeiss Optical Works. He changed his factory fiom a nine to an eight-hour working day at a date chosen by himself when other conditions were not changing ; and the statistical measurements of output, piece rates, and power consumption which he made before and after the change constitute perhaps the most important single contribution towards a generalized law of industrial fatigue.[1]

And a modern factory is not the only institution in which quasi-experimentation is possible. There, it is true, standardization of working conditions and of output has almost reproduced the standard apparatus and atmosphere of a laboratory. Yet banking, financial, and trading habits and arrangements also tend to at least comparative stability in the modern world, so that if the values of some single factor in the economic situation change heavily, they may exert an influence so predominant over that of all other factors that these latter may in practice be neglected.

Such " quasi-experimental " conditions were realized, according to Taussig (summarizing Viner),[2] in the Canadian financial and trading system between 1900 and 1913 :

" a single influence—namely, borrowing on a great scale—was affecting the international trade of the country, and the modifications caused by this influence can be traced with quite unusual accuracy. I state the

---

[1] Florence, *Economics of Fatigue and Unrest*, p. 226. See also, Goldmark, *Fatigue and Efficiency*.

[2] Taussig, *International Trade*, Chapter 19 ; Viner, *Canada's Balance of International Indebtedness*, 1900–1913.

case somewhat too strongly in saying that the one influence alone was in operation ; there were others, beside that of the great borrowings ; but this last preponderated so enormously that the others could have but little effect in confusing the situation. In essentials the case is of a kind rare in economic experience, in that a single force was at work under conditions which enable us to trace its effects with certainty. The series of phenomena come as close to the conditions of an experiment—the deliberate isolation of a given force—as economic history can well supply."

Thanks to the new condition of Canadian borrowing on a large scale (totalling $2,500,000,000 between 1900 and 1913), Taussig, following Viner, is confidently able to trace effects upon the balance of trade (an excess of commodity imports over exports of $1,300,000,000 in the 13 years as against a previous excess of exports), upon the gold inflow, and consequently the demand liabilities of Canadian banks (deposits plus notes increased 300% between 1900 and 1913), and finally upon the price level especially of domestic goods (a rise in prices of domestic goods of 62% between 1900 and 1913 as against a rise in the prices of similar goods in the U.S.A. of only 23%).

Beside actual or comparative uniformity in conditions, there is another feature of the laboratory which appears in many workaday institutions of modern Western civilization. I refer to the probability that overt orders will actually be carried out, and that when conditions are changed it is at the fiat, definitely recorded, of some human director. In short, control is effective.

If a factory is scheduled to work two four-hour shifts, say from 8 to 12 a.m. and 1 to 5 p.m., those hours will be kept (with certain exceptions, e.g. for acute illness, merely proving the rule) by all those reporting for work. This fact of ordered or controlled performance helps considerably in interpreting the train of causation. Statistics have shown that the shorter the hours of work the greater the hourly rate of output. But it is open to the captious critic to insinuate the question whether the rate of output was greater because the hours were shorter, or whether hours were not shorter because the rate of output was higher. If the worker were allowed to work any hours he liked, as he was, under the commission or outwork system, he might well knock off work earlier on days in which he worked faster, i.e. made a greater output per hour. But under the factory system the hours of work from day to day are known to be determined without reference to rate of output, and daily variations in output if correlated with variations in hours must, if there is any direct relation, be a result not a cause.

Wherever it is possible, the investigator of economic and political events should follow the laboratory experimenter and arrange for a system of double control. Suppose the effect of a new social policy is being tried ; it is often not sufficient for scientific purposes to make observations before and after its introduction. The results observed after the introduction of the policy may be simply due to changes after that date in relevant conditions quite unconnected with the new policy ; they are results that would have occurred anyhow. It is advisable, therefore, to separate the subjects during the whole period of observation into two groups and to apply the new policy only to one of those groups. Four sets of data are thus obtained. The hypothetically causal character at issue—the new policy—is present only in one set. The other three sets are all " controls," " checking " the interpretation of results.

The method of control is familiar, of course, in physiological circles. In Mr. Sinclair Lewis' novel of that name, Martin Arrowsmith is called in to stem the ravages of plague in a West Indian island with a vaccine that he has developed. He is a scientist, however, not a mere welfare worker, and is determined only to vaccinate half the population, picking these at random, and leaving the remaining half as controls. For suppose all had been vaccinated and the plague ceased, two interpretations would have been possible : (a) that the vaccine was efficacious, (b) that the plague had at the moment of vaccination run its course, and would have ceased anyhow.

With half the population unvaccinated results would decide which interpretation was true. If the plague ceased both among the unvaccinated and the vaccinated, interpretation (b) is indicated. If the plague ceased only among the vaccinated, or to a greater extent among the vaccinated than among the unvaccinated, then it is interpretation (a) that is the more probable.

An approach to such double control is feasible in political, industrial, and economic activities wherever similar institutions are to hand within some of which a definite change can be introduced at a given time without altering conditions in the others. Several of the States of the American Union or several English towns are stable enough in their own life, and similar enough when their life is compared, to warrant the expression legislative experimentation when one or more of the group but not the others adopt specific new laws or bye-laws. We may speak of the Carlisle (Eng.) experiment in the control of the liquor traffic, or the Wisconsin (U.S.A.) experiment in social legislation. In an otherwise stable civic life Carlisle adopts a unique revolutionary policy. Subsequent events in Carlisle may then be compared with events there before the date of the change, and the comparative results compared in turn with comparative results before and after that date in the towns not making any change. If, say, crime diminished in Carlisle but diminished equally in the other towns, nothing can be proved as to the effect of liquor control. There was a general increase in sobriety at that date, perhaps, regardless of specific policies. But if Carlisle was unique in the degree to which crime fell as well as unique in carrying out the policy of liquor control then a basis of inference is established. We possess the makings of a causal interpretation by means of *regional* comparison.

The limits to the use of the experimental method in economics and political science are due to a lack of control of the relevant and important conditions, and the pitfalls and fallacies involved in generalizing from such experiments may be summed up as FALLACIES OF MAL-CONTROL.

There may be a long lag, a lengthy period of adaptation between the inauguration of the new conditions and the appearance of " results," and during this period further novelties may occur among the conditions, novelties that are beyond the control of the investigator.

Further, if persons know they are being experimented with they may, according to circumstances, be inordinately enthusiastic, sullen, or self-conscious, and may thus render generalization and application to conditions of ordinary life impossible. Though it sounds the right and noble thing to do and is generally advocated, it is for this reason unscientific to " enlist the workers' co-operation " when carrying out any new industrial policy.[1] And the same difficulty attends generalizations from politico-economic experiments in new socialistic communities[2] : the members are not typical agriculturists ; they are inordinately keen that their experiments shall be a success ; on the other hand, they are to some extent highly strung intellectuals finding routine work difficult to continue for years on end. Criticized as part of a scientific experiment, the feelings of the " subjects " are evidently mal-controlled.

§5 *Summary : The Form and Limits of Statistical Investigation*

When economists speak of other things being equal, cæteris paribus, they appear to be referring to a natural situation where all

---

[1] See Section IV in the *Second Report of the Committee of the British Association on Fatigue*, 1916.

[2] J. N. Keynes, *Scope and Method of Political Economy*, p. 186.

P

possibly relevant characters, other than those to be associated, remain constant. But under actual economic and political conditions a situation, however carefully selected, is hardly ever likely to show no variations in relevant conditions affecting the issue. The " Stationary State " of " static " economics is admittedly a convenient fiction,—convenient certainly for teaching general principles to those without much experience of the variegated, puzzling, and often contradictory facts, and convenient *possibly* to the deductive analyst in his search for underlying tendencies.

But to the statistician, the inductive annalist, " other things being equal " usually denotes not a state of nature from which to argue, but an artificial construction at which to arrive (and lucky at that !) after the most strenuous efforts. The real situation which he can and has described is not a static state but a *dynamic* flux or welter of forces—tides, ebbing and flowing, permanent currents, occasional storms, and rhythmic waves,[1] out of which the forces involved in the issue must be artfully and arbitrarily isolated, and the conditions extraneous but relevant to the issue somehow or other eliminated.

When the question is one of causal relationship the complicated form in which statistics ultimately rests its case is usually an association-issue, in which ratios indicating the values of one character of an item are placed side by side with ratios indicating the values of another character of the same item when certain conditions are (by selection) *found*, or (by control) *kept* constant. This formulation is usually arrived at, and preceded by, a combination of the processes of mathematical correction, and of isolation of factors by means of partial associations and quasi-experiment : processes usually suggested by the field statistician.

Suppose the issue is how far, if at all, R, the number of persons unemployed in various quarter-years, is caused by N1, a fall in the general level of prices. N1 is represented by an index of wholesale prices n ; R is indicated by an index (r) of unemployment among Trade Unionists only, and only a sample r1, being the Unions of certain industries, can be observed. Besides N1 there are three other relevant conditions, N2, N3, N4, plausibly affecting R and r1, and the influence of these is eliminated in various ways. N2 is the number of men in the Unions observed and r1 may be simply divided by N2 to form a percentage of unemployed. N3 is the empirically known standard monthly fluctuation in the percentage

---

[1] Economic literature is full of sea metaphors. Cf. Marshall, *passim*.

of unemployment, and is subtracted from the actual percentage to form a corrected figure.

N4 is the occurrence of a strike in the course of the same month in another but allied industry that will render a considerable number of men in industries rı involuntarily idle.

To isolate this " accident " the only plan is to *select* months when such strikes did not occur and to avoid months such as April, May, June, 1921, or May to December 1926, when great strikes occurred in the basic Coal Industry affecting almost all other industries of the country.

TABLE XIIIᴇ

SYNCHRONISM OF FLUCTUATIONS IN INDICES OF PRICES AND UNEMPLOYMENT

THE ITEM (Central Month in each Quarter)	THE FIRST CHARACTER (PRICES) N1 (n) Wholesale Price Index Number (Board of Trade), Base Year 1913	THE SECOND CHARACTER (UNEMPLOYMENT)					
		R (rı) Number of Men Unemployed in Trade Unions of Particular Industries	N2 Number in the Unions	R/N2 % Unemployed	N3 Seasonal Flux	N4 A Strike in Allied Trade	Significant Index of Proportion Unemployed $\frac{rı}{N2} - N3$
920 May	325	16,689	1,572,085	1·1	−·4	–	1·5
,, Aug.	313	26,709	1,669,257	1·6	·0	–	1·6
,, Nov.	287	60,298	1,611,756	3·7	·0	–	3·7
921 Feb.	225	130,815	1,533,973	8·5	+·2	–	8·3
,, May	202	298,144	1,342,725	22·2	−·4	Coal Strike	–
,, Aug.	190	234,864	1,419,530	16·5	·0	–	16·5
,, Nov.	173	228,484	1,432,659	15·9	·0	–	15·9

Further conditions relevant to changes in the unemployed percentage might be (N5) a change in the definition of unemployed such as occurred under the English National Unemployment Scheme in 1924 under the Labour Government, and again in 1925 under the Conservative Government; but for simplicity's sake this additional disturbing factor will be neglected.

The statistical approach to the issue, whether or not variations in the price-level (N) affect the level of unemployment (R), lies, therefore, through a comparison or correlation of the index number of prices N with the " significant " index differential $\frac{rı}{N2} - N3$ for selected months.

The result of such a comparison looks interesting; there is a continual and heavy fall in the index of prices which is particularly violent between November 1920 and February 1921, and this is accompanied till August 1921 by a continuous rise in the significant index of unemployment which is most severe between November 1920 and August 1921. But " results " do not concern us for the present.

CHAPTER XIV

NON-STATISTICAL ANALYSIS AND INTERPRETATION

§1 *The Law of Evidence*

THE statistical association of the values of two characters is *some* ground for inferring *some* causal relation, when the variations in the values of all the other relevant characters in the field have been duly allowed for. In economics and the social sciences the situations are so complex, and control and measurement of the factors so difficult, that statistical correlation—the method of concomitant variations—can scarcely ever be accepted as conclusively demonstrating the exact causal relations. Corroboration, as the lawyers would say, is required by prudence if not by law, and we must enquire what other grounds there may be for forming conclusions as to causal relationships.

Non-statistical grounds for inferring a particular causal relationship between two characters can most easily be illustrated from the practice of the law courts. The law courts are continually engaged in a search after causes and facts relevant to some issue, and since it is the causes of an individual single occurrence and not mass phenomena that are sought, resort cannot be had to statistical methods.

In a trial for murder the prosecution seeks to establish that death was caused by the deliberate act of the accused; this is clearly a theory of cause and effect. Let a case be supposed where no person claims to have seen the deed done, and that failing such direct evidence, the prosecution rests its case upon inference from circumstantial evidence.

" A man is found slain, suspicion attaches to one of his neighbours and the suspected man is put on his trial for murder. No one beheld the deed, save the man who is now dead, and the man whoever he was, who slew him. The deceased made no statement about it to any living person, and the prisoner has disclosed nothing. Here, the act of murder, which is the fact in issue, cannot be proved by direct evidence; it must be proved if at all by inference from other facts. The prosecution will be entitled to prove as relevant all facts which may tend to show that the prisoner had a motive for the murder, that he expressed an intention to commit it, that he made preparation, and that he had opportunity."[1]

Let it be supposed further that expert medical evidence has shown death to be by a particular poison taken at a particular hour. The prosecution adduces the relevant facts that the prisoner " made preparation " by purchasing the said poison at a certain shop, " had opportunity " to administer it by being near the scene of the tragedy about the hour of its occurrence, " had a motive " in that the deceased had annoyed the neighbourhood by blocking a local footpath, and had sent respectable and respected villagers to jail as poachers, and had also been wont to make disparaging allusions to the prisoner's parentage. Facts are also adduced by the prosecution to show that at the local ale-house the prisoner on several occasions expressed his intention of " doing the deceased in."

The defence, on the other hand, brings forward the prisoner's hitherto blameless reputation and conduct, and maintains that there was no adequate personal motive for the crime and that his " expressed intention " was simply " talking big " for the purpose of currying favour and acquiring prestige.

The arguments by which such legal issues are decided are paralleled in the social sciences by the non-statistical reasons that suggest plausible hypotheses as to causal relationship, or explain and interpret statistical associations and correlations ; and this reasoning is subject to the same dangers and fallacies.

§2 *Arguments Derived from Allied Sciences*

Take first the calling of the medical expert. Many of the so-called economic laws, which I prefer to regard as mere hypotheses, are *derived* from the laws of other sciences just as the medical expert is called in for the post-mortem diagnosis. Lawyers take it for granted that when a physiological chemist says death was by poison, or strangulation, he knows what he is talking about, just as economists pretend to accept an agricultural expert's conclusions that repeated doses of capital and labour applied to a given field will eventually produce a decreasing return. Or again, diseases are accepted by politicians, and legalized, as occupational, if these diseases are " distinctly more prevalent among workers in certain occupations than among people in general, *and* if this greater prevalence established statistically can be specifically accounted for by physiological analysis as well."[2]

[1] Wills, *On Evidence*, 1907, p. 62.
[2] Florence, *Economics of Fatigue and Unrest*, p. 326.

The danger in the acceptance of the conclusions of one science by exponents of other sciences is that these conclusions may be imperfectly understood. Professor Marshall thought that it was physiologically established that fish was a nerve rather than a muscle food, and he thought it worth while to consider " the great increase during a whole generation of the demand for fish which might result from the rapid growth of a high-strung artisan population making little use of their muscles."[1] A specialist in one subject is all too likely to swallow the conclusions of mere cranks or out-of-date plagiarists in other subjects. This danger is particularly threatening to English savants since the classical education they have received at their public schools does not enlighten them as to recent scientific conclusions. " Mr. Gladstone," says Mr. H. G. Wells, " went to Eton and Christchurch and never recovered."[2] And, certainly, political science and economics have too readily accepted and clung to outworn psychological theories.[3] Colonials, Americans, and those Englishmen who have had the nonsense knocked back into them that was so carefully knocked out at public schools, or who, like Straker,[4] have been brought up at Polytechnics, are likely to be better informed on general science. They will be able to interject the conclusions of modern physiology, biology, and anthropology, or experimental psychology into their investigations at relevant points.

Professor Graham Wallas has enlightened and enlivened political science with his knowledge of modern psychology, and Thorstein Veblen has attempted to do the same by economics. There is clearly much information that economics should derive from psychology, but the two disciplines have not yet affected a synthesis. The Weber-Fechner law in psychology cannot be brought into line with the economic law of diminishing utility,[5] nor can decreasing return in industry to repeated doses of labour quite be identified with work curves and laws of industrial fatigue.[6]

If economists and industrial and political scientists cannot be induced to study the conclusions of modern psychology, perhaps psychologists might try to understand political and economic conclusions, problems, and conceptions,[7] and to apply the special experimental technique of psychology to their corroboration, solution, or precise formulation. In the study by questionnaire of

---

[1] *Principles*, Book V, v, §4. [2] *Outline of History*, pp. 427, 430.
[3] Cf. McDougall, *Social Psychology*.
[4] G. Bernard Shaw, *Man and Superman*.
[5] Dickinson, *Economic Motives*, pp. 232–4.
[6] See below, Chapter XVII §4.
[7] Duly purged of their ethical and utilitarian *sous-entendre*.

the business man's mentality and processes of thought[1] a beginning is being made of great importance to economists; and further political and economic problems in which the psychologists' co-operation is urgently needed are, as outlined elsewhere, the limits of division of labour, and the real costs of bearing financial risk.[2]

§3 Common-Sense Experience and Introspection

But the sort of common sense that guides a jury, may, it is contended, be more important than mere knowledge derived from other sciences and from the expert opinion of others, and it is upon common sense that we must ultimately rely for correct inferences. What any and every man knows by common sense may be considered as obtained from two sources : (a) his experience based on observation of how other people seem to act under similar circumstances to those laid before him, and (b) his knowledge of how he himself would feel and act under such circumstances. In both cases the argument is one of analogy, an inference from an apparently similar case, but the analogy may be obtained either (a) by observation and experience of others, or (b) by introspection.

(a) In each of several departments of a large American factory, I found that month by month the frequency of accidents and first-aid cases was higher, the higher the proportion of newly hired men admitted in the current month. But this did not tell me *qua* statistician whether the increase of accidents in any month was due to an increase in the proportion of newly hired men or, conversely, whether the increased proportion of men new to their jobs was not the result of increased accidents.[3] Conceivably the accidents might have frightened the patients and eye-witnesses so much that they left and had to be replaced by new employees. Common sense had to be appealed to and common sense in this case is based on our general experience. In the course of our observation of others whom we assume to be a fair sample of humanity, we have noticed that men new to an occupation commit mistakes of all kinds and that any one of such mistakes might lead to a definite accident. Increase in accidents is therefore quite likely to be due to increased "dilution" of the working force by new hands. The opposite

---

[1] *Reports of the National Institute of Industrial Psychology,* 1926, 1927.
[2] Chapters XIX §3 and XVIII §4.
[3] The possibility that more men had to be hired to replace those actually incapacitated by the injuries received is excluded by the minor nature of the great majority of the injuries involved. In few cases was there any question of even temporary incapacitation.

theory that dilution is due to accidents may, moreover, be discounted by common-sense considerations. It does not tally with common experience that an accident to X deters Y, Z, or X himself; the lesson of experience is rather that industrial workers are, or perhaps have to be, rather unduly careless of their safety. This inference as to the train of causation is reached by methods parallel to the jury's probable refusal to attach much significance to the prisoner's threats. Observation and experience of others tells them that however law-abiding a man may be, and however sound his reputation, he is inclined to boast of his law-breaking intentions if stimulated by appropriated liquids and an appreciative audience. These errors and accidents of judgment must be largely discounted. Experience of their fellow-beings may also suggest to the jury that men do not risk hanging for the sake merely of avenging wrongs done to the community as a whole. Landlords are not often found to be murdered for closing footpaths or for prosecuting others, though they might be for casting aspersions on a man's family tree.

Many errors and fallacies are committed in the name of common sense. The word is often used to fill a vacuum in knowledge that should have been admitted and left a vacuum. The name is " taken in vain " to cover the imaginings of an arm-chair philosopher with little experience of industrial, economic, or political life. His common-sense observations are too often a mere impression of the occasional aspects of life that happen to have struck him, with as much relation to the whole observable situation as an impressionist picture to its subject. But even where common sense is the result of a fairly wide experience and consideration of the motives and behaviour of others, there are *besetting fallacies*. First of all, the " others " observed, particularly if one moves in academic circles, may be far from a typical sample of humanity. Secondly, where common sense is a semi-conscious conclusion from analogous experience, it must be recognized that human beings are often likely, when semi-conscious, to experience what they want to experience and to be blind to what they won't see. According to their predisposition an optimist will see pink, a pessimist black, where the object was merely greyish. Many authors will apply *common sense* to problems liable to yield statistical answers repugnant to their peace of mind ; and the *common-sense* answer to these problems will often show a tendency to give comfort to themselves and their readers. It is a comfortable maxim of political science that men will not live long without liberty, that sooner or alter men are bound to rise against tyrants, etc. ; but though history is often appealed to, to " tell us " this, it is doubtful if a statistical enquiry into tyrannies would show any very high frequency of revolts.

It is noticeable that while the poor are continually subjected to statistical enquiries into their family budgets, wages, hours of work, the behaviour of the rich is described and accounted for by common sense. This has some justification in that the poor are mass phenomena and therefore more reliably converted into statistics, and also in the fact that most social enquirers move in middle, if not upper-class circles and therefore know more of well-to-do habits and motives. Yet economists or political scientists have not, after all, the experience of family solicitors, father confessors, psychoanalysts, or even that of general practitioners in a " residential " district, and they are inclined to place too much confidence in their penetration. The rich and middle-class person should be investigated like " labour " and the poor, as a puzzling problem ;— not privileged as " one of us " and exempt from statistical enquiry. To nine-tenths of the country's population, it is not labour but the capitalist that appears as the problem. Though odious, comparison of the same events among rich and poor, e.g. death rates, expenditure on " sundries," leisure time, is particularly significant. But such comparisons have been mysteriously neglected.[1]

If statistics are not available and resort must be had to commonsense analysis, the utmost precaution should be taken to avoid impressionism and incomplete and one-sided observation. Psychoanalysts make it a rule to be psycho-analysed themselves before setting up a practice, and economists and political scientists who rely on common-sense analogies certainly ought to have the psychological, economic, and political basis of their particular common sense laid bare at least to themselves.

(b) To revert to the supposititious murder case. If the deceased was heard to have made disparaging remarks about the prisoner's parentage, the probability that the prisoner killed him is likely to be considered greater than if such remarks were not in evidence. This " common-sense " attitude of the jury rests at least partly on introspection ; each juryman probably knows his own liability to " lose control " if personally insulted ; and economists and the sociologists also (though with less cause than a juryman) regard their personal feelings as typical of mankind. The man in the street, who is also a juryman, knows, if he is honest with himself, that however good a reputation he may have, and however inadequate a motive to murder, there are times when one is unduly provoked. Evidence of general good character and of lack of motive

[1] Cf. Florence, *Economics of Fatigue and Unrest*, p. 243.

may occasionally have to be overruled. Similarly the economist and political scientist, who is so largely by virtue of his powers of reasoning, imagines all men to be as reasonable as he. This assumption has admittedly been a fertile source of social and political theory ; particularly that of the rationalist and utilitarian school. Introspection has also introduced many " explanations " of statistical correlations. The fall of output with an increase of hours has been hailed as establishing the fatigue the intellectual investigator would himself feel if working in the monotony and noise of a modern factory.

The dangers of introspection were brought home to me very forcibly when attempting to write a book that could claim to be of general application on this question of industrial fatigue and unrest. I had duly noted my own particular feelings of fatigue and unrest whenever they seemed to recur regularly (i.e. to be correlated with) certain quite definite circumstances. But after talking the matter over with colleagues or with industrial workers, these feelings appeared to be idiosyncrasies and eccentricities of my own not generally shared. I feel most sleepy, for instance, not immediately after, but about an hour and a half after finishing midday lunch or dinner ; I am bored and feel inefficient when performing a job that requires both manual labour and *some* thinking like carpentering, wrapping parcels, carving a joint, or rock-climbing, though I am quite content to do *either* pure arm-chair thinking or pure manual routine and drudgery like sweeping a floor, digging a trench, or walking rhythmically up a mountain valley. Here my own feelings seemed definitely at variance with those of most of mankind that I was trying to describe.

Can I therefore take any of my own feelings however definitely they may recur under similar circumstances as in any way representative ? When discussing quality of output and the occurrence of accidents, I should have liked to mention that I find myself playing the fiddle and playing tennis worst, not when I am absent-mindedly " carrying on " (a condition that is, alas, all too frequent) but when I am returning from this condition to fuller consciousness. At school part of my duties as præpostor used to consist in repeating a simple standardized grace before and after dinner, and I generally performed this either completely conscious or completely unconscious of what I was saying. On one occasion, however, I returned from unconsciousness to consciousness in the midst of the performance and created a " show " by failing to recall the form of words of the grace. But this individual experience of the inception of industrial accidents or pieces of " spoiled work,"

though intriguing, is quite possibly not true for mankind generally ;
and the same may be said of my own feelings and comparative
efficiency after exercising or sleeping, smoking, drinking coffee or
tea, as also alcohol. In short, the outcome of my introspection did
not seem proper in a book designed to elucidate the results of
various working and living conditions upon the efficiency of man
" in the mass."

" The economist," wrote Dr. Marshall (and the same is true of
the political scientist), " has little concern with particular incidents
in the lives of individuals. He studies rather ' the course of action
that may be expected under certain conditions from the members of
an industrial group,' . . . in these broad results the variety and the
fickleness of individual action are merged in the comparatively
regular aggregate of the action of many."[1]

§4   *Arguments from General Presumption*

Finally, in the mock-murder case there is the incriminating
circumstance of the purchase of the poison and the circumstance
of the proximity of the accused to the deceased's house. The case
for the prosecution will probably be a step-by-step description of
the events leading up to the supposed murder. The evidences are
mere patches, but they will be pieced together by means of certain
assumptions in the manner familiar to readers of " Sherlock
Holmes "; though Holmes, of course, would show that the construction which the Inspector (and Watson and the reader) had leapt to
was entirely erroneous. Now it is this step-by-step argumentation
from general presumptions that economic theory chiefly relies upon ;
but often unfortunately without specifying each of the several
steps severally. The original quantity theory of money states that
the transactions using money and the velocity of circulation of
money remaining constant, prices tend to vary exactly as the
quantity of money available. Some statistical corroboration can
be found in the fact that in countries using gold as a monetary
basis, prices did in general rise and fall during the nineteenth
century as the production and stock of gold increased or decreased.
But it would very greatly raise the probability of the theory if the
gold could actually have been traced from its source of production
at the mine into the pockets of those directly responsible for increasing the price ; if the whole chain of events could be linked up and
the exact *modus operandi* of the process laid bare step by step.

[1] Marshall, III, iii, §5.

The step-by-step method in economics is often a pure construction; i.e. not one of the steps may have been actually observed, but each is constructed by certain general presumptions out of the previous step. The chief presumption of economics is that of the Economic Man, though knowledge, mobility, divisibility, and competition more or less perfect is often presumed also.[1] Occasionally natural facts also supplement the deductive argument. A typical example of an argument constructed step by step by reference to general presumption is the theory of value applied to joint supplies.

TABLE XIVa

ANALYSIS OF THE STEPS IN THE THEORY OF JOINT SUPPLY

Step in theoretical construction	Type of presumption
1. If more wheat is demanded and stocks get exhausted wheat dealers will raise the prices of wheat.	The Presumption of the Economic Man and of knowledge. (Statistical Correlation possible.)
2. If higher prices can be obtained by dealers higher prices can be obtained *from* the dealers by the wheat growers.	The Presumption of Competition on the Market. (Statistical Correlation possible.)
3. Higher prices for the growers will cause them to plant more wheat so that each may obtain maximum aggregate profit for himself.	The Presumption of the Economic Man. (Statistical Correlation possible.)
4. Wheat and straw are jointly produced ; more wheat cannot be produced without more straw.	Law of Nature.
5. If more straw is supplied with no change in demand dealers will lower the price of straw so as to dispose of the stock for maximum aggregate profit.	The Presumption of the Economic Man. (Statistical Correlation possible.)

A Summary of the steps in the argument duly co-ordinated may be given in a table of indentation :

More wheat demanded
   R Wheat dealers raise the price of wheat
      R Wheat growers obtain higher prices
         r More wheat planted
            o Maximum aggregate profit
         r More straw produced
            r Lower prices of straw
            o To dispose of stock.

It is seldom the case that economists actually plot out the steps as I have done in Table XIVa and ask of each step the grounds for

[1] See below, Chapter XV §4.

the presumption.   There is a tendency to merge steps 1, 2, and 3 so as to read " if more wheat is demanded . . . the growers will plant more wheat," an elliptical statement which, I have found, leaves the impression upon the guileless student's mind that the producer is a kind philanthropist who is shocked by the prospect of demands going unsatisfied and graciously produces more to fill the poor man's stomach.[1]

Nor is the sequence of steps 1, 2, and 3 so certain as to justify their merger for research, if not for teaching purposes.   If dealers combined when an increase in the demand for wheat manifested itself, they might raise prices and at the same time resist any attempt of the grower to get more for his wheat ; or again growers might agree (as they have in rubber production) to restrict their output and *keep* prices high instead of eventually spoiling the market.

The law of evidence recognizes that the presumptive links that bind together the chain of reasoning are of less or greater certainty. Examples cited by Wills of *conclusive presumptions of law* are that an infant under the age of seven years cannot be guilty of felony, and that a boy under the age of fourteen is unable to commit the crime of rape.   Rebuttable and less certain presumptions of law or fact include the familiar " presumption of innocence, by which it is deemed that a person is innocent until proof to the contrary has been given " and also the legal rule that " a married woman who in the presence of her husband commits a theft or receives stolen goods knowing them to be stolen, is presumed to have acted under his coercion."   But whatever the degree of validity of an argument, that degree of validity is probably made more certain by dis-tinguishing separate steps within the argument and considering the degree of validity of each of those steps.

Hence the importance of tracing each successive generation of possible or plausible cause-and-effects in a genealogical tree such as Table XIIA, or in a table of indentation such as is given at the foot of Table XIVA or in Table XIIc.   Each heading represents

---

[1] This goodwill upon earth view of business practice is strengthened by its habitual adoption among business men in their public pronouncements.
" Why are the prices of tea rising ? " asked the *Daily Herald* representative of a Mincing Lane broker.   His answer, chronicled on July 29, 1924, was that ever-increasing demands are overtaking supplies and this *alarms* him. " Tea merchants are alarmed because France and Italy have doubled their consumption of tea since last year.   America and our colonies, too, are more exacting in their demands."   Possibly the said merchants were excluded from dealings outside the British Isles ; otherwise the expression of a seller's alarm at the increasing popularity of his goods can only be regarded as part of a publicity campaign.

one stage of the argument and the connection between each heading represented by a line or branch of the tree or by a symbol, is a step forward (or back) in the argument that would correspond roughly to a paragraph in a systematically thought-out literary version.

§5 *Argument by Mathematical Deduction*

One further sort of non-statistical link in a chain of reasoning should perhaps be distinguished, that of *a priori* mathematical deduction. Beginning with the simple processes of subtraction, addition, division, and multiplication, this deductive method extends through the calculation of discount and compound interest to algebra, the differential calculus, and the devices of the higher mathematics generally.

It does not, for instance, require statistical observation to show that a country's increase (or decrease) in population between two years will be the (immigration+births)−(emigration+deaths) that occurred in the intervening period. And calculations of this kind may be considered the prototype of the very frequent discussions that occur in economics and the social sciences generally about the logical relation between accumulations or stocks on the one hand, which (like population) are measured AT any given time by a census, audit, or inventory, and a flow of continually occurring events, on the other, which (like births, deaths, or migration) are measured DURING any given period. When flow is expressed as a proportion of stock (as in the birth *rate*) or stock as a proportion of the flow, the mathematical properties and relationships of such ratios demonstrable *a priori* are by no means obvious at first sight. They often appear paradoxical, and mathematical reasoning is required to disabuse the lay reader of a fallacy. If the birth rate is falling it does *not* follow that the absolute number of births is falling, so long as the birth rate is still above the death rate and population (the denominator of the birth rate) is increasing. This *a priori* contention can be verified statistically from the experience of England and Wales. The birth rate began to fall in 1876 but the absolute number of births went on rising till 1903.

A ratio with the flow of events, income, or outgo as the numerator, and the stock as the denominator, is frequently used in economics and industry under the name *Turnover Rate*. The Turnover Rate of a business is the

$\begin{cases} \text{Sales of goods effected during a period, } \textit{divided by} \\ \text{Stock of goods held at any moment within the period} \end{cases}$

and the rate of Labour Turnover of a factory is the ratio

$$\left\{\frac{\text{The number of employees leaving and replaced during a period}}{\text{The number of employees AT any moment within the period.}}\right.$$

The expression Velocity of Circulation that has won fame in connection with the theory of money, is only another way of saying turnover. While the stock turns over, the flow circulates. In both cases the rate is calculable by dividing the stock into the flow for any specific period, or is calculable by measuring the exact period within which stock=flow. This " period of circulation "[1] follows mathematically from the turnover or velocity rate without independent statistical calculation ; if the flow per year is twice the stock and the annual rate of turnover 200%, the period when turnover=stock is, *a priori*, half the year.

Mathematical considerations also loom large in the choice of methods of computing index numbers to measure tendencies (see above, X §2). Index numbers computed by taking the arithmetic mean of item-prices are, for instance, not reversible. The arithmetic mean of a rise, between two years, of 100 to 174 in one item and of a fall from 100 to 50 in another item, shows a *rise* to 112. But if the second year is taken as the base, the arithmetic mean will show a *fall* between the same two years. The index number for the *second* year is 100 ; the index number for the *first* year[2] is (57+200) ÷2=128½. An average in the form of a geometric mean[3] avoids this non-reversibility. Whether index numbers are calculated backwards or forwards a fall of about 7% between the first and second year is indicated :

| | Base the First Year | | Base the Second Year | |
	First Year	Second Year	First Year	Second Year
Item A . . .	100	174	57	100
Item B . . .	100	50	200	100
Arithmetic Mean .	100	112	128½	100
Geometric Mean .	100	93[4]	107[5]	100

Mathematical deduction is thus often necessary in criticism of certain statistical methods of argument as well as in building up arguments without the aid of statistics. And in the fusion that is here advocated, of statistical and non-statistical methods of investigation, reasoning from inherent mathematical properties must often be resorted to along with the other sources of non-statistical

[1] E.g. Robertson, *Banking Policy and the Price Level.*
[2] Reciprocal of 174=(100÷174)=57·4.
[3] Glossary §4.
[4] $\sqrt{174 \times 50}$.
[5] $\sqrt{57 \times 200}$.

argument : other sciences, experience and introspection, and general presumption. With every possible basis of argument, statistical as well as non-statistical, at our disposal, we may proceed, in Part IV, to review the field of economic and political theory.

PART FOUR

SKETCH FOR A STATISTICAL ECONOMICS AND POLITICS

CHAPTER XV

MODIFICATION OF THE CONCEPTS AND ASSUMPTIONS OF ECONOMIC THEORY

§1 *The Fusion of Economic Theory with Statistics*

THE proper study of mankind is man, but attempts at scientific study in this direction have largely broken down owing to faulty "liaison" work between the non-statistical and the statistical methods of approach. The causes for this neglect are somewhat obscure and seem to call for an historical and psychological diagnosis too recondite to be undertaken by the layman. The results, however, are patent. The mathematical statistician is out of touch with the expert in a special field, and the experts, whether economists, political scientists, or sociologists, generally fail to make use of statistical methods and busy themselves with repeating the same unverified hypotheses, or pitting one equally unverified hypothesis against another.

The economist usually looks at the important factors and gets them orientated in correct perspective[1] but does not define or classify them consistently or measure them accurately,[2] while the statistician often looks at the wrong or at unimportant factors, but defines, classifies, and measures them with meticulous care. One is isolated from the other. The economist starts out with a knowledge of the context of economic data, and walks towards a place that he knows to be of great interest; but he is liable to lose his way if he is not a statistician, for want of statistical sextant, watch, and compass. The mathematical statistician starts out complete with sextant, watch, and compass in the shape of correlation coefficients, index numbers, probable error formulæ (Chapters VI–IX), or such higher mathematical devices as harmonic analysis; but

---

[1] Chapter XI §4.   [2] Chapter X §1.

unfortunately he has not enquired into the configuration or history of the country to be traversed and walks most efficiently to a quite unattractive, uninteresting, and often obvious spot.

Clearly the economist who knows the source and significance of the numerical data and who is conversant with the circumstances of its collection, and the statistician who knows how to summarize those figures must both work in collaboration, or one man must be both economist and statistician.

Professor H. L. Moore in his *Laws of Wages, Forecasting the Yield and the Price of Cotton*, and other works, Professor Wesley Mitchell in his *Business Cycles* (1927), and Professor Taussig in his *International Trade* (1928), have actually carried out this plan of fusing statistics and economics.[1]   Professor Cassel used this fusion in developing the theory of Purchasing Power Parity ; and though, in discussing the theory of wages,[2] he confines himself " to making clear the general outline of such a theory," he holds that " the work of filling this up with a detailed description, based upon a comprehensive mass of facts (which are unfortunately still too scanty), must be left to special research."

Professor Pigou in his recent *Industrial Fluctuations*, part of the argument of which is given above in Chapter XII, reasons admittedly by a combined use of common-sense and statistical data, such as unemployment percentages, price and output of crops, rates of discount, bank clearings, changes in bank credits and the proportion of reserves to liabilities.   And in meeting the criticism that the economic laws of increasing and diminishing returns are simply empty boxes, Professor Pigou[3] urges the training up of more men of the calibre of Jevons, equally at home in the more intricate parts of economic analysis and in modern statistical technique or, failing that, collaboration between economists, statisticians, and business men. " Economists unaided cannot fill their empty boxes because they lack the necessary realistic knowledge, and business men unaided cannot fill them because they do not know where or what the boxes are."

Marshall is notably helpful in pointing out the difficulties a statistician would encounter, and the methods he may adopt in the field when collecting facts about economic characters such as the demand curve[4] or the curve of supply prices.   He is constantly worrying how his arguments and conceptions, such as consumers'

---

[1] Further recent attempts at fusion include J. W. F. Rowe, *Wages in Practice and Theory*, H. Schultze, *Statistical Laws of Demand and Supply*.
[2] *The Theory of Social Economy*, Chapter VIII.
[3] *Ec. Jl.*, Dec. 1922.   [4] See below, Chapter XVII §3.

surplus, may be tested, verified, amplified, and made useful by the collection and analysis of statistical material.[1] Finally, I have ventured even to claim Malthus as one who fused theory and statistics to form a scientific law. His theory of population may be presented in a genealogical tree such as I have described in Chapter XII,[2] and his statistics are drawn from the birth rates and death rates of a series or " mass " of peoples living, or who have lived, all over the world.

Yet a statistical economics based on the fusion of theory with measured observations has still a long way to go. In England there is small prospect of men trained both in economic analysis and statistical technique, or of the collaboration of business men. English students in economics are with very few exceptions not trained in statistics, and statisticians seem to have little conception of economics if the controversies on over-population may be taken as a random sample. And as for the business men, what Dibblee[3] wrote in 1912 is as true as ever : " The few men who hold the threads of the great realities of business are too much concerned to keep their knowledge for their own profit to have any regard for general ideas. Their instinct in dealing with the mere investigator and observer is to cover up their tracks as far as possible and encourage his general confusion of ideas. The only theories for which they have any use are those which will turn the stream of business in their own direction."

Economics is thus liable to remain isolated from economic statistics, and to be confined to the excogitation of plausible theories that *appear* reasonable, but may have little relation to the facts. This is not entirely due to the business man's non-co-operation nor is the non-appearance of another Jevons entirely due to faulty training. The fault lies also with the nature of economic theory. If the economist wants to turn his plausibilities into probabilities he must express his theory in such terms, that facts can be observed and statistics collected and summarized to fit into, and to prove or disprove that theory. His theory must be amenable to statistical treatment. Bearing in mind the technique of statistical measurement and fieldwork described in Chapters V to XIV, he should regard his theory either as a working hypothesis by the light of which to classify and orientate his data or else as a possible

---

[1] E.g. *Principles of Economics*, Book VI, iii ; Book III, vi, 4.

[2] Florence, *Over-Population—Theory and Statistics*, Diagram, p. 18.

[3] *The Laws of Supply and Demand*. See also Lowes Dickinson, " Publicity and Industrial Accounts," and Macrosty, " Submerged Information," *J.R.S.S.*, May 1924, and Part I, 1927. For use of what banking statistics exist, see works of Allyn Young and T. E. Gregory.

interpretation of data already summarized. In the next two chapters I shall set forth (XVI) the sort of data the economist starts out with and the process of their classification and summarization and shall sketch (XVII) the method of orientation and interpretation indicated by economic theory. But in this present chapter I shall first indicate the sort of theoretical conceptions and principles that are likely to prove useful in the orientation and interpretation of the variable and interrelated data facing the realistic economist.

Statistical investigations have shown (Chapter VI) the wide dispersion and skew distribution of the values of characters ; have shown (Chapter VIII) the waywardness of economic progress and regress ; and have shown (Chapter IX) the variability in the quantitative degree of correlation of any two or more characters, the more or less dependence between them. Clearly if a given quality or quantity of a character or a given tendency or relation is to be assumed the widest allowance must be made for " accidental " modification and deviation. Finally, statistical measures have shown (Chapter VII) the uncertainty of all variation, the danger of dogmatism, and the need of speaking of possibilities, plausibilities, and improbabilities, rather than certainties and the impossible. " Rigid," " mechanistic," " fixed," " inflexible," " immutable," " sacred," " eternal," are epithets often applied to the assumptions and conceptions of classical economics by friends and foes alike, and they all point to a practice of assigning an invariable character to economic items, and invariable independence or dependence as between two or more characters under discussion. There is too much black and white, too little shading off by degrees. Economic assumptions reached by introspection and supposed common-sense observation (Chapter XIV), may by the exercise of logical ratiocination produce conclusions quite true *of those assumptions*. But since these assumed principles may not in fact actuate the majority of mankind, nor the conditions in fact prevail in the existing situation, the economist's conclusions are not practically very interesting.

The economist who wishes to be an object of serious interest must be prepared to modify his stolid assumptions and conceptions. If we make use of the terminology defined and employed in Chapters V–XIV we may classify the requisite modifications in economic theory as four :

(1) The realization of the variability of single economic *characters* and *items*.

(2) The realization of the variety of the *relationship* of economic characters.

(3) The realization of the variety of economic *conditions*.

(4) The realization of the variety of *relationship* between economic *characters* and *conditions*.

These four requisites will be discussed and illustrated in successive sections, §2, §3, §4, §5.

§2   *The Variability of Single Economic Characters and Items*

The first requisite to enable economist to collaborate with statistician is a realization of the variability of economic characters and items. Economic conceptions must become more adjustable and flexible to tally with the varieties of economic experience and with the variable world which they attempt to describe.

If economics is to adopt the proposed course, of a flexible theory adapted to the complexities of real economic life, the first modification is to note the quantitative and qualitative differences in economic characters and items. The theoretical economist has for certain purposes lumped (or " classed ") together all sorts of persons, things, and activities, and named them by the same word, as " commodities " or " factors of production." For other purposes and in other contexts the contents of these classes are far from homogeneous. The factor-of-production " labour," and various " sorts of labour," may not behave like the factor-of-production capital or machines in response to higher remuneration or longer hours of work, and the idiosyncrasies of its reaction must be separately measured.

Similarly the terms of exchange or the costs of production of different sorts of exchangeable, must be observed and measured on their own merits, not merely deduced from general principles of exchange. The admitted fallaciousness of the iron law of wages and Senior's profit-hour, are a danger-signal of this pitfall of assuming quantitative and qualitative invariability in single economic items and characters classed under the same name. The fallacy involved is an example of the logician's fallacy of accident of which the converse has (Chapter XI §3) already been cited.

The fallacy of accident " consists in inferring of the subject with an accident that which was premised of the subject only." The example quoted in logical text-books of the last four hundred years[1] is " what you bought yesterday, you eat to-day ; you bought raw meat yesterday ; therefore, you eat raw meat to-day." Here, says Jevons, the assertion in the conclusion is made of meat with the accidental quality of rawness added, where the first premise

[1] De Morgan, *Formal Logic*.

evidently speaks of the substance of the meat without regard to its accidental condition.

Most economic " subjects " have " accidental qualities " added, and the theoretical procedure of assuming certain " essential " qualities as axioms or dogmas, and arguing from these to particular events, has exposed deductive economics over and over again to fallacies of accident.

The fallacy of the iron law of wages was based on two dogmas of economics.

(I) " A rise in price tends sooner or later to decrease demand and to increase supply. Conversely a fall in price tends sooner or later to increase demand and to decrease supply."[1]

According to the iron law of wages, higher wages, a rise in the price of labour, gives encouragement to an increase in the supply of labourers in the form of additional children.

(II) " When supply exceeds demand the price tends to fall."[2] The increased supply of labour that higher wages called into being results ultimately in a fall of wages. The labourer is where he started, paid at that natural price which, in Ricardo's words, purchases " the quantity of food, necessaries and conveniences become essential to him from habit."[3]

If instead of dogmatizing we look at the facts statistically recorded, it is found that labourers with higher wages have smaller families than labourers with lower wages.[4] There seems to be some " accidental quality " in labour withstanding the logical application of the economic law.

" To one who had been taught to believe," wrote Charles Booth in the midst of his statistical enquiries into the *Life and Labour of the People in London*, " that every increment of income and security would inevitably be accompanied by additional children in working-class families, it was disconcerting to discover that the greater the poverty and overcrowding, and especially the greater the insecurity of the livelihood, the more reckless became the breeding of children ; whilst every increment in income, and especially every rise in the regularity and the security of the income in working-class families, was found to be accompanied, according to the statistics, by a more successful control of the birth rate."[5]

---

[1] This is Henderson's Law II, in his *Supply and Demand* published in 1922. In fairness to modern economic theory, it should be stated that Henderson explicitly modifies this statement later when dealing with labour.

[2] Part of Henderson's Law I.   [3] Ricardo, *Principles*, Chapter V.

[4] Pigou, *Economics of Welfare*, Part I, Chapter IV.

[5] Quoted by Sir Josiah Stamp in the *Statistical Verification of Social and Economic Theory*.

We still find economists assuming that additional income will normally stimulate the supply of babies *if* this income is an " offer, on behalf of the State, of deliberate and overt bounties upon the acquisition of large families." " This class of addition to the income of the poor," writes Pigou,[1] " has, of course, a strong tendency to augment population." It is of the utmost importance to practical politics to-day to measure the strength of this tendency. Under the terms " the Endowment of Motherhood," " Family Allowances," " Family Income Insurance," *et al.*, proposals are put forward to pay sums of money to families specifically in respect of each dependent child. Is this going to result in a higher birth rate and larger families ? Most theoretical economists, bound by the " Principles " of their doctrine, say (or assume) " Yes." But the statistical economist if he existed would first look at the precise figure of the allowance proposed. The most usual figure put forward is 5s. for the first child, 3s. for each subsequent child. Most authorities agree, however, that 5s. a week for each child (and probably more for the first) is, on the strictest economy, the lowest figure which a child would cost. Hence on " subsequent " children a family would be " down " at least 2s., and if parents were really economic men and women it would still by no means follow that they would engage in child-rearing as a paying proposition.[2]

We must turn from theory to statistical precedents.

Pigou points out that such a bounty on children was in effect given under the Old Poor Law in the United Kingdom, but a recent statistical study of the historical facts[3] is far from making this positive correlation of bounties and children a matter of course. In fact, a negative correlation is suggested, though I do not think proven.

Statistical investigations show labour to be a veritable bundle of " accidents." Senior, Professor of Political Economy at Oxford, accepted the general premise that the output of a factory was simply a multiple of the hours of work. If the annual return of a mill working an $11\frac{1}{2}$-hour day is goods worth £115,000, " each of the twenty-three half-hours of work produces $\frac{5}{115}$ths or one twenty-third."[4] One hour taken away by the factory legislation then

---

[1] *Economics of Welfare*, Part I, Chapter IV.

[2] They might possibly learn to think of children in economic terms and to count the cost for the first time ; thus the allowance for each child *might* actually reduce the number of children born below the number that would have been born without such allowance.

[3] Blackmore and Mellonie, *Family Endowment and the Birth Rate in the Early 19th Century*. Economic History Series No. 2, *Ec. Jl.*, 1927.

[4] *Letters on the Factory Acts*, London, 1837.

proposed from an 11½-hour working day would thus reduce output by two twenty-thirds. But this two twenty-thirds of the output was that which paid the (supposed) net profit of 10% on the capital invested. Hence the proposed factory law meant ruin to the entrepreneur.

Senior failed to allow for the " accident," so common to labour, that is called fatigue.

In 1913, some eighty years after Senior wrote, economists assembled in Section F of the British Association for the Advancement of Science had the then quite novel idea of collecting statistics of the precise effect of hours upon output, instead of dogmatizing about it. In the subsequent report which I had the honour of drafting, it was found doubtful whether the removal of one-ninth of the working hours, let alone one eleven and a half[th], would decrease output at all.[1]

The fallacies of the iron law of wages and of the profit-making hour rest, first of all, upon a failure to distinguish varieties of the class " means of production " and varieties of the class " products." They are founded on strict logical syllogisms ;

(1) The amount produced is in proportion to the time the means of production are at work. Labour is a means of production. Therefore the amount Labour produces is in proportion to the time it is at work.

(2) The supply of all exchangeable commodities and products increases when the price paid increases. Labour is an exchangeable commodity or product and wages its price. Therefore the supply of Labour increases with an increase in wages.

But Labour is a commodity (means of production or product) with the " accidental " qualities of (a) fatigue, (b) self-control. Labour may not behave like a machine uniformly from hour to hour, and babies may not be produced, as other products, at a price.

Secondly, the mistake was made in both cases of taking the uniform non-variable variety as the type of the whole class, to the exclusion of the human and more variable variety of producer or product.

The fallacies to which non-statistical deductive economics is prone are not all diagnosed so easily. But these often-quoted fallacies of classical economics which, though derelict, still float about dangerously in the sea of economic controversy, may be taken as a text and a warning. They are types of fallacy to which

---

[1] Committee of British Association on *Fatigue from the Economic Standpoint*, Report published 1915.
Cf. Florence, *Economics of Fatigue and Unrest*, Chapter VIII.

a deductive theory of economics is heir, and congenitally pre-disposed ; fallacies arising out of an often not realized, unconscious, assumption of invariability or homogeneousness in the items and characters classed together.

§3   *The Variability of the Relationship between Economic Characters*

The second modification to enable economic theory to co-operate with statistical observation and measurement is the realization of the variable relation between economic characters.

Recent developments in economics, at least since Jevons and Marshall popularized mathematical conceptions, are gradually qualifying economic theory to play the rôle of co-operation in this respect.   The economist now thinks arithmetically and geometri-cally in terms of units and points, sums, products and areas, net differences, margins and ratios.   The relations between his chief characters appear as algebraic functions or graphical curves.   He does not speak of the demand or supply of anything flatly as either so or so much, but looks at demand and supply as graphs, the amount demanded or supplied depending upon, " being a function of," the exact price asked or offered.   The demand and the supply are regarded, in fact, as variable amounts increasing and diminish-ing, " varying," with variations in price.

This variation is not expected to be exactly proportionate but may have any " elasticity " more or less than unity.   This variable variability is now, in fact, the kernel of the economist's thought as it always has been that of the statistician's.   Though the demand curve is taken as invariably inclined in one direction, i.e. the more the price the less demanded at that price, the *supply* curve may fall in accordance with the conception of increasing return (the more supplied the less the supply price), or rise in accordance with the conception of decreasing return, or remain horizontal in ac-cordance with the conception of constant return.[1]

These mathematical conceptions, though they do not in them-selves constitute laws in the sense of propositions, are helpful in interpreting observed measurements and avoid many popular and bourgeois fallacies.   They provide boxes of more or less precision into which to file the statistical records if and when obtained ; and they give the statistician working hypotheses in interpreting the immediate causes of price variations.

[1] Chapter XVI §7.

This co-variability of one economic character, say the price of an exchangeable or of a factor of production, with other characters at issue, say the amount of that exchangeable demanded and available on the market, is now admitted in the theory of the mathematical school that " thinks in curves."

The notion of equilibrium brought home by Marshall himself in the metaphor of the balls in a bowl each dependent for its position upon the position of all, clearly envisages the simultaneous, interacting causes present in economic phenomena. If among three balls resting in a bowl one, representing, say, the supply or stocks of an article on the market, is changed in position or removed, it affects the position of both the other balls. In the same way changes in supply will effect changes in the price of the article and in the amounts demanded at that price.

But this admission of co-variability of the chief economic characters does not always find expression when it is a question of filling the many little boxes, and the economist's conclusions often become as arid, unhelpful, and pitted with falls in pronouncing upon specific cases as though he never thought in curves or positions of equilibrium.

An example is displayed in the economist's treatment of the merchant or middleman, wholesale or retail. The several useful or at least " vendible " functions of the middleman are detailed, such as storage of goods and " their transfer as and when they are required, into the hands of those that require them,"[1] bearing risks and uncertainty, often forecasting and interpreting the desires of the consumers for the inspiration of the manufacturer, and sometimes stimulating those desires by advertising.

For these functions the merchant is paid a price, and if that price is expressed as so much per year per individual middleman, it often does not *appear* excessive. The economist is wary of pronouncing whether any specific income is really excessive, i.e. more than is required to get the merchants' functions supplied in suitable quantities. But with such sentiments as, " the middleman stands between producer and consumer, but not to obstruct ; if his profits are a toll, it is a toll levied not at a toll-bar on an otherwise open road, but a toll for the use of a very necessary bridge,"[2] he is liable to neglect the variable relation or co-variation of price of individual middlemen with their number. Owing to the *curve* of diminishing utility or productivity individual profits should fall with numbers. Many merchants may not get much income individually, but the question is whether fewer merchants with less total, but the same

---

[1] Robertson, *Control of Industry*.   [2] Clay, *Economics for the General Reader*.

individual, income might not provide as efficient a service. The law of substitution does not work (as in the case of employed labour) through human agency (i.e. the employer). The independent middleman cannot be dismissed and left unemployed as soon as his services are not wanted, and he may parasitically " hang on."

Marshall was " wise " to this and issued the warning I suggest.[1] " In some cases, the number of middlemen is in excess of the real requirements of their work ; and they earn goodly incomes by large additions to the prices of comparatively small quantities of goods that pass through their hands." But recent English statistical evidence is yet more specific.

The Departmental Committee appointed by the Ministry of Agriculture and Fisheries in 1922 and presided over by Lord Linlithgow, made several searching statistical investigations into the *Distribution and Prices of Agricultural Produce*. Their final report (Par. 16) states definitely that " in some trades there are now too many profit-making agencies engaged in the process of distribution."

Two summarizing paragraphs may be quoted from their interim report on milk and milk products :

224. The present (1923) nominal retail margin of 8d. per gallon (of milk) *in London* is not at present more than is necessary to provide a living for the small retailer who relies entirely on the sale of milk for his livelihood. He plies his trade regularly and is bound by contracts to purchase wholesale supplies at fixed prices. His continued existence seems to be satisfying to public opinion, but having regard to the dominant position occupied by the Milk Combine, he cannot be regarded as an effective competitive agent.

238. The United Dairies could retail milk at a lower price than at present, but the effect would be to exterminate the small retailer dealing only in milk who lives on the edge of the profit margin. It is important that the position thus reached in the London milk trade should be realized and understood.

The need and demand for storers, transferers, and risk-bearers is unquestionably strong up to a certain number, but beyond that may fall heavily. The economist would probably be the first to agree to this application of the hypothesis of variable (i.e. diminishing) utility. But if the economist does " realize and understand " such a possible and statistically recorded trade position, he does not always expound it very clearly to his readers. He leaves the general impression that the merchant distributor is burdened with functions so many and various that his profit, whatever it is, must be " pretty

[1] *Industry and Trade*, Book III, XII §3.

fair." There is the less excuse for this neglect of the variable relation between numbers of middlemen and their price in that the exact profits made (on turnover or capital) for specified and definite functions are being disclosed by a series of statistical investigations into the marketing of specific articles both in England and America.[1] In spite of these readily available statistics the economists' discussion is still confined to a vague and vapid " qualitative " listing of functions, qualitatively distinguished without reference to the possible *quantitative* over-supply of those " services " at the profits exacted.

§4   *The Variability of Economic Conditions and Premises*

The conception of curves and variability generally, must clearly proceed further to a third modification in the interest of adjustment to the real complexities of economic life. The assumption of a fair normal profit by the middleman ignores the possibility of any sort of agreements or tacit understandings to maintain profit, or the possibility of inefficiency in fulfilling middlemen's functions and services. In short the assumption of a normal profit as a just remuneration for necessary work rests upon assumptions of invariable underlying conditions such as competition, and a norm of business acumen.

The equilibrated balls of amount supplied, amount demanded, and price, rest not in a solid standard bowl but in a canvas bag on a swift-flowing current blown hither and thither by a changing wind and nibbled at by politician fishes.

" Nowhere do (economists) seem to be handling really defined standards," complains Mr. H. G. Wells,[2] and he compares economic dissertations with Alice in Wonderland's Game of Croquet " when the mallets were flamingoes and the balls were hedgehogs and

---

[1] (a) *Ministry of Agriculture and Fisheries*. Besides the Linlithgow reports quoted, there have recently been published Reports on Agricultural Economics, esp. No. 6, 7, 9, 10, on the marketing and trade of specific articles.

(b) *Report of the Royal Commission on Food Prices*, 1925, and special reports by the Food Council.

(c) *Reports of the National Distribution Conference*, Chamber of Commerce, Washington.

(d) *Reports of the Bureau of Business Research*, under the direction of Horace Secrist into Retail Clothing Stores, Meat Stores ; North-western University, Chicago.

(e) *Harvard Committee on Business Research*.

(f) *Report of the Royal Commission on the Coal Industry*, 1925, esp. Chapter VIII on Distribution.

[2] *A Modern Utopia*, Chapter III.

crawled away, and the hoops were soldiers and kept getting up and walking about."

The demand is not merely a variable in that the amount demanded varies elastically or inelastically with price at any given moment ; it is also a variable from time to time according to underlying variations in purchasing power and in the tastes, habits, and needs of the consuming public and manufacturer.   The whole demand curve showing the momentary correlation or co-variation of price and amount may be pushed up or down or scrunched into another form.   Similarly the whole curve of supply prices showing the co-variation of amount supplied with price, may alter in level or shape as the lapse of time at first allows more (or less) production from existing plant, then allows more (or less) plant to be adjusted to production.   The temporary supply curve alters into a normal short-run and then a normal long-run curve of supply prices.

Economic theory since Marshall blazed the trail has admitted that the issue of prices cannot be considered abstractedly in " any " period.   The period that is being thought of must be stated as at least one of four alternate cases :   temporary equilibrium on the market, normal short period, normal long period, and secular trend. But the abstraction of the characters at issue, say profits and numbers of middlemen, from their context is still clung to in considering many another underlying condition such as the degree of competition or monopoly and the middlemen's level of intelligence.

To use Marshall's own metaphor, such contextual factors are still " impounded."   This abstraction or impounding is, however, now regarded as merely temporary and to be followed by a process of disabstraction, a sort of gradual goal-delivery from the pound where the conditions were first kept fixed and out of sight.[1]

The plea put forward in justification of the method of deducing from impounded conditions that are not measured is that factors must be taken one at a time.   " It is assumed," complains Professor H. L. Moore,[2] " that the concrete problem of the relation of price and supply of a commodity will be simplified by attacking first the constituent elements of the question rather than by attacking directly the problem in its full concreteness. . . ."   At first sight this seems like the method of isolation of factors advocated above (Chapter XIII) ; but it is a similarity with a difference.

It is as though the question of the effect of hours of labour upon output were first considered in vacuo, all other things, for instance light or type of work, being impounded and for the while neglected.

---

[1] *Principles of Economics*, V, v §§3, 4.
[2] *Economic Cycles*, p. 66.   See also pp. 67 and 68.

But no such vacuous situation can ever be found in reality. There is either light, no light, or some degree of natural or artificial light ; and there must be some type of work in hand. There is not necessarily any normal light or normal work, and the relation of hours of labour to output must be considered under various conditions and types of lighting and occupation. The situation may be so selected as to manifest constant degrees of lighting throughout the place or period. Similar occupations may be combined in a group[1] to give an hour's output relation *true* of that group. But that is very different from impounding and neglecting light and occupation and abstracting the hours-output issue therefrom.

The chief conditions which even modern Economics takes for granted as assumptions may be listed as follows :

(1) Reasonable knowledge of market conditions by those engaged in buying and selling.

(2) Fair mobility of labour and capital in adjusting itself to demand ; though if immobility is held to exist new laws can be worked out, e.g. the theory of international trade.

(3) Real competition among buyers and among sellers ; though, if monopoly is held to exist on one side only, new sets of economic laws can be framed to suit.

(4) Divisibility of the commodity into enough units consumed and produced to make quantitative calculation and " balancing " possible.

(5) A more or less stationary state, where (though they may all be increasing in volume) " by far the most important conditions of production and consumption, of exchange and distribution will remain of the same quality, and in the same general relations to one another."[2]

Now a statistically conscious economics would attempt to measure the degree of knowledge of trade opportunities, mobility, competition, divisibility, and stationariness in any economic situation. And laws would be worked for specified " grades " or ranges of such degrees. Economists have already done this for mobility and competition, though the grades are too black or white : complete monopoly or immobility as against complete competition and mobility. " Competition," writes Professor Maurice Clark, " is a varied and elastic thing. . . . Agreements, understandings, and the sentiment against ' spoiling the market ' all play a part in restraining competition, and are limited in their turn by some of the various forms of potential competition. Some of the forces of

---

[1] Florence, *Economics of Fatigue and Unrest*, pp. 235-40.
[2] Marshall, *Principles of Economics*, V, v, 3.

potential competition do not begin to act until the earnings of the capital engaged in the business are materially above the minimum rate necessary to attract free capital; while some of the forces of active competition continue to act even after prices are below the level necessary to cover operating expenses."[1]

The assumption of competition plus business acumen among competing entrepreneurs leads to the almost automatic conclusion that price must be equal to the cost of production (including cost of marketing)[2] in the long run. But since the degree of monopolistic control exercised in fixing the price of any one article bought and sold here and now is seldom investigated, any more than the frequency distribution of brains among entrepreneurs,[3] the economists' conclusion is arid. As in the case of the classical Iron Law of Wages, and Senior's theory of the profitable hour the economist has not sufficiently studied the " accidence ": the incidence of business folly, the frequency of varieties of price-fixing method, and the " accident " of monopoly or semi-monopoly.

The exception that proves the rule of his assumption of mobility is the economist's law of international trade. The theory of international trade holds that even though in one country labour might be applied more advantageously than in another country in producing *everything*, yet trade will be exchanged between them. The more efficient country will import those things to which its labour (though more advantageously applicable than in the other country) is more advantageously applicable to a *lesser* extent, and will export those things to which its labour is more advantageously applicable to a *greater* extent. It will specialize (see Chapter IX §2) on what it can do most better, or most cheaper. This law of comparative costs assumes, however, immobility at least of labour, if not capital. For otherwise labour would migrate *en masse* to the country where it was more advantageously applicable to everything and where presumably it could earn higher wages generally.

" Countries " are assumed to be places between which mobility of labour (called in that case emigration or immigration) and to some extent mobility of capital are negligible; and originally countries were taken as the only case of such immobility. Recently, however, economics has admitted that international conditions are (to quote the phrase Marshall used in another connection) only

---

[1] *The Economics of Overhead Costs*, p. 461.

[2] Though this inclusion is seldom stated explicitly enough to make it clear to, say, intelligent, business men.

[3] *Psychologists*, however, are carrying out research work on the " psychological make-up of higher business executives." Cf. Annual Reports of the National Institute of Industrial Psychology, 1926, 1927.

R

" one species of a large genus." There is immobility of labour
between the " non-competing " classes such as the professions on
the one hand and artisans on the other[1] ; there is immobility
between town and country,[2] and one place and another within the
same country ; *and* there is immobility of labour exemplified in a
low labour turnover between different organized institutions like
industrial plants. Finally, and partly as a result of these immobili-
ties, there is immobility of labour (also capital) between whole
industries.

The resources *within one country* may be " mal-distributed" as
between different lines of investment, that is, added amounts of
labour and capital may not be so distributed or applied as to yield
equivalent increases in return in all uses. A tendency to such
equivalent return cannot be assumed, but must either be shown by
direct statistical measures such as equivalent increases in product
per head in one industry as compared with another, associated with
equivalent increases in horse power and other measures of capital
employed,[3] or else the tendency must be deduced from an assumption of a " sufficient " degree of mobility.

The assumption of mobility of factors of production at least
within a single country, combined with the principle of the economic
man,[4] leads to the conclusion that reductions in real wages will
move adult labour out of overcrowded industries over-supplied
with labour into more highly paid employments, and conversely
of increases in real wages. But the recent history of labour in (*a*)
the English coal-mining and unsheltered industries and (*b*) domestic
service, seems to throw doubt upon the universal application of
these conclusions. If continued unemployment is a measure of an
over-supply of labour, and a continuance of situations vacant a
measure of an under-supply, mobility seems in fact most incomplete,
and it becomes essential to estimate the *degree* of mobility ;—a
degree that is likely to lie somewhere between the complete mobility
theoretically assumed within a country, and the complete immobility
assumed between countries.

Now statistical methods can undoubtedly distinguish several
grades of mobility between absolute mobility and absolute immobility in each of the forms of mobility : international migration,
and class, place, industrial, and institutional mobility. Some occu-

---

[1] Taussig, *Principles of Economics*.
[2] M. H. Dobb, *The Economic Development of Russia*.
[3] These statistical measures are used by Benham (*The Prosperity of
Australia*, pp. 146–62) as a criterion to show that Australian protection has
produced *mal-distribution* of resources.
[4] See below, Chapter XVII §1.

pations and industries will show greater mobility than others,[1] and various grades of mobility will be shown by the population of different countries at different times. Class, place, and institutional mobility is probably higher in the United States than the United Kingdom[2] (with important effects upon the supply of competent entrepreneurs and upon welfare work designed to hold employees in the employment of the firm) ; and to some industries like coal-mining labour seems to " stick," however intense the negative stimulus, i.e. however low wages and conditions of work may fall. Here the supply is not " equalized " to the demand by the action of price, and to one writing in England in 1929 there appears a tendency to a permanent unemployment of 10% to 20% of miners.

Economists have also begun to question the propriety of assuming a normal stationary or even uniform progress of trade, and are busy contemplating the trade cycle. Here the supremacy of statistical methods is admitted. Clearly price may be determined one way during the boom phase of a cycle and quite another in the slump phase, just as in Bernard Shaw's *The Doctor's Dilemma* Sir " Collie " Ridgeon's vaccine cured the patient in one phase, as shown by the opsonic index, and killed him in another.

Wide variations in the knowledge of contracting parties to an exchange is also grudgingly admitted, notably in the sweated trades. The wages here may not be equal to the marginal productivity of the worker because the worker does not know how much he or she is " worth " economically and does not ask for the true economic wage. In fact, unless wage bargains are concluded collectively by Trade Unions or are organized by the State, as through Wage or " Trades " Boards (and the extent of such practices can be statistically ascertained), ordinary economic laws break down.

Economists have, of course, not neglected the *possibility* of degrees of monopoly, immobility, and ignorance (I deal with indivisibility later) ;[3] but their attention to such deviations from their assumed norm has often been little better than lip-service. Under the phrase friction or stickiness they are called upon as important neighbours

---

[1] E.g. for wide differences in labour turnover of different occupations, see Brissenden, "Occupational Incidence of Labour Mobility," *J.A.S.A.*, Dec. 1923.

[2] For comparative statistics of labour turnover in English and American industry during the war and just after, see Florence, *Economics of Fatigue and Unrest*, Chapter VI. In certain Western States of America like Oregon there is actually a " problem " of the " Automobile Floater " described as an invasion of families in automobiles applying for work in harvesting all sorts of fruit and vegetables. See *U.S. Monthly Labour Review*, October 1925.

[3] Chapter XVIII §§1 and 2.

and then dropped as inconvenient bores. Statistically conscious economics must cultivate them and get better acquainted.

Nor is it enough to discuss the effect upon the economic characters at issue of various *possible* grades or varieties of conditions. The frequency of occurrence of those grades or varieties should be ascertained, and those most frequent or likely to be most frequent most discussed. The modern economist is too much inclined to canvass all the possible cases, A, B, Alpha, Omega, and " not-A," " not-B," " not-Alpha," etc., without real enquiry as to whether A or not-A, etc., actually exist to any extent worth worrying about. The variety of economic conditions appears to me quite wide enough without fussing about non-existent types and classes and boxes in which there is nothing to file.[1] Instead of *analysing* the possible boxes, it is best to begin with the facts and *classify* them. Otherwise, though there may be laws true of some given box, there may be no actual phenomena discoverable to file into that box.

§5   The Variability of Relationship between Economic Characters and Conditions

The conception of variability may finally be extended to the relation between the relevant factors and the main characters at issue. While economists argue with the help of the stationary state, they impose this limitation upon themselves that the " other things " or conditions assumed to remain equal in value must be absolutely independent of the things or characters primarily at issue.[2]

This self-imposed proviso has enabled them to expose, without the aid of statistics, fallacies such as the wages fund theory, a skeleton that ranks with the iron law in the economists' cupboard. But I am inclined to think that, thoroughly and logically applied, this proviso would damn all economic laws as possibly fallacious.

If one sets about it one can always think out *a priori* some possible or plausible causal relationship between the characters primarily at issue, and the conditions that are supposed to remain equal. I would, therefore, relax this proviso on the *a priori* side of the argument, but in accordance with my general policy of combining *a priori* with *a posteriori* methods of proof, I would enquire more strictly whether the speculative possibilities or plausibilities

---

[1] See above, Chapter X §1.

[2] Cf. Dr. J. N. Keynes, *Scope and Method of Political Economy*, Chapter VII, esp. pp. 218 ff., 4th edition.

were in fact probable. A preliminary statistical investigation should be made as to how far the " other things " are in fact significantly dependent. Hand in hand with the more rigid *a posteriori* examination whether " other " factors really are independent and manifest the values that are assumed *a priori*, I advocate a less rigid *a priori* exclusion of all factors whose values *might* not remain equal and might be " dependent."

The wages-fund theory assumed that all wages were paid out of the capital that " employs " labour, and that the amount of this capital was independent, that is, in no way related to labour. All economists now deny this " independence." The fund that employs labour is a continuous flow, one of whose sources is the efficiency of any given supply of labour ; but the wages-fund looked only at the relation between a supposedly fixed fund and the given supply of labour, not its output. The theory, in Cairnes' words, was that " the rate of wages other things being equal varies inversely with the supply of labour." But as Marshall points out,[1] " an increase of labour must increase the national dividend, which is one of the causes that govern wages ; and therefore if the supply of labour increases, other things *cannot* be equal."

Many modern economic theories involving " other things being equal " are hardly free from this same fallacy of assuming their " other " things to be independent of the things primarily under discussion. In the quantity theory of money, velocity of circulation is certainly affected by the quantity of money when this increases rapidly and prices are rapidly rising[2] ; and therefore it is, under the economist's own self-denying ordinance, fallacious to say that *other things being equal* changes in prices are exactly proportional to changes in the quantity of money.

The orthodox theory that, other things such as bargaining power equal, wages are equal to the net marginal productivity of labour, also infringes the proviso that the other things must be independent factors. Variations in wages will, by varying the labourer's financial reserve, and his standard of living, change his bargaining power and ambitions. Low wages and low bargaining power are interdependent.

It is held by certain strict economic logicians that the theory of over-population is also fallacious in this sense of assuming inconsistent conditions. When population increases, other relevant factors like capital cannot be supposed to remain constant. Increase in population will result in a greater supply of labour, greater supply involves cheaper labour, cheaper labour may involve greater profits,

---

[1] *Principles of Economics*, Appendix J §2.   [2] Cf. Lehfeld, *Money*.

and greater profits may involve the accumulation of more capital that entrepreneurs can invest or use in their own business. Thus the classical theory that low wages could be attributed to over-population cannot according to this view be proved, since more capital may be thrown into industry as an indirect consequence of increased population, and labour may thus become more productive and likely to be more in demand and higher paid.

The proviso that all the other things supposed to remain equal must be shown *a priori* absolutely independent of the things primarily at issue, e.g. population and wages, should, I maintain, go as impossibilist. There are few economic phenomena that are not in some degree possibly interdependent. In its place I suggest the proviso, in keeping with the principles of the isolation of factors, that a situation should be so SELECTED that the " other things " remain for the while IN FACT approximately equal, or the effects of their variation under CONTROL, at least while the characters at issue vary within given limits.

In meeting the criticism of the strict logicians upon the theory of population, it might be admitted that though more population possibly involved cheaper labour and therefore higher profits to entrepreneurs and therefore a greater supply of capital put back into the business at the same supply price, yet the additional supply of capital might be so small as to be negligible ; or it might be contended that cheaper labour would also involve a desire on the part of entrepreneurs to substitute labour for machines and would therefore involve a lower demand for capital. And this new situation with both lower supply prices and lower demand prices for capital, might have the net result of an equilibrium oscillating approximately about the same amount of capital as before. The amount of capital may IN FACT remain approximately equal not because it is independent of population, but because there is only slight, negligible dependence, or because there are two contrary lines of dependence of approximately equal importance—a state of affairs that may be called counter-dependence.[1]

This conception of counter-dependence may be thought too slovenly and rough. Yet a precedent may be cited from accepted theory : the conception of constant return.

" If the actions of the laws of increasing and diminishing return are balanced we have the law of constant return. . . . It may happen that

---

[1] The reasons for considering such counter-dependence plausible in this case of population are detailed and illustrated diagramatically in my Irrthümer einer Wirtschaftstheorie ohne statistische Grundlage, *Archiv für Sozialwissenschaft und Sozialpolitik*, Vol. 59, No. 3.

an increase in the aggregate production of blankets diminishes the proportionate difficulty of manufacturing by just as much as it increases that of raising the raw material. In that case the actions of the laws of diminishing and of increasing return would just neutralize one another ; and blankets would conform to the law of constant return."[1]

Most economic propositions involving " other things being equal " would be disallowed if only absolutely independent " other things " are admitted ; and the first step to avoid inapplicability to actual events is thus to drop or at least modify the proviso. If there is a possibility that the other factors may not be independent of the main issue, a preliminary statistical investigation should be made into the probable form of co-variation of other things with the characters at issue. If there is possible dependence, but this is, on investigation, found slight enough to be considered negligible for the relevant variation of the characters at issue ; or if a counter-dependence is discoverable owing to equally important relationships tending in opposite directions like " the actions of the laws of increasing and diminishing return " cancelling out or " neutralizing " into constant return, then the other conditions may, as a working hypothesis, be considered to remain equal. We must abandon a proviso designed to make economics fool-proof, but demanding a state of perfect independence among economic characters and conditions that is in fact utopian.

§6 Summary : The Rôle of Economic Theory

An economic theory that thinks in terms of variable characters and factors and of variable relations between those characters and factors has an important rôle to play in statistical investigation ; the rôle that I have distinguished in Chapters X to XIV as that of fieldwork. Theory is particularly necessary during the process of generalization (Chapter XI) in judging what circumstances and factors are relevant and what are irrelevant to any particular issue, and in advancing causal interpretations that cannot be reached statistically to explain statistically found relations. By collaboration of statistical investigation and theoretical speculation, merely possible or plausible hypotheses, subject to fallacy, may be transmuted into improbabilities or probabilities of high degree.

The theoretical economist may help the statistical observer of facts and events in much the same way as Dr. Keynes[2] thought he might help the historian.

[1] Marshall, *Principles of Economics*, IV, xiii, 2.
[2] *Scope and Method*, 4th edition, p. 285.

" A knowledge of theory, i.e. of previously established general propositions relating to economic phenomena, teaches the historian what kinds of facts are likely to have an important economic bearing. . . . Industrial phenomena are exceedingly complex, and unless we know what special facts to look for, it is quite possible that some of the most vital circumstances may fail to attract our notice. Knowledge of cause and effect in the economic world is, accordingly, of assistance for discriminating between the facts to be specially noted and those that may without risk of error be disregarded."

. Economic theory has always shunned the superficial and looked " through the sign to the thing signified,"[1] and has been of the utmost service in exploding the economic fallacies of the superficial " façade " observations and nomenclature of the man in the street, whether he be bourgeois or proletarian. But I feel that economics should not stop at exposing the popular interpretation of chance facts.

The ways of human behaviour are variegated, changeable, uncertain, and juxtaposed in unexpected combination. Statistical methods have been specially devised for the summary measurement of the variable and composite things, events, and situations displayed in human society. And economics should, through a flexible theory conscious of the variability of the facts surveyed, endeavour to help statistics in correctly measuring and interpreting these facts in the light of all the circumstances of the field of study. The original numerical data available are limited, and it is only by selection and control of the factors and conditions suggested as relevant by expert economic fieldwork that one can avoid spurious and nonsense correlations, and all the *non-sequiturs* of coincidence and co-accident type. In the present state of statistical information on human affairs, it is usually impossible to argue that because characters are observed to be correlated statistically or to tend in parallel or exactly opposite directions, therefore there is a causal relation, much less that there is some PARTICULAR causal relation.

You can prove anything by statistics is a common gibe. But " its contrary is more nearly true," says Yule.[2] " You can never prove anything by statistics. The statistician is dealing with the most complex cases of multiple causation. He may show that the facts are in accordance with this hypothesis or that. But it is quite another thing to show that all other possible hypotheses are

---

[1] Address to Dr. Marshall on his eightieth birthday, *Ec. Jl.*, September 1922.
[2] Report No. 28 of the Industrial Fatigue Research Board.

excluded and that the facts do not admit of any interpretation other than the particular one he may have in mind."

" Sensible investigators," according to Keynes,[1] " only employ the correlation coefficient to test or confirm conclusions at which they have arrived on other grounds." If economic generalizations aspire to become probabilities, a flexible theory must be fused with economic statistics, (1) to distinguish the non-essential and irrelevant from the essential and relevant factors, circumstances, and causes,—to orientate the statistician ; (2) to provide theoretical conclusions, arrived at on sensible grounds other than statistical, as plausible working hypotheses that may interpret, explain, or throw light upon statistical investigations.

The following chapters will be devoted to practical details for implementing this fusion. A structure may eventually be built up in which concrete facts statistically measured may be held in due position by a flexible framework of theory ; and as we must all have slogans nowadays to advertise our ideas, let us call the main theme of these chapters, that of ferro-concrete Economics.

---

[1] *A Treatise on Probability*, p. 426. See also for tacit use of other grounds to (1) refute or (2) support apparent empirical laws, Chapters XXV §7 and Chapter XXIX, esp. §12.

CHAPTER XVI

THE MEASUREMENT OF ECONOMIC VARIATIONS

§0   *The Plan of Procedure*

THE orthodox theory of economics may be provisionally accepted
as the iron framework on which to build up a concrete statistical
economics if, conscious of the complexity and variability of economic
phenomena, modifications are made in at least four respects.
These modifications were described in consecutive sections of the
last chapter. But the application and use of theory even when
thus modified must proceed gradually, and this chapter deals
section by section with the steps necessary to measure the variable
economic facts so as to bring them into relation with the modified
variability-conscious theory.

(I) (§§1 and 2) The statistical economist's starting-point should
be the objectively observed and usually measurable facts of exchange. This implies a focusing upon objective characteristics at
the outset in place of vague psychological elements such as real
cost, utility, or maximum satisfaction, thus reversing the usual
order. These psychological elements will, however, in company
with physical and institutional characters, play a large rôle in the
final dénouement.

(II) (§3) The facts forming the chief focus of economics are the
prices, wages, profits, interest rates, etc., at which persons exchange
various amounts of goods, services, or factors of production. The
units in which variations in amounts, such as an increased supply
of " labour " or an increased productivity generally, are to be
reckoned must be carefully selected and defined, classified, and
analysed.

(III) (§§4, 5, 6) The variability that was found to be the leading
feature of economic transactions can be summarized, in accordance
with the methods prescribed in Chapters VI–VIII, as a distribution
of the different values of a single character, or as a general tendency
over time or (e.g. localization) space ; " dynamic " tendencies over
time such as trade cycles, and secular trends have recently indeed
been the special preoccupation of statistical economists.

(IV) (§7) The Principles of Economics, however, are chiefly

concerned with the " static " relationship between the values of two or more characters of a set of items, say rènt and productivity of item pieces of land at any given time or place, and laws are framed to describe these relations. But these " static " laws, too, whether conceptional, or propositional, may be formulated in statistical language as correlation issues.

§1   *The Economic Starting-Points*

Most economic text-books set out with so-called " fundamental " economic forces and characteristics such as the principle of substitution, utility, marginal utility, consumers' surplus, real costs, before they tackle what are taken to be the necessary and inevitable results of compounding these elementary forces, namely, actually observable values in exchange or prices. I propose to reverse this process and start with the observable, and often accurately measurable, facts.

A beginning has already been made in this proposed revolution. Works like W. T. Layton's *Introduction to the Study of Prices*, and Wesley Mitchell's *Business Cycles*, or Sir William Beveridge's *Unemployment*, begin with the actual facts or real situations *before* they attempt to explain these phenomena by means of the Quantity theory of Money, the theory of the Reserve of Labour, the Marginal Productivity, or any other theory.

This method of approach is akin to the " case " or problem method so widely mooted in America. Actual cases or situations are observed, and the question or problem is put why or how things come to be as they are. Why and how comes it that English daily newspapers are now sold at 1d. or 2d. the copy ; or that heavy hogs cost $8·90 at Chicago in August of 1924,[1] or that there are some three sheep for every four head of (human) population in England to-day and only one for three in the U.S.A. ; or that there were 35% unemployed among shipbuilders in England between 1922 and 1926 ?

This approach is in marked contrast to the excogitary or speculative method which posits certain fundamental assumptions and principles, and asks how they would work out in usually imaginary cases or situations. The order I advocate begins with the overt manifest phenomena,—facts, events, deeds, terms of exchange ; and tries to investigate, interpret, and explain these phenomena after they have been accurately measured and summarized.

---

[1] Charles F. Sarle, "Forecasting the Price of Hogs," *American Economic Review*, September 1925.

The economic facts with which I propose to start may be regarded as varieties of human reactions[1] to stimuli. As set forth in Chapter III the peculiarly economic transaction is that of EXCHANGING.

Exchange involves two parties. Where money is in use, the party exchanging money for goods or services is called the BUYER, the party exchanging goods or services for money is called the SELLER. The buyer's stimulus is various amounts of goods or services, and his reaction the payment of various amounts of money. The seller's stimulus is various amounts of money, and his reaction various amounts of goods or services. It is usual, however, to express the money stimulus or reaction not as total amount (i.e. in Marshall's terminology " outlays "), but as amount of money PER UNIT of goods or service, i.e. as a PRICE. Each exchange transaction has thus two measurable " elementary " character-istics or dimensions which we call the " terms of exchange," showing wide yet accurately measurable variations :

(1) The amount of service, goods, or use of goods that persons exchange.

(2) The price *per unit of* such services or goods that persons pay, or obtain in exchange.

These are elementary characteristics since the other measurable characters can be formed out of them. Persons' incomes (wages, rents, interest, etc.) and expenditure are the prices they obtain and pay respectively multiplied by the units of services or goods sold or lent, and bought or borrowed respectively.

While text-books of " Economic Principles " admit the im-portance of values in exchange, i.e. prices, and usually devote a whole book to the subject, they often omit even a mention of the amounts exchanged as one of the terms of exchange. Professor Pigou actually has carefully to explain half-way through his *Industrial Fluctuations*[2] that if A and B exchange apples for oranges both may give one another " better terms of exchange " without altering the price of apples in oranges or oranges in apples, by the mere fact of increasing the number of apples and oranges exchanged.

When the price at which any article exchanges is known, it does not tell us the amount of that article to which the act of exchanging was applied. The wage at which men are employed does not tell

---

[1] This psycho-physiological terminology needs no apology to-day. It is used by so strict an economist as Prof. Cassel (*Social Theory*, Vol. I, pp. 80 and 265) in explaining such pure economics as the notion of elasticity of demand and the theory of rent.

[2] Op. cit., p. 172.

us necessarily how many men were employed and how many unemployed. In the ordinary diagram used by economists the price actually paid by buyers and sellers is shown by the vertical height of a horizontal line (PP in Table XVIIA) drawn right across the diagram so that it represents the price of any amount exchanged (e.g. 1, 2, 3 . . . 13, 14, 15, in Table XVIIA), and knowledge of the height of this horizontal line does not tell us the amounts exchanged at that price. The confusion caused by this abstraction of the price aspect (the vertical height of the horizontal line) from the total value (the whole area) is apparent when economist meets business man on any commission of enquiry.[1] Business men think chiefly of the total value of their sales and the *total* profit to be derived therefrom, and only incidentally as a means of profit, of the price at which each sale is effected.

The increasing attention paid by economists to the actual amounts exchanged and produced and consumed is manifested in measurements of, or plans for measuring, the National Income or Dividend.

These estimates are becoming an integral part of lecture courses at Cambridge following perhaps Professor Pigou's original example in his *Wealth and Welfare* published in 1911, and appearing subsequently in amplified form under the title *Economics of Welfare.* Except for a preliminary discussion as a " Fundamental Notion " in Book II, Marshall does not refer to the National Income or Dividend in his *Principles* till the introductory chapter to Book VI, devoted to distribution ; but Pigou makes the National Dividend the starting-point and pivot of his whole argument. The three main parts of his original work discuss :

(A) The total aggregate Magnitude of the National Dividend ;

(B) The equality or inequality of its Distribution among classes of persons, e.g. rich and poor within the nation ;

(C) The regularity or fluctuation of the Dividend from time to time.

Meanwhile statisticians have been at work actually measuring the amounts of income thus aggregated, distributed, and fluctuating.

(A) The aggregate *magnitude* of the National Income or Dividend is measured either from the Census of Production or Income-tax Returns, supplemented (for those below the taxable minimum) by wage statistics, estimates of small traders' profits, etc.

---

[1] E.g. *The Colwyn Commission on National Debt and Taxation.* See D. H. Robertson, " The Colwyn Committee, the Income Tax and the Price Level," *Ec. Jl.*, December 1927.

This is the starting-point of Bowley's *Division of the Product of Industry* brought up to date in Bowley and Stamp's *National Income in* 1924 (published 1927).

(B) The actual *distribution* of income among classes of individuals is distinct from the theory of distribution discussed by the economist. The *theory* is an attempt to explain rates of pay in exchange for " land," " labour," " capital," " enterprise " ; it is a study of part of the distributing process. The actual distribution measures the amounts of income accruing to persons " rich " or " poor " as such, whatever the factor or factors in production that they represent, if any.[1] It is a statistical conception in very essence, and the facts gathered from income-tax returns, a wage census, etc., can be presented in a *soi-disant* frequency " distribution " like Table VIc.

The amounts of various articles actually consumed by *specific classes* of the community have by the collection of family budgets also formed a starting-point of investigations. Charles Booth's *Life and Labour of the People of London*, Mr. Seebohm Rowntree's *Poverty*, and Bowley and Burnett-Hurst's *Livelihood and Poverty* are the leading instances of statistical investigation of this type. Here the interest lies not in comparing different classes of incomes, but in measuring the position of any one class in relation to an absolute poverty line where income from all sources is insufficient to secure adequate nourishment (measured perhaps in calories),[2] housing, and clothing for the maintenance of life or efficiency.

(C) The now familiar subject of Trade Fluctuations (i.e. variations from time to time) is also primarily a question of the amount of articles of various kinds that are exchanged. The word " trade," in fact, usually stands for *amounts* " traded " or exchanged measured either in total value or physical volume. Statistics of such amounts of trade (volume or value) may be based on censuses of production, periodical returns of production of specified articles, export and import statistics, the values or volume of goods carried by railways and so on.[3]

(D) Transcending the National Dividend is the subject of International Trade. Here again the word Trade stands for amounts exchanged or traded, measured either in value or volume.

The prices of any article entering into international trade tend to be the same in the several trade centres, allowance being made for

---

[1] Income from inheritance or pensions, for instance, is not paid for any part in production.

[2] See above, Chapter X §2.

[3] For English experience see Rowe, *The Physical Volume of Production*, London and Cambridge Economic Service. See below, §6, for list of indices of trade that have been used.

cost of transport. Hence the opening question is not price-variation but why particular goods are exported or imported, and why *in the amounts* to which they are exported or imported. This is the question to which the law of comparative costs attempts an answer in the form that a country tends to export those commodities in greater amounts in which it has a comparative advantage.[1]

To sum up this preliminary discussion. Four types of data can be distinguished from which the statistical economist can start his investigation :

(1) The prices or exchange values of units of different goods or services that are exchanged.

(2) The rate of payment made to units of the various factors of production.

(3) The total amounts of different goods or services that are exchanged. " Trade " measured either in physical volume or in total values, i.e. the product of volume and prices per unit.

(4) The total amount of income paid to the different factors of production.

Data (3) and (4) have not customarily been dealt with by the *theoretical* economist[2] except in the case of international trade, and with this exception the approach to these problems has been statistical, not theoretical. No change in starting-point need therefore be discussed. But in case of (1) prices, and (2) rate of payments of factors of production, a change of venue is needed and the new starting-point in the discussion of prices and payments requires further elucidation.

§2   The Starting-Point of Prices and Payments

Casually taking up an ordinary retailer's price list I read :

A fine-gauge mercerised lisle stocking with lace clock in various colours, sizes 8½ to 10½	2/-
Pure linen damask table-cloths, size about 68 × 72 ins. . . .	10/-
Patent leather Oxford shoes for men, sizes 6–12	20/-
Helene, lipstick (light or dark)	4/1
Desiccated cocoanut per 3 lb..	1/6

Presuming that sales are actually effected at these prices, the problem that arises is why the situation at one time, place, and commercial establishment[3] is such that customers' outlay in money is the same, namely £1, for 10 said stockings, or 2 said table-cloths,

---

[1] See above, Chapter XV §4.

[2] See below (§7) for subjects the laws of economics *do* deal with.

[3] July 4 to 9, 1927, Brompton Road, Harrod's Stores, to be exact.

or 1 pair said shoes, or (roughly) 5 such lipsticks, or 40 lbs. of desiccated cocoanut. These are the sort of facts that worry (or should worry) the economist. They should form the starting-point of his investigations into prices of values in exchange.

If he should find the explanation of the prices of such variegated articles as I have picked out at random too complicated, the economist may select for comparison the prices of different sizes of the same article or different articles meeting similar wants or made of similar stuff; say, for comparison with ladies' " mercerised lisle stockings," gents.' fancy socks also of mercerised lisle. Or he may start with exactly the same article in different shops in different towns or at different times. But, however he groups and compares them, the economist's original data should be the price reactions of buyers and sellers in exchanging goods and services.

Similarly in the purchase and sale or hiring of factors of production the actual rates of payment passing hands should be the statistical economist's starting-point. But the orthodox and familiar " distribution of wealth " among the four theoretically distinguished payments for factors of production (rent " for " the land or the " original and indestructible properties of the soil," interest for waiting, profit for enterprise, and wages for labour) does not tally with statistical data.[1] The only classes of payment or income distinguishable by statisticians such as Professor Bowley and Sir Josiah Stamp, in their *National Income in* 1924, are: the income of wage earners, salaried classes, independent workers, employers, farmers, and professional classes[2]; and the income *from* lands and buildings, Government securities, dividends, pensions.[3] Wage earners are certainly examples of the economist's " Labour," and holders of debenture shares examples of the economist's capitalists; but the salaried class are partly labour, partly management. Independent workers are a compound of labour and management, employers a compound of management and capital. Landlords, again, are partly capitalists providing farm buildings and improvements.

Rates of payment for Labour, Capital, Land, Management (and Enterprise) can thus not form a statistically measurable starting-point. The provision of Capital, Management, and Enterprise are services each of which are not necessarily performed exclusively and in isolation by one person, or for one distinguishable form of payment.

The distinction that the statistician does find it possible to make

---

[1] See below, Chapter XVIII §3.
[2] Op. cit., Table, p. 12.   [3] Op. cit., Table, p. 46.

among income recipients and sources of income, hinges largely on the ascertainable legal terms of the contract of employment or investment, or on status in the employment relation. Thus the statistician can get closer to a distinction based on the nature of the " factor " for which payment is made, by distinguishing the precise legal or contractual basis upon which the payment is reckoned (if there *is* any basis), i.e. time worked, work done, or capital lent.

TABLE XVIA

ANALYSIS OF THE CLASSES OF PAYMENTS TO FACTORS OF PRODUCTION

The distinct kinds of rates of payment actually changing hands can be classified according to their contractual or non-contractual characteristics as follows :

I.   Rate of Income charged by contract or custom :

   A : *For time worked :*
       (*a*) Daily or weekly time wages.
       (*b*) Monthly, quarterly, or yearly *salary*.

   B : *For work done :*
       Piece wages.
       Commissions on sales.
       Tips.
       Fees.

   C : *For Capital or other Property Lent or Owned :*
       Debenture interest.
       Discount rates.
       Interest on Government Stock or Bonds.
       Rents (according to Contract).

II.   Rate of Income arising by force of circumstance :
       (Difference or " margin " between Revenue and Expenditure divided by Turnover, Capital, or Time Worked per Person.)
       Rate of Profit of Single Entrepreneur.
       Rate of Dividend on Joint Stock Capital.

It is impossible *at the start* to say more than this as to what a payment is " for." That a certain payment is *for* enterprise, or *for* " waiting," or *for* " the original and indestructible properties of the soil," is in fact a hypothetical construction. We must examine the precise type of work or service of the recipients of different incomes before a conclusion can be reached.

The sort of data which confront the statistical economist may be illustrated from the apparently simple case of wages or salaries for work. The variations even for any one time, country, and industry are at least of three types :

(1) Wide variations in income for *different kinds* of work, manag-

s

ing, supervising, or manual. While an English general manager's annual income might be calculated in thousands of pounds, a supervisor or foreman would usually get somewhat less than half a thousand, while a manual worker's annual income is a matter of only a hundred pounds or two.

(2) Variations in income per hour (week or year) for work of the *same kind*, e.g. manual work, but for different species of this kind of work.   Table XVIB refers purely to the wages of the manual labour in one industry of one country,[1] yet sawyers (a skilled trade) get on the average 88 cents an hour, setters 46 cents, labourers only 31 cents.

(3) Variations in personal income for the same kind and species of work in the same place at the same time. Any one " setter " may get as little as 10–20 cents or as much as 60–70 cents. Any one " labourer " may get as little as under 10 cents or as much as over a dollar an hour. This latter variation is shown very clearly in Table VIB as well as Table XVIB. The women charging buttons, cf. Table VIB, were on a straight piece rate, so that the variations in output there shown are identical with variations in earnings.

Now variation (3), as between persons performing the same species of work in the same place, is largely accounted for by individual differences in productivity. There may be persons of representative efficiency (say, levels 4 and 5) in Table VIA, but there are extremes of personal efficiency and inefficiency. This is admitted by economic theory, but subsequently neglected except in allusions to *rents of natural ability*.

Work of all sorts is limited by human capacity. No man can do more than a certain amount of work per year, and if he has two trades the more he does of one trade the less he will do of the other. This is not so of the ownership of capital, apart from its administration. A capitalist may receive almost any amount per year according to the amount of his capital and the changes in its value. He may have his capital invested in many different trades and he may combine the ownership of capital (or land) with work. Statisticians may therefore draw a significant distinction between two primary forms of income : Earnings of Work and Income from Ownership.[2] The former can be reckoned (as a start) in units of income *per period*

---

[1] This form of tabulation is that adopted by the U.S. Department of Labour for measuring the wages and hours of work of a wide range of American industries. Table XVIB is an abridgement of Bulletin No. 413, Table 10. Similar tabulations for different American industries at various dates have appeared up to the present writing (1928) in at least fifty-five such Bulletins.

[2] Professor Cannan takes this as the primary distinction in his *Wealth*, Chapter IX.

TABLE XVIb

AVERAGE AND DISTRIBUTION OF EARNINGS PER HOUR FOR 43,176 EMPLOYEES IN EIGHT TYPICAL OCCUPATIONS

AMERICAN SAW-MILLS, 1925[1]

Number of Employees Observed	Occupation	Average (Arithmetic Mean) Wage in Cents	Under 10 cents	10 to 20 cents	20 to 30 cents	30 to 40 cents	40 to 50 cents	50 to 60 cents	60 to 70 cents	70 to 80 cents	80 to 90 cents	90 to $1.00	Over $1
644	Sawyers	87·7	—	—	—	1	3	13	40	134	145	173	135
911	Edgermen	46·8	—	3	53	220	339	118	94	46	22	6	10
832	Setters	45·8	—	3	35	226	266	176	89	35	1	—	1
600	Trimmer Operators	40·9	—	7	105	182	174	64	32	20	16	—	—
1,535	Machine Feeders (planing mills)	39·0	—	40	426	347	318	336	52	10	2	1	3
786	Saw Tailers on Head Saws	34·9	—	22	304	200	151	95	14	—	—	—	—
1,170	Doggers	33·2	—	12	527	324	173	122	12	—	—	—	—
36,698	Labourers	30·9	24	3,519	16,851	7,061	6,603	2,105	265	54	89	15	72
43,176	Total	32·9	24	3,606	18,301	8,561	8,027	3,029	598	299	275	195	221

[1] Bulletin No. 413, Table 10, U.S. Department of Labour.

of work, but the latter must be calculated in income *per unit of property* (land or capital) per period.

I say " as a start," because pay per period of work does not consider intensity and the type of work, nor income per period per unit of property the elements of administrative work connected with investing property and the risk of losing the property. These considerations come later when we compare the variations disclosed, and interpret them in terms of the physio-psychological efforts and sacrifices involved (Chapter XVIII).

The payment known as a rate of profits straddles across this dichotomy of incomes into earned and investment incomes. It is not, like wages or salaries, a rate per piece of work done or per hour, day, month, year worked; nor yet, like interest, is it a rate per unit of capital invested. And at first sight we are unable to say for what units of service, rates of profit are paid. This initial difficulty is, however, becoming less important with the growth of joint-stock and other public companies. In one-man businesses and in partnerships, profit is usually a payment both for the investment of capital *and* for the work of management. But in joint-stock companies managers are paid a salary, directors a fee, while the residual amount of profit left after subtracting certain charges[1] is definitely assigned as *dividend* to ordinary and preference shareholders who have done no " work " beyond choosing and reviewing their investments. In so far as profit is the earnings of management it appears as salaries or fees; in so far as it is the " reward " for investing property and taking a risk of its loss it appears as a dividend; and accordingly the statistical starting-points in the discussion of profits-rates are salaries per period of time and dividends per capital invested and risked.

§3 *The Definition of Amounts Exchanged*

If economists must be urged to look upon actual prices, rates of payment, and amounts exchanged as their starting-point and general *point d'appui*, they must clearly be warned against building or treating these foundations lightly. A statistical investigator who is counting and classifying amounts of items, i.e. distributing items into specific classes, has to decide of each item into which class to " file " it. Classes must therefore not only be so selected and defined (1) that they are significant and relevant to the point at issue, but also (2) that items may be distributed or assigned to

---

[1] See below, §3.

one class or another without any worry and uncertainty, and without divergence between different investigators.

The concrete things or services exchanged in various amounts against money are not uniform in quality or size, and if they are to be classed as so much desiccated cocoanut, stockings, cattle, houses, factories, labour, or degrees of productive efficiency, an agreement must be reached as to the quality (or quantity) of a characteristic that is to "qualify" items for inclusion in that class and as to the various sizes and dimensions that are to be distinguished (if any) in assigning quantitative value.

Houses might be sized or evaluated by number of rooms, but then one large room may often provide more accommodation than two small ones ; and in any case statistical investigators like Seebohm Rowntree found difficulty in settling whether a pantry or coal-hole was or was not a room. Zizek in his *Fünf Hauptprobleme der Statistischen Methodenlehre* points out that there are many definitions that an economist has to accept ready made or even at second hand from lawyers, Government departments, or business men which are not significant for his purposes. Moreover, the official definitions (e.g. of houses or industrial establishments, see above, Chapter X §1) may often not tally.

These official conceptions and classifications and their divergences may prevent the economist finding "what he wants" in official statistics, and will certainly mar international comparisons if it does not make them impossible ; and the economist ought to be loud in demanding the standardization of statistical classes and in proclaiming his wants, where these are obtainable by other statistically measurable classifications or conceptions. For the economist has an important rôle to play in statistical economics if he can so select and define the items, characters and units and classes of value which he employs in his argument that they may be *both* measurable in statistics and of economic significance.

The need for defining what the amount of an exchangeable is to consist in has been thoroughly recognized in the case of money. Money is in general defined with reference to its acceptability in payment for goods or in discharge of other kinds of business obligation. Lists and diagrams[1] of types of money are made out, and types are admitted to vary in their degree of acceptability. But somewhere or other a definite line is drawn between what is to be counted as money and what is not to be so counted. Robertson does, Fisher does not, include bank cheques or deposits as money. Currency or circulating media is the inclusive term that Fisher

---

[1] E.g. Robertson, *Money*, Chapter III.

uses to refer to any type of property right which, whether *generally* acceptable or not, " does actually for its chief purpose and use, serve as a means of exchange."

Economists are also devoting themselves to a specification of the items to be included in the National Income. The statistician, though he can add up the money incomes of all persons in any community, may not thereby reach any very significant or comparable estimate of the National Dividend. The controversies that rage as to what items to include and what to exclude in this census of wealth appear to me a sign that economists are beginning to play the rôle of orientation that I have sketched out. They are getting their teeth into the facts collected about actual incomes and masticating this nutritive food, instead of chewing gum. The result of mastication and digestion is to learn what foods are wanted and how they should be served, and the economist who sits down to a diet of figures is in a position to help the statistician in selecting and classifying the facts and characteristics that ought to be observed.

The statistician dealing with economic activities, whether he be a census taker, administrative official, or cost accountant, must co-operate by accepting this help.

" The development of accountancy with the evolution of industry and society," writes Sir Josiah Stamp,[1] " is going to be better if its received principles are shot through with light from other angles than the legal, the financial and the technical. Think of the economic conception of capital as distinct from income, and then deliberate upon the sorry figure that is cut in the light of it by our modern fetish of a ' safe ' or ' sound ' balance-sheet, which lies in almost every line and yet is approved professionally because it overstates no assets and understates no liabilities, while it has valuable premises written down to negligible figures and reserves hidden in innumerable places, or profits ' held up ' and ' tucked away.' ' The truth, the whole truth, and nothing but the truth,' cannot be derived from the modern balance-sheet, so vaunted for its prudence ; but prudence is just as possible without departing from what a balance-sheet ought to be—a faithful record of the employment of the total capital invested in the business, whether as an original outlay or retained profits, from which the *true* rate of profit on invested capital can be determined."

A conception of what amounts are to be counted as profit is clearly required as the numerator for the *rates* of profit (on capital or turnover, etc.)[2] that appear of such economic significance. Profit is the result of a subtraction sum : it is not the gross proceeds or output value of a business, but this gross total minus some money

[1] *Current Problems in Finance and Government*, p. 14.
[2] See above, Chapter X §3.

costs. But *what* costs are to be subtracted and what words are to be used to refer to the result of subtracting some costs rather than others cannot apparently be agreed upon. No more important example of the method of defining concretely the kinds of income whose amounts are to be measured can be cited.

It is certainly agreed that (1) the prime cost of raw material must be subtracted, and the result is called in the official British Census of Production the Net Output. Since, however, output suggests physical, not monetary, units, and we are speaking of the net exchange value of the output commercially disposable, I prefer the term net proceeds.

The next most usual items to subtract are : (2) the prime costs of tools and supplies, e.g. the stores and timber of the coal-mining industry ; (3) the partially supplementary cost of power for driving machines, etc. ; (4) the prime or supplementary costs of repairs, depreciation, and obsolescence ; (5) the prime costs of royalties and the supplementary costs of rent on land. The subtraction of these further items leaves what Sir Josiah Stamp distinguishes as the *economic return*, the " net fund out of which has to come the reward of the factors of production in the industry itself—viz. the workers in that industry, the owners of the capital, or, in rough language, the division into wages and profits."[1]

Next (6) wages and salaries may be subtracted. This leaves what is commonly referred to in business circles as Operating or Gross Profit.[2]

Next (7) interest on bank loans, debentures, etc. ; (8) insurance and (9) taxes are subtracted leaving the *Net Profit*, part of which may in a company be (10) paid as directors' fees, part (11) declared as dividends, and part (12) put by to reserves and re-investment in the business.

Practice varies widely and my analysis may not correspond with the policy accepted in the best or most typical business circles. All I urge, however, is a standard nomenclature that will indicate precisely how the amount of " profit " was obtained, i.e. of what precise subtractions it is the residual. These subtractions may have to be specified by sheer enumeration, e.g. by specifying the numbers I have just prefixed to the several classes of cost. But whatever system of names or symbols is adopted let us have one system only for economists and business statisticians alike.

[1] Op. cit.
[2] Prof. Edie distinguishes between the two, and makes gross profit to refer to any net proceeds (*Economics*, p. 202). The inclusion of wages in any kind of profit appears to me contrary to common usage, however.

So far I have mainly been criticizing practical statisticians such as the accountant for lack of co-operation with the economist. But there is the converse point of view of the statistician. Economists have not in their choice of terms or in their definitions been considerate of the statisticians' potentialities and limitations. They have failed to familiarize themselves with the " language and types of statistical measurement " and have not allowed sufficiently for the circumscribed " conditions " of the statisticians' activity.[1]

Issues that are statistically measurable involve the counting of " items " which manifest with varying " frequency " various values (qualities or quantities) of one or more " characters."[2] The economist should, if possible, so select and define his chief " characters " that various qualities or quantities are easily distinguished and that the frequencies of the items that manifest these values can easily be counted. The economist who thus selects and defines his units will meet the statistician half-way.

Land, Labour, Capital, and Management form as fine-looking a body of chapter headings as any short-novelist may yearn for, but the use of these terms without specifying of what units the amount of land, labour, capital, or management is to consist, is apt to lead to hasty generalization and dangerous half-truths. When the supply of labour is discussed economic arguments seem to visualize lumps, or shall we say doses, infallibly conjured up in any convenient quantity. The very *different sources* of additional labour clearly distinguishable in statistical descriptions are : (1) extra working hours or extra intensity of work by a given number of persons ; (2) transference of adults from other occupations or from unoccupied classes, over and above those transferring from the given occupation into idleness, another occupation, or unpaid work, e.g. women at marriage ; (3) excess of young persons coming into the labour market mostly from school, over and above persons dying, or retiring from paid work through ill-health, to secure a pension, etc.

These different sources are in the heat of the argument not always distinguished.[3] Yet the effect on supply of, say, increasing the wages in any occupation unquestionably differs greatly from source to source. The supply from source (1) is known to react positively under some circumstances, i.e. to rise ; to fall under other circum-

---

[1] Heading of Chapter V, and V §1 above.
[2] Chapter V §2, Chapter X §4.
[3] It should be noted, however, that Prof. Cassel in his *Theory of Social Economy* is careful to distinguish in separate sections (Chapter VIII §36 and §37) the Supply of Labour as Determined by the Number of Workers ; and the Supply of Labour as Determined by the Supply of Work per Worker.

stances.[1] The supply from source (2) is probably invariably increased by a higher wage. The supply from source (3) can only be immediately affected by a higher wage, through the shortening of the school career, or the postponement of the retirement of old persons. Increased number of births is obviously slow (fifteen to twenty years) to affect the number of young persons coming on the labour market, and births may remain quite unaffected by the change in wage. Deaths and retirement through ill-health are much more likely to be affected by wage changes, though, curiously enough, economists seldom seize upon this statistically demonstrable[2] aspect of their theories.

Labour, in short, is hardly a homogeneous class of amounts exchanged reacting homogeneously to wage changes, and the impossibility of defining it as a single statistical item or character should be a healthy check to abstract argument.

But even when the economist concentrates upon the " labour " of a given number of labourers, apart from additions to their number, he is apt to slur over the precise units in which greater or less labour is to be reckoned. More or less intensity of labour appears at first sight measurable in units of product, i.e. the productivity of the given group. When women's wages are compared to men's the lower rate of the former is held to be due to women's lower productivity. When it is then pointed out that women on piece rates get a lower wage per piece than men, the unit of productivity is said to be measured not merely in the units of output but in the quality of the output, the amount produced per machine and the shouldering of overhead charges generally, in the degree of employability at an emergency,[3] in the amount of time lost by sickness and accident, and in the chance of continuing at the same employment (as shown by labour turnover) or of being promoted to foremanship, etc. etc.

It is only after specifications are drawn up of the precise reference of the units in which characters are to be measured that statisticians can help economists. If productivity were specified as the stable *maintenance* of a maximum *quantity* and *quality* of *output* without *accidents* or *ill-health* under given material and mechanical conditions, different persons' productivity could be compared at different times or places in units of lost time, output, days of illness, spoiled work, and frequency or severity rates of accident to men or equip-

[1] Florence, *Economics of Fatigue and Unrest*, pp. 261–3.
[2] Op. cit., Chapter XI.
[3] " Men . . . can be put on night-work and can be sworn at more comfortably.'' Cf. Pigou, *Economics of Welfare*, 1st edition, p. 523.

ment.   Or, adopting Marshall's view that by "productive" economists usually refer to things productive of further amounts of production, the statistician may set apart as productive such economic activities as have been statistically observed to result in greater output, and less lost time, spoiled work, accidents, ill-health, or labour turnover.   Thus the eight-hour working day may under certain circumstances be called more "productive" than the ten-hour day, and similarly welfare work, higher wages, and motion study may often rank as productive.   And though stimulating the production of, say, Rolls-Royces, spats, and caviare, just as much as his thrifty brother stimulates the production of clogs, fish and chips, and traction engines, the spendthrift stands condemned on this definition as unproductive.   These Rolls-Royces, spats, and caviares, when consumed, can be shown not to lead to the further tangible increases in output, health, or industrial prosperity that results from the use and consumption, to an equivalent amount, of fish and chips, clogs, and traction engines.

When the economist proceeds to consider efficiency which takes into consideration the cost of producing as well as productivity itself, he must help the statistician by specifying (1) whose cost is to be considered ; e.g. is the cost of an accident to an employee to be measured merely by the money compensation payable by the employer ?   (2) In what units the cost is to be valued, whether in money or in human effort and sacrifice, including perhaps the risk of industrial disease and accident.   (3) How the relation of cost to product is to be expressed.   Is the cost of production to be divided into the product and expressed as a ratio, or subtracted from it to leave a "margin" or net return like profit, or is the relation more complicated ?   England produces only about a fifth of the wheat she consumes, but produces it at about 16·6 quintals to the hectare, i.e. at a high efficiency ratio as against the United States' 9·9 quintals to the hectare[1] which feeds, however, her whole population. Is the present English procedure a more or a less efficient wheat production than if half the wheat consumed at home were grown at home at, say, 20 bushels instead of 35 bushels to the acre ?   Till answers to these questions are agreed upon it is questionable whether the words efficient and efficiency have really serviceable definitions.

§4   *The Variations in Prices and Amounts Exchanged*

The next point to realize is that economics does not concern itself with individual transactions—the fact that at 11 a.m. on a

[1] *International Statistical Year Book.*   Average for 1920–24.

certain day Mrs. Jones bought three pair fine-gauge stockings from Messrs. Harrod's at 2s. the pair—but with the average price and the total amount of any goods or service exchanged within a specified period and market, when all transactions in that particular article within that period and region are massed. If the period and the region are sufficiently restricted to form a MARKET " in which buyers and sellers are in such free intercourse with one another that the prices of the same goods (and services) tend to equality easily and quickly,"[1] then the theoretical economist assumes that taking all transactions in one article *en masse, one,* or a narrow range of price will clearly predominate.

" Economists study the actions of individuals, but study them in relation to *social* rather than individual life ; and therefore concern themselves but little with personal peculiarities of temper and character. They watch carefully the conduct of a whole class of people, sometimes the whole of a nation, sometimes only those living in a certain district, more often those engaged in some particular trade at some time and place : and by the aid of statistics, or in other ways, they ascertain how much money on the average . . . "[2] But when the reactions (of any particular character) of a mass of people are observed they usually appear to the statistician quantitatively or qualitatively of great variety. The (male) poet's familiar theme of female capriciousness appears, in the cold light of scientific observation, true of both sexes. Hence the average must not be allowed to eclipse the frequency distribution. The frequency distributions of different varieties of hours that men work, or of output that women produce (shown in Tables VID and VIB), are typical examples of human reactions that may or may not be fairly represented by an average.

Moreover, uncertainty broods over all these forms of variation and we can seldom predict how far a given form of variation will be reproduced under apparently identical conditions. The theoretical economist is inclined to claim a certain degree of stability in some aspects of human behaviour due to a predominant economic motive among a large proportion of economic agents. But this cannot be accepted *a priori* independently of statistical investigations, and if in reality this motive does not predominate over all others it is likely to add to the instability of the variation.

The output of men working for piece wages might be expected, if all the piece workers were striving for maximum income, to show

---

[1] Part of Cournot's definition of a market quoted by Marshall, *Principles of Economics*, V, i §2.
[2] Marshall, *Principles of Economics*, I, ii §7.

(like Table VIB) a normal distribution consonant with the normal distribution of abilities. But if a certain section of the workers have another objective, e.g. to restrict themselves to a given conventional output,[1] we may find skew curves with a mode but not an average at that objective. And where any article is bought by consumers who look for the cheapest price, and also by consumers who like to boast of paying a high price, then perhaps we may observe a bimodal distribution in the prices paid for the same article.

However variable the facts he starts with, the statistical economist must, by frequency distributions, averages, measures of deviation, tendency, correlation, or in some other way summarize his multitudinous data in the statistical language and measures set forth in Chapters V to XI. He must find if he can some regularity in irregularity.

The variations that must be summarized are either (1) variations in different items (at one given time or place, or during one given period) of the SAME single character (i.e. wages and salaries of different or the same kind of individual workers as Table XVIB) ; or else they are (2) " tendencies " in the whole distribution of values of one character (possibly represented by an average value) over time or place ; or (3) they may be correlated variations of two or more characters. These three types of economic variation corresponding to the issues whose statistical summarization was discussed in Chapters VI, VIII, and IX, will be considered in the next three sections, 5, 6, and 7.

§5   *Summary of the Distribution of Values of a Single Character*

Economists must start with the fact of a distribution of values and a mere average of those values, rather than with the thought of one unique normal value to which everything " approximates." Unbearably unsettling as it may seem, they must learn to question whether there is a normal rate of profits at which enterprise requiring equal effort and risk is remunerated in all industries ; and even to ask whether there really is only one price at which a given article exchanges in any actual market. At present questions such as these are inhibited, and the idea of variety in true rates of profit or in prices of one article in one market is so shelved that the economists do not even dare to speak of an average variety. This

---

[1] See Florence, *Economics of Fatigue and Unrest*, p. 223.

is due partly to a healthy respect for the uncertainty, inconstancy, and instability of economic events.   It is only " in the famous fiction of the stationary state " where population and wealth are either stationary or growing at a constant rate, where there is no scarcity of land, where methods of production and the conditions of trade change but little, and the character of man himself is a constant quantity, that " average price and normal price are convertible terms."[1]   But the avoidance of any mention of average is also due to the cautious policy of letting sleeping dogs lie.   Once statistical calculation is started the difficulties of precision become all too obvious.

When the economist assumes that the same kind of article is exchanged at one unique price in a market he is thinking of articles as specific as pots, pans, or stockings of definite quality.   This equality of prices of *the same article* is difficult enough for the statistician to take for granted in view of the price discrimination of monopolists and the possible policies of makers and merchants of proprietary articles, of setting at " market price plus " or " market price minus."[2]   But when the discussion shifts to exchange value of factors of production, the " kinds " of factors that are distinguished are very broad classes indeed and difficulties multiply. It is not a question of the price of the labour of driving a van of definite load, or of shaving a customer, or the price of lending money for, say, rubber growing.   The theoretical discussion usually starts with the price of labour in general, and the price of enterprise and capital in general.   In the course of the discussion sub-kinds of labour, such as unskilled, skilled, and professional, and sub-kinds of capital taking varying degrees of risk may be distinguished.   But the *general* proposition is carefully enunciated by Marshall that competition tends to equalize wages in occupations in the same neighbourhood that are of the same difficulty, and require an equal exertion of ability and efficiency.[3]   Parallel to this assumption that efficiency wages tend to equality, is the assumption that though sub-species of capital and management may be distinguished according to the degree of risk, trouble, and sacrifice, yet there is here also a broad tendency for *net* interest[4] and profits[5] per risk taken, and work done, and sacrifice made, to tend to equality in different trades.

---

[1] Marshall, *Principles of Economics*, V, v, §§2, 3, 4.
[2] A. W. Shaw, *Some Problems in Market Distribution*, pp. 47, 52, 59.
[3] *Principles of Economics*, VI, iii, 2.   [4] Op. cit. VI, vi, 5.
[5] Op. cit. VI, viii, 2.   Marshall carefully discusses the wage bill, the capital of the enterprise, and the turnover, as possible measures of risk taken and work done.   See above, Chapter X §1.

What steps have economists taken to verify these assumptions by summary measurement of the actual facts ? Have they established, as Prof. H. L. Moore has tried to do in his *Laws of Wages*, that there is a normal curve in the distribution of, say, wages which might justify reference to an average wage ? A glance at Table XVIIB shows that such a more or less symmetrical distribution with a distinct average value only appears probable where occupations are separated off fairly minutely. The most frequent or modal[1] range of values for the total of employees in sawmills is 20 to 30 cents per hour ; 18,281 employees receive a wage in this range of values and no other equal range of value is received by more than 8561 men.

But the arithmetic mean value[2] of the wages of all employees listed is 32·9 cents. There is thus a considerable positive skew,[3] and it would be hard to specify an average representative wage. Within the separate occupations, on the other hand, it can be seen that the arithmetic mean (column 2) does sometimes fall within the modal range of values. The arithmetic mean wage of edgermen, for instance, is 46·8 cents per hour, and the modal range of wages 40 to 50 cents, and a similar indication of a symmetrical distribution[4] is observable in the case of setters. As a rule, however, there is the same positive skew as for the total of employees. The arithmetic mean wages for sawyers is 87·7 cents, their modal wage 90 to 100 cents ; the arithmetic mean wage for machine feeders is 39 cents, their modal wage 20 to 30 cents, and so on. Furthermore, apart from their skew distribution each occupation shows a wide deviation of the item-wages paid to individuals from the average wage for the occupation. In the case of machine feeders, for instance, the mean deviation[5] from the arithmetic mean of 39·0 cents per hour is 11·5 and the coefficient of dispersion[6] thus 29·5%.

Some recognition of the distribution of items over classes or grades of value in place of one normal value which all items called by the same name tend to manifest, is gradually and peacefully permeating the economic theory of wages. Economists used to speak of the general level of wages, but this begs the question whether there is any general level at all. The existence of grades of labour is now admitted, but the grades conventionally adopted are not based, as they should be, empirically, upon a review of the actual distribution of wages. The classes or grades are not formed by more or less discreet groups of wage values showing, possibly

---

[1] Glossary §5.
[3] Glossary §15.
[5] Glossary §11.

[2] Glossary §4.
[4] Glossary §15.
[6] Glossary §13.

modes of their own within a multimodal total distribution,[1] but are grades like (1) automatic and (2) responsible manual labour, (3) automatic and (4) responsible brain workers,[2] distinguished by preconceived criteria of what might plausibly lead to wage differentiation, and repeated *ad nauseam* without independent investigation by author after author.

To sum up. Statistical economics recognizes that though there may be in any one industry a latent tendency toward one representative type of business or firm, and though there may be in any one market a tendency toward one price for one kind of article, and one level of wages for one kind of work, and one rate of interest for one kind of loan and so forth, yet in fact there is a more or less wide distribution of types and values. Statistics must therefore set out to measure the form and deviation of such a distribution, and must by observation decide whether an average value may fairly represent the distribution, or whether, owing to the high coefficient of dispersion, or to the appearance of two or more modes, or of a skew form of distribution, one average, or an average at all, is not misleading. If several modes appear, as they probably will in the case of wages, when women and children on the one hand, and foremen and supervisors on the other, are included in the group, then separate grades with distinct average values of their own must be empirically distinguished.

§6 *Summary of the Time Tendencies of a Single Character or Set of Characters*

Simple illustrations of statistical methods of summarizing so-called time series together with the similarly measurable geographical place distributions were given in Chapter VIII. These summarizations take the form of measures of span, amplitude, regularity, and rhythm, and the original data are usually first reduced to index numbers giving the precise comparative values and changes.

The economically important characteristics that are measured, usually in index numbers,[3] to show these temporal variations are in the first place the characteristics already distinguished (§1) as *primarily* economic, though they may be grouped slightly differently:

(I) The price or rate per unit at which exchange is effected.

(II) The total physical amounts or *volume* of trade of exchange-

---

[1] Like the hours of labour in Table VID.
[2] First distinguished by Giddings, *Political Science Quarterly*, Vol. II.
[3] See above, Chapters VIII and X §2.

units (*a*) exchanged, etc., *during* a period or (*b*) outstanding *at* a point of time.

(III) The total value of trade or amounts of income (price or rate × physical amount) of exchangeable units (goods, services, factors of production), (*a*) exchanged, etc., during a period, or (*b*) outstanding at a point of time.

Finally (IV) there are certain standard ratios between total values or amounts such as sales turnover, bank's reserve ratios, etc. ; and (V) certain institutional facts and events may also form a " time-series " of interest to the economist.

Table XVIc groups the time series of data into these five classes. Series in Class I are used chiefly for measuring changes in the power of money in purchasing various types of exchangeable (see below, Chapter XVII §4). Series in Classes II and III (and sometimes in the other classes) are used for measuring Trade (or " Industrial " or " Business ") Fluctuations.

The Trade or Business *Cycle* is of course only one tendency among a number of others, such as the secular trend and seasonal variation, which statistics attempt to " analyse out " of the course of fluctuation in general (see Table VIIID and Chapter VIII). Mitchell, in fact, considers that what we can get from the statistician are " the residual fluctuations of many American and some foreign time series after the secular trends and the seasonal fluctuations have been eliminated." The cyclical fluctuation simply forms part of this residue.[1] In this measurement of trade fluctuations generally, the most modern practice, as described by Mitchell, insists upon monthly or at least quarterly (not merely yearly) data[2] and recognizes that " weighted arithmetic means of relatives (i.e. index numbers) are less desirable price indexes for most uses than relatives made from aggregates of actual prices weighted by physical quantities."[3]

Perhaps the earliest attempt to distinguish *seasonal fluctuation* by means of statistics is Jevons' paper *On the Study of Periodic Commercial Fluctuations*, read before the British Association in 1862. In that paper Jevons mentions earlier work by Gilbart on bank-note circulation, and by Babbage on the statistics of the Clearing House, but otherwise he considers it " surprising what little work has already been done in this way." Jevons himself uses statistics of the average monthly rates of discount, number of bankruptcies, price of consols, and price of wheat. In a later paper, read before the Statistical Society in 1866, Jevons described in

---

[1] *Business Cycles*, p. 256. See also pp. 2, 454.
[2] Op. cit., p. 260.   [3] Op. cit., p. 316.

TABLE XVIc

INDEX CHARACTERS MEASURING BUSINESS TRENDS AND FLUCTUATIONS

I *Prices and rates of exchange.*
Wholesale and Retail prices of goods.
Cost of Living of Working-class families.
Freight rates.
Prices of stocks and shares.
Wage-rates.
Interest-rates.
Discount-rates.
Dividends.
Foreign Exchange Rates.

II (A)   *Amounts* (Physical) *exchanged* (or prepared for exchange), produced, or consumed *during a period of time.*
Physical Consumption, e.g. Barrels of Beer, Units of Electricity, etc.
Physical Production, e.g. Pig-iron, Coal.
Amounts of Traffic, e.g. Ton-Miles of Railway, Letters, Ships entering and leaving Port.
Export and Import Volume.

II (B)   *Amounts* (Physical) *Measured at one point of time.*
Stocks of goods.
Crop Reports.
Unemployment.
Furnaces in Blast, etc.

III (A)   *TOTAL VALUES Exchanged, etc., during a period of time.*
Export and Import Values.
Retail Sales.
Bank Clearings.
Life Insurance Policies.
Expenditure on Advertising.
New Capital Issues.
Shares Exchanged.
Money or real Incomes, e.g. Earnings of Labour, Total Profits.

III (B)   *TOTAL VALUES Measured at one point of time.*
Total value of Stocks held.
Treasury Bills Outstanding.
Bank and Currency Notes Outstanding.
Bank Deposits, Discounts.

IV   *Ratios between Total Values or Amounts.*
Percentage of Unemployment.
Sales Turnover.
Velocity and Turnover of Bank Deposits.
Central Banks Gold Reserve Ratio.
Banks ratio of cash to Deposits.

V   *Institutional Changes.*
Business Failures.
" Social Consequences," Poor Relief, Migration, Births and Deaths, etc.
Taxes.

T

greater detail *The Frequent Autumnal Pressure in the Money Market and the Action of the Bank of England.*

Jevons, however, is better known for his statistical enquiry into a supposed decennial *cyclical fluctuation* that he tried to explain in terms of sun spots. Sir William Herschel who had suggested this hypothesis in 1801 had tried to trace the connection with the sun's spots in the price of corn, unsuccessfully, in Jevons' opinion. Jevons in his paper before the British Association, 1878, supplies much fuller statistical data and makes special use of bankruptcies, annual exports to India, and exports from American colonies to England, traced back to 1700. He thus foreshadowed the multitudinous modern indices of business cycles that are formed out of fluctuations in a number or composite set of differently weighted item characters. The Harvard Committee on Economic Research measure fluctuations in English business by an index composed of exports of British produce, unemployment, bank-clearings of five provincial towns, and blast furnaces in blast, thus mixing several index characters of the amount and the total value group (Table XVIc, Groups II and III).[1]

An alternative measure of business fluctuation is that of business profit. The amount of profit (Group III) is generally used rather than any rate of profit (Group I). Belshaw draws attention to the *profit cycle in agriculture*[2] and Sir Josiah Stamp[3] has shown the wide amplitude of fluctuations in the profits of coal-mining, gas, railway companies and some textile trades, and draws important conclusions. For instance, " the fluctuations in the profits of (cotton) spinning are very violent. The deviation of the price from the trend of prices is 14·4% on the average price, but the deviation of profit is 154 per cent, or nearly eleven times as great (standard deviation taken).[4] Reckoned by another method also, it is ten times as great (average deviation). It may fairly be said the fluctuations in profits are ten times as great as fluctuations in prices."

The statistical study of the *secular trend* was first attempted through measurement of prices, and the progress of the working class in "real" wages and the amount of meat, wheat, bread, etc. consumed.

Thomas Tooke's *History of Prices* goes back to 1793 and was revised and continued by Newmarch down to 1856. But as Jevons points out,[5] " Tooke and other writers on the subject of prices were

---

[1] For an excellent summary of the various composite measures of trade fluctuations actually in use see Mitchell, *Business Cycles*, pp. 271 ff., 343 ff. Mitchell also gives a summary of conclusions (up to 1927) as regards span, amplitude, and rhythm of cycles.
[2] *Ec. Jl.*, March 1926.   [3] *J.R.S.S.*, 1918.   [4] See Glossary §11.
[5] *Investigations in Currency and Finance*, p. 120.

in want of some method of reducing their tables of prices, and eliciting the general facts contained in them," and to Jevons belongs the credit of working out an index number to measure price fluctuations in general.

Sir Robert Giffen chose the *Progress of the Working Classes in the Last Half Century* for his inaugural address as President of the Statistical Society in 1883, and added *Further Notes on the Progress of the Working Classes* before the same Society in 1886. Professor Bowley's *Wages in the United Kingdom in the Nineteenth Century* gives a most detailed review of the trend in several important industries. And as a wider survey of working-class progress Thorold Rogers' *Six Centuries of Work and Wages* published in 1884 is, of course, a classic of economic history using quantitative measures.

Fluctuations from time to time in these economic characteristics are not necessarily studied in isolation. *Synchronous* fluctuations in two or more characters may be set side by side for comparison, as was done in Table XIIIE above, with or without calculating a coefficient of correlation.[1] Or, comparison and correlation may be made between fluctuations of one or more characters at one time with fluctuations of another or other characters at a later or earlier time. If a high degree of correlation is established in the fluctuations of two characters with a constant gap of so many years or months between them, one character is said to have a LAG (or LEAD) of so many months or years behind (or before) the other.

For this correlation of synchronous or constantly lagging or leading fluctuations in different characters several methods may be used:

(1) The absolute or percentage change of the value for one period, as compared with the preceding (or succeeding) period, may be calculated for each character and these changes correlated.

(2) The general secular trend may be eliminated by the various devices described above (Chapter VIII), and the deviations of the values of each character from their secular trend correlated to find the co-variation *ratio* and the degree or coefficient of correlation.

Thus Stamp in his paper before the Royal Statistical Society on the *Effect of Trade Fluctuations upon Profits*[2] compares synchronous annual deviations from the linear trend of coal profits, tonnage, and prices, and finds that " the change in profits due to a change in price had been three times as great as the price change, i.e. that a 1% fluctuation in price was accompanied by a 3% fluctuation in profit. But in the case of a unit variation in output, the change in

---

[1] For the difficulties and fallacies of correlation of time series see Yule, *J.R.S.S.*, January 1926.
[2] *J.R.S.S.*, 1918.

profit was only quite a small fraction over unity. In these investigations all the coefficients of correlation were very high."

The correlation between railway profits and the price of coal was negative, but high and significant ; i.e. if the price of coal was markedly increased, then the railway profits were clearly less in the following year—a lag of a year giving the most marked correlation. The deviation of railway profits from the trend was about one-quarter of the opposite deviation of coal prices. Gas profits had a similar negative correlation with coal prices, and the deviation about two-thirds in amplitude.

The precise period of the lag or lead is often the chief point at issue. There is much discussion among statisticians on the precise order of events marking any one phase of the cycle. Which is the statistically measurable change that comes first and at what distance in time or " lag " will the changes in the other characters follow suit ? The investigations of Dr. E. C. Snow, for instance, seem to show[1] that at the violent crisis and depression of 1920–22 in Great Britain the import of raw materials and the prices of industrial shares were first affected ; then at a distance of one or two months' wholesale price index numbers and the percentage of unemployment ; then after a lag of another two or three months the export of manufactures.[2]

For the period 1903 to 1914 in the U.S.A., Professor Persons,[3] using the Harvard University index of general business conditions, for which he is largely responsible, found that the cyclical fluctuation of the curve of *speculation* (measured by yields of ten railroad bonds, prices of industrial stocks, prices of twenty railroad bonds, bank clearings in New York City) led, by eight months on the average, the cyclical fluctuation of the curve of *business* (measured by pig-iron production, outside clearings, Bradstreets' price index, Bureau of Labour Statistics' price index, reserves of New York City banks) which in turn led, by four months on the average, the cyclical fluctuations of the curve of *money rates* (measured by rate on 4 to 6 months' paper, rate on 60 to 90 day paper, loans of New York City banks, deposits of New York City banks).

The fact that some series rise or fall before others may lead to the discovery of causal relations, and this is especially important in facilitating the forecasting and prediction of probable tendencies.

[1] *J.R.S.S.*, May 1923.
[2] This is an extremely rough summary merely designed to show the kind of conclusions that statistics may show. For accurate details the reader must refer to the paper itself. See also for England, C. D. Whetham, " The Economic Lag of Agriculture," *J.R.S.S.*, December 1925.
[3] Mitchell, *Business Cycles*, pp. 325 and 293.

" Of the three groups of series used in the Harvard University index of general business conditions, that of speculation during the period 1903–1914 generally rose or fell before the ' business ' group, and the business group before the money group, also the period of lag between the movements of these different groups showed a rough correspondence at different dates.   In the depressions and booms of the business cycles which took place during the pre-war period, this general correlation of movements was evident.   After the war, although certain changes were necessary in the statistical data used, the same general succession of movements has been shown to exist."

" From the point of view of predicting future conditions, the Harvard University Committee regards the movement in opposite directions of the speculation group and the money group as indicating a change in general business conditions.   If the speculation curve is rising and the money curve is falling considerably, an improvement in business is probable.   If money rates are rising and the speculation curve falling, business is likely to change for the worse."[1]

§7   Formulation of Economic Laws Correlating Several Characters

Most of the so-called laws of theoretical economics are association, or correlation issues as described in Chapter IX, rather than the frequency distributions (expounded in Chapter VI), or the tendencies over time or place (described in Chapter VIII).   The frequency curve of one character is considered merely descriptive and unworthy of theory, while the neglect of time tendencies follows from the self-denying ordinance whereby economists restrict themselves to the " stationary state."   " Other things being equal " is practically synonymous with " at any given moment or place."   When economists use the word " tendency " they do not refer to actual developments in time, dynamic growths or changes, but simply to some law of co-variation or regression line (Chapter VIII) or curve to which the facts and values at issue are expected to approximate, if other conditions remain stable.   This has led to much misunderstanding of economic doctrines.   The tendency to over-population in particular has been criticized by medical men, statisticians, publicists, and ecclesiastics because they supposed that it prophesied future developments, whether other things remained equal or not. Repeatedly it is affirmed by those who should be better read that Malthus' " prognostications " have been completely " exploded " by the fact that while England's population increased throughout

---

[1] *Economic Barometers*, I.L.O.   Studies and Reports, N 5.   See, however, Karl Karsen's criticism of the basis of the Harvard Committee's predictions, *J.A.S.A.*, December 1926, and the rejoinder of the Harvard Committee.

the nineteenth century, her total wealth or means of subsistence increased still faster. But economists made no prophecies of the future course of events. The " tendency " to which they pointed was what the statistical economist may formulate as a negative correlation between heads and wealth per head, other relevant characters such as inventions and discoveries remaining constant. The *more* the heads the *less* the wealth per head. This tendency may equally well be expressed as a state of over-population in which any decrease in population (as occurred at the Black Death, for instance) would lead to a *smaller* decrease in the community's total means of subsistence and therefore to greater wealth per head.[1] The economist can always cap his critics by suggesting that wealth per head in England, say in 1929, would have been still greater than it is, but for England's Victorian orgy of fecundity.

Economic laws or " curves " of correlation-issue type may be either what Professor Edgeworth[2] distinguishes as " concepts," or what he calls " propositions." Laws in the sense of concepts merely state possible quantitative relations between two or more characters without specifying to what economic transactions the concept may apply. The outstanding examples, apart from high or low degrees of elasticity of demand, are increasing, constant, or decreasing return conditions of supply. Any one exchangeable may fall into any one of a large number of conceptual " boxes " according as it obeys any of various " laws " of variable or constant return. But the concept, e.g. of highly or moderately increasing constant or decreasing return, is merely a box, is merely a *possible* relationship, and does not tell us what data to class therein.

Here lies an important opportunity for the statistician to collaborate with the economist by filling the empty boxes representing theoretical laws. For the more realistically minded economists have indicated certain observable and measurable characters as tests of an increasing, constant, or decreasing return industry, and have at least given us the *means* for correct boxing and filing. Marshall, indeed, gives us an admirable instance of getting down to earth at this point. " Supplementary costs are, as a rule, larger relatively to prime costs for things that obey the law of increasing return than for other things ; because their production needs the investment of a large capital in material appliances and in building up trade connection."[3] Prime costs are those that vary proportionately with the units of output, and supplementary costs those

---

[1] Cf. my *Over-population—Theory and Statistics*, p. 10.
[2] *Papers relating to Political Economy*, Vol. I, pp. 61 ff.
[3] *Principles of Economics*, Book V, xii §2.

that do not; so that the conception (or "character") of primeness or supplementariness is measurable in the form of a statistical correlation. And, further, the actual costs of most industries can definitely be classified into files of various degrees of primeness and supplementariness.[1]

But before the statistician takes to classing and filing industries outside the limited range of constant return, he must understand the refinements in the economist's formulæ of increasing and diminishing return. The law of constant return refers to a non-correlation between amount produced and cost per unit, and the statistician may class under constant return all cases that approximate to this by showing negligible degrees of correlation. Classification of cases under increasing and decreasing return is, however, more difficult.

The law (or conception) of decreasing cost, or, as it is more usually called, that of increasing return, has been expressed in two theoretically distinct and alternate formulæ, that of (a) average, and that of (b) marginal returns. (a) The more the amount of any exchangeable men produce, the more the *average* return to a unit of (combined) expenses when factors of production are substituted one for the other to obtain the most appropriate combination. (b) The more the amount of any exchangeable men produce, the more is *added to the total return* by an additional unit of (combined) expenses when factors of production are substituted one for the other to obtain the most appropriate combination. In both cases the hypothesis is a *positive* correlation between the amount produced and (a) the average return, or (b) the addition made in the total return (i.e. the "marginal" return) by an additional unit of expenses.

The law (or conception) of increasing cost, or as it is more usually called, that of decreasing return, is also expressed in these two distinct and alternative formulæ, and the exact wording can be obtained by substituting in formula (A) the "less" for the "more" the average return, and in formula (B) "the less is added" for "the more is added." Here the hypothetical correlation is *negative*.

These laws emerge from concepts into propositions when they are stated to apply to specific industries. The law of increasing return either in form A or form B is usually held to be true of manufacturing industries that have undergone their "industrial revolution." But it is doubtful whether the law of *decreasing* return *in either of the forms given above* applies to any existing industry.

The law of decreasing return that is supposed to apply to agricultural industries should be worded differently and has a

[1] See below, XVII §7.

correspondingly different law of increasing return to set against it, at least as a concept.

These laws, distinguished from those already formulated, are the laws of decreasing or increasing returns *to any one, or some factors when other factors remain constant* ; or as I propose to call them, the laws of decreasing or increasing *factorial* return.[1]

Here again it may be the *average* return per unit (or dose) of the variable factor or factors that varies (as enunciated by Marshall, *Principles of Economics*, IV, iii, §1, or Carver, *Distribution of Wealth*) ; or alternatively it may be the *marginal* return that varies, i.e. the total return from specified units minus the total return from units numbering one unit less.[2]

As a propositional law, decreasing factorial return (the negative correlation of returns and additional units of some factors) is the more frequent in theory and probably in fact. This abandons the assumption that factors of production are, or can be, substituted one for another to an unlimited extent and combined in any proportions desired.

The proposition states that the concept of decreasing factorial return applies to products of the land in a settled country, since fertile and accessible land is in fact scarce and limited in amount, and the assumption of constancy in some factor or factors is thereby realized. The concept is taken to apply also in the " short " period to every branch of industry. Marshall speaks of the " almost universal law that the term Normal being taken to refer to a short period of time, *an increase in the amount demanded raises the normal supply price.*"[3] While certain factors of production, such as factory buildings and machines, cannot be increased in this short period any more than land, other factors, like hours of labour and individual labourers, can be added as doses to the constant " plant " factors, and will plausibly obtain decreasing (factorial) return.

The statistician will want to know more definitely (cf. §3) what the units are in which the return is to be measured, whether monetary, physical, or psychological,[4] and his calculations as to the applicability of the law will certainly be different according as the law of *increasing* return is one of increasing marginal returns, increasing

---

[1] To distinguish it from *factorial* return the concept first considered of return to factors combined in any proportion may be referred to as *general* return.

[2] This seems to be the precise measure used by Marshall in footnote to *Principles of Economics*, IV, iii, §2.

[3] Op. cit., V, v, §4.

[4] Cf. Florence, *Economics and Human Behaviour*, and below, Chapter XVIII §6.

average returns, increasing marginal factorial returns, or increasing average factorial returns. But the point that I am content to conclude with here is that these fundamental laws can, and should be, formulated as statistical correlation issues, i.e. as laws of a " co-variation " of two (or more) characters.

CHAPTER XVII

THE INTERPRETATION OF ECONOMIC VARIATIONS

§1 *The Hypotheses of Economic Theory*

IN Chapter XV modifications were indicated that would prepare economic theory and its apparatus of thought to fuse with economic statistics ; in Chapter XVI the steps were indicated that would bring economic statistics into relation with theory. It remains in this chapter to effect the fusion.

It is as hypothetical but plausible interpretations or " explanations "[1] of the correlation laws or other summaries of the facts, that the theoretical " principles " neglected in Chapter XVI now find their place. These economic notions are mainly psychological and can mostly be taken as corollaries or sub-assumptions of the psychological assumption of the economic man.

Social psychologists have attacked this " conception of human nature constructed in all good faith by certain eighteenth-century philosophers which is now no longer exactly believed in." But " because nothing else has taken its place (it) still exercises a kind of shadowy authority in a hypothetical universe."[2] The creature of instincts, most clearly manifest perhaps in the sporting individual purchasing costly fishing, hunting, or shooting rights and tackle, is a " scientific fiction " no more convenient for deductive purposes nor more truthful to workaday life, than the economic man who still flourishes in Cambridge lecture-rooms. In spite of suggestions by Prof. Walton Hamilton in the *New Republic*[3] one does not see an Oxford School of Economics arising on the foundation of instinctive man.

" The exploitation by the psychological school of a ' normal ' instinctive animal for deductive purposes, stands condemned as no better scientifically than the orthodox use, for the same purpose, of a ' normal ' economic man.

" The way out of the dilemma," to continue the quotation, " is

---

[1] In the sense used and expounded in Chapters XII to XIV.
[2] Graham Wallas, *Human Nature in Politics*, p. 128.
[3] Review of Henderson's *Supply and Demand*, 1922.

to drop deduction from *any* a priori view of human nature as the main source of economic knowledge."[1]

The economic man may be regarded as one who, however ignorantly, calculates, and balances his wants against their cost. Without exploring into the nature of those wants or assuming that his ultimate objective is always wealth, we may take this human calculator simply as one who seeks his wants as economically as he can, i.e. with the least cost, in whatever terms he measures cost. This hypothesis may possibly or plausibly explain (or suggest) inductions from statistical observations.

Utility is the quality in anything that stimulates the reaction in a man of wanting or seeking. To give utility any ulterior reaction such as pleasure, satisfaction-in-consumption, or moral benefit in or to the consumer, is to transcend quite unnecessarily the scope of economics. Similarly costs, or more accurately *real* costs, are all and any sorts of aversions, checks, or " negative " stimuli against the reaction of working or saving. Both utility and cost affect economic events only indirectly through demand price (i.e. vendibility) or supply price. " A demand for goods, if it is to have an economic significance, must be backed up by ability to pay," writes Professor Cassel.[2] It is only such wants to such amounts as men are willing to pay a price for, and such costs as they are willing to undergo for a price, that really affect the terms of actual exchange transactions.

The *economic man* is one who prefers to buy any given thing cheaper rather than dearer, and prefers to sell any given thing dearer rather than cheaper. Whatever the economic man exchanges he chooses to lose as little, and to gain as many units as he can.[3]

In a "money economy" one of the sets of units exchanged is always money ; but on the other side of the bargain the choice may not be between more or fewer units of *one* article at any one time, but (1) between various amounts of several kinds of exchangeable, (2) between amounts of one or more exchangeable now or in the future, (3) between amounts of different qualities of the same exchangeable. The principles upon which the economic man is supposed to model his behaviour in each of these cases are the principles of (1) substitution, (2) anticipation, (3) selection. The principle of substitution is that most explicitly enunciated by the economist, but the two further principles subsumed under the

---

[1] Florence, *Economics and Human Behaviour*, p. 112.
[2] *Money* and *Foreign Exchange after* 1914, p. 55.
[3] The economic man is presented and brought home most notoriously, perhaps, in Adam Smith's advocacy of piece wages for the academic profession. *Wealth of Nations*, Book V, Chapter I.

general principle of the economic man are implicitly used in the arguments of economists, and they should be explicitly recognized and separately distinguished so that their actual existence may be brought to the test of observation and statistical measurement. When observation and measurement are called in it should be clearly recognized that the economist need not, and usually does not, maintain that all men are all-economic all the time. There is merely some " sufficient proportion of persons " making a " sufficient proportion of their purchases or sales by calculating cost and utility and balancing one against the other."[1]

(1) The principle of substitution states that in distributing any given amount of money over various amounts of several kinds of exchangeable, a consumer or producer will so substitute units of one exchangeable for units of another that he incurs a minimum of cost and gets a maximum of return or satisfaction. The principle of substitution thus refers to a calculation between amounts of different exchangeables at any one time.

(2) But man may also calculate about the different times of buying or selling amounts of the same (or different) exchangeables and may prefer to lose satisfaction now that he may get more later. This I shall call the principle of forethought or *anticipation*. It is admitted explicitly in economic text-books when discussing saving and the discounting of future satisfaction, but is implicit in many other applications of economic reasoning.

The principle of anticipation is of the utmost importance in guarding against a fallacious interpretation of correlations found between economic characters. In particular it avoids the fallacy of *post hoc ergo propter hoc*. The foreign exchange rate of countries that have inconvertible paper money is said to be determined by the purchasing power parity of the two currencies. " When two currencies have undergone inflation, the normal rate of exchange will be equal to the old rate multiplied by the quotient of the degree of inflation in the one country and in the other." This is " the new parity between the currencies . . . towards which in spite of all temporary fluctuations the exchange-rates will always tend."[2] The degree of inflation in either country can be measured statistically in index numbers of general prices, hence the purchasing power parity is statistically obtainable.

Let us follow Cassel's instructions for finding the normal rate of exchange of dollars against pound sterling in the *third quarter of*

[1] Florence, *Economics and Human Behaviour*, p. 16. See also Henderson, *Supply and Demand*, pp. 45–6.
[2] Cassel, *Money and Foreign Exchange since* 1914.

1924. The old pre-war rate of exchange was 4·866, and this multiplied by the quotient of the degree of inflation between 1913 and 1924 third quarter in England (Board of Trade general index=165) and in America (Bureau of Labour wholesale index=149) is 4·866 × [149÷165]=4·39. The actual average of daily rates of exchange of dollars against pound sterling in the third quarter of 1924 was 4·44, which certainly may be said to " tend " toward Cassel's normal rate of exchange. But statistical investigation cannot *prove* that it is the relative degree of inflation of one country as against another that causes the exchange rate to be the value it is and not vice versa. In fact, the exchange rate of a country's currency may fall *before* a fresh issue of currency by its government, and before a rise in its index of internal prices, and it has been argued that for that reason the fall in the exchange rates which come earlier cannot be the result of the inflationary issue of currency that came later. This criticism of the purchasing power parity theory might be cogent if it were not that inflation (or deflation) is often *anticipated*, and that people (not necessarily mere " speculators ") tend to sell the foreign currency they expect will be inflated or to buy the currency they expect will be deflated.

In the *last* as compared with the third quarter of 1924 inflation, as measured by general price index number, increased an equal number of points in both England (165 to 170) and America (149 to 154), and though the percentage increase is of course not quite the same, on Cassel's calculation the normal rate of exchange should have remained very near the third quarter's " parity " of $4·39. In fact, however, the average of actual daily rates of exchange tended *away* from this to $4·60.

This " over-valuation " of the pound sterling (i.e. a higher actual exchange rate than the " normal " rate of the purchasing power parity theory) was anticipating a deflation and return to the gold standard in England that actually took place in the second quarter of 1925.

Similarly, it is sometimes held that since the rent a farmer or shopkeeper has to pay for his land or site is settled *before* he produces or sells on that land, the proceeds obtained from the *subsequent* produce or sales, which admittedly are usually correlated positively with the rent, cannot be the cause of that rent and may rather be its result. Economic theory supposes, however, that landlord and farmer, or landlord and shopkeeper both think ahead as to what the proceeds are likely to be, and it is their estimates of the future that determine the bargain. Thus rent is determined by proceeds (i.e. units sold × price of units) not vice versa.

Larger purchases of Jaeger underwear are associated with autumn days, and winter " lags " behind ; but no one supposes that it is money spent on Jaegers that causes winter to come on. Man, as he is found in the trading and exchanging countries of the world, anticipates, thinks, and plans ahead. What is expected as the last phase determines the present.

(3) Calculations about units of different kinds of exchangeables and about exchangeables now and in the future, jostle in the mind of economic man with calculations about the different specimens of the same kind of exchangeable, when these specimens vary in quality. Here the principle is taken as so obvious that it is not even mentioned and has no name generally agreed upon, though it sometimes appears as the principle of competition. Economic man, it is tacitly presumed, is aware of differences in quality and his higgling will be based upon the precise consequences he expects from such differences.

Where differences in quality lead to *measurable* difference in quantity, as qualities of the means of production lead to different amounts of product, economic man will be able to measure these differences and will calculate accordingly. If the prices of the several qualities are the same he will select the more productive qualities and he will persist in selecting them even if their prices are greater up to the point where the difference in price paid exactly counterbalances the difference in the value of the product obtained. This principle, which I shall call the principle of selection, is the second basis upon which rests the theory of rent. If land were free or the same price were charged for all acres, the economic man would, on the principle of " selection," select the more fertile and accessible rather than the less fertile and accessible land. Land of high fertility and convenient site is limited ; hence combining the two principles of anticipation and selection, economic man will be prepared to offer a money value for land with these scarce differential advantages up to that value that will (when subtracted from his net proceeds[1]) just give him a return or profit equal to that of other farmers making equal efforts. This money value that should thus equitably handicap each farmer is the economic " rent."

The statistical test of the theory of rent would involve land valuation to measure the natural productive capacity and convenience of site of the different acres or plots of land under cultivation or habitation. But even if this were accomplished and a positive correlation established, say, between productivity (in quantity and economic values) and rent charges, the difficulty is to

[1] Cf. analysis of profits above, p. 263.

prove that it is the total value of the produce that governs or causes the rent and not vice versa. This difficulty, as in the case of the theory of purchasing power parity, can be overcome only by resort to the psychological hypotheses of economic man.

Besides these three principles guiding the economic man's behaviour, economics presumes upon one other basic proposition. The Law of Diminishing Utility, put in the form of a correlation issue, states that the more units men have or get of any exchangeable, the less they want (at that time) additional units. This law is NOT subsumed by the presumption of an economic man and would not be upset if economic man proved a fiction. Even a pig may be fed up, " satiated," and probably gets less than twice as excited over twenty units of its food than it does over ten units put before it. The grounds for holding diminishing utility to be true are physiological or psychological, and by rights the law should be an example of knowledge derived from other sciences. Actually I have not been able to find this " law " stated in any psychological or physiological text-book,[1] and though the law is not confined to the economic man, it does seem to be confined to the economist's man. It is certainly more likely to be true when under conditions of unequal and positively skewed distribution of wealth, economic demand is at issue, rather than mere want. The law, in the form that the more units are put up for sale the less the price that will carry all of them off, is true not merely because wants become satiated, but also because poorer social strata must be " tapped."

At least two corollaries have been derived from this Law of Diminishing Utility, that of the consumer's surplus and that of marginal utility. The former is not in practice used to further strictly economic analysis into the " terms of exchange," is highly contentious,[2] and had best not detain us. Marginal utility, on the other hand, often appears as the corner-stone, and the very namesake, of modern " Marginalist " economics. The word derives from the conception of a buyer on the margin of doubt whether to purchase or not to purchase[3] additional units of an exchangeable. It assumes (1) calculation, and the balancing of a want against the price asked, and (2) a diminishing degree of want with additional

---

[1] Chapter XIV §2. The reason is, possibly, that the precise rate of diminution in want has not yet been discovered for any single object, and physiologist and psychologist may scorn to call anything a law that cannot be given any exact numerical " co-variation ratio."

[2] See *Economica*, Nos. 10 and 11, controversy between Professors Cannan and McGregor.

[3] Margin here means a " borderland," not as in the margin of profit, or the unspent margin, or the margin of a printed page, an " edge " or *additional* something.

units, so that eventually there must be some unit that is so little wanted that the balance is tipped against buying it.

So much misunderstanding has arisen as to the significance of marginal utility, however, that I am inclined to advise a statistical economist to be chary of its use. At least he must be quite clear that no responsible economist of the Cambridge School believes or has said either (1) that marginal utility determines price,[1] or (2) that, except possibly in the case of land, the marginal unit is inferior in quality or in any way inherently distinguishable from other units.

(1) It is one of the cardinal defects of Prof. Cassel's *Theory of Social Economy* that he entirely misrepresents Marshall on this point.[2] There is no excuse, since no one could be more emphatic than Marshall himself (*Principles of Economics*, V, viii, 5, marginal heading) : " *Marginal uses and costs do not govern value but are governed together with value by the general relations of demand and supply.*" The point of using the phrase is the very realistic consideration that it is difficult to explain the price of any one unit of an exchangeable by direct reference to its particular supply price or demand price. For that particular unit the buyer or consumer may have been willing to pay more and the seller or producer to receive less. But by the economist's assumption, the price of all units of the same exchangeable is, in any one market, the same. Hence the price of any one unit must be determined or " governed " by the conditions affecting the number of units as a whole, and it is " *at the margin* " or borderline amount of units just exchanged where an amount just greater would not be exchanged that these conditions are most clearly indicated. If I may use an orthodox diagram, such as Table XVIIA, the point is that to explain the price O P at which, say, unit 10 changes hands, we must run our eyes along the whole set of 14 units that have actually changed hands. The price of the 14th unit is clearly determined jointly by the demand and supply curves, DD and SS.

(2) The marginal shepherd discussed by Marshall is assumed to be a man of normal efficiency only called marginal " because his employment is marginal."[3]   The marginal unit of labour is *not to*

---

[1] Taussig and many American disciples of Marshall have, I admit, gone wrong here. Cf. Taussig, *Principles of Economics*, Chapter 47, 1st edition : " The marginal contribution from any grade or group of labour determines the remuneration of all within that grade." See also Prof. Hobhouse, *Economica*, November 1924, in an alleged account of the views of the Cambridge School : " Each factor has its value determined by its marginal net product."

[2] *Theory of Social Economy*, Vol. 1, pp. 82, 83, 301.

[3] *Principles of Economics*, VI §7.

be conceived as inferior in quality. This misconception was exhibited notably by Mr. and Mrs. Sidney Webb when they identified the marginal labourer with an industrial invalid or pauper. They were duly chastised in a Marshallean footnote[1]; but if this reference of marginal is to be considered a misconception, it should be noticed that a similar reference is rife among disciples of the orthodox school when discussing land or mines. " Marginal land," writes H. D. Henderson, " will be land which yields a decent profit to a decent farmer, as well as a gross rent to the landowner, sufficient to compensate him for his capital outlay, but nothing further." Or,

TABLE XVIIA

GRAPHIC PRESENTATION OF DEMAND AND SUPPLY SCHEDULES

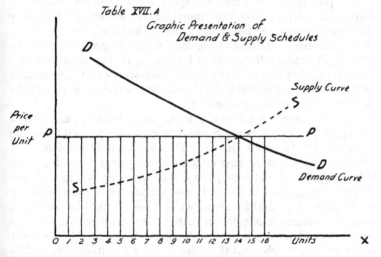

again, " we can speak of a marginal farm, which we should conceive as the least fertile and worst situated farm which it is just worth while to cultivate."[2]

Marginal is a useful adjective to the statistical economist (and is bound up with his interest in amounts exchanged as well as prices) when it refers to the result of a subtraction of measurable amounts from measurable amounts, at the margin. Thus the marginal return from 14 or r productive units is the total return from the 14 or r productive units minus the total return from 13 or $r-1$ productive

---

[1] Op. cit., VI, xiii §8.
[2] *Supply and Demand*, p. 60. See also pp. 54, 55 for the use of marginal applied to the mines.

U

units. And the marginal expenses of any number of units r produced is the total expenses of the r units produced, minus the total expenses of $r-1$ units produced. Returns and expenses can be calculated either in money or physical output ; but utility to the buyer and real costs to the seller or producer cannot be so calculated, and mention of marginal utility and marginal (real) cost will be eschewed for this reason, as well as for the apparent confusion in the orthodox use of marginal.

The principles subsumed in the presumption of the economic man, together with the Law of Diminishing Utility, form the chief connecting *links* in the step-by-step argument so common in economics and illustrated in Chapter XIV by the case of the theory of Joint Supply.

The principles are derived largely from common sense, i.e. individual introspection and individual observation,[1] but they might with advantage be subject to statistical tests. For instance, do farmers really cultivate more land with any given crop and to some degree *substitute* that crop for others, if they *anticipate* that the price of that crop will rise ? An interesting chart presented in the report of the Agricultural Tribunal[2] lends statistical support to these principles of the economic man.

" The causes which led to the decline in arable land, and also to the modifications of farming practice consequent on it, may be summed up in the word ' prices.' The chart shows the influence of prices on the wheat acreage of the following year, from the years 1868 to 1913. The highest price (1868) corresponds also with the highest acreage, and the lowest price (1894) corresponds with the lowest acreage, and although between these limits there are years when the correlation of price and acreage is not perfect there can be no question about it over the whole series of years. There cannot be the slightest doubt that the price of any agricultural commodity controls the quantity produced."

But anticipation of farmers and business men may not always be accurate and there is statistical evidence of certain tendencies toward inaccuracy in estimating interest.

" Suppose that the conditions of real demand and supply at the time the contract is made point to a 5 per cent real rate of interest for one year. If lenders and borrowers both expect prices to be unaltered at the end of the year, the contract will be made at the rate of 5 per cent. If both sides expect prices to have risen 10 per cent, it will be made at (approximately) 15 per cent. If one side expects prices to have risen 10 per cent, and the other expects them to have

---

[1] Chapter XIV, above.   [2] *Final Report*, Cmd. 2145, p. 305.

risen 5 per cent, it will be made at some rate intermediate between 10 per cent and 15 per cent, the exact rate depending on (1) which side expects the 10 per cent and which the 5 per cent rise, and (2) the elasticity of the demanders' demand for capital in relation to the elasticity of suppliers' supply of it. Correct foresight on both sides would necessarily lead to a money rate truly representing a 5 per cent real rate ; and incorrect foresight on both sides, provided that one erred by excess and the other by defect, *might* do this. In actual fact, however, experience shows that the joint judgment of the market almost always under-estimates future price changes, and does not make sufficient allowance for them. Thus, supposing 5 per cent to be the real rate of interest at which contracts aim, when prices are rising they will almost always hit a real rate of less than 5 per cent, and, when prices are falling, a real rate of more than 5 per cent. The evidence which Professor Irving Fisher has collected leaves no doubt that this is so."[1]

To sum up. The objective data defined, summarized, and correlated as prescribed in Chapter XVI must be interpreted with the aid of economic theory. Correlations cannot prove any causal relations, and such economic theory as has stood the test of time must often be appealed to for a possible explanation of the causal relationships underlying statistically found distributions, tendencies, and correlation tables. Thus statistics' fidelity to facts may be fused with the tried orientation of an economic theory that has gradually learned to think in terms of variables and curves, and to avoid many popular *non-sequiturs*, false comparisons, and spurious connections.

Economic theories are based implicitly on certain psychological principles and laws of substitution, anticipation, selection, diminishing utility, etc. But objective statistical economics must be explicit about these principles and laws, must recognize the occasions when argument rests upon them, and must, wherever possible, test their truth.

§2 Theory and Statistics of Demand and Supply

The opening proposition in economic theory is that when, at the price ruling, the amount demanded exceeds the amount supplied, the price tends to rise. Conversely, when supply exceeds demand, the price tends to fall. Ultimately price tends to that " *equilibrium* " price at which the amount demanded at that price is equal to the amount supplied at that price.[2]

[1] Pigou, *Industrial Fluctuations*, pp. 157–8.
[2] Henderson, *Supply and Demand*, Laws I and III.

This proposition is based entirely on the hypothesis of the economic man (discussed in §1), and the law of diminishing utility. Suppose demand for any exchangeable at some given price to be greater than its supply at that price. A " sufficient proportion " of sellers will presumably anticipate that they can charge a higher price without diminishing the amount sold, and without having supplies left on their hands, and will prefer a price higher than that " given." Hence with demand greater than supply prices will rise. Conversely, if the supply of any exchangeable at some given price is greater than its demand. The sellers will sooner or later " anticipate " supplies being left on their hands, and since they prefer some price rather than none, they will lower their price in the belief that, by the law of diminishing utility, a lower price will carry off a larger supply. Each individual economic man seeks to gain as much and to lose as little as he can by means of substitution, anticipation, and selection. In the terminology of Chapter XII these are the P (policies) to obtain his supposed O (or objective) of maximum net gain. Yet supply and demand are conceived as determining prices and value in exchange automatically. They are blind natural forces (" N ") having unintentional results (" R ") upon prices. For under the conditions of competition that are assumed, there is no one person or organized body of persons successfully controlling, for their particular net gain, either the prices or the total amount produced of any exchangeable article.

In attempting to interpret and explain the complexities of economic behaviour, we must take this opening law of supply and demand as a preliminary hypothesis, and range the possible causal factors of the price of any exchangeable, into those affecting demand, and those affecting supply.

The laws enunciated in text-books of Economic Principles do not seek to explain either variations in price over different times and places nor variations in the *amounts* exchanged, with the one exception of the law of comparative costs in international trade.[1]

---

[1] I mention all the chief propositional laws dealt with in *Principles of Economics* in one place or other of this work. For purposes of inspection they may be brought together here as (1) the law of diminishing utility (or demand), Chapter XVII §§1 and 3 ; (2) the laws of increasing return and decreasing (factorial) return, Chapter XVI §7 ; (3) the law or theory of population, Chapter XVI §7 ; (4) the law of equilibrium of demand and supply under competition, Chapter XVII §2 ; (5) the law of exchange value under competition in the long run, Chapter XVII §6 ; (6) the law of exchange value of articles in joint demand or joint supply, Chapter XIV §4 ; (7) the law of exchange value under monopoly, Chapter XVII §6 ; (8) the law or theory of rent, Chapter XVII §1 ; (9) the law or theory of distribution, i.e. of wages, interest, and profits, Chapter XVII §§2, 5 ; (10) the quantity theory of money, Chapter XVII §§3, 4; (11) the theory of comparative costs in international trade, Chapter

Economic laws in the sense of propositions are, according to the view already advanced, mainly attempts to explain and interpret the several types of difference and variation in price or payment per unit at one time and place that were listed in Chapter XVI §2. We now start out to explain these variations by correlating or associating them with differences and variations in (a) demand and (b) supply.

Economic propositions may therefore be cast in the form that variations (or differences) in the price of the same or similar things are due to variations (or differences) in their demand and in their supply. Specifically the *more* that is demanded or the *less* supplied the higher the price ; the less that is demanded or the more supplied the lower the price. This negative (inverse) correlation of supply and price is illustrated statistically in the *real* case of Indian corn in the U.S.A from 1866 to 1911 (see Table IXF), by comparing percentage changes in amount produced from one year to another with contemporary percentage changes in the price of corn.

" Prices," moreover, do not refer merely to the values or prices of goods or specific services offered for sale, but also to the exchange value of money, and to the " income " or " pay " of units of the factors of production.

The same formulation of the law of equilibrium is possible in this latter problem of *Distribution*. When, at the rate of wages, interest, profits, etc., ruling, the amount demanded exceeds the amount supplied, the rate tends to rise. Conversely, when supply exceeds demand, the rate tends to fall. Ultimately the pay (wages, interest, profit, etc.) of a unit of any factor of production tends toward the equilibrium rate of pay at the margin or borderline amount just exchanged, where (see §1 and diagram) the amount demanded at that rate is equal to the amount supplied at that rate. And this orthodox formulation may be similarly expressed in terms of a statistical contingency, correlation, or co-variation.

The more the demand for any class of labour, capital, enterprise, or land, and the less the supply of those " factors " the higher the wage, interest, profit, or rent. These rates of pay are positively correlated with or contingent upon the demand for, and negatively

XV §4 ; (12) the theory of purchasing power parities in the international exchanges, Chapter XVII §1.

All except possibly (11) and (3) deal with values or rates of exchange, whether of articles, factors of production, or (10) and (12) money.

Laws (4), (5), (6), (7), (10), and (12) deal with the value or rates in exchange of articles and money ; laws (8) and (9) deal with the value or rates in exchange of factors of production ; laws (1) and (2) deal with demand and return *per unit* produced for exchange.

correlated with or contingent upon the supply of, their respective factor of production.

But these propositions are merely the opening of the game and I have compared them with the chessman's gambit.[1] They might also be compared to a bottle-neck pass, that is a mere means of entering the fertile plain of economic thought.

To say that differences and variations in the value of goods, money, services, labour, capital, enterprise, and land are due to the fact that they vary with demand and supply is rather a hollow solution unless we know what is the supply and conditions of supply, and what is the demand and the conditions of demand for these different exchangeables. In short, the so-called law of demand and supply merely forwards our enquiry into specific channels, and these channels lead in many cases to statistically ascertainable facts.

The following diagram (Table XVIIʙ) appears to me to indicate roughly the directions in which statistical investigation would proceed under the auspices of economic theory, in order to explain and interpret the *values* (not amounts) in exchange, with which economic principles are chiefly concerned.

TABLE XVIIʙ

ANALYSIS OF FACTORS IN THE THEORY OF EXCHANGE VALUE

Differences or Variations in the Prices (or Values in Exchange) of similar or the same Articles are determined by their :

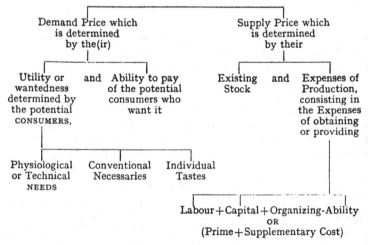

---

[1] *Economics and Human Behaviour*, p. 15.

§3 *The Measurable Conditions of Demand*

Demand refers to various amounts of an article for units of which persons are able and willing to offer specified amounts of other articles (usually a demand price in money) *in exchange.*

The notion of the Demand Schedule can be expressed as a correlation regression line or curve.[1] Each specific amount is taken to be conjoined at any one time with a specific demand price or vendibility at which units of it will be demanded ; and *the Law of Diminishing Utility* (which should properly be called the hypothesis of diminishing demand price or diminishing vendibility) can be stated in the form that the amount demanded and demand price are always negatively or *inversely* correlated, i.e. the greater the amount the less the demand price. If any given variation in price payable (e.g. doubling) tends to be associated with an exactly (inversely) proportionate variation in the amount demanded (e.g. halving) the demand is said to have an elasticity of unity. In this *datum line* case, the aggregate demand or " outlay " (price per unit × number of units) remains constant for all amounts of units demanded. If there is a variation in the amount (units) demanded more than proportionate to the variation in the price, and outlay (units × price) rises as price falls, then demand is said to be elastic or highly elastic. If there is a variation in the amount (units) demanded less than proportionate to the variation in the price, and outlay (units × price) falls as price falls, then demand is said to be inelastic.

These alternative conceptual boxes (see above, Chapter XVI §7) should be filled by means of statistical investigation.

One of the most thorough attempts to estimate statistically the specific demand for various amounts of an exchangeable at various prices, i.e. to give reality to such a curve as DD in the Table XVIIA, was made in England in the case of electricity. The method adopted is different from that ordinarily envisaged by theoretical treatises, in that the co-variation of price and amounts sold occurs over different local *areas*. The official committee on the *Supply of Electrical Energy* presents a chart to show the relation between the average price of electricity supplied to consumers by some 261 item-undertakings, and the number of electrical units sold by these undertakings per head of population in the area[2] they

---

[1] See Chapter IX §5.

[2] This division by the head of population in the area served eliminates the disturbing factor that any price being given, the greater the population of the area the more units will be sold, and helps to isolate the relation between units sold and price by *correction of index*. See Chapter X §3.

cover.   Table XVIIc presents the results as a statistical correlation table.

TABLE XVIIc

DEMAND SCHEDULE FOR ELECTRICITY : RELATIONSHIP OF PRICE AND AMOUNT OF ELECTRICITY DEMANDED[1]

Average Price Charged per Unit		Number of undertakings selling specified amounts of units (ranges of 50) per head of population in their area							
Range	Mid-point	0 to 50 units	50 to 100	100 to 150	150 to 200	200 to 250	250 to 300	Over 300	Total
6¼d. to 10d.		49							49
5¾d. to 6¼d.	6d.	9	3						12
5¼d. to 5¾d.	5½d.	12	1						13
4¾d. to 5¼d.	5d.	12	2						14
4¼d. to 4¾d.	4½d.	14	4						18
3¾d. to 4¼d.	4d.	10	6						16
3¼d. to 3¾d.	3½d.	16	12	3					31
2¾d. to 3¼d.	3d.	5	5	1					11
2¼d. to 2¾d.	2½d.	2	14	7					23
1¾d. to 2¼d.	2d.	–	14	16	4	1			35
1¼d. to 1¾d.	1½d.	–	2	13	8	7	1	1	32
¾d. to 1¼d.	1d.	–	–	–	1	1	3	2	7
All Ranges		129	63	40	13	9	4	3	261

Thus among the twelve undertakings selling their electricity at prices between 5¾d. and 6¼d. per unit, nine sell between 0 and 50 units only and three sell between 50 and 100 units per head of population in their area.   At the other end of the scale, seven undertakings sold their units at an average price of ¾d. to 1¼d. Of these one sold 150 to 200 units per head, another 200 to 250 units, three others 250 to 300, and yet two others over 300 units per head.

The " scatter " of items over the table is wide, but the committee felt justified in drawing a definite regression curve to summarize the co-variation of price and units sold, from which the deviations of the items are not unreasonable.   This curve shows the number of units sold per head as rising consistently as price per unit falls. In the words of the Report :

" Where the average price is 8d. to 10d. the number of units sold per head of population is 20.   At an average price of 4d. the number of units has risen to 50.   At 2d. the units sold are 140 ; and there-after the number rises rapidly with each decrease of price."

The formal demand schedule which such a regression line repre-sents is worth stating in full.   At a price of 6d. the units sold per

[1] Report of Committee on *the Supply of Electrical Energy*, 1926.

head are 29 ; at 5½d. the units sold are 31 ; at 5d. the units sold are about 35 ; at 4½d. about 40 ; at 4d. about 50 ; at 3½d. about 60 ; at 3d. about 70 ; at 2½d. about 90 ; at 2d. about 140 ; at 1½d. about 220 ; at 1d. about 600.

At the higher prices the demand appears to have an elasticity roughly of unity. A fall of ⅙th in price from 6d. to 5d. is associated with a proportionate rise of roughly a sixth in the demand, from 29 to 35 units per head. At lower prices, however, the demand has an elasticity of more than unity. A fall of price from 3d. to 2d. is associated with a doubling in the units sold, from 70 to 140 a head ; and a halving of the price from 2d. to 1d. is associated with more than a fourfold increase in units sold, from 140 to 600.

Other attempts to measure the demand curve statistically have been made in connection with estimates of the effects of indirect taxation, customs, excise, etc., in restricting the consumption of taxed articles such as spirits, cigars, etc.[1] The demand for a taxed article may have an elasticity so much more than unity that a rise in the rate of tax, and consequently the price, will check demand and consumption heavily enough to reduce the total revenue from the tax. Other very practical applications of statistics in estimating the demand curve occur in modern sales' management, particularly in marketing and advertising policy. Statistics of past performance are compared with statistics of possible performance in the matter of consumption of the goods to be sold in various areas or classes of the community. The limit to possible performance is the satiation or saturation point where no further reduction in price will increase sales. The questions for investigation include: " How big is your total possible market ? What proportion have you already secured ? What extent of trade distribution (e.g. distribution to retailers) have you secured ? How do your competitors' sales compare with your own ? Who uses and can be made to use your produce ? " The statistical answers to these questions are obtained from published documents, official or otherwise, or else by house-to-house or shop-to-shop visitations, and many advertising agencies, such as the Walter Thompson Company of New York or Pritchard Partners[2] in England, will make " market investigations " in which samples of possible customers are selected if possible *at random* (Chapter X §4) and their wants and wealth scrutinized.

---

[1] See K. M. Williamson, "The Effects of Varying the Tax on Spirits," *J.A.S.A.*, December 1920.

[2] See Walter Thompson Co., *Population and Distribution*, and the exhibits of Pritchard Partners at the Olympia Exhibition, London 1927.

Marshall has rendered great service to the *rapprochement* of statistics and economic theory by forcefully pointing out the difficulties in ascertaining how prices vary with variations in amount on sale, apart from other variations.[1] Changes in amount can be observed only at different places or at different times over a period. During any period there may be changes (i) in the purchasing power of money units, (ii) in the general prosperity and total means of purchasing at the disposal of the community, (iii) in the gradual growth of population and wealth, (iv) in fashion, taste, and habit. These changes are aggravated in the case of durable exchangeables like furniture and clothing where purchase is made for consumption over protracted periods and where replacement can be postponed. Nevertheless Marshall shows that some at least of these difficulties are not insurmountable. Correction can be made for change (i) through index numbers (cf. Chapter X §§2 and 3). The importance of change (ii) is less, he thinks, than is generally supposed, and allowance is made for it by " comparing the prices and the consumption of as many things as possible." For change (iii) " an easy numerical correction can be made when the facts are known." Change (iv) is more difficult to control but could probably be avoided by selecting staple articles.

" Though the theory of demand is yet in its infancy, we can already see that it may be possible to collect and arrange statistics of consumption in such a way as to throw light on difficult questions of great importance to public well-being."[2] But Marshall was perhaps a little premature in telling us in the first book of his Principles[3] that " by the aid of statistics or in other ways, they (economists) ascertain how much money on the average the members of the particular group they are watching are just willing to pay as the price of a certain thing which they desire."

Following Table XVIIB, demand for any exchangeable depends upon (*a*) the *utility* of the exchangeable,—that is, the degree to which it is wanted, and (*b*) the *means* of purchasing the exchangeable at the disposal of those who want it. The so-called Law of Diminishing Utility is probably true in fact less because of (*a*) the gradual psycho-physiological satiation of individual wants, than because of (*b*) the statistically measurable unequal distribution of wealth of the type shown in Table VIc.

The following characteristics in the consumption of exchangeables are plausibly suggested by theory as causal factors (NN)[4] of the

---

[1] *Principles of Economics*, Book III, iv, 6.
[2] Op. cit., III, i §2.   [3] Op. cit., I, ii §7.
[4] See Chapter XII §5 for reference of Symbols.

elasticity of demand. Many of these characteristics can be formulated as statistical correlations.

(N I) Any exchangeable in joint demand with others, like tyres with motor-car parts, the consumption of which is positively correlated with the consumption of other articles in certain proportions, has an inelastic demand. Physiological, technical, or conventional *necessities* are simply special cases of this generalization. Food, housing, and clothing are in joint demand and all of them derived from the " want to live." *Within each income-class* they tend to be consumed in the same proportion by all families.

From budget studies of the Belgian Statistical Commission in 1852 and 1854, Ernst Engel formulated four laws of consumption. The first two of those empirical laws were that the poorer a family (1) the more they spend on food proportionately to other forms of consumption and (2) the less on education, recreation, luxuries, etc. The third and fourth laws are that approximately the same proportion is spent on clothing, and on rent, fuel, and light. While Engel's first and second laws have been substantiated by more recent statistics, it would seem as though the proportionate expenditure on fuel and light was (like that on food) higher among the poorer families while clothing, like recreation, was lower.

Little statistical investigation has been made among the bourgeois, but what results have appeared in the United States show that rent and payment for housing formed a higher proportion of expenditure among the richer classes. The proportion spent on clothing follows a more complicated law of co-variation. It appears to rise, " to co-vary positively," with rising incomes, up to a point, but then as incomes rise further to fall, to " co-vary " negatively. Apparently a point of satiation is reached in middle-class incomes, where more clothes proportionately to income cannot be " piled on."[1] But however the proportions vary as between classes, *within the class they are more or less fixed* and of low deviation. In England before the war, for instance, item working-class families agreed closely in spending 60% of their total expenditure on food, 12% on clothing, 16% on house rents, 8% on fuel and light, and 4% on " sundries."

(N II) Any exchangeable in composite supply with another as an alternative, whose consumption is inversely correlated with that of the others, like tea with coffee, is likely to have a highly elastic demand. If price rises even a little the alternate is likely to be demanded instead. Such a substitution of one alternative for another and the consequent elasticity of demand for either, can be

[1] For statistical findings see Edie, *Economics*, Chapter VI.

shown statistically in workmen's budgets in the case of butter and margarine, and occurs whenever a highly advertised article is put on the market to fight an unadvertised or only *slightly advertised* rival.

The demand for *money* and for factors of production is treated by economic theory in precisely the same manner as the demand for any other sort of exchangeable, though the demand may arise from very different circumstances.

The demand for money differs from the demand for goods and services, or the demand for factors of production, in that it cannot usefully be expressed in terms of money, i.e. in terms of itself. Instead of x units of goods, services, or factors having a demand price of y £, s., or d., we must now deal in terms of pounds, shillings, or pence having not a demand price but a (real) *demand value* of so many goods, services, and/or factors. In this unfamiliar atmosphere we must be doubly careful not to confuse (*a*) the total aggregate demand for money, i.e. the *outlay* of goods, etc., for money, and (*b*) the demand for *units* of money, that is, the (real) exchange *rate*, or purchases offered for *one* unit.

The basis of the demand for money is the need or want on the part of buyers for a medium of exchange that will be accepted at sight by the seller of any good, service, or factor of production. The immediate ownership of this medium, however, brings in no income. If money is in the owner's pocket or even on current (" checking ") account at his bank he gets no interest ; hence the demand for money is not without limits. An economic man will, in fact, keep as small a proportion of his resources in this liquid but unremunerative form as he can, and the aggregate demand for money will tend to be some definite fixed proportion of his total resources in goods, services, and/or factors of production.

If these total resources are constant, the aggregate demand or outlay for money in terms of resources remains constant whatever the number of *units* of money there are. This implies that the more units of money there are to " add up " to this constant aggregate demand, the less proportionately will be the demand for each unit, which is only another way of saying that the demand for *units* of money has an elasticity of unity (as defined above, page 295), and that as the amounts of units of money vary, so proportionately will the real exchange-rate of each unit vary, *inversely*. Doubling of the quantity of units of money will halve the real value or " purchasing power " of each of them. The purchasing power of a unit of money thus depends chiefly on the supply of units of money, and the statistical verification of this all-important quantity theory of money will therefore be taken up (§4) in connection with the supply side.

As the demand for units of money is derived from their measurable work of exchanging, so the demand for units of any *factor of production* is derived from the measurable amount of production associated with that unit. " The chief *demand* for capital arises from its productiveness, from the services which it renders." " Wages tend to equal the net product of labour ; its marginal productivity rules the demand price for it."[1]

In general, the demand for (i.e. the rate of pay that is offered for) one unit among a number of similar units of labour or any other factor of production, is determined by the difference its addition to or subtraction from employment would make to the (discounted) value of the total production of all the number. If the number of units employed is r, the " marginal " productivity (or value of production) of any one unit can be measured objectively as the total (value of) production of r units minus the total (value of) production of $r-1$ units.[2]

It is doubtful whether it can ever be proved by mass statistics that the pay offered to any factor of production is always *equal* to the marginal productivity of that factor. Precise equality could only be demonstrated by intensive investigation, or by a virtual experiment in a carefully selected or controlled situation (see Chapter XIII §4) where the value added by the employment of additional units is ascertainable. This would not be possible, say, in the case of labour in a large factory where goods pass from hand to hand without any exchange and pricing as they pass ; and if only a small workshop were selected, providing one specific service, e.g. repairing of shoes, it might be difficult to prove that such a firm was representative of the industry as a whole.

In short, the causes underlying the demand for factors of production can be discovered only by a judicious fusion of statistical measurement, that approaches, though it may not exactly hit the point, with relevant theoretical orientation and interpretation.

Increased *value of* production associated with higher, or decreased value of production associated with lower rates of interest, wages, and profit, can be shown statistically in the correlation of fluctua-

[1] Marshall, *Principles of Economics*, VI, ii §3.
[2] See above, §1. The marginal wage-earner as conceived by the theoretical economist is the man just, or just not, employed. He is not the last man among the unemployed who might be employed in the given trade or occupation. Departure from this terminological convention (see e.g. Rowe, *Wages in Practice and Theory*, Chapter XII) is likely to lead to misapplication of statistical data to the theoretical position.

tions in these characters over time,—i.e. in their synchronous or lagged co-variation. The co-variation of the prices of coal and of coal *profits* found by Sir Josiah Stamp has already been mentioned. Professor H. L. Moore, investigating data extending from 1847 to 1897, finds that in the case of " the great industry of coal-mining in France : (1) the fluctuation in the mean daily rate of wages varies directly with the fluctuation in the mean value of the product of the labourer ; (2) the coefficient measuring the degree of association between the percentage variation in the rate of wages and the percentage variation in the mean value of the daily product per labourer has the very high value of $r = \cdot 843$." This Professor Moore cites as " a first approximation to the theoretical principle that the rate of wages varies directly with the marginal productivity of labour,"[1] and he takes care to eliminate the secular trend. Without this precaution the correlation over such a long period might be spurious ; variations both in wages and value of output might of course be due to variations in the value of money.

These statistical correlations do not of course settle whether increased value of production *causes* increases in the payments of factors of production or vice versa. But the theory of distribution maintains that if this co-variation of value of product and pay of a factor of production does not take place, then, as a result (assuming the conditions of supply to remain constant), the same number of units of that factor of production will not be employed. An increase of pay of any factor relatively to or " per " value of product, e.g. pay rising, value of product constant, will cause a less amount of the factor to be employed, *how much less* depending upon the elasticity of the demand, just as a rise in price per unit of goods or services will cause less of it to be bought. And the elasticity of demand for factors of production will be affected by the same considerations as to whether it is in joint demand or composite supply. By definition factors of production are in joint demand for production, and hence each tends to have an inelastic demand. But in so far as factors are in composite supply and can be substituted one for another, as machinery (and capital) or scientific management (organizing ability) for labour, factors tend to have an elastic demand.

In the case of the factor labour, Benham[2] has brought this theory to the statistical test by comparing the average money wages, the average money value of production, and the percentage of un-employed in Queensland for successive years 1916 to 1924. " It

---

[1] *Laws of Wages*, Chapter III.
[2] *The Prosperity of Australia*, pp. 209–13.

would be hard to find a clearer proof of our thesis. From 1916 to 1921 the rate of wages was continuously increasing *relatively to the value produced per worker*, and consequently unemployment was continuously increasing also. In 1922 the value produced per worker was little higher than in the previous year but the percentage of unemployment fell from 15·5 to 10·0. What relieved the situation was *not* more favourable seasons or other causes beyond human control, but a lowering of average wages by about 3 per cent. In 1923 and 1924 the value produced per worker continued to increase relatively to average wages per worker and the percentage of unemployment continued to decline."

Where the value of production and its variation is not ascertainable, economists may link up statistics and theory by showing an increase in the percentage of unemployment among " would-be wage earners " associated with a rise in real wages or vice versa, productivity being assumed, or roughly estimated, as constant. Professor Pigou,[1] improving on Professor Rueff, calculates a real wage index number for England, by dividing the index number of money wages by the Ministry of Labour cost of living index, and finds the "consilience" of this curve with that of unemployment to be extremely close. The more real wages fall or rise the more the unemployment percentage falls or rises. The number of workers demanded and their price appear to be negatively correlated.

These statistics only show the elasticity of the demand for labour, or the variation of the amount of labour demanded with variation in labour's price or wage for any specified productivity of labour. It does not follow that unemployment will " co-vary " if there are other concomitant changes such as a fall in the number of would-be wage earners either through a fall in the past birth rate or transference to other industries. Whatever mal-distribution there may be between industries is, when discussing the demand side, taken as given.[2]

§4 *The Measurable Conditions of Supply*

Going over to the Supply side and combining conditions therewith with conditions on the Demand side, the propositions of Economics that set forth the causal relationships depend upon the period or length of run involved.

[1] *Ec. Jl.*, September 1927.
[2] See Prof. H. Clay's reply to Prof. Pigou, *Ec. Jl.*, March 1928.

"Four classes stand out. In each, price is governed by the relations between demand and supply. As regards market prices, Supply is taken to mean the stock of the commodity in question which is on hand or at all events ' in sight.' As regards *normal* prices, when the term Normal is taken to relate to short periods of a few months or a year, Supply means broadly what can be produced for the price in question with the existing stock of plant, personal and impersonal, in the given time. As regards normal prices when the term Normal is to refer to long periods of several years, Supply means what can be produced by plant, which itself can be remuneratively produced and applied within the given time ; while lastly, there are very gradual or Secular movements of normal price, caused by the gradual growth of knowledge, of population and of capital, and the changing conditions of demand and supply from one generation to another."[1]

These four classes are not distinguished by any hard-and-fast limits of time. Short periods, for instance, might consist, as Marshall suggests, of a few months or of a year, and I shall refer to " runs " instead of, or in addition to, " periods " (i.e. short-*run* and long-*run* conditions) to make this indefiniteness plain. The statisticians' distinction already mentioned between casual, seasonal, cyclical, and secular periods of business fluctuation *cannot* be taken, except perhaps in the case of secular periods, as in any way displacing the period or " runs " of economic theory.

Secular movements are admittedly beyond the pale of isolated " pure " economic theory. They can only be studied by the so-called dynamic economics that brings statistical methods to its aid. The secular growth of population, and growth of capital are commonplaces of statistical enquiry since the institution of official Censuses of Population or Production, or such private estimates as those of Giffen.[2] As to the " changing conditions of demand and supply from one generation to another," that again is a matter for statistical enquiries of the type described in Chapter XVI §6 and lies beyond the unaided powers of economic theory. Theory confines itself, therefore, to the three shorter periods or " runs " as three alternative cases (M A, M B, or M C).[3]

The price or exchange value of any exchangeable and the amount of it exchanged depends

(M A :) In temporary equilibrium,

---

[1] Marshall, *Principles of Economics*, V, v §8.
[2] Ibid., IV, vii, §11, note on the Statistics of the growth of Wealth.
[3] Cf. Chapter XII for choice of these symbols.

upon (N I) its demand and (N II) the available stocks on the market.

(M B :) In the normal short period,
upon (N I) its demand, and (N II) the cost of supplying it from the available means of production.

(M C :) In the normal long period,
upon (N I) its demand, and (N II) the expense of production when the means of production have been appropriately adjusted.

(A) In *temporary equilibrium* the causes underlying the price of any exchangeable on the supply side are the existing stocks of that exchangeable, and these are often measurable and measured.

The London-Cambridge Economic Service, for instance, estimate, usually month by month, the stocks existing throughout the world of such staple commodities as cotton, copper, tin, lead, spelter, rubber, sugar, tea, coffee, petroleum, nitrate, and wheat in standard units of tons, lbs., bales, bags, barrels, quarters.

Or again, the U.S. Federal Reserve Bulletin gives the stocks existing at specific times of such agricultural commodities as corn (maize), cotton seed, cheese, apples, butter, frozen poultry, beef, pork, lard, eggs, tobacco ; or such industrial commodities as coal, gasolene, timber of various sorts, bricks, cotton goods and fabrics, raw wool, raw silk, hosiery, knit underwear, leather, rubber tyres and tubes, wood pulp, paper, etc.

When time is so short that no supplies additional to the stock on the market can be secured, the statistical calculation of the amount of those stocks is clearly of dominating interest. To say that in this temporary period " the price is governed by demand " can only be excused if the stock is taken for granted. In a fish market, as Marshall points out, " the value of fish for the day is governed almost exclusively by the stock on the slabs in relation to the demand." To discuss the price of fish observed on the actual day, abstractly leaving the actual supply out of account, is as fatuous as to leave the cost of production out of account in discussion of a long-run price. " We might as reasonably dispute whether it is the upper or the nether blade of a pair of scissors that cuts a piece of paper, as whether value is governed by utility or cost of production. It is true that when one blade is held still, and the cutting is effected by moving the other, we may say with careless brevity that the cutting is done by the second ; but the statement is not strictly accurate, and is to be excused only so long as it claims to be merely a popular and not a strictly scientific account of what happens."[1]

[1] Marshall, *Principles of Economics*, V, iii §7.

x

In the case of money and circulating media generally where the elasticity of demand tends, as we have seen, to be unity, the supply of units is all-important in determining the exchange value per unit. To measure the supply of money is not, however, a simple matter. Money is not like food or fuel, goods that are immediately consumed, nor yet, though durable, does it, like clothes, pianos, etc., remain more or less permanently in possession of its owner. It *circulates* from one person to another in exchange for the goods, services, and factors of production they buy or sell, and the velocity with which it circulates varies from time to time and from situation to situation. The supply of money available in any community over a given period, is thus the product of the total stock of money and its velocity of circulation over that period. If M be this stock and V its velocity of circulation, the quantity theory of money, as formulated by Irving Fisher (among many other economists' formulations)[1] is that the value (i.e. purchasing power) of a unit of money is equal to T (the transactions that " demand " money over a given period) divided by M V, the supply of money in the course of the same period.

The quantity theory of money has been subjected to statistical test more thoroughly perhaps than any other of the doctrines of classical economics, and in his *Scope and Method* Dr. Keynes singles out " the extent of the evils resulting from bad currency regulations " as obviously suitable for inductive study.

A much-discussed attempt at statistical verification of the quantity theory as applied to the U.S.A. from 1896 to 1909 is undertaken in Irving Fisher's *Purchasing Power of Money*.[2] The stock of circulating media (or money in Robertson's wide sense) is taken to consist of " M " *common* money, metallic or paper and " M[1] " bank deposits. Fisher measures M as the total amount of money (coin and paper) outside the " hoard " of the federal treasury and outside the " reserve " of the banks of deposit and discount. He measures M[1] as those individual bank deposits that are subject to cheque. Fisher then derives V[1] by dividing M[1] (already found) into M[1]V[1], the total value of cheques drawn, as calculated by Professor Kemmerer. The calculation of V is more difficult since money withdrawn from banks, unlike cheques, may circulate more than once. But Fisher shows that (1) in actual fact much money circulates out of banks only once ; (2) that when money is paid for wages it

---

[1] E.g. Keynes, *Monetary Reform*, Chapter III §1. Pigou, *Essays in Applied Economics*, XVI. Lavington, *Capital Market*, Chapter V.

[2] Chapters XI and XII are devoted to Statistical Verification, and the Appendix to Chapter XII, pp. 430–93, gives full details of the statistical methods of calculation.

usually circulates twice; and (3) that only rarely does it circulate three or more times before completing its circuit back to the banks.

Hence banking statistics, once the proportion paid for wages is estimated, can be used to calculate V as they were used to calculate V^1. M, already known, is divided into MV, the "amount of exchanges effected" which can be calculated as equal to the total money deposited in banks, plus the total money wages paid, plus a small miscellaneous item.

Changes in *demand* for money due to changes in transactions, Fisher also calculated statistically by reference to the physical volume of trade in various lines. Fisher's figures are based on data for 44 articles of internal commerce, 23 articles of import and 25 of export, sales of stocks, railroad freight carried, and letters sent through the post.

Finally, the value or purchasing power of money itself is the inverse of the statistically measurable general index number of prices. If the value of money$=\dfrac{T}{MV+M^1V^1}$, it follows that P, the prices index,$=\dfrac{MV+M^1V^1}{T}$. All the terms of this equation are statistically measurable, and the quantity theory is thus amenable of quantitative proof. Fisher compares each year's P as a ratio to the *preceding* year's P, and each year's $\dfrac{MV+M^1V^1}{T}$ also as a ratio to the *preceding* year's, and then compares these comparative ratios. He finds that for each year from 1897 to 1909 in the U.S.A. the ratios tend to rise and fall together, to "co-vary positively," the coefficient of correlation being ·57.

Mitchell, discussing this method,[1] warns us that neither the theory nor the correlation proves that variations in $\dfrac{MV+M^1V^1}{T}$ *cause* variations in P. In certain phases of the business cycle, P (with T) may be the "active" not the passive factor. Furthermore, since ' of the payments $(MV+M^1V^1)$ made to-day, the bulk are payments for goods transferred (T) some time ago, at prices (P) most of which were agreed upon still earlier"; . . . "the payments made on a *given day* are most unlikely to equal the prices then current times the transfers then in process. But the equation of exchange $PT=MV+M^1V^1$ or $P=\dfrac{MV+M^1V^1}{T}$) is substantially valid for periods such as a year or more."

[1] *Business Cycles*, pp. 128–39.

(B) *In the normal short period* the economist's focus shifts from the stocks of the exchangeables actually existing to the possibility of producing more units of the exchangeable from the existing factors of production. Here the notion of elasticity of supply is relevant and parallel to that of the elasticity of demand. The elasticity of the supply of a product is the proportion to which total supply from any given fixed stock of factors of production will be increased (or decreased) in response to the stimulus (or check) of a price increased (or decreased) in any given proportion.

And similarly to the case of demand, there are certain characteristics in the consumption and production of any exchangeable, that theory plausibly suggests as causal factors (N N)[1] in its elasticity of supply. These characters can be formulated and measured as statistical correlations.

(N I) Any exchangeable in joint supply with another or others (like straw with wheat), the production of the two or more being positively correlated, tends to have an inelastic supply.

(N II) Where any exchangeable is in composite demand for several uses like leather used for shoes or saddlery, the consumption of one use of which (e.g. shoes) is negatively correlated with the other use or uses (e.g. saddles), there the elasticity of supply of any one use is likely to be high. A given rise in the stimulus of price, e.g. for saddles, is likely to transfer leather away from shoes in large quantities. In considering industries making articles for widely different markets (as shoes and saddles), but using the same raw materials (which may be limited by nature), this transference and new distribution of resources is of great practical significance.

It is important to realize that the supply whose elasticity is measured, and which, jointly with demand, determines prices, still consists partly in the existing stocks held by dealers and ready for exchange. In the case of *durable* articles, the existing stock may indeed be considerably greater than even a year's production, and the elasticity of supply low in consequence. This is probably true of most industrial metals and even of houses ; i.e. a year's production of houses may be less than the number of houses offered for sale and in the estate agent's hands at any one time within the year. Hence statistics of existing stocks, and the velocity of their circulation, remain important for many articles even in the short normal period.

This predominance of dealers' stocks over annual production is undoubtedly true of gold. The metal is of great durability.

Professor Cassel calculates that during the years 1850 to 1910 there was a loss of only 0·2% of the stock each year ; and more than

---

[1] See above §3, p. 299.

half the stocks of gold in the world are held by bankers and government treasuries as a basis for internal monetary circulation and circulation in foreign exchange. Lehfeldt estimates the stock of gold " available for money " in 1921 as £2,060,000,000, of which (in 1923) £1,877,000,000 was known to be in banks and national treasuries, and an additional small amount in active circulation. The total production of gold for all uses, for arts and hoards as well as money, he calculates as £75,000,000 per annum at the present time (1926). Thus, even if all the new annual production were added to that part of the stocks of gold that is known to be held for monetary purposes only, it would increase that stock by some fraction approximating to $\frac{75}{1877}$, i.e. 4%.[1]

Existing stocks usually statistically measurable remain, as we have said, exceedingly important even in the short *normal* period. However, a marginal heading and paragraph from Marshall's *Principles*[2] may turn our attention to the new circumstances introduced in the short normal run,—namely, the possibility of adding to the existing stock by new production from existing appliances of production.

" *For* (normal) *short periods the stock of appliances of production are practically fixed but their employment varies with demand.* The immediate effect of the expectation of a high price is to cause people to bring into active work all their appliances of production and to work them full time and perhaps overtime. The supply price is then the money cost of production of that part of the produce which forces the undertaker to hire such inefficient labour (perhaps tired by working overtime) at so high a price, and to put himself and others to so much strain and inconvenience that he is on the margin of doubt whether it is worth his while to do it or not."

This paragraph presents clearly the theoretical interpretation of the *modus operandi* whereby supply can be increased in the short normal run. Labourers, entrepreneurs, and capital equipment or land already employed can work or be worked harder and longer, labourers and entrepreneur, capital and equipment and land unemployed can be brought into employment, and to some extent labourers, entrepreneurs, land, and equipment can be transferred from other industries.

[1] These calculations must be read in their context of a gold standard then (1920–22) existing in the U.S.A., and an ideal of a gold standard hoped for as an eventual policy in and by other countries. For the gold situation previous to the war, see Cassel's *Theory of Social Economy*, Book III. Cassel calculates that the new supplies of gold produced annually were some 3% of the gold stock used.
[2] *Principles of Economics*, V, v §6.

If labourers, entrepreneurs, capital equipment, or land were originally working below full capacity, returns to successive doses of them may at first be increasing or at least constant. But after an optimum point in working given factors of production, decreasing returns will result, if the other factors or some of the other factors are not also increased by successive doses.

In the case of all four factors, labour, the entrepreneur, land, and capital equipment, one theoretical explanation or interpretation of decreasing returns to successive doses of any one of them, will lie in the forced selection of less naturally efficient hands, brains, soils and sites, and tools.

In such a sudden short-period increase in demand like that for munitions of war in 1914–18, the existing distribution of ability, and persons of working age generally, among the population was clearly paramount to the possibility of creating a new generation of workers. Existing man-power was statistically registered and docketed, and recourse had, even for the heaviest of jobs, to available women, youths, and old men. The lower grades of intelligence, denoted as subnormal in Table VIA above, were also probably more fully exploited.

The census of the existing resources in human ability given in statistics of the population of working ages, is paralleled by the necessity of taking stock in the short period of existing resources in material equipment and plant. Statistics are available of a country's wealth in general,[1] and statistics are often issued of a specific industry's productive capacity, which may be more, or less, fully utilized. The capacity of British steel works has, for instance, been calculated as eight millions of tons of steel in 1913, twelve millions of tons in 1923. The actual production, however, while something like 7·7 millions in 1913 was only about 8·5 millions, i.e. 70% of capacity, in 1923.[2]

In the case of two factors of production, labour and the entrepreneur, a second, additional, explanation of decreasing returns in the short period will lie in the industrial fatigue to which harder and longer work subjects the human organism. The incidence of this limiting " check " has been observed and tested by statistical methods with a fair degree of success,[3] once the fieldwork difficulties described above (Chapters X and XI) are overcome.

Finally, in the case of one factor, labour, a further (third) check

[1] See, for instance, Carr-Saunders and Jones, *Social Structure of England and Wales*, Chapter X ; and, for the U.S.A., Mitchell, *Business Cycles*, Chapter II, ii 4.

[2] Layton and others, *Is Unemployment Inevitable?* pp. 14 and 256.

[3] See Florence, *Economics of Fatigue and Unrest*, esp. Chapter VIII.

becomes obvious in sheer overcrowding, getting into one another's way, bad ventilation and so on.

When labour is the variable factor, therefore, three types of theoretical explanation may be advanced to account for inelastic supply and diminishing (factorial) return :

(1) wide deviations in the distribution of ability as shown in Table VIA,

(2) correlation of falling productivity with longer hours,

(3) lower productivity with less space per man.

And these explanations are all susceptible of statistical testing.

(C) *In the normal long-run* period the causes underlying the price of any exchangeable depends chiefly, on the supply side, not upon the existing plant but upon the cost or expenses of production when the plant and other means of production have had time to adjust themselves to demand. But this " time of adjustment " obviously varies for the production of different exchangeables. " There is no hard and sharp line of division between ' long ' and ' short ' periods. Nature has drawn no such lines in the economic conditions of actual life," wrote Marshall,[1] and "the periods required to adapt the several factors of production to the demand may be very different." But the theoretical economist has been content as a rule to leave the matter in a conceptual condition, without attempting to find the " long-run period " for any particular commodity except to point out that land can never, by definition, be adjusted or adapted. The theoretical explanation of diminishing returns in the short period to any factor of production, that lay in the forced selection of less capable units, remains true of land (though not the other factors) in the *long* period.

Different acres of land differ widely and *measurably* in fertility and site value. Land of high fertility and convenient site has in statistical language a limited frequency, or is, plainly speaking, *scarce*. These properties are by definition of land indestructible and original. They cannot be diminished or added to, i.e. they are perfectly inadjustable even in the longest periods. Where land is required as a factor of production and forms a substantial part of the expenses of production, increased output and accessibility can only be obtained either by intensive cultivation and road, railway, or ship building, that is, by applying more capital and labour to or near the same land, plausibly bringing on diminishing (factorial) returns from the land factor ; or by extensive cultivation, that is, by having recourse to lands of inferior fertility and accessibility.

[1] *Principles of Economics,* V, v §8.

In either case average or marginal expenses are increased, and the prices of exchangeables requiring land as a factor of production must, in the long run, rise to cover this additional expense in the cost of production.

Various attempts have been made to verify this theoretical hypothesis of diminishing return in the long-run period by reference to statistics, though hitherto without much success. One product of the land only is usually selected, namely, wheat ; but any potential rise in the cost of production of wheat over time, due to growing scarcity of fertile and accessible land, is usually counteracted by progress in the use of machinery. Other foodstuff products being less uniform in their growth are not so amenable to the application of new mechanical inventions, and therefore a composite price index number of *several* food products eliminates disturbing factors more successfully. Furthermore, since England subsists largely on food imported from a distance, English prices of foodstuffs are heavily influenced by the secular trend of progress in the application of invention to *transport* facilities. Hence, the selection of a composite index of American food and raw material prices is likely to leave " other things equal " most successfully of all.

Table XVIID shows that prices of food and raw materials rose considerably more between 1890 and 1916 (from 52·4 to 100) than the prices of the articles manufactured *out of these identical raw materials*. If there is increasing return in the production of raw materials, these statistics of price changes certainly suggest a *less* increasing return in the production of raw materials than of corresponding manufactured articles, and possibly open up a fruitful line of research into the effects of comparative inadjustability of land and natural resources.

TABLE XVIID

WHOLESALE PRICE INDICES (1916 = 100 IN U.S.A.) OF IDENTICAL COMMODITIES IN RAW AND MANUFACTURED STATE[1]

	Raw state (average of prices of 27 articles)	Manufactured state (average of prices of 71 articles)
1890–94	52·4	63·6
1895–99	48·8	56·6
1900–04	60·4	65·2
1905–09	67·4	71·0
1910–14	76·6	76·0
1916	100	100

[1] Based on *Bulletin* 226, *U.S. Dept. of Labour*, Table 7.

§5 *The Adjustability or Scarcity of Supply*

Land and natural resources, as Marshall remarks in connection with rents from land, are simply a species of a large genus, and instruments of production might be ranked in order of inadjustability, putting land at the top with an adjustability of O.

The supply of labourers in so far as it depends on births would come a good second, as hardly less inadjustable and less responsive to prices than the supply of land. Hence, the possibility of over-population, both food-growing land and food-needing persons being liable to get " out of harmony " until restored by famine death rates.

This raises the question whether the permanent scarcity of capable units (and their diminishing return if overcrowded or exploited), which is the leading feature of land, is not true also of some of the other factors of production, and whether the principle of scarcity is not the dominating fact of economic life.

Scarcity has always exercised economists, and the principle of scarcity has recently been proclaimed the dominating determinant of economic life by Professor Cassel. I am not aware, however, that any economist has yet troubled to look up the dictionary (even the " Concise " Oxford Dictionary will do) and to remark that the adjective is assigned two senses, one corresponding to the noun scarcity, the other said to correspond with the noun scarceness.

Scarce : Insufficient for the demand or need, not plentiful, scanty (usu. pred., and of food, money, or other necessaries of life) ; whence *scarcity* n (*of*, or abs. =dearth of food) ; seldom met with, rare, hard to find, (a s. book, moth ; make oneself s. colloq. retire, make off, keep out of the way), whence scarceness n.

Now scarce*ness* is a physical property that can be measured statistically. There are exactly so many copies of a scarce book or specimens of a scarce moth, but scarcity in the sense of supply insufficient for the demand is coterminous with economics' almost universal (see Chapter XVII §2) bottle-neck approach to its problems. I strongly suspect that when Professor Cassel speaks so blithely of the principle of scarcity he is making the best of both senses. He gets credit for explaining the difficulties of economics in terms of the simpler conception, and at the same time he is not wrong because he sometimes qualifies scarcity as scarcity relatively to wants,[1] and

---

[1] " We give the name ' economic ' only to those activities which are conducted under the condition that the possible satisfaction of wants is limited. As the means of satisfying wants are usually available only in a limited quantity, whereas the wants of civilized human beings as a whole are unlimited, the means are usually *scarce* relatively to the wants. It is only means of this

this is identical with the orthodox introduction to economic reasoning.

The more easily measured fact that statistical economics must start with is scarce-ness, the actual existing number or amounts of units of factors or production available and suppliable whether demanded much, little, or not at all. This scarce-ness is identical with statistical frequency and can be measured accordingly. In the short run, it has been argued (XVII §4), the *existing* units of factors of production are all-important and can be measured statistically through censuses of occupation, production, and wealth, inventories of stock, etc. In the short run more production can only be obtained by working these existing factors harder, while less production entails under-employing these existing factors or leaving them unemployed. But in the long run it is supposed that varying amounts of production, as required, can be secured by increasing or decreasing the supply of the factors of production themselves. Statistical measurement must shift, therefore, from a mere inventory or census of existing amounts of the factors of production to an estimate of the long-period impulses, " supply prices " or other stimuli required to overcome, to the required extent, any aversion from work that may exist in the mind (or breast) of producers or potential producers. To be employed, a factor of production must be demanded at a price at or above its supply price ; hence the employment of all existing units and of sufficient units in the future to maintain the " stationary state " (XV §4) requires such an adjust-ment of the schedules or curves of demand and supply prices, that these curves intersect at a price that will impel demanders to employ, and suppliers to seek employment, in sufficient amounts to absorb actual supplies, and to ensure either stationary production, or pro-duction changing at a stationary rate. In so far as these long-run adjustments in the factors of production can be secured by variation in their rate of pay, the pay that will result in this sufficient employ-ment of labour, capital, and enterprise is known as the normal wage, the normal rate of interest, the normal rate of profit. But in real life there is no stationary state, and the conditions of production and consumption, of exchange and distribution, are variable and uncertain. It is only occasionally in certain selected or scientifically controlled situations (Chapters XIII §§3 and 4) that *normal* rates of pay can be statistically observed and summarized as an average.[1]

kind that pertain to the economy : only scarce means are economic means. Hence the entire economy is conducted on the understanding that the means are scarce ; it is, in this sense, governed by the ' principle of scarcity.' "
Cassel, *The Theory of Social Economy*, First Book, Chapter I.
    [1] See Marshall, *Principles of Economics*, V, v §4, esp. last paragraph.

The demand for factors of production varies with the *varying* value of their product (Chapter XVII §3), and statistics can only discover *what various amounts of labour, capital, and enterprise will be called out by various rates of wages, interest, and profits actually offered* by the inconstant unstationary demand.

As a first step in such discovery the statistical economist must know (1) the co-variations that have actually occurred at different times and in different situations in the rates of pay and the amounts of labour, capital, and enterprise (amounts and rates of pay being used as defined in Chapter XVI §3) ; and must estimate (2) the possible sources of further amounts of labour, enterprise, and capital that may enter into the long-run adjustment, in response, at least, to the probable variations in pay near the present level.

No general assumption is made of permanent scarcity. It is not true of labour (within limits) or of enterprise or capital that they do not respond to economic stimulus in the form of increased price. Greater capacity and willingness on the part of labour (though not a greater number of labourers in the long run) may be created, *and scarcity overcome* by variations in incentive, wages, and training. Higher wages result in higher feeding and housing, and this is likely to result in higher working capacity and hence higher output and lower labour turnover and lost time. This theory of the economy of high wages is obviously capable of being subjected to statistical tests, though the opportunity first seized by Lord Brassey in his *Work and Wages* has not been used as much as it might.[1]

The relation of variations in the average value or the distribution of profits, salaries, and dividends, or rates of profits (defined in Chapters X §3 and XVI §3) with variations in the supply of *entrepreneurs* and *risk-takers*, is also statistically measurable. But both the statistical co-variation and correlation of wages and the supply of labour, and the statistical co-variation and correlation of profits and the supply of entrepreneurs, must be *interpreted* with the help of psychological considerations coupled with knowledge of institutional circumstances, and the matter is taken up in discussing (Chapter XVIII §§3 and 4) the psycho-physiological and institutional basis of economics. The supply of *capital* is probably adjusted more immediately and automatically, and some possibly fruitful lines of statistical investigation may be sketched out here.

The adjustment of the supply of capital upward to an increasing rate of interest, depends largely upon an increase in the income of the community that is invested instead of spent ; in short, the degree

---

[1] See Florence, *Economics of Fatigue and Unrest,* Chapter VIII.

of the community's underspending. This underspending in turn depends upon a number of conditions, several of which are statistically measurable.

Statistical distinctions cannot be based upon people's intentions, but information can be collected in any given period about the customary or original amount of wealth in the form of money (a) spent and (b) received by individuals, and about the current or new amounts of wealth (c) spent and (d) received as income by individuals.

The difference $b-a$ I shall call the amount of *original* underspending; $d-c$ the amount of *current* underspending; $\dfrac{d-c}{b-a}$ or $(d-c)-(b-a)$ the current variation (increase or decrease) in underspending. These variations in underspending may be due to *changes* in spending (changes in the way c compares with a), or changes in receipts or earnings (i.e. changes in the way d compares with b). It is usually the current variation only that enters into practical problems, and in the following outline of the statistically measurable sources of the supply of new capital attention may be concentrated upon the measurement of these changes in " underspending." For the sake of simplicity I suppose an *increase* of capital, the overcoming of a scarcity of capital to be the result, the causes of which are to be measured. The causes involved (see Table XVIIF) are partly deliberate policies (denoted P) for some intentional object (O) and partly automatic, spontaneous, or natural (and denoted N).[1]

TABLE XVIIF

ANALYSIS OF FACTORS EFFECTING INCREASE IN SUPPLY OF CAPITAL

P I   Intentional Decrease in Spending (i.e. Saving).
    O 1   To profit by rise in rate of interest.
      2   To secure (a) Capital sum or (b) Fixed Income at later date by payment of Insurance Premiums.
      3   To meet needs of own business (Re-investment).

P II   Intentional Increase in Earnings or other Receipts.
    O 1   To profit by rise in rates of entrepreneurs' profit, managers' salaries, etc.
      2   To invest or insure against additional liabilities (e.g. on marriage).

N I   Automatic Decrease in Spending.
    N 1   Fall in retail prices and cost of living.   Original standard of living maintained.

N II   Automatic Increase in Earnings or other Receipts.
    N 1   Rise in money income, especially profits, higher salaries, and loanable funds of richer classes.   Original standard of living maintained.

[1] For explanation of symbols see Chapter XII.

Most of these causal factors are statistically measurable. Nominal market variations in the rate of interest (P I O I) are known and published from day to day, and it only remains to convert nominal into " real " rates of interest (see above, §1) by correction for changes in the (expected) purchasing power of money while the capital is on loan. The market rates of interest that are significant for our purpose consist in the yield on fixed interest securities such as government stock or debentures or preference shares, and the yield on ordinary shares. The percentage " yield " is the actual amount of money obtained annually in interest or dividend by investing at any given moment £100 in cash at the current market price of stock on the Stock Exchange. If the owner of capital is only indirectly an investor through depositing money in a bank, he may be influenced by variations in bankers' deposit rates ; hence these should also be taken into account and measured.

Variations (P I O 2) in the amount and rate of premium paid or insurance carried are also ascertainable ; and the amounts (P I $O3$) put back into the business are estimated from time to time. For Great Britain this was estimated by the Board of Inland Revenue[1] after deducting income-tax as 96 million £ in 1912, 164 million £ in 1922, and 168 million £ in 1923. Variations (P II $O1$) (N II $N1$) in salaries and profits of those who can afford to underspend are also calculable and have been[2] calculated ; and variations (N I N 1) in retail prices and the cost of living are measured by appropriate index numbers.

To affect new production, the wealth invested, thanks to underspending, must be translated into physical machines, buildings, and other equipment ; and the statistician must attempt to measure technical as well as financial adjustability.

With our Victorian belief in industrial progress, adjustment of capital is habitually thought of as adjustment upward. But postwar difficulties in the English cotton and iron and steel industries indicate the practical need for considering downward as well as upward possibilities. The degree of adjustability *downward* clearly depends upon the durability of the plant. If not more than 5% of factory buildings and heavy machinery perish by mere exposure, etc., apart from wear and tear in the course of a year, no decrease, however large, in the price of their products can result in more than a 5% adjustment of these factors downward. Furthermore, even if progress is assumed, the durability of most capital equipment

---

[1] Report on the *Colwyn Committee on National Debt and Taxation*. Refers to gross reinvestment of *companies* only.
[2] Bowley and Stamp, *The National Income* 1924, Chapter VI.

entails only a small new overall increase of equipment to maintain the ordinary rate of net progress, and it will require a comparatively long period materially to accelerate that rate of progress.

Mitchell[1] supposes a case in which one-tenth of the equipment in operation wears out every year. The replacement met by the machine-building industries would therefore normally be 100 when the stock of machines was 1000. To this may be added, for purposes of illustration—a low estimate—5 extra machines made per year for a progressive 5 per thousand (0·5%) increase in industry.

Now suppose that the demand for the products of the machine increased 10% instead of 0·5% and a total of 1100 machines are required instead of 1005.

The machine-building industry would so have to adjust itself that it could produce its normal output of 105 plus the additional 95. And this virtual doubling of output might well be impossible within, say, a period of a year.

This point is familiar in discussion of the variability from year to year in the amount of production of industries making machines and industrial equipment generally. It is not usually seen, however, that this variation is conditioned by the assumption of a low replacement and progress rate due to the *durability* of most equipment and existing facilities for production.

"During depression and early revival the equipment-building trades get little business except what is provided by the replacement demand. When the demand for products has reached the stage where it promises soon to exceed the capacity of existing facilities, however, the equipment trades experience a sudden and intense boom."[2]

This boom would not be so sudden or intense if equipment-building industries were accustomed to replacing 50%, i.e. 500 of the existing stock of 1000 machines (as well as adding 5 machines or 0·5% for progress) rather than the 10% that is held to be the average proportion. In that case a demand for an additional 95 machines would entail an expansion of only $\frac{500+5+95}{500+5}$, roughly one-fifth, instead of a doubling.

The facts, however, of modern manufacturing industry are that in anticipation of demand a durable capital equipment is required that needs only fractional replacement and increase in any year. The equipment-building industries (that also require a durable equipment) need only be organized to produce this fractional

[1] *Business Cycles and Unemployment*, Chapter I.   [2] Loc. cit.

replacement plus some additional percentage for progress. The stock of equipment and the stock of appliances for producing new equipment is, relatively speaking, fixed, and can neither be easily adjusted upward to meet sudden increases in progress nor yet downward to meet retrogression like that experienced in England after 1920.

To sum up. Though one cannot speak of permanent scarcity in the sense of a limited absolutely inadjustable frequency, the conditions of supply, even where land is not an important factor of production, may thus often be highly inadjustable and the long-period conditions when expenses of production determine supply, long delayed.

During these " short-run," but in respect of actual time often protracted periods, capital, enterprise, skilled labour, and other factors of production will receive payments governed by the demand for their product on the one hand, and their existing supplies rather than their price or cost of adjustment on the other. These payments will not be the *normal* rates of interest, profit, and wages, that classical economics assumed on the basis of the supposed cost of adjustment of these factors of production in the stationary state, but will be *quasi-rents* that can only be estimated and accounted for on the basis of positive information about the actual supply of the factors. *It always remains important, therefore, for the economist to have statistical information as to existing stocks in dealers' hands and existing supplies of factors and appliances of production.*

With this warning as to their limited applicability, and the many degrees of scarcity and adjustability, we may proceed to consider long-period results.

§6   The Long-Run Theory of Demand and Supply

In the normal long-run period the main law of economics is that in industry under competition the exchange value or price of units of any aggregate volume of production is equal to the marginal cost of production of a representative firm " which is managed with normal ability, and which has normal access to the economies external and internal which belong to that aggregate volume of production."[1] This theory is demonstrated by reference to the principles of the economic man in much the same way as the more general law of equilibrium of supply and demand. Its proof is a formal *reductio ad absurdum*.

There are three possible situations : that exchange value (or selling price) is above, below, or equal to the marginal[2] cost of

---

[1] Marshall, *Principles of Economics*, IV, xiii §2.
[2] Marginal is used in the statistically measurable sense explained above, §1. The marginal cost of r units is the cost of $r - (r-1)$ or of $(r+1) - r$ units.

production of the representative firm (including, of course, normal profit to the entrepreneur).

If the exchange value or price per unit of any given amount were below marginal cost of production of the representative firm, some individuals, at least among a group of economic men, would not go on producing at all and others might not produce as much. The consequent fall in the supply of products would, by the law of diminishing utility, enable those remaining in business to obtain higher prices.

If the exchange value or price per unit of any given amount were above marginal cost of production of the representative firm (including normal profits), most individuals among the group of competing economic men would produce more, and their ranks might be swelled (supposing competition and a long enough run) by new entrepreneurs. The subsequent rise in the supply of their product would, by the law of diminishing utility, force all to lower the sale price.

In short, both the situation of an exchange value or sale price *below* and the situation of a sale price *above* marginal cost of production is, in the long run, impossible and absurd under competitive conditions, and stable equilibrium can only be found where sale price (or exchange value)=marginal cost.

But these laws and this automatic determinism are not invariable. When there is not competition but monopoly, the monopolist determines either the price charged or the amount exchanged (though not both). And his deliberate purpose as an economic man must be to get his revenue well above cost of production.

The economic law of price under monopoly is that the " owner of a monopoly (will) adjust the supply to the demand in such a way as to afford him the greatest possible total *net* revenue[1] ; " that is, gross profit (see above, p. 263) " over and above what may be fairly allowed as earnings of management, interest, and insurance against risk."[2]

Whether price is equal to (marginal) cost of production, and whether there is really a maximum monopoly revenue, can only be statistically verified (1) if we know the demand schedule for the monopolized product, and (2) if we can measure the actual costs of production.

This compels the economist to define clearly exactly what he refers to by cost ; and it will be found that when the economist

---

[1] Marshall, *Principles of Economics*, V, xiv §2.
[2] See Jenks and Clark, *The Trust Problem*, Chapter IX, for a statistical investigation how far monopoly has in fact raised prices.

states that prices will in the long run and under competition be equal to the cost of production, he includes items like a normal profit to the entrepreneur that most business men do not call costs, and he excludes items like economic rent and direct taxes (e.g. income tax) that business men are inclined to include in costs. Economic theory, before it can be tackled by statistics, must state specifically what are the costs which price is supposed, under competition, to equal, or under monopoly to exceed.

Unfortunately, instead of thus defining what he classes as costs, the economist often darkens counsel by introducing what is merely a definition as a law. When the economist says that rent does not enter into the cost of production he simply means, as Flux most clearly puts it, that rent does not enter into " that cost of production which determines or at any rate registers value."[1]

It is only when the items that are selected and defined as costs are fully specified that statistics of the sum of all these costs can be collected for the purpose of correlation with prices, and that the truth of the economist's law can be tested directly by this correlation, or indirectly and negatively by attempting to show that there is no correlation with price in the items specifically excluded from costs.

Income-tax is not part of the production costs in the eyes of the economist's law, and it has been shown statistically that comparing the financial year of low income-tax 1912-13 with the year of high income-tax 1922-23, there is " no evidence of any increased rate of profit on turnover such as would be necessary to yield the same net reward per unit when account is taken of the 328 per cent increase in the rate of income-tax." Mr. W. H. Coates, part of whose evidence before the Colwyn Committee is thus summarized, concludes that there is difficulty in " tracing any influence of the rate of income-tax on prices through the medium of the rate of interest."[2]

" The data at the disposal of Mr. Coates," writes Mr. J. M. Keynes,[3] " have enabled for the first time the à priori conclusion of the economists (as to the incidence of income-tax) to be subjected to a statistical test . . . from which it emerges undamaged." Income-tax is not a cost of production shifted, by affecting price, on to the shoulders of the consumers.

Once we have ascertained what the costs are, of which the economist speaks, and what they are not, we may accept as a

---

[1] Flux, *Economic Principles*, p. 110.
[2] Report of the *Colwyn Committee on National Debt and Taxation*, p. 164.
[3] *Ec. Jl.*, June 1927. But see criticism of Mr. Coates' argument by Mr. D. H. Robertson, *Ec. Jl.*, December 1927.

plausible working hypothesis the law that the price of any specific exchangeable is, in the long run and under competition, equal to its marginal cost of production in a representative firm.

When discussing the theory of distribution it was suggested (XVI §2) that only by intensive investigations carried out under selected and controlled conditions could statistics find that the payments of factors were *equal* to marginal productivity. The same is true of marginal cost. Mass statistics can probably show only a " co-variation " of price with cost of production. But when it is realized that marginal costs are usually taken to be variable, either diminishing or increasing, then the statisticians' co-variation is clearly an important first step in the verification of the theory. If price does not vary with varying marginal costs or is negatively correlated, then price clearly cannot be identical with marginal costs. A high positive correlation, though it does not prove the identity of price and marginal cost, is certainly a condition of that identity.

Price, then, is equal to or varies with variations in the marginal cost of production. But how does the cost of production of any specific article under discussion vary ? Is it produced under the laws of increasing, or of constant, or of decreasing return that were distinguished in Chapter XVI §7 ? The investigation must clearly shift to the analysis and statistical measurement of the actual cost or expenses involved in production within a representative firm.

§7 *Investigation of the Expenses of Production*

The expenses of production, average or marginal, of any exchangeable, may, as set forth above, be variable or constant for different amounts of the exchangeable. Whether expenses are increasing (and returns decreasing), or whether expenses are decreasing (and returns increasing), or whether the cost is approximately constant, can be decided only after measuring the elements of expense involved in the production of the specific exchangeable under discussion.

In order to produce goods, and even such services as railway transport, for exchange under modern conditions, many different kinds of subsidiary exchanges must be undertaken. The entrepreneur of a manufacturing business must buy raw material from mining or agricultural businesses, and he must buy or hire machines from engineering firms, buildings and land from contractors, land from " realtors," and must often borrow capital from banks and the investing public, and must hire labour and sometimes power and lighting. The terms of these subsidiary exchange transactions are known and measurable so that the expenses of production can be analysed according to the relative importance of the several factors of production that are bought.

Different industries, manufacturing, transport, commercial, will show wide variations in the distribution of their total expense over these different factors of production, and consequently the prices of their products will be very variously affected by any given rise, say, in the wages of the labour they employ, or in the interest on the capital they use. It is useless to generalize about the effect on the price of the products of variations in the price of any factor of production, until the economist knows the amount of money spent on that factor relative to other factors in producing that particular product.[1] This is a subject that English economists have tended to avoid mainly, I think, owing to lack of funds for such kinds of investigation and the oysterish secretiveness of English business men. Exceptions to this rule of secretiveness in British Industry are Mr. Stanley Unwin's analysis of the cost of books,[2] the enforced publication of railway costs, and the statistical surveys of British industry published by the Balfour Committee.[3]

There are plenty of examples of this " factorial " expense analysis in America where neither funds nor publicity are lacking. We may mention (1) the work of Secrist and the Bureau of Business Research (North-Western University) into the expenses of retail clothing shops classified by rent for buildings and land, wages, advertising expense; (2) the general investigation of Federal government departments into (a) the tanning, leather and shoe industry,[4] (b) the pottery industry,[5] (c) the economics of the construction industry.[6] Attention may also be drawn to the attempt by the League of Nations to estimate Labour Cost in Agriculture.[7]

A second sort of distinction between the various expenses of production is that between prime and supplementary expenses. Prime expenses are those that vary exactly proportionately with the amount of output, like paper and ink in newspaper production. Supplementary expenses are those, like the wages of compositors or the type they use, that do not vary proportionately, and this

---

[1] Marshall gives a brief analysis of factors in Supply Price, *Principles of Economics*, V, iii §5.

[2] *The Truth about Publishing.*

[3] Committee on Industry and Trade, *Factors in Industrial and Commercial Efficiency*, etc. etc.

[4] The broad results of some of the earlier American investigations were shown in Table 5 of my *Economics of Fatigue and Unrest*.

[5] *Dept. of Commerce*, Miscellaneous Series No. 21.

[6] *U.S. Dept. of Labour*, 1919. [7] International Economic Conference, 1927.

distinction is essentially statistical in nature. With any given organization prime expenses vary proportionately (1 to 1) with output. Supplementary expenses also co-vary, but not in 1 to 1 ratio.

The line of demarcation between prime and supplementary expenses varies with the length of time under consideration. Some parts of the equipment and plant, such as the tools, are less durable than others, such as machinery and buildings. One tool may last for only six months, other items of the plant, say the machines, may have a life of ten years; others, say buildings, have a life of fifty years. As industrial accounts are usually made up for a period of a year, the use of machines and buildings would appear in the annual depreciation account (except in so far as they were patched and repaired in the course of the year) as supplementary expenses, but tools as prime costs.

Usually a firm or a local industry produces more than one specific exchangeable and some expenses will be common to several exchangeables. The limiting case is that of joint products like straw and wheat, or chemical by-products whose expenses up to the point where the production of the two can be separated are common in their entirety. If these " *common* expenses " cannot at all, or cannot easily be assigned to each separate article, they are in business practice classed with supplementary expenses as " overhead " costs in contradistinction to direct costs.[1]

The two sets of classes formed according as expenses (1) relate to different factors of production, or (2) are prime or supplementary, appear statistically to be more or less " independent." That is to say, there are expenses for the factor labour that are prime and expenses for labour that are supplementary; there are expenses for the factor machinery that are prime and expenses for machinery that are supplementary, and so on. This is demonstrable by a table of double entry, like Table XVIIG,[2] in which I distinguish not merely prime from supplementary expenses, but moderately supplementary from highly supplementary. The moderately supplementary expenses are not correlated with output like the prime expenses as 1 to 1, but might have a co-variation ratio of, say, 8 to 10, while the highly supplementary expenses might have a correlation ratio with output of, say, 1 to 2. The object of the threefold classification is simply to warn the reader against any hard-and-fast understanding of " Supplementary."

---

[1] This point is not always made clear, and we find overhead costs taken as the practical man's equivalent for the theoretical economist's supplementary costs. In fact, it covers more than that.

[2] Planned to cover the first eight classes of cost cited p. 263, *q.v.*

According to Marshall's doctrine, " supplementary costs are, as a rule, larger relatively to prime costs for things that obey the law of increasing return than for other things." This analysis of expense items should help materially, therefore, in filing specific industries that belong there into the increasing return " box."

TABLE XVIIG

ANALYSIS OF EXPENSES OF PRODUCTION

Prime Costs	Moderately Supplementary Costs	Highly Supplementary Costs
	Circulating Capital (Tools and Supplies.	*Raw Materials)*
Tools and Supplies for actual work	Power for Heat, Light, Ventilation	Interest on Bank Loans
Raw Material	Supplies for Maintenance "in condition"	
	Power for Driving Machine shafting	
	Fixed Capital (The Plant)	
Depreciation for Wear and Tear by Work		Interest on Debentures
(Royalty on Machines, e.g. Boot and Shoe industry)		Rent for Land or Site
		Depreciation for Wear and Tear by exposure
		Obsolescence
	Management	
Foreman's Commission on Output	Sub-foremen on Weekly Wage	Manager, Office Staff, Foremen on Salaries
	Labour	
Wage. Salesmen on Direct Labour on a Commission	Utility Men Watchmen	Salesmen on Salary
	Risk-Bearing	
	Accident Compensation	Fire, etc., Insurance

The *Structure* or organization, as contrasted with the Expenses of the industry, is the second direction in which the investigator may look to find how the production of a large number of units results in increasing returns.

Economic theory distinguishes two kinds of economy " arising from an increase in the scale of production to which a representative firm has access ": external and internal economies. External economies are " those dependent on the general development of the industry "; internal economies " those dependent on the resources of the individual houses of business engaged in (the industry), on their organization and the efficiency of their management."

These "individual houses of business" are usually called *firms* and may or may not control more than one local establishment, i.e. a *plant* or *factory ;* and there are clearly additional "inner-internal" economies within a *firm* that is co-extensive with one *plant* as against a *firm* of similar size that is a combination of plants. Moreover, many if not most of the external economies arise as a result of the *local* concentration of the industry.[1] I am therefore inclined to consider the increasing returns that follow from these internal or external economies as returns arising mainly from : (I) the increased scale of production, the increased number of units made or sold, per firm or unit of administration,—*the administrative concentration ;* (II) the increased scale of production of a locality or geographically concentrated area,—*the local concentration.*

The concentration of an industry within the premises of one firm, i.e. in a factory or plant, is a *combination of these two elements and needs no separate method of measurement.* The combination simply cumulates the economies derived from its two components.

(I) *The number of units made and sold per firm.* The relative amount of any one product provided and sold per single administratively centred firm or single combination of firms, may be measured by dividing the number of such administrative units into the number of persons or the value of the capital employed in the industry as a whole, or into the amount or value of the product of the industry as a whole (see Chapter X §2). This will give the *average* amount of labour, capital, or business per firm. But unless the distribution of the sizes of businesses is one of symmetrical normal probability with not too wide a deviation, this "average" scale of production will be far from representative. The skew and deviation (see Glossary §§11, 15) is great even in such an industry of standard small businesses as the Lancashire cotton industry,[2] and the representative firm can only be measured as a firm within some fairly wide *range* of size.

From Table XVIIj, showing the yearly output of 613 British coal-mining undertakings, it would certainly be difficult to establish any representative size except within the widest limits. Almost exactly half have an output from 5 thousand to 200 thousand tons, and the median size would be somewhat under 200 thousand tons of coal per year. But since there are only 10 undertakings with

---

[1] I.e. the presence in the same town of firms that are auxiliary to the firm in question, as banks, builders, machine specialists, haulage contractors, are to a manufacturing firm.

[2] Chapman and Ashton, *J.R.S.S.*, April 1924.

annual output less than 5 thousand tons and 296 with an output of 200 thousand tons or over, the average arithmetic mean output per undertaking is considerably higher, namely 350 thousand tons. Median and arithmetic mean show wide differences and neither can be used to represent any typical *size* of firm. But the representative size of a firm might be measured in another way. Of the 215,052,000 tons of coal mined in Great Britain between January and June 1925 (Table XVIIJ) we can see by adding the first four figures in col. 3 that 98,904,000 tons were mined in undertakings with a yearly output of less than 600,000 tons, and 97,016,000 tons (the sum of the last three figures in col. 3) in undertakings with a yearly output of more than 800,000 tons. The undertaking that is representatively sized in the sense that *half the tonnage was raised from bigger and half from smaller firms* must have an output of something between 600,000 and 800,000 tons.

(II) *Measurement of local concentration.* The measurement of the concentration of a particular industry in one or a few places or areas is more difficult than the measurement of administrative concentration owing to the uncertainty as to the frontiers of a place or area. The required measure cannot be as direct as the *absolute* number of employees of that industry, or the absolute value of the capital or product of that industry in the " average " area, nor can it be the frequency distribution of areas containing specified numbers of employees or values of capital or product. The required measure must be the relative concentration.

This is an essentially statistical notion akin to the association table (e.g. Table IXA). The degree of concentration of the woollen and worsted industry in the Bradford or Leeds area, for instance, is manifest by *comparing* the proportion of all persons returned as occupied in that industry in Leeds or Bradford, with the proportion so occupied in the country (or world) as a whole.

Under the National Unemployment Insurance Act a grand total of 11,514,000 persons were insured in Britain in December 1924 as industrially occupied : of these 260,890, or 2·3%, were returned as occupied in the woollen and worsted industry. In Bradford a total of 122,170 were insured as industrially occupied ; of these 63,490, or over 50%, were returned as occupied in the woollen and worsted industry. In Leeds a total of 127,740 were insured as industrially occupied : of these 5201, or some 4%, were returned as occupied in the woollen and worsted industry. The conclusion is that the woollen and worsted industry is highly concentrated in Bradford with twenty-three times the national proportion, but only slightly so in Leeds with not twice the national proportion.

TABLE XVIIʜ

MEASUREMENT OF THE DEGREE OF LOCALIZATION OF THE WOOLLEN
AND WORSTED INDUSTRY IN BRADFORD

	Number Insured against Unemployment	
	Specified Locality	All Localities
	↑	↑
	(Bradford)	(England)
In Specified Industry	(A)	(B)
(Wool and Worsted)	63,490	260,890
	(C)	(D)
In All Industries	122,170	11,514,000

Local Concentration in Bradford is measured by the Ratio :

$$\frac{A}{C} \ (=52\cdot0\%) \div \frac{B}{D} \ (=2\cdot3\%)=22\cdot6$$

Once the degree of administrative and local concentration is measured, we may proceed to correlate variations in this character with variations in return, measured, let us say, by the margin of profit or loss per unit of output. The instance of correlation of degrees of *administrative* concentration and profit most familiar to English readers is probably the correlation table in the Report of the Commission on the Coal Industry reproduced as Table XVIIⱼ.

Such a correlation showing a definite tendency for the heavy losses to be confined to the smaller undertakings, cannot be accepted by itself as a proof of the law of increasing return. It merely, as the official report remarks, " supports the general advantage of larger units of production."

Statistical demonstration must be combined with theoretical reasoning. The sort of theoretical reasoning for " the advantages " of large-scale production in any given industry is familiar enough, but since it is often muddled and confused the line of argument requires restatement for the purpose of statistical verification.

This restatement may take the form of a table of indentation (of the kind suggested in Chapter XII) tracing and co-ordinating the plausible and probable results (symbol " R ") of any increase of production in any industry of given organization.

The chief headings of Table XVIIᴋ are based upon the two statistically measurable characteristics already discussed of greater production per firm and greater production per locality either taken severally or in combination. Five possible lines of argument can thus be developed according as increase of production is supposed or found by measurement to imply (R I) greater production per firm OR

TABLE XVIIJ

CORRELATION OF LOSSES AND PROFITS WITH SIZE OF UNDERTAKING

Coal Mining, Great Britain, January to June 1925[1]

Total No. of Undertakings making a specified Loss (−) or Profit (+) per ton

Yearly Output in 1000 tons of Coal Disposable Commercially	No. of Undertakings	Total 1,000 of tonnage raised	−7s. & over	−5s. & under −7s.	−3s. & under −5s.	−1s. & under −3s.	Between −1s. & +1s.	+1s. & under +3s.	+3s. & under +5s.	+5s. & under +7s.	+7s. & over
Under 5	10	32	5	—	2	—	2	—	1	—	—
5 and under 200	307	27,360	28	16	39	73	83	48	9	5	6
200 ,, 400	126	36,394	2	5	13	39	38	14	14	1	—
400 ,, 600	72	35,118	—	—	2	25	29	12	4	—	—
600 ,, 800	28	19,132	—	—	—	9	13	4	2	—	—
800 ,, 1000	20	17,992	—	—	—	6	10	2	2	—	—
1000 ,, 2000	42	56,280	—	—	2	10	14	15	—	1	—
2000 and over	8	22,744	—	—	—	1	4	3	—	—	—
Total	613	215,052	35	21	58	163	193	98	32	7	6

[1] Report of the Royal Commission on the Coal Industry, 1926.

per locality ; (R II) greater production specifically per locality and not per firm ; (R III) greater production specifically per firm and not per locality ; (R IV) greater production BOTH per firm and per locality ; (R V) greater production generally but not necessarily either greater production per firm or per locality.

Each of these lines of argument (or at least the first four) must be considered in turn.

The greater the production in number of units of any article that is made (R I) EITHER in one locality (which may be a whole country), OR by one firm, the more probable (or at least plausible) it is that there will be a full use ($R\,I$) of specialized processes (mechanical, chemical, etc.) and ($R\,2$) of specialized human ability of all sorts, including specialists in research. The technical and physical conditions of full use of specialists are discussed in Chapter XVIII §§1 and 2, and the organizational and quasi-political conditions in Chapter XX §5. Both mechanical and human division of labour are plausibly argued to result in specific economies (r i, r ii, r iii) if certain physical conditions, such as (n i) uniformity, (n ii) divisibility, are present, and if the organization reaches a certain size. But first, according to our plan, we must illustrate the statistical methods of ascertaining the facts as to specialization.

The use of specialized *machinery* can be indicated *directly* by the consumption of power measured in so much horse-power or kilowatts, and the use of machines compared to direct labour can be shown in the ratio of horse-power to man-power, i.e. to the number of wage earners employed. In America " in 1880 this ratio was 1·25 (3,410,000 horse-power to 2,733,000 wage earners) ; in 1900, 1·99."[1] Division of labour and the use of specialized *human ability* is indicated directly by the number of different operations performed by different groups of individuals in any one industry. In the American shoe-making industry of to-day, for instance, a useful pair of shoes develops from a few scraps of leather after they have passed through four separate departments of the factory and undergone no less than 239 operations.[2]

The use of special machines and processes is indicated *indirectly* by high capital expenses that swell the supplementary costs, and the division of labour and specialization in a staff is also liable to swell supplementary costs. Where chemical processes require expensive supplies with which to perform them, the direct material cost may also rise. A lowering of the *direct labour* cost in relation

---

[1] Florence, *Economics of Fatigue and Unrest*, p. 26.
[2] For the full discussion of this and other methods of measuring division of labour see below, Chapter XIX §3.

to overhead expenses, or to all other expenses, is perhaps the most exact single test of the degree of technical or human specialization.[1]

Among a group of men working with simple tools, each of whom makes a single pair of shoes unaided, practically all the expenses are prime and relate to labour. The expenses of the business, with the exception of a little rent and a little capital spent on lasts and leather, are all direct labour costs and strictly proportionate to the number of shoes turned out. But an industry like that of the railways, relying very greatly on mechanical plant and rolling stock, shows a very high proportion of expenses for capital. Ripley gives 27% of total annual expenses as the fixed charges, mainly interest on capital, for the railroads of the United States. These charges are all supplementary and he estimates another 40·5% as due to further supplementary expenses, comprising maintenance of way and structures (10%), maintenance of movable equipment (7·5%), conducting transportation (20%), and general expense (3%). Prime expenses are merely 32·5% of the total expense.[2]

Another method of indicating the extent of the use of machines and chemical processes is the proportion the value of the capital bears to that of the *net* annual output. The English Census of Production of 1907 estimates this proportion as follows for different industries :

Industry	Proportion : Capital to Net Annual Value of Output
Mining (U.K.)	1·3
Cotton (U.K., quoted from Chapman)	2⅜
Cotton (U.S.A., 1909)	3·2
Iron, Steel, and Engineering (U.K.)	2¼
„ „ „ (U.S.A., 1909)	2·6

To continue the analysis. In addition to the specialization that may occur (R I) *either* from a greater number of units made by one administratively concentrated *firm or* in one geographically concentrated *locality*, there are certain results peculiar to (R II) local concentration, and other results peculiar (R III) to administrative concentration.

Local concentration, i.e. greater production per locality (but not administrative concentration of plants geographically scattered), results (R 2) in economy of transport between successive operations

[1] See Florence, *Economics of Fatigue and Unrest*, Table 5, p. 134. On the test of " Percentage Overhead to Labour " the Canning and Tanning industries appear most specialized technically and humanly ; the coal-mining industry least so. But Labour Costs vary widely in different mills of the same industry.
[2] *Railroads, Rates and Regulation*, p. 55. For analysis of English railway expenses see Acworth, *Railway Economics*.

in production. By-products, if heavy, can be taken to the neigh-bouring factory of another firm but not to a distant factory of the same firm. Where industry is locally concentrating it will permit that locality to be selected for concentration which is nearest to more or less intransportable or immobile factors of production like minerals and $(R\ I)$ traditionally skilled inhabitants.[1]

This economy is analogous to that of using the different natural abilities of man which results from specialization. Both places and persons are differentiated and vary in productive capacity. Local concentration and specialization both permit the assignment of work to the most suitable variate.

Administrative concentration, i.e. greater production per firm (but not local concentration of plants under a different administra-tion) will result in the economy $(R\ I)$ of bulk buying and selling (including advertising) ; in economies $(R\ 2)$ in reserve funds or stocks of all kinds for, as we know (Chapter VIII), uncertainty becomes less the larger the number of items dealt with and to that extent credit stands higher the larger the administrative concern ; and lastly in possible integration $(R\ 3)$ of by-processes.

Where a larger factory presents both local AND administrative concentration (R IV), additional *cumulative* economies arise in the full use of specialized processes and men that are both working simultaneously and co-ordinated in one spot.   There is easier supervision $(R\ 2)$ that is adaptable at a moment's notice to un-expected circumstances or tactical advantages that may arise. One set of premises is more localized than properties that adjoin, however closely, so that cost of transport tends to a minimum $(R\ I)$, so much so that materials may (e.g. in an iron and steel plant) be transported in liquid and molten form between integrated processes, thus saving the reheating of the solid pigs in which iron must be transported to *separate* steel plants.   Transport, in fact, can be planned rationally as the *routing* of materials from process and specialist to process and specialist, without stoppage to reheat, or to load for transport, a stoppage which in the case of heavy by-products might well have been prohibitive.

The lines of argument to be used in " explaining " or interpreting increasing returns in conjunction with statistical measures may now be summed up. This summary runs parallel with Table XVIIK

---

[1] " The characteristic of manufacturing industries which makes them offer the best illustrations of the advantages of production on a large scale, is their power of choosing freely the locality in which they will do their work. They are thus contrasted . . . with agriculture and other extractive industries (mining, quarrying, fishing, etc.), the geographical distribution of which is determined by nature." Marshall, *Principles of Economics*, IV, xi §1.

TABLE XVIIK

ANALYSIS OF RESULTS OR IMPLICATIONS (R) OF AN INCREASE OF
PRODUCTION IN ANY INDUSTRY

R I   GREATER PRODUCTION PER FIRM OR PER LOCALITY

    R 1   *Full Use of Special Machines and Processes*

        r i   Economy of labour
        r ii   Economy of time
        r iii   Economy of materials
        n i   Physical Uniformity of materials
        n ii   Physical Divisibility of materials and equipment

    R 2   *Full Use of Specialized Human Ability (Division of Labour and Function)*

        r i   Use of different native abilities of men
           n   Differentiation of native ability
        r ii   Acquisition of skill by practice
        r iii   Economy of working continuously at one special job
           n   Physiological Endurance of monotony

R II   GREATER PRODUCTION PER LOCALITY

    R 1   *Lower or No Cost of Transport of Specialized Labour and Ability*
    R 2   *Lower Transport Cost of Materials to Specialized Machinery*

R III   GREATER PRODUCTION PER FIRM

    R 1   *Lower Administrative Costs per Unit in Buying and Selling*
    R 2   *Lower Proportion of Financial Reserve*
    R 3   *Elimination of Buying and Selling by possible Integration*

R IV   GREATER PRODUCTION PER LOCALITY AND FIRM

    R 1   *Minimum Transport and " Routing" Cost of Materials (No reheating)*
    R 2   *Efficiency (lower costs) of Supervision*

R V   GREATER PRODUCTION GENERALLY, BUT NEITHER GREATER PER FIRM OR LOCALITY

(Purely External Economies)

and carries the argument further into psycho-physiological territory than the foregoing text.

The economy or increasing return from (R I) a greater production per firm OR locality is explicable by reference to its result in permitting full use of specialization, technical or human. These two explanatory results in their turn are theoretically, and could be statistically, explained by reference to the economies that the use of special machines and processes effect in labour, time, and materials, and to the economies that division of labour or human specialization effects in the use of the different natural abilities of man, in the acquisition of skill through practice, and in the continuousness of work. All these ultimate results depend upon physical (and probably also physiological or psychological) characters that act as enabling or, after a point of maximum return, disabling conditions. The substitution of machinery for human labour depends, for instance, upon (n i) the uniformity and (n ii) the divisibility of the materials to be worked; and the extent to which the division of labour can result in the use of differentiated ability must depend (n) upon the extent of differentiation as displayed in Table VIA; in particular, the number of differentiated geniuses that are able to control large-scale firms. Similarly the extent to which continuousness of work can be carried depends upon (n) human endurance of repetition and monotony. The statistical measurement and wide importance of these physical and psycho-physiological factors will be discussed in Chapter XVIII, and Chapter XIX §§3, 4.

Returning to the further immediate results of an increase of production in any industry, economic theory holds that the economy or increasing return from (R II) a greater production per locality (apart from the size of firms) is explicable mainly by reference to its result in lowering costs of transport. The economy or increasing return from (R III) a greater production per firm (apart from localization) is explicable mainly by reference to its result in lowering administrative and financial costs. There are further economies explicable (R IV) from the result of both localization and increasing size of firms, and finally some (R V) economy is possible, like extra return from the establishment of trade journals, by sheer increase in production without any increase in local or administrative concentration.

The reduction of transport and administrative costs, etc., resulting from greater production have limiting physical and psycho-physiological causes just as much as specialization human and technical; the physical intransportability of certain goods is a clear case in point. Hence on all sides the law of increasing return drives us back, like the law of decreasing return (above, §4) and the law of diminishing utility (above, §1) upon physical and psycho-physiological factors. The next chapter will be devoted to consideration of the statistical measurability of these fundamental physical and psycho-physiological characters and conditions.

CHAPTER XVIII

THE PHYSICAL AND PSYCHO-PHYSIOLOGICAL BASIS OF ECONOMIC VARIATION

§1 *The Economic Importance of Physical Qualities*

STATISTICAL economics that does not wish to shut its eyes to the part economic activities play in human behaviour and technical achievement as a whole,[1] must endeavour to anchor its complicated argument to the tangible basis of such physical, psychological, and institutional items and characters as can themselves be accurately measured.

Much has been written of the economic interpretation of history, but here I beg to urge a physical interpretation of economics. Professor Carver points out that the economic struggle is an effort to attain to a harmony between man and nature which does not naturally exist, and the notion of " scarcity," used so often by economists, implies limitations imposed by the actual amount and distribution of natural resources upon the ever-recurring wants of man in the matter of food, clothing, shelter, and so on. But taking natural resources and human wants as " given," and observing how this situation works itself out, economists find physical limitations—the same inkling of ultimately increasing cost, of a sort of Malthusian check—confronting them, at every turn. We may take the significant physical and natural characters first.

Numerous references to the importance of physical characters have already been made in the last three chapters, notably to the importance of mobility in Chapter XV §4, and of durability in Chapter XVII §5 ; and a third physical character, divisibility, was cited (XV §4) as one of the underlying assumptions of economic theory. This continual reference to the physical basis of economics is not an idiosyncrasy of my own, as citations from Marshall[2] may abundantly prove.

" There are many special causes which may widen or narrow the market of any particular commodity : but nearly all those things for which there is a very wide market are in universal demand, and capable of being easily and exactly described . . . so that they can be bought and sold by persons at a distance from one another and at a distance

---

[1] Chapter IV.   [2] *Principles of Economics*, V, i §4.

also from the commodities. If necessary samples can be taken of them which are truly representative : and they can even be ' graded ' so that the purchaser may be secure that what he buys will come up to a given standard. . . . Commodities for which there is a very wide market must also be such as will bear a long carriage : they must be somewhat durable, and their value must be considerable in proportion to their bulk."

" Textile materials are delivered by nature in standardized primary forms, well suited for massive change into standardized finished products. Cotton, wool and other fibres are fine homogeneous cylinders of different shapes. Cotton is flat, wool is round ; but both lend themselves to be laid out in orderly array by machinery and thus to be spun into yarn."[1]

" There is no doubt that greatly increased efficiency can be attained through division of labour in those occupations in which there is much demand for mere manual skill. . . . Anyone who has to perform the same set of operations day after day *on things of exactly the same shape*, gradually learns to move his fingers exactly as they are wanted, by almost automatic action and with greater rapidity than would be possible if every movement had to wait for a deliberate instruction of the will."[2]

And the classical doctrine as to the commodity to be used as money involves, amongst others, several *physical* qualities :

" Economists quite generally agree that the commodity selected to serve as money should have the following qualities : (1) value, (2) durability, (3) portability, (4) homogeneity, (5) divisibility, (6) cognizability, and (7) stability of value."[3]

These texts exemplify the importance attached by economists to such physical characters as durability, portability or mobility, homogeneity and gradability, divisibility and cognizibility. And these characters may be almost indefinitely analysed or combined to form further physical characters of great economic significance.

High mobility in an exchangeable of any given value involves, for instance, compact shape and light weight. When compactness is combined with durability there results the character of storability clearly important in reducing rents, interest, and wages of watchmen, and in determining how much a producer can make for stock. For durability involves not only freedom from putrescence, rust, or moth, but absence of inflammability, fragility, etc. Immobility, indivisibility, absence of uniformity make new production slow and thus determine the length of the economists' " long period," before which the conditions of supply cannot adjust themselves to a change in demand (Chapter XVII §5).

[1] *Industry and Trade*, I, iv §1.
[2] *Principles of Economics*, IV, ix §2.
[3] Seager, *Principles of Economics*, p. 325.

We must proceed, however, from scattered problems of economics to a more thorough study of two particular economic problems in which physical characters play an important part : the problem why certain industries are concentrated in one LOCALITY rather than another ; and the problem why certain industrial activities are concentrated (in the boom phase of the trade cycle) at one TIME rather than another.

We have already dealt (VIII §6, XVII §7) with the measurement and economic importance of the local concentration of industry. Localization is the heaping up of business transactions and business organization at any place, and implies that items, unlike farms and agricultural market towns, are not evenly scattered throughout the scale of values, are not evenly " spread out," in short, over the " distance values."

This statistical calculation may be applied to situations distinguished in time as well as place. The boom phase of a trade cycle is an example of a heaping up of business transactions at that particular time.

Once such local or temporal concentration or heaping up is demonstrated, but not before, the second question arises why concentration occurs at *particular* places or times. This secondary problem of place is that usually indicated by the familiar word *localization*, but I should prefer to refer to it as the problem of the specific LOCATION of concentrated industries.

The solution of the problem is very largely in terms of the degree of physical transportability of the factors of production, particularly raw material and fuel, labour, and atmospheric conditions, and the degree of transportability of the product.

The word industry is generally used and thought of as referring exclusively to (1) manufacturing industry where a more or less transportable raw material is converted into a more or less transportable product. But in a wider sense it includes (2) industries like hair-dressing, repair work, catering, transport, and dealing and retailing that do not convert raw material into product, and consist merely in providing services. Other industries (3) like agriculture, mining, and fishing have as their raw material intransportable soil, rocks, or sea, and their work consists in extracting a transportable product. Other industries (4) like building and engineering have, on the contrary, an intransportable product embedded or fixed in the land but transportable raw material. Finally (5) there are industries where raw material is less important than other factors of production like labour or atmospheric conditions and where these factors are not transportable. Health resorts and the Lanca-

z

shire cotton industry are located where intransportable atmospheric conditions are favourable, and university teaching and other skilled trades take place where tradition has fixed the skilled labour. In international trade the locating of industry within the borders of certain countries is largely due to the character and energies of the population, though the relative abundance of "embedded" materials is also important.

Mining, agriculture, and fishing (group 3) must clearly be located "at" the raw material, and building and service industries (groups 2 and 4) at "market" where people live and are served. But where, as in manufactures, raw material, fuel, and other factors of production are all more or less transportable and products more or less transportable also, the location of any industry should (in theory) be nearer the market or nearer the raw material and other factors of production according to the gain or loss of transportability in the course of manufacture. Where raw material like malt and hops (or coal) are more transportable than the product beer (or gas), the brewing industry (or gas works) will be found near the place of consumption, i.e. in most towns. Where raw material or fuel like iron ore and coal is less transportable than the product pig iron or steel ingots, the iron and steel industry will tend to "locate" near its material resources. The measurable character transportability is thus the key to the problem of location.

The parallel problem of timing,—why the observed *temporal* concentration of business should occur at particular seasons of the year or in particular years, is likewise partially soluble in terms of physical characteristics. Seasons vary in temperature, sunshine, and rainfall, and this results in seasonal variations of *supply* of agricultural crops, etc., and in seasonal variations of *demand* for clothes, fuel, shelter, and to some extent food. Years also vary in weather and this results in the harvest variations that, according to one school of cycle-analysts, is the predominant cause of trade fluctuations.

But seasonal and annual variations in production and demand would not affect the economic life of the market so deeply if so many important economic exchangeables were not perishable.

"Market supply," writes Mitchell,[1] "is kept far steadier than the rate at which goods subject to strong seasonal influence are produced. This steadiness is a triumph of economic planning. It is won by arranging compensatory seasonal variations in the activities which intervene between producing and consuming. The processes of preserving, storing, transporting and distributing goods

[1] *Business Cycles*, p. 237.

are purposely made to vary in such a way that a highly unstable rate of production is converted into a fairly even rate of market supply, or into a rate of market supply which varies with seasonal changes in demand."

But there are limits to these possibilities of preserving, making for stock, and of stabilizing market supply or adjusting it to demand. And the limits are largely imposed by the perishability and the impossibility of storing certain goods, and all services. Vegetables and fruit ripening in the summer must be canned or consumed forthwith, and eggs and milk whose production also varies from season to season cannot long be preserved even with modern cold storage and refrigator methods. Similarly heavy clothes are not worth buying ahead to meet demand at some distant winter date since moth and mildew may corrupt them while in storage at home. The supply of services must certainly be contemporaneous with the demand for them. A man cannot have his hair cut in advance of his need, nor can restaurants cook appetizing dishes except (at most) a few hours before they are wanted.

In determining the temporal incidence of business activity, lack of durability is often aided and abetted by a difficulty in packing away certain articles " snugly " enough. Clothes may not be kept in store for future use partly because of their possible decay and partly because they take up too much room ; and amounts produced for stock are clearly limited by the warehousing space at the producers' disposal, no less than by the stocks' possible perishability.

The joint force of physical perishability, i.e. physical lack of durability, and lack of compactness might be summed up as the physical quality of instorability. The analogy of this storability's part in the seasonal fluctuations of industry and transportability's part in the localization of industry is striking. Factors of production differ in fertility and productivity generally from place to place and from time to time. In spite of all economic planning this affects local and seasonal (or periodic) concentration of industry because the goods produced are often intransportable and unstorable. Intransportable materials must be worked up near the *place* where they are extracted from the earth ; perishable and unstorable foodstuffs must be consumed near the *time* when they are harvested.

On the other hand, *durable* and storable articles run the risk of obsolescence. A durable article yielding services over a number of years is in the course of its long life more likely to be exposed to unexpected fluctuations in conditions than perishable short-lived articles. Economic uncertainty may be expected, in fact, to be greatest where storability (or durability), transportability (or immobility), and one other physical character already mentioned— indivisibility—are present. If durability leads to a lack of adjustability amidst the temporal variations of the industrial cycle and trend, and immobility to a lack of adjustability amidst the spatial redistributions in the location of industry, indivisibility leads to a lack of adjustability to changes in demand in time or place. An indivisible outfit of a certain size is inadjustable to changing amounts in demand even though, like a circus tent, it be perishable and movable. The audience may shrink or expand, but in either case the whole tent must be pitched in spite of gaping voids or overcrowding and turning away.

Now much modern industrial equipment, such as railway plant, mines, factories, housing machines,—and department stores, shows the combination of characters cited above ; it is durable, immobile, *and* indivisible. Hence the continual presence of risk and uncertainty in modern economic life. And the more complicated and indivisible the plant, the more apparently efficient, the greater its inadjustability to unfavourable conjunctures of all kinds.

§2 *The Statistical Measurability of Physical Characters*

Durability, portability, gradability, divisibility, are admittedly important characters in economic life and economic theory ; and they are characters that can be measured objectively along a scale of degrees and of which statistics can eminently be formed.

The degree of portability is largely a question of (1) overall volume[1] measurable in, say, cubic feet, and of (2) weight measurable, say, in pounds. The degree of durability is measurable in the life, say the number of days, the article remains fit for consumption.

The degree of gradability is not measurable in direct physical units but is essentially a statistical conception. To be relatively gradable, an exchangeable article must obey at least two conditions already indicated in the qualities of cognoscibility and homogeneity. The character or characters according to which it is to be graded must be objectively measurable, recognizable, and " cognoscible " in units of weight, size, etc., *and* the quantities of such units that are manifested should fall into a few prevalent homogeneous modes or types.

If a few staple or standard quantities have a great relative

---

[1] A compact article is of course easier to transport, as well as to store, than one with protrusions and odd in shape.

frequency, if there is one or several distinct modes in the distribution of any physical character of an article, the article is gradable ; if there are no such prevalent types or modes the article is not so gradable.

The degree of divisibility is a question of the comparative economic value of each unit of an article that is complete in itself ready for use or consumption, independently of other units. One guinea's worth of cloth, oranges, tea leaves, pocket knives, and soap, is divisible into several pieces of cloth or soap, and several oranges, tea leaves, pocket knives. And when the cloth or soap is thus cut up or the oranges, tea leaves, etc., taken severally, the total value of the several pieces is much the same as the undivided whole. But a guinea pair of trousers is more valuable than the sum of its parts and is thus comparatively indivisible. There is no demand, or a comparatively low demand, for a single trouser leg. This may be thought simply the result of fashion's convention and hardly a physical character of leg-wear ; if so the case of machines or animals that physically cannot work without a whole set of parts is perhaps more to the point. The degree of divisibility is thus indicated by the number of conventionally or technically determined organic units, independently consumable or usable without loss of value, that can be purchased for any given sum.

An exact measure of divisibility would probably be particularly difficult to define and obtain, but there are of course difficulties and pitfalls in measuring the other physical characters also. If durability is measured in the life of an object, it is evident that an object does not die at any one discernible time, and a definition of the precise state of putrescence or failure in working capacity which shall count as death requires careful definition. The business man has already tackled this difficulty in his estimates of the yearly depreciation ; for to write off, say, 5% for the annual depreciation of his equipment, implies an estimate of a life of twenty years for that plant.

§3 *The Psycho-physiological Substratum*

In the course of their arguments economists make the psychological assumption of an economic man who " substitutes," " anticipates," " selects," in rational ways. They also assume on the demand side the psychological law of diminishing utility, and on the supply side they make the assumption that most payments for factors of production, their short and long-run supply prices (Chapter XVII §5), can ultimately be accounted for by the " real " cost incurred in physiological and psychological effort and sacrifice. Utilities are balanced against real costs and men will buy only if the utility of the purchase exceeds or does not fall short of the cost, and will sell only if the " real cost " of what they sell falls short of or does not exceed the utility of the price they charge.

On the demand side, the economists' utility refers simply to the quality of being wanted or, more precisely, to the degree to which an article is wanted ; and the economists' cost refers simply to various physiological and psychological aversions against producing, or rather (since to some extent some people like work) to a balance of aversions over wants toward producing.[1] This leaves the question open as to the type of weights thrown into the balance. Ultimately, before proceeding to prophesy or to interpret results, the nature of man's wants and aversions must be known. For this purpose there must be a psychology of consumption and production that is experimental or observational ; for to assume " reasonable " wants and " reasonable " aversions as did the earlier economists is simply to project one's own wants and aversion (found by intro-spection) upon possibly alien ground.

On the demand and consumption side the situation in which exchangeables are bought by the ultimate consumer and the " trade " must be clearly envisaged and the economist correctly orientated. Nowadays consumables are not as a rule bought drop by drop, unit by unit, dose by dose (like beer in bars, or à la carte portions in restaurants) at the moment when they are consumed, but are bought in bulk as totals, for future consumption. Hence their " utility " or " wantedness " at purchase is possibly different from their utility in consumption. At purchase the economic man must anticipate various degrees of utility at different moments of consumption in the future, and the law of diminishing utility could, I think, be substantiated by showing that the ordinary purchases are made in varying " bulks " or totals to satisfy the diminishing frequencies of various intensities of wanting that are anticipated in the future. It is not the actual case, as some students of economics are led to suppose, that the housewife purchasing oranges gets satiated at the time of purchase, swallowing one orange after another. Modern institutions are such that she purchases totals ahead, perhaps for three days or a week's spread of consumption, and that when oranges, let us say, are expensive, she limits the total amounts purchased to a number that will " hit the high spots " only ; that will satisfy only the direst wants that she expects in the course of the " consumption spread." The consumer,

[1] See the definitions, pp. 78–86, in my *Economics and Human Behaviour*.

in short, thinks in terms of, and compares, *totals*, not units. The same is probably true of the producer employing masses of labour and capital.

The supply as well as the demand side of his analysis leads the economist to interpret the surface facts of exchange (under modern conditions and institutions) in terms of the psycho-physiological states of human producers and consumers. This process of delving through a series of levels down to that of human nature is on the side of production set forth by Marshall more definitely than any other economist. Certainly this part of his teaching has been the most subject to criticism by fellow-economists, notably Professor Cassel[1] and his own disciple H. D. Henderson.[2]

Yet the delving to find the psychological roots of economic behaviour seems to me of the utmost importance and help in interpreting statistically established facts and relations, and nowhere is this psycho-physiological interpretation more important than in the economics of production. It permits us to link up the findings of a scientific statistical economics with those of the growing science of industrial psychology,—itself largely statistical in method. The mutual aid of independent sciences that has been such a fertile source of development in our knowledge generally (cf. Chapter XIV §2), can thus be used to further economic research. But in appealing to psycho-physiological theory, the precaution must be taken that the superstructure of the plant should not be deduced *in toto* from its psycho-physiological root. This precaution has already been discussed; our starting-point is not to be psychological costs any more than psychological utility, but manifest observable facts.

The usual division of incomes into rents, wages, profits, and interest is not, as we have shown (XVI §2), a convenient starting-point of fact for statistical investigation. These divisions represent payments for four different elements that are all necessary factors for carrying on industry under modern conditions : land, labour, enterprise, and capital. The supply of at least three of these factors involves distinguishable types of psycho-physiological cost : manual exertion ; thought and risk-taking ; and sacrifice, waiting, or " abstinence " ; yet the payment of these factors is seldom found, in fact, independently of some payments for at least one of the other factors.

" Pure elements are seldom isolated from all others by nature either in the physical or moral world. Pure rent in the strict sense

[1] *The Theory of Social Economy,* p. 286.
[2] *Supply and Demand,* esp. last chapter.

of the term is scarcely ever met with : nearly all income from land contains more or less important elements which are derived from efforts invested in building houses and sheds, in draining the land and so on. But economists have learnt to recognize diversity of nature in those composite things to which the names of rent, profits, wages, etc., are given in popular language ; they have learnt that there is an element of true rent in the composite product that is commonly called wages, an element of true earnings in what is commonly called rent, and so on."[1]

The greatest difficulty in isolating the " pure elements " occurs in the case of the composite payment to which the name profit is " given in popular language." The next section will accordingly be devoted to the psychological basis of this profit, to be followed (§5) by a similar analysis of the basis of wages.

§4   *The Psychology of Profit and Interest Variations*

Profits are on the surface a residual difference or " margin " arrived at by the cost accountant after a series of subtractions from the total gross revenue of a business.[2] This gross profit that in the case of joint-stock companies is paid out as dividends to ordinary shareholders, is not analysed by cautious economists except in the long run. In the short period all gross profit, that is all the revenue of a business over and above out-of-pocket expenses, can only be lumped together as a quasi-rent which is, theoretically considered, the result of temporary variations (or fixity) in the demand and supply of the products made, or in the scarcity or abundance of the means required for production.

In the long run, however, dividends are held by economists to comprise payments for several elements of cost, that are not always found separated ready for direct measurement. The *persons* who invest in speculative shares must of necessity risk as well as lend their capital, and in their choice of investment must be performing some mental work. Here the distinction between interest, profits for risk, and earnings of (investment) management is clearly psychological, the kind of effort or sacrifice made by the payee.

An individual in receipt of dividends on an ordinary share is supposed to be paid something (1) as net " interest " to overcome a " real " cost or aversion in postponing consumption, to induce waiting and saving instead of spending ; something (2) as pure or net " profits " to overcome a real cost or aversion in taking certain

---

[1] Marshall, *Principles of Economics*, V, ix §4.
[2] See Chapter XVI §3.

kinds of risk instead of playing safe ; and (3) something as earnings of management to overcome a real cost or aversion in labouring to choose between investing in one industry, country, and firm, rather than another. But all that the statistician can usually see is the paying over of dividends, the rest is hypothetical.

The economist is ready with the same type of hypothesis to explain each supposed element with which he explains actual wage levels and net interest. Man is on the whole averse to risk-taking, or at least averse to the type of risk presented in business enterprise as distinct from the type of risk presented by the race course. Though he may like (and in the long run *pay* the race-course bookmaker to present him with) a slight chance of a great gain combined with a heavy chance of a small loss, he is averse to a slight chance of a great loss coupled with a heavy chance of a little gain. And this latter, so the theory runs, is the distribution of chances presented by business.[1]

Now statistical analysis may help theory first by attempting to discover, by process of *selection and control*, the net payment for any one element such as risk isolated from the others, and may help theory, secondly, by testing the psychological hypotheses as to what are man's aversions.

We may select for comparison first various rates of interest (using interest in the widest sense of that word) upon loans of various kinds in all of which payment of interest and recovery of loan are practically certain. On the whole the rate of interest is lower the more liquid the loan, i.e. the shorter the period or " term " for which the loan is contracted. Interest on loans from day to day usually commands a lower rate than on short loans that are " at call " for periods usually not exceeding a week. These rates, known in the City as money rates rather than interest, are in turn lower than the discount rate on bills maturing in three (or six) months, and this discount rate is lower in its turn than the rate of interest (technically so-called) on irredeemable Government stock such as Consols. The actual average rates prevailing in four post-war years may be quoted from Lavington.[2]

	Average Rates per cent per annum London, 1919–1922
Day-to-day money	3·44
Short Loans	3·90
Three months' Bills	4·54
Yield on Consols	4·90

[1] See above, Chapter VIII, and Henderson, *Supply and Demand*, Chapter VII.
[2] *Economica*, November 1924.

Lavington himself states clearly the psychological explanation which may interpret these rates in terms of the lender's psychological attitude.

" Every lender, however strong his financial situation, is exposed to the incidence of imperfectly foreseen emergencies and opportunities which he can meet effectively only if his capital is readily recoverable from the uses in which he employs it. As a lender, therefore, his ideal situation is one in which his capital is invested in uses from which he can withdraw it at any time convenient to himself. Hence, in order to secure themselves against imperfectly foreseen contingencies, bankers and private persons alike will be willing to supply at least a part of their capital for such uses at rates of interest exceptionally favourable to the borrower."

" The greater willingness of lenders to lend (and the less willingness of borrowers to borrow) for short periods rather than long, work on rates in the same direction and lead to the expectation that rates of interest will be at their minimum for loans repayable on demand and will rise as the period of supply lengthens."

The rates of interest hitherto quoted were for loans on which payment of interest and recovery of loan were practically certain. But the lenders appear also to have a psychological aversion to uncertainty in this matter. To test the lender's preference for " security," statisticians may select for observation the insurance premiums individuals are prepared to pay purely to be relieved of risk (their demand price for relief from risk), or may observe the margin of profit obtained by those bearing risk of loss (the supply price for taking risks). This margin may be found in the case of securities of equally long terms by comparing rates of interest obtainable on what are considered safe or gilt-edged investments such as Government stock or industrial debentures, with *dividends* on such (1) preference shares, (2) preferred ordinary shares, (3) ordinary shares, and (4) deferred ordinary shares where loss is measurable in past experience.

The rates of dividend in single years for item-companies becomes more variable and uncertain as we progress from class of security (1) to (4). But if the average rate of dividend is calculated over a long enough period for a sufficient number of companies, it is progressively higher the more variable in dividend payment the class of security. This higher average payment for greater variability and uncertainty rates may seem a mere matter of common sense that it is unnecessary to test statistically. Yet if we consider the phenomenon of Monte Carlo or betting on English race courses, it looks as though a large section of human society, so far from being averse, *wanted* to take risks and to be financially insecure and uncertain.

A man will continue to put money on a horse or on a particular jockey when the average return is almost certain to be negative and not a money gain at all. Many newspapers publish from time to time the net results up to that date of investing £1 at the beginning of the season on each of the mounts of the leading jockeys. It is usually the case that every one such line of investment brings a loss. Taking one such calculation at random (e.g. *The Times*, July 1925), only one jockey out of the fourteen leading names gave any positive return on the investment of £1 and that return was £1 13s. 7d. The *losses* on each of the other thirteen leading jockeys ranged from £10 1s. 3d. to £105 13s. 4d.

Though the average expectable eventuality is thus a loss we know that the betting public is most numerous ; the attractiveness or " utility " of betting (to use utility according to the economist's definition) must be due to the odd chance that big prizes are to be won in some particular race. This consideration leads to the second part of the economist's hypothesis, namely that man is not attracted to invest in business for no—or a negative—average reward, because it is the few heavy *losses*, not the many moderate gains that are spectacular in their extent.

Some statistical testing of this plausible theoretical hypothesis, interpreting the need for payment to those who bear risk, was undertaken in Chapter VII. The figures there quoted did not appear to make the plausible hypothesis very probable. So far from rates of profit of a multitude of business undertakings showing a negatively skewed distribution with many slight gains over average, and a few heavy losses, the opposite appeared to be generally the case. Theory was thus driven back to the position that " the risk of getting no profit at all, though this is only a few points below the average of, say, 5%, may be as painful (or aversive) to a business man as, say, 20% profit (15 points above average) is pleasant (or attractive)."

In short, the theory is speaking in *psychological* terms of utilities and costs, wants and aversion, and the statistical test should attempt to isolate the psychological factors.

What distribution of risk is most aversive and repugnant to human nature might be tested statistically much as an advertiser tests what goods and what " copy " describing those goods are the opposite of repugnant. Various prizes, 1st, 2nd, 3rd, consolation, etc., might be advertised in a scheme for a lottery in which fines of various amounts should also figure. The test of psychological repugnance or attractiveness in the *distribution* of prizes and fines, would be the total subscriptions raised or tickets sold in relation to the total amount offered in prizes minus fines. The psychological theory advanced by economists is that a larger subscription list could be secured by a few big prizes and many small counterbalancing fines, rather than by a few big fines, not, however, necessarily as big as the prizes, and many counterbalancing small prizes.

The first of these schemes, that with a few large prizes, corresponds to the situation at Monte Carlo, in State lotteries, and on the race course ; the second of these schemes, with many small prizes and a few big losses, corresponds *according to theory* with the distribution of business risks.   But it has yet to be statistically proved (1) that this distribution is unattractive and repugnant to human nature, and (2) that business profits and losses really distribute themselves as theoretically supposed.

§5   *The Psycho-physiology of Wage Variations*

Wages correspond much more closely to payment for an element of psychological cost than profits.   The wages actually paid are not generally a compound of payments for different factors of production, and wages need not be split up by the economist according to the type of psycho-physiological cost incurred.

The main " real cost " or " discommodity " of labour Marshall considers to " arise from bodily or mental fatigue."

The intensity of this discommodity, whatever its form, " nearly always increases with the severity and duration of labour," and statistics that attempt to measure fatigue fit in with Marshall's theory by demonstrating the correlation, negative, e.g. in the case of output, positive, e.g. in that of accidents, with hours of work and with the heaviness of work.   But effort and fatigue are not the only costs of labour.   There is further discommodity arising, according to Marshall, from labour " being carried on in unhealthy surroundings or with unwelcome associates or from its occupying time that is wanted for recreation or for social and intellectual pursuits." Labour is exchanged as a commodity on the labour market, but it is peculiar in that the seller of labour retains property in himself and has to present himself at the place where his work is required.   And owing to his " perishability " and usual lack of reserve funds, a labourer has to take what conditions he finds at his work place. Hence these working conditions are often as important as the actual hours and type of work in stimulating or checking the supply of work (productivity) from given workers, or the supply (numbers) of workers moving into any industry.   Statisticians are therefore looking at very relevant conditions when they attempt to correlate indices of labour efficiency (such as the output, spoiled work, and accidents of a given number of workers, or the lost time and labour turnover by which the number of effective workers diminishes) with the physical and social environment of the factory as well as with hours and various types of work.

The psycho-physiological basis, fully stated, of the efficiency of labour is the capacity and willingness to work. It is " through the intermediacy of," i.e. by affecting capacity and willingness, that variations in the industrial environment and other terms of employment are most probably correlated with variations in efficiency.[1]

A man or woman's *capacity* for work is to some extent inborn and cannot be stimulated or possibly even checked except within limits. Those classified at the bottom of Table VIA could probably never be capable craftsmen however much stimulated. Moreover, even where the capacity of any individual is subject to wide variation, it is not fatigue only that will check it, but a lack of training or practice. Hence among the checks to working capacity we must include not only (I) fatigue defined as a tendency for capacity to decrease with increased activity, but (2) inexperience, where capacity will tend to increase with increased activity, and (3) inborn capacity, which will be inexorably different for different individuals (see Table VIA), and for any one individual will vary inexorably with age.

To include various states of *unwillingness* to work, a comprehensive and intelligible word is, in my view, industrial unrest. Some working conditions foster unrest and other conditions (i.e. incentives) would stimulate willingness and tend to overcome this unrest. " Every occupation," writes Marshall, " involves other disadvantages besides the fatigue of the work required in it, and every occupation offers other advantages besides the receipt of money wages." The balance disposing to work constitutes the net advantages that were alluded to in Chapter IV (§3). Many of these encouragements and discouragements, incentives or deterrents, other than wages on the one hand, and the hours and type of work and industrial environment leading to fatigue on the other hand, are statistically measurable, in particular several that Adam Smith distinguishes as " the principal circumstances which make up for a small pecuniary gain in some employments and counterbalance a great one in others " : constancy or inconstancy of employment, for instance, through statistics of unemployment ; probability or improbability of success, through the comparative frequency of eventual high income among persons pursuing the employment or

[1] Florence, *Economics of Fatigue and Unrest*, Chapters IV (" The Theory of Fatigue and Unrest ") and XII.

through statistics of the rapidity of promotion ; easiness and cheapness, or the difficulty and expense of learning, by actual expense incurred[1] or lapse of time before full earnings are obtained. Besides these " principal circumstances " of Adam Smith, at least two other sets of similar circumstances are directly measurable : (1) health and safety, through statistics of the frequency and severity of accidents, of occupational diseases, and of the comparative occupational mortality, and (2) degree of leisure allowed, by the length of hours worked, number of holidays on pay, etc.

Other circumstances, such as Adam Smith's " agreeableness or disagreeableness of the employments themselves, and the small or great trust which must be reposed in those who exercise them," are more difficult to measure directly. But in some occupations it would not be impossible to think out objective indices of degrees of the intensity or load of the work (e.g. tons of coal shovelled by stokers on various railways, cubic measure of earth shovelled by navvies, foot-pounds of energy expended by boiler-makers, etc.[2]), or even to distinguish degrees of the monotony or irritation in work that most psychologists consider such an important influence in modern industry. Monotony is a feeling that is evoked chiefly by the frequency and regularity of repetition of any job and its continuousness. Frequency and regularity can, as I have suggested elsewhere,[3] be measured, (1) by the average amount of product per man per day, and (2) by the average deviation or coefficient of dispersion of the whole series of repetitions. Continuousness or lack of intermittence is also a matter of observation. The pauses that occur in the course of work can be timed, care being taken to distinguish true rest-pauses, where no attention is required to the work in hand, from being " on duty " waiting for a cue or other eventuality.[4] Irritation is a feeling evoked very largely by irregularity, such as that of the time-incidence of telephone calls upon the operator at the telephone exchange. Here again the statistical measure of the deviation can be used.

These possible " disagreeablenesses " inherent in the nature of the work may be coupled with others incidental to the employment, such as the lack of sociability mentioned (in Chapter IV) as plausibly repugnant to the factory workers. Statistics may enumerate and

[1] See, for instance, "Cost of Preparation for Teaching," U.S. Monthly Labour Review, November, 1925.
[2] See above, Chapter X, §2 for Professor Sargent's calibration of intensity of effort in terms of climbing.
[3] Florence, Use of Factory Statistics in the Investigation of Industrial Fatigue, Columbia Studies, Chapter XV.
[4] Loc. cit.

compare the number, if any, of people met and/or spoken to in the course of a typical period of work in various occupations and may grade occupations accordingly. " The small or great trust reposed in persons exercising different employments " is also a matter of degree. An objective comparison can be drawn between the rank and file employee, only receiving orders, one like a foreman receiving and giving orders, and others only *giving* orders, or quite independent like peasant proprietors. It has already been suggested (Chapter IV §3) that a man will sacrifice something in income to be his own master and possibly the master of others, and statistics recently published of independent farmers' incomes in America[1] go to show that they often compare unfavourably with agricultural " hired men's " wages when the farmers' additional work of management is taken into account.

With all these statistical facts at our command, we may draw up a sort of balance-sheet for various occupations placing the circum-stances to which the worker may plausibly be considered averse, e.g. low wages, long hours, monotonous, irregular, or heavy work, poor ventilation, expensive training, periods of unemployment, infrequency of success, numerous accidents, high disease and death rates, dependence and unsociability, etc., on the liability side ; and circumstances that the worker may plausibly be supposed to want, e.g. high wages, short hours, sociability, etc., on the asset side. If this be done for a sufficient number of occupations between which labour is mobile, i.e. within the same social grade, and various weights are given to specific degrees of success, danger, unemploy-ment, etc., an adjustment could experimentally be reached, such that the balance of wants satisfied (by wages or otherwise) over aversions (Marshall's " true reward " or " net-advantages ") should be the same for each such occupation.

Such a balancing would allow the economist to estimate much more precisely the nature of men's aversions, or disutilities as he calls them, the weights men throw into the scale against producing and for which they require an equivalence in wages to compensate and recompense them.

§6 Summary : The Contributory Institutional Basis of Economics

Whether or not it can be established by the co-operation of statistics and theory that elements on the physio-psychological

---

[1] " Farmers' Incomes," quoted in *U.S. Monthly Labour Review*, February 1925.

level are the ultimate cause of the surface economic phenomena of prices or rates of pay, and of amounts and aggregate values exchanged, the three levels, pecuniary, physical, and psychological, in terms of which economics speaks must always be kept in mind. They occur and recur in almost every economic issue.

In what terms, for instance, shall the gain from international trade be reckoned ? The gain cannot be in the pecuniary terms, for the *payments* must balance. The aggregate economic value of a country's exports, goods, services, bullion, and capital, etc., must, in the long run, be equal to the aggregate value of her imports, for imports can only be paid for by exports. But the gain may be taken to consist in more favourable " barter terms." A country may get (i.e. import) the same amount of physical units of goods, services, capital, or bullion in exchange for a less amount (exported) of her physical units. This, however, is not necessarily the final touchstone of " gain." The country may have worked harder to produce that less amount of physical units. America may get the same amount of manufactured goods from England in exchange for a 10% less amount of wheat and thus gain physically in barter terms ; and yet that diminished quantity of exported wheat may have cost America more (greater home consumption, law of diminishing returns) in labour effort than the original quantity. Can this be called a gain for America ? For one physical unit of wheat, America gets more English manufactured goods, but for one psycho-physiological effort unit she gets less.

Two problems are thus presented by the three " levels " of our economic analysis. (1) To keep clearly in mind what level is referred to, (2) to interpret the facts of one level in terms of another, in particular to relate economic values on the pecuniary level to values on the physical and psychological level. This problem of interpretation is ultimately the more important, but it cannot be solved without settling the first problem nor can it be tackled without the aid of statistical correlation.

And here one other set of variations must be referred to that may help to interpret the facts by relation with *economic* values, namely, *institutional* circumstances. The importance of an institutional interpretation of economics was put forward in Chapter IV at the very outset of this treatise, and the more thoroughly the apparatus of economic theory is exploited the more surely we " come up against " institutional factors. In the outline of the factors determining exchange value (Table XVIIA), the demand side is reduced to physiological or technical needs, conventional necessaries, and individual taste, and also to differences in the wealth of consumers.

On the supply side the factors are reduced to existing stocks, and expenses of obtaining labour, capital, and organizing ability. Now most of these factors are ultimately subject to institutional conditions. By an institution we referred, be it remembered, both to " an organized society or group of persons," and to " a social custom like the institution of marriage."[1]

Conventional necessaries are by definition a matter of custom or habit, and the standard of living of any class of persons is largely built up of such habitual forms of consumption. In this case purchase is made without much conscious calculation of utility. Custom through the notion of a fair wage, or a fair rate of profit or interest, also affects the expenses of labour, capital, and organizing ability. Some writers, in fact, go so far as to maintain that the market rate of interest is only paid because lenders and borrowers are accustomed to that rate and regard it as a right or natural standard. The expenses of labour, organizing ability, and capital are also heavily influenced by societies such as Trade Unions, the Stock Exchange, professional and employers' associations and types of business organizations (joint-stock company, private business, co-operation, etc.), and finally by the organization and government of the State. Where these institutions restrict the supply of those factors of production the wages of labour and the salaries and fees of organizers and business advisers include elements of *institutional rent*. The effect of institutions of all kinds upon wages was cited (in Chapter IV) as the clearest illustration of the need for the institutional interpretation of economics, and among such institutions were included the family and social stratification into " classes." This social stratification, in fact, lies behind much of the difference in wealth that partly determines the demand schedule.

Now these institutions that are, in the ultimate analysis, so important to any economic theory that applies itself to interpreting the facts, are often either statistical in essence or else statistically describable. A habit or custom is some action that occurs comparatively frequently, precisely a statistical " mode " (Glossary §5). The standard of living is that adopted most commonly by a given group or class of person ; a customary fair day's wage or fair rate of interest or profit will tend to be the modal wage or rate of interest or profit or at least will be a narrow range of values measurable in a low coefficient of dispersion (Glossary §13). Stratification, again, is statistically measurable as a distribution

---

[1] Chapter IV §1.

with a wide deviation of values, heavily skewed, or with several modes.

The possibilities of statistical investigation of institutions in the sense of organized societies will, however, be left to the next two chapters ; it is a question, as we have maintained, for the Political Sciences to deal with.

CHAPTER XIX

THE FRAMEWORK AND DATA OF STATISTICAL POLITICS

§1 *The Analysis of Political Relations*

An important distinction was drawn in Chapter III between Political Economics or Administrative Science, Economic Politics or the study of industrial organization, and Political Science proper or the study of the organization of States possessing compulsory power. In the sketch for a statistical political science that is contained in this and the following chapter we shall focus principally upon the latter two branches, which have so much in common[1] ; we shall concentrate, in short, upon the study of organization of all kinds, industrial as well as State or " civic "[2] organization. Political economics or administrative science will, however, be touched upon incidentally (e.g. XIX §2 · 2, §2 · 3) chiefly as providing characters that can be correlated (e.g. XX §7 · 1, §7 · 2) with organizational characters.

The present chapter is an attempt to provide for statistical politics the analytic framework, and the apparatus of thought, that economic theory (when suitably modified as suggested in Chapter XV) already provides for statistical economics. That this framework is suitable for a statistical content will constantly be demonstrated by reference to the possibilities of numerical enumeration.

§1 · 1 Social Transactions, Functionings, and Structure

In Chapter III an analysis was roughly sketched of humdrum mundane organization that excites no particular reverence or any other emotion which might interfere with cold-blooded scientific investigation. Yet the activities manifested by a plain industrial firm or factory are closely analogous to the so-called political, or organizational, activities of the State, and the activities of both can be observed and measured by the aid of the same analysis.

If we begin by observing the facts of any one society, say the

---

[1] See Table IIIA.
[2] Civic may be used as the adjective corresponding to the substantive " State."

industrial firm or the civic State, we find[1] that they refer to qualities and quantities of three characters-in-chief of that society :

First, what that society does, how it acts and " behaves " as a whole, its external work, labour, or transactions, such as exchanging goods or apprehending thieves.

Second, how that external work is carried out in the internal functioning or procedure of the groups or parties within that Society, say the government and the subjects, or the management and the employees.

Third, the structure of the society and its parts ; the number of men and the number of parts of which the society consists.

Unconsciously, by force of circumstances and without remarking the universal application of their analysis to all societies, most political scientists have in fact classified their data according to at least two of these three characters-in-chief. Sidney and Beatrice Webb's *Industrial Democracy* is divided into Part I : Trade Union *Structure* ; Part II : Trade Union *Function*. Sidgwick's *Elements of Politics* has " two main divisions, one concerned with the Functions of Government, and the other mainly with its Structure."

Even official circles have distinguished, though by different names, the structure, transactions, and functioning of a " Company." In an official publication of the War Office (*Infantry Training*, 1905, Part II : The Training of the Company, Sections 59 and 60) will be found the following instructions about (1) the organization (or structure) of the Company ; (2) the object of Company drill (the transactions of the Company as a whole unit in relation to the larger units) ; and (3) " Drill. General Rules " (the functioning of the parts within the Company).

" *Organization of the Company*. A company is permanently divided into two half-companies, the right and left, each under a subaltern, when available. Each half-company is permanently divided into two sections, each under a non-commissioned officer. They will be numbered from one to four.

A section is permanently divided into two squads, each under a non-commissioned officer, or selected private. They will be numbered from one to eight.

Object of Company Drill. The object of company drill is : First to enable the company, when it takes its place in the battalion, to carry out any movement or formation the commanding officer may prescribe, whether laid down in this manual or improvised to meet the circumstances of the moment, without hesitation or confusion. Second, to render the company capable of independent action when detached from the battalion.

[1] Chapter III §4.

DRILL. *General Rules*. The company may be formed as follows :—
   (i.) In line.
   (ii.) In company column (i.e. column of sections).
   (iii.) In column of half-companies.
   (iv.) In column of fours."

Here the War Office have (unconsciously I am sure) grouped their instructions according to the chief characters to which I have called attention. The " Organization " of the Company is the aspect of any society that I shall call its structure ; the " Object " of Company Drill is the external aspect that I shall call its transactions ; and Company Drill itself is the inner working of the Company that I shall call the functioning or procedure of any society.

I have selected these names (1) structure, (2) functioning or procedure, and (3) transactions, because they exclude ethical or moral implications and turn attention in cases (2) and (3) to the behaviour aspect.

And in case these names should come to denote other meanings, Greek symbols may be adopted which, being used only in the scientific writings, may exercise a steadying influence.

I suggest,

  ϵ for ἔργον (an action or performance ; a work ; a task) as in ergograph ; to represent transaction.

  ϕ for φύσις, as in physiology, to represent functioning or procedure ;

  μ for μορφή (form), as in morphology, to represent structure.

Now each of these social characters-in-chief have been vaguely distinguished by the old political theorists, but only under the most bewildering multiplicity of names ; one character has not merely been called by as many names as a royal prince, but different characters often have acquired the same name, like twins " for simplicity." Thus the *transaction* of a society is also known as its field, sphere, province, domain, scope, function, powers, object, aim, end, ideal, work.

The *functioning* or *procedure* of a society is known *also* as its working, powers, function,[1] or work, in addition to its action,

---

[1] Function has many other, and often confusing references besides the two mentioned here of the external activity or transaction of a group and its internal mechanism or procedure. A person's function may refer to what he ought to do ; or what he is normally supposed to do. Both these references are excluded here. The first has the moral implication we rejected in Chapter I ; the second may not tally with the man's actual doings in which we are primarily interested. Function is also used to refer merely to occupation. A " functional analysis " of a group of persons is identical with their occupaional analysis, and it is less confusing to use the word occupational. Functional

mechanism, machinery, *modus operandi*, etc. The *structure* has had fewer baptisms, but has been called composition, substance, organization, form.

The confusion caused by this wealth of synonym can be illustrated both in theoretical and practical politics. Political theories ever since Montesquieu have advocated that the procedure of legislating, adjudicating, and administration should be performed by different people, and this doctrine has been labelled the Separation of Powers. Some time later it was discovered that in Federal States the transactions or province of government had to be divided up between the unitary States and the Federation ; in the U.S.A., for instance, the Federal Government has foreign affairs as its province, and unitary States have labour legislation. But " province " and " power " were interchangeable terms, and this discovery in Federalism was actually tending to be also called the " Separation of Powers " when some one coined the phrase *Distribution of Powers*. The quaintness of this system of terms lies in the fact that two names, Distribution and Separation, here have the *one* meaning of allotment among different persons, while *one* name, Power, has the two different references of the Province (or transactions) of a State and of the Functioning or procedure of that State.

Ordinary practical politicians in England hardly distinguish a socialist from a democrat or a republican. All three are supposed to want a revolution in government and to be Bolshevist. If theorists cannot find names to distinguish between the procedure of government and the province of government, practical politicians need hardly bother to know that the democrat as such may merely want more people included in the governmental structure through the referendum, the recall, or the initiative ; while the socialist as such merely wants an extension in the transactions of government whomever the government may consist of. The transactions of the old Czarist Russian State included management of the railways and ownership of huge tracts of land—it was technically a socialist, but not therefore a democratic government. In structure, the

is also coming into use to denote integral ; a " functional interpretation," e.g. in anthropology, is one taking into account psychological, economic, and all other relevant considerations. But integral, as used in Chapter IV, seems the less ambiguous word. Function is also used to refer to mathematical dependence. " Death rates are a function of occupation " means that a group's death rates depend upon, or are a result of, or co-vary with, that group's occupation.

Less hard-worked synonyms can be found for all these references of the term function, and, with the exception of the title of Chapter I to " prove the rule," I have, as far as possible, avoided the use of the word in these connections

United States government is democratic, but by its *laisser-faire* policy it restricts its province and stamps itself as extremely unsocialistic.

The chaos in terminology is due in the main to the fact that the godparents bestowing the names failed to understand that transactions, procedure (functioning), and structure, are all relative to a particular society and that the transacting of one society might be the functioning of another. There can be no transacting, functioning (procedure), or structure without something that acts, functions (or proceeds), and is constructed ; these headings are characters that societies possess, and which, obviously, can have no existence apart from particular societies.

Further, these three headings are very particular characters ; they are characters without which we cannot think of societies existing. Just as every object has some sort of colour and shape, every society has some transactions, procedure, and structure, and the recognition of these characters is due rather to human ways of thinking than to any peculiarity of the thing thought of.

§1 · 2 Structural Analysis

The structural analysis of any society into individuals and groups of individuals may be made quite arbitrarily, for convenience of observing, comparing, and generalizing about the Society's varieties of functional and transactional activities. Structural analysis simply indicates the persons and groups of persons within a society whose inter-relations are to be measured. It brings to light the sub-societies within that society acting as " parties " in its procedure or transactions.

Each of the " parties " disclosed by investigation into the structure of any society may be considered as a whole society, which, in its turn, may be split into parties and so on, till at last every party consists of one individual person, and the whole original society may be viewed structurally as a sum of individuals, though, functionally, their interactions will no doubt have been found most various. Thus to return to the military example, the Company may be split up structurally into sections, squads, and privates till the whole Company appears as so many *men*. Further analysis is not the business of the political scientist, but of the psychologist, physiologist, and anatomist.

The transaction of any one society must, on the other hand, be ultimately reducible to the functioning of a super-ordinate society that includes it. Any inter-relation of men may always be considered as the internal action, functioning, or procedure of a society that includes those men as its parties.

Once determined upon, therefore, the same scheme of super-ordinate, co-ordinate, and sub-ordinate or constituent[1] structures should be consistently used in the discussion, and the same super-, co-, or sub-structure thought of as the standpoint.

If we focus upon a factory which is only one of many sub-ordinate factories comprised in a firm, the transaction or external relations would refer to the relations between the factory and its super-ordinate firm or between the various co-ordinate factories within the firm; but if in the course of discussion we alter the standpoint to that of this super-ordinate firm, transactions would refer to the exchange relation of that firm with other independent firms or with individual consumers or producers on the market.

When the French nation fights the German nation it is for the French an external action, but for the Europe that includes both nations it is an internal action, functioning, or procedure. The military column of sections is, from the standpoint of the Company, an internal action or functioning; from the standpoint of the section it is an external action or transaction. Similarly the external action of the Company is the " taking of its place " in *battalion* drill as a party to the battalion's functioning. In discussing the government of States we must not switch our structural standpoint from, say, the legislature to the whole government. The transaction or external relations of the legislature are its relations with the judicature, executive, and electorate; the transactions or external relations of the whole super-ordinate government are its relations to the governed; and it is the inward relations (functioning or procedure) of the government that corresponds with the external relations of the legislature and other constituent parties within the government.

Apart from some specific social structure that is taken as the standpoint, the use of distinctions such as transactions and procedure is not merely meaningless but confusing. Hence the importance of a consistent preliminary structural analysis.

Political science, as I conceive it, is not directly concerned with transactions as such but with structure and the functioning or procedure of structures.

Transactions may be performed by single individuals and may

---

[1] Sub-ordinate used in this connection should not imply being ruled, but simply being a part of a larger (super-ordinate) society. Constituent might be used as a synonym, but unfortunately there is no corresponding synonym for super-ordinate. To avoid confusion with subordinate meaning inferior, I shall spell sub-ordinate, the opposite of super-ordinate, with a hyphen.

affect only material nature. It is only when such transactions can be regarded as the functioning or procedure of some super-ordinate society, that they attract the notice of political science. For the scope of political science in the sense of the study of organization is the inter-relations and contacts of persons and bodies of persons, the actions and behaviour of individual persons or bodies of persons toward one another,[1] and the total of inter-related persons or bodies of persons must form a larger super-ordinate society of which the inter-relations of the constituent persons or bodies of persons are merely functionings.

These inter-relations of men to men *within* any society, i.e. its functioning or procedure, were compared in Chapter III to the physiological functions of the structures within the body, and three predominant types of functional relations were distinguished :

(1) The relation of ruling or governing, the behaviour of government or rulers *vis-à-vis* the governed or ruled who are under that rule.

(2) The work-relations of sharing of work or co-operation " between " or " among " persons or bodies of persons in their several activities.

(3) The relation of manning or staffing. The recruitment, entry, and exit of persons " in and out " of the society and its constituent structures.

The series of activities known as managing or employing is analogous to governing and is a social functioning that I shall consider equally a *form* of *ruling* but without the element of compulsion. In industry, persons either ruled under, or forming part of one management, are usually called a FIRM, just as persons ruled under and forming part of one government are called a STATE. All persons who are thus customarily or habitually in relations of rule under one common ruler, whether a single person or a group of persons, I shall call AN ORGANIZATION.

The inclusion of the adverb habitually or customarily points to the " statistically-to-be-determined " nature of an organization. An organization can only be effective if it is in some degree stable in the sense that the persons under one rule remain under that rule for a certain minimum of time. This stability is measurable either (a) by the average time (or frequency distribution of times) spent by individuals in that organization, e.g. their length of tenure, or (b) by the labour turnover rate or velocity $= \dfrac{\text{Number Leaving}}{\text{Total Population}}$ per given period, usually a year.

[1] See Chapter III.

Now modern Nation-States are in this sense very stable. The majority of nationals stay nationals of the same State throughout their life. They enter the organization by the fact of birth and leave the organization by the fact of death. It is only a small minority that enter by artificial naturalization, or leave by naturalization into another State.

The manning of the State is in this sense virtually automatic and impersonal. But absence of human agency is not true of the manning of the firm, and this peculiarity which the firm shares with most other organized societies is one reason for studying the industrial firm side by side with the State. In the firm manning is a relation between persons. Manning, or as it is colloquially known, hiring and firing, is in fact performed by the ruler party which thereby becomes more than a managing party and grows into an employing party. Considerations of space forbid the devotion of separate sections to manning relations within the whole *personnel* of the firm as logical thoroughness demands. Apart from indicating analogies, manning will only be considered (§6) in so far as it occurs *within the government* of the Firm or State as exhibited in the appointment, dismissal, or resignation of managers, officials, members of legislative bodies, and other rulers.

§1 · 3 The Institution or Body of Persons

A factory consists in a number of persons meeting together more or less continuously or recurrently at the same time and place. There are observable working premises within a measurable local area, and observable working hours within specified times. The whole number of persons may be dismissed at any moment through closing down, or a new factory may be set up and " constituted," thus calling together a whole new body of persons at a given time and place.

Both factory and firm are organizations of persons, but the factory is in addition a body of persons and thus distinct from a firm comprising several factories, in that all the members of a *firm* do not necessarily meet together simultaneously and recurrently at a stated time or place. This distinction is a necessary preliminary to the analysis of political structure if we are to avoid confusion.

An organization, as already defined, refers to a number of persons or groups of persons in more or less habitual (permanent or recurrent) relations of rule. But an organization of which the constituent organs are persons attending or " mustering " more or less habitually (permanently or recurrently) at one time and place may be specifically named a *body of men*.

Akin to a factory body are Houses of Parliament, the Cabinet, a Judicial Court, Committees, and so on. All these groups of persons meeting more or less continuously, or recurrently, and simultaneously at some place and time are " bodies of persons," and the more or less of simultaneity and of recurrence or continuousness in their meeting is a matter of statistical determination.

The degree of effectiveness in the mustering of individual persons at a given place or time can be measured statistically by the attendance records or the rate of absence and the degree of punctuality, etc. Though the body known as the British House of Commons consists of a definite number of persons, the attendance may vary from the full 100% attendance to a bare QUORUM, i.e. the legal minimum limit. This limit may be either a definite absolute number of persons or a specific proportion of the total number.

In the body of persons known as an Industrial Factory statistics of absence are a regular feature of a well-ordered system of *personnel* records, and statistical correlations have been established between the variations in absenteeism and the hours of labour, seasons of the year, type of worker employed, etc.[1] Absenteeism under adverse conditions may rise as high as 20% ; that is, one person out of five may be absent at any one time, or one hour out of every five scheduled for work may be lost. Just as when turnover approaches 100% per day and no one stays within the given relation of rule longer than a day, an organization becomes in fact no organization ; so, as absence approaches 100% and no one ever turns up at the given time and place, a body of persons becomes in fact no body of persons.

Given that persons muster or attend at a given time or place continuously and *effectively enough* to pass as a " body of persons," they will be observed to act in certain customary relations toward one another. But these, we shall find, resemble so closely the relations of ruling, of work-sharing, and of manning that will be dealt with as the *functioning* of the State or Firm or of the Government or Management ruling the State or Firm, that no separate analysis need be made. The various relations of individual persons within a body of persons can be observed and classified side by side with the similar relations of bodies of persons or individual persons within *any* organization.

These simultaneously and recurrently meeting " bodies of persons " will be found to act and be acted upon partly collectively

[1] Florence, *Economics of Fatigue and Unrest*, Chapter VII.

as an integral body, partly as a number of related individuals or members.

In the *manning* relations they may be summoned and dissolved collectively as a body ; or each member may be appointed and dismissed individually, as by a by-election for filling a vacancy in the House of Commons.

In the *rule* relations the whole body of persons may exercise rule as does any Board of Directors of a firm or the British Cabinet ; but for the very purpose of making the individual members *act as one man* with the natural coherence, decision, and unanimity of a single person, there are rules of procedure within the body, enforced just as orders are enforced among individuals in the State or Firm as a whole.   Members of bodies are ordered to muster by ruling members, as members of the English House of Commons by the party whips ; they are prohibited from interrupting debates or speaking on subjects out of order by the ruling of a chairman ; and there is impulsion or compulsion exercised, in suspension or ex-pulsion from membership, payment of fines, or forfeiture of salary.

In the *work-sharing* relations the body of persons may specialize as a body, for example a judicial court specializes in trying in-dividual cases as against passing general laws.   But within the body of persons there may be individual specialization, for example the case of an orchestra with individuals playing different instru-ments ; or there may be specialization by individuals and sub-bodies, for example judge, and counsel, and jury—a sub-body of twelve individual persons.

In short, the external or internal relations and contacts of *a body of persons* will not be treated as peculiar, but can be classified as either ruling or manning or work-sharing relations.   The only difference from the case of a group of persons that is not a body is that bodies must be considered in two aspects, individual and collective.

§1 · 4 The Plan of Discussion in Succeeding Sections

Political science, to resume the main discussion, is interested in the acts or behaviour of men toward men, their mutual inter-relations and reciprocal contacts ; the orders, punishments, votes, verdicts, appointments, dismissals, passing transitively from men to men, and the meetings and discussions between men, that form part of their relations of ruling, manning, and sharing of work.

But before these acts and this behaviour can be objectively

measured, it must be made clear *who* are the participants referred to as agents and patients of these acts and contacts. Structural analysis of a group or society into parts or parties is necessary in order to make manifest what are the interactions between the structural parties, " the interstructural relations," that are to be measured.

Now the State and the Firm are specific social structures consisting of so and so many persons, measurable, and measured in population statistics of States, and in statistics such as the frequency of different sizes of establishments given in Table VA.

I shall take the persons within the State to be grouped, amongst other ways, into two sub-structures or parties—the government and the governed ; and the persons within the Business Firm to be grouped into two sub-structures or parties—the employer and the employed. I shall then examine, in §2, the relation of governing and managing or employing that is observable in their mutual interaction. In §3 I shall consider the other groupings of the persons within the State or Firm and the political or business world generally, with the object of examining the work-sharing relation that is observable in their mutual interaction. In §4 I shall proceed to a structural analysis of the governing and employing (or managing) *party* (distinguished in §2) with a view to examining the functional relationship, the mutual interaction, of the several parties or sub-structures, if any, disclosed *within* the government.

A difference is observable in the relations between States and the relations between Firms ; a difference that justifies our focusing upon both in turn. While the political world is sub-divided more or less territorially into national States, the business world is divided up functionally into firms specializing in different kinds of work and it is the " work relations " that are of the greatest interest. It is as a chief instance of ruling customs that I cite (§2) the relation between the structure of government as a whole and the governed as a whole within the State. But as a chief instance of customs of work-sharing and their statistical measurability I cite (§3) the relation between firms and between individuals in the business world as a whole, before proceeding, in §6, to apply this analysis of work-relations to the State government.

§2   The Rule Relation

In observing the relations of ruling I shall deal mainly with two types of organization, the State and the business firm. For purposes of observation the State or the firm must be defined in terms of this very functioning of rule. A State or a firm is a number of men *ruled* (*governed*, or *managed-and-employed*) in common by the *same* individual governor and employer-manager or group of governors and managers. It is not as a transacting unit with some vague " duty to " or " function in " the outside world, but as an observably functioning, interacting, group of men within which men rule and employ, and are ruled and employed, that I define State and Firm. True, the State and firm perform certain external transactions. The firm as a whole exchanges goods and services on the market either with individual customers or other firms, and the State engages as a whole in international relations for peace or war abroad, and is held[1] to secure order and mutual toleration and to further industry and education at home. But these transactions are not the functionings of any wider super-ordinate organized society, and according to the limits laid down (Chapter III and above, §1) go beyond the scope of political science.

The State and the firm are sovereign in this sense, that they are not part of any wider organization ruling them, they are a group of persons ruled by a government or management that is not in its turn governed or managed.

People often speak of firms belonging to an industry as though an industry were a definite super-ordinate organization. But pursuant to our definition of organization, an industry cannot be so classed. An industry can only be defined in some such way as any kind of transaction for exchange (production, distribution, services, etc.) usually specialized in by a group of firms who do not usually perform other transactions. Thus transport or coal-mining is an " industry " because there are special transporting or coal-mining firms who do not perform much of any other transaction, though they may provide a fraction of hotel accommodation, or coking and gas production.

Our analysis of rule relations will not be concerned with the relations of firms or men to the industry. In the market relations between separate firms, just as in the international relations between political States, there is as yet anarchy and competition modified, now and then, here and there, by agreements, a League of Nations, alliances, ententes (Kartells, Pools, etc.), Combines and Trusts, and variously organized attempts to obtain hegemony, or to obtain monopoly within an industry the effectiveness of which can be measured statistically by the proportion of output that is " controlled." The normal relation is still exchange or " diplomatic " relations subject to crises and wars, not orderly rule.

[1] Holland, *Jurisprudence*, Chapter on " Public Law."

§2 · 1   Rule Relations of Ordering and Finance.

The primary relations of rule may be observed in the relation between individual persons within a body of persons meeting simultaneously. Government is not effective unless some person or persons are set aside at least for the time being to do the governing, and such bodies may thus be viewed as consisting of two parties, the rulers and the ruled, even if the ruler is only a chairman, an orchestra conductor, a steering committee, a captain, or a referee.

The ruler party within the body of persons may be loosely defined. It may be one man or body of men one day or in one con- text, another man or body of men on another occasion. And on any one occasion the ruler party is not necessarily solely a ruler. Most chairmen, for instance, may give casting votes and thus join in the decision as well as ruling the debate upon some proposal. Moreover, the ruler party, whoever it consists in, may be to some extent subject to the rules. Yet the fact remains that there *are* rules, orders, or commands issued or interpreted by some sort of chairman, as the rules of procedure (who may speak, what subjects are out of order, etc.) by the Speaker of the House of Commons. Attached to these rules or orders are certain sanctions stimulating or inducing members of the body to obey them, a financial incentive or penalties such as suspension, expulsion, fining, etc. Where a financial incentive is paid or expenses are involved in inflicting a penalty, a second relation is added possibly involving further compulsion,—that of obtaining a revenue to defray costs.

The same two elements involving terms of compulsion in the rule relation between the ruler on the one side and the ruled or the whole membership on the other side, is also clearly observable in any organization wider than a mere body of persons, if the ruler party consists of one autocrat. The relation of an autocrat in govern- ing a State or managing a firm consists : (1) in issuing rules, orders, or commands with some " sanction " to stimulate members to carry out these orders, and (2) in financing or defraying costs. The element (2) might be unnecessary if the State government could (as it practically does in the case of compulsory military or jury service) avoid the payment of financial remuneration. But in modern States the applicability of compulsory non-remunerated service is limited.

Where in any organization that is more than one body of persons meeting simultaneously, there is a multitude of rulers, the relations are more complicated. The rules may be " substantive " in the sense of ordering the relations of all members of the State, i.e.

relations among the ruled; or they may be constitutional or adjective rules in the sense that they (*a*) order the relation of members of the government (the ruler party) toward one another or toward ruled persons, or (*b*) order (as in the sacrosanctity of the Roman Tribune or the modern contempt of court, *lèse-majesté*, etc.) the relation of the ruled to the ruler. Members of the ruler party are sometimes privileged, i.e. immune from the substantive rules (and the stimulation to obey them) applying to members of the State, generally.[1] For instance, in the U.S.A. members of the legislature, and in Britain members of Parliament, can be arrested while the session is in progress only for indictable offences, and in Britain this privilege was even extended to members' servants (case of Smalley, 1576). There is also immunity, granted in special cases, from taxation. But whatever the modifications, the same two rule relations that involve terms of compulsion remain as elements : (1) finance and (2) issuing orders, " laws," or commands.

Law is the word preferred by political scientists. " Law," writes Sidgwick, " is a body of rules intended to control the conduct of members of a political society, for the violation of which penalties may be expected to be inflicted by the authority of the government of that society, and which, therefore, may be regarded as imposed by government."[2] But the word order is perhaps preferable as a wider term, including rules issued to individuals as well as general rules.[3]

§2 · 2   The Variety of Procedure in Ordering and Financing

Both ordering and financing can conceivably be done in various ways ; and, in fact, the State does order and finance its transactions by alternate procedures measurably distinguished.

Let us suppose that the State wants better drains in its towns, and that since individual effort has failed, the State decides to include the provision of drains among its transactions.   Having

---

[1] This may possibly be justified pragmatically as avoiding interference with the procedure of ruling. More often it is a vestigial remain of the doctrine that the Sovereign can do no wrong and that the State government is the Sovereign (see Laski, *Grammar of Politics*, p. 396).

[2] *Elements of Politics*, Chapter III.

[3] The word command, by the analogy with the economist's word demand, may be taken to exclude orders connected with the government's procedure of finance.   Demand is primarily an order on the part of a buyer (coupled with a money stimulus) for the provision or performance of specific amounts of goods, services, or acts ; it is not a seller's bid for money.   Similarly, while government *finance* is the order to pay money, government *commands* will be taken to be orders (coupled with the sanction of compulsion) to perform, or to refrain from performing, specific non-financial services or acts.

announced their decision the government will next have to stimulate people to obey the order to build the drains. This may be done in three ways :

(a) By criminal law : the government may proclaim that anyone whose drains smell or are otherwise defective shall be punished, and may employ inspectors to " nose " around.

(b) By civil law : the government may proclaim that any person who can show that the smell of a neighbour's drain annoys him may procure " compensation " from that neighbour.

(c) The government may just *pay* managers and labourers to make and repair the drains.

The first two methods may be classed as compulsion or " inducement by punishment " ; the instigator of punishment being in case (a) the State government, in case (b) any member of the State. The third method may be called " inducement by payment." The term payment should not, in this case, be confined to money payment, but may include payment in board and lodging or in the net advantage of, say, the social prestige of title or uniform.[1] Inducement by payment plus, perhaps, some net advantages[2] is the usual method of stimulating the performance of orders in the industrial firm. The employee (or managee) of the firm is paid a wage or salary. If he is fractious and refuses obedience to orders he is dismissed from his employment (and the need for further obedience), but then forfeits the receipt of wage or salary in the future.

Whatever the alternate policy of ordering adopted, the government will have to *finance* or *defray the expenses* incurred in building or in making men build the drains. The wages of drain builders or the salaries of judges and police will eventually have to come out of the pockets of members of the State. And two observably different financial policies are possible.

(a) Let those members of the State who use the drains or gain by the threat of punishing bad drainage, pay the makers or the threateners ; this may be termed the financial policy of *State trading*.

(b) Let the government of the State grant payment for making drains or for threatening punishment and then let it recoup itself by levying taxes. This may be termed the financial policy of *grant and tax*.

Similarly, in the case of the industrial firm, the whole ruling procedure is only complete when the employer has found the wealth wherewith to defray the payment of wages to those carrying out his orders. Here the necessary wealth is generally secured, by the

---

[1] See below, Chapter XX §7 · 2.   [2] See Chapter XVIII.

2B

trading method, out of the pockets of the consumer or customers who pay a price in voluntary exchange for the goods or service the firm is producing. It is, indeed, in the stimulation of the ruled to carry out orders and the defrayment of expenses, that the chief distinction between the industrial society and the State arises.

In the firm or factory men are stimulated to obey orders by means of pay offered in exchange, while in the State men may be stimulated to obey orders by civil or criminal compulsion as well. It is a distinction in the *terms* of the stimulus to obedience of rules, not in the organization of the ruling. Similarly, in the industrial firm, expenses are defrayed by setting a price on the goods or services exchanged, such that the total return (price × units sold) will balance or more than balance expenses. The State on the other hand may or may not adopt this price policy.[1] Here again, the distinction lies in the terms of the financial transaction, not in the organization or procedure of that transaction.

In Chapter III these two aspects of social life, the *terms* of the stimulus or check to action, and the *organization* of action or quiescence, were distinguished as fundamental enough to call for two distinct sciences :

(1) Administrative science or political economics measuring and investigating the terms, the relation of stimulus to reaction.

(2) The science of organization, economic or political " politics," measuring and investigating the organization of ruling and other human activities.

In the next two sub-sections (§2 · 3 and §2 · 4) we shall outline examples of statistical methods applied to administrative science in solving the question of (1) the terms of the stimulus to obey orders, and (2) the terms of financial recoupment for the costs of ruling.

§2 · 3   Degree of Deterrence of Specific Terms of Compulsion

Table XIXA is an example of a statistical investigation applied to the terms of penalties and traces the effect of various kinds of penalties or absence of penalty (i.e. discharge) on the reappearance in court of the penalized person in two " sample " towns. In the first column for each town are the absolute number of juveniles who reappeared within two years after the specified kind of penalty (or absence of penalty) was meted out. In the third column the percentage of reappearance in any ONE year is worked out for comparative purposes by halving the reappearance figure in column 1

[1] See below, §2 · 4.

(since this refers to TWO years) and dividing by the average annual number *originally* dealt with as given in column 2. Thus, 42 juveniles in Town A reappeared in the courts in the course of two years after detention had been meted out, or 21 per single year. Since 48 was the average number detained per year, the percentage of reappearance for any one year was $21 \div 48$ or $43 \cdot 75\%$.

" Statistics in this matter," says the Juvenile Organizations Committee of the Board of Education, from whose report the Table is quoted, " can only be approximate, and hasty conclusions must be avoided, for many factors have to be taken into consideration . . . the large number of reappearances after birching is remarkable, but due allowance must be made for the fact that it is usually the bad type of boy who is whipped. Some of these seem to return whatever the punishment. The same explanation may apply to

TABLE XIXA

COMPARATIVE EFFECT OF VARIOUS PENALTIES ON JUVENILE OFFENDERS

Forms (*QUALITY*) of Penalty	Total No. of Re-appear-ances within two years	*Town A* Av. No. originally dealt with per year	Percentage of Re-appear-ances in any one year	Total No. of Re-appear-ances within two years	*Town B* Av. No. originally dealt with per year	Percentage of Re-appear-ances in any one year
Detention	42	48	43·75	—	—	—
Birch	421	524	40·17	19	50	19·00
Discharge	577	1082	26·66	49	162	15·12
Probation	75	155	24·19	44	93	23·66
Fine	—	—	—	109	308	17·65
Binding Over	21	94	11·17	10	15	33·30

the cases who have been under detention for short periods, for these are bad cases also."

" But when allowance has been made for these facts, there still remains a difference in the after-results of various forms of treatment which must be acknowledged and considered."

In particular the more drastic penal terms of detention and birching appear to have the least success as a deterrent in Town A, and are no greater a deterrent than fine or discharge in Town B.

§2 · 4 The Measurement of Various Public Finance Procedures

Two administrative policies of finance are available for the government of the State : (A) the *trading* and (B) the *tax and grant* system respectively.

(A) The trading system is to the economist the simpler of the two.

It occurs whenever the State government is stepping into the shoes of the private business man, and wherever government and the subject are related as supplier to demander. An individual requires to communicate by letter with another individual. To carry the letter he pays the State government so and so much in stamps, just as he might pay the private railway company to carry a parcel. In this financial procedure the revenue of the State takes the same forms as the gross proceeds of the private business man.

(B) In the tax and grant system, on the other hand, there is no exchange. The State government is here generally represented, on the one hand, by the tax-gatherer who extracts wealth without offering any immediate equivalent, and on the other hand by such administrators as the Postmaster-General, who may grant old age pensions, again without demanding any wealth in exchange.

The tax is not necessarily gathered where the grant will benefit. In the English tax system the revenue from different taxes is collected in one lump by the Chancellor of the Exchequer and his minions, and then distributed to the separate " granting " departments of Education, War, Admiralty, etc.

In some cases what may be called a special tax such as the Petrol or Horse-Power Tax on motor-cars may be levied for a specific purpose, i.e. improvement of roads, and the class that pays is the class that benefits. But it still remains true that taxation is payment by a whole class and granting is payment to a whole class ; to the single individual the tax and the grant may not be equal.

To make the taxing side of this system practicable, one condition is essential to the State government,—the power of compulsion either by punishing, or by securing damages or compensation. People will not contribute voluntarily to State funds ; English history is fertile in experiments along this line, interesting to the psychologist, no doubt, but necessarily disappointing to the optimist experimenting. Henry VII, for instance, instituted " benefices " whereby the plutocrats of the day were enabled to help their country. Persuasive agents scoured the country. One of these was Cardinal Morton, whose methods of persuasion are thus described in the unaffected style of S. R. Gardiner. " If he (Cardinal Morton) addressed himself to one who lived in good style, he told him that his mode of living showed that he could afford to give money to the King. If he had to do with one who appeared to be economical, he told him that he must have saved and could therefore afford to give money to the King."

Another interesting experiment of the same sort was tried in the case of the Poor Law. In 1536 it was enacted that the poor be publicly relieved from a common fund to which all who cared might contribute. All does not seem to have gone well, however. In 1555 the local Bishop is required to exhort and persuade his flock to contribute. In 1563 the obstinate were to be handed over to the justices of the peace. Finally, in 1597, all were to be taxed whether willing or not, and such as refused were distrained or sent to jail.

The experience of Morton and his " fork " and of the Elizabethan bishops, not to mention modern Trade Unions, and the Distress Committees of 1905, only confirm what our knowledge of human psychology would suggest ; namely, the inadequacy of voluntary charitable gifts to maintain a large or regular State revenue.

The two contrasted financial procedures of trading and of tax and granting are not mutually exclusive. It is possible to combine them either (1) in raising the general revenue of the State, or (2) in raising revenue to defray particular transactions.

(1) The general revenue of all modern States is raised by both methods of procedure. Hence, for any specific purpose, a price may be charged under the trading procedure high enough to yield a surplus over and above expense incurred, and this surplus devoted to the relief of taxation and the endowment of grants for other purposes.

In many trading transactions the State obtains a high surplus. In the years immediately preceding 1914 the profit on the Prussian State Railways was in the neighbourhood of £28,000,000, and the British Post Office often (e.g. in 1924) reports a large profit. This profit is due partly to the economies of a large-scale production, partly to the State's higher credit and lower rate of interest, but more particularly to a monopoly, often established legally by the State itself. Thus most States allow no competitors to the Post Office ; and the French State is the sole manufacturer of matches in France, while foreign competitors are heavily taxed.

(2) In financing (defraying) *a particular service* the two systems can be combined, by giving each a share in raising the revenue for that purpose. The State Insurance for Health and Unemployment in Great Britain and Ireland is financed partly by a grant from taxes, partly by premiums paid (compulsorily) by the individuals benefited which are thus less than business premiums would be.

Other instances are the so-called " nominal " charges made for entrance to museums, public concerts, etc. Nominal here means that the charge is below the price that would cover expenditure or that would yield average business profits.

In all, four varieties of procedure may thus be distinguished. They may be measured statistically along one scale of value according to whether revenue is (I) nil, (II) falls short of, (III) equals approximately, or (IV) exceeds expenditure. The character in respect of which thèse ranges of value occur may be called the budgetary equilibrium, and the measurement may, of course, be made finer by increasing the number of ranges, grades, or degrees by which revenue falls short of, or exceeds, expenditure.

Setting aside the voluntary tax system as impracticable, and all " penalty " revenues from fines as insufficient, it will be found that these four varieties of the trading and the tax-and-grant procedure cover most of the revenue side of Public Finance. Many economists have differentiated loans and taxes, but a loan is, after all, only revenue anticipated, and the question still remains, how that revenue is to be finally secured. The problem still remains whether the interest or repayment of the loan is to be paid out of taxes or out of a trade revenue. In the long run the two procedures and four varieties still cover the ground, and that by cutting right across loans.

In measuring what is the actual variety of financial policy adopted by the State, the statistics of municipal transactions are readily available. Among English municipalities and local authorities as a whole the provision of markets, of gas, and of tramways and light railways, was, in 1907-8, run at a clear profit of at least 7% on turnover, while the provision of harbours and docks, and of water, was run at a definite loss.[1] The former undertakings can thus be said to have been financed on policy IV, while the latter were financed on policy II. Electricity was provided, taking the average of all local authorities and municipalities, at a profit of only 3½% on turnover, and the financial procedure here may be classed perhaps as policy III. The total profits or losses involved in the undertakings of English *Boroughs* only, may be seen in Table XIXB, column 4.

But the possible fallacies of generalizing too harshly from average or total results is shown clearly in the first three columns of the table, where the item boroughs are distributed for each kind of undertaking according as they in fact pursued financial policy II, III, or IV. In no kind of undertaking do all the boroughs appear in one or even two columns only. In every kind of undertaking all three policies were observed.

Further possible fallacies in making use of these financial statistics are pointed out by Knoop.[2]

" The capital accounts may have been inadequately debited with

[1] Knoop, *Principles and Methods of Municipal Trading*, Chapter XII p. 308.
[2] Op. cit., p. 307.

expenditure incurred in connection with the trading departments, in consequence of which their loan charges would be reduced ; a proper share of the general expenses of the municipality may not have been charged to the trading departments and the provision made for depreciation may be quite insufficient. In this way the annual expenditure of the undertakings would be checked which would make their financial position appear unduly favourable.

" On the other hand, if the trading departments have supplied other municipal departments with services or commodities at less than the usual prices, or even free of charge, their receipts would be diminished to that extent and the return would show their financial position to be less favourable than it really was."

TABLE XIXb

FINANCIAL POLICY OF MUNICIPAL UNDERTAKINGS

Accounts of Councils of Boroughs (other than Metropolitan Boroughs) *in England and Wales*, 1908–9

	Number of Boroughs which			
Undertakings	(under policy II) assisted the specified undertaking out of rates	(under policy III) neither assisted nor received relief	(under policy IV) received sums in relief of rates out of specified undertaking	Total excess (+) or deficiency (−) on specified undertakings
Tramways and Light Railways	32	38	19	+£229,000
Water Supply	63	108	51	−£136,000
Gas Supply	2	34	69	+£450,000
Electricity Supply	34	81	37	+£62,000

§2 · 5 Measurable Elements in Discussion and Formal Rule Activities

Two primary relations of rulers with ruled were analysed in §2 · 1 as (1) rulers ordering or commanding ruled persons or members of the rule-society generally to act or not to act in certain ways on pain of certain penalties, and (2) rulers extracting from the ruled the means whereby to defray the costs of " ordering " by charging them a price or a tax. This analysis was found particularly important in problems of political economics or administrative science dealing with the terms of penalties, or the terms of taxation or trade. We may now proceed to an analysis more important in the science of political *organization*.

Orders may apply specifically to individuals ordering a particular person to do or not to do this or to pay that, or may be *general* laws ordering *all* persons in a certain situation to do or not to do this or that or to pay this or that. If orders are general " laws," but not otherwise, the distinction so familiar in text-books of political science between legislation, execution, and adjudication is relevant. There will probably be persons or bodies of persons to pass the general law ; other persons to execute it in particular cases ; and others to interpret the law, i.e. to test, often by an elaborate trial, whether the general law applies in specific individual cases, and whether and to what extent punishment is due to those accused of infringing the general law.

But the preliminary generalization of orders as " laws " is by no means universal and invariable in modern States, as witness Martial Law ; and even where there is a generalization it is not invariably performed by the particular persons or bodies of persons known as the " legislature." Laws of some degree of generality may be given out by the so-called executive through proclamation or orders in council. In short, the difference between the executive and legislature is not determined *a priori*. *Practice* may vary in the degree of discretion given to the executive, and executive officers may even be given judicial or quasi-judicial authority.[1] As Laski shows, " The decisions of the U.S. Secretary of Labour in all immigration cases are final so that, for instance, a Japanese born in America could be excluded from the United States on his return from a visit to Canada on the fiat of an executive department."[2]

In many arbitration proceedings and in Common Law as against Statute Law, laws are given out by the same persons or body of persons who adjudicate. In so far as custom regulates people's behaviour, there is no precise general law-giving at all, and legislation and adjudication may sometimes be lumped together as we have already suggested the lumping together of legislation with execution, and adjudication with execution.

Now it is for statistical investigation to discover how far these theoretical distinctions between various activities of the government are in fact separate organizational relations, interactions, or " contacts " between rulers and ruled, and whether there are not other more definitely observable distinctions. As a preliminary I am inclined to distinguish only two sorts of interactions of governments as a whole, and the governed (or the State) as a whole *vis-à-vis* one another in modern more or less democratic States.

I   Discussion between rulers and ruled.

II   Formal acts of State procedure.

In treatises of political science government is usually considered entirely from the standpoint of the governing party, and governing

---

[1] See Marriot, *Mechanism of the Modern State.*
[2] Laski, *Grammar of Politics*, p. 389, citing U.S. v. Ju Toy 198, U.S. 253.

procedure is analysed simply as a series of formal activities,—legislative, judicial, and executive. In fact, however, the relations of governed and government are less one-sided as well as less of an ordered stereotyped series. The governed either (1) individually, or (2) in *ad hoc* organizations like the Women Suffrage Societies that urged a change in the electoral law to give votes for women in England, or (3) in more or less permanent organizations like the political parties (whose activities such as nominating candidates through caucuses and primary elections, are legally recognized and controlled in most American States[1]), may bring pressure to bear on government by the airing of grievances, agitation, political campaigns, passing resolutions, canvassing and lobbying, petitions, deputations ; and no realistic political science can neglect the influence of political propaganda conducted through the medium of meetings, bribery, newspapers, or violence.

Hence a contact between ruler and ruled parties to include in the real procedure of governing, is the activity of propaganda, or to use a word with a wider reference, the activity of discussion. This discussion is more definitely part of the process of ruling than the activities of legislation, execution, and adjudication recognized in political treatises. Though partly performed within the government (e.g. in the debates of the legislature and in trials in court[2]), it is in modern States also an interaction of government as a whole and the governed as a whole ; it is a number of overt acts or utterances by which the ordinary person impinges upon or is impinged upon by the State government, and not a mere interaction of the different organs (e.g. King, Lords, and Commons) *within* the government.

§2 · 6   The Measurement of Discussion

The right of the subject to petition the Crown is an old constitutional device in England, and *ad hoc* organizations of subjects naturally arose out of this right. But in contemporary democratic States, the most influential organs of discussion continuously engaged in suggesting and urging changes or the *status quo*, are probably the political parties and the newspapers.

The essential activity of the POLITICAL PARTY, as Laski[3] points out, is the selection of the precise problems to be discussed, the building, as the Americans put it, of a specific party " platform."

These political propaganda societies form a study in themselves for political statistics. The mere number of effective parties is of

---

[1] Beard, *American Government and Politics*, Chapter VII.
[2] See below, §6.   [3] *Grammar of Politics*, p. 312.

great political importance (compare the two-party system of Britain in the 18th and 19th centuries, or the U.S.A. almost throughout its history, with the three-party system of Britain to-day, and the multiplicity of political groups of France and Germany). And party structure (membership and subsidiary organs) and procedure, government (including finance), methods of manning and staffing, and subdivision and distribution of labour, are all amenable to the same sort of measurement as the structure and procedure of the State.

In modern States the NEWSPAPER is perhaps an equally important method of forming public opinion, and significant statistics might be collected of the ownership of and sources of revenue of these overt publications. If a separate statistical study were made in England, attention would be worth directing at the present moment to the dwindling number of newspapers per population, and the increased influence of a few newspapers ; to the combination of several newspapers virtually under one rule, and the increased influence of fewer ownerships ; and to the increasing revenue obtained from advertisement and the probably increasing influence of advertisers.

The realistic statistical study of methods of political discussion has yet to be developed in the world of State government, but in the world of business firms where employment is an analogous relation to government, TRADE UNIONS appear as organizations of the " ruled " employee, and much statistical information is to hand as to the structure and functioning of these organizations and the varieties and results of their transactions in bringing pressure to bear on employers. Table IXc, for instance, correlates the success of strikes in obtaining the industrial " laws " the employees advocated, with a measure of the predominance of Trade Unionists among all employees.

Though collective bargains might fail to be effective were it not for the threat of strike, Trade Unions effect changes in industrial law much more frequently by peaceful collective bargaining than by actual resort to the strike. This effective though negative control (which applies sometimes to the manning of the firm and its ruling party, e.g. the appointment and dismissal of foreman, though more usually to the ruling of the firm) might be found by the aid of statistical investigation to be so regular and habitual that Trade Unions could be considered as raised to the status of an organic part of the ruling party. Trade Unions, however, do not yet participate effectively in the financing of the firm, and for the present we may continue to consider them as an organization of the ruled party.

As such, Trade Unionists elect, dismiss, and pay their representatives just as constituents do their members of Parliament. These representatives sit together, have a chairman, and certain rules of procedure just like the House of Commons. The officials of the Union are given some definite work, such as to make arrangements with the employer, and have powers of taxing or fining members. This exactly parallels the external work or transaction, and the rule procedure of the State, and can be observed and measured by the same scientific methods.

" The rules of all unions, from the earliest times down to the present day, contain clauses empowering the fining of disobedient members, the alternative to paying the fine being expulsion from the Union. The development of the Friendly Society side of Trade Unionism incidentally makes this sanction a penalty of very real weight, and one which can be easily enforced. To this pecuniary loss may, moreover, be added the incidents of outlawry. When a Union includes the bulk of the workmen in any industry, its members invariably refuse to work alongside a man who has been expelled from the Union for ' working contrary to the interests of the trade.' In such a case expulsion from the Union may easily mean expulsion from the trade."[1]

§2 · 7 The Measurement of Formal Activities in Rule Organization

Adjudication or trial is the formal activity of the governing party that impinges upon the governed persons in greatest complication, and it may be observed as a series of contacts between the State government or ruler party represented by police and judicial authorities on the one side, and the ruled individual on the other.

Judicial procedure in modern European states takes two forms, criminal and civil. Translated into observable terms this refers to the recurrence of two distinguishable series of contacts or behaviour patterns, one stimulated or " set going " by one sort of (unlawful) act on the part of the ruled individual ; the other by another sort of (unlawful) act on his part.

In the *criminal procedure* or pattern, the State, represented by the police or judicial authority,

(1) initiates proceedings for some unlawful action by arresting the individual and subjecting him to a preliminary investigation by Grand Jury or Magistrate ;

[1] Sidney and Beatrice Webb, *Industrial Democracy*, Part II, Chapter II, edition 1902, p. 207.

(2) Summons him to court if committed by the preliminary investigation ;

(3) Usually, though not necessarily, prosecutes him in court, and usually through the Public Prosecutor.

(4) To this the accused individual puts in a defence.

(5) The State then judges him and sentences him if found guilty.

(6) Executes the sentence of the court upon him.

In *civil procedure* the ruler party confine their activities to (2) summons, (5) judgment and sentence (assessment of damages) if any, and (6) execution of sentence (damages) if the loser of the action does not of his own will pay the damages.

These " pattern " rule relations between government (denoted " G ") and individual (denoted " I ") are shown in Table XIXc and compared with other procedures ancient and modern. The modern procedure of (1) arbitration, (2) conciliation, and (3) mediation, are pattern systems of stimulating persons to act or not to act in certain ways in which the main functioning of the government or its representative is respectively (1) to pass judgment, (2) to summon the disputing parties, or (3) to initiate proceedings usually as a preventive measure. Here the judicial process may be quite independent of any governmental order or threat of punishment. The primitive systems of judicial procedure in the top rows of the table will be referred to later.[1]

If the whole ruling procedure be looked upon as different kinds of recurrent behaviour patterns, the recurrences may be admitted to vary in frequency, completeness, and intensity. Owing to this variability investigation of the procedure would necessarily take a statistical form in at least three particulars which may be visualized as dealing respectively with :

(1) The relative frequency of recurrence of the different patterns.

(2) The frequency with which patterns are completed or partially completed.

(3) The intensity of the pattern or parts of the pattern.

(1) Statistics may measure the number of procedures started for different offences, especially in relation (a) to the unlawful offences of the same kind known to have been committed, or (b) in relation to the number of the population, or of any class or sex within the population.

For instance, the number of arrests and trials under any given law or series of laws defining specific crimes could be compared with

[1] Chapter XX §9 · 1.

TABLE XIXc

FORM OF TABLE SHOWING OBSERVABLE JUDICIAL DIVISION OF LABOUR
BETWEEN INDIVIDUAL (I) AND GOVERNMENT (G) UNDER VARIOUS
SYSTEMS

SYSTEMS of JUDICIAL PROCEDURE	Initiation of Individual Case	Summons of Parties	Accusation	Defence	Judgment and Sentence	Execution of Sentence
Self-Redress . .	I	—	—	—	—	I
Controlled or Assisted Self-Redress . .	I	G	—	—	G	I
Arbitration . .	—	—	—	—	G	G or I
Conciliation . .	—	G	—	—	—	—
Mediation . .	G	—	—	—	—	—
Modern Civil . .	I	G	I	I	G	G
Modern Criminal (Public Justice) . .	G	G	G	I	G	G

the number of such crimes known to have occurred. In England
and Wales in 1925, 113,986 indictable offences were known by the
police to have occurred. For these 57,543 persons were tried.
Comparing the sex incidence among committals for trial Giffen
shows[1] that during 1897, 87·6% of the individuals committed in
England were men, a higher proportion than the percentage of
males among industrial employees, who would be more exposed to
the temptation of stealing, etc., than those not employed.

In civil proceedings the comparative proportion of suits brought
would measure the degree of *litigiousness* of the community as well
as its lawlessness, and Giffen points to the frequency distribution of
plaints in the County Courts brought for various amounts. In
England during 1896, for instance, " of 1,119,420 plaints entered
1,105,981 were for amounts not exceeding £20, only 1220 for
amounts exceeding £50, the average amount per plaint being just
under £3."[2]

(2) Statistics also throw light on the length to which the cases
were carried—how far the procedure proceeded in each individual
case. Percentages may be worked out of the cases duly initiated
which stopped at summons or proceeded to prosecution but were
not defended ; were defended and not sentenced ; were sentenced
but pardoned, or had the sentence partially remitted, i.e. were not
fully executed.

Giffen quotes from the criminal statistics of England and Wales
to the effect that in 1897 convictions were 79·3% of total committals
for trial,[3] that is to say, of the cases actually summoned to trial

---

[1] *Statistics*, Chapter XV.   [2] Op. cit., Chapter XV.
[3] Op. cit., p. 382.

20·7% were not sentenced and did not proceed beyond judgment to execution.

Statistics may also compute the number of appeals and their proportion to the cases in the court of first instance. For example, according to Beard[1] during the five years from 1898 to 1902 inclusive about 11,000 persons were convicted of felonies in New York County, of whom less than nine in a thousand took an appeal, and of these less than a third were successful.

(3) Statistics are also available on the significant subject of the amount of money spent by the parties concerned in prosecution and defence ; and the proportion which that money formed of damages.

In cases of industrial accident for which compensation is claimed under the employers' liability law the injured workman, or his relations if he was killed, are the plaintiffs, his employer the defendant. Crystal Eastman[2] gives the following American statistical experiences :

(i) Experience of 327 New York State firms employing 125,995 persons. Of $192,538 paid out by employers in connection with accident claims (including premiums to insurance companies) $104,642 only was actually paid to the men injured in those accidents. And of this $104,642, it was estimated from a large sample that 22·7% went to plaintiffs' fees and costs.

(ii) Forty-six cases of workmen killed in Erie County during 1907 and 1908.

Percentage of Total Lawyers' Fees to Total Compensation

26 cases where settlement without suit . . .	17·1%
17 cases where settlement out of court after suit .	30·0%
3 cases where damages recovered	34·2%

(iii) Fifty-one cases investigated by the New York Employer's Liability Commission ; percentage of lawyers' fees to compensation :

Less than 25%	.	14 cases
25% to 49·9%	.	23 cases
50% and over	.	14 cases

The significance of these statistics lies in the burden thrown on the poor man as plaintiff or defendant.

" In theory," writes C. F. G. Masterman,[3] " the Courts are open to every subject. In practice the power to obtain redress is limited

---

[1] *American Government and Politics.*
[2] *Work Accidents and the Law* (Russel Sage Foundation), 1910.
[3] *How England is Governed*, edition 1921, p. 178.

by the power to pay legal expenses." Recognition of this actual limitation has led to the institution of a Public Defender on the principle of the Public Prosecutor in Denmark, Scotland, and some other countries, and its advocacy in many others.[1]

§3 Work-Sharing Relations

Where persons or whole nations perform several kinds of work, such as the production of food and raw materials, and also manufactured articles, the definition of specialization or the division of labour has been shown in Chapter IX §2 to be essentially a matter of statistical measurement by means of the theory of association. Division of labour implies that one kind (or specific combination of kinds) of work is performed comparatively more frequently by a certain person or group of persons than chance or independent distribution of the total of work of all kinds would theoretically assume. This definition, as we shall see (§6), has important practical applications where the relation of *groups* of persons or government organs are concerned. But in modern political and industrial organization, with its tendency to extreme specialization among its manual and clerical workers, the majority of such *individual* persons can be observed to specialize in certain " jobs " or occupations without the need of the statistical test. The interest shifts from the possible division of labour between groups to the measurement of the comparative degree or extent of individual specialization WITHIN different groups, when the number of persons in the whole group is known and also the number of separate divisions of labour.

§3 · 1 Diffusion of Labour and Varieties of Division of Labour

The opposite of specialization or division of labour is " diffusion " of labour. In this case every person or group of persons is either, like the " general " servant or " mixed " farmer, performing the same act, or performing several sorts of acts *mixed in about the same proportions*. One person or group of persons may be performing a *greater*, or *less*, total of work in general than another person or group of persons, but his actions are of the same simple or composite quality.

At any particular moment the persons forming a Rugby football scrum may be acting differently, but if person A, though *generally* more active, does not in the long run and on the whole tend to act

---

[1] Laski, *Grammar of Politics*, p. 566.

differently in quality or kind from B, or B from A, and the work of each tends to be of the same kind, e.g. " shoving," we cannot say that there is specialization or division of labour among the forwards in the scrum.   There is the opposite relation of diffusion of labour among the individual forwards.   On the other hand, regular division of labour or specialization is observable between these forwards as a whole and the half-backs, the three-quarter backs, and the full-backs of the football team as a whole.

Diffusion of labour and division of labour is the primary distinction in the distribution or sharing of work between persons.   When labour is diffused men may combine *en masse* as the forwards in a Rugby football scrum, or they may work side by side independent but orderly as a military squad, or they may compete like two grocers in the same street or like two opposing political parties in Parliament.   The labour or transaction of providing biscuits, sausages, jam, and groceries generally, is " diffused " among the grocers ;   the labour and transaction of discussing some proposed law or in coming to a decision by vote is diffused among the members of opposite parties.   The prime distinction is not rivalry or combination but the relation between men like general grocers or general practitioners, tending to act similarly doing various amounts of the same simple or composite work, and the relation of men tending to act dissimilarly, to specialize, and to do various amounts of different work like a team or crew.

Where men do different work the division of labour may follow various systems.

The possible relations of persons or groups of persons dividing their labour in industry are usually described as either vertical or horizontal.   Vertical division of labour is said to occur in industry when each specific person or group of persons performs a successive stage, such as cattle raising, tanning, shoe making ;   or iron mining, smelting, engineering; or, more generally, extraction, manufacturing, marketing.   The notion of horizontality in social relations is less clear.   Sometimes, as in " horizontal combination," the notion refers to persons or groups of persons performing precisely identical transactions possibly, though not necessarily, in different localities or markets.   If there is such a specific difference of locality we may speak of territorial division of labour ;   otherwise this reference of horizontal is a reference to mere diffusion, not division of labour at all.   But horizontal division of labour also refers to the case where each person or group of persons performs different acts at the same stage.   These different acts *may* be performed at the same time and place simultaneously, as in the work of a team, gang, or crew ;   but not necessarily. The acts of making the uppers, making the heels, and making the soles of shoes are all at the same stage of preparing for assembly into shoes, and therefore horizontally divided, but they need not be performed at the same place nor yet at the same time.

In actual practice, any one person in industry will find him or herself in certain respects part of a system of diffusion of labour, in certain respects a vertical specialist, and in yet other respects a horizontal specialist. The labour of charging buttons was diffused among the fourteen women whose output is given in Table VIB, but as a group these fourteen women were specializing in one vertical stage of brass button making side by side with other groups working up other brass products. Thus specialization is always present whatever the *number* of persons among whom the same vertical stage or horizontal division of labour is diffused.

§3 · 2 The Statistical Measure of Industrial Specialization

The comparative degree of vertical and horizontal division of labour may be measured by the number of divisions, i.e. stages or horizontally related operations, habitually performed by different individual persons.

The case has already (Chapter XVII) been cited of the American shoe-making industry where a " pair of shoes is made from the raw leather by different groups of men working at 239 different operations." These groups are either horizontally divided as by the division between 13 groups working on the heel, and the 63 groups working on the sole leather, or the 37 groups working on the uppers ; or vertically divided as by the division between these three departments and the next stage of assembly or manufacturing with its 126 operations. Within the manufacturing department there is further vertical division, as for instance, between the groups of men working on the different processes of bottoming, finishing, treeing, and packing.

The degree of division of labour or specialization may also be statistically measured by the number of times a man repeats his special operation per hour, or any other given period of time. In the typical shoe factory under discussion the average time taken for the material to pass through each process together with the due proportion of the time spent by day-workers and those engaged in organization was for each pair of shoes 85·75 minutes, of which ·83 minutes represents the time of day-work and organization in the four departments. Apart from these eight general activities (two in each department) there are the 239 specialized processes.

The average time spent on each pair of shoes at each specialized process or division of labour is thus $\dfrac{85\cdot75-9\cdot83}{239}$ minutes$=\dfrac{75\cdot92\times60}{239}$ seconds $=19\cdot1$ seconds, or almost exactly one-third of a minute. In other words, the average specializing shoe employee repeats his operation three times a minute or 180 times an hour.

But this average of time spent—one-third of a minute per pair or 33 minutes per hundred pairs—is derived from a distribution of very wide dispersion heavily skewed positively (see Glossary §15). Table XIXD gives the details for one, the heeling, department of the shoe factory.

The minutes spent per hundred pairs given in column 1 range for the different special divisions of labour all the way from 2·75 in the case of top-lift skiving, to 167·17 in the case of heel-building. Column 2 gives the number of pairs worked on per hour. This is derived by dividing the figures in column 1 into 60×100. Thus " rough sorting " takes 13·44 minutes per 100 pair, and from this it follows that in the course of an hour of sixty minutes $\dfrac{60\cdot00}{13\cdot44}\times100$ single pairs will be made, i.e. 446·43. These two columns are both reproduced from an official bulletin.[1] The further columns in the

TABLE XIXd

SHARING OF LABOUR IN HEELING DEPARTMENT OF SHOE FACTORY

	(1) Minutes per 100 Pairs	(2) Number of Pairs worked on per hour	(3) Number of Men among whom work diffused (hypothetical)	(4) Number done per hour by number of Men specified in col. 3
Heeling-stock, skivers, sorters, etc.	58·65	102·30	20	2046
Heel builders . .	167·17	35·89	56	2010
Rough sorters . .	13·44	446·43	4	1786
Heel gougers . .	5·66	1060·07	2	2120
Heel skivers . .	4·72	1271·19	2	2542
Heel compressors .	9·03	664·45	3	1993
Heel sorters . .	8·80	681·82	3	2045
Top-lift graders. .	3·44	1744·19	1	1774
Top-lift skivers .	2·75	2181·82	1	2182
Top-lift compressors .	8·66	692·84	3	2078
Top-lift sorters .	6·73	891·53	2	1783
Top-lift casers . .	5·70	1052·63	2	2106
Heel casers . .	5·70	1052·63	2	2106
Day-work . .	48·73	123·13	16	—
Organization . .	58·99	101·71	20	—
Total . .	—	—	137	—

[1] *Bulletin of the U.S. Department of Labour*, No. 232.

table which are derived from the first two columns will be referred to shortly.

The number of repetitions of any operation per hour is a measure of the degree of division of labour that is not generally easily obtainable and requires an intensive study of factory organization. And the measure first suggested, i.e. the bare number of separate divisions of labour or occupations specialized in, is unsatisfactory in that the absolute number of separate divisions depends partly on the size of the particular plant, firm (or group of plants), or industry (group of firms) under discussion. A small industry where five hundred men were employed in twenty-five different operations would certainly be considered to have developed division of labour to a higher pitch than another, larger scale industry where ten thousand men were employed in forty occupations. In the first case each division of work is diffused on the average among 500÷25, i.e. 20 men ; in the latter case each division of work is diffused on the average among 10,000÷40, i.e. 250 men. If diffusion of labour is the opposite of division of labour the latter case, though comprising 40 as against 25 divisions of labour, is less divided. Again, where two industries or groups of occupations are compared one of which is comprised within the other, like boots and shoes within the making of apparel and clothing, the sub-ordinate group must necessarily comprise fewer divisions but is not necessarily less specializing.

This would suggest the diffusion of labour, i.e. the average number of men among whom each division of labour is distributed, as an index of the degree of specialization. The finer the division of labour or the finer the specialization the fewer the number of men doing the same sort of job.

This measure is roughly equivalent to the time-taken-per-unit-of-work measure. In Table XIXd, column 2, it was noticed that the number of pairs of shoes worked on per hour was very different for different divisions of labour. The heel builder can build the heels of only 35·89 pairs in the hour while the " rough sorter " can rough sort 446·43, or about 13 times as many. Clearly more heel builders are required in the factory department than rough sorters and *more to precisely that extent to which heel-building is* slower than rough sorting, i.e. about 13 times as many. When all the specialized operations in the department are taken into account with their varying speed of performance, the required number of men among whom the labour of each division is to be diffused will have to be something like the hypothetical figures in column 3. Only by this degree of diffusion of labour can about the same number (e.g. about

2000 pairs of shoes, as shown in column 4) be completed in a given time (e.g. an hour) by *each* and *all* of the labour divisions in the department.

The total number of men in the whole department required for this more or less balanced production where each hour produces a finished quota is 137,[1] and since there are fifteen separate divisions of labour the average diffusion of labour is $137 \div 15 = 9 \cdot 1$.

The diffusion is likely to be lower the greater the number of divisions like top-lift graders and skivers performing the job in only a short time and requiring for a balanced production only one man. Diffusion is thus an inverse measure of the degree of specialization as measured in time taken.

But this measure is not always satisfactory either. Suppose two plants A and B both performing exactly the same transaction.

	Divisions of Labour	Total Employees	Employees per Division of Labour
Plant A . . .	100	1000	10
Plant B . . .	120	1320	11

Can it be said that Plant A with its 10 employees per work division as against the 11 of Plant B shows the finer division of labour ?

It is evident that for some purposes the average number of men per division of labour is the better index of the degree of specialization but not for other purposes. In selecting one or other of two practicable methods of measuring the degree of division of labour, (*a*) the number of divisions and (*b*) the average diffusion, the following plan may be adopted.

In comparing plants or firms in the same industry performing the same sort of labour or transactions or in comparing the same industries in different countries, and in general, wherever groups are compared among whom the same sort of labour is distributed,—compare the degree of specialization within them mainly by means of the number of divisions observed. The average diffusion would merely measure the scale of the operation.

In comparing plants, firms, or industries performing different work, particularly in comparing parts of an industry to the whole, and generally wherever groups are compared among whom the labour or transactions of the business world as a whole is divided, —compare the degree of specialization within the several groups

---

[1] If production need be balanced only over the day or the week, so large a number of specialists is, of course, not required.

mainly by means of the diffusion, i.e. the average number of employees-per-division index.

§3 · 3   The Measure of Specialization over Whole Industries

Thus, gingerly, the question has been approached how far the degree of division as against diffusion of labour can be measured over a wide area such as the whole of an industry, not merely one plant or firm.

An industry consists of a group of firms[1] and " the industry to which each individual is classed " is determined, in the prefatory words of the English census, " by reference to the business in, or for the purposes of which his occupation was followed. Where the individual was himself an employer or was ' working on his own account ' his business or profession has been regarded as the industry ; but in the most usual case of individuals working for an employer, it is the nature of the employer's business which has determined the industry under which such cases have been classified."

The form or questionnaire circulated for the census also asks a person to state his occupation defined as " the precise branch of Profession, Trade, Manufacture, Service, etc.   Where the occupation is connected with Trade or Manufacture, the reply should be sufficient to show the particular kind of Work done stating, where applicable, the material worked in and the Article made or dealt in, if any."   Clearly occupation is roughly equivalent to a broadly conceived division of labour.

In English industry the number of separate occupations or divisions of labour that are distinct enough to receive a separate name are now specified in the *Classification of Occupations* ; 29,106 different names appear, though, owing to the naming of the same occupation differently in different districts, these are said to refer only to 16,837 distinct occupations.

There will be many more different divisions of labour, such as the shoe-making operations listed in Table XIXD, than there are different occupations.   But, for the purpose of comparing whole industries or large groups or orders of occupations, the number of occupations within them may be taken as a rough index of the number of divisions of labour, on the assumption that the number of occupations and of divisions " co-vary " in the different industries more or less proportionately.

The distinction between industry and occupation and the way

---

[1] See definition above, §2.

an industry is subdivided into occupations must be clearly envisaged by the statistician if he is not to fail in " orientation." A man whose occupation is gardening but who is employed on the Cathedral close by the Dean and Chapter is classed under the industry of " religion," one of the group of professions distinguished by the census. Similarly the occupation of a college bedmaker is personal service, but her industry is that of education. The occupations of men employed by a railway company in (1) locomotive building shops, (2) the booking office, (3) railway hotels, are : (1) metal working, (2) clerical, and (3) personal service, but the industry of all of them is transport.

Some industries clearly include many occupations that seem at first sight foreign to them, like the railway transport industry clerks ; and the same occupation, e.g. that of metal working, will occur in many different industries, not only in the metal industries. But there are a great many industries where this cross classification occurs only to a negligible extent, and here the group or order of occupations formed in the occupation census can be identified with a corresponding industry. At least ten such large groups or orders of occupations roughly identical with an industry may be distinguished, none of which occupy or employ less than some 300,000 persons.

These groups or orders of occupations (corresponding approximately with an industry) that are distinguished in the 1921 English Census of Occupations may now be graded according to the degree of division of labour that they exhibit. On the plan enunciated above, the main test placing them into grades A, B, and C is the average diffusion of persons per occupation ; the greater the number of persons among whom one and the same occupation is diffused, the less fine the division of labour. But the bare number of occupations within the group of occupations or industry may be used as a minor test grading the group of occupations or industry as a, b, or c. The diffusion = No. of occupations ÷ No. so occupied, to nearest ten.

Grade Aa or Ab.   Average diffusion of labour 500 or less individuals per occupation.   Number of occupations distinguished by name (a) over 1100, (b) 600–1100.

1. Textile Workers. Number so occupied	.	.	.	980,928
Round No. of Names of Occupations	.	.	.	2200
Approx. Diffusion of Men per Occupation	.	.	.	450
2. Railway Workers. Number so occupied	.	.	.	315,999
Round No. of Names of Occupations	.	.	.	640
Approx. Diffusion of Men per Occupation	.	.	.	490

3. Makers of and Workers in Paper. Number so occupied   .   278,371
   Round No. of Names of Occupations   .   .   .   1,120
   Approx. Diffusion of Men per Occupation   .   .   .   250

4. Professional Occupations (excluding Teachers). Number   .   389,236
   Round No. of Names of Occupations   .   .   .   870
   Approx. Diffusion of Men per Occupation   .   .   .   450

Middle Grade B. Average diffusion of labour between 500 and 2000 individuals
per occupation. Number of occupations distinguished by name (b)
between 600 and 1100.

5. Builders, etc. Number so occupied   505,278
   Round No. of Names of Occupations   600
   Approx. Diffusion of Men per Occupation   .   .   840

6. Coal and Shale Mining Occupations. Number   .   .   .   993,468
   Round No. of Names of Occupations   .   .   .   920
   Approx. Diffusion of Men per Occupation   .   .   1080

7. Makers of Textile Goods and Dress (Clothing Industry). Number   836,686
   Round No. of Names of Occupations   1080
   Approx. Diffusion of Men per Occupation   .   .   .   770

Grade Cb or Cc. Average diffusion of labour more than 2000 individuals per
occupation. Number of occupations distinguished by name (b) 600–1100,
(c) less than 600.

8. Agricultural Occupations. Number so occupied   .   .   1,254,350
   Round No. of Names of Occupations   .   .   .   480
   Approx. Diffusion of Men per Occupation   .   .   2610

9. Commercial, etc. Occupations. Number so occupied   .   .   1,559,176
   Round No. of Names of Occupations   .   .   .   560
   Approx. Diffusion of Men per Occupation   .   .   .   2780

10. Engaged in Personal Service. Number so occupied   .   .   2,016,369
    Round No. of Names of Occupations   .   .   .   800
    Approx. Diffusion of Men per Occupation   .   .   .   2520

§3 · 4 The Theoretical Interpretation of the Statistics of Specialization

The facts about the specialization of individual persons and the
division or distribution of labour between them that are statistically measurable in industry through official censuses or intensive
investigations of factory organization, may be interpreted and
explained provisionally in the light of psychological and technical
knowledge. If the industrial statistics are found to have a basis in
human nature their conclusions can be carried over into State
politics or into the political aspect of any society.

Why does modern industry display such a high degree of specialization ? The usual answer, first formulated by Adam Smith, is that

specialization results in greater efficiency due, as set forth in Table XVIIK, to its results in

(i) Using the different native abilities of men,
(ii) allowing men to acquire skill by constant practice,
(iii) the economy in freedom from interruption of working continuously at one special job.

Now each of these supposed and quite plausible results ought to be isolated and tested under control in the psychological laboratory. Many factors already observed by psychologists are involved, for example : the practice and learning curve, the distribution and variety of human abilities, rhythm, and monotony.

(1) The Practice and Learning Curve. Do learners increase their output more rapidly from day to day on specialized operations taking little time, rather than on non-specialized operations ? This may be tested by experiment in the laboratory, or statistics may be compared of the proportion of all divisions of labour or operations requiring different amounts of learning (a) in a highly subdivided factory, (b) in a less subdivided and more " diffused " factory. In an American metal factory, distinctly of type (a), operations were divided into those called unskilled that required no previous experience for proficiency, those called semi-skilled requiring one month's experience, and those called skilled requiring over a year's experience. Such a classification may perhaps provide a basis for a standard nomenclature and basis of comparison.

(2) The Distribution and Variety of Human Abilities has been measured by psychologists and statisticians and some of the results appear in Table VIA. This table refers solely to variations in *general* intelligence, but experimental psychologists also devote themselves to the measurement of individual variations in specific abilities, e.g. motor ability, eyesight, tactile discrimination.

(3) Freedom from interruption and continuity of work permits of rhythm, and it is largely through rhythmic working that the greater efficiency assumed by Adam Smith takes place.

" If the same job is continued without interruption the operator acquires a rhythm of motion which accelerates the task and probably tends to decrease the accumulation of fatigue." Rhythm also can be, and has been, minutely measured and studied in the isolation and the controlled conditions of the laboratory.[1]

(4) Working against the influence of practice and learning, of variety of human abilities and of rhythm, is *monotony*. Human beings have a certain intolerance for the frequent repetition of the same actions. Prof. Münsterberg, it is true, considered that the

[1] See *U.S. Public Health Bulletin*, No. 106.

worker, however subdivided his work, never felt boredom, since he could always distinguish minute differences in his materials that were quite invisible to the layman. If he were turning out ten thousand pens a day he would, so to speak, know each pen by name as a shepherd knows individual sheep which to the outsider appear identical. This optimistic theory of Münsterberg still awaits statistical verification. We are accustomed to expect variety in human nature and it is plausible to suppose that there is variety in respect of tolerance for monotony. For some people monotony probably limits their effective degree of specialization,[1] for some it does not.

(5) Side by side with intolerance of monotony as setting a limit to specialization, is the need for a *coherence* in a series or set of operations that can be obtained only by concentrating all those operations *upon* one man or one body of men. This coherence, important as it is in business management, is particularly important in the organs of State government that have to arrive at a definite decision.

The general effects of specialization are clearly matters for laboratory experiment.[2] A simple piece of work like dispatching multigraphed form letters might be divided into sub-processes of signing the letters, folding the letters, addressing the envelopes, and sticking-on-the-stamp-cum-sealing the envelope. Then the question is whether (when conditions are selected or controlled so as to be constant) more letters are dispatched in the long run and on the average by many persons, by, say, four persons or groups of persons each doing their special bit, or by the whole work being diffused. And if the output of groups that divide their labour is greater, what is the limit to the efficiency of this division and specialization? Could more letters be dispatched if a separate individual or group licked the stamp, and another individual or group licked the envelope, etc. ?

§3 · 5 The Measure of Organizational Specialization between Groups of Persons

The method of combining statistical measurement and theoretical and psychological explanation or interpretation may be taken as the prototype of scientific investigation into the specialization and distribution of labour between whole organizations of persons.

---

[1] See Urwick, *Organising a Sales Office*, Chapter III, for a practical experiment in *de-specialization*.
[2] Or intensive observation. See Report No. 52, Industrial Fatigue Research Board.

We have so far considered only the case (M I) of subdivision of labour *among individual persons* within the plant, firm, or industry as a whole.

But similar subdivision arises in other cases, namely

M II : Among plants within the firm.

M III : Among firms within a Trust or Combine.

M IV : Among local authorities within the Central State.

M V : Among primary States within a Federation of States.

The similarity and analogy of industrial case M II and " civic " case M IV on the one hand, and industrial case M III and " civic " M V is evident. Both the plants of a firm (M II) and the local authorities of a State (M IV) are co-ordinated by that firm or State. Certain transactions are delegated to them and there is division of labour horizontal and vertical between central and local authorities or plants, with usually territorial division between the several local authorities and the several local shops and stations of the distributive industries of retailing and transporting.

The firms within a Combine, Association, or Kartell (M III) and the primary States within a Federation (M V) arrive at their division of labour by process of mutual agreement rather than delegation. The name Trust is applied either to a combine of firms comparable to a federal State, or else simply to very large and possibly monopolistic single firms not requiring specific study as distinct from smaller unitary firms. In so far as Trust refers to a Combine it is comparable to a Federation of States in the fact that there must be some written articles of agreement, some constitutional law, defining what are to be the transactions performed by the central State or business organization (e.g. the marketing organization of the Kartell) and what the transactions performed by the constituent States or firms. In political States, for instance, the central federation usually transacts foreign affairs, declares war, keeps an army and navy ; the unit States police and maintain order and security, and also carry out education. Finance is often shared ; the *United* States taxes imports and exports, but did not, until 1913, levy income-tax. The division of labour arrived at between the central federation and the unitary States or firms is thus usually horizontal rather than vertical. Between each of the unitary States the distribution of labour is usually territorial division, and between each of the unitary firms either territorial division (each firm specializing in one local market), or simply diffusion of labour without particular specialization.

Thus in all cases M II, III, IV, and V the same kinds of work relations occur as in case M I : division of labour—vertical, territorial, or horizontal ; and diffusion of labour. The same statistical methods of discovering the degree of specialization may be used ; and interpretation of the degree and kinds of work relations discovered might follow on the same psychological lines. Some of the topics of statistical investigation may be indicated.

Local government (apart from the local execution of national laws) implies a sharing of labour AMONG local States and raises many important questions that can be answered by statistical measurement.

(1) What are the number of co-ordinate local authorities into which the country is subdivided ? In France there are 90 departments, in England and Wales 62 administrative counties (including London) and 83 County Boroughs. In the U.S. there are 49 States, including the District of Columbia. What is the average diffusion of population per local authority ? The median population of the States in the U.S. was 1,574,449 in 1910, since this was the population of Arkansas, 25th State in order of population.

(2) How equally is the labour or transactions of the central State distributed among the local States ?

Though in the United States of America the median population of the States was 1,574,449, the actual population of the different States (which are also the constituencies for election to the Federal Senate) varied in 1910 from 145,965 (Wyoming) to 9,113,614 (New York) ; this would, incidentally, give a voter in Wyoming some 63 times the weight of a New Yorker in the U.S. Senate. The interquartile range of State-population was from a round number of 580,000 between the 36th and 37th States in order of population, to a round number of 2,350,000 between the 12th and 13th States in order of population. The interquartile range was thus in 1910 about 1,770,000, making a coefficient of dispersion (formula Glossary §13) of $\dfrac{1,770,000 \div 2}{\frac{1}{2} (2,350,000 + 580,000)} = 60\cdot 4\%.$

This measure of deviation allows the inequality in size of the local divisions of different nations, e.g. the French departments or the English counties, to be compared and contrasted.

(3) Division of transaction, between the central and the local States' procedure. Is there any specialization ?

The " degree of specialization " between English local authorities and the national State may be measured by the proportion of (a) local expenditure, (b) national expenditure (excluding interest on loans and war pensions, etc.), spent on the several broad classes of transactions of State.

In Table XIXe the local expenditure refers to England and

Wales only, the national expenditure to Great Britain ; but since both columns are expressed as a percentage distribution of the total expense, and this distribution over various kinds of expenditure does not differ significantly in Scotland as compared to England, the difference in the source of the figures is negligible.

It is clear that while the central or national State specializes in war and foreign affairs, the local authorities specialize in health and housing, roads and bridges, in the sense (indicated above, and in Chapter VIII) that of any equivalent amount spent, say £100, by the national and by the local States, a greater proportion is spent by the local than by the national States on health and housing, namely, £21·4 as against £5·2, and on roads, namely £19·6 as against £5·3 ; while a greater proportion will be spent by the

TABLE XIXʙ

HORIZONTAL DIVISION OF LABOUR BETWEEN NATIONAL AND LOCAL
AUTHORITIES

Transaction	Distribution of Total Expenditure in specified Transactions		
	Local (a)	National (b)	
	% of total expenditure	% of all	% of Home Transactions only
Police, Law, and Justice . .	7·4	3·7	6·3
Relief of Poor, Pensions, and Insurance	18·4	15·8	26·9 (c)
Health and Housing . . .	21·4 (a)	5·2	8·8 (d)
Roads, Bridges	19·6	5·3	9·0
Education, Science, Art, Libraries, etc.	21·2	16·6	28·3
War and Foreign Affairs . .	—	41·3	— (e)
Other or Unclassified . . .	3·7	3·1	5·3
General Administrative Expense .	8·3	9·0	15·4 (f)
	100·0 (g)	100·0 (h)	100·0

Notes : (a) The whole column is quoted from *Britain's Industrial Future*, Table 39, except that three allied items have been added together to form the percentage for Health and Housing.

(b) Actual expenditure for 1924–25 obtained from statistical abstract for the U.K. (Cmd. 2620), Table No. 3.

(c) Health and Unemployment Insurance+Old Age Pensions.

(d) Health, Labour, and Insurance—Health and Unemployment Insurance.

(e) Army+Navy+Air Force+Foreign and Colonial Services.

(f) Public Works and Buildings+Salaries and Expenses of Civil Dep.+ Customs and Excise+Inland Revenue Expenses.

(g) Actual expenditure (local)=£153,000,000.

(h) Actual expenditure (national)=£294,000,000. This is composed of the " Total Supply Services "=£402,000,000, *minus* Post Office Services (=£50 m.) and Non-effective and Miscellaneous Services, mostly War Pensions (=£100 m.) *plus* Old Age Pensions (=£26 m.) and Road Fund (=£16 m.), £402—150+42 millions=£294 millions.

national State on war and foreign affairs, namely £41·3 as against nil. Local specialization in other transactions of State is more apparent than real since the high proportion the national State spends on war and foreign affairs overshadows all else. If this expense were neglected and the amount spent by the national State on the various home transactions expressed as a percentage of total home expenses as in column 3, the central State would appear to spend a greater proportion of its total (home) expenditure on relief of poor, pensions and insurance, and on education, science, art, etc., than does the local State.

Similar statistics could show whether this horizontal division is true of other national States and their local subdivisions, and a set of such statistics might lead to important empirical generalizations as to the functions, i.e. transactions, of local authorities.

§4   *The Structure of Government*

The structural analysis or morphology of the governing party (the " government ") of a State, or of the managing and employing party (the management or employerate) of a firm consists of a description of the government's or management's *Size* and *Constitution*.

(1) *Size*. A government or management may consist of a few persons or many persons, and according to this statistically measurable distinction Aristotle divided governments into Monarchies or Tyrannies ; Aristocracies or Oligarchies ; and Democracies.

The sub-distinction is ethical ; tyrannies were bad monarchies, oligarchies bad aristocracies. But the main distinction is the *number* of the rulers, and an advocate of statistical methods can thus claim to derive his doctrine from the highest sources. He may extend Aristotle's statistical test to the government of joint-stock companies, consumers' co-operative societies, and in fact all organized societies, and may refine upon it by preferring the *proportion* of the total population that are rulers as the index of the degree of democracy rather than the bare number of the rulers. But the real difficulty, as is so often the case, lies in the fieldwork. How define a ruler or member of the ruling party ? Shall a vote for the Parliamentary representative confer rulership ? Or the power to vote in a plebiscite or referendum ?

I distinguish the activity of ruling from that of manning ; hence unless otherwise specified, I exclude voting for a man from the ruling procedure, and a person need not be counted among the rulers if his activity merely consisted in voting for one person

rather than another. On the other hand, voting or being allowed
to vote for proposed laws, as in the case of the referendum and
initiative, e.g. in Switzerland, might qualify a man as a member of
the ruler party.

Here again the statistical conception of variability may be called
in. Persons may be conceived as more or less rulers and the
degree of their rulership would be measured statistically, for instance, by the number of proposed laws submitted to referendum
compared to proposed laws not so submitted ; and by the number
of men voting in such referendum.

A man to whom proposed laws were submitted but seldom, and
who hardly ever voted even when they were so submitted, would
not be much of a ruler. Laski tells us that the initiative and referendum as practised in the American States and Switzerland " rarely
enlist much popular interest ; on the average, about half as many
persons vote in them as will vote for persons in a general election
for office."[1]

Hence the initiative and referendum though in theory making
for a highly democratic government may in fact not alter the size
of the government substantially.

(2) *Constitution*. The governing or managing may be carried
out by one individual man or by one body of men, or it may be
done by several individual men or by several bodies of men or by
individual men and bodies of men. Five constitutional possibilities
are presented :

(A) Government or Management by One Person. E.g. an auto-
cracy or unlimited Monarchy in the State. Within any body
of persons, one chairman or president may exercise sole
discretion in interpretation of rules, e.g. the Speaker of the
House of Commons.

(B) Government or Management by One Body of Persons.
E.g. the rule of an executive committee.

(C) Government or Management by Several Individual Persons.
E.g. a bureaucracy.

(D) Government or Management by Several Bodies of Persons.

(E) Government or Management by Several Bodies of Persons
and Individual Persons. This is the case of the constitutions
of modern national States.

In all constitutions that include bodies of persons the precise
number of individual men in the constituent bodies should be

---

[1] *Grammar of Politics*, p. 321.

specified.   Different names are customarily given to governing bodies of different sizes, i.e. consisting of various numbers of members.   The word Committee, Board, or Commission usually refers to a smaller body than Council, and Council to a smaller body than Assembly or Congress.   The mere size of a body of persons measured in the number of individuals composing it is by no means to be neglected, as will be shown later.

This completes the study of government or management structure. We have reduced politics to the individual man and need not go further since that would lead us into individual psychology or human anatomy and physiology.   Governing and managing are a series of relations or contacts between different human beings ; politics is not concerned with the mind and body *within* one human being.

If we were viewing government or management at one instant or if government or management were suddenly petrified, nothing could be said of its nature except its structure.   In the same way we can study only the structure or anatomy of a dead man but not the physiology, because his structural organs have ceased to function. But in governments and managements that are living and working there is far more to be studied than mere structure.

Let us suppose the five hypothetical structures we have cited to be in full working order.   What are the facts, beyond those about structure, and the rule procedure considered in §2, which we should want to know in the case of each ?

For the sake of simplicity we may reduce each of the five hypothetical structural cases we have cited to two, by considering both one governing person and one body of persons (which on a statistical reckoning meets sufficiently simultaneously and sufficiently continuously or recurrently) to be just one " organ " of government. These bodies of persons though appearing as lumps in the porridge preventing easy digestion, require special chewing.   Eventually, however, the whole structure can be reduced to its component atoms—i.e. the individual person, by reconsidering (as suggested in §1) the body of persons in its aspect as a group of individual persons in relations of rule, manning, and work-sharing, not collectively as one " organ."   What then are the facts beyond those of structure and ruling which we should want to know ?

Structure of Government or Ruler-Party Cases A and B.
One Organ : One Person or One Body of Persons.
Functional Problems of Procedure.
  How is this one person or body of persons appointed ?
  How is this one person or body of persons dismissed ?

In short, how did he or they get there and how long will he or they stay ?

Structure of Government or Ruler-Party Cases C, D, and E.

Several Organs : Persons or Bodies of Persons.

Functional Problems of Procedure.

What are the relations of the several governing organs, persons or bodies of persons ?

How is each person or body of persons appointed and dismissed ? (Problem of Cases A and B).

It is evident that there are but two separate sets of problems :

(I) Problems of Structural Cases A and B, repeated in Cases C, D, and E. The appointment and dismissal of ruling organs. Methods by which the government or the management is manned. In short, the MANNING procedure.

(II) Problems peculiar to Structural Cases C, D, E. The relations of the several ruling organs. These relations are mainly, as we shall see, the division or diffusion of labour already considered, in short the WORK-SHARING procedure.

I shall consider MANNING relations in §5 and WORK-SHARING relations among rulers in §6.

But what of the structure of the organization among the manag*ed* and govern*ed*, the structure of Trade Unions and political parties ? The answer of realistic science already indicated (§2), is that these organizations have the same possible classes of structure and the same functional problems of procedure as the organization of the ruler party ; and the political study of one is also the political study of the other.

§5   *Manning Relations*

Manning includes the two opposite events of appointment and dismissal. Each of these events may occur by four different classes of procedure : I " own choice " of person appointed or dismissed ; II appointment or dismissal by choice of others ; III appointment or dismissal by circumstances more or less of own choice ; IV appointment or dismissal by circumstances beyond own choice.

In the following analysis designed to build up an apparatus of thought and to form a framework for statistical investigation, various specific procedures of appointment and dismissal are listed separately under these four main classes. These various procedures are not necessarily alternative, however, but may be found combined. Thus in the appointment to specific offices, circumstances (IV) " beyond control " of age, sex, mentality, race, and heredity may all be factors ; and these circumstances beyond control may be, and often are, combined with (III) circumstances of own choice, with (II) choice of others, and (I) own choice.   Such combinations should form a special subject for statistical investigations with a view to establishing pattern systems of appointment and dismissal ; but here we are content to call attention to actual procedures that may either be alternative or may be supplementary elements in one pattern.

A. APPOINTMENT

I   *Appointment by Own Choice*

The choice of the person appointed may be assumed except in cases of compulsory service, such as military service in France and other continental European States, compulsory jury service in England, etc.

II   *Appointment by Choice of Others*

The distinction of greatest practical importance turns upon the number of persons making the choice, a statistically measurable character.   The personal and circumstantial qualifications tending, in fact, to appointment are very different, as described below, if the appointment is by ELECTION of many, or the NOMINATION of one or a very few, or the CO-OPTION of a moderate number of persons.

(1) *By choice of one person or a body of persons numerically very few (say* 2—20), who are usually already part of the government or management.

The procedure of NOMINATION observable in the choice of Cabinet Ministers in Britain by the Prime Minister ; the choice of judges in Britain and the majority of European states by the Cabinet, Minister of Justice or Lord Chancellor ; the choice of Senators in Italy, Canada, and of new peers in England by the Executive ; the choice of industrial managers by the Board of Directors of a joint-stock company.

(2) *By choice of a body of persons numerically few (say* 5-20). When the choice is in the hands of members of the same body of persons (e.g. a Committee, Board, or even Council) to which appointment refers, the term CO-OPTION is applied.

The procedure of *co-option* is observable in the appointment of aldermen on local councils in England, and the appointment of members of sub-committees of such councils.

(3) *By choice of a group or body of persons moderately numerous say* 100–1000).

2D

The choosers are often a "largish" group of persons already holding office and forming part of the government, as in the case of the French President appointed by the members of the Senate and of the Chamber sitting together. This procedure may be referred to as OFFICIAL ELECTION. The procedure of INDIRECT ELECTION is another, alternative procedure. By this plan the choosers may themselves be chosen for no other transaction than to make the election, as in the case of the appointment of the U.S. President by a College of Electors who have in their turn been elected. Here statistical investigation shows that the members of the College of Electors seldom vote for any candidate different from the persons chosen by their political party. There is, in fact, no "choice" on their part. But whether this ineffectiveness applies to all cases of indirect election remains to be investigated.

The two procedures of official election and indirect election may be observed combined as in the choosing of French Senators.

(4) *By choice of a multitude of persons (say over 1000), who are usually performing no rule transaction and are not in this sense participating in the government or management.*

This is the procedure of DIRECT POPULAR ELECTION in large "constituencies" observable in the majority of modern national States in manning at least one house of the legislature. The so-called House of Commons, Chamber of Deputies, House of Representatives, etc., are elected directly by voters who have no (other) part in ruling.

III   *Appointment by Circumstances More or Less of Own Choice*

(1) *Expenditure*

Where appointment is by election the candidate spending most money in the course of the election shows, in England, a slight tendency to be successfully elected (see Chapter XIII §3). There is a legal limit to the amount that may be spent. Expenditure beyond this limit if proved in court of law would disqualify. This limit is occasionally overstepped with legal consequences, and probably overstepped in a further number of cases without legal action.

(2) *Marriage*

Where appointment is by election, to be the wife of a living or deceased M.P. appears a qualification-in-fact for appointment as M.P. The proportion of women M.P.'s in these circumstances is (in 1928) far greater than the proportion of wives of M.P.'s to women, in Great Britain at large.

(3) *Occupation*

Listing the occupations of British M.P.'s from 1832 to 1867 (see Table IXB) there is shown a distinct tendency for persons in certain occupations and professions to stand a better chance of election than persons in other occupations. For instance, 708, or 8·45% of all members of Parliament during those years (totalling 8382) were lawyers, 11·15% army or navy men, and 47·3% landowners. Compared with the proportion of lawyers, army and navy men, and landowners in the population in general, this points to a much higher probability of men in those occupations being elected M.P.'s than of men in other occupations. Though manual workers were far more numerous in the country at large than men in all the professional occupations added together, until the dawn of the twentieth century manual worker M.P.'s like John Burns were rare. The following of a manual occupation was a clear factual disqualification for Parliament.

(4) *The Ownership of Wealth*

In Britain up to 1918 no person who did not pay rent or own a house, and no person in receipt of poor relief could legally vote for members of Parliament. At present, though legally the very poorest may vote, they may not in fact have the means, such as a motor-car, for getting to the polling booth conveniently (e.g. dry if it is raining) and may not be offered the means unless they are likely to vote as the means-owner urges them.

A property qualification is still legally necessary in Britain for service on the Grand Jury.

(5) *Residence*

In the U.S.A. all candidates for election to the House of Representatives and Senate, must by law live in the geographical area of the constituency.[1] In Britain and other countries without this legal restriction statistical investigation would probably show that residents have an advantage *in fact* over non-residents.

(6) *Membership and Activity in some Particular Organization*

Membership in the Roman Catholic Church disqualified by law for membership in the House of Commons in the eighteenth century, and in fact has disqualified for the U.S. Presidency from its inception till the present time (1929).

Membership of and activity in the political party is perhaps the most important unofficial avenue to office.

---

[1] For important consequences of this restriction see Laski, *Grammar of Politics*, Chapter Eight, III.

" The Office of Justice of the Peace," writes Laski,[1] " becomes what Mr. H. G. Wells has aptly termed a ' Knighthood of the underlings.' It is used to recognize inferior political service of which the quality is not sufficient for greater recompense. It becomes a minor note like the Order of the British Empire ; and an important Member of Parliament will secure it for his useful henchman much in the way that the fox is given to the hounds after a day's run."[1]

This qualification for appointment to office under the title of the " Spoils System," is of far more frequent occurrence in America than England. Probably there, many of the lower paid Civil Service appointments would be statistically traceable to " party " services.

(7) *Holding Office other than appointed to*

Legally the holding of another office more often disqualifies than qualifies. In Britain no subordinate minister (civil servant) or clergyman of the Church of England can legally be a member of Parliament. In the U.S.A. no member of the Cabinet can legally be a member of the House of Representatives or the Senate or *vice versa*. But there are legal arrangements to the contrary. In Britain certain bishops are appointed to the House of Lords EX OFFICIO ; in the U.S. the Vice-President is chairman of the Senate, ex officio, etc.

The principle of " To him that hath shall be given " is not confined to such constitutional arrangements, and there are plenty of examples of political Pooh-Bahs whose several offices were not necessarily joined as a matter of law. But statistical investigation to-day would be most significant on this head in the world of big business where the plan of interlocking directorates enables one man to be a director of, and thus to combine, a number of firms. Such a " pluralist " is often regarded as better qualified for any new appointment than another who does not combine in his person the same number of interests.

(8) *Antecedent Holding of some Office*

The method of PROMOTION from an office subordinate to that appointed to, is very frequently the case among governmental offices, but there are some important exceptions, especially in the Judicature.

" No one can study the history of appointments to the higher posts," writes Laski, of Judgeships in superior courts, especially in the United States, " without the sense that there is too little relation

---

[1] Op. cit., p. 561.

between them and membership of the inferior courts. A man who accepts a federal district judgeship in America practically excludes himself from the Supreme Court, and in England men distinguished in politics who decide upon a Judicial career, usually go straight to such a position as the Mastership of the Rolls, or the House of Lords."[1]

The political appointment of English judges as against appointment by promotion Laski demonstrates in the following statistical computation covering the years 1832 to 1906.[2]

" Out of the 139 judges appointed in that period, eighty were members of the House of Commons at the time of their nomination ; eleven others had been candidates for Parliament, six of them on more than one occasion. Of the eighty who thus reached the Bench by the avenue of the House of Commons, no less than thirty-three had been either Attorney or Solicitor-General. Excluding from these men who became Lords Chancellor in this period, no less than fourteen were made, not merely ordinary judges, but heads of the court to which they were called. It is not, for instance, insignificant that, with one exception, every English chief justice for the last sixty years has been an ex-Attorney-General ; and even the exception is explained by the notorious fact that his successor could not be spared by the Government of the day when the vacancy occurred. Eight of the judges who had occupied political office before appointment later returned to politics as Lords Chancellor ; though it should be added in fairness that no such case has occurred in the last half-century. Of the eighty judges who left Parliament for the Bench sixty-three were appointed by their own party while in office ; the remainder are cases where an opponent was selected by the Lord Chancellor of the day. It is also significant that the average age of judges appointed from among Members of Parliament was less by six years than the age of those chosen solely with reference to their position at the Bar."

When appointment is made purely by virtue of the longest tenure of the subordinate position, it is known as promotion by SENIORITY. This is the most usual procedure in the military, naval, and to a lesser extent the Civil Services.

The antecedent office qualifying in fact for appointment may not be one immediately subordinate nor yet one logically connected with that to which appointment is made. S. Herbert[3] analyses the antecedent career of all the United States Presidents, classifying their actual qualification for the Presidency as either experience in legislatures, such as qualifies the British Prime Ministers, or as executive experience. He finds 17 Presidents to have had legislative qualification, 10 executive, and concludes that most Presidents have had some legislative experience, and in a majority of cases their

[1] *Grammar of Politics,* p. 549.
[2] *Michigan Law Review,* April 1926.   [3] *Economica,* No. 17.

most important contribution to political life has been made in that sphere. But no less than five Presidents never sat in a legislative assembly, and the minority in whose cases executive experience predominated was *respectable* both numerically and qualitatively. There is, therefore, a sharp divergency in practice as well as form between the British and American systems of qualification.

(9) *Educational Antecedents*

General Education : In Britain Laski shows that of the 306 Cabinet Ministers from 1801 to 1924, 27% were educated at Eton, 12% at Harrow. Since not 1% of the population are educated at these institutions, this indicates a specific statistical tendency.[1]

How far can this statistical tendency be explained as the result of superior knowledge imparted by these institutions, how far as the result of the superior manner and speech among the classes patronising them ?

Technical Education :   Judges are in Britain usually trained professional lawyers who have passed " Bar " examinations. Exceptions where " laymen " or " amateurs " sit on the Bench are the English Justices of the Peace.[2]

IV   *Appointment by Circumstances Beyond Own Choice*

(1) *Age :* Electoral laws usually put a limit to the youthfulness of candidates for office ; e.g. no U.S. Senator may be under 30, nor Representative under 25, but above that age an interesting frequency distribution might be tabulated of (*a*) candidates for office, (*b*) successful candidates.

Rice[3] traces the average age of U.S. Congressmen in every (biennial) Congress from 1790 to 1924 and finds that the general tendency was a fall in average age until about the year 1850, then a rise. In the Congresses lasting from 1803 to 1811, for instance, the average age of Congressmen was nearly 44, in the Congresses between 1843 and 1851 it was about 41, but in the Congresses between 1917 and 1925 it was about 50. Laski[4] gives a table of the age of entry into the British Cabinet and of the age of entry of eventual Cabinet Ministers into the House of Commons.

(2) *Sex :* In some States women are legally debarred from holding certain offices. Where they are not legally debarred, the statistical

---

[1] See also Sidney Low, *Governance of England*, Chapter X, " The Limitations of Democracy."

[2] See Sidgwick, *Elements of Politics*, p. 490, for discussion of this variety of appointment.

[3] *Quantitative Methods in Politics*, Chapter XXI.

[4] *American Political Science Review*, February 1928.

	Age of Entrance		
	1801 to 1867	1867 to 1905	1905 to 1924
Aristocrats into House of Commons	25·6	26·5	29·0
Aristocrats into Cabinet	45·9	43·4	44·5
Commoners into House of Commons	35·9	38·7	40·0
Commoners into Cabinet	55·0	52·7	54·4

proportion of women to men is worth establishing. In 1929 (June) this proportion was 2·3% among members of the British House of Commons as against well over 100% among voters.

(3) *Mentality:* Those certified as insane are, as a rule, specifically debarred from office by law, but within this limit the statistical distribution of, e.g. members of Parliament over the mental grades distinguished in Table VIA would prove interesting. The English Civil Service is largely recruited by examinations of mental ability, and scientific management recommends the vocational selection of candidates for positions in industry through special psychological tests of their mental capacity.

(4) *Race:* Several of the Southern States of the U.S.A. have devised special qualifications for voters, including the due payment of all taxes required of them, and ability to read and understand and interpret the constitution of the State. According to Beard, " negroes often have great difficulty in giving a ' reasonable ' interpretation to the satisfaction of the registration officers."

" The effect of these Southern limitations on the negro vote can be gathered from the published statistics for South Carolina and Mississippi. It appears that in those States there were 350,769 adult male negroes in 1900, and that the total Republican vote (in both States) in the national election of that year was only 5443. At a rough guess perhaps 2000 of this number were cast by white men, and the conclusion (since negroes would for historical reasons not vote Democratic) is that about ninety-nine negroes out of every hundred failed to vote for President in those States."[1]

(5) *Heredity or kinship:* The hereditary principle is that on which accession to the English Kingship is *usually* based. This has not been 100% true, however. In fact, since William the Conqueror the purely hereditary cases have been more like 90%. Notable exceptions were the accession of Henry IV, Henry VII, George I. And the hereditary principle itself has numerous variants of varying statistical frequency, differing from the English plan of primogeniture, such as the " Salic " Law of France, prohibiting the accession of women and men descended through a woman, *Borough*

[1] *American Government and Politics*, p. 457.

English or inheritance of the youngest son, *Gavelkind* or succession by many heirs, etc.   Seats in the British House of Lords are a hereditary legal right in certain families, and seats in the British Cabinet, and to some extent in the House of Commons, though not legally, yet actually have been more or less a perquisite of certain kith and kin.   From 1801 to 1924, 60% of members of the Cabinet were, according to Laski[1] aristocrats, i.e. sons of men with hereditary titles.   These " scions " (as shown in the table above, illustrating the factor of AGE) entered the Cabinet and the Commons some ten years younger than sons of Commoners.

Managers and directors of business also tend to be appointed in Britain on hereditary or kinship principles.   Fathers appoint their sons, or uncles their nephews to " jobs " in their own firms.   How far a person with family connections has a greater chance of appointment, other things being equal, than one unconnected, is clearly an important matter for statistical enquiry.

NEPOTISM, deriving its name from the practice of medieval Popes in preferring their so-called nephews to Bishoprics or Cardinals' Hats, is condemned as corrupt when practised by State officials. But when practised by private capitalist employers it is considered natural and justified as undertaken at the employer's own financial risk.   It may be noted, however, that National wealth is diminished equally whether subordinate managers are appointed on the principle of Kinship (regardless of their efficiency), by private or by public administrators.

B.   DISMISSAL

I and III   *By Own Choice ; or Circumstances More or Less of Own Choice*

In the case of industrial employment, the wage-earning employee who leaves on his own initiative is said (by Americans) to QUIT. Civil Servants and salaried employees who act similarly are said to RESIGN.   The statistical proportion of cases quitting for various reasons has been investigated in labour turnover studies.   Quitting or resigning may be due to unavoidable circumstances beyond one's own choice (considered under IV later) or to avoidable circumstances more or less of one's own choice.   These cases include :

(1)   *Acceptance of Other Office*

Members of the U.S. House of Representatives legally resign on being appointed members of the Cabinet.

[1] " The Personnel of the English Cabinet," *American Political Science Review*, February 1928.

(2) *Marriage in Case of Women*

This is a " burning question " in England as regards school teachers. Practice is divided. Only a certain statistical proportion of local authorities make marriage a circumstance leading to the dismissal of women school teachers.

II *Dismissal by Choice of Others*

(1) *By choice of one person or numerically very few persons usually part of the government or management.*

The procedure of DISCHARGE corresponding to that of nomination in appointment (II 1).

This is the procedure usual in industrial employment and in subordinate political positions (the Civil Service). Statistical investigation has shown[1] that cases of discharge of industrial employees were considerably fewer than cases of quitting except in times of industrial depression when lay-offs (i.e. discharges purely for want of work) might be heavy.

(2) *By choice of members of the same body of persons to which office-holder belongs.*

This procedure, corresponding to that of co-option in appointment (II 2) is infrequent, but has occurred in the British Cabinet in so far as a Minister has not been dropped entirely on the initiative of the Prime Minister. The process when it occurs is usually camouflaged by conferring some dignity on the " de-opted " member, that kicks him " upstairs."

(3) *By choice of numerous persons already forming part of the government,* the procedure corresponding to that of official election in appointment (II 3).

The President of the U.S. may legally be dismissed by IMPEACHMENT before the Senate, acting as a high court, and presided over by the Justice of the Supreme Court. *In fact*, in the case of only one (Andrew Johnson) among the presidents of the United States between 1789 and 1928 were impeachment proceedings initiated (in 1868), and he was acquitted.

The British Cabinet is dismissed collectively by adverse vote of the House of Commons.

(4) *By choice of a multitude of persons or bodies of persons performing no (other) rule transaction* and not in that sense participating in the government or management.

The procedure of RECALL corresponding to that of election in

---

[1] Florence, *Economics of Fatigue and Unrest*, Chapter VI.

appointment (II 4) is a legal possibility in several American State and City governments for the dismissal of the administrative and judicial officials, usually such as are appointed by election. In fact, however, as statistically observable, the possibilities have not been very frequently exploited.[1]

(5) *Murder or execution.*

Assassination is not infrequent in the case of hereditary kings and of presidents of republics. Of the 37 British Sovereigns since William I dismissal by assassination or execution occurred in at least five cases (i.e. 13% of cases) : Edward II, Richard II, Henry VI, Edward V, Charles I. Of the *thirty* Presidents of the United States, 10% have been assassinated. The importance of these percentages lies in the possibility that more than a certain statistical proportion of assassinations would make any given office unacceptable.

IV   *Dismissal by Circumstance Beyond Own Choice*

(1) *Natural Death or Ill-health.*

Mortality Statistics may test the theory that persons holding responsible office have less than the average expectation of life of persons of their age.

(2) *Lapse of Time since Birth* (i.e. *Age*).

After a certain age officials often retire on a pension. The importance of the precise numerically measurable legal limit, as well as the precise actual average age or distribution of ages at which officials retire short of this legal limit is stressed by Laski. Dicey, whom he quotes, points out the age of judges.   " If a statute is apt to reproduce the public opinion, not so much of to-day as of yesterday, judge-made law occasionally represents the opinion of the day before yesterday."[2]

(3) *Lapse of Time since Appointment ;*
Case M A : Individual Office-Holder.

The President of the U.S. retires automatically, or to be specific, meteorologically, after the lapse of four years since his assumption of office. Except for assassination or natural death this generalization has not been broken. He may stand for the four-year office a second time, but after the lapse of eight years in office he does not (in FACT but not in LAW) get appointed to the office again.

The legal terms of office of the Governors of the several States of America showed in 1913 a " bimodal " distribution.[3]

---

[1] Beard, *American Government and Politics*, Chapter XXIII.
[2] *Law and Opinion*, p. 369.
[3] Beard, *American Government and Politics*, Chapter XXIV.

Term : one year :   1 State (Massachusetts)
            two years :   23 States
            three years :   1 State (New Jersey)
            four years :   23 States

Case M B : Individual Member of a Body of Persons.

The lapse of time between original appointment and retirement of individual members of the legislatures varies greatly (1) within the same legislature and (2) as between different legislatures. Some members leave for a while and are then reappointed. The importance of this statistically measurable rate of turnover is brought out by Laski.[1]

" It is notorious that in assemblies like the American House of Representatives, where what may be termed the legislative turnover is enormous, much of the wastage of time, and not a little of the lack of public esteem, are due to the fact that they are, so to say, almost new assemblies at each epoch of their renewed power. Much of the strength of a chamber like the House of Commons has come from the fact that its leading figures have, over long years, been distinguished actors there. The thirty years' membership of Edmund Burke, the sixty years' service of Mr. Gladstone, the forty years' of Mr. Disraeli, all meant an incomparable insight into the technique of government."

Rice[2] has traced the average previous experience of U.S. Congressmen from 1790 to 1924 and finds a gradual shortening of the previous term of office from an average of 1·44 (two-year) terms per member between 1803 and 1811, to an average of 0·90 terms per member in the Congresses between 1843 and 1851. After this period, however, the average of previous terms grew to 2·71 in the Congresses between 1917 and 1925.

Case M C : A Body of Persons Collectively.

The frequency of the dissolution of French Cabinets since 1871 is admittedly an important factor in French politics that can be statistically measured.

The British House of Commons dissolve collectively " as a body," if Parliament has lasted five years. From 1715 to 1911 this legal limit was seven years, from 1690 to 1714 three years. Below the legal limit the average duration and the frequency distribution of durations can only be statistically summarized. On the other hand, the U.S. House of Representatives legally dissolves after a lapse of two years neither more nor less, and statistical measurement is unnecessary.

[1] Op. cit., p. 341.   [2] *Quantitative Methods in Politics*, Chapter XXI.

§6   *Rule-Sharing Relations*

1   Governmental Division and Diffusion of Labour

The observable contacts of ruling and ruled persons within a State or firm have already (§2) been discussed. These contacts whether formal activities or mere discussion were such as might occur though the ruling party consisted only of one man. In the actual fact of modern Nation-States and the modern joint-stock company, the ruler party which rules the State and the firm consists of a more complicated structure. It is composed of a number of men, and between these men more or less recurrent, habitual, and customary relations and contacts are observable that need statistical measurement for their accurate summarization. Customs occur and recur that imply division or diffusion of labour among the rulers, and the analysis already made of such work-sharing relations must be used as an essential framework to statistical measurement and generalization. The first, fundamental, question is, how far generalizations can be formulated at all to the effect that there is specialization and division of labour, horizontal or vertical, or that there is diffusion of labour.

The labour of ruling or governing consists in the State government as a whole performing a number of transactions. If certain structural organs of the government are observed to perform certain kinds of transactions of State as a recurrent " pattern," comparatively more frequently than the chance or independent distribution of the total of transactions among all organs would theoretically assume, and if other organs perform other kinds of transactions comparatively more frequently ; then statistical investigation allows the conclusion that there is (horizontal) division of labour and that the given organs of government specialize horizontally.[1] Or again if certain structural organs of the government are observed to perform certain stages of all transactions comparatively frequently as a recurrent pattern, then statistical investigation allows the conclusion that there is vertical division of labour and that the given organs of government specialize vertically.

If observation and statistical investigation discloses no such recurrent division of labour, then the generalization can be hazarded that labour is diffused.

The cases M I, II, III, IV, V already considered in §3 were all cases of division or diffusion of labour among individuals or organizations WITHIN a whole organization or integral rule-unit like a

[1] See Chapter IX §2, and above, Chapter XIX §3.

State or firm. We now proceed to consider case M VI division or diffusion of labour among *individual persons or bodies of persons within the ruling party, within the government or management of the State, firm, or plant or* of any other organization.

The alternate systems or patterns that are possible in dividing the labour of ruling among any number of ruling organs would, of course, be multitudinous, but it is up to statistical investigation to find what are (1) *the actual* customs in the matter of division of labour between ruling organs when a comparative study is made of all the transactions of one State-government, firm-management, etc., and when the practice of different State-governments, firm-managements, etc., is compared ; and what are (2) the most frequent types of customs. Such a study would first involve the question whether there is any regular, recurrent specialization at all, such that any one organ is associated with a greater proportion or frequency of certain kinds of work, than would be expected on independent probability and chance distribution, and if so what is the degree of association. And once a significant degree of association appears the case, statistical political science may proceed to enquire how many and what organs are distinguishable as specializing to various degrees according to this statistical test.

Two sorts of observable contacts or relations between rulers and ruled involved in the procedure of ruling were distinguished (§2) : formal acts on the part of rulers and ruled ; and discussion between them. Where the structure of the ruling party consists of several persons or bodies of persons, both these sorts of contacts may be observed as occurring and recurring *within* the ruling party.

§6 · 2   Division and Diffusion of Formal Activities

Certain frequently recurrent patterns or " systems " of diffusion, or of vertical or horizontal division of labour among government organs in the formal acts of government have attracted the special notice of political scientists. They have been given a specific name, owing either to their *actual* existence and frequent occurrence or to their being frequently advocated.

The Separation of Powers is a pattern or system of recurrent customs in which the persons or bodies of persons passing general laws (the legislature) are different from the persons or bodies of persons executing those laws (the executive), and from the persons or bodies of persons testing the application of those laws to particular cases (the judiciary). The main *habitat* of this arrangement in full working order is the United States of America.

The Cabinet System is a set of customs in which, while preserving the separation of the Judiciary, the body of persons (the Cabinet) which controls the execution of laws also initiates and controls the passing of those laws. Apart from the separation of the Judicature these two systems of sharing formal acts of ruling or governing may be regarded, in the terms used in §3, as a vertical division of labour between individual persons and bodies of persons within the government. Each item transaction usually passes successively through the same recurrent formal stages. In the British Cabinet system the usual stages and the persons or bodies of persons customarily performing those stages, are roughly as follows :

1. Initiation of Laws :   Cabinet.

2. Discussion and " Passage   The House of Commons steered
   of Laws " :   by Cabinet Ministers.

3. Execution :   Cabinet Ministers and the Civil
                              Service.

At each vertical stage the number of persons among whom the labour is shared becomes greater : a dozen or so Cabinet Ministers, hundreds of members of Parliament, and hundreds of thousands of Civil Servants. The comparative numbers of persons at different vertical stages among whom labour is divided or diffused can be shown diagrammatically by a pyramid with narrow top and broad base. Among the Cabinet at the top and among members of

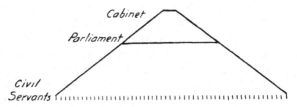

Parliament in the middle, labour is diffused generally, and the number of diffusees or " generals " is indicated by the width of the straight line. Proceeding vertically downwards, however, Civil Servants of the central government divide their labour horizontally into departments and the width representing their number may be divided into compartments.

Table XIXf compares in more detail the vertical division of labour

as between governmental organs in Britain (column 2) for ordinary and (column 3) for financial transactions of State ; and as between governmental organs in the U.S.A. for ordinary (column 4) and (column 5) constitutional transactions of State. The several stages distinguished in column 1 are not pre-ordained *a priori* but, as will be seen from one or another of the other columns, are observably distinguished in that they are performed (in one or other procedure or transaction) by different organs of government. The test of the vertical division of rule is empirical.

The separation of powers is shown graphically in column 3 by the fact that the legislative organs (L) alone are associated with the earlier stages of law-making and the organ E with the later executive stage. The peculiarity of the Cabinet System on the other hand is shown in columns 1 and 2 by a sort of circular division of labour : A law starts by being initiated by the executive organ (E) and ends in being executed by the same organ.

The finance relation between government and governed, when it consists in taxation compulsorily levied, involves, just like an ordinary " command,"[1] a threat of punishment and in the majority of modern States the same precautions are taken only to tax a person under a general " law " that may be interpreted in his case by a judicial court. This financial transaction is divided vertically between legislature, executive and judicature just like an ordinary substantive law. In most State governments, however, the actual statistically observable distribution of the finance procedure, among the legislative and executive organs varies slightly from that customary for non-financial transaction as illustrated in the British procedure column (2) of Table XIXF.

Constitutional transactions ordering the relation of members of the government toward one another (see §2 · 1) follow in Britain, under the system of the so-called *flexible* constitution, the same stages as the ordinary transactions of State, and at each stage are performed by (divided or diffused among) the same persons or bodies of persons ; but in the United States of America and in the majority of States the Constitution is said to be *rigid* in that a different variety of procedure is followed in enacting constitutional laws. There are four legally *possible* ways of amending the United States Constitution, but in actual practice only one procedure has been used,—that tabulated in column 4 of Table XIXF. All the seventeen amendments to the U.S. Constitution that came into force between 1789 and 1913 were first initiated (and discussed) as

---

[1] See footnote, Chapter XIX §2 · 1.

a resolution in the United States Congress (and some of them amended in the course of discussion between the two Houses), and were then ratified by a two-thirds majority of both Houses of Congress and three-quarters of the States.

TABLE XIX$_F$

ALTERNATIVE PROCEDURES OF LEGISLATION AND EXECUTION OF LAWS
EXHIBITING VERTICAL DIVISION OF RULING

	BRITAIN		U.S.A.	
	Constitutional and Ordinary Laws	Finance Laws	Ordinary and Finance Laws	Constitutional Laws
Initiation and Drafting	E (or L)	E	L (Majority of Committee of Congress)	L
Amendment . .	L^1 and L^2	L^1 (only)	L	L
Discussion . .	L^1 and L^2	L^1 and L^2	L	L
Ratification, "*Passage*"	L^1 (Parliament Act of 1911)	L^1	(L^1 and L^2) (J$^▲$ law to be constitutional)	⅔ majority severally in L^1 and L^2 *plus* ¾ of States
Suspension . .	L^2 (for 18 mths.)	—	E till ⅔ majority severally in L^1 and L^2	—
Execution . .	E	E	E	

Legend : L=Organ(s) called Legislature
L^1 Lower House
L^2 Upper or Second House, Senate, Lords, etc.
J=Organ(s) called Judiciary
J$^▲$ Supreme or High Court
E=Organ(s) called Executive : Cabinet, President.

The distinction between financial and non-financial legislation in Britain and that between ordinary and constitutional laws in the United States is in the nature of an empirically formed horizontal division of labour. But horizontal division of ruling is developed most highly in the various executive departments of State and to a lesser extent in the various judicatures with distinct " jurisdictions "—criminal cases, civil cases, divorce cases, etc. Statistical investigations could show how far different State-governments of the same order of size hit upon the same sort and number of executive and judicial divisions ; and the measures of the degree of specialization elaborated in §3 might usefully be applied. Before theories are advanced as to the *raison d'être* of the several divisions of government, some rough statistical computation of this kind should certainly be undertaken as to the actual " *être* " and state of the matter.

§6 · 3   Division and Diffusion of Discussion

In any real observation of the politics of modern Nation-States, discussion between rulers and ruled must be studied alongside of formal activity (§2 · 5). Similarly the relation of discussion *among* the rulers when these are many (relations unduly neglected in text-books of political science) must, when possible, be measured statistically. Discussion among rulers manifest the same measurable divisions and diffusion of labour.

Horizontal division of the labour of discussion within a ruler body is observable in the sub-committees on education, lighting and paving and other special subjects, of the larger general council of English local authorities, and is observable also in the committees of a larger assembly such as the U.S. or French Legislatures.

Vertical division of the labour of discussion is observable among different State-governments in the series of activities connected with the passing of each several law. First by appointing commissions (royal or otherwise), committees of enquiry, etc., the government often adds advisers to its numbers who are either experts on the subject of the proposed law or who represent the persons whose interest the proposed law may touch.[1] After this *probouleutic* or investigatory stage the law is formulated in a definite form, such as a " bill," before discussion starts. Some one person usually puts forward a motion or amendment which initiates the third stage of " debate." As a sequel to debate, the fourth stage of reaching a decision may be observably distinguished and this decision is sometimes, in a fifth distinct stage, revised.

Analogous to these five vertically divided stages in legislation are the vertical stages in Judicial procedure and also in the procedure of manning by popular choice, i.e. by election. Thus in a statistical approach these vertical stages of discussion might be isolated from the other activities of government for separate comparative study. That is to say all item-cases of discussion diffused among persons in whatever place or at whatever time the discussions occur and whatever the procedure—whether legislative, judicial, or electoral—may be brought together, their varieties and similarities measured. The comparability of similar vertical stages in different contexts is particularly striking in the diffusion of labour among rulers and among electors respectively in the vertical stage

[1] See Laski, *Grammar of Politics*, p. 332, for advocacy of an extension of such advisory bodies.

2E

of debating and coming to a decision and will be studied in detail in §6 · 5.

TABLE XIXɢ

VERTICAL DIVISION OF LABOUR IN DISCUSSION WITHIN THE RULING PARTY

Stages common to three columns ·	Legislative Assemblies	Court of Law	Elections
1. *Investigation*	Royal Commissions, etc.	Police enquiries	Consideration of Candidates by Party Organization
2. *Initiation*.	A few sponsors initiate bill— First Reading	Preparation of brief. Presentation of case	Small group of persons sign Nomination of Candidates
3. *Debate*	Debate. Committee Stage	Pleadings, prosecution and defence, by barristers	Candidates indulge in canvassing and Election Addresses
4. *Decision*	"The Division" of whole House	Judgment by the Court	Electors (or some of them) vote, polling for one or other candidate
5. *Revision*	Conference between Houses	Appeal to High Court	Re-count by Returning Officers

§6 · 4   Statistics of Rule Division

When the division of labour between members of a government or ruling party is looked upon as different kinds of recurrent behaviour patterns, the recurrences of which may vary in (1) frequency, (2) completeness, and (3) intensity (compare §2 · 7), investigation must obviously take a statistical form.

(1) Light is often thrown upon the character and outlook of the ruling party, by measuring the class of transactions or subjects upon which laws are most frequently passed by the legislature for subsequent execution.

In England to-day (1920–28 at least) such social legislation as Unemployment Insurance Acts seem to take pride of place ; but in other times the suppression of free speech or the protection of landlords' game and sporting rights against poachers, or sumptuary laws penalizing " swank " in clothes and diet among the lower classes can be statistically observed as the more frequent.   In modern France laws changing the constitutional procedure appear more frequent compared to other laws than is statistically the case in Britain.

(2) Proposals for laws duly initiated may fall by the wayside ; or laws, though passed, may remain ineffective and dead letters as far as their execution goes.

Statistical investigation is thus required to measure the number or proportion of bills or laws failing to pass any of the vertical stages given in Table XIXF. For instance, (i) the number of laws ratified by the U.S. legislature (L^1 and L^2) that were subsequently declared unconstitutional by the Supreme Court (J^A), or (ii) the number of resolutions amending the Constitution (a) initiated in the U.S. Congress and (b) ratified by both Houses of the U.S. Congress (L^1 and L^2) that were (c) actually added to the Constitution. Finer[1] states that up to 1890 the statistical figures were (a) 1900, (b) 19, and (c) 15. Significant statistics of a similar kind might be collected in Britain of the proportion of proposals of (a) a Liberal government, (b) a Conservative government, that failed to pass the House of Lords previous to the change in the vetoing power of the Lords decreed in 1911.

If some proposals do not get beyond the legislature, others do not start there at all but arise with the executive. The King in Parliament, according to Laski[2] will, on the average, pass some eighty statutes each year, while the number of orders and rules made by the executive will be about thirty times as many. These orders will be of varying degrees of generality not merely applying to one case, e.g. one individual ; and mark a deviation from the specialization of the legislative organ in the passing of laws which is exercising the foremost political scientists in Britain.

(3) The intensity of the performance of any vertical or horizontal division of ruling may be measured by the time spent in discussion. Where a body of persons within the government engage in public discussion it is possible to measure objectively and statistically the *time taken* to discuss the different transactions of the government in a way not possible where either (a) only one man is " thinking out " his policy or (b) a body of men is discussing policy in secret. There may be legal limits to the time of discussion after which some sort of closure or guillotine is applied, but within these limits wide variation is observable and must be measurable by statistical investigation.

Henderson and Laski[3] have made statistical computation of the number of hours of (House of Commons) time during 1910, 1911, 1914, 1919, and 1922–3 devoted to debates on matters of central government and local government respectively. The proportion

---

[1] *Foreign Governments at Work*, p. 62.
[2] *Grammar of Politics*, p. 389. [3] *Economica*, No. 13.

for the whole series of years averages 74% for central as against 26% for local affairs, and these proportions are fairly stable in the course of the several years. In any one year the proportion of time spent on central administration is never less than 64% nor more than 86%. Henderson and Laski have also measured the distribution of the discussion in the House of Commons between central and local transactions through the number of answers given to questions in the House. A few answers were not specifically local or central in reference, but the proportion of oral answers that were specifically central as against local in reference were, for the Parliamentary year 1912–13, 64% as against 33% ; and, for the year 1922–3, 76·5% as against 19·9%. The proportion of *written* answers that were specifically central as against local in reference were, for 1912–13, 58% as against 42%, and for 1922–3, 74·8% as against 24·9%. The conclusion drawn by the authors from these observations is that local questions do not occupy Parliamentary time to the extent sometimes supposed by those advocating devolution, and that comparatively little time would be gained by transferring local transactions to special local legislatures.

§6 · 5   Statistics of Rule and Manning Diffusion

In the activity of ruling a State, as contrasted with that of managing a firm, special importance attaches to the diffusion of labour in discussion. The compulsory sanction of State laws necessitates particularly careful consideration of different persons' points of view before the law is passed and made enforceable. In modern democratic States these points of view are elicited by the more or less popular election of " representative " legislatures. Discussion, consisting of a group of persons debating and arriving at some decision, thus occurs and recurs at two points ; in the course of the popular election, and in the proceedings of the representative legislatures.

A statistical investigation that is so obvious that no political scientist has apparently troubled to make it, is to tabulate in a frequency distribution the number of members of each of the legislative bodies of all State governments. Such a tabulation would probably show a definite upper limit to the size of a legislative body at about 800 members, and a less definite lower limit would also probably appear, depending partly on the size of the population of the country represented.

The statistical facts once established, theoretical, psycho-physiological, and sociological interpretations are in order to explain at least the nether and upper limit to the number of persons within a deliberative legislative body.

" No legislature," writes Laski, " should be so small that its representatives cannot, from the size of their constituencies, have genuine personal relations with the electorate : no legislature should be so large that effective debate is impossible for its members. A body of more than six hundred members, like the House of Commons, obviously means either such a limitation of debate that no argument can be properly put, or the restriction of debate to a handful of members, while the rest remain silent auditors. But it has been the experience of every system that if the mass of its members are compelled to silence they will not long remain auditors." Presumably the statistical absence rate at, or rather from, debates may rise to such a degree that the body is no longer an effective body at all.

In addition to psychological limits there is a *physiological* upper limit to the number of individuals meeting simultaneously at one time and place as a body among whom discussion is diffused, in man's powers of hearing.

The technical invention of the loud speaker, though it increases the size of an audience that can hear a few selected men, will probably not help in the activity of mutual discussion. On the other hand, there is in addition to adequacy of representation, a further psychological lower limit to a legislative assembly of a State, in that State's idea of what is due architecturally to its own dignity.

Graham Wallas[1] describes graphically the sort of considerations that might solve the problem.

" The main elements of the problem are that the hall should be large enough to accommodate with dignity a number of members sufficient both for the representation of interests and the carrying out of committee work, and not too large for each member to listen without strain to a debate. The resultant size will represent a compromise among these elements, accommodating a number smaller than would be desirable if the need of representation and dignity alone were to be considered, and larger than it would be if the convenience of debate alone were considered.

A body of economists could agree to plot out or imagine a succession of ' curves ' representing the advantage to be obtained from each additional unit of size in dignity, adequacy of representation, supply of members for committee work, healthiness, etc., and the disadvantage of each additional unit of size as affecting convenience of debate, etc. The curves of dignity and adequacy might be the result of direct estimation. The curve of marginal convenience in audibility would be founded upon actual ' polygons of variation ' recording measurements

[1] *Human Nature in Politics*, Chapter V.

of the distance at which a sufficient number of individuals of the classes and ages expected could hear and make themselves heard in a room of that shape. The economists might further, after discussion, agree on the relative importance of each element to the final decision, and might give effect to their agreement by the familiar statistical device of 'weighting.'

The answer would perhaps provide fourteen square feet on the floor in a room twenty-six feet high for each of three hundred and seventeen members. There would, when the answer was settled, be a ' marginal ' man in point of hearing (representing, perhaps, an average healthy man of seventy-four), who would be unable or just able to hear the ' marginal ' man in point of clearness of speech—who might represent (on a polygon specially drawn up by the Oxford Professor of Biology) the least audible but two of the tutors at Balliol. The marginal point on the curve of the decreasing utility of successive increments of members from the point of view of committee work might show, perhaps, that such work must either be reduced to a point far below that which is usual in national parliaments, or must be done very largely by persons not members of the assembly itself. The æsthetic curve of dignity might be cut at the point where the President of the Society of British Architects could just be induced not to write to *The Times*.

Any discussion which took place on such lines, even although the curves were mere forms of speech, would be real and practical. Instead of one man reiterating that the Parliament Hall of a great empire ought to represent the dignity of its task, and another man answering that a debating assembly which cannot debate is of no use, both would be forced to ask ' How much dignity ? ' and ' How much debating convenience ? ' "

A priori the relation of discussion diffused among rulers and electors might have been supposed such as to force all the individuals discussing to form one body of persons where, as in trials at law, arguments can be met or where (as in legislatures) proposals can be amended, debated, and altered *on the spot*, among persons in physical contact. Yet in fact the majority of legislatures of the central government of a State, and even of the unit States of a Federation (as in America) are separated on the British model into two bodies, two Houses or " Chambers." One body whose *personnel* is modelled on the British House of Commons is usually called a House of Representatives, or of Delegates ; the other whose *personnel* is not modelled on the British House of Lords is usually called a Senate. The " diffusion " of discussion beyond one single body is also observable in the referendum or initiative and in the manning relations when officials and representatives are elected by popular vote. Here voters divide up more or less thoroughly into separate " Constituencies," usually upon a territorial basis. The division is most thorough and fine when for every representative there is one separate constituency, but the division may be various degrees less thorough according as two, three, four or any higher number of representatives or delegates are voted for in the same constituency.

" Before the invention of writing," says Graham Wallas,[1] " a man who engaged in serious and continued thought did so either while dealing in solitude and silence with material provided by his own memory and imagination, or while forming one of an arguing group who constantly provided each other with new facts and diverted in new directions the course of each other's mental associations." But since the invention of writing, and especially printing, voting for men and proposals is done by writing on printed ballot-papers or questionnaires, and discussion (debate and decision) is not necessarily performed by persons organized as one body.

The realistic observation and statistical measurement of the diffusion of labour in discussion (debate and decision) should not be confined, therefore, to the relation of persons within one body. Where more than one body is formed, as in constituencies for the manning of the legislature, statistics have played a most important practical rôle. " The idea of the decennial census seems to be an American product. The provision for representation in the Lower House of Congress, in accordance with population, made a census indispensable, and hence, this was provided for in the Consti-tution, and the first census was taken in 1790. Slightly over a decade later (in 1801), England, too, adopted a similar plan of enumeration."[2]

The precise clause in the American Constitution runs to the effect that " representatives shall be apportioned among the several States according to their respective numbers, counting the whole number of persons in each State, excluding Indians not taxed," and the difficulties connected with an apportionment such that each constituency should be equal in numbers " as nearly as may be " have greatly exercised theoretical statisticians.[3]

In countries where there is no precise or written constitutional ruling on the matter, constituencies may vary very greatly in the number of voters, and the notorious situation in England previous

---

[1] *The Great Society*, Chapter XI.
[2] Though not for the same purpose. King, *Elements of Statistical Method*, Chapter I.
[3] *Journal of the American Statistical Association ;* September 1921, E. V. Huntingdon, " A New Method of Apportionment of Representatives " ; December 1921, F. W. Owens, " On the Apportionment of Representatives " ; and " Report upon the Apportionment of Representatives."

to the passing of the Electoral Reform Act of 1832 only differs in degree from situations in several States to-day.

Among the statistics referring to the diffusion of political discussion seven series may be distinguished. *Statistics Series 1* would consist in measures of the deviation in size of the numerous constituencies into which electors for representatives may be grouped. If the deviation is high and constituencies very unequal, representatives clearly differ in their degree of representativeness. This difference is sometimes taken account of, as in votes for the Trade Union Congress, by " weighting " the vote of each representative according to the number of " constituents " (i.e. the number in the Trade Union) which he is representing.

When incorporated into one body the relation of persons doing the identical labour of discussion (including debating and deciding) upon matters of State are analogous to a " squad " of soldiers or a " force " of policemen or firemen, or a staff of shop assistants, each of whom is ready to do the same sort of work. Members of the force or staff are " on duty," but may not actually have the opportunity or be called upon to keep order, to quench fires, or to sell goods ; similarly, members of a legislature may, or may not, speak or vote.

In manning by election on the part of a number of voters (§5) or in the procedure of the initiative or referendum each voter usually *has* the opportunity of participating in the discussion and the decision. He is usually canvassed personally, he is invited to free meetings, and he has the right to cast his vote for whatever candidate or proposal he pleases ; *but the opportunity may or may not be seized.* This variability in voters' behaviour requires at least two further series of statistical computations for its measurement.

Statistics Series 2 measures passive participation : the proportion of qualified persons among whom discussion is diffused, who attended political meetings, were canvassed in person, etc. etc., in the course of an election or referendum campaign, or who as members of a governmental body were present at its debates, spoke themselves, etc. This computation would measure the degree of interest, attention, popular feeling, etc., evoked on various questions, or at least the importance attached to such questions by the party managers,—matter that has not been very successfully excogitated by political philosophers *a priori*.

Statistics Series 3 would measure active participation, the proportion of persons among whom discussion is diffused (e.g. those entitled to vote) who actually " went to the poll " or took part in a " division."

Rice, for instance, computes the " per cent of eligible votes cast " in presidential election in 21 Northern States of the U.S.A. as 87·2% in 1880 and 82·2% in 1900 ; but in 1920, after the admission of women to the vote, the percentage fell according to his calculation to 56·3%.[1]

When the activity of *making a decision* is diffused among a number of persons, the policy or person decided upon is in modern governments definitely a matter of *numerical computation*. Except in such cases as the jury or the Cabinet, unanimity among all the " diffusees " is not required. Instead, the decision may be determined by one of at least three procedures :

(A) A majority of all the diffusees (usually any number over half but sometimes two-thirds or three-quarters) *actually present or voting*.

(B) A majority of *all* the diffusees, usually any number over half but sometimes two-thirds or three-quarters, whether present and voting or not.

(C) If not a majority then a *plurality of the diffusees*, i.e. the greatest number of persons among whom the decision is diffused who agree in their decision.[2] Where there are more than two candidates in an election even a majority of just over half the persons voting may not be possible.

Where decisions are thus arrived at by diffusion among a number of persons, various further statistical computations are an important *index to the degree of decisiveness or preponderance of one kind of decision compared with another*.

Statistics Series 4 : The comparative number of persons voting for each of the candidates or for or against any proposal and, therefore, the precise majority of the candidate or measure that was " decided upon."

The frequency distribution of various degrees of majority or minority for any party in item constituencies shows significant features. Rice[3] tabulated 566 item counties in eight Western American States according to the percentage of total votes in each county given to Mr. La Follette, the Progressive Presidential candidate in 1924. The distribution approximated to a normal probability curve[4] with a mode at the class of percentage 30·0–34·9%.

---

[1] *Quantitative Methods in Politics*, p. 246. The " fieldwork " difficulties in measuring the total of eligible voters are described, pp. 243–246, and the whole Chapter (XVII) is denoted " The Growth and Decline of Political Attention."

[2] " In elections, a plurality of votes is when one candidate has more votes than any other, but less than half of the whole number of votes given. It is thus distinguished from a majority which is more than half of the whole number." *Webster's Dictionary*.

[3] Op. cit., Chapter VIII. [4] See Glossary §18.

In other " regions," notably Philadelphia, Rice found a heavily skewed bimodal[1] curve, and he suggests that this bimodality in a city known to be relatively homogeneous in population suggests a " politics " in the narrow (and nasty) sense of the word where election officials do not hesitate to tamper with the voting. This sinister interpretation is borne out by selecting the wards known to be controlled by the Republican " machine," and distributing the item election districts within these wards in respect of the percentage of Democratic votes recorded. Sixty-one out of 155 districts show *less than* 4% of Democratic votes to total vote.[2]

Statistics Series 5 : The number of persons elected to " represent " the several constituencies who were members of each of the different political parties. Table VIIIB, illustrating the political swing of the pendulum during the nineteenth century in Britain, is an example of this important type of statistics.

The course of Parliamentary politics in nineteenth-century Britain is only one example of such a swing of the pendulum. Further examples appear in the history of the United States. W. E. Macdonald and Rice[3] examining the election statistics in the States of New York since 1807, New Jersey since 1844, Pennsylvania since 1790, and Ohio since 1803, claim to detect a tendency for the swing to increase in amplitude as time proceeds. To account for this *increase* in amplitude, Rice[4] refers to the increase in the area of social contacts. Owing to universal education and the extension of transport facilities, newspapers, cinematographs, broadcasting, etc., " a mass tendency by the electorate to favour one candidate rather than others would *carry its influence farther* in more recent than in earlier times."

To explain the statistically observed phenomenon of the swing of the pendulum *generally*, the following reasons are adduced by Rice[5] in an article on " The Political Vote as a Frequency Distribution of Opinion."

" There is no reason to suppose that the political opinions held by individuals do not follow the normal frequency distribution[6] which is characteristic of more easily measurable mental characteristics or products. . . . Modern political society, however, resorts to a crude measurement of opinion by means of the vote. With this device, opinions which would normally be distributed continuously are consolidated into a discreet series, containing but two classes. . . . We may cite the various positions taken upon the question of public ownership. At one extreme the anarchist holds for complete individualism, at the

---

[1] See Chapter VI §5.   [2] *Quantitative Methods in Politics*, p. 110.
[3] Op. cit., Chapters XX and XXI.
[4] Op. cit., p. 305.   [5] *J.A.S.A.*, March 1924.   [6] See Glossary §18.

other extreme the socialist would place all industry under State control. In the middle ranges of opinion are to be found those who would nationalize the railways ; those who would add coal mines to railways ; those who would add to these the packing plants and the flour mills. It is probable that individual and class interests help to determine the particular industries or services which the individual would be willing to have publicly owned. Hence as to any particular industry, opinion might be multi-modal or skewed. It remains probable that the thoroughgoingness of public-ownership opinion in the abstract remains normal in distribution.

If political opinions are distributed in the normal manner that we have suggested, it is probable that radical changes in public opinion occur less frequently than is usually supposed. The relative strength of parties at election time may be changed in either of two ways : In the first, the points at which the issues are drawn may remain constant. Hence, a comparatively slight shift of the modal opinion may bring about a transfer of power from one party to another that appears superficially as a ' sweeping verdict at the polls.' Nevertheless, the shift is most likely to have taken place within the central quartiles of the distribution where opinion most nearly approaches indifference. Subsequent events usually prove in such a case that the changes of opinion were not profound or thoroughgoing. Opinions lightly held are easily changed. Thus the fickleness of public opinion that is so frequently observed may be a phenomenon representing the comparative indifference of the central portions of the distribution of opinion.

In the second case, opinions may remain distributed in the same way, but the points at which the issues are drawn may be shifted. When this occurs, it is usually the result of manœuvring for advantage on the part of politicians and party leaders. Old issues are presented in a new light, so that in effect the opinions of the electorate are re-classified and new class limits are established. Any new shift of party strength between two elections in which the same issues are presented probably involves both of these occurrences."

Another American writer, Prof. Merriam, bears out this thesis by advancing specific though hypothetical figures for a " normal " frequency curve in the distribution of opinion between the two classical parties of America. The largest class of voters appears in the middle values as independents or independent partisans.

Hypothetical Distribution of 24,500,000 Voters in U.S.A.[1]

Republican	Organization	250,000
	Strong Partisans	3,000,000
	Independent Partisans	6,000,000
Independent		6,000,000
Democratic	Independent Partisans	6,000,000
	Strong Partisans	3,000,000
	Organization	250,000

Statistics Series 6 : The total number of persons voting in the

[1] Merriam, *The American Party System.*

country as a whole (i.e. in all the constituencies added together) for candidates of each of the different political parties.

The degree of preponderance or relative strength of the different parties as measured by statistics series 5 and series 6 often differs widely, a disparity that forms part of the case for Proportional Representation. Sir Richard Martin, in his presidential address to the Royal Statistical Society (quoted Chapter VIII §5), described the disproportionate effect upon the distribution of representatives between the political parties when only 5% or only 10% of the electors changed sides in each constituency ; and other statistical investigations tend to show that the thoroughgoing division of voters into constituencies each of which only returns one representative, leads to greater disparity in the party distribution of votes as between the country as a whole and the elected representatives, than does less thorough division with larger constituencies voting for several representatives.

Statistics Series 7 : Consistency of individuals in their votes.

Finally, where the identity of each voter is known, statistics may throw light on the important question of the consistency of individuals in their decisions. How far the same persons are always found to vote " as one man " on the same side, as against the practice of *cross-voting*. Answers to this question would show the degree of what party politicians call " party loyalty " and of what independent commentators call " machine " politics.

Statistical measures or indices of " cohesion " and " likeness between groups " among the votes of legislators in divisions, or roll-calls, have been worked out by Rice[1] and applied to the political parties, groups, or " blocs " in the New York State Assembly of 1921, the U.S. Senate in the Sixty-eighth Congress, and the small, and therefore statistically more easily managed, New Jersey Senate in 1914. In this latter case several *blocs* were detected, some of them cutting across party lines, and certain common characters pertaining to the individual members of such *blocs* were indicated, such as affiliation to Masonic order, or Irish ancestry.

But here we are trespassing on the main territory of Chapter XX, the correlation of two or more political characters, and the limits to the present chapter are passed.

[1] Op. cit., Chapters XV and XVI.

CHAPTER XX

§0   *Introduction*

THE statistical approach in economics set forth in Chapters XV to XVIII made use of the orthodox system of economic theory as an iron framework on which to build. In political science, on the other hand, there is no such theoretical framework that can be usefully employed. Ethical and moral implications have not yet been exorcised and there is little trace of the notion of flexible and variable characters and conditions such as economic theory now admits (Chapter XV). Hence, in Chapter XIX I have been compelled to build my own framework and apparatus of thought. No specific theories or laws were put forward, but an attempt was made so to select and define terms, and so to orientate the investigator that the field would be prepared for statistical measurement.

Many of the terms of the old political science walked the plank and were cast overboard ; and since recourse was had to a systematic nomenclature such as Roget's Thesaurus provides, I may say that I have hoist my own *jolly Roget*.

The justification of this piracy lies in the booty, and in this chapter I propose to show how the conceptions and terms introduced in Chapter XIX enable important generalizations made by statistical summarizations to be combined with non-statistical interpretation and reasoning.

The *new* political science embodying these generalizations is *indicative*, not optative or ethical in mood ; *inductive*, starting with observation of item facts, not deductive and speculative ; *realistic* and observant of actual practice and customs instead of legal fictions ; *comparative* rather than snobbish or impressionistic in observing all possible cases of similar practice among all sorts of groups and organizations besides the State ; and finally, the new political science attempts to use numerical measurement and to be statistical, not in the original sense of STATE-istical, compiling isolated facts about the State, but in the new sense of summarizing variations and interrelations numerically. Numerical summarization of different issues are, as classified in Chapters VI, VIII, and IX: the frequency distribution and, if possible, the average of variations of a single character; time and space tendencies in the variations of these characters; and associations and correlations of variations in two or more of these characters. Chapter XIX isolated the essentially political characters such as structure, and the procedures and transactions of ruling, work-sharing and manning, and illustrated the possibilities of measuring the statistical frequency of various structures, procedures, and transactions. This chapter, after a brief review of the need for measures of distribution (§1) and time-tendency (§2) in political science, is chiefly devoted to the statistical association or correlation of political characters as forming, when combined with psychological interpretation, the chief basis for generalizations and laws of political science.

§1 *Summary of the Distribution of a Single Political Character*

At first sight of a treatise on political science the facts about the State that are taken as the focus of political science appear unique, invariable, and not requiring statistical analysis. Only one State is described at any one time (usually the State of which the author is a member), and it has one set of laws to which, for anything said to the contrary, the behaviour of everyone conforms. One hundred per cent of the people conform 100% of the time. There is no suggestion of varying frequency except, perhaps, for the slight deviation represented by " crime."

As against this invariability, such conceptions as the comparative frequency of occurrence and recurrence, comparative degrees of completeness, and varying degrees of intensity put forward and illustrated in the last chapter, stand out in the sharpest contrast. These conceptions clearly call for a statistical approach, and the summarization of item facts by the calculation of frequency distributions, general tendencies, and correlation.

The original item of statistical political science is primarily the individual person, and the chief character upon which the political sciences focus are the acts of individual persons towards one another. Where an act is looked at from the point of view, not of the performance of an agent, but as the experience of a patient, acts will appear, if unusual and not frequently recurring, as something " happening " to the patient, or if usual and frequently current as his " lot "; and such " haps " and " lots " as are not identical with an action of a person, but are " acts of God " or " natural events," may not be clearly distinguished.

Typical starting-points of a statistical political science are thus the item number of persons that live in such and such places or are members, pay subscriptions, own allegiance to such and such organizations ; the item number of persons whose " hap " or " lot " it is that they are born, die, enjoy such and such incomes, have accidents happen to them ; the item number of persons that ply such and such trades and occupations ; the item number of persons going to school, voting, striking ; the number of persons punished for crimes by specific authorized persons, etc. etc.

About some of these activities there may be no State law to which all must conform ; about others, such as going to school when below a certain age, and not committing certain acts scheduled as crimes, there may be universally applicable laws. But do all individuals obey them ?

The United States of America has a law, and a Constitutional Amendment at that, prohibiting the manufacture or sale of alcoholic beverages. Now you may bring a horse (or an American citizen) to water, but you can't make him drink. Nor can you make *all* young men fight by passing compulsory military service acts. Nor can you prevent some persons stealing, murdering, evading taxes, etc., and statistical measurement is thus called for in summarizing (1) the variable extent to which laws are known to have been disobeyed by the population as a whole in spite of the penalties attached. There are (2) further variables, further " matters of degree " for statistics to measure, in the proportion, by no means generally 100%, of total crimes or unlawful acts known to have been committed (a) for which some person or persons have been judicially tried, (b) for which some person or persons have been judicially convicted. The number of crimes or other unlawful acts for which persons were *not* convicted or tried in any period, say a year, compared with the total number of crimes committed in that period, should be stated when an assertion is made that persons doing such and such things must undergo such and such legal proceedings.

(3) Further variability in State politics is introduced by the fact that some laws are optional in the sense that they give certain persons or groups of persons like local authorities the right to perform acts, which they may or may not perform. Thus it is not accurate to say that all adults vote, nor very illuminating to say that most or some adults vote in any particular election. A statistical statement is called for to the effect that $x\%$ vote.

(4) Some of the characters manifested by the persons who are the items observed may be quantitative characters having numerical

values. Thus item persons may be distributed according to whether they pay subscriptions and thus are members of clubs, churches, lodges, factories, etc., of larger, middling, or smaller membership. There is then a frequency distribution of persons over or among measurable sizes of societies. Even if some compulsory State laws may prescribe a quantitative limit like the compulsory attendance at school until a certain minimum age, or not working in factories above a certain maximum of hours per week, or not speeding in motor cars above a certain maximum of miles per hour, there are still many quantitative variations on the " right " and " wrong " side of the law. A person may speed so many miles per hour, or work so many hours, or leave school at such and such ages below or above the prescribed limit. An accurate presentation of the facts is still bound to take the form of frequency distribution. Persons must be distributed according as they work, speed, or stay at school to various quantitatively measured degrees round the legal limit. In so far as the law is not broken it does not really impose one form of conduct but simply imposes a limit, and within that limit conduct may show the utmost variety. If the illegal conduct is regarded as a negative variation the whole distribution of varieties will tend to show a positive skew. The conduct is NOT necessarily uniform.

The original item of statistical political science is, however, not always the person. The act, hap, or lot is the next most usual item. Where the statistical item is not a person but an act, hap, or lot the character may refer to persons. Acts, haps, or lots may be characterized as having a value of so many persons. So and so many accidents, crimes, or illegal acts involved such and such or so many persons ; so and so many factories contained so and so many persons. Or the character may refer to the act itself, its " intensity " as measured by money, by time spent, or by the terms of a penalty. So and so many crimes got so and so many years' imprisonment ; legislative discussion on such and such topics occupied so many days ; to obtain compensation for various injuries workmen spent so and so many pounds.[1]

In short, even within one system of laws (e.g. in one State) it is not accurate to say that such and such things are done or not done, or that persons must behave or refrain from behaving in certain definite ways. When the individual cases are observed they are often found not to tally uniformly with the legal programme, and this variability necessitates statistical measurement if the facts are to be generalized.

The need for a statistical approach becomes yet more apparent

[1] See above, Chapter XIX §2 · 3, §6 · 3.

when political science extends its scope (1) to embrace a comparative study of other sovereign States besides the author's, and the international relations between these States ; (2) to include local government and the study of non-sovereign States ; (3) to embrace all social organizations, whether they exercise compulsory powers or not. The statistical item in this case is usually the group or society of persons. Item States, item local subdivision of State, item party organizations, item Trade Unions or business firms, will, in their procedures and structures, differ from or resemble other item organizations of the same or of a different kind. Wherever possible statistical measures must be used to describe and summarize accurately the resemblances and variations in the structural and functional characters of such societies.

§2   Summary of Political Tendencies through Time

It is in the attempt to discover general political tendencies through time that the observational inductive method has hitherto been most popular. The meticulous examination of item cases and the classification of a mass of observations according to variations in their inherent characteristics has been carried on in England with a minimum of deductive speculation by a school of famous constitutional historians like Stubbs and Maitland, among whom Sir John Seeley was perhaps the most school-conscious.

" You will see that this mass of observation of which I speak is neither more nor less than what we call history. All that perplexity about the object of their labours which besets historians, all that perplexity about their method which hampers those who would form a political science, disappear together if we regard history as the mass of facts, brought together by observers who were but half conscious of what they were doing, out of which our inductive science of states is to be constructed." [1]

In history books we are accustomed to find the mass of facts arranged more or less chronologically, as indeed the facts were arranged in the chronicles or records from which histories are written. But the first requisite for statistical measurement is that like should be compared with like, and that the events or instances brought together should manifest variations and values of the same character. A topical classification is thus called for. All the facts about one particular institution, one particular structure, procedure, or kind of transaction must be grouped together as items in one field of observation. That done, the statistician may confine his attention to the tendencies and changes in the values, quantities or

[1] *Introduction to Political Science,* Lecture I.

qualities, of one specific character. The same types of changes or of time-tendencies may be distinguished in political and constitutional life as in economic activity. There are political cycles and political trends often combined, but capable of being isolated.

A similar CYCLE can often be observed in the histories of all individual instances of one particular sort of institution. A mass of item-occurrences collected of one particular sort of tax, or a number of instances collected of one particular sort of organization, such as a municipal corporation, a guild, or a joint-stock company, may show similarities in the course of the life of that institution. Within each kind of institution the instances may more or less agree and an average typical sort of life-cycle with phases of growth, and decay, or of birth, maturity, and death may perhaps be established. Thus many medieval taxes agree in showing a tendency to ossification or stereotyping of total yield. The total sum obtained from the English medieval tax called tenths and fifteenths, nominally a tenth of the movable property of boroughs and one-fifteenth of the movable property of counties, remained, in spite of the growing value of movable property, at a fixed aggregate sum. About 1334 the yield of item impositions of the tax was, according to Cunningham,[1] nearly £39,000, " and from that time onwards a fifteenth and a tenth became a mere fiscal expression for a grant of about £39,000." And several other medieval taxes in Europe and taxes at all times in Asia, seem to show the same stereotyping tendency. Similarly we may trace the falling numerical proportion of all citizens included in town guilds as each guild reached middle age. Or to come to modern times, we may show statistically the typical life-cycle of a joint-stock company, tracing the proceedings whereby the bulk of joint-stock companies are conceived, born by promotion and underwriting, and presented to the public ; we may measure the proportion that die by bankruptcy ; and among such as die we may trace statistically the proportion that are resurrected by reorganization or else pass into the receiver's hands.

The measurement of generally occurring phases in the life-cycle of a specified kind of institutions is one task for statistical politics. Another task is to take at first only one instance of any institution but by a long series of measurements to establish a number of recurrencies of a cycle in the course of that one institution's history. An example of such a statistical investigation into cycles applied to the institution known as the House of Commons, is furnished by the measurement of the political pendulum in nineteenth-century England given in Chapter VIII §5 and Table VIIIB.

[1] *Growth of English Industry and Commerce*, 4th edition. p. 296.

Political TRENDS when the discoverer of them approves of their direction are often called progress, and the idea of a more or less definite and possibly definable line of progress has exercised the mind of political scientists ever since Turgot attacked Voltaire's cyclical view of the history of civilization. At first the particular lines of progress that were proclaimed were generalizations based entirely on deductions either by introspection, from the author's own consciousness, or by analogy, from the generalizations of other sciences. In contrast to such " philosophies of history " or such doctrines of human evolution based on the conclusions of natural science, are " inductions " generalized from a minute scrutiny of the facts of human development as recorded by ethnology, archæology, anthropology, and the documentary researches of historians after eliminating random accidents and cycles. Working deliberately on these lines Müller-Lyer[1] claims that " social development progresses in a definite and definable direction, and that it proceeds according to clearly recognized laws," and backs his claim by formulating eight such laws, all summarized in a ninth, dealing with the " organization of labour " (i.e. economic organization) alone. Most if not all of those laws are trends amenable to statistical measurement. There are laws of integration and concentration, and three further laws may be cited verbatim.

(1) The law of size or agglomeration. " In the same way as men tend to unite into groups, so these groups have the tendency to combine in increasingly greater social and economic forms. At first there were small independent hordes which roamed over wide regions, later the hordes united into tribes, then the tribes into nations, the nations into great states, and finally the great states into gigantic political systems."

(2) The law of co-operation. " Simple co-operation (*diffusion of labour* in my terminology) such as that employed in building the Egyptian pyramids always merges into division of labour."

(3) The law of differentiation. Müller-Lyer[2] makes differentiation " in which different individuals devote themselves more or less exclusively to their various callings " equivalent to my *specialization*, and the law runs : " In every economic body there exists the tendency to differentiate more and more between the various forces contained in it."

Whether the tendency in question is a trend or a cycle, investigation may take a scientific form with critique of sources, accurate

---

[1] *The History of Social Development,* Book III, Chapter VI English translation, E. C. and H. A. Lake.
[2] Op. cit., p. 153.

observation and careful fieldwork, and yet, of course, not be statistical. The facts observed, though quantitative in character, may not be measured, or the facts may not manifest the quantitative characters capable of measurement. That many political characters are quantitative in character has abundantly been shown. Scientific, political, or constitutional history might certainly gain in accuracy if changes in such quantitative characters as the size of political bodies or the degree of division of labour or the financial expenditure or revenue of government were measured in specific figures.

Changes in our time in the *sizes* of industrial organizations such as plants and firms, have been discussed and summarized for Germany and America, and a tendency to concentration or integration observed and measured.[1] The same tendency would probably be observed in other countries to-day by collecting the same sort of industrial statistics ; and the same approach applied to the European States of the Middle Ages, to local areas of government, to Trade Unions, to churches, would discover tendencies toward integration or disintegration. Variations in the size of a single institution may also be traced over periods of time, as Maitland has done in estimating the number of members of the House of Commons (together with the number of shires and boroughs they represented), through three long periods of English history.[2]

Tendencies to *specialization* or differentiation are measurable by the tests of the degree of division of labour suggested in XIX §3. English constitutional history exhibits this trend clearly and measurably in the horizontal differentiation of the old *Curia Regis*, first into separate administrative and separate judicial bodies, and then into several law courts such as the King's Bench, the Common Pleas, the Exchequer, each transacting different kinds of business.

Lack of quantitative character is, however, no bar to the statistical approach. It remains important to measure the frequency of occurrence of items that may only be qualitatively characterized. The gradual growth of a custom *means* the increasing frequency of occurrence of some form of behaviour, and study of such a growth must be statistical.

If the behaviour is a system or pattern of facts we may note the growing frequency of item cases manifesting such complete pattern until the pattern becomes a regular routine,[3] hard to break. The successive " vertical " acts of initiating, amending, discussing,

---

[1] Cf. Chapter V §3.

[2] *The Constitutional History of England*, edition of 1909, pp. 173–5.

[3] For importance of political routine, see e.g. Stubbs, *Constitutional History*, Vol. II, p. 419.

passing, and executing laws exhibited in Table XIXf were but gradually evolved in various countries, and this evolution can be traced accurately only by statistics of the frequency of that particular system or pattern of government procedure from period to period.

Separate structures of government may be singled out and the growth in frequency measured of the functioning of that given structure or organ of government within the whole procedure of government, as time proceeds. If there is a measurably *less* frequent functioning of a given organ, the organ may ultimately, like the human appendix and the limited monarch, become *vestigiary*.

Or a specific function in the government procedure may be given, and one different structure after another may be observed transacting that given function, one structure succeeding or being substituted for another. In England the specific transactions of the pre-Conquest Earl were akin to those of the sheriffs in the twelfth century, but gradually in the course of the fifteenth century these functions fell into the hands of the justices of the peace.[1] Advice to the King was another function that changed hands until, passing through the hands of the Privy Council, it rested in those of the Cabinet,[2] and the precise process or trend of change can most accurately be studied by measuring, at least during the transition period, the comparative frequency with which advice was sought from or given by one organ and another.

The growth in frequency may be for some country in general, or a spread may be measured from one region or context to another. Thus in medieval England the jurisdiction of the King's court may be measurably shown to have spread or *radiated* from cases arising solely among the King's servants and, later, tenants, to cases arising on the King's highway or in places like markets under the King's special protection till finally the whole country was "irradiated."

Processes such as stereotyping, radiation, integration, differentiation, substitution may be observed, measured, and summarized as general tendencies repeated in the cases of numerous item institutions, and numerous item countries and epochs ; and the very growth of political custom might be found generally to trace a peculiar curve, like, say, a learning curve, beginning with one isolated "generative" case[3] (e.g. the model Parliament[4] of 1295),

[1] Maitland, *Constitutional History of England*, pp. 41, 232–4.
[2] Maitland, op. cit., pp. 190–203, 256, 390–4.
[3] Giddings, *Scientific Study of Human Society*, p. 99.
[4] Maitland, op. cit., p. 76. "Of course one such assembly as that of 1295 might well have been a solitary event which the historian would note on passing as an anomaly. . . . It is only in the light of what was at that time

then growing rapidly in the frequency of its recurrences, then ceding or reaching a *treppe* when frequency per period is stationary, then experiencing acceleration of frequency till complete regularity is reached when the particular variety of custom under investigation becomes the only variety that occurs.

To instance a quantitative character, the most definite meaning that can be attached to the Industrial Revolution as a technical achievement, is that during certain years, in England about 1720 to 1870, in the United States from 1870 to the present day, the rate of growth in the amount of production *accelerated* rapidly. In the years previous to the English and American Industrial Revolution growth was relatively slow ; and in the years after the English Revolution the *rate* of acceleration decreased when compared with that of the revolutionary years.[1]

The violent controversy conducted with terms usually meaningless and referenceless as to when the Industrial Revolution ended, if at all—and whether indeed there was any such event—might be settled (or might never have arisen) if the statistical frame of mind were cultivated among economic and political historians, and some such definite statistical test employed.

In short, whether the items observed have quantitative or qualitative characters, the statistical approach is called for not only in measuring the change in frequency of items manifesting any character from time to time (or it may be from place to place, see Chapter VIII §6), but also in comparing *the rates* of changes and the *continuity* of changes in the frequency itself.

§3   *Summary Association or Correlation of Political Characters*

The chief contribution of statistics to political science as it is to economics,[2] is the measurement of association or correlation among political, as economic, *characters*. These statistical associations or correlations may not prove or disprove anything when taken alone, but when fused with a more or less plausible political theory which may interpret or explain their findings, generalizations or " laws " of political science may be said to be established of some degree of probability.

What are the precise characters that may thus be correlated as a

future history, that the parliaments of Edward's last years have their vast importance. However, we know as a matter of fact that they did form precedents ; that parliaments formed on the model of 1295 were constantly held during the coming centuries."

[1] *The Integration of Industrial Operation*, U.S. Census Monographs. Diagram, p. 29, shows the American curve clearly.

[2] See Chapter XVI §7.

step in the discovery of political " laws " ? The analysis or framework put forward and illustrated in Chapter XIX provides the basis for the statistician's orientation. When a society or group of persons is the statistical item manifesting and thus coupling two or more characters[1] that may be measured and correlated, the characters must pertain to the society's (1) structure, (2) functionings, or (3) transactions. These words are liable to be used loosely, and I have assigned them the Greek letters (1) μ for $\mu o \rho \phi \eta$, (2) ϕ for $\phi \upsilon \sigma \iota \varsigma$, and (3) ϵ for $\dot{\epsilon} \rho \gamma o \nu$ to pin down the reference I wish them to have and to hold in my apparatus of thought.

The structure or anatomy of a living organism consists of a number of constituent organs. Similarly the structure of a society consists in other (sub-ordinate) societies (sub-societies or parties) such that the inner functioning of the larger inclusive or super-ordinate society will appear as the external transactions of the constituent sub-ordinate societies. The Greek letters used as symbols may thus conveniently appear as capitals when referring to the structure (M), function (Φ) or transaction (E) of the super-ordinate or inclusive society but as small letters when referring to the structure (μ), functioning (ϕ), or transactions (ϵ) of the sub-ordinate or component society.

Carrying this orientation a step further, I distinguished three sorts of functioning or transaction (functioning on the part of the super-ordinate, transactions on the part of the sub-ordinate society) : ruling, work-sharing, manning.

The statistical association or correlation of political characters to which our analysis points the way may, therefore, be of the following sorts :

I Association or correlation of the structure (M) (especially size) of one society with the structure (μ) of its sub-ordinate parts, or for short correlation of $M\mu$ type. Analogy : size of whole animal and size of internal organs.

II Association or correlation of the structural size (μ) of any one society with its functioning (ϕ). For short correlation of $\mu\phi$ type. Analogy : one variety of size or anatomy of an animal associated with one particular variety of metabolism.

III Association or correlation of one sort of functioning or procedure (ϕ) of any society with another sort of functioning or procedure (ϕ) of the same society. For short correlation of $\phi\phi$ type. For instance, a society like a firm within which men rule and are ruled in a certain way may also manifest a certain work-sharing procedure or manning procedure. Analogy : one organism with

[1] See Chapter V.

one particular variety of nervous system may relatively frequently also manifest a particular variety of digestive functioning.

IV   Association or correlation of some sort of functioning of one society (ϕ) or its structure (μ) or its structure *and* functioning ($\mu\phi$) with the transactions of that society (ϵ) corresponding to the functioning of a super-ordinate society (Φ). For short correlation of $\phi\epsilon$, $\mu\epsilon$, or $\mu\phi\epsilon$ type.   Analogy : one particular type of external behaviour in an animal may tend to be associated with some particular type of anatomy or physiology in that animal.

V   Association or correlation of one kind with another kind of transaction in so far as performed by one and the same society or sub-ordinate party. For short correlation of $\epsilon\epsilon$ type. For instance, the ruling party's transaction of rule may be associated with a particular work-share transacted by the same party. In the super-ordinate industrial society known as the firm, the party transacting rule and " controlling " is (under the capitalist system) also the party whose transaction or work-share is the provision of capital. Analogy : one organ of the body may serve two purposes in the functioning of the body as a whole.

Examples of the possibility of each of these types of associations or correlations I, II, III, IV, V will be taken up in §§ 4, 5, 6, 7 and 8.

§4   *Association of the Sizes of Super and Sub-Societies*

Is there a positive correlation between the number of persons employed per local plant, factory, shop, mine, etc., and the total number of persons employed by a firm controlling and including one or several such local plants ? This local plant of a firm cannot contain more persons than the firm itself, but the average-sized constituent plant, if there is more than one, may contain any fraction, larger or smaller, of the firm's population.

Negative correlation between the size of firms and their subsidiary plants is observable to the naked eye when, in the case of multiple shops, banks, financial combines, and Kartells, the " branches " or subsidiary plants continue to employ relatively few persons, or even to employ fewer persons ; while the super-ordinate firms or combines by multiplication of such small branches and subsidiaries employ larger and larger numbers of persons.

A statistical summary of the situation as a whole as against a few such easily observable cases, is still lacking in all countries. An official American census monograph[1] approaches nearest, by telling us the average number of establishments (and the distribution of

---

[1] *The Integration of Industrial Operation*, 1924, Chapter VII.

the numbers) found in " central-office groups " or combinations in fourteen groups of industries, but the monograph does not tell us the size of the establishments concerned. Clearly, however, a statistical computation of the number of wage earners (1) per central-office combination and (2) per establishment thus combined, would have been feasible.

The same problem could be approached differently by computing for a number of item industries the average size of establishment whether combined or not, and the average size of firm whether a combination or not. The number of persons employed per " establishment," e.g. local operating unit—mill plant, etc.[1]—is given in the American Census of Production for two hundred and fifty different industries ; but the number of persons employed per firm, combine, or unit of control in each industry is not given. It has been calculated for a few industries in America and elsewhere by the intensive investigation of private students,[2] but for general comparison with the extensive statistics of size of establishment we are compelled to use rough and indirect indices. One such rough index of the size of firms is the ratio of wage earners employed in any industry to " proprietors and other firm members." The U.S. Census of Manufactures gives the number of proprietors and of other firm members together with the number of wage earners per establishment for the same two hundred and fifty item industries, and thus allows us to compare every five years changes in the number of wage earners to proprietors or other firm members with changes in the number of wage earners per establishment in the same industry, and allows us also to note for any one year how far industries with a large number of wage earners per establishment are also industries with a large number of wage earners per " proprietor and other firm member."

A serious flaw in this latter character as an index of the size of the firm is the influence of the relevant and therefore disturbing factor[3] of incorporation. When a firm of given size changes from an individual property or partnership to a joint-stock company or corporation it has no longer any proprietors or firm members, i.e. partners, at all.[4] Hence differences and changes in wage earners

---

[1] For definition of establishment, see above, Chapter X.

[2] For instance, Chapman & Ashton, for the British Cotton Industry, Shimmin for the British Wool Industry. *Stat. Jl.*, April 1914, Jan. 1926.

[3] See above, Chapter XI.

[4] The American Census of Manufactures, though it gives the number of establishments and the number of wage earners ruled by a corporation, unfortunately does not tell us the number of corporations or the number of partnerships as against the number of partners, and we cannot, as we should, add the number of corporations to the number of partnerships and individual

per proprietor or firm members is an index not merely of differences and changes in the factor of size of the firm but also of differences and changes in the factor " form of ruling procedure."

However, incorporation is probably itself indicative of a larger size of firm (corporations can be shown statistically to own on the average larger plants than individual proprietors and partnerships), so that, whether or not incorporation has supervened, more wage earners per proprietor or firm members may continue to be regarded as a rough index of the size of firms.

Now this index is far from showing a positive correlation or association with the size of establishment. Whether the two hundred and fifty different industries are tabulated as item-cases, or the same industry for different years, the higher rate of wage earners per proprietor and firm member is relatively often found manifested by an industry (or year) that manifests a comparatively low rate of wage earners per establishment.

Positive correlation and exact co-variation of the size of establishment and the size of firm is probably true enough of the smaller sizes of manufacturing establishment and firm. The distribution of sizes is as we know (U.S. Census) negatively skewed, with a multitude of very small establishments that would be more or less identical and co-extensive with a firm, but with a few large, and with yet fewer very large establishments. Some of these larger establishments are combined under one firm, some are not, and it is at this upper end of the scale that size of firm probably no longer co-varies precisely with size of plant.

These divergencies show the danger of confusing establishment or plant with the firm. The confusion might not be of any great practical or scientific importance if firm and plant, though different in kind, agreed and were positively correlated in their variations of size as between different industries and different periods. But with the statistical evidence against a high positive correlation the confusion in the writings of even the most authoritative economists

proprietors. In the American Census of Mines, on the other hand, there is in the enumeration of " operators " at least an approach to enumeration of firms. In the anthracite coal mining there were in 1900, for instance, 334 mines owned by 119 operators, in iron ore mining 525 mines with 332 operators, etc. " Operators " may consist in (1) individuals, (2) firms and limited partnerships, (3) incorporated companies, (4) others, including the State and co-operative enterprise, or (5) combinations, of which there were 118 in iron ore mining. The category of combination was introduced in the 1900 census for certain classes of mines (e.g. iron) and manufactures (e.g. iron and steel products, with 40 combinations owning 447 " plants "), but the category does not appear in the subsequent census. It is to some extent replaced by the " central-office groups " of the 1919 census.

as to the type of organization or structure referred to in such expressions as the representative firm, shows the need even for pure economists to consider the " political " distinction between the rule unit or firm, and the mere working body, plant, or establishment.

" It is not so easy to say whether Marshall was thinking of a representative plant or technical production unit or a representative business organization. In the *Principles* he gives the impression of referring to the latter . . . but against this must be put a passage in *Industry and Trade*, in which he distinctly asserts that the establishment or plant best suggests the ' command possessed by it of the economies of production. Economies of marketing are often better represented by statistics of businesses, but on the whole the establishment is doubtless the best unit '."[1]

And many who have popularized Marshall have failed in the same way to distinguish two politically very different types of organization.[2]

The lack of positive statistical correlation between size of firm and size of plant can theoretically be interpreted by reference to the plausible causes of increase in the size of firms. One main cause of increased size of firm may be the increased size of the plant the firm is to control, but another main cause is the desire for monopoly over the market or at least greater marketing efficiency. This second line of causation does not necessarily imply larger establishments but may imply the combination of existing plants and the control of one firm over more establishments of about the original or even less than the original size. If a few firms are trying to compete with one another in all markets, as the joint-stock banks in England are to-day (1928), growth in firms may be associated with plants (i.e. branch banks) averaging smaller in size than before.

The question of the correlation of the sizes of super and subordinate societies has significance also in the politics of the State. A unitary central State is usually split up into sub-ordinate local authorities and a federal State consists of a number of constituent sub-States. The important question arises whether with the growth in population of the central State or among States of comparatively large population, (A) more local authorities or constituent sub-States will be formed, each with about the same population; or

---

[1] L. Robbins, *Ec. Jl.*, Sept. 1928.
[2] E.g. " In each of these industries at any given time there is a certain size of business plant which under average management is most conducive to economical production. This may be designated as the *representative firm*." Seager, *Principles of Economics*, Chapter X.

whether (B) the local authorities or constituent sub-States will remain about the same in number but each with increased population. In the language of statistics, alternative *A* constitutes a *negative* correlation of size of super-ordinate and size of subordinate structure ; alternative *B* constitutes a *positive* correlation. But there may be some " law " of regression short of complete negative or complete positive tendencies.

Once Case A or Case B, or modification of them is statistically established, theoretical interpretation would be worth attempting. Case A might be explained as due to the fact that not more than a certain number of persons can be governed under one authority. Aristotle thought that no State *should* contain more citizens than would be reached simultaneously by one voice, a number physically ascertainable. If that were true to-day the increase in population of central States would be associated with a greater number of local authorities within it and the geographical area of local government would tend to become smaller with the greater density of population per square mile. Case B might be explained by the development of technical inventions (broadcasting, telegraph, railways, trams), whereby more persons can be reached by the voice " area " of the law than heretofore ; or else might be explained by increasing law-abidingness of persons, requiring less legal authority per person. But the point I wish to stress is that statistical investigation is feasible and should precede speculative interpretation.

§5   *Association of Size with Division of Labour of Societies and Organizations*

Organizations of all kinds manifest two quantitative characters, size (i.e. the number of persons they contain), and distribution (diffusion or division) of labour. Each of these characters are quantitative variables with a scale of values or degrees, and the apparatus of thought elaborated in Chapter XIX permits us to ask whether, observing a large number of plants, firms, or industries as items, there appears in general a positive correlation of the size of a local industrial " plant " or the size of an industrial firm or the size of a whole industry, with the degree of the division of labour within it as against diffusion of labour ?

It is usually held that division of labour is dependent upon the size or area of the market, and this assumption was made in Chapter XVII §7 when tracing the theoretical arguments for the " advantages " of large-scale production. Greater production per firm or per locality (R I in Table XVIIκ) or per industry was taken to result in $R\,2$, full use of specialized human ability (i.e. division of labour). But this association of comparatively great production per firm or per plant or per industry with division of labour is not absolute or inherent and must be measured in some degree or coefficient of association.

In the case of the association of division of labour with the size of an INDUSTRY, it can be seen from XIX §3 · 3 that industries equally large in the sense of employing an approximately equal number of persons are not equally or anything like equally sub-divided into separate occupations. In England, agriculture, the coal-mining industry, and the textile industry all employ about a million persons, but the distinguishable number of occupations in each industry is roughly 480, 920, and 2200 respectively. But we shall not pursue the measurement of the precise correlation between division of labour and industry. An industry, as we have said, is not strictly an organization at all in the sense of a rule-unit. We may turn to the correlation of division of labour with the organization (in the strict sense of the term) called a firm.

In England an indirect statistical measure of the size of industrial and business FIRMS may be obtained in the form of the proportion of those occupied in various groups of occupations who were of the status of employers or were " working on their own account."[1] This class of person is distinguished in the English Occupation Census, though not, unfortunately, in the Census of Industries. But where (see XIX §3 · 3) an industry is more or less identical in *personnel* with a group of occupations as formed in the census we may distinguish three " scales " of firm.

I   Where the employers (including " own accountists ") number about, or less than, 1 in a 100 of the total occupied. So measured the large-scale firm with comparatively many employees per employer appears to be usual and perhaps representative in the instance of the textile industry or group of occupations, the coal industry, and railways.

II   Where employers (including " own accountists ") number from 1 to 20 per 100 of the total occupied. The average rate of employers to total occupied or total employed in the industry is within these limits in the instance of the building industry (or builders' group of occupations), in the clothing industry (or makers of textile group of occupations), and the paper and printing industry (or paper and printing group of occupations).

---

[1] The same difficulty occurs in using the English as in the American Census. A joint-stock company though a firm may cease to contain anyone of the status of employer, see above, §4.

III Where the employers (including " own accountists ") number more than 20 per 100 or one-fifth of the total occupied. The average rate of employers to total occupied or total employed in the industry is above this limit, in the instance of agriculture (or agricultural occupations), commerce and finance (or commercial finance and insurance occupations), professions, excluding education (or professional occupations, excluding teachers) ; and would be above this limit in the instance of personal service if the mistresses of domestic servants were officially included, as they logically should, among the employers.

When this classification according to size of firm is taken in conjunction with the grading according to degree of division of labour (XIX §2) it would be possible to tabulate industries or groups of occupation in an association or contingency table according to three quantities, grades or scales of two characters ; Grades A, B, C, in respect of the character subdivision of labour, Scales I, II, III, in respect of size of firm.

Table XXA so tabulates the ten industries (or groups of occupation) that we have cited, as a foretaste of the method advocated. Many more industries would have to be tabulated before any positive conclusions could be reached, but it is suggestive to notice that though the Table shows a distinct regression line from top left (A I high subdivision, large firm) diagonally to bottom right (C III little subdivision, small firm), not all industries " toe the line." In the coal industry the large firm is found associated with medium subdivision. In the printing and paper industry high subdivision of labour is associated with only medium size of firm. And in the professions there is an example of very small firms with a high division of labour.

A positive correlation contingency or association seems, therefore, indicated between subdivision and large scale of firm, but only to " some " degree.

The correlation of size of PLANT or ESTABLISHMENT with the degree of division of labour cannot be computed for Great Britain since the British Census does not enquire into the number of men employed in each plant. This enquiry is, however, made in the United States' Census of Manufacture (as well as in Germany and other European countries) and there would be no difficulty in classing industries in respect of size of plant, just as they have been classified in respect of division of labour and size of firm (i.e. number of employers per 100 employees).

If we refer to the United States' Census of Manufactures where the precise number of wage earners per establishment is directly

TABLE XXA

FORM OF TABLE WITH INSTANCES TO SHOW ASSOCIATION OR CONTINGENCY
BETWEEN SCALE OF FIRM AND DEGREE OF DIVISION OF LABOUR

Grade of Subdivision	Scale of Firm		
	I : *Large*	II : *Medium*	III : *Small*
A *High and Fine*	Textile Railways	Paper and Print- ing, etc.	Professions
B *Medium*	Coal	Makers of Textiles (i.e. Clothing) Builders	
C *Low and Coarse*			Agriculture Commerce Personal Service

stated, it will be found that in 1914 the average (arithmetic means) for all manufactures was 25 wage earners per establishment or plant. But a wide variation is observable in the average size of establishment in different industries. To take a few industries that employed over a 100,000 wage earners. Bread and bakers, printing and publishing, and tobacco, consisted of establishments averaging less than 13 wage earners each ; while petroleum refining, cotton, boots and shoes, steelworks and rolling mills, consisted of establishments averaging more than 100 wage earners each. Clearly there is wide quantitative variation, allowing for precise correlation of size of establishment with size of firm or subdivision of labour.

The association or positive correlation of larger firms, larger plants, and more minute division of labour statistically approached in §§4 and 5 constitutes the precise statistical measure of the " political " or organizational aspect as against the technical aspect[1] of the *Industrial Revolution*. Where statistical conceptions are absent it is often assumed that the three qualities of large firms, large plants, and fine division of labour necessarily occur in combination. In fact, however, association of larger firms and larger plants is not to be assumed (§3), and as Table XXA shows the combination of the large-scale firm and fine subdivision is far from a universal law also. The industries are not all scattered along the diagonal regression line.

Division of labour, scale of firm, and probably scale of plant too, must at the outset be considered independent variables, each of which, taken alone, can plausibly be argued to have increased

[1] See above, §2.

efficiency and can, perhaps, by statistical investigation be shown to have actually done so. Subsequently statistical investigation may or may not find these variables to be in some degree correlated.

In so far as a comparatively high degree of correlation can be shown statistically the next stage of investigation would be to " interpret " these statistically determined political or " organizational " results, that is, to explain them in terms of causes or in terms of *more general* laws.

A technical explanation[1] would probably lie, for instance, in the increased use of machinery (a factor statistically measurable in horse-power, value of equipment, etc.). Increased use of machinery requires (1) larger capital equipment employed under one management and plausibly, therefore, larger firms ; (2) larger capital equipment employed under one roof and, therefore, larger plants ; and (3) the constant attention of one man to the few standard operations that the machine itself can perform, i.e. minute specialization and division of labour on the part of the *personnel*.

The association or correlation shown in Table XXA of the degree of subdivision with the size of organization among item industries, may be extended as a general working hypothesis to State politics and indeed all politics. It is plausible to suppose that the smaller the number of the population under a local or central government the more the act or labour of governing will be found diffused and not subdivided and specialized. This theory if substantiated would have an important bearing on the creation or combination of local government areas. In substantiating such a theory statistical investigation such as I have outlined in industrial politics would be combined with theoretical reasoning applicable both to industrial and State politics.

On the theoretical side the analysis of division and diffusion of labour (made in Chapter XIX §2) now enables us to show almost mathematically the reason why the larger the scale of production, the more *fully* specialists can be used. The argument is based on the fact that for a *balanced production* some, highly specialized, processes may only be diffused among one or a few persons while less specialized processes may require diffusion among a great number. One example of this is the actual organization of the heeling department of the shoe factory displayed in Table XIXD. But the full significance of this unequal diffusion may be brought out more clearly by picturing an office organization. Different methods of dividing and diffusing work are continually exercising

---

[1] For other, economic, explanations see Chapter XVII §7.

practical business organizers as an important factor in industrial efficiency, and the more rational and rationalizing among them[1] draw up charts to show the relative position of each kind of job and the number of persons among whom that job is diffused. A line downward usually indicates a relation of rule. The position at the top (the position of the father in a genealogical tree) is that of the ruler or chief ; the position at the bottom of the line that of the person subject to his rule. Where lines tend thus to run downward a hierarchical military or " staff " type of organization is indicated, where each successive grade of persons takes orders from the superior grade on all subjects. On the other hand, where lines tend to run across the chart, a " functional " type of organization is indicated where systematic division of labour (usually horizontal) has been introduced. Each man or group of men performs his special function or subject without arbitrary interference therein. The number of men within each grade or group among whom the same work or " subjects " are diffused are often indicated by dots, or the number may be stated in figures.

Let us apply this growing practice of systematic charting to a semi-fictitious government department dealing with conciliation and the investigation of industrial disputes. Founded on the facts of Ministries of Labour we may suppose the labour of such a branch of the Civil Service to be divided across under one general secretary into conciliation and investigation sub-departments ; and the investigation sub-department downward into pure investigation, statistical computation, and typing of reports.

To perform the full and exact amount of labour required, the *personnel* might be fully employed if it consisted of seven conciliators, supplemented by five investigators, to enquire into the causes of friction when conciliation failed. These investigators would require three computers, one of whom, however, had to spend half his time at the telephone answering enquiries, and would also require the full time of two typists. The scheme of organization would be charted as follows :

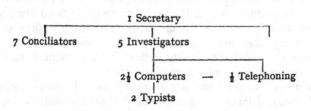

$$
\begin{array}{ccc}
& \text{1 Secretary} & \\
\text{7 Conciliators} & \text{5 Investigators} & \\
& 2\tfrac{1}{2}\text{ Computers} & - \quad \tfrac{1}{2}\text{ Telephoning} \\
& \text{2 Typists} &
\end{array}
$$

[1] E.g. L. Urwick, *Organizing a Sales Office*, esp. Chapter III.

2G

Now let us suppose an economy campaign of the " Geddes Axe " type, followed by orders to shut down to half the amount of labour in conciliation and investigation. The total *personnel* numbered eighteen and is to the axe-wielder clearly divisible by two. Certainly the typists can be reduced from two to one ; but the five special investigators must either be reduced to two, employing the remaining typist only ⅘ths of her time, or may be left at three, when they will require the time of 1 and ⅕th typists and will overwork only one. Similarly the work of the three computers and the seven conciliators, not to mention that of the one supervising secretary, will be " out of balance " unless they cease specializing for the full time.

This simple illustration introduces us to the principle that *the smaller the scale of operation and the fewer the total number of persons dividing and diffusing their labour, the less chance there is of all of them being fully made use of as specialists.* Had the work and the total *personnel* of this government department been doubled there could have been five fully employed specialist computers and one specialist at meeting telephone enquiries instead of a computer spending half his time off his job.

The principle explaining and interpreting the statistically observed association of high subdivision of labour with large-scale organization is that of *multiples,* summed up in the words of Babbage.

" When (from the peculiar nature of the produce of each manufactory) the number of processes into which it is most advantageous to divide it is ascertained, as well as the number of individuals to be employed, then all other manufactories which do not employ a direct multiple of this number, will produce the article at a greater cost."[1]

§6 *Integration ; or Association of Rule With Work-Sharing Procedure of Societies*

The political and business worlds exhibit what may be called the superimposition of one kind of functioning or procedure (ϕ) upon another kind (φ). Though the main, characteristic, functionings, or procedures within the business society (its ϕ) are those of division and diffusion of labour—work relations in short—parts of this society also manifest certain rule-relations.   Some work-relations are sometimes closely knit under one common employer, or in other words included within one FIRM.

Within or " under " the firm's employment, the sharing (division or diffusion) of labour does not cease but is modified.   It is, so to

---

[1] Babbage, *Economy of Manufactures,* Chapter XXI.

speak, muffled like the noise of a train passing through a tunnel. The puffing is going on, but to hear it you must get inside the superimposed tunnel and investigate the relations inside the firm.

In what precise way, then, is work-sharing modified or muffled by the superimposition of the rule-relations known as employment ? Or to put it in a more familiar way, how is work-sharing modified by *integration* of certain shares within one rule unit ?

The diffusion of labour will no longer entail Competition. When by the process called horizontal integration two similar bookstores become included under one employer their respective shares of the transaction of bookselling will be deliberately allotted to them ; each will cater for a territorially or otherwise divided market as prearranged by their common employer. Competition may thus be defined in the terms I am using as " work-sharing " between workers within different employment units, or simply as *Unruled Work-Sharing*.

The division of labour integrated within one system of employment will also involve a different connection between the bodies of persons dividing up transactions. Instead of the cash nexus or exchange nexus, there will be substituted a *deliberately arranged* distribution of the different jobs among the different bodies within the combination. Whereas formerly the payment for each share in some work was a " price " or a " profit-margin," the payment *within the employment unit*, i.e. the firm, consists in a wage or a salary. Inclusion under one employment therefore seems to have modified " sharing " of work to this extent that the shares become prearranged by human rule or control and not directly dependent on the economic circumstances of the market.

In this superimposition of particular rule-relations upon particular work-relations, or integration of particular work-relations in one rule-unit, certain prevailing associations or systems may be statistically discoverable. *Typically*, both (a) factory or establishment and (b) the firm, consisting of employers (the ruler-and-manner party) and employed (the ruled and manned party), will tend to include certain specializing work-sharers whose shares are in specific relations to one another of horizontal or vertical division of labour, and will tend to include other work-sharers.

When specialists with vertically related " divisions " of work are included within one organization, and are ruled by a common employer, the economist speaks of Vertical Integration. When persons doing the same work or specialists with horizontally or territorially related jobs are included within one (ruling) organization and are ruled by a common employer the economist speaks of Horizontal Integration. The economist is inclined to confine these expressions to relations in process of being set up between already existing firms or factories within a newly created firm or factory. If instead of taking the existing organizations as given he were to enquire into the nature of the original unit, the firm or factory, he would see that these groups of persons that are so prevalent that he often overlooks them, are in themselves associations of high frequency between certain specific rule-relations and certain specific work-relations.

(*a*) Typical Work-Relations within the Factory or Establishment.

Within the body of persons called a *factory*, plant, or establishment, the rule procedure between its structural parts is that of employment which usually includes the procedure of hiring and firing, issuing orders, and paying wages and salaries. A statistical investigation of factories would show, I think, that the specialists usually comprised within this rule organization under a common local manager were, since the advent of mechanical inventions, (1) specialists providing the mechanical power to drive the machines (the engine-room staff), (2) specialists designing, maintaining, and repairing the machines and buildings (patternmakers, mechanics, tool-setters, and other craftsmen), (3) routine manual workers operating the machines or working by hand, (4) routine brain-workers (clerks) and the office staff, recording, accounting, writing letters, etc., and (5) the executive or administrative workers (foremen, managers, etc.), and custodians.

The percentage of total employees who were general labourers, or who specialized in these various activities within an American metal plant that I investigated in 1920, were as follows :

Design, maintenance, repair (crafts)	.	.	.	15·6
Routine manual workers	.	.	.	.	59·7
Routine brain workers	.	.	.	.	3·9
General labour	.	.	.	.	.	16·3
Custodial	.	.	.	.	.	.	2·5
Executives (administrative) .	.	.	.	.	2·0
Total	.	.	.	.	.	.	100·0

These several groups of specialists are in the relation the economist calls joint demand. They are not divided up vertically or territorially but horizontally, being all engaged at the same stage of the productive process. Statistical investigation could probably establish the proposition that persons who divide up labour and

" specialize " horizontally tend to group as a body into one rule organization, if the several divisions of labour or specialities are in joint demand. There would, however, be significant deviations from this law. Factories often obtain their power, heat, and light and their water supply from an outside organization, e.g. a municipal power-station or water-works, and such deviations point to the prevalence of certain auxiliary services used in common by all factories.

This " common service " is admitted in the appellation " public utility " services, and one interpretation of the (probably statistically ascertainable) fact of their independent ruling or control is that these service industries are usually most economically managed if they are large-scale *monopolies* providing the same service for all firms. But the fact that they are usually independently ruled should first be statistically established before theoretical interpretations are advanced.

The divisions of labour mentioned so far as included under one rule, within the factory, are not formed vertically or territorially, they are horizontal divisions. The specialists referred to are all working at one stage of production and in one place. But the factory group may also include specialists working at different *vertical* stages. There may be separate iron-making and separate steel-making plants or combined plants ; separate cotton-spinning " sheds " and cotton-weaving " mills " or combined factories, and so on. The fact that there are cases both of " integration " within one factory and of separation into different factories of the SAME vertical stages in any one industry makes the enquiry necessarily statistical. No invariable rule can be laid down and " laws " must be in the form : such and such vertical work-divisions are (a) included under the rule of one plant in $x\%$ of cases, are independent in $y\%$ of cases.

(b) Typical Work-Relations within the Firm

Within the *firms* who exchange goods and services on the outside market the rule-relation includes not only the employment relations or the supervision of the employment relations, but also financing. Statistical investigation would probably show that in the case of most " item " firms, the rule-relations extended over the horizontally divided work (not necessarily done in the same place) of (1) lending capital, and (2) buying raw materials, machines, land and buildings, as well as (3) over the several work divisions already distinguished as comprised within the factory body.

These are horizontal divisions of labour ; but there are other horizontal divisions that statistical investigation would probably show to be provided by independent specialists (individuals or firms) and that are not included within the organization of one general firm ; such are promotion, banking and legal services, insurance against fire or accidents to employees, and advice on advertising.

A synthesis of the industrial and occupational censuses of 1921 undertaken by the English census authorities[1] shows clearly that certain types of occupation, notably draughtsmen and clerks, professional staff and general labourers were included in nearly all manufacturing industries and in the transport industry too, in addition to the occupations mainly associated with the industry, for instance, production, repair and maintenance with manufacture, or transport occupations with the transport industry. Thus among a thousand persons employed in the manufacturing industries, 55 persons were draughtsmen or clerks, 28 were occupied in transport and communication, and 28 also were in commerce, finance, or professional occupations.

Side by side with this occupational integration goes an industrial integration. Firms may combine not only various sorts of occupation and divisions of labour but also various sorts of industry. And statistical investigation may answer the question, what kinds of relation subsist between the industries thus integrated. The U.S. Census monograph on the *Integration of Industrial Operation* traces statistically the extent of combination under one central-office operation of establishments manufacturing or providing (1) joint products, (2) by-products, (3) dissimilar products of similar processes, such as canning or preserving all sorts of food-products, (4) complementary products or different lines of manufacturing converging in a single final product, (5) auxiliary services and commodities, such as printing or fuel, (6) dissimilar products for the same market. Of these varieties of integrative structure, (1) joint products with 427 instances, and (6) dissimilar products for the same market with 233 instances, were found to be the most frequent. Of the other varieties, 169 instances were observed of (5) auxiliary services and commodities ; 159 of (4) complementary products ; 154 of (3) dissimilar products of similar processes ; 125 of (2) by-products. Forty-seven instances were also observed of central offices combining establishments making unrelated products with no apparent " rational functional basis for existence."

But the most frequent variety (903 instances) of relationship among different industries combined under one central office was

[1] Table 1, Census of Industries.

the *vertical* relationship where establishments made " successive " products. Statistical measures may be devised in greater detail to enquire to what degree this vertical combination or integration is carried within one firm or combination, and whether any predominant types are discoverable. Firms are to be found controlling extraction of their raw material, transport to manufacture (e.g. the U.S. Steel Corporation's lake steamers), manufacture in all stages, transport of product (e.g. the Standard Oil Corporation's pipe lines, and motor lorries privately owned), and finally even controlling wholesale and retail distribution to consumers in their own shops. But here again vertical integration may not be complete ; it may apply only to a statistically determinable proportion of the values dealt in. The statistics of the Consumers' Co-operative Societies

Integration within the Consumers Co-operative Movement

Stages

Manufacturing

Wholesaling

Retailing

1 2 3 4 5 6

Each column represents about £28.000.000 worth of retail sales. Total of six columns about £164.000.000.

allow a rough picture (see note, p. 456) of degree of integration. In 1923 the retail sales of Co-operative Societies in England, Wales, and Scotland amounted to £164,000,000. Of these sales of retail Co-operative Societies about one-sixth, or £28,000,000, equalled the value of goods made by themselves. Out of six lines starting from a base that marks the retailing stage one, accordingly, may be continued upwards uninterruptedly through the wholesale and manufacturing stage. Another sixth of the goods value, i.e. £28,000,000, was obtained wholesale from the Co-operative Wholesale Society, who manufactured the goods themselves. The vertical line marking the vertical integration is accordingly, in this second of the six lines, interrupted between the wholesale and retail stages but continued through wholesale and manufacturing stages. The third and fourth lines also continue, interrupted between wholesale and retail stages to mark provision by the Co-operative *Wholesale* Society, but are not continued upwards into the manufacturing stage because the wholesale society in the case of about two-sixths of the goods value retailed, obtained the goods from manufacturers and producers outside the Co-operative movement. Similarly lines 5 and 6, representing another two-sixths of the retail sales, show by stopping at the retail stage that the goods were obtained from wholesalers outside the Co-operative movement.[1]

The work-relations within and between *firms*, when investigated, disclose (as did the investigation of relations between local plants) the existence of independent organizations specializing in certain *vertical* stages for the common service or public utility of *all* industries. Railways, for instance, transport the materials and products for all industries and are Common Carriers in fact as well as law. Roads, telegraph and telephone facilities, and the Post Office provide transport and communication for the materials, services, and products of all kinds of firms. And department stores " provide universally " by retail the products of all sorts of manufacturing and productive industries.

Similar problems occur in State government. The executive is subdivided horizontally into departments each charged with different work. These executive departments are societies manifesting a rule procedure between a ruler party (e.g. the Minister in charge) and a ruled party of Civil Servants, but they are also societies manifesting the procedure of sharing work; and the question arises what precise work-shares are to be associated with (i.e. included within) the various item departments upon which one single rule is superimposed. This question is touched upon by Laski discussing (*Grammar of Politics*, p. 369) administrative organization. He argues that among other types of work-divisions within each department (1) " there must . . . always be a minister responsible to the legislative assembly for the work of a department "; (2) " there must, secondly, be special provision in each department for adequate financial supervision," and (3) " not less vital than any of these is the importance of making special provision for research and inquiry." These three subdivisions of labour are in horizontal relations and in joint demand, and show a remarkable analogy to the subdivision within the large-scale firm of (1) directors responsible to the shareholders, (2) the finance or treasurer's department, (3) the research department, e.g. in the chemical industry.

---

[1] This " picture " follows the Balfour Committee's Summary (*Factors in Efficiency*, p. 16), but *under*states the degree of integration by counting products and whole-sales at *wholesale* prices only.

But before analogies are used as a basis of argument or any other theoretical reasoning applied, the actual facts of executive organization must be observed and wherever possible the integration of certain work-shares within executive departments measured statistically. There are a multitude of item cases to observe in the several governmental departments of the numerous central and local States of the world. These item departments manifest, like the item firms or factories, the functional characters of a common rule and of a sharing of work. The question that statistical investigation may, and as we have shown can, approach is whether any particular values (qualities or varieties and quantities or degrees) of rule are superimposed on any particular values (qualities or varieties and quantities or degrees) of work-sharing. Similarly statistical investigation may throw light on the question whether any particular varieties of rule procedure are associated in scope with any particular varieties of manning procedure. Is it a true generalization of modern societies, for instance, that the democratic manning procedure by the popular election of a representative State government is specifically associated with ruling by political compulsion, while the autocratic manning of the management of a firm is specifically associated with ruling by economic impulsion ?

§7   *Association of Varieties of Transactions with Varieties of Procedure*

A problem very frequently met with in political science occurs where item societies or organizations of one particular sort manifest varieties in two characters, one relating to their external transactions, the other to their internal functioning or procedure. The organization known as the State, for example, has transactions of many different qualities or varieties, and also has a variety of financial procedures in performing these transactions. The problem to solve is whether any particular variety or varieties of internal procedure are associated or correlated with any particular variety or varieties of transaction.

First we shall tackle (§7 · 1) the problem what various transactions of the State are, and might be, financed by the alternative procedures. But the statistical method of association fused with theoretical interpretation applied to this question could equally well be applied to the questions (§7 · 2) what transactions of the State were, and might be, ordered or " commanded " by the alternative procedures of (*a*) compulsion civil or criminal, or (*b*) impulsion by money payment or the conferring of honours, prestige, etc. ; or to the question (§7 · 3) what transactions in general were, and might be, performed by the State (adopting *any* procedure) as against performance by private persons ; or to the question not applied to the case of the State but to the case of the State government (§7 · 4), as to what transactions in general are, and might be, performed by an organ of the government being, say, manned by a particular alternative variety of procedure.

§7 · 1   Transactions Associated with Various Public Finance Procedures

Two opposite financial methods of procedure that the State government could adopt, the tax-and-grant and the trading policy, were described above; and we may now proceed to trace the association of these varieties of the State's financial procedure (ϕ) with particular transactions of the State (ϵ).

First it must be remembered that the two financial systems of procedure can be, and are mixed, so as to produce at least four varieties (PP) measurable along a scale in respect of budgetary equilibrium :

P I : No price charged. Transaction performed free for consumer and expenses entirely recouped out of taxation.

P II : Price charged, but nominal, *below* cost incurred.   Loss made up out of taxation.

P III : Price charged at cost. Neither recoupment from or relief to taxation.

P IV : Price charged above cost and surplus used to relieve taxation in general.

In attempting to correlate the particular variety of financial procedure with variety of transaction it must be made clear that I am not dealing here with what is, or might be, the transactions of the State, as against that of private enterprise—that question is taken up in §7 · 3.   What I am discussing is, *given* a certain class of transaction of the State government, how will that government finance it ? I shall, in fact, deal only with transactions that have been or actually are performed by the State government in England or abroad.

In the tabular statement of associations that follows only the probable conclusions are given to what should be a statistical review of the facts on the lines illustrated in Chapter XIX §2. Every State and local authority would constitute a " case " or item and the cases might not always agree in their association. One State might make trading profit, another a trading loss, another not trade at all but grant and tax in respect to the same transaction, just as British local authorities were found to vary in the budgetary equilibrium of their services of water supply or tramways (§2 · 4). The tabular statement classifies each transaction under one policy or another merely as a result of very preliminary observation. The tabulation is, in fact, put forward only as an example of the sort of conclusions to which political statistics might lead, as a result of observation and measurement of the practice of States and local authorities throughout the civilized world. The transactions are classified and numbered according to the system adopted previously in Table XIXe, and interest attaches to the further question how far transactions in the same *class* have the same financial system applied to them.

P I : The " tax and grant " system appears generally associated with the expenses of the following State transactions.

1. *Justice.*
    Prisons.
    Industrial arbitration.
    Constabulary and police.

2. *Relief of Poverty.*
    Old age pensions.
    Asylums.

3. *Health and Sanitation.*
    Sewage disposal.
    Inspection of factories, etc.

4. *Industrial Aid.*
    Street lighting and lighthouses.
    Roads and bridges.
    Coinage, where no mintage or seigneurage charged.

5. *Educational.*
    Schools (elementary).
    Libraries (public).
    Parks, etc.

6. *Foreign Affairs.*
    Armaments.
    Diplomacy.

P II : In the following transactions States are often found half trading, half tax-and-granting, the selling price being " *nominal* " (i.e. insufficient to defray whole expense). The precise proportion of loss can be statistically determined.

1. *Justice.*
    Court proceedings (partially covered by payment of " costs ").

2. *Relief of Poverty.*
    Insurance (health and unemployment).
    Hospitals (abroad).

3. *Health and Sanitation.*
> Houses (building by local authorities with subsidy).
> Water supply (or policy P III for England, see §2·4).
> Public baths and lavatories.

4. *Industrial Aid.*
> Harbours and docks (see §2 · 4).
> Canalization of rivers.

5. *Educational.*
> Schools (secondary and university).
> State theatres, etc.
> Museums.

P III : The practice of States shows that where States do perform these transactions, they are generally found to " trade at cost " in the following instances :

4. *Industrial Aid Class.*
> Transport and communication.
> Posts, telegraphs, telephones (occasionally policy P II).
> Railways (occasionally policy P II).
> Tramways (or policy P II for England, see §2 · 4).
> Ferries.
> Ships (United States, Australia).
> Provision of markets.
> Supply of electricity (for England, see §2 · 4).
> Coinage (where only mintage costs charged).

P IV : The practice of States, finally, shows that States generally " trade with profit " in the following transactions, in cases marked * usually at monopoly profit.

4. *Industrial Aid Class.*
> Gas (at least in England, see §2 · 4).

7. *Private Consumption Class.*
> *Salt.
> *Matches.
> *Tobacco.
> *Alcoholic drinks.
> *Betting (e.g. State lotteries).

8. *Leasing of land, mines, etc., for private exploitation.*

Can this particular association of certain varieties of State transaction with certain varieties of financial procedure observed in the cases of a number of item States be in any way explained or interpreted on grounds of theory or common sense ?

On an *a priori* deduction from psychology the trade system would seem the more reasonable. By that method—

(1) Payment is in some proportion to the want satisfied or at any rate to the expected satisfaction. If a man makes use of telegraphic communication he pays (in Britain, 1928) 1/– or upward ; but by

the tax-and-grant system, a cyclist using and getting satisfaction from good roads pays no more than any other man equally taxable.

(2) The trade system, again, secures the maximum of satisfaction from a given sum of money. Let us suppose Mr. Jones has 1/- to spend on his weekly half-holiday, and that under a trading finance he will spend 3d. at the museum, 6d. at the public baths, and 3d. on tramways. But under the tax-and-grant system his 1/- will be appropriated in taxes by the municipality and in exchange he will, perhaps, be offered a free concert not to his taste, and free tramways to get there which he will not use.

(3) Trading, further, avoids the expense and unpleasantness of the compulsion to pay up taxes, the only practicable substitute for a trade revenue.

What, then, are the factors (N.N.) *that theory may plausibly advance to explain the application of the tax-and-grant system to certain transactions and class of transactions of the government ?*

N I   Those who are to be served cannot pay for the service. The poor to be relieved, are by hypothesis too poor to pay for their relief. Similarly elementary schools and legal proceedings can never quite be made to pay their way, because of the poverty of scholars and litigants.

N II   The expense involved outweighs the trading receipts. An attempt to collect trade-revenue would cause, in certain transactions, an expense that might swallow all the revenue secured.

If a gate were built across Oxford Street and toll extracted by the London County Council from all passers-by, not only would a large staff of officials and policemen be required, but the trade of London might suffer out of all proportion to the revenue from the tolls. This is the factor that, plausibly, associates the tax-and-grant system with roads, lighthouses, and lighting.

Bridges, on the other hand, form such a convenient bottle-neck trap, that the temptation to get a revenue from bridge tolls has often proved irresistible.

N III   The direct satisfaction derived from State expenditure by particular persons is incapable of assessment by those persons.

If armaments are of the nature of an insurance premium paid by the whole nation against the risk of invasion, it is impossible to predict the actuarial chance of loss by invasion of any one person, and therefore for any person to decide the premium he is willing to pay. Similarly of police protection and public sanitation, which can be considered insurance premiums against crime and disease that benefit a whole district ; it is impossible to measure to what degree each individual in the district is benefited.

N IV   The power of ethical *discrimination* which is secured by taxing and granting. The State may wish to encourage one kind of work at the expense of another, or one class of person at the expense of another class. This can be effected by taxing what is objected to and granting to whatever is cherished.

The tax-and-grant system allows the legislator to discriminate according to his own particular ethical outlook, just because the source of revenue is different from the object of its expenditure. The trade system, though it may efficiently run what statesmen consider " good " projects, such as museums, will do so at the expense of the " good " men who wish to enter, being forced to extract from them a 1/– fee or so. With a tax-and-grant system the " good " museum habitué would be relieved of payment at the expense, perhaps, of the " bad " public-house habitué, just as in fact the gambler at Monte Carlo paid for the Prince of Monaco's oceanographic research.

The particular system of finance applied to any State transaction by the State would usually, of course, be accountable to several of the above factors. The ethical factor particularly would generally be found present in all State grants, since the State government would hardly " endow " objects it did not approve of. This ethical factor may, however, be present to a greater or lesser degree. It is the principal factor present (1) wherever the government performs free services, but *could* quite practically raise some revenue from trading, as in the case of educative services, such as museums and parks ; (2) wherever the government is found taxing a special class of things, e.g. alcoholic liquors, though other classes, e.g. bread or cloth, would yield more revenue in proportion to trouble in collection and assessment.

To sum up. I distinguished, XIX §2 · 4, two elemental methods of financing (or defraying) the expenditure of the State government. If this expense were on account of coinage, the first method would be known as mintage, where " the fee demanded by the government is exactly equal to the cost of coinage." The second method would be known as gratuitous coinage " when the government, as in England, does the work of coining without making any charge." These two methods I have called *in general* the " trading " and the " tax-and-grant " systems respectively. Variations on the two are found where, as in coining, a *trade* surplus or " seigniorage " is devoted to relieve general taxes or where, as in the English Insurance Act, both methods contribute *specifically* to the payment of benefits.

In this section I have investigated which system of finance is associated with what class of transactions of the State. From the table containing the particular facts, one may generalize that the complete tax-and-grant system is associated with class (6) of State transactions, namely foreign affairs ; the complete or partial tax-and-grant system with classes (1), (2), (3), (4), and (5) of State transactions, namely justice, relief of poverty, health, industrial aid and education ; the trade at cost system with class (4) industrial aid ; and the trade with profit system in none of these classes, but rather with private consumption. It is significant that the one apparent exception, the gas supply, is to-day more a matter of private consumption for cooking, heating, and lighting than an industrial aid.

Considerations of human psychology would presume the trade system to be the more convenient form of finance ; why are so many sorts of transactions thus excepted ? The reasons may be classified under two heads, practical and ethical. These non-trading transactions either yield no tangible gross revenue, or none that would make worth while the cost of collection, or none that those who benefit could assess ; *and/or* the transactions are thought meet for encouragement often at the expense of transactions considered, in the judgment of statesmen, bad.

Many will think this argumentation somewhat gratuitous. The thing is so obvious ; the government will finance their *proper* functions by taxing, and the " public services " they will perform on a business basis. My defence is a counter-attack. Proper functions and public service beg the question. Proper functions mean to most people the transactions financed by taxing ; public service the transactions financed by trading. So the criticism merely runs, " the government will finance by taxing what they finance by taxing, and will finance by trading what they finance by trading " !

§7 · 2   Wage versus Prestige ; or Transactions Associated with Various Pay Procedures of States

The importance attached to this type of association is indicated in discussions of the alternative methods of procuring jurymen. ' It is important," writes Laski, " that the juror should be adequately remunerated. Anyone who has sat on a jury for any length of time will have realized that after a period what concerns the jurymen is neither the evidence nor the result of the case, but the very different question of when they will be able to return to their usual routine."[1]

[1] *Grammar of Politics*, p. 560.

Sidgwick discusses the pros and cons of compulsory military service and of a " general obligation to render " service *free*, for " the maintenance of order and for the prevention of detection and punishment of crime," and he raises the question also,[1] whether land may be compulsorily purchased by the State as against obtaining the land by offering the (possibly inflated) market price.

The statistical approach to this question is the same as the approach to the question of finance. That question dealt with the State as a seller at various prices from nil to cost plus ; this question deals with the State as a buyer at various prices from nil to market price or possibly beyond. The same sort of grading into isotropic varieties might be adopted in classing the various procedures (PP).

P I.   *Price Nil or Nominal, Prestige Nil.*
      E.g. Compulsory Military Service.
      Jury Service.

P II.   *Price Nil, but Prestige Conferred.*
      E.g. Justices of Peace.
      Local Councillors.

P III. *Nominal Price well below Market, plus Prestige.*
      E.g. Members of Parliament, salary £400.

P IV.   *Price just below Market, no Prestige.*
      E.g. Compulsory Land Purchase.

P V.   *Market Price, no Prestige.*
      E.g. Stipendiary Magistrates.

The kind of transactions performed to various " extents " in different item countries or localities by each of these grades of policy may then be tabulated to show which of these procedures is " generally " associated with what sorts of transaction.

In modern England we are accustomed to find one definite method of procedure associated with one type of transaction and no other method used, the result being an identification of transaction and procedure. If England to-day, however, is compared with Anglo-Saxon England or with modern foreign constitutions it will be found that the same transaction of the State is performed by quite different methods of procedure. Modern Britain hopes to defend the frontiers of its Empire by employing hired troops, not always of English, Scotch, or Irish extraction. Modern France defends its frontiers by proclaiming that all men over a certain age and physically fit shall be punished if they do not join the rmy

[1] *Elements of Politics*, Chapters XI, XII.

The English voluntary system of recruiting may be classed as procedure P V, the French system as procedure P I.

Variety of procedure requiring statistical approach is also observable in the inducements offered to members of the legislature. It was only in 1911 that Britain changed from policy P II to P III by allowing members of Parliament £400 a year ; members of local councils are still unpaid. The observable results are summarized by Laski (op. cit., p. 416). Many of these results, i.e. the comparative expenditure on drains, education, roads and libraries, and the comparative frequency of the types of person with which councils are manned, are amenable to, and would gain in precision by, statistical measurement.

" If we maintain the principle of unpaid work, we shall always find that membership of these local bodies will be predominantly representative of the richer classes in the community ; and the standards of their performance will accordingly be set, not by the needs of the area, but by the desire of those classes to make local government as cheap as possible. They will provide excellent drainage but inadequate education, good roads but poor libraries. . . . And local government based on the unpaid member has, the world over, somehow seemed to accrete to itself a variety of persons—small contractors, publicans, shopkeepers and the like—whose disinterested zeal for the public welfare has been less apparent in the quality of work done than in their pronouncement of intention. Even in England, the home of the unpaid representative, we have seen the need for remunerating the mayor of many boroughs ; and we have begun to pay expenses incurred in the performance of their duties by members of committees on Insurance and War Pensions."

The simpler forms of crime are dealt with by magistrates who in England may (as stipendiary magistrates) or may not (as Justices of Peace) be paid a salary. Here is an opportunity for the statistical measurement of quantitative differences in the same sort of transaction, and for bringing these measurements into association with the variety of procedure.

Penal reformers have drawn attention to the variation of sentence within the maximum legal limit for the same offence that is observed when comparing one magistrate with another. Where the sentence is of the same sort, i.e. fines or periods of imprisonment, statistics collected from a large number of local areas could work out a coefficient of dispersion (or an average deviation) in the sentences of (a) unpaid justices of the peace with (b) stipendiary magistrates, for the same offence, and could compare the degree of " capriciousness " of the generality of magistrates paid (or not paid) under the two alternative varieties of procedure.

2H

§7 · 3   Nationalization ; or Transactions Associated with State Procedures in General

The question of State versus Private performance of transactions is the well-worn theme of Socialism versus *laissez-faire* which has hitherto been fought out mainly on theoretical *a priori* considerations. Economists and social philosophers enunciate certain basic principles and deduce from these what industries should be " let alone " and what should be State controlled. The statistical approach would be to observe and investigate the multitude of cases, items, or instances of State-performed and privately performed transactions in various countries, noting especially the variable types of State and private procedure and organization adopted. Socialism already exists in various transactions and the practical question is how far and where and when to extend or contract it.

In the case of State transactions the variety of *financial procedure* has already (§7 · 1) been observed and investigated inductively, and this in itself clarifies and gives an important lead to the wider question. Private enterprise does not appear to perform transactions for which no price can be charged, nor transactions for which only a price below cost can in the long run be obtained. Hence transactions performed through financial procedures marked P I, P II must be performed by the State. The only controversial question is about transactions capable of the trade procedures P III or P IV.

The variety of State organization, i.e. organization of varying structure and functioning, for performing trading transactions, has been pointed out in the Liberal Industrial Enquiry of 1928. There is not one universal type of organization such as (1) a central government department or a municipal sub-committee ; but (2) various *ad hoc* organizations both for specific national transactions (like the British Broadcasting Corporation or the Central Electricity Board), and for specific local transactions (as, in the London area, the Port of London Authority, the Thames Conservancy, and the Metropolitan Water Board) ; there is also (3) the plan of regulating private organizations. These " semi-public institutions " to which a monopoly may be granted, present, according to Sidgwick,[1] a useful machinery for supplying certain social wants better than the unaided and unregulated action of private persons would supply them, without unduly increasing the responsibilities of the government. Sidgwick cites the English railway company which " is

[1] *Elements of Politics*, Chapter XIX.

granted a special power of compulsorily purchasing the land that it requires, and in return for this privilege is required to conform to regulations laid down by the legislature in respect of the rates that it charges for the conveyance of goods and passengers." Similarly the Bank of England " is enabled to perform the public function of providing an important part of the medium of exchange in England, through its special privilege of issuing notes that may be legally tendered in payment of all debts of money, provided that such notes are expressed to be payable to bearer on demand, and are actually paid by the bank in legal coin whenever demand is made."

Thus it is not a question of black and white, State procedure or not State procedure, but rather what specific variety of procedure between absolute bureaucratic rule and unfettered private control is associated or associable with specific transactions.

The statistical approach consists in first observing and classifying the facts as to the performance of various transactions by various procedures public, semi-public, or private, and then interpreting the actual associations observed. Certain characteristics absent from or common to the transactions publicly, semi-publicly, or privately performed may be discovered. The characteristic that prices cannot be charged to consumers so as to cover expenses is generally absent from transactions privately performed. On the other hand States appear to avoid transactions which, though they will probably yield a profit over cost, may possibly involve financial loss in individual cases. Though the State in many countries provides matches, alcoholic drink, tobacco, and insurance, where the conditions of demand and supply are stable, standardized, and calculable, the State does not so often transact the business of agricultural production or the provision of clothes, where nature and human nature are capricious in their supplies and demands, and where financial risks must be taken. Transactions publicly or semi-publicly performed for a price covering cost usually show the common character of involving a routine rather than an enterprising management. A further character common to transactions performed by the State at or above cost price appears to be the " common service " nature of the transaction in the sense used in §6, where the transaction (such as transport, communication, lighting) serves many different industries and interests, very often (as in the case of military railways) including the interests of the State government itself.

If theoretical interpretations such as these tally with the actual associations statistically observed in one country or another, they may suggest further specific transactions as suitable for State procedure owing to their possessing characters associated with that class of State procedures. It is for this reason that the question may be put in the conditional as well as the indicative mood as, what transactions does *or might* the State perform by means of the various alternative procedures objectively distinguished ?

§7 · 4   Second Chambers ; or Transactions Associated with Various Manning Procedures of Government Organs

Hitherto the association investigated has been that of the procedure with the transaction of States, but the same sort of association may be investigated within the *ruler party*. Is there, for instance, any association between the particular structure and procedure of an organ of government and its particular transaction ?

In the government of *industrial* affairs, Mr. and Mrs. Sidney Webb point out the different structure and procedure of organs interpreting an agreement (i.e. performing quasi-judicial transactions) and organs making a new agreement (i.e. performing quasi-legislative transactions).

" The expediency of having separate machinery for the essentially different processes of interpreting an existing agreement and concluding a new one is, we think, clearly demonstrated. For one of these two processes, the application and interpretation of an existing agreement, a joint committee (of representatives chosen by the employers and employed) is a cumbrous and awkward device. . . . Unconsciously and, as it were, instinctively (the Lancashire cotton operatives) have felt their way to a form of machinery for Collective Bargaining which uses the representative element where the representative element is needed, whilst on the other hand, it employs the professional expert for work at which the mere representative would be out of place. . . .

The meeting of the salaried professional experts on each side deals only with questions of interpretation, that is, the application to particular jobs, or particular processes, of the existing general agreements accepted by both sides. When it comes to concluding or revising the general agreement itself . . . we find the machinery for Collective Bargaining taking the form of a joint committee composed of a certain number of representatives of each side."[1]

When it comes to the organs of State-government, Temperley in his *Senates and Upper Chambers* points to a very clear association between the " composition " (or manning) of these chambers and their actual " powers " or transactions within the government. After a detailed inductive survey of Upper Chambers in the British Colonies he writes,[2] " Generally power seems to be enjoyed by the Upper Chamber in proportion as its composition is democratized . . . it is generally admitted that Nominee Upper Chambers are far

---

[1] *Industrial Democracy*, Part II, Chapter II.   [2] Op. cit., p. 62.

inferior in power to Elective ones." Of Upper Chambers on the Continent of Europe (and of America) he writes,[1] " a general survey of these Upper Chambers which are purely Elective in their composition shows that these bodies, as a whole, preserve a much more decided financial equality with the Lower House. This fact . . . corresponds to what has been observed in the practice of the State Legislatures of America."

In the matter of non-financial laws Temperley found ten States of Europe admitting both Cabinet responsibility and Parliamentary responsibility and therefore comparable with England. Four of these, Hungary, Italy, Portugal, and Spain (in 1910), had

" Senates in which the Nominated or Hereditary element is dominant, and the whole tendency of the Cabinet and Parliamentary system is to reduce the power of the Upper Chambers accordingly. All four have had a chequered Parliamentary career in the past, but in all four of them it may now be said, that the Lower House is, in practice, the chief power which shapes and initiates the ordinary laws ; and that in disputes between the Chambers, the Upper one usually suffers. With regard to the six States, in which the Upper Chamber is Elective, the case is very different. In two of them, Norway and Holland, the Upper Chamber is legally inferior to the Lower in matters of ordinary legislation ; the ordinary legislative powers of all the others (Sweden, Denmark, France and Belgium) are fully equal to those of the Lower Chamber. The right of the Upper Chamber to veto foreign treaties and commercial agreements is usually also preserved. . . . In Denmark the Upper House has preserved much greater powers in ordinary legislation than in finance, and has vetoed important Bills in quite recent times ; and in Sweden, while the Upper Chamber has shown more caution, its powers remain considerable. In none of the Elective States is the inferiority of the Upper Chamber in ordinary legislation so pronounced as in the case of money Bills, nor has the attempt to reduce and to emasculate these other powers been anything like so evident. All the Elective Senates illustrate the general truth that, so long as a people is satisfied as to the democratic origin of the Upper House, it is not very particular about restricting its powers."[2]

Plausible psychological interpretations are given by the author of his carefully tabulated[3] facts such as " the profound colonial conviction that a man or a body is only to be trusted when it is freely and directly chosen by the people as a whole."[4] There are underlying characteristics of human nature at work, and even if the legal paper constitution does not give an elected Second Chamber much power in its transactions with the other organs of the government, the observed facts and unwritten customs may follow human nature rather than the formal constitution. The respect which his

[1] Op. cit., p. 103.
[2] Op. cit., p. 110.
[3] Op. cit., Appendix.
[4] Op. cit., p. 62.

constituents show for a man by returning him to the Second Chamber will not allow mere legal technicalities to interfere with the scope of his transactions and those of his similarly elected colleagues.

§8   The Control of Industry ; or the Association of Varieties of Transactions in one Society

If a wide historical survey is made of types of industrial organization it will be found that certain combinations or associations of rule and work transactions by parties within the firm have had or do now have a high frequency, a greater frequency that might be expected on mere independent probability when elements in the combination have an equal *a priori* chance of appearing. These comparatively frequent combinations may be called types or systems. Just as a military man who is a Tory, or a legal luminary who is a Liberal (see Table IXB) is typical, so it will be found that the capitalist or the co-operative or some other system of industrial rule and control is typical in certain circumstances.

What are these typical systems of industrial rule or control ? The systems differ in respect both of (1) work relations and (2) rule and manning or " employment " relations, and in Table XXB these differences are shown in respect of both sorts of relations. (1) The number of separate persons or groups of persons specializing in the transaction of consuming, manual work, managing, owning, etc., is shown by the number of letters A, B, C, D, etc. In the household system there is production only for use ; and the same group of persons, the household, are consumers, workers, and owners rolled into one. The craft system, represented to-day by the peasant proprietor, is a trading system in which the worker produces most of his goods for exchange and the consumer or customer with whom he (B) exchanges is a separate person (A). The craftsman is, however, worker and owner rolled into one though he may employ special journeymen workers (C). Under the capitalist system the consumer remains a separate person, and the owner (or capitalist) (B) is usually a different person from the worker (C). In the earlier capitalist system most owners are their own managers or administrators and use their own capital ; but in the later capitalist system organized in the joint-stock company, statistical investigation would probably show that there are usually specialized administrative staffs paid by salary (D) and that capital owners are, in most cases, divided into (E) debenture stock holders whose transactions are purely those of lending since their capital and interest is secure short of bankruptcy, and (F) ordinary share-holders whose transactions are that of lending with risk of loss of interest and capital.

These transactions are shares in the work of the firm. But some of the parties transacting these special work-shares are also per-forming rule-transactions, and whoever among these parties to the work of the firm is statistically observable as being, in the majority of cases, the active ruler or employer is given an (R) in the Table.

If we put the question, to the later capitalist system for instance, which of the specialists usually do the employing, the appointing and dismissing, the ordering, paying and financing so similar to the activities of a State government, an apt answer may be found in a work on *Business Organization* by Lewis M. Haney.[1] " The organization of the ownership and administration of a business is generally the ' *corporate* ' *organization*, and where this is the case the corporation may be regarded as a sort of political machine for enabling the stockholders to govern their property. Within the sphere of the Corporation (*anglicé* Joint-Stock Company) so regarded, we find authority *concentrated* and directed, much as in a political unit, the body of stockholders being roughly comparable to the voters in a democracy, the directors to a parliament, the executive head to a prime minister, and other executive officers to his cabinet." Ultimately, therefore, the " manners " and rulers are the share-holders, i.e. the capital owners ; though their power is exercised only through the Directors and the Executive.

Where the national or municipal States " trade," System VIII in the Table, it is the State government and ultimately the voters that are the employers ; and similarly of non-remunerative State services, such as policing, roadmaking, administration of justice. Between State and policeman the relations of employment—appointment, commanding, payment—exist just as between capitalist and his employees. State business is performed through salaried managers (D) and the capital raised either by loans on the security of the government's bonds or by taxes. Since recourse must be had to taxes if interest on the bonds cannot be paid out of trading revenue, the taxpayer is in somewhat the same position as the ordinary risk-taking shareholders (F) of the latter-day capitalist system.

An employer and ruler party consisting of manual or routine workers is found at least in theory in *Producers' Co-operation* or the *Productive Associations*. English statistics show,[2] however,

---

[1] Chapter XVII, p. 263, edition 1912.
[2] See annual review in *Labour Gazette*, Ministry of Labour.

that in practice most of the members of these associations who hold the capital are not working in the establishment in which the capital is invested. The capital is in fact held and the managers elected mainly by outside sympathizers either individuals or other societies.

To the question which of the specialists A, B, C, D, E, or F dividing the labour of industry within an employing group or firm might transact employing or ruling, the *possible* answers would be as many as the number of specialists, *plus* (since specialists might combine in ruling, see System V) as many as the number of possible combinations of specialists. But the actual systems that exist or have existed are far less in number and as far as historical Europe is concerned are all listed in bleak outline in Table XXB.[1]

TABLE XXB

ASSOCIATION OF RULING (R) WITH SPECIFIC FUNCTIONS OR WORK-SHARES IN DIFFERENT SYSTEMS OF INDUSTRIAL CONTROL

System	Consumer	Manual or Routine Worker	Manager	Owner Secure	Risk-taker
I HOUSEHOLD	A	A	A	A	A
II CRAFT (Peasant Proprietor)	A	BC(R)	B(R)	B(R)	B(R)
III EARLY CAPITALIST	A	C	B(R)	B(R)	B(R)
IV LATER CAPITALIST	A	C	D	E	F(R)
V CO-PARTNERSHIP SCHEMES	A	C(R)	D(R)	E	F(R)
VI CONSUMERS' CO-OPERATIVE	A	C	D	A(R)	A(R)
VII PRODUCERS' CO-OPERATION (Productive Associations)	A	C	C (and outside sympathizers)		
VIII STATE-TRADING	A	C	D	STATE (Bondholder)	STATE (Taxpayer)

But the statistician is not satisfied with a mere list. He must know the actual comparative frequency of the various systems of association actually observed.

[1] Bleak, because realistic political science cannot be satisfied with the bare statement that, say in the later capitalist system, the risk-takers *only* are " (R) " rulers. Though workers are not incorporated in the body of Directors as under Co-partnership schemes (System V), they do exercise some measure of at least negative rule through Trade Unions. And the State also, through factory laws, wages, or Trade Boards, takes a part in ruling or at least *regulating* the modern capitalist.

The comparative frequency of the different systems of rule may be measured statistically in several ways :

I   (1) the number or proportion of firms or plants or (2) the number of wage earners ruled under each different system.   For instance, the U.S. Census of Manufactures, 1914, tells us that 51·6% of establishments or 10·1% of wage earners were under individual ownership (early capitalist) and that 28·3% of establishments or 80·3% of wage earners were under corporation ownership (later capitalist).   It is evident, incidentally, that there is a (positive) association of larger-sized plants and corporate ownership.   The remaining establishments were mostly under ownership of a " firm," i.e. partnership.

II   The amount of capital owned under each system of rule. The Liberal Industrial Enquiry of 1927[1] gives, for instance, the amounts of capital, compared to the total capital in the country owned by State-controlled or partially State-controlled systems.

III   The value of the sales or produce effected under each system :   The British Consumers' Co-operative Societies retailed in 1923, £164,000,000 of goods.   In the United States of America during 1909 the value added by manufacture in establishments individually owned was 968 millions of dollars ; in establishments owned by firms (i.e. partnerships, etc.) 951 millions of dollars ; in establishments owned by corporations (i.e. joint-stock companies) 6,582 millions of dollars.

Whatever system of measuring the frequency is adopted, it is clear that the capitalist (early or late) systems predominate in the industrial control of modern Western countries and that of the two, the *later* capitalist system of joint-stock type controls the destinies of more men, more capital, and more goods (and increasingly so year by year) than the earlier capitalist system.   Nevertheless statistics also show that the capitalist system is merely an alternative to strong rival systems of procedure.

§9   *Association of Political with Economic and Sociological Characters*

The five types of association or correlation discussed in §3 to §8 do not exhaust the possibilities of statistical association in political science, but they will serve as examples of what can and should be done if political science is to emerge out of the limbo of moral philosophy and into the light of a more or less exact science.

[1] *Britain's Industrial Future.*

And if it is to be useful as well as exact, political science must transcend politics proper and associate with economics and general sociology.

The limits to the scope of political science were set (in §1, see also Chapter III) at the individual person at one extreme, and the inner functioning of some super-ordinate society, or at least its transactions with other persons, at the other extreme. It is, strictly speaking, beyond the scope of political science to find correlations or associations of specific varieties of structure or functioning with technical achievements or *general* sociological conditions; but (as was said in Chapter IV) though the social system must at first be studied piecemeal, it should ultimately be considered as a whole. And some of the most practically useful contributions of the new statistical politics will be the association or correlation of measured political characters with measured characters of wider reference.

Statistically measured political activities may be correlated with statistically measured economic or sociological circumstances, to test or check theories about the *causes* of various political activities (§9 · 1), or to test or check theories about the *results* (§9 · 2) of various political activities.

§9 · 1   Correlated Economic and Sociological Factors

Measured economic or sociological characters interpreted by authorities as causes or conditions of measured variations in political characters are of many sorts and varieties, but considerations of space compel us to cite statistical investigations of the " political " results of only three sorts of economic or sociological factors : the business cycle, the social stratification of peoples into classes and sections, and the stage of material culture reached by a people as a whole.

The business cycle has been brought into relation with problems of politics in the sense of administrative science, in the correlation of variations in business prosperity with variations in the amount of crime.

Ogburn and Thomas[1] compare their carefully worked out index of the business cycle in America with " the number of convictions for criminal offences in Courts of Record of the State of New York in the years 1870 to 1920." In both cases the coefficient of correlation and its probable error is calculated after elimination of the normal secular trend.[2] They conclude that,

---

[1] *J.A.S.A.*, September 1922.   [2] See Chapters VIII §7 and X §3.

" in most of the depressions the number of convictions is above the normal, as indicated by the trend, and in most of the periods of prosperity the number of convictions is less. The coefficient of correlation is $-\cdot35\pm\cdot08$; when the trend for the data on convictions is for nine-year moving averages the correlation is the same, $-\cdot32$. With a one-year lag the coefficient of correlation is smaller, $-\cdot24$.

The conclusion that there is an increase in convictions for crime in business depression is corroborated by Davies, who correlated the annual admissions to New York State prisons, 1896–1915, with wholesale prices and found a correlation of $-\cdot41\pm\cdot13$.

The Secretary of State of New York in his report publishes an analysis of the number of convictions, and one of the series is the number of convictions for offences against the person, exclusive of offences against property with violence. It is interesting to inquire whether such offences against the person are correlated with business conditions. The coefficient of correlation is negative, though small, $-\cdot12\pm\cdot09$.

Our conclusion is, therefore, that although the records of crime statistics are not wholly satisfactory, there does appear to be some negative correlation between convictions for crime and the business cycle, and this conclusion has been corroborated by another investigation from different data."

Voting statistics afford a promising field for the statistical verification, modification, or nullification of the economic interpretation of politics. Ogburn and Goltra[1] have, for instance, applied the method of partial correlation[2] to statistics of votes in 26 initiative and referendum measures submitted in Oregon, to elucidate the difference, if any, in the political views of men and women. And the social stratification of a people into classes has been brought into relation with problems of political science in a somewhat simpler statistical analysis of votes.

Ogburn and Peterson give an analysis of the different " sides " on which five social classes,—upper, middle, labouring, city, and rural—voted in initiatives and referenda held in the State of Oregon between 1910 and 1914. The voters selected as samples of these classes are distinguished mainly by their place of residence, but occupation is used as a secondary test.

City class, votes in Portland, the largest town of the State.

Rural class, votes in twenty counties in no one of which was there a town having as many inhabitants as 3000 in 1910.

Upper class, votes in the electoral precincts constituting the residence section of the wealthiest people of Portland.

Middle and labouring class, votes cast in specific electoral precincts of Portland.[3]

[1] *Political Science Quarterly*, September 1919.
[2] See above, Chapters IX §6, XIII §3.
[3] " Political Thought of Social Classes," *Political Science Quarterly*, June 1916.

The percentage of the sample persons from each class voting for
each of all the 103 item measures submitted from 1910 to 1914 is
tabulated. Among these measures 26 are distinguished as " related
to the larger social movements " and " either radical or progressive." The difference in opinion is calculated as the arithmetic
difference between the percentages. " If 32 out of every 100 city
voters want suffrage for women, and 46 out of every 100 rural
voters want it, then the difference between these two numbers, 14,
may be said to measure the difference in the viewpoint of the city
and the country on women's suffrage."

TABLE XXc

DIFFERENCES IN THE VOTE OF DIFFERENT SOCIAL CLASSES IN
REFERENDA AND INTITIATIVES

Oregon 1910 *to* 1914

		ALL (103) Measures	Progressive Measures (26)
Upper and labouring	. .	14	20
Middle and labouring	. .	12	17
Upper and middle .	. .	6	7
Upper and rural .	. .	11	9
Labouring and rural	. .	11	14
City and rural	. .	8	6

The *a posteriori* results of this analysis given in Table XXc
agree in direction, though possibly not in force and degree, with
a priori economic interpretation. The greatest difference in voting
lies between the upper or richest and the labouring or poorest
classes ; and this difference is greatest when progressive measures
are voted upon that would be supposed to benefit the poor but
not the rich. The authors' main conclusion, however, is that the

" figures indicate that the differences between the social classes are not
so great as many have been led to suspect. Capital (the upper class)
and labour agree in eighty pairs out of every hundred on the most
radical and progressive legislation that has come before the Oregon
voters during five years. The points of agreement far outweigh the
points of difference. The heterogeneity of Oregon society does not
seem to have proven a serious obstacle to the problem of government.
The figures show little indication of class conflict nor do they point to
a revolution. They rather point toward harmony and show a considerable ability on the part of the social classes to get along together."

A somewhat opposite generalization is justified by the research
of Dr. Ambler into the politico-economic history of the State of
Virginia between 1776 and 1861. In a series of maps he displays
the direction of the vote of the representatives or delegates of the
several counties or electoral divisions within the State, on a number

of proposals, or for rival candidates for office. In almost every case the State is split across, along a line running from south-west to north-east, and this political variation (culminating in the carving out of the new State of West Virginia) between the north-western territory and the south-eastern can be correlated with distinct geographical, economic, and sociological differences. The north-west is mountainous and mineral producing, and settled by small farmers; the south-east, " Tide-water " and " Piedmont " district is flat, approachable by sea, tobacco-growing, and settled by large slave-owning proprietors of plantations at the apex of a socially stratified community.

An example of the statistical association of political characters with sociological or economic conditions going yet further back into history is furnished by the monograph of Hobhouse, Wheeler, and Ginsberg entitled *The Material Culture and Social Institutions of the Simpler Peoples*, which the authors themselves denominate an " essay in correlation."

The material culture of the simpler peoples is a character which the authors grade into seven varieties. The peoples may be hunters, agriculturists, or pastoral. The hunters may be (1) lower hunters, (2) higher or independent hunters ; the agriculturists (3) incipient, (5) pure, or (7) highest agriculturists ; and the pastoral peoples (4) lower or (6) higher.

The distinction between the lower and higher hunters is that the lower but not the higher " live very largely by gathering fruits and nuts, digging roots, collecting shellfish and devouring reptiles, insects and vermin, have no permanent dwelling . . . no spinning and weaving except in the form of plaiting, no pottery, no metal, and very poor canoes and no domestic animals except the dog and possibly a few pets." The dependent hunters who may be classed with the higher hunters, are hill and jungle tribes principally in India and the Malay region, who

" do not practise any agriculture and cannot be called pastoral. . . . They live on the outskirts of villages, come into the markets, sell jungle products, possibly serve the villagers in various ways, and sometimes are hunters rather in the sense in which thieves, gypsies and brigands may be so called rather than in any other."

The agriculturist peoples are subdivided into the three classes according to the following objective tests:

" (1) Incipient Agriculture or A^1. Subsistence depends largely on hunting or gathering. Women do the field work. The digging stick is the chief implement used. Culture is nomadic. No animals except poultry, perhaps a few pigs. No metal. Textile industries and pottery rudimentary, and houses very variable. No specialized trade, but some barter of natural products.

(2) Agriculture—pure or A². Main subsistence, agriculture. Pottery, spinning and weaving, but not as specialized industries. Substantial houses of timber. No large cattle or flocks, but pigs and small animals. Animals not used in agriculture. No trade except as above.

(3) Highest Agriculture or A³. Flocks and herds and draught cattle. The plough. Irrigation, manuring, and some rotation of crops. Specialized industries. Metal ; woodwork ; textile. Regular trade."

The pastoral stage the authors regard as an alternative development from the hunting stage not necessarily anterior or posterior to agriculture. In the first division of pastoralists " there is little or no agriculture and but a slight development of other arts " in the second division " where agriculture is developed or is practised by a serf or tributary people, metal is in use, and war, trade, or handicrafts are well developed."

The seven grades or stages of material culture distinguished by these objective tests are then correlated with classes of certain institutions. That is to say some four hundred of item peoples are tabulated as cases both in respect of their grade of material culture and of their institutions.[1] Of these the institutions that interest the political scientist are those connected with government and justice.

The task of grouping governmental and judicial institutions in accordance with the transition from unorganized to organized justice presented considerable difficulties, and the authors of the monograph adopt two alternative classifications. In compiling Table XXᴅ I have used their classification A which places in class I peoples manifesting the institution of Retaliation, no Law, and Regulated or Expiatory Fight (Self-Redress), and places in class II peoples having " Assisted or Controlled Private Justice and those in which some private offences are publicly punished. These may be combined with Retaliation or Composition." To this class are added the numerous cases in which there is a definite system of Public Justice covering all or most ordinary offences, yet Self-help is still a recognized institution—the two, in fact, existing side by side. In class III are placed those peoples among whom Public Justice is the regular system, although Composition may be allowed.[2]

Alongside procedures of public justice Table XIXᴄ indicates the

[1] The classification presented many of the fieldwork difficulties described in Chapter X. For the precise basis of classification adopted, reference should be made to the monograph itself.
[2] Op. cit., Chapter II.

relationship implied by more primitive institutions between the aggrieved individual (" I ") (or the group acting collectively on his behalf), and the chief or other representative of government (G). Under the system of self-redress the individual who feels himself aggrieved simply *executes sentence* upon the supposed aggressor by retaliation, by taking compensation or composition in goods, or by prescribed (regulated or expiatory) form of fighting.

Under the system of controlled or assisted self-redress the injured party *initiates* the proceedings and *executes* the sentence, but he may call in the chief or some officer (G) to help him in *summoning* the person he accuses, and may have to obtain a judgment which may take the form of composition before he proceeds to execute sentence.

Table XXᴅ gives the percentage of all peoples at each stage of economic development who manifest one or other of the three stages of *judicial* development. A definite line of regression or co-variation is noticeable : 90% of lower hunting peoples but only 16% of the highest agricultural peoples are also primitive (class I) justice peoples ; 41% of the highest agricultural peoples and 48% of the higher pastoral peoples are also highly developed (class III) justice peoples. If classes II and III are added the percentage of item peoples with these more developed systems of judicial procedure is seen to rise *continuously* as we pass from the grades of less developed to those of more developed economic systems.

The economic interpretation of political institutions, if it is not taken to explain everything but only some or possibly many things is, as suggested in Chapter IV, unduly neglected as an hypothesis.

TABLE XXᴅ

CORRELATION OF VARIETIES OF JUDICIAL PROCEDURE WITH VARIETIES
OF ECONOMIC DEVELOPMENT

Stage of Economic (Technical) Development	Percentage cases at each Economic Stage			
	Self-Redress or No Law (Private Justice)	Assisted or Con-trolled Private Justice Co-existence of Public Justice and Self-help	Public Regular Justice	Columns II+III
	I	II	III	
Lower Hunters (L.H.) . .	90	10	0	10
Higher and Dependent Hunters (H.H. and D.H.) . .	78	16	06	22
Incipient Agriculture (A¹) .	58	22	20	42
Lower Pastoral (P¹) . .	44	40	16	56
Agriculture-pure (A²) . .	41	35	24	59
Higher Pastoral (P²) . .	32	19	48	67
Highest Agriculture (A³) .	16	42	41	83

Political history has been written chiefly by the well-to-do with independent means or a fixed salary and little sense of the importance of economics to the average man. Political history has often been written by men with a classical education, often clergymen, with little theoretical knowledge of economics and a certain contempt for economic activity as material and dishonourable. Even the modern sociologist does not appear to consider economics as part of his " shop " and is often woefully ignorant of the conclusions of economics. Yet the science of economics may throw considerable light on problems of its less statistically developed sister sciences, and the likelihood of some influence of, e.g. vested interests, lobbying or graft upon legislation, or of poverty or riches upon voting, is not to be ignored merely because they are influences unworthy of man.

But there is no need to confine the interpretation of statistical results to economic hypothesis. Together with the extension of the facts to be collected by political science and the statistical measurement of their variety and co-variation may come the widening of the psychological causal interpretation. We need no longer assume man to be rational either in politics or in economics, nor, if rational, necessarily to aim at unrestricted freedom[1] or unlimited wealth. The theory of man as largely imitative developed by Bagehot in his *Physics and Politics*, or of man as largely intuitive and instinctive set out by Graham Wallas, or of man as a biological product,[2] may be used as working hypotheses ; or if man be rational his aim might be assumed for working purposes to be not freedom or economic advantage but power.[3]

My thesis is not that all deduction from the assumed character of man should be dropped, but that such deduction should be used in conjunction with inductive and statistical investigation. Statistics of human behaviour show such variation and uncertainty, and inductive inference is so beset with probable error that *a priori* deduction must be used as corroborative evidence or even as the original working hypothesis. The possibility of such deduction must indeed be regarded as a positive advantage that the human sciences have over the natural sciences. We cannot enter into the mind of an atom, a rock, a buttercup, or even a butterfly ; but we do have enough similarity in our mental make-up and should gain enough experience of our fellows in the course of a life not too much

---

[1] See *Encyclopædia Britannica*, edition 11, article *Sociology*, for an example of sheer deduction from assumptions, to the effect that permanent conquest is impossible by a militarist State.

[2] Bateson, *Biological Fact and the Structure of Society.*

[3] Catlin, *The Science and Method of Politics.*

confined to arm and other professorial chairs, to make it possible, in Sidgwick's words, to "assume certain general characteristics of social man," and to deduce therefrom.

§9 · 2 Correlated Sociological Consequences

Taking leave of measured political activities correlated and interpreted as caused *by* social circumstances we may, finally, turn to political activities correlated as hypothetical causes *of* social circumstances.

Measurable sociological *results* of political activities to which importance is publicly attached are :

1. Statistics of Health and Safety. General death rates or average length of life ; infant mortality ; mortality from specific diseases, or suicide ; sickness, morbidity rates. Rate of industrial or non-industrial accidents fatal or non-fatal.

2. Statistics of Poverty. Proportion of "paupers" in receipt of State relief or charity ; proportion of families below physiologically determined subsistence level (e.g. the Rowntree poverty line). Special manifestations of poverty : housing shortage and overcrowding.

3. Statistics of Education and Mental Ability. Proportion of illiterates ; proportion reaching given school standards ; examination results, proportion completing school, college, university career ; proportion being educated in various degrees at various ages. Proportion feeble-minded, detained in lunatic asylums, etc.[1]

4. Statistics of Crime and "Morality."

These "sociological" statistics are often used as tests of the success of any political policy. Success may be defined in the elementary terms and symbols suggested in Chapter XII as the occurrence of a result (R) which was the object (O) of a deliberate policy (P). When the result actually obtained corresponds to the object (i.e. when O=, or is positively correlated with, R) then there is certainly a plausible theoretical case for claiming success. But this use of statistics is only admissible on certain conditions.

(1) The object or aim of the policy (the (O) of the (P)) must have been openly asserted or must be attested by some other objective evidence.

(2) No other possibly fortuitous cause, or causes can account for the result "R."

---

[1] It is interesting to note that in England and Wales the population of lunatic asylums is about the same as that of universities. The amenability of educational activities to statistical approach is indicated by the number of books devoted to statistical methods as applied solely to education. E.g. H. O. Rugg, *Statistical Methods Applied to Education.* A text-book for students of Education in the quantitative study of school problems.

It is only when such conditions are satisfied that it becomes possible to measure success and the degree of success in the correlation of the object of the policy with the result actually occurring.

Jevons was perhaps the first to point out the importance of correlating political policy with observed statistics instead of relying on theory and " metaphysics."

" The parent in theory was the best educational guardian of the child ; but, if the result was no education at all, there was no ground for the theory. In this case, again, the State dispersed metaphysics by stepping in and ordering the child to be educated."[1]

" It is no doubt a gross interference with that metaphysical entity, the liberty of the subject, to prevent a man from working with phosphorus as he pleases. But if it can be shown by unquestionable statistics and the unimpeachable evidence of scientific men that working with phosphorus leads to a dreadful disease, easily preventable by a small change of procedure, then I hold that the Legislature is *prima facie* justified in obliging the man to make this small change."[2]

Modern political science has on the whole followed Jevons in its insistence upon comparative, and if possible, numerical data.

" If we could know annually in each measurable department of the national life the comparative achievement of each local authority, we should go far towards stimulating competition in achievement and in providing ourselves with an index to what should be the standard of minimum service exacted from local bodies by the State. We could compare library systems and the degree to which their use was organized ; the number of children in each area who passed from primary to secondary schools and from secondary schools to the university ; we could see what service was made available for the sick in Durham and compare it with kindred service in Winchester ; we could measure the reduction in cost to the consumer of tramway services in Cincinnati and Cleveland ; we could get reports upon the local museums of Boston and Glasgow. What Mr. and Mrs. Webb have called ' the impartial qualitative assessment of each town as a whole ' seems to me a really urgent task if its government is to approach adequacy."[3]

" The importance of the interests of consumers has been underestimated," writes Marshall[4] in a series of marginal headings, " because direct personal experience seldom helps much towards forming correct estimates of them, and our public statistics are not yet properly organized."   And he proceeds in his text :

" Much of the failure and much of the injustice in which economic policies of governments have resulted have been due to the want of statistical measurement. . . . The few get their way, although if statistical measures of the interests involved were available, it might prove

[1] *The State in Relation to Labour*, Chapter I.   [2] Loc. cit.
[3] Laski, *Grammar of Politics*, p. 428.
[4] *Principles of Economics*, V, xiv §8.

that the aggregate of the interests of the few was only a tenth or a hundredth part of the aggregate of the interests of the silent many. . . . The rapid growth of collective interests and the increasing tendency towards collective actions in economic affairs make it every day more important that we should know what quantitative measures of public interest are most needed and what statistics are required for them, and that we should set ourselves to obtain these statistics."

Applied to industrial organization the idea has been expressed as *statistical control*, and forms part of the whole movement toward scientific management and rationalization. The up-to-date business manager uses statistics as a test of efficiency and success in gaining his object in every department. He uses statistics in his cost-accounting; he uses statistics in calculating his financial and operating ratios giving the proportion of total expense going to administrative cost; he uses statistics in assessing the prospective and actual response to his advertisement and marketing policy; he uses statistics in testing by correlation with labour turnover, absence, output, or accidents, the efficacy of his labour policy and welfare work. "Statistical Methods," so writes an American business leader, " are tied up with—are a function of—the good management methods."

In public and private finance, too, statistical control is becoming a matter of course. The banker in granting credits keeps an eye on the numerical ratio of his reserves to his deposits and tends to work to some constant standard ratio; while the treasury official, if he be a Sir Josiah Stamp,[1] may detect tax evasion through a discrepancy in the frequency curve of the actual returns for each income-class when compared with the corresponding regression curve statistically established by Professor Pareto.

Statistical control may, some day, form part of a rationalization of political organization. At present, however, the correlation of political procedure with sociological statistics is still in infancy—or infantile.

Few politicians, however up-to-date, seriously compare statistical results, except perhaps votes, when originating, adopting, or modifying political and constitutional structure or procedure. Yet once a statesman knows what he wants or what the public want, once the optative of the practical syllogism (Chapter III) is given, it is to statistically summarized experience that he should turn to find the policy for producing that desired result, and for avoiding different or even opposite results. That policy once initiated, statistical records and summaries should keep statesmen and public

---

[1] Stamp, *Wealth and Taxable Capacity*, p. 82.

continuously informed of its " working." Blue books, to be sure, are usually heavy writing and seldom light reading, and such a statistical initiation and consummation devoutly to be wished, calls for education in the beauties and conveniences of the statistical approach. May this treatise be of help to writer and reader !

CHAPTER XXI

A Table of Cross-references

THE headings adopted follow the conventional order of subjects dealt with in economic (and to a less extent political) text-books to which reference was made in Chapter III, §2. They are numbered and organized as follows:

1 Scope and Method of Economics
2 Demand
3 Supply : Factors of Production
4 Supply : Forms of Industrial Organization
5 Supply : Cost and Efficiency of Production
6 Value : Independent Values under Competition
7 Value : Dependent Values under Competition
8 Value : Conditions under Monopoly
9 Distribution : Distribution and the National Dividend
10 Distribution : Rent
11 Distribution : Wages and Unemployment
12 Distribution : Wages ; Conditions of Employment and Organization of Labour
13 Distribution : Interest
14 Distribution : Profits
15 Mechanism of Exchange : Money
16 Mechanism of Exchange : Banking
17 International Trade
18 Industrial Fluctuations
19 Political Economics or Administrative Science
20 Political Science or Organization of the State

Subjects we have classified (Chapter III) as forming part of the science of Economic Politics (or industrial organization) occur under headings 4, 12, and 16. The subjects coming under headings 19 and 20 are also explained in Chapter III.

1 SCOPE AND METHOD OF ECONOMICS
  Scope of Economics
    Conventional Definitions   III §2, IV §5
    Relation of Economics to Political Science III §§1, 2, Table IIIA
    Relation of Economics and Political   XIV §2
      Science to Psychology

  Assumptions of Economics   III §2
    The Market   XVI §5
    Mobility   XV §4

To find page of section referred to v. Contents, pp. ix-xxii.

To find page of section referred to v. Contents, pp. ix-xxii.

To find page of section referred to v. Contents, pp. ix–xxii.

To find page of section referred to *v.* Contents, pp. ix–xxii.

To find page of section referred to *v.* Contents, pp. ix–xxii.

GLOSSARY OF ELEMENTARY STATISTICAL TERMS

§1. Statistics deals with numbers ("sets," "series," "masses") of observed ITEMS manifesting characters whose values may or may not be quantitatively measurable. The character colour of the item hair has values red, black, brown not quantitatively measurable; but the character length has values that are quantitatively measurable along a "scale." If not quantitatively measurable the character is referred to as an ATTRIBUTE; if quantitatively measurable as a VARIABLE. Whether quantitatively characterized or not, items may be considered of different degrees of importance, in which case their values can be WEIGHTED through multiplication by some exact measure of their relative importance.

§2. Where items are variables with quantitative characters (but not otherwise) the statistician can summarize the distribution of values of each such quantitative character by means of averages and other standard positions of incidence (§3–§9), by means of measures of dispersion (§10–§13), and by means of measures of skewness and of the form of distribution (§14–§18). Items that are attributes with only qualitative characters do not permit of statistical summarizations of their values, but statistical measurement is possible of the relative numerical frequency of the association of such attributes. This is taken up in §21.

§3. The AVERAGE sums up in a single number the most representative, typical, value or position (along the scale) upon which the whole distribution of item-values centres. The averages found in common use are Arithmetic and Geometric Means, the Mode and the Median.

§4. THE ARITHMETIC MEAN (A.M.) is the sum of the values of the items divided by the number of items. It is often spoken of as THE average *par excellence*. Of fourteen items 3, 4, 4, 5, 5, 5, 5, 6, 6, 6, 7, 8, 12, 22, the sum is 98 and the arithmetic mean $98/14 = 7$. The GEOMETRIC MEAN is the nth root of the product of the values of n items; while the arithmetic mean of 2 and 18 is 10, the geometric mean is $\sqrt{2 \times 18} = \sqrt{36} = 6$. For positive numbers the geometric is in fact always lower than the arithmetic mean; of the fourteen items already cited it is $\sqrt[14]{3 \times 4^2 \times 5^4 \times 6^3 \times 7 \times 8 \times 12 \times 22} = 6\cdot08$. Where each item-value is to be weighted differently (see §2) the WEIGHTED ARITHMETIC MEAN is obtained by multiplying each item-value once, twice, thrice, etc., according to whether it is not weighted (i.e. weighted only by one), weighted by two, three, etc., and dividing the sum of the products by the total number of multipliers used. Similarly, the WEIGHTED GEOMETRIC MEAN is the nth root of the product of values multiplied by weights, where n is the total number of multipliers.

§5. THE MODE is the single value manifested by the greatest number of items. It is that value of which there are most instances. Of the fourteen items 3, 4, 4, 5, 5, 5, 5, 6, 6, 6, 7, 8, 12, 22, four have a value

495

of 5, and as four is the greatest number of items manifesting any *one* value, the mode is 5. Though approximating most nearly to the notion of a typical value, the value of the mode is often difficult to ascertain exactly and the mode cannot well be used as a basis of further calculation.

§6.   THE MEDIAN is the value on each side of which are half the items when the items are listed or ranked in order of the magnitude of their values. It is the value of the item in the middle of the list, or where the number of items is even it is conventionally taken as the value half-way between that of the *two* middle items. Of the fourteen items 3, 4, 4, 5, 5, 5, 5, 6, 6, 6, 7, 8, 12, 22, half (i.e. seven) have values at or below 5 and half have values at or above 6. The median is therefore between 5 and 6—approximately $5\frac{1}{2}$. A WEIGHTED MEDIAN is obtained by listing each item-value once, twice, three times, etc., according to the weight assigned to it, and *then* finding the value of the item in the middle of the list.

§7.   It may not be one typical or representative central value upon or around which the whole distribution of item-values tends to fall that is required but SOME OTHER POSITION ALONG THE SCALE OF VALUES. By the same methods of listing or ranking item-values in order of magnitude whereby the median is found, standard points of incidence can be settled upon, other than that of the item value half-way along the ranks. Of such points of incidence or " positional values " those most frequently used are the Quartiles, the Deciles, and the Percentiles.

§8   When items are ranked in order of the magnitude of their values (lowest value first) THE UPPER QUARTILE (Q_3) is the value of the item three-quarters of the way along the ranks. Three-quarters of the item-values will be equal to or *smaller* than Q_3, one-quarter equal to or *greater* than Q_3. THE LOWER QUARTILE (Q_1) is the value of the item one-quarter of the way along the ranks. One-quarter of the item values will be equal to or smaller than Q_1, three-quarters equal to or greater than Q_1.

The middle quartile Q_2 is identical with the median.

Of the fourteen item-values 3, 4, 4, 5, 5, 5, 5, 6, 6, 6, 7, 8, 12, 22 : Q_3 is the value of the $(\frac{3}{4} \times 14 + \frac{1}{2})$th item, that is the 11th item in order, namely 7 ; Q_1 is the value of the $(\frac{1}{4} \times 14 + \frac{1}{2})$th item, that is of the 4th item in order, namely 5.[1]

---

[1] The general formula for finding the median and quartile items among n items ranked in order of their magnitude is

$$\text{Median} \qquad \frac{n}{2} + \frac{1}{2}$$

$$\text{Lower Quartile} \qquad \frac{n}{4} + \frac{1}{2}$$

$$\text{Upper Quartile} \qquad \frac{3n}{4} + \frac{1}{2}$$

The inclusion of the $\frac{1}{2}$ in the formula—a relatively unimportant matter as n becomes larger—is due to our practice of indicating any space along the line in language by the position of its further boundary, which, accurately speaking, is half the space beyond the centre of the space. Thus we refer to a child as being in his fourth year when actually his age is anywhere between three and

§9 When items are ranked in order of the magnitude of their values, the DECILES are the values of the items every tenth of the way along the ranks, the PERCENTILES are the values of the items every hundredth of the way along the ranks. The fifth decile (D 5) or the 50th percentile are identical with the median. Nine-tenths of the item values will be equal to or *smaller* than, one-tenth equal to or *greater* than the ninth decile (D 9), or the ninetieth percentile. One-tenth of the item values will be equal to or smaller than, nine-tenths equal to or greater than the first decile (D 1), or the tenth percentile.

§10 The DISPERSION measure, or measure of VARIATION sums up in a single number the degree of homogeneity or conformity of the distribution of item values to the average. It indicates how far the average is really typical and representative. Dispersion measures in common use are the mean (or average) and the standard deviations, and the semi-interquartile range.

§11 THE MEAN DEVIATION (M.D.), also named AVERAGE DEVIATION (A.D.), is the arithmetic mean of the item-deviations from some average value, all signs (+ or −) being considered positive (+). The form of average from which the deviations of the item values are calculated is usually either the median or the arithmetic mean.

THE STANDARD DEVIATION or ROOT MEAN SQUARE DEVIATION (S.D. or σ) is the square root of the arithmetic mean of the squares of the item deviations. These item deviations are always the deviations of the item values from their arithmetic mean.

For the fourteen items 3, 4, 4, 5, 5, 5, 5, 6, 6, 6, 7, 8, 12, 22, these measures of dispersion may be obtained as follows :

Value of Item	Deviation of Item from Mean	Square of Deviation	Deviation from Median	
3	(−) 4	16	(−) $2\frac{1}{2}$	Mean Deviation from
4	(−) 3	9	(−) $1\frac{1}{2}$	Arithmetic Mean :
4	(−) 3	9	(−) $1\frac{1}{2}$	$42/14 = 3$
5	(−) 2	4	(−) $\frac{1}{2}$	Mean Deviation from
5	(−) 2	4	(−) $\frac{1}{2}$	Median : $36/14 = 2\cdot57$
5	(−) 2	4	(−) $\frac{1}{2}$	Standard Deviation
5	(−) 2	4	(−) $\frac{1}{2}$	from A.M. :
6	(−) 1	1	(+) $\frac{1}{2}$	
6	(−) 1	1	(+) $\frac{1}{2}$	$\sqrt{\dfrac{304}{14}} = 4\cdot66$
6	(−) 1	1	(+) $\frac{1}{2}$	
7	0	0	(+) $1\frac{1}{2}$	
8	(+) 1	1	(+) $2\frac{1}{2}$	
12	(+) 5	25	(+) $6\frac{1}{2}$	
22	(+) 15	225	(+) $16\frac{1}{2}$	
	42	304	36	

four and averages three and a half. Hence to indicate in language any space along a line (or list of equal spaces), we must add half a space to the actual middle of the space. See my note, *J.A.S.A.*, September 1920, p. 302.

If (number of items ÷ 4) + $\frac{1}{2}$, or 3 (number of items ÷ 4) + $\frac{1}{2}$ is not a full number and lies between items listed with different values, Q^3 and Q^1 must be calculated by adding to the value of the item just below (for Q^3) three-quarters, or (for Q^1) one-quarter of the interval between that value and the value of the item just above. Where values are not exact but ranges or grades, intrapolation may be used. See Table VIc ; also Bowley, *Elements of Statistics*, Pt. I, VE.

2K

§12 THE SEMI-INTERQUARTILE RANGE (" Q ") is the difference in value of the upper and lower quartile divided by two.

The INTERQUARTILE RANGE just includes or " covers " half the item values above and half the item values below the median. Roughly, half the items should have values deviating from the median by not more than the semi-interquartile range in either direction (+ or −).

Since in the illustrative set of item values Q 1 is 5, Q 3 is 7 (§8) the semi-interquartile range is $\frac{7-5}{2} = 1$.

§13 THE RELATIVE DISPERSION. Where it is desired to compare the measure of dispersion in one series of items with that of another series, allowance must be made for the fact that the size of the average value of each series affects the size of the dispersion measure. If we multiplied all the values in the series cited above by ten, the dispersion measure would rise with the average tenfold, yet *relatively* to the average the dispersion is the same. To obtain the *relative* variation of a series of items " COEFFICIENTS OF DISPERSION " have been devised.

The following coefficients of dispersion are most commonly used. All the component terms have already been defined. The coefficients all vary within the limits 0 and 1, so that the widest possible relative deviation is measured as 1 and no deviation as 0.

(A) The Mean Deviation divided by the Arithmetic Mean
Using the example cited above this would be 3/7 = ·43.

(B) The Standard Deviation divided by the Arithmetic Mean
Using the example cited above this would be 4·66/7 = ·67.

(C) The Semi-Interquartile Range divided by the Median, or rather (to avoid any chance of the coefficient exceeding 1) divided by the Arithmetic Mean of the upper and lower Quartiles.

Using the example cited above this would be $\frac{1}{\text{A.M. of 7 and 5}} = \frac{1}{6} = \cdot 17$

§14 The FREQUENCY TABLE OR CURVE[1] gives the entire picture of the distribution of item values in some more or less summary form. It shows the number of items having values within specified limits, i.e. it shows the frequency of occurrence of any, or particular values along the relevant scale of values.

Detailed Values	Distribution Frequency	Summarized Distribution Ranges of Value	Frequency
3	1	Over 2 up to 4	3
4	2		
5	4	Over 4 up to 6	7
6	3		
7	1	Over 6 up to 8	2
8	1		
12	1	Over 8	2
22	1		

If there is a large variety of different values it is convenient to class together neighbouring values into grades or ranges within well-defined limits falling at equal INTERVALS. If values between the limits over 4

[1] For method of presentation of frequency curve see Chapter V §4.

up to 6, over 6 up to 8, over 8 up to 10 are classed together the distance or " interval " between the limits is 2 throughout the scale.

§15 The frequency curve cannot be described in a single number as the average or dispersion measure can, but certain CHARACTERISTICS OF ITS SHAPE can be summarily measured. A curve is either symmetrical about its average or not. If symmetrical then the values of the three types of average—mean, median and mode—will coincide. If not symmetrical a curve is said to be skewed positively or negatively. With a positive skew, the plus deviations are more extreme and are on the average higher than the minus deviations, as in the Table of §11, and the upper quartile is further from the median than the lower quartile ; with a negative skew the reverse is the case. The arithmetic mean (A.M.) is always pulled away from the mode in the direction of the skew, and the difference (A.M.—mode) is therefore positive when the skew is positive, negative when the skew is negative. The median is usually found to be two-thirds of the way from mode to arithmetic mean ; i.e. A.M. − mode = 3 (A.M. − median).

§16 The exact degree of SKEWNESS is expressed relatively to the (absolute) dispersion, as a coefficient. The element that is measured is either the divergence in value of the three different types of average (as in Coefficient A below); or else the difference in deviation from the median of the upper and lower quartile (as in Coefficient B) or of any two items holding the same relative position at either end when items are listed in order of their values, as the deciles used in Coefficient C.

The following COEFFICIENTS OF SKEWNESS are most commonly used ; all the component terms have already been defined. A symmetrical distribution with no skew will have a coefficient of 0, and extremely skewed distributions will have coefficients close to $+1$ if positively, and close to -1 if negatively skewed.

(A) The difference between the arithmetic mean and mode (or, see §15, three times the difference between the arithmetic mean and the median) divided by the standard deviation.

In the example cited above this would be $\dfrac{3(7-5\frac{1}{2})}{4\cdot 66} = +\cdot 97$.

(B) The deviation of the upper minus the deviation of the lower quartile from the median, divided by the difference of the quartiles (the interquartile range). The numerator $(Q_3 - M) - (M - Q_1)$ is more easily calculated as $Q_3 + Q_1 - 2M$.

In the example cited above this would be $\dfrac{7+5-11}{7-5} = \frac{1}{2}$ or $+\cdot 50$.

(C) The deviation of the ninth decile from the median minus the deviation of the first decile from the median, divided by the difference of the deciles. The numerator $(D_9 - M) - (M - D_1)$ is more easily calculated as $D_9 + D_1 - 2M$.

This measure of skewness takes account of eight-tenths of all the values and thus includes values outside the interquartile range. It is useful if a distribution is symmetrical near the average, but skew when comparing the higher and lower values.

§17 A rough measure of the FORM OF ANY DISTRIBUTION can be given by citing the values of all the deciles ; or simply by citing the first (or lower) decile, the first (or lower) quartile, the median, the third (or upper) quartile and the ninth (or upper) decile. The deviation will be narrower the lower the *range* of value between the quartiles (or deciles) when compared with the average value of the items as shown by the median or the value half-way between the quartiles. The skew will be the greater the more the range of value between upper quartile or decile and median differs from the range between lower quartile or decile and median.

§18   A particular type of the symmetrical frequency curve according to which certain characteristics of man, such as his height, seem to be distributed, is known as the NORMAL DISTRIBUTION or NORMAL CURVE because it is the result that will most probably occur by chance, where the values actually distributed are themselves the sum or chance combination of a number of component characters each varying in value independently one of another—a situation that is considered Normal. If one die is thrown each of the values 1, 2, 3, 4, 5, and 6 will probably in the long run be as frequent as another. But if two dice are thrown, the value of one varying independently of the value of the other, the sum of the values will not show any equal frequency at each of the possible values from 2 to 12. While only one sum or combination, namely 1 + 1, can add up to 2, and only one sum or combination, namely 6 + 6, can add up to 12, six sums or combinations of the values of the two dice can produce 7, namely 1 + 6, 2 + 5, 3 + 4, 4 + 3, 5 + 2, 6 + 1.

The probable frequency of occurrence of each and all of the possible combination values in the course of 36 throws is as follows : Value of 2 once, value of 3 twice, of 4 thrice, of 5 four times, of 6 five times, of 7 six times, of 8 five times, of 9 four times, of 10 thrice, of 11 twice, of 12 once. This, though only a rough approximation because of the small number of possible values and the presence of only two component variables, may be taken as a simplified example of the normal probability distribution.

A further example of the constancy of relations between different measures of deviation when values are distributed " normally " is that the semi-interquartile range (see §12) is ·6745 of the standard deviation (" σ " or S.D.) and ·845 of the average deviation (A.D.).

Once the average (mean = median = mode) and the deviation therefrom is known, this curve can be drawn ex-hypothesi. For instance, if the lower quartile is −1, and the upper quartile +1 from the average, then the lower decile should be about −1·92 and the upper decile +1·92 from the average. In short, if the values of half the items in a normal distribution do not deviate more than + or −1 from the average value, then the values of eight-tenths of the items will not deviate more than + or −1·92 from average.

Instead of calculating what exact fraction of a multiple of the interquartile range the value of the interdecile range will be, we may calculate the exact proportion of items whose values will be included within any integral multiple of the interquartile range. In the normal distribution, 82·26% of all items should have values deviating not more than twice the semi-interquartile range (Q) from average, and 95·70% of all items should have values deviating not more than 3 Q from the average.

The various relationships holding of this normal distribution may be tabulated for reference :

Proportion of items	have, in a normal distribution, plus or minus deviations (" errors ") from average of a value not more (or less) than :—
50% (Q3−Q1)	Q= ·6745 S.D.= ·845 A.D.
80% (D9−D1)	1·92Q=1·2950 S.D.=1·622 A.D.
82·26%	2Q=1·3490 S.D.=1·690 A.D.
95·70%	3Q=2·0235 S.D.=2·535 A.D.

§19 If values are expected to be distributed according to the normal probability curve, then it becomes possible to PREDICT or ESTIMATE from a comparatively small SAMPLE the limits within which summary values (such as the standard deviation, the coefficient of correlation, but more especially the arithmetic mean type of average) of the whole generality of items will MORE OR LESS CERTAINLY fall.

The measure of the degree of uncertainty or unreliability will obviously vary positively with the deviation measure of the observed sample distribution, but negatively (or inversely) with the number of items observed. When the dispersion of observed sample item values is comparatively wide and the deviation measure high, the limits within which the general average of the whole distribution can be estimated with any given certainty and reliability from the sample average must be comparatively wide too. The reliability or certainty depends in the first place, therefore, on the observed deviation ; it also depends on the number of items observed in the sample. An average of a few items is less reliable than an average of many items, and the limits of the estimated general average must be wider. The traditional measure of unreliability called the PROBABLE ERROR takes the semi-interquartile range Q (above, §12) as the measure of deviation and divides it by the square root of the number of items in the observed sample. This probable error added or subtracted to the averages gives the limits within which or outside which there is an *equal probability* that a value will occur purely as a result of chance.

Since Q is ·6745 of the standard deviation (S.D.) the formula of probable error can be written

$$P.E. = \frac{·6745 \text{ S.D.}}{\sqrt{\text{number of items observed.}}}$$

If the fourteen items (of §11) are taken as merely a sample of a much larger whole distribution of values presumed to be of normal probability form, then the probable error of the arithmetic mean (7) would be stated as follows :

$$7·00 \pm \frac{·6745 \, (4·66)}{\sqrt{14}}$$
$$= 7·00 \pm ·84$$

That is to say, the general average of the whole distribution is *as likely as not* to fall between the limits 7·84 and 6·16. If the limits are widened by taking a multiple of the probable error (say, twice or three times), then instead of equal probability of the general average falling inside there is practical certainty. The table in §18 shows that if any estimate or prediction is likely to be right in 50% of the cases where limits are imposed by a probable error of x above and below sample average, the estimate or prediction is likely to be right in 82·26% of the cases where the limits are twice this probable error (i.e. $2x$) above and below the sample average, and the prediction is likely to be right in 95·7% of cases where the limits are three times this probable error (i.e. $3x$). A corollary is that any value outside those limits of $3x$ above and below sample average is unlikely to be due to chance and must be attributed to some *significant* difference.

§20 RELATIONSHIP (Association) BETWEEN CHARACTERS. The frequency distribution lists the number of items having various values or ranges of values of one particular character. But most items have more than one character and it is often required to measure the nature and degree of relationship, if any, between the values of one character and the values of another character manifested by the same set of items.

The statistical item is not necessarily some one nameable thing, but may be any set of circumstances observed or considered conjointly, any context or " conjuncture " ; the various circumstances or members of the context or conjuncture being the characters whose relationship is at issue.

Two or more characters conjointly manifested by any item may be related or unrelated, or (in alternative synonymous words) may be said to be dependent or independent.

One character is *unrelated* to or *independent* of another if its value (quality or quantity) in any item tends in no degree to vary with variations in the values of the other character or characters conjointly manifested by the same item. Otherwise it is *related* or *dependent*.

A relation between characters may be either positive (congruent) or negative (inverse). It is positive if a comparatively high value tends in some degree to occur in one character when the value of the other character is comparatively high and similarly of low values. The relation is negative if a comparatively high value tends to occur in some degree in one character when the other character has a comparatively low value or vice versa.

Different sets of words are used according as (*a*) the characters are both attributes with only two alternative qualitative values each ; (*b*) both are variables with quantitative values reckoned in numbers of units ; or (*c*) one character is a variable, the other a " duo-qualitative " attribute, or both or one are multi-qualitative attributes. By multi-qualitative I refer to an attribute that has more than two specified qualities or " varieties." These several qualities are often quasi-quantitative in that they can be ranked in isotropic order off-hand, as very thin, thin, fat, fatter, fattest.

In case (*a*) if there is a relation between qualitative characters (ATTRIBUTES), it is usual to speak of the *qualities* (or less accurately the characters) being associated or disassociated. Though colour of eyes and tint of hair may be said to be related it is more usual to speak of some particular colour (e.g. brown eyes) being *associated* with some particular tint (e.g. dark hair) or disassociated with some other particular tint (e.g. fair hair).[1] If the characters (attributes) are unrelated or " independent " and the qualities neither associated (nor disassociated) they are said to be unassociated or non-associated.

[1] Yule, *Introduction to the Theory of Statistics*, Part I.

(b) When quantitative characters (VARIABLES) are related they are said to be either positively or negatively *correlated*. When quantitative characters are independent and unrelated they may be called uncorrelated or non-correlated.

(c) When qualitative characters are related to quantitative, or both or one character is multi-qualitative, they may be said to be either positively or negatively *contingent*.

When there is independence and neither positive nor negative contingency, the characters may be called uncontingent or non-contingent.

Where quantitative and quasi-quantitative characters are involved, positive contingency and positive correlation can be stated in the form " the more . . . the more . . .", or " the less . . . the less . . ."; negative contingency and negative correlation in the form " the more . . . the less . . ." or " the less . . . the more. . . ."

The terminology that is used may be tabulated systematically as in Chapter IX, §1.

§21 THE ASSOCIATION TABLE. Suppose the fourteen values given as an illustration in §11 to be breadths, but that the exact breadth is not given. All that is known is that the ten items with values from 3 to 6 are narrower than average, while the four items with values above 7 are wider than average. Suppose also that of the ten narrow items eight can be described only as of a length shorter than average and two only as longer ; and that among the four wide items one can only be described as shorter than average, three only as longer. With such vague descriptions it might be thought that statistical methods were useless, since there are no numbers to be dealt with. But this neglects the fact of the variable number or frequencies of items manifesting the four possible combinations of qualities.

> 8 are narrow and short items.
> 2 are narrow and long items.
> 1 is a wide and short item.
> 3 are wide and long items.

Important questions that statistical methods may attempt to answer are how far the relatively large number (or high frequency) of items in which narrowness and shortness, or width and length are combined constitute a definite tendency to association, and how far the relatively small number (or low frequency) of items in which narrowness and length, or width and shortness are combined constitute a definite tendency to disassociation. If we know that an item is short, are the chances favourable to its also being narrow and unfavourable to its being wide, and if so, what are the exact chances ? Similarly what are the probabilities (if any) that a long item will be wide and not narrow ? Or to put the question yet more briefly, how far is shortness ASSOCIATED with narrowness and length with width ?

If narrowness and shortness tended neither to be associated nor disassociated but quite *independent* characters, then a certain theoretical proportion of narrow items should also be short and a certain theoretical proportion also long, namely—exactly that proportion in which all (narrow *and* wide) items are distributed between short and long ; in his case 9 and 5, or $\frac{9}{14}$ths of the total of items short and $\frac{5}{14}$ths of the total items long. Of the 10 *narrow* items $\frac{9}{14}$ths or $6\frac{3}{7}$ items should be short, $\frac{5}{7}$ths, i.e. $3\frac{1}{2}$ items should be long. Similarly, among the 4 wide items, $\frac{9}{14}$ths or $2\frac{4}{7}$ items should be short, $\frac{5}{9}$ths or $1\frac{3}{7}$ items should be long.

MODEL ASSOCIATION TABLE

	Narrower than Average (Values 3 to 6)	Wider than Average (Values 7 to 22)	Total Items
Shorter than Average	Actual 8 Items Theoretical $6\frac{4}{7}$ Items (Difference $+ 1\frac{4}{7}$)	Actual 1 Item Theoretical $2\frac{4}{7}$ Items (Difference $- 1\frac{4}{7}$)	9
Longer than Average	Actual 2 Items Theoretical $3\frac{4}{7}$ Items (Difference $- 1\frac{4}{7}$)	Actual 3 Items Theoretical $1\frac{3}{7}$ Items (Difference $+ 1\frac{4}{7}$)	5
Total Items	10	4	14

§22 Comparing actual to theoretical distribution a difference of $1\frac{4}{7}$ will be seen in all four boxes of the Table. Where the difference has a + sign the qualities manifested are combined in more items than theoretically expected and can be considered more or less associated ; where the difference is negative, qualities are more or less disassociated. This common *difference* between the actual distribution and that *theoretically* worked out on the basis of complete independence or non-relation, is used as a measure of the exact degree of positive or negative association of the qualities.

When there is complete independence the common difference is clearly 0, but if it is to serve as a coefficient this common difference must not vary beyond some well-defined limits such as $+1$ or -1 when there is complete positive or negative association, complete association or disassociation.

The usual formula for obtaining such a COEFFICIENT OF ASSOCIATION is to *multiply the common difference by the total number of items and divide this by the sum of the products of frequencies with a plus, and of frequencies with a minus common difference.*

In the table the coefficient of association between length and width, or shortness and narrowness is $\dfrac{+1\frac{4}{7} \times 14}{(8 \times 3) + (2 \times 1)} = +\dfrac{22}{26} = +\ \cdot 846$; the qualities are markedly associated positively. Between length and narrowness, and width and shortness the coefficient is $-\cdot846$; the qualities are markedly disassociated or negatively associated.

It will be noticed that the frequencies with a common difference of the same sign are situated diagonally across the association table and their products, whose sum is the denominator of the coefficient, may be referred to as the cross-products.

The common difference multiplied by the total number of items will always be found equal to the difference of the cross-products. In the Table, $1\frac{4}{7} \times 14 = (8 \times 3) - (1 \times 2)$.

The formula may therefore be written for short

$$\frac{\textit{The difference of the cross-products}}{\textit{The sum of the cross-products}}$$

The coefficient is clearly o when the theoretical distribution assuming complete independence (non-association) of qualities agrees with the *actual* distribution and the common difference is o ; and for the following reasons it cannot exceed + or −1.

When there is complete association one cross-product will be o. (E.g.: If there is complete association of length and width there will be *no* short-and-wide items and no long-and-narrow items, and the product of short-wide items and long-narrow items is o. Complete association of length and width, in fact, implies complete disassociation of length and narrowness.)

With complete (positive) association between two qualities the coefficient will therefore be

$$\frac{\text{Cross-product (of frequencies of items with associated qualities)} - \text{o}}{\text{Cross-product (of frequencies of items with associated qualities)} + \text{o}} = +1$$

With complete disassociation (i.e. negative association) between two qualities the coefficient will be

$$\frac{\text{o} - \text{Cross-product (of frequencies of items with associated qualities)}}{\text{o} + \text{Cross-product (of frequencies of items with associated qualities)}} = -1$$

§23 CONTINGENCY : The method of fixing the degree of association between attributes described in §22 can be extended to cases where one of the characters is a variable, or to cases where more than two rough classes or ranges of values (qualities or quantities) are distinguished in one or both of the characters studied. If items are distinguished as long, medium and short, and also as very wide, wide, narrow and very narrow, the actual distribution of items of the three lengths over the four widths must be compared to the distribution to be theoretically expected if length and width varied independently. The proportion of all long items should on the theory of independence, be the same in all four categories of width. Similarly the proportion of medium and of short items should not be greater or less in one width category than another, and the difference must be noted between the actual and such a theoretical distribution. These differences between the actual and theoretical number of items distributed will not be one *same* " common " difference, and the method of measuring the coefficient of *contingency* though similar in principle is different in practice to the method of measuring the coefficient of association.

Each particular difference (some negative, some positive) should be squared and the square divided by the particular theoretical number of items involved if the characters were independent. These quotients may be called the relative differences and the coefficient of contingency, denoted C, is

$$C = \sqrt{\frac{\text{Sum of the relative differences}}{\text{Total number of items} + \text{Sum of the relative differences}}}.$$

An example of the use of this coefficient is given in Chapter IX, §§3 and 4.

This coefficient clearly cannot be greater than 1 however great the sum of the relative differences, and approaches o when the actual frequencies tend towards the distribution to be expected as probable on the theory of independence ; that is, when the particular differences, and consequently the relative differences, tend to 0.

§24 CORRELATION : Each of the items given in §11 with variable characters manifesting values measurable as a specific quantity of units may have more than one such *variable* characteristic, and the two variables may be *correlated*. If the values already given are taken to be breadths given to the nearest inch, each item may also have its length measured in inches. Suppose the fourteen items have such a second characteristic.

Item with value (e.g. breadth) 3 has second value (e.g. length) 9.

Two items with value 4 have second values 12, 13.

Four items with value 5 have second values 11, 12, 13, 16.

Three items with value 6 have second values 13, 15, 16.

Item with value   7 has second value 15.

Item with value   8 has second value 18.

Item with value 12 has second value 25.

Item with value 22 has second value 36.

The coefficient of correlation (r) is (in words) *the arithmetic mean of the products of the deviations of the two characters of each item from their arithmetic mean, divided by the product of the standard deviations of the two characters.*

Since the arithmetic mean is the sum of values divided by the number of items, this may be written

$$r = \frac{\text{Sum of the products of the deviations of each item}}{\text{Number of items} \times \text{Product of S.D. of the two characters.}}$$

A table for working out the coefficient of correlation in our illustrative case would run as follows :

MODEL CORRELATION TABLE

| Items | Original Values | | Deviations from Average (Arithmetic Mean) | | | | Products of (Original) Deviations xy |
| | Breadths | Lengths | Breadths | | Lengths | | |
			Original x	Squared x^2	Original y	Squared y^2	
(1)	3	9	−4	16	−7	49	28
(2)	4	12	−3	9	−4	16	12
(3)	4	13	−3	9	−3	9	9
(4)	5	13	−2	4	−3	9	6
(5)	5	12	−2	4	−4	16	8
(6)	5	11	−2	4	−5	25	10
(7)	5	16	−2	4	0	0	0
(8)	6	16	−1	1	0	0	0
(9)	6	13	−1	1	−3	9	3
(10)	6	15	−1	1	−1	1	1
(11)	7	15	0	0	−1	1	0
(12)	8	18	+1	1	+2	4	2
(13)	12	25	+5	25	+9	81	45
(14)	22	36	+15	225	+20	400	300
Total				304		620	424
Average	7	16					

The standard deviation of the breadths (symbol σ^x) is

$$\sqrt{\frac{304}{14}} = \sqrt{21 \cdot 7} = 4 \cdot 66$$

The standard deviation of the lengths (symbol σ_y) is

$$\sqrt{\frac{620}{14}} = \sqrt{44 \cdot 3} = 6 \cdot 65$$

The coefficient of correlation is (in symbols) $\dfrac{\Sigma(xy)}{N\sigma^{xy}}$

$$= \frac{424}{14(4 \cdot 66 \times 6 \cdot 65)} = +0 \cdot 97$$

ALPHABETICAL INDEX

Printed in the United States
by Baker & Taylor Publisher Services